The Fall and Rise of Freedom of Contract

The Fall and Rise of Freedom of Contract

Edited by F. H. Buckley

Duke University Press   Durham and London 1999

© 1999 Duke University Press
All rights reserved
Printed in the United States of America on acid-free paper ∞
Typeset in Trump Mediaeval by Wilsted & Taylor Publishing Services
Library of Congress Cataloging-in-Publication Data appear
on the last printed page of this book.

FOR SAUL SCHWARTZ

Contents

Preface   *xi*

Introduction   F. H. BUCKLEY   *1*

I   Free Bargaining and Formalism

Contracts Small and Contract Large: Contract Law
through the Lens of Laissez-Faire   RICHARD A. EPSTEIN   *25*

The Decline of Formality in Contract Law   ERIC A. POSNER   *61*

External Critiques of Laissez-Faire Contract Values
MICHAEL J. TREBILCOCK   *78*

In Defense of the Old Order   TIMOTHY J. MURIS   *93*

The Limits of Freedom of Contract in the Age of
Laissez-Faire Constitutionalism   GREGORY S. ALEXANDER   *103*

II   Bargaining around Tort Law

Courts and the Tort-Contract Boundary in Product Liability
PAUL H. RUBIN   *119*

Commodifying Liability   ROBERT COOTER   *139*

III   Contracting for Land Use Law

Zoning by Private Contract   ROBERT H. NELSON   *157*

Dealing with the NIMBY Problem   WILLIAM A. FISCHEL   *177*

Devolutionary Proposals and Contractarian Principles
STEVEN J. EAGLE *184*

The (Limited) Ability of Urban Neighbors to Contract for the Provision of
Local Public Goods   ROBERT C. ELLICKSON   *192*

IV   Free Bargaining in Family Law

A Contract Theory of Marriage
ELIZABETH S. SCOTT AND ROBERT E. SCOTT   *201*

Marriage as a Signal   MICHAEL J. TREBILCOCK   *245*

Family Law and Social Norms   ERIC A. POSNER   *256*

Contracting around No-Fault Divorce   MARGARET F. BRINIG   *275*

V   Bargaining around Bankruptcy Reorganization Law

Contracting for Bankruptcy Systems   ALAN SCHWARTZ   *281*

Free Contracting in Bankruptcy   F. H. BUCKLEY   *301*

Free Contracting in Bankruptcy at Home and Abroad
ROBERT K. RASMUSSEN   *311*

VI   Choosing Law by Contract

Contract and Jurisdictional Freedom
BRUCE H. KOBAYASHI AND LARRY E. RIBSTEIN   *325*

A Comment on Contract and Jurisdictional Competition
MICHAEL KLAUSNER   *349*

Choice of Law as a Precommitment Device   GEOFFREY P. MILLER   *357*

Corporate Law as the Paradigm for Contractual Choice of Law
ROBERTA ROMANO   370

Notes   387
Contributors   457
Index   459

The essays in this book were presented at six colloquia sponsored by the George Mason University Law and Economics Center and the Donner Foundation between November 1996 and December 1997. The general theme of the colloquia was the intellectual revival of freedom of contract, after a period of decline in the 1970s.

In North American law schools, the 1970s was a decade of regulatory triumphalism. The most exciting scholarship was in such areas as consumer, securities, and environmental regulation, while in contract law free bargaining was in retreat. Twenty-five years later, the balance is reversed. In contract law, the principle of bargaining freedom enjoys newfound respect, while in regulatory law one begins to perceive the benefits of permitting parties to bargain around mandatory rules.

Why the turnaround? Part of the reason was the practical failure of the progressive political agenda. Entrusting broad authority to enlightened regulators did not produce a Heavenly City. When I arrived in Washington ten years ago, my New Deal liberal neighbors were shocked that cars might be inspected at private Virginia garages, rather than at government facilities like those of the District of Columbia. Few people today have the same faith in government.

Our concern is not raw politics, however, or even empirical results. Instead, we examine the intellectual failure of the progressive attack on free bargaining and free markets. Consumers are not as helpless as they were made out to be; and intrusive legal rules designed to protect them not infrequently left them worse off. Contractarian principles have also been found remarkably robust in areas far afield from contract law, something the contracts scholar who never ventures from his discipline might have missed. This is why much of this book reviews how free bargaining principles might inform the content of private law rules in nontraditional areas such as tort law, land use controls, family law, bankruptcy, and private international law.

Contractarianism is thus the dominant principle in private law and has pushed far back the borders of public law. But it has not erased that border. Law-and-economics offers an explanation for the limits as well as the benefits of free contracting, and both are discussed in the book. For example, same sex marriages and waivers of no-fault divorce rights in Louisiana's "covenant marriages" both involve a contract between two people. Yet few people, even if economically sophisticated, would enforce both contracts. It is not that contractarianism is imperfectly understood, but that reasonable people may disagree about the proper scope of paternalism and the social benefits of traditional marriage legislation.

Notwithstanding the broad focus of the essays, this is above all a book about contract theory. Basic problems of bargaining freedom, such as paternalism, informational failures, and strategic behavior, are discussed throughout. At the same time, specialists in fields other than contract law will be challenged by novel contractarian arguments.

Many of the essays are written from a law-and-economics perspective. The 1970s law teacher who rejected contractarian norms was often deeply ignorant of market processes, and law-and-economics scholars have led the revival in free bargaining principles. However, technical terms are clearly explained, and all of the essays are readily accessible to the contract law generalist.

I owe an enormous debt of gratitude to the Donner Foundation for sponsoring the colloquia and this book. In addition, several of my George Mason colleagues were very helpful throughout, particularly Dean Mark Grady, Peg Brinig, Steve Eagle, Bruce Johnsen, Nelson Lund, Tim Muris, Jeff Parker, and Larry Ribstein. I also owe a great debt to John Giacomini and Susan Wallace of the George Mason Law and Economics Center, who organized the colloquia. I also hasten to thank Miriam Angress of Duke University Press for her unfailing help with the book. Lastly, I owe special thanks to three people—Dean Henry Manne, who first proposed the colloquia; Law and Economics Center Director Bill Lash; and Richard Murphy, who organized the first colloquium and whose tragic death we still mourn.

F. H. B.

The Fall and Rise of Freedom of Contract

Twenty-five years ago, the principle of freedom of contract was everywhere in retreat. In 1974, Grant Gilmore's *The Death of Contract* argued that contractual liability was in decline,[1] with tortious liability taking its place. Gilmore's thesis was echoed by Patrick Atiyah in several books, most notably *The Rise and Fall of Freedom of Contract*.[2] These books were followed by even stronger attacks on freedom of contract by Critical Legal Scholars, who argued for broad interference with personal preferences.

Several themes ran through the attack on contract. First, free bargaining was thought to rest on an antiquated laissez-faire ideology. Because laissez-faire had fostered monopolistic abuses, it was thought, the modern state had wisely restricted the scope of contract. Second, free bargaining was said to serve poorly the consumer's true interests. Consumers were unduly influenced by advertisements and societal prejudices, and unable to choose prudently for themselves. In some cases, consumers know what is in their best interests, but are unable to pursue it because of weakness of will. In other cases, consumers cannot know what their best interests are because of the judgment biases identified in the psychological literature. Third, the parties might fail to reach an agreement because of transaction cost or strategic behavior problems. For example, a group of creditors might be unable to craft a valuable reorganization plan because the gains from the agreement are exceeded by the costs of bargaining. Finally, neoinstitutional theorists have noted that business bargainers often cooperate without formal, legal agreements, and that they frequently waive strict enforcement of contractual terms when their bargains turn sour. "Ah," said the enemies of free bargaining, "We can relax the rules of contract law, and it will not matter very much."

These attacks on free contracting profoundly influenced a generation of law students and lawyers. In the thoroughly modern curriculum of the 1970s law school, the growth courses were in regulatory law, such as consumer protection, while private law courses such as contract shrank. And in the contract class, the palm went to the clever student who could explain why a bargain should *not* be enforced. Unequal bargaining power, exemption clauses, and fundamental breach—these were the modernist banners around which we rallied. It was a simpler time.

How long ago that now seems. Since then, the modernist assault on private law institutions has been answered by three camps of scholars. First, and weakest, are the neoformalists, who object to the modernist's politicization of private law and who propose a return to the traditional ideal of the law as an independent discipline. Next come the Kantians, who posit an abstract and noncontingent right to contract, wrongly denied by the modernists. Lastly, law-and-economics scholars defend free bargaining from a consequentialist perspective. Like the modernists, they do not see the law as an independent discipline and would test legal rules by reference to the social goals they serve. But unlike the modernist, the law-and-economics scholar has a sophisticated understanding of the incentive effects of legal rules.

Neoformalist, Kantian, and consequential theories all seek to provide an explanation for why contracts should be binding, whether in morals or in law. Of the three responses to modernism, only consequentialism (in its law-and-economics form) offers a satisfactory defense of free contracting. The intellectual revival of freedom of contract therefore coincides with the rise of the law-and-economics movement, and this explains why most of the essays in this book are written from that perspective.

The naïve law teacher sometimes says, objecting to positive theories of law and economics, "But I see it from a moral point of view." In doing so, he reveals his ignorance of moral as well as economic theory. Not merely does law-and-economics scholarship offer a compelling normative explanation for free contracting, but rival theories are unpersuasive.

NEOFORMALISM

Neoformalism is not so much a theory as an antitheory of law.[3] For the last sixty years, since the decline of formalism and the rise of legal realism, academics have sought to justify legal institutions by reference to nonlegal theories. Where the formalist strove for an internally consistent set of legal rules, the legal realist proposed to test legal rules by reference to external criteria taken from moral philosophy, politics, economics, sociology, psychology, anthropology, or evolutionary biology. Why was internal consistency the *summa bonum*, asked the realist? The rules of Hell might be perfectly consistent. But after sixty years of theorizing, did we end up with a better set of rules? Burke asked the same question about the political metaphysicians of the French Revolution, and employed "theorist" as a term of contempt. So too, not a few of us might prefer the stock of rules we had before lawyers began to theorize.

Neoformalism harkens back to an earlier era when law was regarded as a dignified, independent discipline. For strategic reasons, it will appeal to those who prefer contract law circa 1920 to the modern version. Yet the neoformalist critique of legal theory is ultimately unsuccessful. Even if the formalist's law were superior to that which succeeded, legal realism might not have had anything to do with the decline. A good many things might contribute to a change in legal rules, and new legal theories do not top the list. But there is a more fundamental objection to neoformalism. Its appeal is founded on a sense of decline, and that decline cannot be observed from within a system of rules. Thus one might prefer Williston's strict contract law rules to more modern principles of fairness, but not because one set of rules has a superior formal structure over another. Instead, the comparison must be based on external criteria, such as those provided by efficiency norms. Put another way, the legal theorist who prefers modern contract law rules will not be persuaded that the move from formalism was anything other than benign. It takes a theory to beat a theory, an "ought" to beat an "ought not."

Now, neoformalism is not entirely without normative theories. It might first be seen as a self-denying ordinance, in which judges are enjoined from theoretical speculation. A court that is permitted to deliberate on social and political theories has a broader grant of authority than one that is bound by narrow, formal rules. Thus, in "The Decline of Formality in Contract Law," Eric Posner ties the move away from formalism to a weakening in the deference that courts paid to legislatures and judicial authorities.

The American skeptic who regards all laws as indeterminate will dispute Posner's "deference thesis." But this is mere parochialism, for English and Canadian courts are clearly more restrained than American ones. Anglo-Canadian courts are less likely to depart from established rules, and their contract law more closely resembles the formalist rules Americans left behind them. Today a Canadian can more profitably read Williston than can an American.

Anglo-Canadian traditions of judicial caution may usefully reduce the agency costs of judicial misbehavior. For economists, "agency" refers to any consensual relationship between two parties in which one, the principal, implicitly bestows authority on the second, the agent, whose decisions may confer benefits or impose costs on the principal.[4] Thus the courts may be seen as agents of all the subjects in a state. Rule-making authority is delegated to courts because they have the expertise to identify and the ability to effect improvements in the law—often more economically than the legislature. Yet the delegation of authority comes at a cost, particularly when the restrictions on judicial innovation are weak. Courts are less accountable than legislatures and less subject to sanction when they embark on a judicial frolic.[5] They may also be less able than legislatures to assess the consequences of a legal change, since appellate advocacy is not a particularly good method of weighing empirical evidence. Neoformalism might therefore commend itself as a bonding device that usefully addresses an agency cost problem of judicial overreaching.

The difficulty with this argument is that neoformalist fetters also impose costs, in the form of forgone benign laws that might have been adopted by a sophisticated and activist bench. Whether the Canadian tradition of judicial reserve is beneficial is therefore an empirical issue, on which reasonable men may differ. The American liberal might be happy with an activist judiciary, and the Canadian liberal might bemoan the conservatism of his country's judges. As judicial norms, activism and conservatism are instrumental values, good insofar as they result in a better stock of laws, and not good in themselves. The prior question is always which set of laws is better. After that, the choice between judicial activism and conservatism takes care of itself. But the formalist cannot tell us which set of laws is superior; that takes a theorist, and an external perspective.

THE RIGHT TO CONTRACT

One must therefore look elsewhere for a satisfactory defense of free contracting. And the second place to which we turn are abstract theories of a right to contract. On such theories, individuals have a right to bind themselves by contract, quite apart from the consequentialist benefits of promissory institutions. We might be wealthier or happier with contract law, but that is beside the point. What matters is that the private law institutions should respect abstract personal rights, including the right to promise and the right to contract. Modern statements of the nonconsequentialist position may be found in Charles Fried's *Contract as Promise*[6] and in the writings of Kantian scholars such as Ernest Weinrib[7] and Peter Benson.[8]

When promising and contract law are analyzed as conventions, however, the defects in the Kantian analysis of contract law are apparent. To describe promising as a convention is not to claim that it is trivial or easily dismantled. Instead, it is to make a claim about language. Promising is a convention in the sense that it could not exist without a set of constitutive rules provided by a language about what counts as a promise and an acceptance.[9] If we lived in a society whose language lacked a word for "promise," the question of breach could never arise.[10] Nor would contract law exist either, without the constitutive rules of promising and of contract.

To see how the Kantian project fails, imagine that our society lacks a convention of promising, and that we are asked to deliberate on whether to adopt one. We might argue that, with promising, our society would be richer, as promisees could rely more strongly on promises. Without promising, the promisee might fail to take steps to exploit an opportunity that the promise presents him. Promisee reliance is further strengthened when legal sanctions are added to moral ones, on the adoption of contract law. But these reasons look to the consequences of adopting a promissory convention, and consequentialist explanations are not available to the Kantian.

When promising games are added to our language, we are able to do one new thing. In the sense that our domain of alternatives has expanded, we might say we are freer. But this does not supply a libertarian justification for promising. Think of a world that lacks the game of baseball, whose members lack the ability to balk, strike out, and steal second base. After baseball is invented, these gaps in the domain of alternatives will be filled, and this will expand our liberty in just the same way. But without an explanation for why one game is better than another, or why promising is superior to hopscotch, this explanation has little purchase. Not every new choice is of equal worth, and if different games are to be evaluated it must be on the basis of their consequences.

The problem with Kantian explanations of promising may be observed from the opposite direction. Suppose that conventions of promising and of contract law exist and that the question for deliberation is whether to abolish them. What reasons for preserving them could the Kantian raise, which did not look to the consequences of doing so? Consider the way in which the doctrine of illegality sets the boundary of contract law. Where a consideration is tainted with illegality, at common law or statute, contracts are unenforceable. But whether a consideration is illegal is a matter of public rather than private law, of social benefits and costs rather than abstract individual rights. Common law courts refuse to enforce immoral contracts because they impose external costs on society, and not because they violate the internal rules of contract law. Now suppose that the social costs of promising were so pernicious that it was entirely banned. In this way, public law might squeeze out the private law of contract. Thus the borders of public law are set by public law, by weighing the public costs and benefits of barring the enforcement of a contract.

This helps to explain why opponents of bargaining freedom might insist on the possibility of public law trumps, and why supporters sometimes resist consequentialist explanations of contract law. But this need not trouble the consequentialist supporter of free bargaining. When barriers to freedom of contract leave us worse off, it is not self-defeating for the consequentialist to resist them. But it is self-defeating for the rights theorist to pick his theories strategically, and to oppose consequentialism because he thinks that one consequence of adopting such theories is a slippery-slope slide toward restrictions on free contracting.

Can the Kantian project be salvaged through indirect means? On consent and reliance theories, contractual obligations might seem to arise from abstract theories of right. However, neither of these theories satisfactorily explains contractual obligations.

On consent theories, those who invoke a convention of promising have implicitly promised to support it, through a prima facie obligation to perform their promises. But how does this duty of support arise? It cannot be because the parties have consented to the convention, for no one has a choice about basic conventions such as promising. There is no exit strategy worth thinking about. Consent theories are also circular, as Hume noted.[11] They posit a promise to obey promises, but do not explain why the first promise is binding.

Reliance theories argue for liability when the promisor intentionally or negligently induces the promisee to rely at his cost. However, this supports only a tortious and not a contractual theory of promissory obligations and cannot account for the full scope of contractual obligations. On reliance theories, promises misfire absent promisee reliance. But contracts are enforceable before promisees rely, and the contractual measure of damages is not set by the reliance interest. As we shall see, the consequentialist has an explanation why this is so; but the reliance theorist has none. Thus he cannot provide a satisfactory account of promising or of contract law, as he can of quasi-promissory institutions like estoppel.[12]

The intellectual failure of neoformalism and of rights-based theories clears the way for a consequentialist account of contract law and promising. Here promissory conventions are evaluated on the basis of their consequences. What then are the consequences of promising games, which make them more valuable than baseball or hopscotch?

Promising is a self-binding strategy, in which the promisor backs up his statement of intention by undertaking to bear a moral sanction on nonperformance (unless he can legitimately avail himself of an excuse). With contract law, the promisor is permitted to bind himself more strongly to perform, by undertaking to bear a legal as well as a moral sanction on breach. In doing so, the promisor places his reputation and assets at risk. However, he might wish to do so for one of two reasons. First, the promisor who seeks to confer a benefit on a friend or relative might fear that, out of weakness of will, he might change his mind before performance unless he increases the costs of nonperformance through his promise.[13] Second, by fettering himself by promises and contracts, the promisor invites stronger promisee reliance. Such reliance may permit the promisee to exploit a valuable investment opportunity, which in turn will permit the latter to make a side payment to the promisor—the consideration—to induce him to incur the burden of the promissory obligation.[14]

If promising and contract law are valuable, it is because we prize these consequences. Why then are they prized? Promisee reliance is sometimes good in itself, for by promoting reliance we create a more trusting world, in which mutual ties are strengthened. But where such ties matter most, with those closest to one, the parties seldom choose to contract. Instead, they rely on natural bonds of affection, strengthened through repeated patterns of cooperation.[15] And in commercial contracts, trust is an instrumental goal, valuable not in itself but for the investment opportunities which it permits the parties to exploit. These material benefits are thus the most important consequences of contract law. They are shared not only by the immediate parties but also by members of their society, for whom life in a prosperous economy is preferable to life in an undeveloped country.

This explains this book's emphasis on the economic analysis of bargaining freedom. More than neoformalism and theories of rights, the consequentialist perspective of the economist accounts for why promissory and contractual institutions are valuable. It is not surprising, therefore, that the intellectual revival of freedom of contract has been led by scholars in the law-and-economics tradition. Many of the best of these scholars are represented in the essays that follow.

II   The Critique of Bargaining Freedom

THE ATTACK ON FORMALISM

In their critique of free bargaining, Gilmore and Atiyah emphasized broad political trends. Formalist contract law rules had come under attack in the twentieth century, at a time when laissez-faire seemed in decline, and the authors concluded that these changes were related. However, they really had very little to say about laissez-faire, notes Richard Epstein in "Contracts Small and Contract Large: Contract Law through the Lens of Laissez-Faire." What concerned them were the finer points of contract law, and not bargaining freedom. That is, the Gilmore-Atiyah critique was directed not at *freedom of contract* but at the *sanctity of contract*. Freedom of contract ("contract large") means laissez-faire: the right to choose one's contracting parties and to bargain with them on any terms one sees fit. Sanctity of contract ("contracts small") is the narrower term, as it does not presuppose full bargaining freedom. Some contracts will, and some will not be enforced. But where they are enforced, the parties are free to stipulate terms, and a mostly efficient set of contract law rules will be supplied.

For Epstein, therefore, the Gilmore-Atiyah critique is small stuff. It leaves alone the grand principle of bargaining freedom and concentrates on the relative minutiae of narrow, formalist rules. Can one imagine improvements on nineteenth-century rules of offer and acceptance? No doubt. But how does this add up to the death or fall of contract? As Epstein notes, "[n]o system has to be perfect to survive, and the perceived defects of the nineteenth-century legal regime can be fixed without any major changes to its overall structure." Besides, the old formalist rules were often quite sophisticated, as a first approximation of an efficient set of rules. And to the extent that they were inconvenient, they were mostly default terms, around which the parties could bargain. Finally, how can a book that celebrates the rise of noncontractual liability sound the death knell of contractual liability? Liability for promissory estoppel does not trump contract law. Instead, "[w]e simply have more routes to promissory liability," with contract liability of central importance and estoppel liability restricted to a few stray promises.

How did we come to make so much of the critique of contract law? Gilmore's principal claim was that: "We are fast approaching the point where, to prevent unjust enrichment, any benefit received by a defendant must be paid for unless it was clearly meant as a gift; where any detriment reasonably incurred by a plaintiff in reliance on a defendant's assurance must be recompensed."[16] From which the next sentence did not follow: "When that point is reached, there is really no longer any visible distinction between liability in contract and liability in tort." What the move from the first to the second claim ignores are the expectation measure of damages and the enforceability of wholly executory contracts where no one has relied. If the promisee can recover an expectation award in contract beyond any reliance damages he may have incurred, even where he has not relied at all, then contractual liability must be broader than tortious liability. And these points are not disputed in *The Death of Contract*.

By contrast, Atiyah more clearly described the fall of contract. He did not assert that executory contracts were unenforceable but hinted that the law was evolving in that direction. He saw arguments for the enforcement of wholly executory contracts as suspect and thought that this might be unfair from a distributional perspective. In any event, he said, most promises are enforced on reliance grounds since they quickly pass from being wholly executory.[17]

These arguments were taken a very long step further in Atiyah's *Promises, Morals, and Law*, which argued that contracts and promises do not impose a moral obligation. They merely certify the existence of a prior obligation and do not create a new liability where none existed before.[18] But if this is so, then everything that is permitted must be obligatory. *PML* is thus the high-water mark of the attack on free bargaining and of contract nihilism, for under it a rising tort law would entirely submerge contract law. *PML* also betrays a very basic misunderstanding of promising. It assumes that promises are content-dependent, with the obligation depending on the thing promised. This is wrong, for the obligation arises from the fact of promising and not the content of the promise.[19] Since then, Atiyah has retreated from these most illiberal views.[20]

EVALUATING THE ATTACK ON FREE BARGAINING

Does Epstein's critique of Gilmore and Atiyah succeed? The decline of formalism has plausibly weakened what Epstein describes as the security of exchange in contract law—the expectation that promises made in a contractual setting will be enforced. The excuses which promisors may invoke to excuse performance, such as unconscionability, misrepresentation, duress, mistake, and breaches of promisee duties of good faith, are much broader in scope today than they were in the nineteenth century. Moreover, the possibility of noncontractual reliance liability may impede contracting when the parties want their liability to sound only in contract. Because promisors fear reliance damages for precontractual negotiations, they might restrict their bargaining endeavors.

Why this happened, and what it means for freedom of contract, is examined in Eric Posner's "The Decline of Formality in Contract Law." Posner first considers, then rejects, what he describes as a "market thesis," under which the decline in formality is attributed to a loss of faith in laissez-faire. In rejecting narrow, formal rules, courts sought to give effect to the intentions of the parties, and not to promote nonmarket goals such as social justice. In addition, English contract law is more formal than American law, and yet laissez-faire sentiments are usually thought to be weaker in England.

Posner next considers the "deference" explanation of the decline of formalism in America. American courts are more interventionist than English ones, and less deferential to legislatures or to a classical conception of contract law. Posner argues that this did not represent a loss of faith in free markets, since the move from the narrow rules of formalism to the broader standards of contemporary American contract law permits a court, in interpreting a contract, to reflect the intentions of the parties more closely.

How did American courts come to shake off the constraints of formalism? Posner discounts political explanations, which posit a sea change in judicial ideology. What ideological theories fail to explain is why an individual judge would care to promote his personal political views, if this would result in a reputational sanction. Instead, Posner advances a reputational explanation, in which individual judges nudge at the edges of legal rules in a quest for judicial status. Which direction this competition might take is almost, though not quite, random. When the rules of contract were still being formed, during the nineteenth century, the palm went to the synthesizers, who could extract specific rules from a mass of case law. But after the work of the synthesizers was done, and there was little to be gained from a restatement of the rules of offer and acceptance, the judicial innovator turned from narrow rules to the Wetlaw of broad standards of fairness and good faith.

Was the move from formalism beneficial? Non-Americans who do business in this country regret the lack of predictability in American litigation, not unlike the way in which Americans fear litigation in countries but lately converted to the rule of law. If so, the foreigner might take heart from Posner's diagnosis of the decline of formalism as a random perturbation. If Posner is correct, the wheel will turn in time, back in the direction of formalism, for once fairness norms are adopted, reputation gains come from renouncing and not reformulating them. There can be only one Lord Denning in a generation or two; after him comes the neoformalist.[21]

A second difficulty with the Epstein thesis is reviewed in Michael Trebilcock's "External Critiques of Laissez-Faire Contract Values." Trebilcock contrasts Atiyah's and Gilmore's "internal critiques" of formalist rules (which do not implicate freedom of contract) with "external critiques" (which more closely trench on free bargaining). Thus the debate over the rules of offer and acceptance is an internal critique, which leaves bargaining freedom undisturbed. By contrast, external critiques, based on information failures, paternalism, commodification, and externalities, would restrict the scope of free bargaining. Law-and-economics scholars have demolished much of the facile anticontractarianism of the 1970s, but they have also given us a more sophisticated understanding of the proper limits of contract.

How serious a blow do these doctrines inflict on freedom of contract? That depends. If they promote efficiency gains, the restrictions will trouble few but the most ardent supporters of bargaining freedom. Nor were bargaining restrictions resisted by nineteenth-century defenders of freedom of contract. As Epstein notes, even Jessel M.R. acknowledged them in *Printing and Numerical Registering Co. v. Sampson*,[22] the locus classicus of the principle of bargaining freedom. Courts have always refused to enforce immoral contracts or contracts in which one party labored under an incapacity. But the Master of the Rolls would have given a narrow scope to those restrictions, and that is what the debate is about, and was about in Jessel's day.

The law-and-economics movement has contributed greatly to this debate, by explaining how restrictions on bargaining freedom may serve efficiency goals and by exploding inefficient barriers to freedom of contract. Take information failures, for example. Some restrictions on bargaining freedom are justified by the wasteful information production costs which consumers would have to incur were the fetters relaxed. One such restriction is U.C.C. § 9-307(1), which provides that a buyer in the ordinary course from a retailer takes free of a perfected security interest that the retailer has given to a prior inventory financer. This is a mandatory rule, which limits how the financer may bargain with the retailer-debtor. But without this restriction, consider the plight of consumers who purchase from the retailer. Lacking easy access to the security agreement, they could never be sure whether the financer had reserved an interest in the goods after their sale by the retailer, and would therefore assume that the financer could repossess them on the retailer's default. This result is manifestly inefficient, as the financer is far better able to monitor the retailer and evaluate his probability of default. It is hard enough for consumers to screen a used car for faults; must they screen the retailer's credit-worthiness as well? So the financer and retailer would wish to cut off the financer's repossession rights after an ordinary course sale. But this cannot be done by private agreement, since the retailer's private loan agreements are hidden from consumers, and since a future secured lender would not be bound by the retailer's pledge to consumers not to grant a security interest. What instead is needed are mandatory barriers, such as those provided by u.c.c. § 9-307(1), to which all parties would willingly agree had they the choice.

Restrictions on free contracting that might be justified in this way are relatively modest. Many of the broader objections to free bargaining have been trenchantly answered by law-and-economics scholars. One such objection was Kessler's attack on standard form contracts. As Timothy Muris's "In Defense of the Old Order" notes, Kessler thought that free enterprise had an "innate" tendency toward monopoly. He had taught in Hitler's Germany and left it only to find a new form of fascism in America: the tyranny of monopoly capitalism that rode roughshod over consumer wishes through standard form contracts.[23] Concentration camps and exemption clauses. No difference, really. From the premier law faculties, these ideas trickled down, imperfectly understood, to lesser schools, and by the 1970s this critique of free bargaining had influenced a generation of contract law teachers. (We can fight fascism too, right here in the classroom!) In an irony worthy of Tom Wolfe, American law schools raised the pillar of private ordering on a Marxist base.

The critics of free markets misunderstood the efficiency goals which standard form contracts serve. As Muris notes, Kessler's critique of market competition is entirely unpersuasive, and there is considerable competition in the provision of standard form terms. Standard form contracts also serve valuable efficiency goals. They eliminate costly dickering over terms and permit the seller to specify terms in far greater detail, either to limit his liability or to extend it through warranty coverage, than if each contract had to be rewritten from scratch. Standard form contracts also address an agency cost problem within the seller, whose sales representatives might be tempted to overpromise the consumer in order to get a sale, but for a standard form exclusion of oral representations and warranties. The critique of standard form contracts also erred by underestimating the ability of consumers to screen for harsh terms. For such screening to be effective, not every consumer must read the contract, and nonscreeners might free ride on a minority of screening consumers.[24]

Does this mean that courts should never intervene to set aside harsh terms of a contract? No. As Elizabeth and Robert Scott note, "contract routinely embraces arguments for limiting itself." Take *Thornborow v. Whitacre*,[25] for example. The defendant borrowed £5 and in return promised to give the plaintiff two grains of rye-corn in the first week, four grains in the second, eight grains in the third, and so on for a year. The defendant argued that there would not be enough rye-corn in the world to satisfy the promise were it enforced, and it was set aside. So some terms should remain unenforceable. But these are the outliers, easily recognized, and very different from the usual terms of a standard form contract. In particular, the fact that a contract term might seem novel, or that its purpose is not immediately clear, no longer suffices to condemn it, as was the case in the law school classes of the 1970s.

Consider next paternalistic fetters on free bargaining. On consequentialist theories, free bargaining need not be an instrumental good, and might be seen as good in itself. Nevertheless, the possibility of bad choices must be troubling to the consequentialist. And to the individual himself. Could we persuade him that, for certain kinds of choices, he will systematically choose poorly, as compared to the choices we would make for him, we might persuade him to give us the power to bind him in the tainted class of choices. This might happen in two kinds of cases. First, the individual might choose poorly because of judgment biases, in which he mishandles probablistic calculations. For example, he might ascribe too small a value to downside risks, or too great a value to upside possibilities. Alternatively, the individual might be free of judgment biases but lack the strength of will to implement a utility-maximizing life plan.

During the 1980s these theories were advanced to justify barriers to free bargaining in a variety of areas. The common law's refusal to enforce immoral contracts might thus be seen as a response to the promisor's weakness of will. Yet the temptation to flush a bit of experimental psychology was often too strong. There are a great many difficulties in relying on experimental results as a basis for policy prescriptions.[26] For example, experimental studies report that individuals misapply the multiplication rule in probability theory when presented with several conjunctive events, overestimating the probability of joint occurrences.[27] In the real world, however, individuals might react to anticipated judgment biases and correct for multiplication mistakes by reducing probability estimates for each separate event. The judgment bias might therefore be self-correcting in ways that escape the notice of experimental economists.

The individual might also address weakness of will problems through self-control strategies. Consider the mandatory fresh start policy of Bankruptcy Code Chapter 7, one of the greatest barriers to free bargaining. Under Chapter 7, individual debtors cannot bargain away their fresh start by waiving their right to shelter future income from creditors through a bankruptcy petition. This has been said to be justified on weakness of will grounds (Stop me before I shop again).[28] Mandatory fresh start policies prevent the debtor from leveraging himself up to the hilt, and thus reduce his ability to mortgage his future to fund present gratification. But the individual who can bind himself by cord or contract may do without mandatory rules. With his cord and earplugs, Ulysses did not need legal rules to protect himself from the Sirens. Similarly, the man who marries and has children adopts a most effective self-control strategy against imprudent borrowing. In particular, present borrowing to purchase a house restricts future choices as strongly as any law. What the paternalist fails to note is that borrowing to purchase durable goods is more likely to be a self-control technique than a weak-willed act and may render restrictions on free bargaining unnecessary.[29]

Does this mean that bargaining fetters can never be justified on paternalist grounds? If so, we should have to relax the ban on the sale of hard drugs, and many would find this objectionable. But how much do extreme cases tell us about general principles? If we would ban the sale of hard drugs, what does this tell us about any of the commodities we might see on any counter of any store of any city in the United States?

Finally, a court might refuse to enforce a contract because of the external costs this would impose on third parties. One example of this is the immoral contracts to which Jessel M.R. referred. Twenty-five years ago, the notion that common law courts should enforce morality was thought passé. The question was entirely settled by H.L A. Hart, who had trounced the Tory Lord Devlin in debate.[30] With the benefit of hindsight, it is less clear that Hart won the debate. Hart's classical liberalism is wonderfully able to produce private wealth but might also be thought to result in the public poverty of a decline in social capital.[31] Should "trash TV" be permitted on the airwaves? Why not, asks the liberal, if viewers can be found. But what this might miss are the costs such programs impose on society at large. That these costs are difficult to weigh does not mean that a zero value should be attributed to them. As Einstein observed, not everything that counts can be counted.

The concern for external costs, and for social capital, also explains the "commodification" barriers Trebilcock describes, where rules of inalienability are imposed to take certain goods out of the stream of commerce because of the social costs their sale would impose. Think of the sale of fetal tissue, for example. Finally, the argument that individual choices might be second-guessed because private preferences are shaped by legal institutions ("endogenous preferences") is also a very Tory argument, insofar as it looks to the state to shape a more moral and civilized society.

Do these add up to a major restriction on bargaining freedom? Likely not, for they operate at the fringes of contract. Few consumer contracts, and almost no commercial contracts, are implicated. Nor are the family debates between social conservatives and libertarians what the Gilmores, Atiyahs, and Kesslers had in mind.[32]

Gregory Alexander's "The Limits of Freedom of Contract in the Age of Laissez-Faire Constitutionalism" is a useful account by a skilled legal historian of the values which shaped legal rules in the era described by Richard Epstein. Without a sense of the world we left behind us, we can too easily commit the historicographical sin of anachronism, looking at past centuries through the prism of twentieth-century ideologies. Thus Professor Alexander rightly criticizes "Progressive" historians for their search for class struggles in early-nineteenth-century America. But a libertarian perspective is also likely to mislead, for the nineteenth-century commitment to free markets was never divorced from a vision of a good society of responsible citizens. Free markets were seen as an instrumental good and valued because they reduced dependency and promoted responsibility. When they conflicted with this socially conservative vision, as they sometimes did, free market theories gave way.

III   Contractarianism in Foreign Fields

Quæ regio in terris nostri non plena laboris?—Aeneid 1.460

While still an Anglican, Cardinal Newman saw a sign of the truth of his faith in the success of its foreign missions. So too, the expansion of free bargaining norms in fields other than contract law, which hitherto were the preserve of mandatory rules, evidences the strength of contractarian principles. The extension of free bargaining principles to novel fields can be traced to the Coase Theorem, which explained why legal rules did not affect outcomes when the parties could bargain around the rules and there were no transaction costs or strategic barriers to an agreement.[33] How easily such bargaining barriers might be surmounted is an empirical problem, of course. Yet the difficulties have sometimes been overestimated in the past, and free bargaining strategies are more robust than has been thought.

Parts II through VI discuss how free bargaining principles might plausibly be extended in tort law, real estate zoning, family law, corporate reorganization law, and conflicts of law.

FREE BARGAINING IN TORT LAW

Paul Rubin argues that consumers should be permitted to waive their right to bring product liability tort claims in "Courts and the Tort-Contract Boundary in Product Liability." Rubin begins by noting that the present set of tort law entitlements is not one for which most consumers would bargain, if given the choice. For example, consumers would wish to waive the right to sue for design defects and would likely bargain away the right to sue for emotional distress and for most punitive damages. Scholars who would refuse to enforce such waivers often point to experimental evidence from the psychological literature to justify paternalistic fetters. But these claims prove too much, for they would justify a far broader interference with individual choice than obtains at present. Such arguments also underestimate the extent to which competitive product markets may narrow the bargaining problem. Finally, these arguments also commit the "Nirvana" fallacy: They compare the *actual* defects on free bargaining with an *ideal* world of contractual screening by juries and judges. In fact, juries and judges are prone to the same heuristic biases as individual consumers, and very plausibly more so. Thus the psychological evidence, so far from justifying paternalistic barriers to free contracting, argues for enforcing waivers of liability in product liability cases.

In "Commodifying Liability," Robert Cooter suggests a novel way in which free bargaining principles might be extended in tort law. At present, champerty barriers restrict the sale of tort claims, apart from such recognized exceptions as insurance subrogation and contingent legal fees. Suppose, Cooter hypothesizes, these barriers were removed, and tort claims could be freely traded, even before the injury. What might well result is a competitive market for claims. Potential consumer plaintiffs would be able to sell off damages claims for emotional distress, for which the possibility of recovery in tort represents an inefficient insurance contract, without sacrificing deterrence goals. Consumers could also purchase their own insurance, where this is cheaper than the third party insurance of tort recovery.

Champerty barriers are ostensibly designed to protect consumers, who might sell their claims at an undervalue to more sophisticated purchasers. However, Cooter is very skeptical that fetters on alienation help uninformed tort plaintiffs. Consumers are best protected not by rules of inalienability, which bar efficient trades, but by competitive markets. While there will be an informational disparity between sellers and buyers about the ex ante value on unmatured tort claims, this will not matter if consumer sellers can free ride on the information provided by prices in competitive markets. It is perverse to prevent competitive markets from emerging, through inalienability rules, in the name of consumer protection.

Cooter speculates that such a regime might reduce litigation levels. But he admits that litigation levels might in fact increase (particularly as compared to a regime where liability waivers are enforced but the sale of tort claims is banned). If so, a possible objection to Cooter's proposal is that an increase in litigation levels might lead to broader substantive tort law rules, if procedural and substantive rules are endogenous. It is perhaps no accident that substantive tort law rules are more generous to plaintiffs in the United States than in England, where procedural rules inhibit litigation.

REAL ESTATE ZONING BY CONTRACT

Robert Cooter noted that his proposal to permit the sale of tort claims resembles the sale of pollution rights. This suggestion, considered extremely radical ten years ago, has more recently been welcomed, and is an example of how free bargaining principles have expanded in environmental and real estate law. Another example of this may be found in private bargaining over land uses.

Land use planning has hitherto been thought the exclusive province of municipal or state zoning law, which polices land uses by imposing building and development restrictions. Mandatory zoning barriers are thought to be needed on the theory that property owners (with purple awnings and weed-filled yards) may impose external costs on their neighbors, and that transaction cost barriers will prevent the parties from addressing the problem by contract. The third party effects might be so broad that the contract would need to bind hundreds of parties, some of whom might bargain for extra compensation as holdouts.

Yet public zoning requirements are often very costly, adding an enormous amount to the price of new home construction, and private bargaining over land use restrictions is not as burdensome as has been thought. In "Zoning by Private Contract," Robert H. Nelson shows how land use restrictions have been specified for a large and growing number of new home purchasers. As of 1992, about 32 million Americans lived in neighborhood associations, formed by a developer who served as an intermediary and internalized the external costs. In this way, the bargaining and holdouts problems for new home developments have been effectively addressed.

In his comment, William A. Fischel discusses the NIMBY costs which arise when "not in my back yard" homeowners oppose property development. NIMBY barriers may be inefficient, since the development decision is made by homeowners who do not share in its benefits. Existing homeowners might then seek an absolute ban on development of new homes, imposing a large cost on new homeowners. Up to now, this has been thought to argue for zoning at the metropolitan level, as in Toronto. But Fischel describes how private contracting might also address these concerns, when new cities such as Columbia, Maryland, are created by a sole developer.

The next two comments discuss a proposal by Robert Nelson to devolve zoning authority down to small neighborhoods, so as to permit existing homeowners to share in the benefits of the neighborhood associations available in brand new homes. Nelson suggests that homeowners in existing neighborhoods be permitted to organize themselves into neighborhood associations with something less than a unanimity requirement. Only in this way, he argues, can the holdout problems of private bargaining be avoided. The case for and against this proposal is made by Robert C. Ellickson and Steven J. Eagle in their comments. In criticizing the proposal, Eagle notes that village Cromwells might outnumber village Hampdens (whom they sometimes resemble), and that greater interference with personal preferences can be expected as the power to bind dissenters devolves downwards. When homeowners consent to these fetters, they may be presumed benign, but not when dissenters are bound against their will. Eagle also notes how neighborhood association might turn into a forum for opportunistic extractions by majority coalitions of homeowners. For his part, Ellickson argues that these costs are exceeded by the gains of block-level land use planning, where "mildly-coercive micro-institutions . . . diminish the role of more coercive cities."

This debate tests the limits of freedom of contract among large groups of bargainers. It usefully shows how barriers to contracting may be overcome when a single developer internalizes transaction costs by assembling the land and building the neighborhood. Where this is more difficult, with an existing block of homes, the choice is between adherence to free bargaining norms or devolutionary principles. In either case, it's a far cry from the scientific management of cities and progressive zoning law.

Even with a thick set of city zoning requirements, homeowners might have a broad range of choice over land uses through private locational decisions. Zoning rules determine what may be done to homes but not where homeowners must live, and they often may choose among many adjacent cities. For example, Washington lawyers might live on a five-acre Potomac estate or in the well-preserved and heavily zoned city of Alexandria, while Washington law students might live in an Adams-Morgan flat or a Ballston apartment. In a mobile society, diversity offers choice, and local zoning rules may expand choices. Thus Alexandria may attract a clientele of homeowners who like Federal period architecture and who support zoning rules to preserve it, while those who resist all zoning rules may commute to distant cul-de-sacs. In either case, free bargaining over locational choice permits the homeowner to select his preferred zoning regime.

For non-Americans, this debate might seem a little parochial. I do not know how many Canadians or Europeans live in a neighborhood association. Far less than the 15 percent figure for Americans, I should think. The reason is not hard to see. Canadian and European inner cites are simply more livable than American ones, and so there is less concern for land use restrictions. Yet the American example, exceptional though it is, shows how private bargaining may substitute for the basic institutions of peace, order, and good government which some American cities no longer provide.

BARGAINING AROUND DIVORCE LAW

In "A Contract Theory of Marriage," Elizabeth and Robert Scott distinguish between two different kinds of liberty interests. In ex post liberty, long-term commitments do not bind the subject and can never deprive him of a fresh start. This is a Rousseauian liberty, which forces the subject to be free. By contrast, under ex ante liberty the subject is free to be forced, since he may waive fresh start rights through long-term agreements.

From a libertarian perspective, ex ante trumps ex post freedom. Under ex ante freedom, the subject who fears he may regret a commitment has the option of refusing to undertake it. Under ex post freedom, the subject is deprived of rights to plan his future life. Unless a convincing case can be made for fetters of free choice, such as those proposed by paternalists, ex ante freedoms should be conceded.

The contribution of law-and-economics to the debate is to identify the costs of refusing to enforce long-term commitments on ex post theories. The costs of forgone long-term commitments are no different in kind from the benefits of short-term ones. In both cases, the promisor's willingness to incur liability for breach invites stronger promisee reliance. Where the promise is not binding, the promisee might simply abandon the contract, with the result that bargaining gains are lost. Alternatively, the promisee might demand more costly substitutes for contracting. For example, the promisor might be asked to provide a pledge or hostage that he will surrender on nonperformance.

Modern legal systems fetter ex ante bargaining freedom through fresh start rights in bankruptcy (discussed in part V) and through no-fault divorce laws (discussed in part IV). Divorce rights offer a particularly useful way of analyzing differences between ex ante and ex post liberty interests. In an ex ante marriage bargain, each party will recognize that he might subsequently seek to exit the union to marry someone else. But he might have to waive this right to persuade the other party to marry him, and might be quite happy to do so for a similar waiver from his fiancée. If divorce rights can be waived in this way, ex ante freedoms dominate ex post ones. But the ex ante bargain will likely contain a set of narrower conditions whose breach permits exit from the marriage. For example, both parties would likely wish to provide for exit rights on traditional annulment grounds, such as nonconsummation.

Even with these benefits, not every couple will seek a covenant marriage. But the question is not which regime will prove more popular but why couples who seek a stronger bond should not have the option to do so. Where different kinds of contracts are uneasily yoked together, a common legal regime might satisfy no one. One law for the lion and ox might not be oppression, but imposing a common regime on both would assuredly be inefficient.

From this one draws three conclusions. First, marriage and divorce law may without difficulty be analyzed through the prism of contracting. Family lawyers sometimes argue that marriage is a covenant and not a contract, but this is a distinction without a difference. Second, no-fault divorce law restricts free contracting in marriage and is therefore suspect absent plausible reasons for bargaining fetters. Third, the contractarian approach to marriage is deeply moral, since it respects the desires of the parties to bind themselves to each other. By contrast, ex post divorce rights force the parties against their wishes to be free, and weaken a haven in a heartless world.[34]

It is sometimes thought that divorce law does not affect divorce levels, since the law cannot keep the parties together when they want to separate.[35] But this amounts to a misunderstanding of the Coase Theorem, which teaches only that, at the moment when the parties contemplate divorce, legal rules will not keep them together. From an ex ante perspective, however, unilateral divorce rights will affect divorce levels in several ways. First, some couples will simply not marry without the assurance of more stable legal rights. Second, the parties will bind themselves more closely together through marriage-specific investments (of which children are the greatest) when the possibility of divorce recedes. Through such investments, divorce becomes costlier and less likely. (These two arguments are precisely the same as those made by Alan Schwartz in part V on the costs of fresh start rights in bankruptcy.) Third, when the probability of divorce lessens in these ways, the parties may more safely form emotional bonds to each other. The temptation to stray will weaken, and small slights will more easily be ignored.

If long-term marriage commitments offer these benefits, how can divorce law fetters on free contracting in marriage be justified? Elizabeth and Robert Scott note that standard arguments for paternalistic fetters are particularly unpersuasive here, and in any event argue only for a cooling-off period, such as that already provided by marriage banns. However, both they and Michael Trebilcock argue for restrictions on marriage agreements to preserve the signal provided by marriage itself. With fifty-seven varieties of marriage, it would mean less to be married—and less still with fifty-seven thousand varieties.

This is a signaling explanation for restrictions on free contracting in marriage. However, signaling arguments might as easily justify the abolition of no-fault divorces, which weakened the marriage signal when they were introduced. Moreover, as Trebilcock notes, it is difficult to see how marriage signals are greatly weakened if the parties are given the right to waive divorce rights in a Louisiana covenant marriage. Giving the parties a small menu of options will moreover provide better information about the kind of marriage most parties desire.

Signaling theories provide a second argument for restrictions on bargaining freedom in marriage. Given the ex ante choice between an exacting and a lax divorce regime, the parties might select the former even though both prefer the latter. Doing so is rational if selecting the more highly valued lax option is taken to signal private information about the party and his expectations for the marriage. For example, both parties might privately want to reserve a right of divorce for adultery but might fear that insisting on this might signal doubts about the future spouse. This is an "oversignaling" explanation for restrictions on free contracting.

Oversignaling theories are difficult to evaluate. Since one cannot tell how strong the impulse to oversignal might be, the argument provides weak support for policy prescriptions. In addition, where both options are offered to the parties, they might also undersignal by proposing the lax regime through a mistaken sense of generosity, even though both prefer the stronger one. (I won't change, but she might, and I won't want to hold her to a marriage when she wants out.) If one option is to be excluded, then, which is it to be? Finally, to the extent that oversignaling effects are anticipated, the parties might seek to address them by asking family members to negotiate terms on their behalf. This was how marriage bargains were made not so long ago, and might be again with a return to free bargaining. (Not soon enough, for some parents.)

If bargaining fetters are to be imposed, the social conservative who seeks to strengthen the institution of marriage is more likely to support a ban on no-fault divorce rights. In that case, only the covenant marriage option would be available. But such strategies are self-defeating if raising the hurdles simply means that fewer couples will clear them. If the restrictions on divorce are those that the parties would have selected themselves, barriers to free contracting are irrelevant. And if the restrictions are stronger than the ones the parties would have chosen, some might decide not to marry. Those who do will also find themselves relying less on the religious institutions (described by Eric Posner), whose more exacting vows substitute for lax legal promises in no-fault regimes. The social conservative might therefore find himself satisfied with the covenant marriage option, and contractarianism might offer a means of ending a battle in our cultural wars.

This is not to say that social conservatives and contractarians will always agree. For example, the contractarian who is agnostic about the social benefits of marriage might support nontraditional forms of marriage, such as homosexual unions, which the social conservative would oppose. For social conservatives, the restriction to heterosexual unions is best seen as a method by which the state, through expressive rules, signals its support for child rearing and future generations, through barriers so mild that they were scarcely seen as discriminatory until recently.

CORPORATE REORGANIZATION BY CONTRACT

Many countries prop up their failing businesses, often through highly inefficient legislation. Some countries nationalize or subsidize the failing firms. Others penalize foreign competitors through tariff barriers. The peculiarly American contribution is Chapter 11, one of the most restrictive bankruptcy reorganization laws ever devised. By filing a bankruptcy petition, an American business debtor can forestall creditor repossessory remedies for years. And there is no way for debtors to precommit against an opportunistic filing, through an ex ante contractual waiver of Chapter 11.

In "Contracting for Bankruptcy Systems," Alan Schwartz discusses the costs that such rules may impose. On default, firms might either be liquidated under Chapter 7 or reorganized under Chapter 11. Liquidation is efficient when firm assets are worth more under a divestiture; reorganization is value-increasing when firm assets are worth more kept together by the firm. The Bankruptcy Code leaves the liquidate vs. reorganize choice to firm managers, who can be expected to choose strategically so as to maximize their private gains. Since liquidation means job loss for the managers, they will seldom fail to reorganize even where this is inefficient. Creditors will anticipate management's opportunistic behavior and will discount the promise of repayment. Because of this, the firm will not be able to finance some profitable opportunities. The resulting underinvestment costs represent a deadweight efficiency loss. To some extent, these costs are reduced by the prospect of ex post renegotiation, where creditors "bribe" firm managers to adopt an efficient liquidation. However, Schwartz shows how some underinvestment costs may remain. His solution is to permit the parties to opt out of Chapter 11.

In "Free Contracting in Bankruptcy," I suggest a second way in which the parties might address management misbehavior through free bargaining. If the parties could waive Chapter 11, they could agree to transfer control of the firm to creditors on default, and this would police management misbehavior more effectively than Schwartz's incentive strategies. This was how bankruptcy reorganizations were conducted under the Canadian private receivership, since the Canadian Bankruptcy Act did not stay the hand of repossessing secured lenders prior to 1991. The private receivership was a regime of free contracting and property rights which barriers to free contracting deny American lenders and borrowers.

Robert Rasmussen suggests two further ways in which bankruptcy reorganization law might be liberalized in "Free Contracting in Bankruptcy at Home and Abroad." For liberalization at home, Rasmussen proposes a "menu" approach, in which the parties are permitted to elect their reorganization law from a menu of possible options. One such option might include the present Chapter 11, but other menu choices might involve more restrictive reorganization regimes, such as the private receivership. The choice might be enshrined in the debtor's charter documents, so as to avoid the problem of subsequent parties without notice. For liberalization abroad, Rasmussen suggests that debtors be permitted to elect to be bound by the reorganization laws of foreign states, on the model of choice-of-law clauses in commercial agreements, or state chartering in corporate law. As in the market for state charters, Rasmussen foresees a race to the top, where the parties will elect to be governed by the state with the most efficient reorganization law.

CHOOSING LAW BY CONTRACT

The suggestion that bargaining freedom might be extended to private international law is the theme of the last part. In "Contract and Jurisdictional Freedom," Bruce Kobayashi and Larry Ribstein discuss how bargainers might elect the state whose law will govern their contract, and thereby avoid inefficient legal regimes. In particular, Kobayashi and Ribstein discuss how bargainers may choose corporate, unincorporated association, and franchise law by contract. Exit strategies of this kind usefully permit bargainers to choose the set of legal rules best suited for them. In addition, choice-of-law clauses impose a pressure on the states themselves to eliminate inefficient rules, since exit imposes a cost on them. The result is a race to the top, in which the winner is the state with the most efficient set of laws as well as greatest balance of trade in cross-border legal work.

Michael Klausner's comment takes on the Kobayashi and Ribstein claim that "lock-in" concerns are not troubling. The benefits associated with a business form depend in part on how many other people use it because of the network benefits of increased legal and judicial familiarity with the form. This may mean that new, superior forms might not be adopted because this would sacrifice the network benefits of the old form—a phenomenon known as "lock-in." Klausner's point is a theoretical one, against which Kobayashi and Ribstein assemble evidence that lock-in problems appeared minor in related business forms. In any event, the lock-in problem does not argue for restrictions on free contracting.

In "Choice of Law as a Precommitment Device," Geoffrey Miller considers a possible objection to the Kobayashi-Ribstein thesis. If a state expects to lose valuable litigation through a choice of forum clause, then why does it enforce such clauses? And why enforce choice-of-law clauses, if they permit the parties to undo an interest-group bargain? Kobayashi and Ribstein give one answer to this puzzle—the exit state may not be able to block exit strategies, since the parties can often structure their contract so that the litigation will take place in the state whose laws they wish to select. In addition, suggests Miller, states might wish to adopt liberal choice-of-forum and choice-of-law rules as a precommitment device, weakening the power of interest group coalitions which might seek to have inefficient laws enacted.

Roberta Romano's comment discusses the race to the top literature in corporate law and suggests an extension to securities law. There is no reason in principle, she argues, why firms should not be permitted to elect their securities law as well as their corporate law regime on incorporation. Though the case for free choice of law is strongest in these fields, Romano also supports the right to choose law by contract for unincorporated associations and franchises.

In sum, bargaining freedom is greatly expanded when the parties may elect the law that will govern their contract. In addition, states have greater incentives to adopt efficient laws when parties may easily exit an inefficient state through choice-of-law clauses. State competition for corporate charters provides the paradigm case of a race to the top; but the lessons from corporate law apply in other areas of law, and argue for the general enforceability of choice-of-law clauses.

Conclusion

We have come a very long way from the unreflective dismissals of bargaining freedom which were current twenty-five years ago. Law-and-economics scholars have shown that broad objections to freedom of contract are untenable, and that narrow restrictions are best understood from an economic perspective. The scope of contract law has also expanded, with novel and interesting contractarian solutions proposed for regulatory problems. Private contracting permits bargainers to exploit the opportunities offered by regulatory inefficiencies in fields once thought the exclusive province of mandatory rules.

The principle of freedom of contract is not without limits, and these have been usefully analyzed by scholars in the law-and-economics tradition. While broad objections to standard form contracts are simply naïve, more focused concerns about information costs, third-party effects, and holdouts suggest the need for continued restrictions on bargaining freedom. Where such limits should be set is a matter on which reasonable men may differ. Yet all will agree that announcements about the fall of bargaining freedom were premature, and, as is evident from these essays, that its rise continues.

I Free Bargaining and Formalism

Contracts Small and Contract Large:
Contract Law through the Lens of Laissez-Faire

RICHARD A. EPSTEIN

I A Fallen Theory?

Laissez-faire capitalism, along with its associated doctrine of freedom of contract, had many stalwart defenders during the nineteenth century. But it has received a rocky reception from many legal and philosophical commentators in the twentieth century. Freedom of contract has often been pronounced "dead on arrival" as an organizing principle for complex contemporary societies. That principle has been said to be insensitive to differences in wealth, status, position, and power that make the exercise of contractual choice a myth for the weak and dispossessed. Within the legal literature, it has been attacked as ignoring the large concentrations of wealth that distort market processes and that trample down the rights of consumers and workers. Modern writers often rejoice in pointing out the intellectual narrowness and class bias of the leading judicial defenders of the principle, of whom Baron Bramwell was surely one.[1]

This sustained attack on laissez-faire political theory has taken place on two levels. The most obvious level addresses grand themes of industrial capitalism and political discontent. These challenges to laissez-faire found their most vivid expression in several contexts: the role of assumption of risk in torts cases,[2] the role of contract and combination in labor cases,[3] antitrust cases, and the requirements of constitutional rates of return for public utilities and other regulated industries.[4] But a second level of concern has also exerted a surprising influence, especially in legal circles. Here freedom of contract has been criticized not only for its social consequences but also, doctrinally and internally, for its unsatisfactory and confused conceptual foundations. Four of the most influential legal critiques of laissez-faire theories have bored at the system from within instead of assaulting it from without. I speak here of Friedrich Kessler's early critique of "Contracts of Adhesion";[5] Grant Gilmore's highly influential set of lectures, *The Death of Contract*;[6] Lawrence Friedman's *Contract Law in America*;[7] and Patrick Atiyah's massive study of contract theory, *The Rise and Fall of Freedom of Contract*.[8]

In these writings the emphasis shifts from contract large to contracts small. Although these authors advert to the major social themes that surround the debate over laissez-faire, they focus on contract doctrines, such as the rules relating to offer and acceptance or consideration, which at first blush are the stuff of lawyer's law, and not the stuff of political controversy and intellectual unrest. They find that the nineteenth-century synthesis of contract law contains errors, confusions, and equivocations that undercut its intellectual vitality. In one sense, these writers have picked odd doctrinal targets for their work, but the influence of their writing calls for a more sustained examination of their position.

This essay therefore has two central objectives. The first of these is to show that the disputes found in classical contract law, and indeed today, operate for the most part at the fringes of any functioning legal system. No system has to be perfect to survive, and the perceived defects of the nineteenth-century legal regime can be fixed without any major changes to its overall structure. This essay's second objective dovetails with the first. It is to establish the internal coherence of the classical system in order to explain why it does withstand the doctrinal and political attacks launched against it.

This essay seeks to discharge these missions by using both a top-down and a bottom-up approach. The bottom-up approach is the worm's-eye view of contracts law that examines such issues as offer and acceptance, consideration, and conditions. The plural "contracts" is used to stress the diversity of doctrinal and technical issues that are incorporated into this overall mosaic. The top-down approach, contract large, uses the singular. It examines the social and intellectual linkages between contract law, writ large, and laissez-faire. The specific doctrines of contract law, which form the core of standard treatises and casebooks, do not bear any simple relationship to the principles of laissez-faire. Much of contract law is compatible with extensive systems of social regulation, both foolish and wise. Accordingly, the efforts of modern writers hostile to laissez-faire—Kessler, Gilmore, Friedman, and Atiyah—falsely posit an intimate connection between the formal doctrines of contract, derogated under the name of formalism, and the political philosophy of laissez-faire. But they cannot bring down laissez-faire by pointing out the perceived inadequacies and rigidities of the nineteenth-century doctrines of offer and acceptance, or consideration. Nor do the twentieth-century doctrinal developments in these areas presage the inevitable rejection of laissez-faire. Indeed, some developments, such as the explicit articulation of the principle of promissory estoppel, are more consistent with freedom of contract than with its rejection.

The received wisdom on this relationship is often otherwise. Friedrich Kessler's influential critique of the contract of adhesion dwelled at great length on the perceived mischief the rules of offer and acceptance generated in insurance contracts. Kessler deplored the outcome when individual insureds were denied coverage because their policies had not been approved by the home office.[9] Yet he never once asked about the centrality of this issue to the overall scheme of insurance regulation or addressed the principled defenses of the earlier rules.[10] Similarly, Grant Gilmore thought that the survival of the larger principle of laissez-faire stood or fell with the nineteenth-century contractual synthesis of offer, acceptance, and consideration.[11] Lawrence Friedman found a still tighter connection between the two sets of principles.

> Basically, then, the "pure" law of contract is an area of what we can call abstract relationships. Pure contract doctrine is blind to details of subject matter and person. It does not ask who buys and who sells, and what is bought and sold. In the law of contract it does not matter whether the subject of the contract is a goat, a horse, a carload of lumber, a stock certificate, or a shoe. As soon as it matters—e.g., if the sale is of heroin, or of votes for governor, or of an "E" Bond, or labor for twenty-five cents an hour—we are in one sense no longer talking about pure contract. In the law of contract, it does not matter if either party is a woman, a man, an Armenian-American, a corporation, the government, or a church. Again, as soon as it does matter—if one party is a minor, or if the transaction is one in which a small auto company sells out to General Motors, or if a seller of legal services happens to be a corporation instead of a partnership or individual—we are no longer talking pure contract. When the relationship of parties to land is involved, this is land law or property law, but not contract. In contract cases land is treated as a commodity on the market, the same as every other commodity, and the rules are supposed to be the same as the rules for horses and cows. If a court says that an insurance contract is "just another contract," or that contracts between the state of Wisconsin and a citizen follow the same rules as any other contracts, the judges are making the same kind of point, are asserting the same abstraction. Contract law is abstraction—what is left in the law relating to agreements when all particularities of person and subject-matter are removed.

> The abstraction is not what people think of when they criticize the law as being too abstract, implying that the law is hyper-technical or unrealistic. (Though often it is.) The abstraction of classical contract law is not unrealistic; it is a deliberate renunciation of the particular, a deliberate relinquishment of the temptation to restrict untrammeled individual autonomy or the completely free market in the name of social policy. The law of contract, therefore, is roughly coextensive with the free market.[12]

Friedman's obvious foil was Christopher Columbus Langdell, the originator of the Socratic method and the author of the first casebook on the law of contract, for which he prepared a companion volume, his well-known *A Summary of the Law of Contracts*.[13] Langdell is a tempting target for any writer, but even so it is dangerous to overstate the connection between Langdell's legal formalism and laissez-faire, or to assume that Langdell's view of the law of contract dominated the judicial writing of the time.

The judges who pondered grand theory also had to make peace with the routine tasks of contractual interpretation, and on these issues they well understood that no market could ever be sustained by the pure theory of contract law standing alone. Contract law must supply default terms for key elements of common transactions both to reduce the costs of forming contracts in the first place and to eliminate uncertainty in contract disputes after the fact. Choosing default terms that lend business efficacy to transactions takes more than abstract principles that transcend commercial categories. It requires good situation sense as well, which the best nineteenth-century judges surely possessed.[14] Ironically, it was Gilmore who devoted far too much energy in *The Death of Contract* to the sterile dispute over whether the development of general contract principles preceded or followed the emergence of law for particular types of contracts, such as sales, partnerships, leases, and mortgages.[15] In so doing, he missed the obviously correct answer, which is that the two sets of rules developed side by side with reference to each other. Every system of contract law needs both, and this parallelism long antedated the nineteenth-century rise of laissez-faire and continues happily after its demise.

It is therefore critical to unpack the larger relationship between contract doctrine and laissez-faire. In order to do so, it is necessary to distinguish clearly among three interrelated concepts. The narrowest idea is *security of exchange*: whenever there is a bargain the party who performs first must be secure in the knowledge that it can enforce the agreement against the other side. The grandest conception is *freedom of contract*, which includes, in addition to the security of exchange, the right to choose one's contracting partners and to trade with them on whatever terms and conditions one sees fit. Midway between them is the doctrine of the *sanctity of contract*. Under this doctrine, the parties may not have perfect freedom to form whatever contract they choose, but once a contract is made, then one side is not free as a matter of course to vary its terms at will, even if he is prepared to compensate the other side for his losses. The sanctity of contract is analogous to the absolute rights of private property in a world devoid of the power of eminent domain. More specifically, sanctity of contract rejects the principle of efficient breach, and for that reason it exerts a powerful hold on classical contract theorists and ordinary traders, both of whom who resist the facile substitution of cash for performance.[16]

Believers in the freedom of contract are committed to both the sanctity of contract and the security of exchange. But the progression does not operate in reverse. It is possible to defend security of exchange and reject both the sanctity and freedom of contract. Or to defend both the security of exchange and the sanctity of contract and still accept limitations on contractual choice. The law may limit an individual's right to choose his trading partners and still provide remedies for the contracts so made. Nineteenth-century English law imposed restrictions against wages paid in kind,[17] and the twentieth-century law requires the payment of some minimum wages, thereby rejecting freedom of contract but accepting security of exchange. The use of specific performance remedies accepts the sanctity of contract but is consistent with the rejection of freedom of contract, when for example land is inalienable by public decree.

Most importantly, most of the law of contract is not about the principle of freedom of contract. The rules of contract formation, interpretation, discharge, and enforcement consonant with a system of laissez-faire apply with undiminished force to the truncated system of contracts that survive scrutiny in the modern regulatory state. The benefits from security of exchange survive in a legal regime that pays less than total homage to freedom of contract. Indeed, it is hard to think of any philosophical or economic reason to abandon security of exchange as a principle of human interaction.[18]

In order to develop these themes, this essay is organized as follows. Section 2 deals with the general theory of laissez-faire in relationship to the principle of freedom of contract. Section 3 uses this framework to examine the law, first of offer and acceptance, and then of consideration. Section 4 takes a closer look at the principle of the sanctity of contract in its relationship to doctrines of necessity and impossibility, unilateral contract modification, and deliberate breach. Section 5 concludes with a brief public policy defense of freedom of contract, as understood by its nineteenth-century defenders.

II   Laissez-Faire through the Eyes of Foe and Friend

Laissez-faire is a general political philosophy that in its popular sense stresses that government should keep its hands off the economy. While that crude formulation evokes the correct mood, laissez-faire does not deny government any place at all in the running of the economy. Quite the opposite, laissez-faire, at least as viewed by its proponents, conceives a role for government in the creation and stabilization of property rights and in the enforcement of voluntary exchanges between adult parties.[19] The belief in freedom of contract does not banish tort law from the legal system: the law of trespass, nuisance, and defamation, insofar as they protect strangers, form a key, regulatory element of the basic system. Laissez-faire is not anarchy. Like other normative theories, it makes explicit substantive judgments about which kinds of regulation work in the common interest and which do not.

The philosophical foundations of laissez-faire rest on an uneasy admixture of natural law and social contract theory. In contrast, its practical side stresses the bad consequences to civil society that flow from ambitious government regimes of taxation and regulation that violate its precepts. The youthful Herbert Spencer, for example, commingled ideas of natural rights, social contract, and social consequences within the confines of a single essay.[20] This intermingling of rights-based, contracts-based, and consequence-based arguments does not reveal a weakness in the philosophical foundations of Spencer's system; indeed most eighteenth- and nineteenth-century writers thought that these three approaches worked in tandem and not in opposition.[21] While Spencer was quite categorical in his delineation of government functions, the common law, to use the felicitous phrase of Aaron Director, softened that position to provide that government actions that went beyond these limited tasks should be evaluated under a presumption of error.[22]

In its heyday, laissez-faire hardly preserved the status quo or glorified the position of the privileged. Rather, it reflected and nurtured strong reformist impulses.[23] Its historical targets were mercantilism and the welter of special privileges and franchises that operated with government favor and support. In their place, laissez-faire displayed a marked affinity for open competition as the engine of social progress, a view that went hand in hand with the principle of freedom of contract.

Freedom of contract has been attacked, of course, for the restrictive assumptions on which it is said to rest. In particular, Patrick Atiyah noted that the system assumed that "the parties dealt with each other 'at arm's length,'" in a regime where neither was bound to offer any information to the other side, and where "the content of the contract, the terms and the price and the subject-matter, are entirely for the parties to settle."[24] Under freedom of contract, all this is said to make sense because individuals are the best judges of what is in their personal interest.[25]

While this stark portrait of common law principles of bargaining freedom surely contains important elements of the truth, it misses out on several elements of the system. First, the rule on "arm's length transactions" was never universal, nor should it have been. Contracts for insurance, for example, were contracts uberrimae fides, about which Judge Bayley wrote in 1828, "I think that in all cases of insurance, whether on ships, house or lives, the underwriter should be informed of every material circumstance within the knowledge of the assured; and that the proper question is, whether any particular circumstance was in fact material, not whether the party believed it to be so."[26] The duty, as codified by statute, applies with special strictness for marine insurance, where "the assured must disclose to the insurer, before the contract is concluded, every material circumstance which is known to the assured, and the assured is deemed to know every circumstance which, in the ordinary course of business, ought to be known by him. If the assured fails to make such disclosure, the insurer may avoid the contract."[27] Such a rule, whether statutory or contractual, makes good sense given the obvious asymmetry of information with respect to the covered risks. Likewise, many of the default terms at contract contain implied warranties of seaworthiness or merchantability, which again match the commercial intuitions of both the nineteenth century and our own.

Nor was the content of the bargain left to the desires of the parties in all cases. Common carriers had long been under an obligation to take all comers, whom they could charge only a reasonable price—not whatever price they wanted.[28] It is both odd and regrettable that neither the supporters nor the detractors of laissez-faire paid much attention to this critical class of institutions in working out their general theories. The failure to note these important institutional exceptions to the basic rule makes laissez-faire appear more extreme than it is— an all too inviting target that its adversaries can then attack for its thoughtless absolutism in defense of individual choice.

Often the criticisms are less focused. Atiyah's prose is characterized by a pervasive undercurrent of skepticism that defies easy summary. Gilmore's vision of laissez-faire comes across at best as tongue-in-cheek, and stands in sharp contrast to the careful treatment that he gives discrete, tricky issues in the law of contracts: "I suppose that laissez-faire economic theory comes down to something like this: If we all do exactly as we please, no doubt everything will work out for the best."[29] And further: "It seems apparent to the twentieth century mind, as perhaps it did not to the nineteenth century, that a system in which everybody is invited to do his own thing, at whatever cost to his neighbor, must work ultimately to the benefit of the rich and powerful, who are in a position to look after themselves, and to act, so to say, as their own self-insurers."[30] Thus the theory is often presented as though individuals are entitled to advance themselves by causing greater harm to their neighbors. Faced with such caricature, I will set out its philosophical presuppositions in a fashion that commends itself to the sympathizers, and not the critics of the theory.

As noted earlier, laissez-faire did not (and still does not) reflect a single intellectual tradition. Natural law theories, contractarianism, and utilitarianism are all mixed together in uncertain proportions. But the elements of this admixture are not randomly thrown together.[31] Utilitarianism may seek to reflect the overall welfare of individuals within society. But so long as utility is not a disembodied spirit, it must find some way to sum utility over separate persons. Voluntary contracts do that job quite well for their participants, and contractarian views seek to find the utility of the group in the hypothetical contracts that its members would accept if transactions costs were low. The two set of solutions tend to converge even though utilitarianism in theory focuses more on outcomes and contractarianism focuses more on process. Within both theories, natural rights fit into the picture as a means to secure the desired social outcomes. A contractarian can hardly take a uniformly hostile view to private contracts; and a utilitarian can hardly fail to see their utility in daily life. Sophisticated utilitarians (and sophisticated contractarians) tend to despair of direct social measurements of utility, and thus seek to find ways in which private actors can express their own preferences, for which a system of property and contract rights offers the best starting point, even if it does not respond fully to the full range of collective action problems found in modern social organizations. These theories thus differ on the extent to which they tolerate social justifications for the limitation on individual rights, but the family preference in favor of strong private rights is nonetheless fairly secure.

This intellectual convergence can be traced in the philosophical literature. Here the most convenient point of departure is Thomas Hobbes's account of ordinary contracts. His initial query was sociological in nature: why do individuals make promises and form contracts in the first place? That question is not answered by stressing the sanctity of the promise. We must first explain why anyone should take the trouble to be bound by a promise in the first place. Hobbes's answer was the self-interest of both parties, each of whom surrenders by agreement something he values less to receive that which he values more. But how does a simple exchange create gain sufficient to justify the cost of transacting? Before the exchange I had a cow and you had a horse. Afterwards I have the horse and you have the cow. Same horse, same cow. So where is the gain? To this skeptical inquiry Hobbes gave an indispensable part of the overall picture: subjective value. Each side has its own unique ranking of goods and services, based on complex private motivations that can be satisfied without giving explanations to others. Thus his famous remark:

> As if it were Injustice to sell dearer than we buy; or to give more to a man than he merits. The value of all things contracted for, is measured by the Appetite of the Contractors: and therefore the just value, is that which they be contented to give. And Merit (besides that which is by Covenant, where the performance on one part, meriteth the performance of the other part and falls under Justice Commutative, not Distributive) is not due by Justice; but is rewarded of Grace only.[32]

Hobbes chose his words, and his targets, carefully. His reference to the commutative and distributive theories of justice is a veiled attack on Aristotle,[33] and his dismissal of the just price takes after the church doctrines of the same name.[34] For Hobbes, the mere fact of making the bargain generated the obligation: measuring return benefit, direct or indirect, was for each party to decide. He did not see, or impose, any independent judgment of what was or not valuable about the property or services exchanged. His choice of the word "appetite" consciously elicited images of subjective desire as the animating force of exchange and the source of mutual gain. We attach different values to the horse and the cow, which our conduct reveals to the world.

Hobbes's position runs through the laissez-faire period. It is implicit in the duel between Justice Pitney and Justice Holmes in *Coppage v. Kansas*,[35] which rightly struck down a law that prohibited "yellow-dog" contracts, whereby an employer could condition the offer of work on the willingness of an employee not to join a union. Pitney's words echo the classical conception of contract (and property) that animated both Hobbes and Hume.

> As to the interest of the employed, it is said by the Kansas Supreme Court to be a matter of common knowledge that "employés, as a rule, are not financially able to be as independent in making contracts for the sale of their labor as are employers in making contracts of purchase thereof." No doubt, wherever the right of private property exists, there must and will be inequalities of fortune; and thus it naturally happens that parties negotiating about a contract are not equally unhampered by circumstances. This applies to all contracts, and not merely to those between employer and employee. Indeed, a little reflection will show that whenever the right of private property and the right of free contract co-exist, each party when contracting is inevitably influenced by the question of whether he has much property, or little, or none; for the contract is made to the very end that each may gain something that he needs or desires more urgently than that which he proposes to give in exchange.[36]

The brief Holmes dissent showed a much weaker understanding of the logic of contract:

> In present conditions a workman not unnaturally may believe that only by belonging to a union can he secure a contract that shall be fair to him. If that belief, whether right or wrong, may be held by a reasonable man, it seems to me that it may be enforced by law in order to establish the equality of position between the parties in which liberty of contract begins.[37]

Yet Holmes offers no independent account of fairness. He does not explain why it depends exclusively on the sentiments of one side to the potential arrangement. Likewise, he does not tell us why contracts cannot secure mutual gain even when the wealth of the parties are unequal at the time of formation. And he surely has no grasp of the threat potential when workers in a group withdraw their labor after the employer has committed extensive capital to the venture. Yet just that risk is inherent in the monopoly position that compulsory unionization creates.

It would, however, be a mistake to assume that all gains from trade derive solely from differences in subjective value. Thus we speak of the sale of "goods" not just because they are chattels, but because they are in fact perceived as "good" by all who observe them. I may prefer the horse to the cow, and you may prefer the reverse. But typically neither of us attaches a negative value to either. I may want your horse because mine has just died. You might be willing to give me your horse because you have an extra in the barn, but have no cow. Markets work because they allow a ranking of preferences by their intensity. This matching of scarcity and superfluity is a very old theme in contract law, and can be found in explicit form, for example, in Justinian's Digest in the opening passages on the law of sale.[38] It was picked up in the political economy literature of the eighteenth century, even before Smith.[39] These dual rationales—subjective value and situational needs—differ on points of detail. The latter refers to things which are desired in and of themselves, but for which a party has an adequate supply. But in dealing with exchanges, the differences between them are unimportant. What matters is that they reinforce each other, by highlighting the different paths to the gains from trade on which so much of liberal theory insists.

So understood, the lifeless abstractions of contract law are not just idle formalisms; they function as a precondition to voluntary exchange, the precursor to mutual gain. Freedom of contract as such does not go to the interpretation of the contracts validly made. It addresses the question of the right to make them, or not make them, in the first place. Freedom of contract therefore is at one with the basic doctrines of property law. The ability not to have offers forced down one's throat is part and parcel of the right to exclude others from your land, or to justify the refusal to hire or be hired. The proposition that made each person the "master of his own offer" does not state what terms an offer should contain, but leaves all parties free to decide what offers to make or reject. Beliefs of this sort were very much a part of the nineteenth-century thought,[40] but, notwithstanding their central substantive importance, they functioned as the backdrop to more specific doctrinal disputes. Most typically, they were not the focus of any sustained doctrinal discussion or dispute.

In this environment, contract law plays an instrumental and facilitative role. Individual intentions must be discerned for promises to be enforced. This separation of freedom of contract from contract law is evident from the topics covered by Langdell in his *Summary of Contracts* published in 1880 as the handmaiden to the 1879 (second edition) of his casebook. His table of contents is most notable for its truncated choice of topics: mutual consent, consideration, and conditions.[41] Mutual consent exhaustively discussed the endless variations on the theme of offer and acceptance. Consideration received still more extensive treatment, both theoretically and with specific topics such as forbearance, compromise, moral consideration, gratuitous bailments, consideration void in part, and executed consideration. The third section parsed the law of conditions precedent, subsequent and concurrent; independent and mutual covenants; and waiver and performance.

These topics, however important, do not come close to exhausting contract law, as Langdell acknowledged in the preface to the first edition.[42] The remarkable list of contemporary omissions includes: frustration, including *Taylor v. Caldwell*;[43] damages, including *Hadley v. Baxendale*;[44] privity, assignment, and third-party beneficiaries, including both *Lawrence v. Fox*[45] and its English rival, *Tweddle v. Atkinson*;[46] restitution for a plaintiff in default, including *Britton v. Turner*[47] from 1834 and its opposite number, *Smith v. Brady*.[48] In addition, Langdell offers no discussion of the public policy limitations on freedom of contract (a subject that does implicate the principles of laissez-faire), nor does he include the oft-quoted judgment of Sir George Jessel: "If there is one thing more than another which public policy requires, it is that men of full age and competent understanding shall have the utmost liberty of contracting and that their contracts, when entered into freely and voluntarily, shall be held sacred and shall be enforced by courts of justice."[49] These omissions cover many cases on which both Gilmore and Atiyah lavish considerable attention.

So the agenda is now fairly set. To what extent do these doctrines form a constituent part of laissez-faire? In order to examine this inquiry, I shall look at a number of discrete doctrinal developments with an eye to showing the separation between contract law as such and the grander theories of laissez-faire.

III From Contract Theory to Contract Law

The next question is how the broad interest in laissez-faire translates into particular contracts doctrine. Here there is no shortcut to dealing with this matter on an issue-by-issue basis.

OFFER AND ACCEPTANCE

Many contract scholars treat offer and acceptance as a linchpin of laissez-faire. One notable battleground has stressed the tension between subjective intention to be bound, under the so-called will theory, and the overt manifestations of intention, under the objective theory of contracts. Do the nineteenth-century theories of laissez-faire incorporate some version of the will theory because of its emphasis on subjective value and individual choice in voluntary exchange? Cheshire and Fifoot, that solid barometer of modern English sensibilities, write in criticism of the ostensible nineteenth-century views: "Agreement, however, is not a mental state but an act, and, as an act, is a matter of inference from conduct," a matter in which "external appearance" plays a central role. This point is one that Baron Bramwell, a chief judicial defender of laissez-faire, was said to have misunderstood. Then, to clinch the argument, Cheshire and Fifoot quote the famous 1478 dictum from Chief Justice Brian: "As for the other conceit, it seems to me that the plea is not good without showing that he has certified the other of his pleasure; for it is common learning that the intent of a man cannot be tried, for the Devil himself knows not the intent of a man." Outward signification of intention is therefore required.[50]

The point, however, has no theoretical bite. Any legal system must deal with errors in communication, both in the transmission of contracts at a distance and with the ordinary slips of the tongue (and pen), a phrase highlighted by Gilmore.[51] These errors in communication by definition could have been avoided by prudent conduct of the speaking or receiving party, or perhaps both. In an ideal world, these errors never crop up because the outward expression of desires corresponds perfectly with one's inner thoughts. Chief Justice Brian's rumination on the devil does not dispute this proposition. It points out the difficulty of *trying* mental states. It does not offer the behavioralist manifesto that banishes mental states from the list of respectable concepts. Brian's only point was that in the case at hand the plaintiff gave no indication of an acceptance.

But what happens when the external words do not match the internal intentions (as proved by other means)? An exchange is not a solipsistic act but involves the cooperation of two or more individuals. Who should bear the costs of error in transmission—the party who made the error or the party forced to rely on those incorrect statements? One sensible rule places the risk of error on the party who makes it, for he is usually, all things considered, in a better position to prevent it. The "objective" theory of contract interpretation simply crystallizes that view that parties are strictly responsible for their errors. But this doctrinal move hardly embodies some philosophical view about the dominance of external appearances. I wish to sell my cow, but say horse by mistake. From the context, you understand that the cow is meant. Now that the error is known to the opposite party, the dual subjective intentions will, or at least should, normally trump the objective slip of the tongue.

The Restatement of Contracts, which once fought this conclusion, has now adopted this sensible view.[52] The objective theory applies only when one party makes a mistake of which the other is ignorant. It does not dispense with mental states in cases where the second party is aware of the first party's mistake,[53] or from objective circumstances has reason to believe that the offer is too good to be true (as when the buyer "snaps up" the seller's offer for a Rolls Royce at $1,600.00 when $160,000 is the market price).[54]

So arrayed, how do these rules prop up laissez-faire? The objective interpretation of words and conduct reduces communication errors and thus helps both parties realize their subjective desires through exchange. No serious defender of laissez-faire could object to the objective theory suitably qualified. Nor could any opponent of laissez-faire. To be sure, people may wish to ban or restrict certain types of transactions by statute or common law rule. But even if some transactions are deemed exploitive or against public policy, why attack them by criticizing the objective theory of contract interpretation? Even the attackers of freedom of contract should support the security of exchange for that subset of voluntary transactions of which they approve. They too should endorse the traditional mix between subjective and objective interpretation.

To see why, consider that great nineteenth-century classic *Raffles v. Wichelhaus*,[55] which arose when the buyer rejected a shipment of cotton, Bombay ex Peerless, on the Liverpool docks at the height of the United States Civil War. The basic contract did not refer specifically to either the December Peerless (the ship intended by the plaintiff-seller) or the October Peerless (the ship intended by the defendant-buyer). The identification of the ship was surely relevant if one ship lost its cargo at sea. The plaintiff argued that, with the cargo safely delivered, the "ex Peerless" term was at best a minor condition of the contract whose breach (if there were breach) did not allow the buyer to reject the cotton from the later ship, even if he had meant to purchase cotton shipped on the earlier one— a view that Gilmore found persuasive[56] and which Brian Simpson found more problematic.[57] But the court treated the term as essential, just as if the ship was the object of sale, and allowed parol evidence to expose the latent ambiguity that defeated consensus.[58]

The numerous post-mortems on the case often pay too much attention to resolving the particular dispute, and not enough attention to its limited institutional significance.[59] Brian Simpson is the notable exception.[60] As he notes, the identification question can be sidestepped by listing either the name of the captain or the registration number of the ship.[61] No matter whether we endorse the objective or subjective theory of contracts, no one profits from commercial surprises. It is better to ensure correspondence between objective manifestation and subjective intent than to be forced to choose between them when a dispute arises.

This need for avoiding slippage between word and thought takes on added urgency in markets where prices fluctuate widely (as they did during the Civil War, owing to the end of the blockade of the American South) and thus open windows for strategic litigation. Accordingly, we should expect members of trade to take quick institutional measures to eliminate the puzzles that give such delight to lawyers. The thick institutional framework that Lisa Bernstein found in the diamond market in New York City is replicated in the English setting.[62] The critical market development was the final report of a specialized commission, adopted in June 1863, that explicitly incorporated customary practices and required arbitration of all disputes in light thereof "by two respectable brokers."[63] The attendant evolution in standard contract terms, moreover, did not stem from one wayward case but from voluntary action in response to the improvement in sailing vessels and their navigational aids. Greater control over sailing vessels made it possible to key contracts not to the date of departure but to the anticipated arrival date, which has far greater commercial significance in planning for resale or use.[64] These arrival contracts in turn lay at the foundation of the emergence of a systematic market in cotton futures in Liverpool by the mid-1870s, a development that Simpson carefully chronicles.[65] How odd it is to look to the small points of contract law when futures markets are a fixture of all modern economies.

CONTRACTS AT A DISTANCE

Long before laissez-faire, legal systems had to fashion rules for contracts made at a distance. Justinian's *Institutes* begins its discussion of the consensual contracts, such as sale, hire, partnership, and mandate (or agency), with the observation that "[p]arties who are not present together, therefore, can form these contracts by letter, for instance, or by messenger."[66] But the *Institutes* do not elaborate the rules of offer and acceptance, for the Romans took the sensible view that agreement was the ultimate issue, which the trier of fact could find for whatever reason seemed sensible (e.g., the joint acceptance of an offer posed by a neutral third party), an approach which does not quite fit into the offer and acceptance model.

The problem of contracting at a distance also lay at the core of the dispute in which Brian C.J. uttered his devilish aphorism. The plaintiff sued the defendant for trespass for the carrying away of goods. Plaintiff and defendant had bargained in London for the sale of corn, barley, and grass found in a distant field for the sum of 3s. 4d. per acre. Defendant went to the site, viewed the corn, and then gathered it for his own use. His defense to the trespass action interposed a contract that he claimed passed title to him, at the latest when he took possession. The plaintiff's objection was merely that the defendant had not communicated his acceptance to the plaintiff prior to taking the corn. Catesby, the defendant's lawyer, kept stressing that his client had unequivocally indicated his acceptance of the goods by taking them from the field, so that the right action should be for the price, as computed, and not for trespass. On his view, the transaction could be understood to be one in which return communication of an acceptance had been waived, given the defendant's unambiguous overt act, just as, centuries later, in the famous smoke ball case, where acceptance was found in using the smoke ball as requested and not in the return communication.[67] So the real issue is who takes the risk of the slippage from delay brought on by physical separation. Why not side with the defendant who wants to expedite contract formation? From the ex ante perspective, the court could treat the London conversation as forming a binding contract, subject to a satisfactory field inspection. Alternatively, the case could be treated as akin to one where the offer leaves it open to the offeree to decide whether to accept by return promise or by performance.[68]

In fairness, Brian feared that hasty acceptance could influence the sequence of performance. The defendant could take now and pay later, and thereby leave plaintiff an unsecured creditor. But even that point is not decisive, for an acceptance by messenger also creates an unsecured obligation without leaving plaintiff the opportunity to bargain further.

The peculiarities of this transaction to one side, Brian was a stout defender of freedom of contract because he recognized that the parties could have initially stipulated that the defendant could have taken the corn if he liked it, subject only to a bare future obligation to pay. In other words, he was quite prepared to enforce fully executory agreements without security, just like the Romans. His only reluctance was to presume that this agreement took that form. So understood this case is not about the philosophical importance of external appearances. It is about default rules for the order of performance, an issue that retains its salience to this day.

At this point it is instructive to contrast Brian's aphorism with Bowen L.J.'s equally famous bon mot: "The state of a man's mind is as much of a fact as the state of his digestion."[69] This clash of maxims is driven by context, not by any fundamental disagreement in worldview. Bowen's comment was made in a fraud case, where invincible human ignorance, if taken seriously, would block any chance of recovery in all fraud cases. The correct approach treats the question of intention as one of fact, difficult but not impossible to prove. Here again we can detect no transformation of attitudes that hinges on the rise or fall of laissez-faire. It is simply a matter of exercising good common sense on matters of proof. Neither defenders nor opponents of laissez-faire hold any brief for fraud.

In most contract-by-correspondence, unlike Brian's case, the offers to buy and sell contemplate an acceptance by mail to set up a future bilateral transaction. The crucial matter—when is the contract formed?—cannot be resolved simply by finding that single moment in time when the subjective intentions of both parties converge. Adopt the mailbox rule, so that the acceptance is binding when posted, and the offeror is bound even if he changed his mind in the interim. But if the return acceptance must reach the original offeror, then, conversely, the offeree is bound even though he changes his mind before the offeror receives, or reads, the reply.

So which rule is preferable when both present reciprocal risks?[70] The first cue comes from freedom of contract: the offeror, as master of his offer, can stipulate that his personal receipt is required, even in the teeth of his own negligence (as by misstating the return address). The offeree who bristles at this condition need not respond at all. That risk in turn should induce the offeror to sweeten the deal by allowing acceptance at some earlier moment. He may take a greater legal risk to increase his chances of landing a desirable deal. Let offerors adopt different strategies, and the courts should respect a divergence that they may not quite understand.

Empirically, however, most litigated cases contain no special provision on offer and acceptance: cases with specific clauses may just have washed out of the system. But so long as explicit terms govern, then all legal rules assume the status of default provisions. The task is finding the rule that gives the best fit in the routine case and thus reduces the need for contracting out. An observed lack of contractual activity should however not be treated as strong evidence that the common law has gravitated to an efficient rule. The risk of miscarried mail could be so small that neither side finds it worth resolving specifically.

What then are those default rules? One situation involves negligence by offeror or offeree, but hopefully not both. The celebrated case of *Adams v. Lindsell*[71] involved a misdirected and delayed offer followed by a prompt acceptance. (Notwithstanding technical changes, the nineteenth-century English post office seemed to outperform its twentieth-century American rival.) The case thus pits a negligent offeror seeking to escape liability from the responsible offeree who in the interim has resold the goods to a third party. On one reading *Adams* merely assigns the risk of an avoidable loss to the party best able to avoid it. It thus sidesteps the trickier "strict liability" cases when the transmission failure is attributable either to bad weather or to post office error. Who bears the risk of third-party misconduct or natural events?

A second reading of *Adams*, however, downplays the admitted negligence of the defendant-offeror and adopts in its stead a general proposition that contracts are formed when the offeree posts an acceptance. Its short opinion deduces the conclusion philosophically by claiming the defendant's position invites a reductio ad absurdam: "no contract could ever be completed by the post. For if the defendant-offeror were not bound by his offer when accepted by the plaintiff till the answer was received, then the plaintiff ought not to be bound by the acceptance until they had received the notification that the defendants had received their answer and assented to it. And so it might go on ad infinitum."[72]

Adams's sin is an unsound deductive formalism. But how is this the fault of laissez-faire? The sensible response for contracts by correspondence is to choose, as best we can, the rule of contract formation that minimizes the costs of error to both parties. This view allows us still to side with the offeree even if the offeror had not been negligent: the risk of error lies with the party who makes the mistake, period.

Langdell strenuously opposed the mailbox rule on the dubious ground that the acceptance should be treated as a counteroffer that was presumed accepted when it reached the offeror.[73] But he never explained why it is wise to recast what was meant as an acceptance into something else. Even so, Langdell showed one flash of insight that, contrary to Gilmore's unflattering portrait, develops a hesitant error-cost analysis of the alternative rules. Langdell did not warm to his subject graciously, but began with an apology for his functional musings: "The true answer to this argument is, that it is irrelevant. . . ."[74] But like a shrewd lawyer, Langdell hedged his bets by asserting that if convenience did count, then the balance of advantage still did not lie with *Adams v. Lindsell*. Hardship in one direction or another is inevitable, so what are the choices?

> Adopting one view, the hardship consists in making one liable on a contract which he is ignorant of having made; adopting the other view, it consists in depriving one of the benefit of a contract which he supposes he has made. Between these two evils the choice would seem to be clear: the former is positive, the latter merely negative; the former imposes a liability to which no limit can be placed; the latter leaves everything *in statu quo*. As to making provision for the contingency of the miscarriage of a letter, this is easy for the person who sends it, while it is practically impossible for the person to whom it is sent.[75]

This passage transforms Langdell into an unwitting precursor of the law-and-economics movement. He urges that the error costs are greater from enforcing the contract than letting it pass. He may be wrong in thinking that the language of "positive" and "negative" losses clinches the idea that the offeree's uncompensated loss from losing the action will be smaller than the amount of damages, especially when *Hadley v. Baxendale* limits recovery. Nor does this proposition easily mesh with Langdell's repeated invocation of the Roman maxim *ut res magis valeat quam pereat*—it is better that the affair be valid than perish.[76] The relevance of error costs, apart from knowledge of their frequency, magnitude, and direction, is not decisive either way. But his second point, that the original offeror has the capacity to shape the rule to his own advantage, retains its persuasive power even today.

This last point led Baron Bramwell to inveigh against the mailbox interpretation of *Adams v. Lindsell* in *British & American Telegraph Co. v. Colson*,[77] which Cheshire and Fifoot chastise for its regrettable tendency "to champion the cause of 'real' consent,"[78] in opposition to the sounder view that finds the mark of contract in external appearances. But can we disagree with Bramwell's preferred rule without questioning his devotion to laissez-faire? *Colson* arose when the post office delivered the plaintiff's acceptance of an allotment of shares to the wrong address. The defendant, when thereafter pressed, refused to take up the subscription and offered a catalog of reasons why the misdelivery occurred: someone else with the same name lived on the same street; the numbers had just been changed; extensive construction was going on nearby to add to the confusion; and a number of his other letters had been similarly misdirected. Bramwell first noted that this case lacked the offeror's negligence found in *Adams v. Lindsell*. He then argued in effect that the offeree is the cheaper cost avoider, so that liability should be postponed until the offeror receives the acceptance: "The sender of the letter [of acceptance] need not use the public post. If he does, he may guard against mistake by sending two letters, or requesting an answer and sending another on a non-receipt of an answer, or by taking other steps to ascertain the arrival or non-arrival of the letter, and to remedy the mischief of the latter event. But the person to whom it is addressed can do absolutely nothing; for by the hypothesis he does not know it has been sent."[79]

This functional argument hardly shows any excessive devotion to some ideal of real, let alone, mystical consent. But however sensible his basic orientation, Bramwell's oversight lies in his claim that the original sender can do nothing, which implicitly places the capacity to avoid harm on one party only. Although the original offeror can do nothing after the offeree receives his letter, he could have protected himself earlier in the process by stating that he will only distribute the shares if confirmation reaches him by a fixed date. The defendant had no reason to couch his solicitation as an offer instead of the so-called "invitation to treat" that becomes binding only when accepted by the solicitor. So in the abstract we really cannot decide who is the cheaper cost avoider after all, or even who is an offeror, and who an offeree.

These difficulties explain the lack of convergence on a single default rule. The correct choice remains problematic even today when scholars have identified the relevant variables. But it is a mistake to tarry too much in the search for optimal solutions, for the twisted history of contracts by correspondence should be taken as yet another illustration of the same institutional truth found in *Raffles*. Once the obviously unsatisfactory rules are eliminated, any variation in the choice of default rules is akin to shifting water from one shoulder to the other. The water is heavy no matter where it comes to rest. The surviving competitors are so evenly balanced that the water weighs about the same no matter which shoulder bears the brunt of the load. However, the central business mission is to reduce the total risk, not to shift its incidence from one shoulder, or one side, to the other. The risk is much reduced today, since phones, faxes, and express services have closed the temporal gap between offer and acceptance. Indeed, when the question does pop up, the context is just as likely to be directed to a jurisdictional or choice-of-law issue, asking whose law governs an admitted agreement.[80]

More generally, the prolonged battle over offer and acceptance has little to do with the rights and wrongs of laissez-faire. Any legal order has to search for the right rule on formation of contracts at a distance in order to promote the security of exchange. Getting that rule right, however, has no direct bearing on the more contentious issue of freedom of contract. As with slips of tongue and pen, the rejection of the doctrines of laissez-faire does not require us to reconsider the mailbox rule or its alternative. No matter how the class of valid contracts is defined, why follow an inefficient rule when only security of exchange is in issue? A modernist need not oppose a rule of offer and acceptance just because Bramwell or Langdell favored it. Parallel conclusions apply to the doctrine of consideration to which we now turn.

CONSIDERATION

The doctrine of consideration occupies a large, if somewhat undeserved, place in the history of Anglo-American contract law. The traditional legal rule holds first that mere, or "bare," promises were unenforceable. This rule in turn requires an account of what acts or forms so clothe a promise as to render it enforceable. Consideration is said to supply the needed raiments.

Early on, the term *consideration* seemed to suggest a diffuse meaning of "cause," which allowed enforcement of promises made for good reason whether or not they formed the part of some bargain.[81] Debates swirled around the enforcement of a promise made in consideration of a future marriage (which were on occasion allowed),[82] or a promise to pay for the receipt of some past unrequested service (for which relief was generally denied).[83]

The tension between the moral obligation to perform these promises and the legal right to ignore them has generated extensive commentary.[84] Perhaps the best explanation is that, in the context of family transactions, these promises will usually be performed except where some change in family circumstances or some hidden form of familial pressure justifies nonperformance. The overbroad rule remains in effect because its error costs are low: promisors want to perform promises borne of natural love and affection, and typically balk only where circumstances are fishy. Since the law cannot improve the background practice, it steers clear of the field. The social sanctions work well even if, perhaps because, the legal sanctions are put to one side. But there is always a hitch: the promisor may die and the executor of the estate may not perform the decedent's promise under pressure from the estate's beneficiaries.

By degrees consideration became less tied to "good reasons" and more tied to the idea of bargain or exchange: the promise was enforceable because it was supported by some return promise or act. At this point the doctrine of consideration was no longer so closely linked to family arrangements. Rather, consideration became a general principle of promissory enforcement. Langdell, for example, used that principle to justify enforcement of promises to perform preexisting duties.[85] In his view, making a second promise does impose real constraints on the promisor "by giving another person the right to compel him to do it, or the right to recover damages against him for not doing it."

The analysis of the preexisting duty controversy in turn raises the larger issue of why allow the executory enforcement of any promises at all. On this question, Langdell has been roundly attacked for being both logically incoherent and necessarily circular.[86] The logical circularity lies in the fact that one has to assume that A's promise is enforceable (for it to be a detriment) in order for B's promise to be enforceable. But A's promise is not enforceable unless by parity of reasoning B's promise is enforceable as well. So the enforcement of each promise is said to presume the validity of the other; hence the validity of neither is established.

This formal objection is a poor way to undercut Langdell's commercial judgment, just as it is a bad way to critique his position on contracts by correspondence. A better approach asks what theory of bargains between A and B promotes overall social convenience. One solution is to say that neither promise is enforceable, eliminating all gains from future trades, to no one's benefit. A second alternative is to hold that the promise of either A or B, but not both, is enforceable. At this point either A or B, and perhaps both, will steer away from transactions that could promise them all pain and no gain, once again frustrating the emergence of trade.

So it hardly takes a shrewd and determined utilitarian to realize that the fourth solution, which Langdell embraced, is best. Where two promises are meant to be part of an integrated transaction, enforcing both preserves the gains from trade, a result that is consistent with laissez-faire and with any other political system that wants to nurture an exchange economy. Langdell's mistake was not in outcome but in tying it to some transcendent legal principle. The wise court thus makes itself the servant of the parties. Since they can be (accurately) presumed to desire enforcement of these bargains, then enforce them, unless there is some strong reason of public policy to do otherwise. If the parties believe that courts are dangerous places to resolve commercial disagreements, then they can specify arbitration, or deny any intention to create legal relations in what otherwise looks to be a standard commercial context.[87] In the end, legal enforcement should not depend on meeting some external norm but should reflect what the parties want. Legal enforcement of bargains becomes a powerful default rule, to which exceptions should be clearly manifested.

Frederick Pollock was alert to the ostensible circularity of consideration, which he called "the secret paradox of the common law." Pollock also rued the proposition that "in fact there is no conclusive reason other than the convenience of so holding."[88] But why is social convenience the mark of a feeble legal theory? Joint convenience supplies ample reason for aligning law to social practice. And the logical objections to the rule have never led anyone to alter or abandon the rule of executory enforcement. The real difficulty lies with placing consideration at the center of the commercial system. A test that examines the intention to create legal relations in commercial contexts is freed of the logical conundrums. And it well tracks the commercial expectations of the parties to most agreements.

To be sure, enforcing executory promises does not settle all doctrinal issues. Our moral instincts become far shakier (as the utilitarian consequences become far less clear) when the debate shifts from the enforcement of promises to the sequence of performance. Must A and B perform simultaneously? Should A perform first? If he must, then what are B's options when A's performance is only partial and not complete. In principle, each variation is a node on some perfect decision tree. But relying on decision trees unintended by the parties is a risky enterprise at best. It invites default rules to specify how B may respond to A's imperfect performance: is B excused from performance, or must B perform as well and settle for a reduction in price, or an action in damages?

Answering these questions takes time and patience. It raises certain questions to which the phrase "sanctity of contract" gives only a partial answer.[89] But for our purposes the basic point is again simple: no political philosophy would consciously set its face against the parties' preference for the enforcement of fully executory, legal promises. Use explicit substantive prohibitions against those contracts—gambling, prostitution, child labor, and drinking were nineteenth-century favorites—disliked for substantive reasons. But do not impair contractual efficiency where freedom of contract is preserved. Enforcing executory exchanges supported by consideration advances the security of exchange, which should be prized in every legal system, regardless of its attitude toward freedom of contract.

Consideration also has its "bad," or at least troublesome side: the refusal to enforce promises not supported by consideration. This nineteenth-century defect was trumpeted first by Gilmore[90] and then, in expanded fashion, by Atiyah.[91] Both insist that the limitations of the classical theory of contract have been overrun on two sides. First, on the detriment side, promissory estoppel today allows for the enforcement of a promise on which the promisee has justly relied. Second, on the benefit side, conferring a benefit on the defendant for which the defendant then promises to pay creates an enforceable obligation. The point holds even where the law of restitution does not permit a plaintiff to recover for the benefit conferred in the absence of the subsequent promise to pay. In tandem these two doctrines have been hailed as a sea change from the narrow theories of responsibility championed by Holmes and Williston to the more enlightened theories of Corbin and Cardozo.[92]

What should be made of this shift? Very little, in the grand scheme of things. First, adding two novel heads of liability does nothing to compromise the enforcement of fully executory bargains. We simply have more routes to promissory liability. Put more baldly, the emergence of promissory estoppel was not suppressed until the 1930s debates over Section 90 of the Restatement. Rather, Corbin insisted that he worked to codify the earlier judicial acceptance of promissory estoppel. Second, these two new theories of liability have scant importance relative to commercial bargains which cover sales, leases, mortgages, partnerships, hire, and countless other collaborative arrangements for mutual gain through voluntary cooperation. Executory enforcement allows both sides to rely on the security of a promise in their committing resources to some common venture, expanding the scope of trade by reducing the likelihood of breach. This universe offers very few occasions to enforce promises under theories of promissory estoppel or, especially, prior benefit. Third, from the vantage of laissez-faire, why place limit on the class of enforceable promises? Lord Mansfield favored enforcing all serious commercial promises (perhaps subject to a writing requirement) wholly without regard to the presence or absence of consideration.[93] The nineteenth-century English reaction notwithstanding,[94] why was Lord Mansfield wrong in theory?

The key question asks why freedom of contract requires any doctrine of consideration at all. Kessler and Gilmore sensed the tension when they wrote: "Freedom of contact, even during the period when laissez-faire had its greatest triumphs, never succeeded in overcoming a deep-rooted suspicion on the part of the common law against the social desirability of enforcing one-sided or gratuitous promises, as contrasted with reciprocal bargains."[95] But why so, at least in the commercial context? The point hardly squares with any basic philosophical commitment to contractual self-determination. Even in the absence of consideration, the defendant must first consent to be bound, and thus cannot be stripped of his primary means of self-protection: do not make promises that you do not intend to keep. And the practical questions of proof are better handled by a writing both for sales and nonbargain transactions. So why oppose any expansion of the class of enforceable promises in the name of freedom of contract?

One reason for this caution is indirect: bare promises commonly fall prey to coercion and manipulation. But although this point has force in family contexts, it hardly follows that the routine informal adjustments in commercial settings should be invalidated on a wholesale basis. The problems run in both directions. Consideration would enforce some transactions that should be cut down, and it cuts down other transactions that should survive. On the first side, it is quite easy to "hold-up" a trading partner in renegotiation without running afoul of the consideration requirement, whose adequacy is, in the tradition of Hobbes, not a judicial issue. The aggressive holdout can happily agree to perform some small additional obligation as the price for extracting some very large payment. Thus, even with doctrine of consideration firmly entrenched, we still need some account of economic duress to deal with cases where the threat to breach a promise is used to secure renegotiation of an existing agreement. All defenders of freedom of contract should be sensitive to this risk.

On the other hand, many so-called bare promises carry no whiff of coercion. In *The Death of Contract*, Gilmore discusses at length the famous renegotiation in *Stilk v. Myrick*,[96] where a portion of the crew had deserted the ship when moored in Cronstadt, a Russian port. In response the captain offered to divide the salary of the deserters among the crew who remained to guide the ship back home. It is doubtful that the desertion of some crew members released others from their obligation. Accordingly, the remaining crew did not extend fresh consideration since they were already bound to provide additional services. Yet it was good business for the captain to promise additional wages to improve the chances of a safe voyage home. The fact that the captain's total wage bill did not increase under the revised agreement negates any risk of untoward extraction. Indeed, whenever the increase in payment offered is proportionate to the increased costs imposed on the original performers, the renegotiation looks as though it helps, not hinders business efficacy. The want of consideration is a poor proxy for holdout behavior, just as presence of consideration is a weak proxy for the absence of holdout behavior. In both cases the task is to trace the pattern of negotiation in relation to the perceived risks. Although occasional errors mar that inquiry, the cases have generally done well.[97] Consideration does not have a bedrock role to play in responding to coercion during contract modification.

We can now put both detriment-based and benefit-based doctrines in perspective. Promissory estoppel allows enforcement of a few stray promises after the plaintiff has performed or changed position. Stated otherwise, courts often suspend the requirement of "mutuality": no longer is the promisor free because the promisee was not bound. Even though mutuality often captures commercial intentions in a world of self-interested behavior, it is only a first approximation, not a sine qua non for rational behavior. Often hopes for indirect benefit and the creation of good generate a desire to create free options in other individuals. A firm offer left open for a definite period of time is one such example. The nature of the interaction generates a level of protection for both sides. The offeror can limit the time that the offer remains open (or the time that goods will be kept "on hold" for a particular customer). Even so, he runs some risk that offer will be rejected, while another sale was foreclosed. So a merchant or trader is likely to make a firm offer only to someone likely to consider it seriously. The additional legal risk yields an increased probability of acceptance. On the other side, an offeree who takes up idle offers spends resources that yield no return. So firm offers are not costless to those who receive them. The process is thus bounded by powerful institutional constraints, so why preclude anyone from making that offer binding unless he receives consideration in exchange? All in all, this expansion of liability should be regarded as compatible with the doctrines of freedom of contract, not as its enemy. The Corbinized world gives a greater scope to promissory liability than the Williston vision, and is in every particular consistent with robust markets. The parties who do not want to be parties to unilateral arrangements do not have to make them.

The overall analysis does not change with benefit-based liability. This boomlet is intimately connected with the well-known case of *Webb v. McGowin*,[98] where an employer promised a small pension to an employee who quite literally put himself in the path of injury to prevent still greater harm to the employer. The promise was serious when made, and honored by the promisor until his death. When his executor, perhaps subject to the familiar family pressures, sought to renege, he was forced to honor the employer's promise. A new Restatement provision, section 89A, was drafted to celebrate the occasion.[99] But this mini-revolution does not deserve to be trumpeted in any larger debate over the role of contract in social affairs. First, the liability in question is promissory: the act of rescue did not generate in and of itself a claim for restitution. Second, the relevant class of cases is so small that it hardly alters the fundamental balance of contract law. Nothing about laissez-faire blocks this expansion of promissory liability, so long as the usual excusing conditions are allowed for this as for other promises.

So once the dust settles it is clear that the developments here bear little relationship to the "death" in *The Death of Contract* or to the "fall" in *The Rise and Fall of Freedom of Contract*. Both of these volumes may cheer the decline of laissez-faire, but only by adopting the odd position that its demise rests in the expansion of promissory liability. Laissez-faire writers focused their fire on rules and regulation that restricted the enforcement of promises, and which allowed states to determine the shape of markets and to set prices and wages for goods and services. The nineteenth-century corn laws, which restricted the entry of grain into Great Britain, were one notable target. To my knowledge, not one of them cared about legal developments that were small in magnitude and favorable in direction. To find any challenge to the traditional laissez-faire doctrines, we have to look to cases that challenge the sanctity of contract. That is the topic of the next section.

IV   The Sanctity of Contract

The previous sections have shown how the security of exchange is a paramount objective for all legal systems, whether or not they embrace laissez-faire. They also examined the extent to which traditional doctrines of offer and acceptance, and consideration, fit into that overall framework. The more distinctive portions of laissez-faire, however, relate to two additional doctrines, one the sanctity of contract and the second its broader and distinctive claim of freedom of contract.

Sanctity of contract is best analyzed in two separate parts. The first examines the set of excuses a defendant may interpose for the nonperformance of a contractual undertaking. The second asks how far a party is entitled to deviate unilaterally (i.e., without the consent of the other party) from a contractual undertaking while still claiming the benefits under that contract. Does laissez-faire require a narrow set of contractual excuses, and exact performance of contractual undertakings?

The scope of permissible excuses is a topic of major importance not only in contract law but also in torts. As early as 1616, *Weaver v. Ward*[100] allowed some form of inevitable accident, narrowly construed, to excuse a defendant from tort liability: the defendant who had to cause harm no matter what he did was excused from the harm in question.[101] In contrast, however, the legal response to promissory obligations has long been somewhat different. In 1647 *Paradine v. Jane*[102] contrasted the tort defendant with the contract defendant:

> where the law creates a duty or charge, and the party is disabled to perform it without any default in him, and hath no remedy over, there the law will excuse him . . . but when the party by his own contract creates a duty or charge upon himself, he is bound to make it good, if he may, notwithstanding any accident by inevitable necessity, because he might have provided against it by his contract. And therefore if the lessee covenant to repair a house, though it be burnt by lightening or thrown down by enemies, yet he ought to repair it.[103]

Public duty and private agreement each have their separate excuses. The law allows excuses, albeit very narrow ones, for public duties (such as guarding prisoners in time of war), on the ground that the law cannot demand any individual to perform the impossible.[104] Indeed, when *Paradine* speaks of the law creating a duty or charge, it is uncertain whether it refers to tort obligations to compensate for harms caused, or, as seems more likely, public obligations to protect against certain forms of harm in some official capacity or role. But this ambiguity does not carry over to contractual duties, where the promisor possesses the right denied to persons burdened with public duties, namely, to bargain on his own behalf.

Even that view has not been consistently followed. For example, the Roman law held those obligations which were truly impossible to perform—such as touching the sky with one's finger—were void ab initio.[105] That legal response has no bite if it only blocks a decree of specific performance, which could not be discharged even if ordered. Rather, its novelty lies in the denial of damages to the promisee, even though the unwise promisor could have protected himself by agreement. That view of objective, or literal, impossibility carried over into the English law before laissez-faire, and is clearly expressed in Powell's 1790 treatise on contractual obligations.[106] The sanctity of contract never required some remedy for the nonperformance of the impossible.

But this conceptual curiosity should not be allowed to conceal the main point. Who would bother to undertake the sterile obligation to touch the sky if he were certain to breach it? Alternatively, who could ever sensibly rely on its promised performance? So it hardly matters whether we enforce a set of promises that are never made, or refuse to enforce them on the ground that they are wholly idle. Either way, the level of observed transactions will be zero. The matter will forever be one of speculation and never of litigation.

In the commercially relevant cases, however, both the Roman and English traditions enforced promises capable of performance, even if it were impossible for this defendant to perform it. The usual example was a promise to convey land in fact owned by another.[107] Now, this promise gives information about capability not apparent from the general nature of things. So all the legal bite comes from treating these promises as categorically enforceable. Wherein lies the attractiveness of so doing? To stress that the promisor could have stipulated for some excuse does not supply the needed philosophical foundations for the rule. Why should promises for the performance of some particular event not be subject to an implied condition of defeasance? These conditions are implicit in many ordinary understandings: who thinks in 1800 or today that physicians guarantee cure instead of making a promise of due care?[108] If these conditions are implicit in some contexts, then why not require the promisee to ask for the ironclad assurances that the crown, or state, does not extract from its subjects or citizens? So understood the default rule of no excuses loses much of its formal appeal, even though it has been numbly repeated countless times since *Paradine*.

But what rule should take its place? The basic truth is that default rules never raise fundamental philosophical issues about the institution of promising: filling gaps or divining intention when the parties are silent is at best a second-order affair. Indeed, so long as the topic is inevitable necessity, the background presumption is not that critical. The correct choice is hard to determine, and any choice may be freely varied by contract. The tort debate between negligence and strict liability has been so closely divided because of the genuine uncertainty as to whether the residual risk in a stranger case should fall on the injurer or injured party, when the defendant has exercised the same level of care that he would take in his own affairs.

With contracts, however, the contexts are much more richly variegated. Even philosophical skeptics of absolute promissory obligations are usually unwilling to discharge many contractual obligations whenever the defendant exercised all reasonable care: the default rule for medical services does not carry over to the payment of money, the delivery of goods, or the construction of a waterproof roof. Usually some higher standard of liability is invoked, even if it is not clear exactly what that standard should be. But the range of permissible variation makes it hard to treat the sanctity of a promise as a necessary precondition for the success of markets, or even as an accurate rendition of the ordinary commercial understandings. Contexts matter. How might these be broken down? One approach is to break down the obstacle to contractual performance into problems whose source lies (1) with the defendant, (2) with the plaintiff, and (3) with a third party or in some act of God. What presumption should be set for each case?

For the first class of cases, the usual view saddles the defendant with the risk of nonperformance. He has the greatest knowledge and control of his capabilities and resources, and it seems odd that he could shift the risk of his nonperformance to the plaintiff who has neither. But some exceptions to this general rule may make sense. If the defendant contracts to draw the plaintiff's portrait, and is killed or disabled thereafter in a road accident, the usual view discharges the basic obligation completely. Who would choose death or serious disability in order to escape a promise which, in the general case, he wants to make and keep?[109] Nor does a release in this context give the promisor an opportunity to enter into some new lucrative engagement. Nor is it likely that an executor or caretaker could paint as well as the original promisor. The release of the obligation thus eliminates some nettlesome litigation and costly damages calculations, without undermining the basic obligation to perform. So the discharge clearly makes sense, whether or not one believes in laissez-faire.

The companion question is whether the death of the paying party also terminates the contract. Here, of course, the ability to pay money is never rendered literally impossible, so the buyer's estate should be able to require the painting of a landscape. But if the contract were for a portrait of the deceased, and the arrangement were executory, then perhaps the deal should be called off—unless the portrait could be painted from photographs or other sources. Of course some compensation might be owed for any reimbursable expenses that the painter incurred in good faith prior to the subject's death, as in Roman law.[110] Perhaps my instinct on some of these variations is wrong, but for the grand questions at hand it hardly matters. We are lost in the sea of implied contracts, as in *The Moorcock*, with an eye toward the business efficacy of the entire arrangement.[111] As the variations become more complex, the intuitions become less robust, which is as it should be when so little is at stake. It is a happy concordance that intuitions on default are strongest in the most frequent cases, and most difficult to resolve in the suits that are selected for litigation.

In the second case, the difficulty is attributable to the default, or at least the conduct, of the plaintiff. Take, for example, a construction contract that calls for the builder to erect a structure on the buyer-owner's lot, which is unbuildable because of some latent defect in the soil. The nineteenth-century cases often denied the builder any portion of the contract price from the landowner if the promised building was not completed,[112] even though some cases that reiterated the *Paradine* theme only demanded strict performance "unless prevented by the act of God, the law, or the other party to the contract."[113] The builder had to firm up the foundations on the owner's site at his own cost.

This approach clearly seems to be wrong. Typically, the landowner has greater knowledge and control over the site and hence should, in the absence of a stipulation to the contrary, take the risk that it will not support his proposed building. That position would allow the builder to recover, if not the full contract price, his actual expenditures plus lost profits until the project is called to a halt. The modern builders' contract is typically written in this fashion unless the builder is charged with the preliminary site investigation. Invoking the maxim that the builder could have protected himself by contract rings hollow; ditto for the owner. But either way, little is at stake for the principle of laissez-faire when a stroke of the pen can reverse an unwise nineteenth-century presumption.

When performance is rendered impossible by the conduct of some third party or an act of God, the analysis becomes more uncertain. The contingency is not within the obvious control of either party, nor is it easy to determine who can predict its occurrence with greater accuracy, or for that matter who can insure against the risk. Indeed, capacities could be split: one party can better insure against the risk that the other is better able to prevent. So what should be done?

For starters, *Paradine*, a case of third-party risk, was correctly decided. The lease transferred possession of land for a limited period of time. The landlord did not owe the tenant any service obligations. Hence the term of years becomes, as an estate in land, the thing sold. Normally the owner of a thing takes the risk of its destruction—res perit domino. The lease creates two owners, the tenant for his term and the landlord for the reversion. The tenant would surely bear the risk of loss for the term if he made a lump-sum purchase of the term. What difference is there if the payments are called rent and staggered over the duration of the lease? The purchaser of the fee simple takes the risk of loss even on an installment sale. Why not follow the same rule for leases? The situation would be different if the landlord had service obligations that were discharged by the destruction of the property, for then the best default rule reduces the rent by the amount of the services paid or discharges the lease entirely. But *Paradine* raises no service issues, so the decision seems right, wholly apart from any question of impossibility.

It is an open question whether the same result carries over to the controversial case of *Hall v. Wright*,[114] where the court refused to release the defendant from his contract to marry the plaintiff even though he could only consummate the marriage at great risk to his own health. Who believes that this condition does not excuse? Do we think that a defendant will fake death or illness to avoid marriage? And why damages if the plaintiff is free to marry another? Baron Pollock, no opponent of freedom of contract, dissented, protesting the false assimilation of personal into commercial contracts.[115] The twentieth-century view to the contrary hardly shakes laissez-faire to its foundations,[116] but turns a sensible dissenting opinion into law.

Even in its own time, *Hall v. Wright* did not establish any blanket prohibition against recognizing implied conditions. *Taylor v. Caldwell*,[117] decided in 1863, invoked an implied condition to defeat the otherwise categorical obligation to pay rent on premises accidentally destroyed before the plaintiff's planned gala. Here the possession of a music hall remained with the landlord; the obligations in question were for a short term—four days of grand concerts and festivities—that look service-intensive. The rule of joint discharge makes each side lick its wounds. But it also gives both sides the strongest incentives to mitigate losses after destruction, and the rule reduces the administrative costs by simplifying the accounting on discharge. Holding that the destruction of the premises be without fault of the defendant guards against the risk of moral hazard, although truth be known, the negligence condition here does not have much bite: what defendant would destroy his own premises to escape a profitable four-day engagement? Any explicit ex ante bargain could easily stipulate that both parties go their separate ways, which also happens when a building is destroyed before the defendant can begin repairs.[118] In any recurrent institutional setting, once bitten, twice shy. In future cases this remote risk will be allocated by contractual terms that either affirm or reject the excusing condition. But no public policy limitations surface. The choice of default provision may provide fertile grist for legal argument, but it has little if any relevance to the grand structure of laissez-faire.

UNILATERAL ALTERATION OF TERMS

Sanctity of contract raises a more urgent theme when a party seeks, not discharge, but unilateral variation from the initial contractual terms. Of course, it is well understood that circumstances may make it impossible to perform a specific undertaking: property may be destroyed before it is conveyed; workers may quit before they discharge their appointed tasks; ships may encounter bad weather. In those cases where the breach is against the will of the promisor, then damages must be substituted for performance. In many cases the parties might seek to protect the expectation of the promise by setting damages that in theory (but rarely in fact) leave the jilted promisee indifferent between performance and breach. But in principle the parties should be able to decide what happens if performance is blocked or made more costly for reasons beyond the promisor's control.

It is at this juncture that some of the most difficult questions of contract law arise. Thus suppose that the defendant can deliver goods that deviate from the contract stipulation by some small degree. No. 2 cotton is substituted for No. 3 cotton. Promised goods are one day late, or must be shipped by rail instead of boat. One obvious response is to use cash allowances to offset the difference, if any, between the performance promised and the performance delivered. Yet to confer this option as of right to the party in breach carries with it this oddity: the party in breach can force the innocent party to take goods or services on new terms to which it never consented—such is the effect of a cash reduction against the late delivery of goods. A belief in the sanctity of contract gives all the cards to the innocent party. Once the defendant does not perform just as promised, the plaintiff as the innocent party has the election to take expectation damages or to throw off the bargain altogether. The familiar refrain is: "Where parties have made an agreement for themselves, the courts ought not to make another one for them."[119] Doubly so, at the insistence of the party in breach.

Will the promisee typically exercise this newfound right of rejection? Truth is, usually he won't. In most cases getting goods late is better than getting no goods at all, so this breach is often waived for just that reason. Where it is not, then a "just in time" inventory policy will set out stringent conditions for suppliers. But every strategy is vulnerable to unfortunate outcomes in at least some cases. Perhaps the market price has broken between promise and delivery, so that the fortuitous opportunity to reject goods allows the plaintiff to insulate himself from the adverse price shifts that would have been his lot if sound goods had been delivered on time[120] or had been shipped in the stipulated way.[121] Recall that *Raffles v. Wichelhaus* was such a case. The "perfect tender" rule developed in the nineteenth-century cases allowed the plaintiff to ditch the losing contract for reasons that had little or nothing to do with the defect in the timing or quality of the goods. By giving the innocent party an undeserved "out," does this rule undermine the security of exchange in the guise of protecting it? Stated otherwise, why does the perfect tender rule become the default position?

Here the choice is close, but some strong argument supports the hard-line position on perfect tender. The first point to note is that our intuitive reaction varies between two extreme cases: in the first, the tendered performance is identical in all relevant respects to the promised performance, notwithstanding some formal deviation in contract terms. That was what happened, for example, in *Jacobs & Young v. Kent*,[122] where Judge Cardozo allowed the defendant to wiggle out of his breach because of the precise equivalence between the Cohoes and the

Reading Pipe. At the other extreme the market price remains dead level, so that any deviation in quality forces the innocent to accept a compromise with the promised goods. Just how much of an offset should be made in these cases if the formica comes in yellow instead of brown? If aesthetic beams are discolored in some public hall?[123] Here the willingness to hold the defendant to the precise terms of the bargain reduces the likelihood of breach in the first place. And the risk that the promisee will take the larger damages (cost of completion, not diminution in market value) and pocket them, could be blocked by having the promisor make the corrections instead of paying over the cash, or by making payment of the cash conditional on the use of the funds to secure corrections. Where the substitute performance is identical to that bargained for, the cases will be few and far between in which the defendant will reject the performance, even to avoid the last installment on the construction price.

The modern efficiency analysis of these outlying cases is inconclusive in the outcome.[124] Taken in the round, it seems that the legal rules should be tailored for the typical situation, stable markets, and not for the atypical volatile ones. The parties are already sensitive to risks of gamesmanship when prices shift rapidly, as they did for the cotton markets in Liverpool. But for that ill, some institutional response is needed, not some doctrinal refinement. So on balance the nineteenth-century rule seems correct after all. But either way, commerce can adapt in ways to overcome any mistakes stemming from the initial use of the wrong presumption.

DELIBERATE BREACH

The Holmesian Heresy. Sanctity of contract becomes a far more tenacious principle whenever the defendant plans a deliberate breach to take advantage of some better contractual opportunity elsewhere. In this context, widespread scorn has been heaped on Justice Holmes's famous aphorism: "The only universal consequence of a legally binding promise is, that the law makes the promisor pay damages if the promised event does not come to pass. In every case it leaves him free from interference until the time for fulfillment has gone by, and therefore free to break his contract if he chooses."[125] Stated in this fashion, the party in breach, not the innocent party, enjoys all the options. How could nineteenth-century law do so strong an about-face after its endorsement of the perfect tender rule? The answer is that it did not.

Entire Contracts. The weakness of Holmes's position is evident from the recurrent nineteenth-century disputes over the wage contracts for hired hands, an issue that Holmes nowhere addresses in *The Common Law.* A farmer hires a worker for an entire year for room and board and a salary of $10 per month. After ten months the hired hand quits and demands payment of $100 for the time already worked. The farmer is usually held not to owe anything, even for the benefit previously received, because the obligation is "entire," and thus need be paid only at the end of the year, much like the modern "bonus."

As early as 1470, Choke, J. denied an action in debt to a priest who chanted for the soul of the departed for only six months, after having promised to do so for a year. "This duty is entire, and he must serve for a year or otherwise he will have no salary; and he cannot have his salary until he has served his term."[126] This rule remained intact until the nineteenth century. Then some cases, most notably *Britton v. Turner*,[127] allowed the action in quantum meruit for the time worked, subject to a deduction for the farmer's additional costs in hiring substitute labor, no small matter for workers who leave just at harvest time when spot wages are highest. Most cases denied recovery to the worker as a plaintiff in breach (but none ever required him to refund the value of room and board received during his stay).[128]

Gilmore, for one, treats the entire contract as a sign of the misguided nineteenth-century synthesis, and much prefers the rule that allows for quasi-contractual relief.[129] Why?[130] Typically, these are not cases of impossibility or anything close to that. The standard doctrine did allow the worker to recover his wages if the farmer's misconduct chased him from his job before the end of service, and it thereby sought to control employer abuse.[131] But the greater risk lay in workers leaving for a short-term gain,[132] and in these cases the customary practice supports the view that only workers who worked out their term could collect the cash bonus.[133] "The plaintiff might as well claim his wages by the month as by the year, by the week as by the month, and by the day or hour as by either."[134] Indeed, it is a mistake to import restitution into contract when the parties have allocated the risk of loss by contract.[135] Restitution works best for the return of money paid under mistake, or the reimbursement of expenditures made in conditions of necessity for the benefit of the defendant. But it should not override contracts whose provisions govern the contingency. The option to negotiate a lower salary for an early departure remains available to workers anxious to try their luck elsewhere. Once again, the courts neither make contracts for the parties nor allow one party to remake a contract in its own image.

Efficient Breach. A second offshoot of the famous Holmes dictum is the now storied doctrine of "efficient breach." The doctrine praises defendants who deliberately breach contracts so long as they pay plaintiff full expectation damages and come away with a net profit to themselves.[136] This idealized argument rests upon a conception of economic efficiency which has the breaching party better off in consequence of its action and the innocent party no worse off, given the compensation. The doctrine is in obvious tension with nineteenth-century thought, which for all its affinities to laissez-faire strongly condemned the Holmes dictum because it allowed the wrongdoer to profit from his own wrong.

That nineteenth-century position is correct both for moral and economic reasons. The wheels of commerce work best when social pressures support the faithful performance of promises with a minimum of legal compulsion and interference. To adopt a rule that invites breach on payment gives rise to the obvious question, how much should be paid, and when? The rule also allows promisors to be the arbiter of when they perform and when they pay, sharply contrary to the global expectations in standard commercial transactions. Theory aside, contract damages, as administered, often fail to bring the plaintiff to the position he would have enjoyed if the transaction were completed. Administrative costs often block suit even for an ironclad case. The contract measure of damages often excludes certain real losses that are not in the joint contemplation of the parties. The experience and contacts gained from one job often provide the gateway to the second, and these indirect gains are lost if expectation damages are calibrated to the discrete transaction.

It is therefore easy to imagine situations where the following inequalities hold: plaintiff's recovery is smaller than the defendant's gain, so the defendant will breach. But defendant's gain in turn is smaller than plaintiff's (uncompensated) losses, so that the breach is inefficient. It should surely give champions of the efficient breach some pause that Lisa Bernstein reports that in trade (in her case through the National Feed and Grain Association) the only breaches that are tolerated are those which are done when the defendant has no prospect of gain but is, for example, unable to obtain needed supplies.[137] With unavoidable breaches, the relationship is preserved, and damages, as determined in arbitration, are used for an offset of loss. But deliberate ones, succumbing to the temptation to breach for gain when performance is possible so disturbs the social fabric within the trading community, creating dislocations up and down the line, that the group response is to drum the opportunist out of the trade. This bifurcated legal response thus captures the deserved ambiguities that shroud the term *opportunity*. To take advantage of opportunities is an unalloyed good. But to be an opportunist (that is, to act in breach of a norm) carries with it the kinds of negative connotations that should never be overlooked.

The doctrine of efficient breach may be faulted on other grounds. By allowing easy exit from contractual undertakings, it may induce people to enter casually into arrangements taken seriously by the other side. As applied, it also allocates all the gains from breach to the party in breach, even if for some reason it gives full compensation. The doctrine encourages individuals to profit from their own wrong, and thus clashes with the moral view of laissez-faire, which aspires to create a commercial atmosphere that reduces the reliance on legal mechanisms by an appeal to a common commercial morality.

To fortify those instincts, the expectation measure is often bolstered by specific performance and injunctions. Holmes had acknowledged the role of the former, but dismissed its moral significance by noting that it was available only in select cases, while damages were the universal remedy.[138] The better explanation is that specific performance is out when parties settle up in cash at the end of the day, as in security markets. Unfortunately, Holmes never discussed the ability to obtain injunctions against employees who wish to work elsewhere or damages for inducement of breach of contract, even though both received judicial support a generation before *The Common Law*.[139]

In sum, laissez-faire may well be a doctrine of individualism and enterprise, but its own strong moral component precluded any ready affirmation of the Holmes dictum. The commercial morality that allows individuals to make contracts of their own choosing cannot allow people to breach those contracts free of moral stain, with only limited legal consequences.

V   The Freedom of Contract

At long last we come to the central battle over freedom of contract, where laissez-faire has its greatest bite. The reach of this principle is measured by the ease with which individual contracts were invalidated on grounds of public policy. Here Sir George Jessel, Master of the Rolls, gave voice to the nineteenth-century view in a dispute that arose out of the assignment of patent rights. The sentence usually quoted reads as follows:

> It must not be forgotten that you are not to extend arbitrarily those rules which say that a given contract is void as being against public policy, because if there is one thing which more than another public policy requires it is that men of full age and competent understanding shall have the utmost liberty of contracting, and that their contracts when entered into freely and voluntarily shall be held sacred and shall be enforced by Courts of justice. Therefore, you have this paramount public policy to consider—that you are not lightly to interfere with this freedom of contract.[140]

The passage that immediately follows, while less quoted, should not be forgotten either:

> Now, there is no doubt public policy may say that a contract to commit a crime, or a contract to give a reward to another to commit a crime, is necessarily void. The decisions have gone further, and contracts to commit an immoral offence, or to give money or reward to another to commit an immoral offence, or to induce another to do something against the general rules of morality, though far more indefinite than the previous class, have always been held to be void. I should be very sorry to extend the doctrine much further.[141]

Exactly what, if anything, is wrong with this statement? Initially, it gets the right balance by defending freedom of contract in the name of public policy, and for good reason. Any contract that improves the lot of both sides will normally improve the position of third parties as well, by offering them expanded business opportunities with individuals of greater wealth. These positive externalities from mutually beneficial exchange are often neglected. Even though contracting parties cannot sue to recover these benefits conferred, any social evaluation of the overall practice must reckon with their impact. So the basic challenge raised under Jessel's framework asks what considerations could overcome the presumption in favor of freedom of contract. Jessel notes right off the bat that the doctrine applies only "to men of full age and competent understanding," for, sitting in a court of equity, he could not categorically insist that contracts are never set aside for undue influence. Jessel also understood the obvious mischief in enforcing contracts that threaten criminal actions against third parties, or even immoral behavior. His one weakness is his failure to confront directly the dangers of monopoly power, against which the common law had already devised some protections, as with common carriers.

Nor does Jessel's defense of freedom of contract depend on incantation devoid of analysis. Indeed, his treatment of the underlying transaction in *Sampson* reveals that he understood fully the subtleties of the matter. The defendant, for £48,750, had assigned his patent rights in a new invention (for numbering and printing tickets consecutively) to the plaintiff. As part of the deal, he also agreed "to enter into a covenant with the said company to assign, as and when required by the company or their directors, all future patent rights, or in the nature of patent rights, which they or any of them may hereafter acquire with respect to the aforesaid inventions, or any of them, or any of a like nature in the United Kingdom, or any part thereof, the Channel Islands, the Isle of Man, or all or any part of the continent of Europe."[142]

Jessel held that the quoted covenant did not violate public policy, but only after a detailed discussion of the incentive effects of the covenant. He was fully aware of the relevant trade-offs. While this covenant acted as a deterrent to future invention, it was also necessary to prevent the patent from becoming worthless to the buyers if the sellers could retain control of some follow-on venture that "exposed them to the instantaneous, or almost instantaneous, competition of the inventor with the benefit of his previous experience."[143] The two forces do cut in opposite directions, but that is hardly a new phenomenon in the law, especially with intellectual property. The creation of the patent monopoly itself involves just such a tension, for in order to induce the creation of the invention in the first place the law blocks its free usage for a stated period of time. Jessel's point was that the parties were best able to consider their combined impact, and he could find no dislocation massive enough to upset a part of the bargain that secured the initial purchase. And he denied that "a man who has obtained money for the future products of his brain will not be ready to produce those products."[144] The defender of freedom of contract was quite prepared to believe that other noneconomic motivations could induce production, or that other contractual arrangements were able to secure it. He was therefore right to recognize both the advantages and shortcomings of this long-term arrangement, without striking down one of its essential components.

The genius and importance of the general maxim is that it offers guidance to judges less skillful than Jessel in deciding cases in which discrete analysis is likely to be cloudy. But by the same token, it does not dispense with efforts to understand both the uses and limitations of that maxim. The key issue that was nowhere addressed in Jessel's argument was that of the role of monopoly in limited freedom of contract. That is surely the dominant social question, and it is possible here to make only a few concluding remarks on this matter that has been canvassed far more thoroughly elsewhere. First, most businesses do not possess monopoly power, and for them the choice of trading partners is the indispensable feature in a system of competition and voluntary exchange, as the nineteenth-century theorists understood. "A party has the right to select and determine with whom he will contract, and cannot have another person thrust upon him without his consent."[145]

Yet the system is not closed. Introduce monopoly power and the presumptions change. And again the legal system responded. The important class of monopolies facing the law were probably those that rose with common carriers and public utilities, areas that underwent explosive growth toward the end of the nineteenth century. On these matters, the common lawyers stuck pretty much to their guns and insisted that these contracts were "affected by the public interest," not in some woolly sense of being important but in a far more specific sense that special rules had to limit the freedom of contract when a single provider sat astride an essential commodity. Yet once again the response to these cases did not originate with laissez-faire but predated it. Sir Matthew Hale surely understood the point when he spoke of the dangers of maritime monopoly.[146] Lord Ellenborough had the same basic insights with respect to customs monopolies.

> There is no doubt that the general principle is favored in both law and justice, that every man may fix what price he pleases upon his own property or the use of it; but if, for a particular purpose, the public have a right to resort to his premises and make use of them, and he have a monopoly in them for that purpose, if he will take the benefit of the monopoly, he must as an equivalent perform the duty attached to it on reasonable terms.[147]

The entire institutional framework is key, if only because it rebuts the charge that laissez-faire was so doctrinaire that it was blind to the dominant social realities of its time.

The issue is surely more closely matched on the question of whether the dangers of monopoly in other sectors of the economy were tolerated under laissez-faire. Michael Trebilcock finds that trend under the English cases that let many horizontal arrangements pass freely by.[148] I am far less sure about his conclusions, thinking that some of these devices had some efficiency justifications, such as the efficient management of divided territories. Ironically, Langdell understood this. When he denounced the Supreme Court for its decision in the *North Pacific* case, he did more than appeal to classical principles of equitable jurisdiction. Rather he argued, and with considerable force, that a system of rate regulation for common carriers was clearly superior to breaking up a large and complex operation under the antitrust law. He wrote, "[T]here was no call for such an act respecting them; that the only way in which railways can do an injury to the general public is by charging unreasonable rates for services which they render, and that for such an injury the state already had an incomparably better remedy than any which the Sherman Anti-Trust Act can furnish, in its unquestioned power to regulate and control railway rates."[149]

But for these purposes we can put these disputes to one side. Even though the most urgent issues under laissez-faire concerned the response to various manifestations of market power, one point remains true: the efforts to undermine laissez-faire by looking to the doctrinal or conceptual foundations of contract law, traditionally understood, should be rejected. When Atiyah, Fifoot, Friedman, Gilmore, and Kessler look into the belly of the beast, they take after Bramwell or Langdell, and they see the insidious remains of an insensitive legal regime out of touch with the social realities. Yet a closer examination of the relevant issues suggests that they frequently fastened on to a sideshow. There are no great conceptual riddles that cannot be solved by traditional techniques. There are no great gaffes that bring the system to its knees. Too much focus on the oddities of legal doctrine leads to a misguided political focus. The great political systems stand or fall on the way in which they respond to grand social problems—the trusts and the utilities.[150] The true political struggles are the large questions of freedom of contract, not the smaller task of fine-tuning the mechanisms of voluntary exchange.

The Decline of Formality in Contract Law

ERIC A. POSNER

Gilmore's *The Death of Contract* has had a peculiar influence on contract law scholarship.[1] Its appearance met with heavy criticism from contracts scholars, but the book has been popular among students and professors and is routinely cited in modern work. The book is more frequently read than two better books with similar themes—Atiyah's *Rise and Fall of Freedom of Contract* and Friedman's *Contract Law in America*.[2] Most recently, participants in a symposium at Northwestern University almost universally condemned Gilmore's thesis, and yet all found something to praise in Gilmore's arguments, although no one agreed on what that something was.[3] This confusion is due, in part, to the considerable confusion of Gilmore's argument, a confusion that also appears in the arguments of Atiyah and Friedman.

This confusion in Gilmore's book results from his use of the word *contract* in multiple, inconsistent ways. Here are some of them: (1) to refer specifically to the "bargain theory" of contract law elaborated by Holmes and Williston; (2) to refer to the use of methodological formalism, exemplified by the approaches of Langdell and Williston; (3) to refer to contract as a doctrinal category, as opposed to, for example, tort; (4) to refer to the various doctrines that composed "contract law" as it existed at the end of the nineteenth century and the beginning of the twentieth century; (5) to refer generally to commercial behavior in a market economy; and (6) to refer to the ideology of laissez-faire. The "death of contract" thus refers not to one death but to six. Although Gilmore can plausibly argue that the bargain theory has less influence now than it did at the end of the nineteenth century, this "death" is logically distinct from the propositions that Gilmore presents as evidence of it or consequences of it: (1) that methodological formalism is dead; (2) that contract has been absorbed by tort; (3) that the consideration doctrine and related doctrines are losing their influence over judges; (4) that the market economy is gradually being replaced by an economy administered by the state; and (5) that the popular commitment to laissez-faire has been replaced by a commitment to the welfare state. Indeed, propositions 1–5 have proven to be remarkably hasty. Methodological formalism survives in a more sophisticated form in some kinds of normative economics; contract and tort are still distinct doctrinal categories; contract doctrines of today bear a strong, though not complete, resemblance to those of one hundred years ago, differing mainly (but significantly) in their degree of formalism; regulation of business has been on the decline for twenty years; and although it is true that laissez-faire enjoys less intellectual and political respectability than it did one hundred years ago, it lives on in a muted and circumscribed form.

If Gilmore was on solid ground when arguing about the decline of the bargain theory, moreover, this claim was not exactly news to anyone even in the early 1970s. It was more or less explicit in the work of scholars like Dawson, Kessler, Corbin, and Fuller, indeed, in the work of the legal realists in the 1920s. So why has Gilmore's book become so influential? Part of the answer lies in Gilmore's daring, his willingness to make generalizations of a grand philosophical and historical character. Most contracts scholars did not connect the decline of the bargain theory to the rise of the welfare state, and those who did, such as Kessler, did so mostly in an implicit and carefully hedged fashion, and they limited their claims to specific doctrines rather than "contracts" as a body of law;[4] or else they saw the bargain theory as a deviation, inspired perhaps by transitory politics, from the evolution of a more sophisticated and humane common law of contract that reached back into the mists of time.[5] But this background work is what made the academy responsive to Gilmore's argument. Gilmore's generalizations had shock value but were at the same time plausible because they drew together threads from earlier scholarship.

Gilmore chose to demonstrate the rise and decline of the bargain theory by discussing a handful of contract doctrines and a handful of old cases. Epstein takes up the challenge by showing that the minor variations in "contracts small" are broadly consistent with laissez-faire.[6] Epstein does not discuss the decline of formality in contract law (which might be called "contracts medium"). Perhaps he does not discuss the decline of contractual formality because this phenomenon was simply a characteristic of the variation in contracts small he identifies, and therefore his discussion of the latter can be applied without modification to the former. I will argue, however, that one gains additional dividends by shifting the focus of the analysis from contracts small to contracts medium. First, the shift in focus forces one to confront the older and more solidly argued work that underlies Gilmore's. Second, it forces one to recognize that there has indeed been a trend in contract law, and that this trend begs for an explanation. So, third, the shift in focus encourages one to supply such an explanation. I will argue that Epstein is correct to reject Gilmore's explanation. There is no reason to believe that the decline of formality in contract law is related to changes in the fortunes of laissez-faire. I will propose and evaluate two other explanations for the decline of formality in contract law, both of which are consistent with but distinct from Epstein's argument.

I The Decline of Formality in Contract Law

Holmes's bargain theory of contract law was more aspirational than historical, but it did a tolerable job of unifying prior doctrine (against Gilmore's view), and it had a great deal of influence on the judicial development of contract law over the next, say, forty years (consistent with Gilmore's view). Holmes's bargain theory was also highly formal.[7] It thus provides a convenient starting place for investigating the meaning of formality in contract law.[8] The formality of Holmes's bargain theory has three components. First, the bargain theory is self-contained: it forbids the court to implement a substantive moral theory of contract law and instead requires the court to follow a series of rules.[9] To understand this point, imagine a law that says "enforce all promises whose nonenforcement would result in injustice." This rule is not quite a tautology: it refers the court to an unarticulated moral theory that explains what promises should be enforced. If the moral theory is sympathetic to laissez-faire, then the application of the rule will result in outcomes that will often differ from the outcomes that would result if the moral theory were not. A more formalistic rule might be "enforce all promises that are supported by bargained-for consideration." As is well known, formalism leads to decisions that are both underinclusive and overinclusive as compared to the decisions that would follow from direct application of the underlying moral theory. The bargain theory, for example, prohibits the enforcement of firm offers and other apparently gratuitous promises that would probably be enforced under the theory of laissez-faire.

Second, the bargain theory is characterized by what might be called "externalism" (sometimes confusingly called "objectivism"): it forbids courts to rest decisions on evaluations of mental states and other unobservable phenomena. Holmes's aversion to laws that require an evaluation of motives[10] led him to argue that the enforceability of promises depends not on whether the promise was *motivated* by consideration, but on whether the parties *recited* that the promise was motivated by consideration;[11] and, more famously, that a promise is for legal purposes a statement that one will pay damages if a specified event does not occur, rather than the expression of a mental state.[12] One possible reason for avoiding laws that refer to mental states is that they make the law unpredictable. A deeper reason is that they allow judges and juries to smuggle in substantive moral theories when adjudicating a contract dispute—in violation of the commitment to self-containment described above.

Third, the bargain theory is axiomatic: it reduces the large number of contract doctrines to a handful of axioms. Holmes argued that the doctrines of fraud, misrepresentation, and mistake could all be derived from the axioms of contract law.[13] A better-known example, which was not proposed by Holmes but was inspired by his approach, is the derivation of the doctrine of duress from the principle of consideration.[14] A promise to perform a preexisting contractual obligation is unenforceable not because of "duress," with its connotations of force and unfairness, which have no place in the bargain theory, but because of lack of consideration. This example shows the close connection between the self-containment of the bargain theory and its axiomatic character: if a doctrine like duress can be derived from the axioms of a system, then it is unnecessary to appeal to a moral theory. (To be sure, this approach, as is well known, stripped the doctrine of duress of perfectly sensible functions, and it made other valuable doctrines of contract law—notably, the doctrine of third-party beneficiaries— virtually incomprehensible.) Holmes's commitment to an axiomatic system of contract law comes perilously close to Langdell's "geometric" approach to contract law, but should not be confused with it. A formal theory like Holmes's must be internally consistent, or else it will produce indeterminate results. However, Holmes did not purport to derive his theory from self-evident premises. Instead, he tried to present it as a unification of existing cases, which themselves emerged from a long history of common law development in response to social needs.[15]

The extent to which Holmes's theory reflected judicial practice at the time is not entirely clear, but what is clear is that judicial practice now is much more distant from the requirements of Holmes's theory than it was a hundred years ago. Let us consider some familiar examples.

Numerous contract doctrines invite judges to apply the underlying moral theory directly to disputes. The best example is the doctrine of promissory estoppel, which requires courts to enforce relied-on promises when necessary to avoid "injustice." A similar doctrine applies this standard to offers. As Corbin pointed out to the drafters of the first Restatement, courts had been applying estoppel arguments to promissory disputes long before the acceptance of the bargain theory, but it is clear that promissory estoppel is a more respectable doctrine now than it was a century ago.

Mental states and other unobservables also play a larger role in contract adjudication than they did when Holmes wrote. The good faith and best efforts rules require courts to evaluate a party's motives for breach. Indeed, most courts never accepted Holmes's theory of consideration, conditioning enforcement on proof that consideration really motivated the promise rather than on proof of a recitation that the consideration motivated the promise,[16] and as a result getting themselves into all sorts of difficulties about what counts as motivation and what counts as "sufficient" (as opposed to "adequate") consideration.

Finally, courts have abandoned the idea that the doctrines of contract law can be derived from the theory of bargained-for consideration. For example, it was gradually realized that the bargain theory could make little sense of the doctrine of third-party beneficiaries. The theory seemed to suggest that beneficiaries could not enforce promises, because they did not supply consideration to the promisor; but the value of promises for the sake of third parties was sufficiently evident that the theoretical objections of the bargain theory could only delay courts' development of the doctrine,[17] and its eventual vindication was a blow to the bargain theory. In other areas, the bargain approach persisted despite the sense that it could not adequately account for many doctrines, with the result that an odd system of parallel tracks now prevails. Courts apply seriatim the doctrine of duress and the preexisting duty rule to disputes over contract modifications; the consideration doctrine and the doctrine of mutuality to disputes over indefinite contracts; the consideration doctrine and promissory estoppel to disputes over firm offers and gratuitous promises; and so on. Confusion persists over whether contracts are unenforceable because the parties *referred* to different things (Holmes's interpretation of *Raffles*[18]) or because they *intended* different things (the doctrine of mutual mistake). In a formal and self-contained system, this profusion of semiconsistent doctrinal categories would not be possible; but when the system is understood to be incomplete, and implicitly to refer to a deeper moral theory, doctrinal conflicts can be tolerated in the vague expectation that they will be resolved as the moral theory slowly comes to light.

These changes together amount to an extraordinary trend in contract law, and they pose a challenge to Epstein's thesis. If Epstein is right that changes in contract doctrine are unrelated to changes in attitudes toward laissez-faire, then how can he explain the trend toward informality? Doesn't the existence of a significant trend suggest larger forces at work, rather than, as Epstein suggested in discussion, contract law "working itself out"; and what more obvious trend than the decline of laissez-faire? To defeat Gilmore's argument decisively, Epstein must present an alternative theory.

II   What Explains the Decline of Formality in Contract Law?

The question to be addressed now is whether the decline of formality in contract law is related to the decline of laissez-faire, or is in fact related to other trends. Before addressing this question, I make a few simplifying assumptions about the package of thought to which the label "laissez-faire" or "freedom of contract" is routinely glued.[19] Laissez-faire originated as a political program committed to the elimination of laws that interfere with the market. But this idea contains an ambiguity. To the extent that laissez-faire refers to government support of competitive markets, this can involve rather vigorous government intervention, not only for the purpose of breaking up monopolies but also for the purpose of enforcing property rights. However, laissez-faire has historically also had a libertarian flavor, detectable in the associated view that the government should regulate private behavior only as a last resort. The first or "economic" component of laissez-faire can be called the "market thesis." This refers to the idea that courts should enforce contracts in a manner that most respects the parties' intentions, or (roughly the same thing) that maximizes the contracts' ex ante value to the parties, or (also roughly the same thing) that maximizes the value of participation in the market.[20] This view can be contrasted with a variety of alternatives: that courts should decide disputes in a manner that redistributes wealth to the poor, or that spreads risks, or that respects autonomy, or that conforms to notions of fairness. The second or "political" component of laissez-faire can be called the "deference thesis" and refers to the idea that, because they have epistemic limitations and perverse incentives, courts and other government actors should regulate contractual behavior in a way that minimizes the chance that state error will cause harm—for example, only when evidence of a market failure is compelling.

The tension between the political and economic sides of laissez-faire is illustrated by the old dispute among laissez-faire theorists over the extent to which the government should break up monopolies and regulate natural monopolies. Some have argued that the government should vigorously regulate monopolies; others have argued that, because monopolies are rare and unstable, and because government intervention is likely to stray, the government should rarely intervene.[21] A similar conflict divides those who want courts to enforce clearly defined property rights and those who want courts to manipulate them in a manner that promotes social welfare. Consider, for example, the conflict between those who support specific performance on the ground that judges cannot competently determine the value of promises and those who support expectation damages on the ground that judges can and that damage awards reduce transaction costs. I suspect the disagreement stems not so much from differing assumptions of judicial competence as from differing attitudes toward government intervention. A laissez-faire theorist of a libertarian or anarchist bent would likely favor political deference in principle, while the welfare-maximizing social engineer would likely reject it in favor of a policy that required government actors to perform discrete cost-benefit analyses.

THE MARKET THESIS

To investigate the connection between laissez-faire and contract formality, let us first consider the relation between laissez-faire and the decline of the self-containment of contract law, illustrated by the rise of promissory estoppel, with its invitation to courts to consult their sense of justice. The way in which promissory estoppel is applied depends on how courts interpret this privilege. A judge who rejects the market thesis could very well use promissory estoppel to transfer wealth ex post to a vulnerable and impoverished promisee who relied on the promise in conflict with the promisor's wishes. Gilmore probably had something like this idea in mind when he associated the rise of promissory estoppel with the decline of laissez-faire. The problem with this idea is that because promissory estoppel leaves the external moral theory indeterminate, it allows the judge to apply to the dispute any moral theory he wants to. A judge could apply an antimarket theory, but he could also apply a promarket theory. Moreover, the evidence suggests that, far from using promissory estoppel as an opportunity to promote social justice, judges use it to support the market. This seems to me the best interpretation of the emerging consensus that judges use promissory estoppel to enforce any "serious" or economically important promise.[22] On this view, promissory estoppel does a better job than the bargain theory at implementing the program of laissez-faire: it allows courts to circumvent the consideration doctrine's restrictions on such value-maximizing promises as firm offers and gift promises.[23] Although the decreasing formality of contract law *could have* resulted from a decreasing commitment to laissez-faire, it did not, as a matter of historical fact.

Similar comments can be made about the relation between laissez-faire and the decline of "externalism" in contract law—the decline in judicial refusal to consider mental states and other unobservable phenomena—illustrated by the rise of the doctrine of good faith, with its invitation to courts to evaluate the motives of the promisor. This invitation, again, did not specify how the courts should evaluate motives. The rise of good faith *could have* reflected judges' increased willingness to hold promisors to a level of integrity that was beyond the requirements of the market—that, for example, promoted human dignity and fair dealing. There is little evidence, however, that this was the case. When Cardozo famously used the idea of good faith to justify enforcement of a routine agency relationship, he enforced a contract that was fully justified on market grounds but that would not have survived application of the bargain theory, as then interpreted.[24] In effect, a mental state of "honesty" or "good faith" becomes a reliable proxy for value-maximizing conduct.

Finally, let us look at the relation between laissez-faire and the decline of the axiomatic character of contract law, illustrated by the eventual rejection by courts of the attempt to absorb the duress doctrine into the preexisting duty rule. Again, there is little reason to believe that the reemergence of duress as a distinct doctrine is necessarily consistent or inconsistent with laissez-faire. Applied in a way that redistributed entitlements, it would have been inconsistent; applied in a way that merely eliminated hold-up problems, it is consistent with laissez-faire. My impression is that the latter approach has predominated. Not even Dawson argued that the duress doctrine should be or had been used to redistribute entitlements; instead, he argued that it should be and had been used to protect bad bargainers against sophisticated practices and to equalize bargaining power.[25] Whether such a use of the duress doctrine would conflict with laissez-faire depends on the competence of courts. If courts can successfully use contract law to undermine monopoly power, then the market component of laissez-faire would permit such a practice just as it has permitted courts to regulate common carriers.

The recent rise of the unconscionability doctrine illustrates some of these ideas. This doctrine received a great deal of criticism early on for being too nebulous, for giving courts too little guidance, for not fitting in with the other doctrines of contract law. This criticism is the criticism of the formalist: (1) the doctrine required direct application of a moral theory, rather than the application of second-order rules; (2) the doctrine, under some interpretations, required analysis of mental states and other hard-to-measure phenomena such as bargaining power; (3) the doctrine was not consistent with the consideration doctrine, instead, in the eyes of some, setting up a competing axiom of fairness. There were two kinds of scholarly response. One was to domesticate the doctrine, making it if not formally derivable from the consideration doctrine, at least consistent with the market approach. "Procedural unconscionability" would refer to defects in bargaining of the sort condemned by the market paradigm, and "substantive unconscionability" would refer to inequality in terms that would be *evidence* of defects in bargaining.[26] The other response was to claim the unconscionability doctrine as an antimarket law, a means for redistributing wealth from rich to poor, or merchant to consumer, for giving the buyer procedural advantages, or for condemning commercial practices that violated intuitions about fair play (especially "coercive" creditor arrangements).[27] It appears that gradually courts adopted the market version of the unconscionability doctrine, while the antimarket applications were made the domain of statutes and regulations.

Another useful example is the treatment of the doctrine of third-party beneficiaries. This doctrine currently allows third-party beneficiaries of a contract to enforce the promise. Although its scope must be limited so as not to create indeterminate liability, the value of this doctrine is clear: it gives the promisee assurance that the beneficiary will obtain performance when the promisee cannot do it himself (hence the importance of the doctrine when the promisee dies). Inasmuch as the doctrine guaranteed judicial enforcement of certain kinds of value-maximizing promises, it was consistent with laissez-faire. But the doctrine conflicted with the bargain theory, because it permitted a person to enforce a promise for which he had not supplied consideration. Recognition of such a right would have violated the self-contained and axiomatic character of contract law. Although the doctrine was recognized prior to the creation of the bargain theory, courts under the sway of the bargain theory subsequently pulled back.[28] The eventual vindication of the doctrine at the expense of the bargain theory, many years later, was a victory for, not a defeat of, laissez-faire.

In sum, the decline of the formality of contract law cannot be taken as evidence of, or as a result of, and still less as a cause of, the decline of the market thesis of laissez-faire as a respectable political position. This argument would not surprise anyone who has noticed that contract law in England has remained more formal than contract law in the United States,[29] while laissez-faire has enjoyed much less popularity in England both as a political philosophy and as an organizing principle of economic institutions. The argument also is a more general version of Epstein's argument: if changes in the formality of contract law have been unrelated to changes in attitude about laissez-faire, then changes in the particular doctrines of contract law—most of them instances of contract law's increasing informality—must also have been unrelated to changes in attitude about laissez-faire. But it also leaves open the question we want to answer: why has contract law become less formal? To answer this question, we investigate another hypothesis.

This second hypothesis turns our focus from the market thesis to the deference thesis. The argument is that the declining formality of contract law is related to a declining commitment to political deference. To understand this argument, note that one powerful argument in favor of formalism rests on skepticism about the ability of courts to adjudicate disputes properly. If courts routinely err in, say, their interpretation of contracts, requiring them to abide by even very crude rules is preferable to allowing them to enforce the underlying moral theory that justifies those rules. The reason is that formality introduces predictability, allowing parties to plan, without sacrificing justice, since judicial incompetence prevents courts from achieving justice under a less formal system.

This theory of formalism was not the focus of the legal realists' critique. The realists attacked formalistic theories of the law and formalistic adjudication for denying the relevance of policy concerns. Even more, they attacked formalism for denying the necessity of justifying the law generally (as well as particular applications) by reference to policy concerns.[30] Perhaps because realists, or at least some of them, believed that formalistic adjudication was simply incoherent and dishonest, they never took seriously the possibility that formalistic laws could serve valid goals. Thus they implicitly assumed that courts could enforce the underlying moral theory (or theories) of the law; that they could evaluate unobservables such as mental states; and that, because doctrines would reflect the moral theory, it was not necessary for them to be collapsed into a set of axioms. Consider, for example, Llewellyn's U.C.C., with its insistent appeals to business practice and good faith, and its refusal to unify doctrine around the principle of consideration. But what was the underlying moral theory of the U.C.C.? The Code was hardly a manifesto of redistribution or fairness—in fact, its solicitude for established business practices amounted to a paean to freedom of contract. Llewellyn objected to the formalism of the bargain theory not because it prevented courts from redistributing wealth, imposing norms of fairness, and protecting the weak from the strong, but because it prevented courts from enforcing value-maximizing contracts.

The hypothesis, then, is that the decline of formality in contract law reflects a decline in judicial commitment to political deference, and as this idea broke apart, judges started applying the value-maximization idea traditionally behind contract law in a more particularized, "informal" way. Hence courts were increasingly willing to enforce firm offers, requirements and output contracts, agency contracts, gratuitous promises, promises for the benefit of third parties—that is, all "serious" promises, even at the expense of the classical conception of the consideration doctrine—by using the doctrines of good faith and promissory estoppel, and by manipulating the consideration doctrine. Now, to establish this theory, one would have to read a lot of cases which I have not read. I simply want to suggest that the cases discussed by Gilmore and others—for example, the "fairness" cases discussed by Friedman[31]—are more consistent with this interpretation than they are with Gilmore's interpretation. Courts have abandoned formalism because it interfered with their ability to read and enforce the parties' intentions, and to punish force and fraud when they rendered intentions invalid, not because it prevented them from implementing an anti-market conception of justice.

What might have caused the decline of the idea of political deference? If, following Gilmore, one looks for major political trends, one might point to the rise of the administrative state, based, at least in part, on the idea that the government has sufficient competence to be able to regulate intimate areas of commercial and personal life. This idea implied confidence not only in the abilities of the bureaucratic agencies of the centralizing state but also in the abilities of the courts. (Indeed, in legal realism one sees a link between enthusiasm for the administrative state and rejection of common law formalism.) Assuming a rise in public confidence in the abilities of courts, it would not be surprising if judges came to share it. This might have led them to stop applying rules in a mechanical, formalistic manner, and instead to evaluate disputes on a case-by-case basis. Formalism is, after all, an acknowledgment of the limitedness of judicial ability; abandonment of that conviction implies that formalism can be shed. Thus, even as intelligent and creative a judge as Cardozo, before this age of judicial hubris, would not have dared, as Traynor later did, to lecture parties on the requirements of public policy and the philosophy of language.[32] The increase in judicial confidence would explain why modern judges have been more willing than their predecessors to condemn contractual behavior on moral terms and to look through the parties' words and into their heads. And yet if, as I have argued, the morality that the judges demanded of the parties was the morality of the market, the decline of political deference is consistent with the persistence of judicial commitment to laissez-faire.

As a final bit of evidence, it is worth observing that when one reads Holmes, Williston, Corbin, and Cardozo, the most striking difference between the first pair and the last pair is not their attitude toward freedom of contract but their attitude toward political deference. Williston, on the one side, expressed skepticism about the idea of freedom of contract, albeit a highly unimaginative form of skepticism.[33] (Holmes's view was too complex to summarize.) Corbin and

Cardozo, on the other, were more critical of the bargain theory's restrictions on courts' ability to enforce the intentions of the parties than of its exclusion of redistributive and other antimarket considerations. Though Corbin's realist tendencies can be seen in his insistence that contract doctrines must be related to policy rather than derived from universal axioms, he seldom made claims about policy, and much of his work—especially his writings on the parol evidence rule[34]—suggests a commitment to enabling courts to enforce contractual intention.[35]

It is worth mentioning that, although the decline of the formality of contract law cannot be taken as a rejection of laissez-faire, it is not necessarily desirable in the eyes of certain kinds of laissez-faire theorists. It did not so much reflect a rejection of the market as an attitude about the best way to support the market. Judges may have thought that the best way to support the market was to enforce contract rights in a highly particularized way—using, one might say, the standards of market behavior rather than the rules of market behavior. But a libertarian might see in this approach a threat to autonomy: if the value of markets consists in their promotion of liberty, as opposed to social welfare, even highly competent courts ought to defer. The rejection of political deference would also upset those who doubt the competence of legal actors and see in custom a repository of wisdom.[36] And although the Benthamite social engineer will celebrate the decline of the formality of contract law if he thinks that judges evaluating a contract ex post can do a better job of picking value-maximizing terms than parties can ex ante, this assumption of judicial super-competence is implausible. The social engineer, unlike the libertarian, however, faces a dilemma. This dilemma occurs whenever discretion is given to an imperfect institution like the judiciary. On the one hand, if courts police the bargaining process with great vigor but overstep the bounds of their competence, they will enforce and strike down the wrong contracts. On the other hand, if courts regulate the bargaining process as little as possible, they will tolerate monopolistic and deceptive practices and other actions inconsistent with the spirit of laissez-faire. Ideally, the courts would exercise the optimal degree of formality—a level of formality that balances its advantages (reduction of unpredictable judicial error) and costs (systematic underinclusiveness and overinclusiveness). The problem is that courts cannot determine what that optimal degree of formality is. There is no natural stopping point between the extremes of formality and informality. Moreover, even if courts could determine the optimal level of formality, it is not clear that they *would*. This raises the problem of judicial incentives.

THE ROLE OF REPUTATION

The failure to discuss the motives of judges, institutional constraints, and other factors relevant to common law change is a conspicuous weakness in Gilmore's arguments. Any theory of doctrinal change should have an account of how and why judges change the doctrine.[37] Gilmore seems to assume that judges absorb general political trends like sponges and then implement them when deciding cases. But this assumption is too simple, ignoring judges' institutional insulation from the political world, their (at least, notional) freedom to decide cases on the basis of personal interests and idiosyncratic moralities, and their concern for their reputation in legal communities. One can take account of these complications, while keeping the analysis relatively tractable, by positing that when judges decide cases they maximize two kinds of utility: (1) personal utility, which refers to the satisfaction they obtain when they decide a case in a way that either is consistent with their conception of justice or advances their personal or political interests; and (2) reputational utility, which refers to the satisfaction they obtain from being known among members of some relevant community as a "good judge."

Theories like Gilmore's fail to explain why judges, even if their views shifted with general trends, would apply those views to the cases. A judge who rejects laissez-faire cannot simply begin striking down unfair contracts without risking a loss of reputation. Even those sympathetic to the judge's views will disapprove of his departure from precedent, and those who disagree with the judge will have lots of ammunition for attacking him. With rare exceptions, judges obtain their reputations from the local legal community and other judges, seldom from the public. So an obviously politically expedient adjudication generates criticism, not applause. By the same reasoning, the political deference thesis could be true only if a general political trend in favor of government (especially, judicial) authority influenced judges, and they could implement their views without risking a loss of reputation. Again, this proposition is possible, but not powerful. The plausibility of the political deference thesis, compared to that of Gilmore's thesis, is just that doctrinal changes are more consistent with the former than with the latter. But we still have not provided an explanation of why judges would seek to change doctrine in this way and, for that matter, whether they could.

The latter point is significant. Judges cannot independently decide to change legal doctrine; they can do so only by deciding cases in a way that other judges find plausible. Nor can judges self-consciously collectively decide to change the law in a general way; institutional barriers stand in the way of such collective action.[38] Not even en banc panels of judges sitting in high courts have a significant influence on the molasseslike creep of the common law. In order to understand how judges change the law, we must say something more about reputational utility.

What does it mean for judges to care about having reputations as good judges? We might suppose that members of the relevant community call judges good who decide cases in the correct way, all things considered. This does not get us very far. But we can make some progress by noting that clearly a judge is *bad* if he decides disputes in a way that furthers his personal or political interests. So in order to be a good judge, a judge must at least avoid deciding disputes on the basis of his personal or political interests. But there is a difference between being a good judge and having a reputation as a good judge. In order to have a reputation as a good judge, a judge must decide cases in such a way that causes people to think that the judge does not decide cases on the basis of personal or political preference, whether in fact he does or not.

The crucial consequence of these assumptions is that only a judge knows whether he truly decides a case by reference to personal interest; no one can know a particular judge's personal interests. What people can do is read a judge's opinions and make a guess about whether the judge is a good type or a bad type. Because of the heterogeneity of factual situations that underlie legal disputes, this guess is often difficult, but it is not impossible. If we suppose that judges care about their reputations, then each judge will feel pressure to decide cases in such a way that causes observers to think that the judge is a good type. If judges did not care at all about personal sources of utility, there would be a well nigh infallible strategy for deciding cases in this way: always follow precedent. If a judge always follows precedent, either it is always the case that the judge's personal interest matches up with precedent or the judge does not always follow his personal interest. Since the former is unlikely, observers will conclude that the judge is not the bad type. The judge might not be a great or even smart or sensitive judge, but at least the observer knows that he does not follow his personal interest, and will give him some credit for that.

Now suppose a continuum: some judges care deeply about their reputations and little about their personal interest; some other judges care deeply about their personal interest and little about their reputations; most judges care about both their reputations and their personal interests. Depending on the proportions, one is likely to see a great deal of, but not complete, conformity with precedent. The argument is roughly as follows.[39] A dispute comes before a judge and seems to be controlled by a prior case. If the judge believes that the prior case was correctly decided, he will follow precedent, since both personal and reputational utility are maximized. If the judge disagrees with the prior case, then he must weigh the reputational cost of departure and the personal cost of conformity. If you suppose that judges' preferences are uniformly distributed over outcomes, then you would expect most (both bad and good) judges to conform to precedent, with only the outliers resisting. The reason is that if everyone assumes that only (or mostly) bad judges deviate from precedent, then judges whose personal outcome is close but not identical to the outcome demanded by precedent gain little personal utility by deviating while losing a lot of reputational utility. (The assumption is reasonable because judges who want to decide a case correctly are more likely to come to the same outcome than judges who want to decide a case in the manner that advances personal or political interests.) Only judges with extreme views on a particular case or with low concern about their reputation will depart from precedent. Finally, as more and more cases follow an early case, the precedent will become so strong and precise that judges cannot evade it in the hope that deviations will be lost in noise; hence even judges who care relatively little about reputation cannot afford the loss of reputational utility that would result from openly violating it.

The argument shows why judges usually adhere to prior decisions, though nothing—no "law," for example—compels them to do so.[40] A judge who violates precedent will not be impeached or fined. In addition, the argument shows how easily error can be built into the law. When new technologies create new legal issues, the first few decisions will have disproportionate influence on the case law. If the first judges are either not competent or more concerned with personal or political commitments than with justice, incorrect decisions can become the law and it may take a long time before the error becomes obvious enough to justify a departure from precedent. Finally, a judge may cautiously try to break with precedents that he thinks are wrong by using legal fictions: the advantage is that he retains deniability in a sense and can return to precedent relatively easily; the disadvantage is that his innovation may be overlooked and thus fail to change precedent.

But I am not so concerned about explaining why judges follow precedent, as about answering the closely related question of why in deciding cases judges adopt more or less formalistic modes of analysis. Recall that judges who care about both personal interests and reputation will be torn between following precedent and departing from it when it is inconsistent with their interests (defined broadly to include moral commitments). Suppose, for example, that a judge believes in the market component of laissez-faire and must decide whether the consideration doctrine bars enforcement of a firm offer. The command of the moral theory and the command of the doctrine conflict. The moral theory may suggest enforcing firm offers "seriously proposed" or "non-negligently relied on," in which case it requires evaluation of motive in conflict with the consideration doctrine. Faced with such a dilemma, some judges will depart from the consideration doctrine, usually sub rosa—for example, by finding consideration to be implied from the promisee's actions—or through the limited application of other doctrines such as promissory estoppel. If, through chance, most of the judges who first confront the problem of the firm offer care relatively more about personal utility than about reputational utility, and are committed to laissez-faire, then their evasions will weaken the formalistic rule; if not, then it will be sustained as the judges, worried about being accused of enforcing personal views, apply the consideration doctrine to strike down firm offers. But take the first alternative: the rule weakens. As the rule becomes vaguer—as increasing exceptions turn it into a standard—judges will not be able to derive reputational utility from adhering to it, because observers will not be able to tell from the judge's decision whether he is acting in conformity to precedent rather than implementing his own views.

We can expect that, at some point before the precedent becomes completely formless, judges who care deeply about their reputations will realize that they can maximize reputational utility, without losing much personal utility, by re-characterizing the formless standard as a specific rule. This process is straightforward. If a precedent resulted from the application of a standard to a particular cluster of facts, a judge can derive a rule from that precedent by generalizing from the specific application. For example, after a judge strikes down a contract with an add-on clause as unconscionable, a later judge interprets the earlier opinion to establish the rule that all add-on clauses are unenforceable—whether or not the earlier judge had this view or stated it. Then the later judge can either enforce or strike down the contract in front of him on the basis of whether it has an add-on clause, and obtain reputational gains from having refrained from following his personal views. Now, he may actually have behaved strategically, and some commentators may catch him at it; but, generally speaking, this judge is in a better position to claim that he is not implementing his own moral theory than the judge who decides a case simply by calling certain conduct "unconscionable."[41]

This story could be complicated in many ways. One could take account of judges who through the intelligence of their opinions have unusually powerful influence over the development of the common law; judges of this kind and others who have a strong desire to influence their colleagues; academic criticism of judges and academic efforts to "restate" the law; legislative reactions to judicial decisions; and so on. But the point is strong enough that these modifications would not significantly change it. That point is that a realistic assessment of judges' motives and the institutional constraints on their behavior precludes simple hypotheses, such as Gilmore's, that connect political and economic trends to judicial action in an uncomplicated way. Of course, they may be heard as a distant echo, but just taking account of reputational concerns, we see that the development of doctrine may follow a logic that can be found only in an understanding of judicial behavior. I have also suggested that the increasing informality of contract law is a random perturbation, a fad rather than a basic trend, that can reverse itself at any time, and that does not reflect general trends with respect to laissez-faire, the market, or political deference. Thus, as between the reputational theory and the political deference theory, I prefer the former. Indeed, the reputational theory is superior in one crucial respect: the political deference theory predicts that all areas of law would advance toward informality, when in fact many areas of the law outside of contract demonstrate the reverse trend, toward increasing formality.[42] Given the insulation with which judges approach different kinds of legal disputes, one can easily imagine doctrinal trends with respect to one kind of dispute moving independently from doctrinal trends with respect to another.

If legal form is subject to buffeting from random forces, we must still explain why the market idea is not. Why is it that the market idea has been more stable than the political deference idea? There are a few possibilities. One is that the political deference idea is not as ideologically charged: although it has some political overtones, it can also be understood as a technical idea about the implementation of policy, rather than policy itself. Modifications in the formality of doctrine do not create obvious winners and losers. The market idea, in contrast, is sufficiently ideologically charged that once judges committed themselves to it, they could not divest themselves of it without risking accusations of engaging in politics, accusations that will be raised by those directly harmed.

Another possibility is that attempts by judges to implement antimarket values through contract adjudication are futile. When a judge strikes down a contract as unfair, future parties will contract around the offending term. Except under special conditions that are unlikely to arise in a predictable manner, courts cannot significantly redistribute wealth or bargaining power by striking down "unfair" contracts, and usually such behavior will simply make people in the more vulnerable class worse off. The gains from this policy are nonexistent or nebulous; the costs are clear to the parties who seek enforcement of the promises, and they will complain loudly. The rapid decline in judicial efforts to implement antimarket values, after the initial excitement generated by *Williams v. Walker-Thomas*[43] and *Henningsen v. Bloomfield Motors*[44] (which are themselves by no means models of judicial candor), suggests that courts are not willing to accept the political costs. Such regulation has been taken up by legislatures, which more than judges have democratic legitimacy.

III   Conclusion

Gilmore's conjecture that the decline of formality resulted from a decline in judges' commitment to laissez-faire is not supported by the evidence. To the contrary, the evidence suggests that (1) modern contract doctrine is consistent with the program of laissez-faire, understood to mean market support, and (2) it is probably more consistent with that program than the bargain theory was. Possibly, the decline of formality resulted from frustration among judges with formal doctrinal categories that interfere with market support, accompanied by increasing confidence among judges in their ability to interpret contracts, detect bargaining abuses, and so on—a confidence, I conjecture, that might have been related to the growth of the administrative state. More likely, the decline of formality is epiphenomenal, resulting from judges' concern for their reputation, a concern that under plausible conditions can lead to self-reinforcing behavior that is unconnected to larger social and political trends. On this theory, the decline of formality, like the rise of formality before it, was just a long-term accident, and may be reversed in the future. Which theory one prefers will depend on one's assumptions about how much judges care about their reputations and on one's inclination to look for grand theories; but both theories are more persuasive than Gilmore's.

External Critiques of Laissez-Faire Contract Values

MICHAEL J. TREBILCOCK

I The Normative Basis

Professor Epstein's essay "Contracts Small and Contract Large" provides a panoramic review of laissez-faire era contract law doctrine as it bears on three related philosophical concepts: freedom of contract, security of exchange, and sanctity of contract. His central thesis is that little or nothing in the contract law doctrine of the period is incapable of being reconciled with a laissez-faire view of the social and economic role of private contracts. There is little or no basis for the claim of incoherence by critics of laissez-faire contract doctrine, such as Friedman, Atiyah, and Gilmore; and in turn little basis for a much more prescriptive role for the legal system in regulating the domain and features of contractual obligations.

In general, I find Epstein's thesis a compelling one. Disagreements over the implications of doctrinal nuances that emerged during this period—such as the relative role of subjective and objective theories of contractual intention, rules relating to contract formation such as the mailbox rule, rules relating to mistakes as to contractual terms, contractual excuses such as the doctrine of frustration, appropriate remedies for contract breach, and the scope and limits of the doctrine of promissory estoppel—seem mostly to implicate in only marginal ways the larger philosophical debates over the virtues and vices of laissez-faire philosophy as to the appropriate social and economic role of private markets and of the institution of contracting that facilitates their operation. Most, if not all, of these legal debates are internal critiques of the coherence of laissez-faire period contract doctrine, and seem to me to amount to little more than clubhouse squabbles among teammates. It is hard to imagine that a single drop of blood could ever have been spilled, or even a single vote in a popular election could ever have turned, on any of these issues. So far as I am aware, repealing the mailbox rule has never appeared on anyone's election platform.

In contrast, the larger and more formidable challenges to laissez-faire philosophy and the role of private markets and private contracting were external challenges that confronted the philosophical values of laissez-faire much more directly. These challenges have always been matters of "high politics" and have had much more enduring and substantial impacts on our political economy and the role that we have assigned to law in circumscribing the domain of private contracts and prescribing features of contracts in general or particular classes of contracts within that domain. Professor Epstein, in his essay, does not address these external critiques. However, surely in any contemporary normative reappraisal of the scope and limits of private ordering, these external critiques must be seriously addressed—indeed, I would argue, taken much more seriously than the internal critiques with which Professor Epstein's essay is primarily concerned.

A foundational issue that must be squarely engaged in evaluating both internal and external critiques of laissez-faire conceptions of the institution of constraining is the relevant normative benchmark against which these critiques should be evaluated. Here, Epstein is surprisingly vague and leaves himself vulnerable to external critiques of laissez-faire philosophy. At the outset of his essay, Epstein states that "Herbert Spencer, for example, commingled ideas of natural rights, social contract, and social consequences within the confines of a single essay. This intermingling of rights-based, contracts-based, and consequence-based arguments does not reveal a weakness in the philosophical foundations of Spencer's system; indeed, most eighteenth- and nineteenth-century writers thought that these three approaches worked in tandem and not in opposition."[1]

As I have argued elsewhere,[2] however, once one abandons a normative theory of the private ordering process that rests on the actual or at least manifested consent of the affected parties (as classical autonomy or libertarian theories espouse), and adopts a consequentialist normative theory of the institution of the contract and the legal rules that should govern it based on some notion of hypothetical consent, the welfare implications of alternative legal rules or regimes chosen on this basis are often inconclusive. This indeterminacy is entailed in Kaldor-Hicks's efficiency analysis, in which it is hypothesized that the particular parties to a specific transaction would have chosen a given legal rule had they addressed their minds to the matter at issue, or that large aggregations of contracting parties would consent to a particular legal regime suggested by efficiency or welfare analysis if they were to be consulted ex ante before their stakes in particular transactions ex post have become clear. Once we are driven into the realm of designing legal rules or regimes by reference to notions of hypothetical consent, the welfare implications of alternative legal regimes, even within an efficiency perspective, are often highly indeterminate. Moreover, the way is now clear for alternative legal regimes grounded not on efficiency considerations as conventionally understood by economists, but on theories of distributive justice of the kind proposed by Rawls and others.[3] In turn, it is far from clear that theories of distributive justice predicated on hypothetical consent generate a very determinate set of implications for the law of contracts.

Charles Fried in his book *Contract as Promise*[4] is much more alert to the political and philosophical dangers of abandoning consent as the basis of contractual obligations than is Epstein. Fried states that "the promise principle, which in this book, I argue is the moral basis of contract law, is that principle by which persons may impose on themselves obligations where none existed before." Fried goes on to argue, after noting historicist critiques of autonomy-based theories of contractual obligation, that "a more insidious set of criticisms denies the coherence of the independent viability of the promise principle. Legal obligation can be imposed only by the community, and so in imposing it, the community must be pursuing its goals and imposing its standards, rather than neutrally endorsing those of the contracting parties." Fried notes that these lines of attack are found recently in the writings of legal scholars such as Patrick Atiyah, Lawrence Friedman, Grant Gilmore, Morton Horowitz, Duncan Kennedy, Anthony Kronman, and Ian McNeil, as well as in philosophical writings.[5] On this view, "the bases of contract law are as many and shifting as the politics of the judicial and legislative process." Fried explicitly distances himself from writers like Richard Posner, "who in denying any independent force to promissory obligation derive such force as the law gives to contracts from social policies such as wealth maximization and efficiency." Strikingly, Fried concludes his book with a statement that is strongly similar to Epstein's closing statement: "The law of contracts, just because it is rooted in promise and so in right and wrong, is a ramifying system of moral judgments working out the entailments of a few primitive principles—primitive principles that determine the terms on which free men and women may stand apart from or combine with each other. These are indeed the laws of freedom."

In the end, I believe that Fried's efforts to sustain a unifying theory of contractual obligation based exclusively on autonomy values is unsuccessful. Within an autonomy-based theory of contractual obligation, difficult questions arise as to when a transaction can be regarded as voluntary or, conversely, coerced. It is difficult to construct an autonomy-based theory of coercion without first constructing a moral baseline (or set of rights) for the party choosing to accept a proposal under constrained circumstances against which the proposal can be evaluated. Similarly, difficulties arise in determining when a contracting party has sufficient information about the contract subject matter or future course of events affecting the value of the contract for a conclusion to be sustained that the choices in question were autonomous. Although contracting choices made with false information or in the absence of highly material information may, at one level, be regarded as nonautonomous, at another level the decision to forgo opportunities to acquire further information may itself be an autonomous choice. Thus it is not obvious how complete a contracting party's information set should be for his choice to be regarded as autonomous.

It can also be argued that a rich conception of individual autonomy entails not only a negative but also a positive theory of liberty. Under a positive theory, the autonomous ability to choose one's own conception of the good life entails access to economic opportunities and resources that makes nondemeaning, self-fulfilling life choices a realistic possibility.[6] For example, with respect to the question of coercion, it might be argued that deliberate exploitation by one party of another party's lack of choices to exact returns that exceed those normally realized in a more competitive environment should be viewed as suspect. Similarly, conscious acquiesence by one contracting party in mistaken and material assumptions made by the other relating to the contract subject matter may be viewed as undermining the autonomy of the latter. More generally, positive theories of liberty can be invoked to justify the adoption of contract doctrines or regimes designed to redistribute resources, and thus effectuate a conception of distributive justice.[7]

In the case of externalities, autonomy values yield an unclear set of implications where the choices or activities of contracting parties impact on the interests or welfare or moral sensibilities of third parties, leading to claims by the latter that their autonomy has been infringed by these contractual choices or activities.[8] In cases of incomplete contracts, the legal system, almost by definition, cannot resolve the incompleteness by reference to the intentions of the parties (subjective or objective) and is compelled to use external reference points. In the end, Fried is required to resort to rather vague social conventions to define the practice of promising and its entailments. Thus his theory appears often to entail a resort to external values to specify when promises should or should not be enforced, rather than deriving an internally generated set of implications exclusively from the premise that contracts rest on individual autonomy and consent. Moreover, as Buckley argues,[9] although promises made within such conventions may be content-independent, the reason we have collectively adopted a social convention of promise-keeping in a broad range of circumstances cannot simply be that the more choices open to individuals the better: we must justify which kinds of additional choices are better than fewer choices of given kinds, which he claims require a consequentialist justification—in his case a utilitarian justification.

Notwithstanding the shortcomings of an autonomy-based theory of contractual obligation, it is far from clear that these problems become any easier by shifting from a theory of contractual obligation based on actual or manifested consent to a theory of contractual obligation based on hypothetical consent. Whether reflected in either utilitarian judgments of the appropriateness of legal rules to constrain the domain of contracting or the legal entailments of contracts within that domain, or in a theory of distributive justice predicated similarly on some theory of hypothetical consent, hypothetical consent rarely yields precise implications. But at least Fried is acutely sensitive to the tensions between autonomy-based theories of contractual obligation and consequentialist theories of various kinds, in a way that Epstein appears not to be. This leaves Epstein more vulnerable, in many respects, than Fried to the shifting political sands of the judicial and legislative process. To the extent that Epstein, like Herbert Spencer, is prepared to rely simultaneously on natural rights, social contract, and social consequences theories of contractual obligation in defending his conception of laissez-faire contract philosophy, then of course he must be prepared to meet critiques—most of them external to contract law—of all three classes of theory. Epstein must also demonstrate a convergence or compatibility among these three classes of theory in supporting his conception of the laissez-faire view of contracting. This is a daunting and probably impossible challenge, which Epstein is largely able to avoid by focusing on internal critiques of laissez-faire contract doctrine. External critiques would not permit these fundamental normative dilemmas to be escaped so lightly. I now turn to a brief review of these critiques.

II Information Failures

In at least two important respects, nineteenth-century courts committed to laissez-faire philosophies of the institution of contracting revealed themselves to be strikingly insensitive to information asymmetries between contracting parties: first, with respect to mistakes as to contractual terms, and second, with respect to mistaken underlying assumptions.

With respect to mistakes as to contractual terms, as Waddams points out, "from the 19th century until recent times an extraordinary status has been accorded the signed document that will be seen in retrospect, it is suggested, to have been excessive."[10] As stated by Mellish L.J. in *Parker v. Southeastern Railway Co.*,[11] "Where an action is brought on a written agreement which is signed by the defendant, the agreement is proved by proving his signature, and, in the absence of fraud it is wholly immaterial that he has not read the agreement and does not know its contents." This proposition was later elevated to the so-called rule in *L'Estrange v. Graucob Ltd.*,[12] where Scrutton L.J. stated, "When a document containing contractual terms is signed then, in the absence of fraud, or, I will add, misrepresentation, the party signing it is bound, and it is wholly immaterial whether he has read the document or not." The sanctity of signed agreements was reinforced by the so-called parol evidence rule—the rule that when a contract has been reduced to writing, extrinsic evidence of verbal understandings is inadmissible to modify the writing. This view is obviously an embarrassment for consent-based or autonomy theories of contractual obligation. While such theories can be better accommodated within an objective theory of contractual intention (and rationalized by reference to pragmatic or utilitarian considerations relating to security of exchange), even objective theories of contractual intention are pressed beyond the bounds of credulity in holding parties bound to contractual terms which they have manifestly not read or understood.[13] While I have been critical of notions of inequality of bargaining power predicated solely on disparities in size, disparities in information as to the contractual terms are a genuine problem. The problem is perhaps at its most acute in the case of standard form contracts. Given positive transaction costs, one assumes that the parties will often not read the terms or, if they do, will not wish to spend significant amounts of time attempting to renegotiate the terms.

Subsequent judicial and academic reactions to the laissez-faire view of the sanctity of signed contracts have been predictable, albeit in many cases ill-conceived. Standard form contracts, in particular, have suffered a bad press from both the judiciary and the legal academy. One line of objection, reflected in writings by Kessler and others,[14] and in judicial decisions such as that of the House of Lords in *Schroeder v. Macaulay*, is that standard form contracts are symptomatic of either monopolization or cartelization. This arguments essentially rests on the "take it or leave it" character of most standard form contractual offerings. However, as I have argued elsewhere,[15] this feature of standard form contracts is as consistent with the benign transaction cost conservation rationale as it is with a monopoly or collusion rationale. Simply observing the fact of standard form contracts yields no meaningful implications as to the underlying competitive structure of the market. Indeed, they are used in many settings where manifestly the market is highly competitive, for example, in dry cleaning stores, hotel registration forms, insurance contracts, and so on. Indeed, even in the absence of standard form contracts, goods are offered on a take-it-or-leave-it basis in some of the most competitive retail markets in the economy, including corner variety stores.

The second source of hostility to standard form contracts—information asymmetries—is clearly more substantial. However, responding to this argument without undermining the transaction cost conservation rationale for standard form contracts is not a simple challenge. Anglo-Canadian courts in recent decades evolved the doctrine of fundamental breach to address this problem, but the doctrine suffered from the opposite vice to the nineteenth-century doctrine of sanctity of signed contracts: overinclusiveness, whereby disclaimer or limitation of liability causes in formal contracts between substantial commercial enterprises were sometimes struck down. More recently, both English and Canadian courts have largely abandoned the doctrine of fundamental breach and instead subjected clauses in standard form contracts, at least in consumer and related contexts, to scrutiny under a general doctrine of unconscionability, although without being particularly forthcoming about the precise criteria of enforceability.

In this respect, I have argued[16] that problems of unfairness resulting from imperfect information are not as severe as they might seem at first sight. To the extent that there is a margin of informed, sophisticated, and aggressive consumers in any given market who understand the terms of the standard form contracts, and who either negotiate over those terms or switch their business readily to competing suppliers offering more favorable terms, they may in fact discipline the entire market, so that infra-marginal consumers can effectively free-ride on the discipline brought to the market by marginal consumers. However, where suppliers are able to discriminate either with respect to terms or performance between marginal and infra-marginal consumers, this generalized discipline will be undermined and there is a clear risk that infra-marginal consumers will be exploited because of their own imperfect knowledge of the contract terms. Here, I have proposed that courts, in evaluating the fairness of standard form contracts, should investigate whether a particular consumer has received a deal that is significantly inferior, in relation either to the explicit terms of the contract or to the performance provided under it, to that realized by marginal consumers in the same market, holding constant the economic as opposed to personal characteristics of consumers in these two classes. In markets which are so badly disrupted by imperfect information that there is no identifiable margin of informed consumers from which appropriate benchmarks can be derived, then judicial intervention in case-by-case litigation seems less appropriate than legislative or regulatory intervention of the kind that has occurred in many jurisdictions, for example, with respect to various classes of door-to-door sales. More generally, this problem exemplifies once again how the extreme position taken by laissez-faire courts on the sanctity of written contracts proved not only unsustainable but counterproductive in eliciting an unreflective and to some extent indiscriminate overreaction by courts and commentators, impeding the formulation of an efficient set of rules to govern the enforceability of standard form contracts.

The second respect in which nineteenth-century laissez-faire courts revealed themselves as insensitive to problems of information asymmetries in the contracting process was with respect to mistaken assumptions as to material facts underlying the contract at the time of its formation, where the true state of affairs was known by one contracting party and misapprehended by the other, to the first party's knowledge. Laissez-faire era courts in general took the view that such mistakes in no way affected the contract. For example, in the famous case of *Smith v. Hughes*,[17] Cockburn C.J. stated, "The question is not what a man of scrupulous morality or nice honour would do under such circumstances. A case of a purchase of an estate, in which there was a mine under the surface, but the fact was unknown to the seller, is one in which a man of tender conscience or high honour would be unwilling to take advantage of the ignorance of the seller, but there can be no doubt that the contract for the sale of the estate would be binding." In *Bell v. Lever Brothers*,[18] Lord Atkin postulated a series of similar examples to similar effect:

> A. agrees to take on lease or to buy from B. an unfurnished dwelling house. The house is in fact uninhabitable. A. would never have entered into the bargain if he had known the fact. A. has no remedy, and the position is the same whether B. knew the facts or not, so long as he made no representation or gave no warranty. A. buys a roadside garage business from B. abutting on a public thoroughfare; unknown to A., but known to B., it has already been decided to construct a bypass road which would divert substantially the whole of the traffic from passing A.'s garage. Again A. has no remedy. All these cases involve hardship on A. and benefit to B., as most people would say, unjustly. They can be supported on the ground that it is of paramount importance that contracts should be observed, and that if parties honestly comply with the essentials of the formation of contracts—i.e., agree in the same terms on the same subject matter—they are bound, and must rely on stipulations of the contract for protection from the effect of facts unknown to them.[19]

This position is almost impossible to reconcile with consent or autonomy-based theory of contractual obligations, given that one party knows that the other party would not have wished to enter into the contract, but for the mistaken assumption. As both Cockburn C.J. and Lord Atkin acknowledged, the legal rule that they espoused was inconsistent with widely held notions of morality and justice. While arguably, as Lord Atkin suggested in *Bell v. Lever Brothers*, pragmatic or utilitarian considerations relating to security of exchange might preclude contracting parties from afterwards arguing that they were induced to contract only by virtue of a mistaken assumption (given the perverse incentive or opportunism problems that permitting such arguments obviously raise), it is far from clear that there is never a case for mandatory disclosure of material facts bearing on the contract subject matter. Indeed, in more recent times, courts have relaxed the nineteenth-century rule in many contexts, both creating numerous exceptions to the parol evidence rule and holding that material nondisclosure in itself may sometimes constitute grounds for contractual invalidation.[20] Legislatures have been much more activist in mandating disclosure requirements in a wide range of contexts or legislating disclaimable or in some cases nondisclaimable implied warranties. Whether some of these responses are again an overreaction to the laissez-faire period position on material nondisclosure is open to debate. Admittedly, formulating efficient duties of disclosure in various contractual contexts poses major analytical and empirical problems,[21] entailing difficult trade-offs between creating incentives to generate information, in the first place, and incentives to transmit it, once generated, thereafter, but this emphasizes once again that neither autonomy nor welfare nor consequentialist values yield easy implications for the choice of appropriate legal rules in many areas of contract law. This necessarily renders the domain contestable in ways which Epstein's wistful invocation of simple laissez-faire values obscures.

III Externalities

Laissez-faire era courts were not oblivious to the problems of externalities, as reflected in the evolution of the tort of nuisance and the rule of strict liability for certain land uses adopted in *Rylands v. Fletcher*,[22] as well as other aspects of tort law such as the developing tort of negligence and the tort of defamation. Even in the contractual sphere, contracts that furthered the conduct of some activity widely viewed as immoral, such as supplying a carriage to a prostitute on credit, were held unenforceable as contrary to public policy.[23] But as both Epstein[24] and I[25] elsewhere acknowledge, externalities are one of the more normatively intractable concepts in defining the permissible domain for private action, including private contracting.

John Stuart Mill advanced his famous "harm to others" principle as a way of sharply delimiting the role of the state in interfering with individual autonomy.[26] Epstein and I share the view that Mill seems to have thought that the harm principle was susceptible of relatively mechanistic and restrictive application and would leave open very large realms of activity for individual freedom of choice and action unconstrained by the views or interests of third parties. However, as Feinberg points out, "Without further specifications, the harm principle may be taken to invite state interference without limits, for virtually every kind of human conduct can affect the interests of others for better or worse to some degree, and thus would properly be the state's business."[27] As Epstein notes, the current view sees externalities everywhere.[28] In effect it isolates one negative consequence of any action on third parties and uses it to justify prohibition of that action—whether by tort, administrative remedy, or criminal prosecution—no matter how large the gains for others. This skewed form of social accounting has a predictable, if perverse result: every action generates some harm under the expanded harm principle.

Both Epstein and I have our favorite examples of the indeterminacy of the harm principle. He rails against requiring owners of wetlands to preserve them without compensation, because of the negative externalities that may be entailed if they were destroyed; interfering in employment relationship through prohibitions on discrimination; requiring that well or young people subsidize the provision of health care to sick or elderly people. For example, Epstein argues in his book *Forbidden Grounds*: "An antidiscrimination law is the antithesis of freedom of contract, a principle that allows all persons to do business with whomever they please for good reason or no reason at all. . . . The first question to be asked in any public debate is *who* shall decide, not *what* shall be decided. On the question of association, the right answer is the private persons who may (or may not) wish to associate, and not the government or the public at large."[29] This view is reflected in the famous (notorious) decision of the Supreme Court of Canada in 1940 in *Christie v. York Corporation*,[30] where a tavern operator had refused to serve a black man because of his color and the latter sued for damages in tort for the humiliation he had suffered. In rejecting his claim, the majority of the Court stated: "We ought to start from the general proposition that the general principle of law . . . is that of complete freedom of commerce. Any merchant is free to deal as he may choose with any members of the public. It is not a question of motives or reasons for deciding to deal or not to deal; he is free to do either."[31] An editorial note accompanying the reported decision renders explicit a common perception of the implications of this decision: "This would appear to be the first authoritative decision on a highly contentious question and is the law's confirmation of the socially enforced inferiority of the coloured races."[32]

Externalities that I find problematic include: pornography, which arguably reinforces negative gender stereotypes about women; prostitution, which might create a public nuisance or cause public offense and (like pornography) might reinforce negative gender stereotypes; hate literature directed at minorities; helmet laws for motorcyclists or seatbelt laws for motorists on the grounds that their risk-taking behavior imposes costs on dependents and the social welfare and public health systems; smoking, where the health effects of secondhand smoke and the costs of smoking to the public health care system may constitute externalities; narcotics such as alcohol, heroine, and cocaine which may increase the incidence of violence toward others, lead to neglect of dependents, increase the incidence of property crimes, or increase the cost of social welfare or public health care systems; and potential extinction of a rare species of whale, the Bengal tiger, or a rare environmental or scenic treasure to which individuals assign a positive existence value even if they never intend to view the endangered species or scenic treasure. Both Epstein and I appear to accept that some form of balancing test is required in order to weigh the costs and benefits of these activities and that in this context theories of individual autonomy and utilitarian- or welfare-based theories of the public good are not nearly as sharply divergent as one might initially suppose. However, at this juncture we part company.

For Epstein:

> the antidote is to recall Mill's optimism and to accentuate the positive and limit the negative. The full range of consequences has to be grasped and evaluated, comprehensively not selectively, not case by case, but by broad categories of cases. When and if that is done, the bottom line will be pretty much as Mill himself understood it: limitations against force (including pollution) and fraud (including defamation). To that is added some concern with monopoly and contracts in restraint of trade, always a source of concern at common law. For the rest, the principle of freedom of action (of speech, religion, contract, and association) should remain as strong and as vibrant as Mill would have it, not in any naive belief that it causes no harm, but in the informed belief that the alternative systems lead to totalitarian excesses that cause far greater harm than any of the ordinary practices they suppress.[33]

For myself, I do not feel nearly the same confidence in my judgments as Epstein does in his in performing the balancing exercises that we both accept need to be undertaken. In many—perhaps most—of the difficult cases cited above, I believe that the balancing exercise will lead to high levels of indeterminacy and disputation. That is to say, the judgments (as with other issues I have discussed in these comments) will be highly contestable. While Epstein may believe that an appeal to simple laissez-faire principles should carry the day, this is an article of faith, indeed an ideological preference, which reflects how he would put his thumb on the scales in making a number of these assessments, but there is nothing in the logic of his position that refutes other weightings of the interests that require to be balanced.

IV Commodification

An uncompromising laissez-faire view of the limits of freedom of contract is likely to take the position that anything can be bought and sold if there is a willing buyer and a willing seller, subject to possible qualifications with respect to problems of monopoly, information failures, and externalities discussed above. Commodification objections to this view would argue, on a number of grounds (some of which are closely related to or elide with an expansive notion of externalities), that some resources or human attributes should lie outside the domain of the market. Laissez-faire era courts were not insensitive to this concern, as reflected in decisions invalidating contracts that were found to promote immoral purposes. Moreover, legislation quite early in the laissez-faire period prohibited slavery and trafficking in slaves in Britain and her colonies, and the Factories Acts enacted in the first part of the nineteenth century prohibited the use of child labor in mines and factories. Moreover, as Arrow has pointed out, a private property–private exchange system depends, for its stability, on the system being nonuniversal.[34] For example, if political, bureaucratic, regulatory, judicial, or law enforcement offices were to be auctioned off to the highest bidder, or police officers, prosecutors, bureaucrats, regulators, or judges could be freely bribed in individual cases, or votes could be freely bought and sold, a system of private property and private exchange would be massively destabilized, as mounting evidence of the economic costs of corruption in developing countries and former command economics currently demonstrates.

In addition, it is often argued that in other contexts to allow full commodification of human attributes or resources is inconsistent with theories of personhood or human flourishing. Karl Polanyi, in his well-known *The Great Transformation*,[35] published in 1944—interestingly at almost precisely the same time as Freidrich Hayek's *The Road to Serfdom*[36]—argued that in most premarket societies the values of reciprocity and redistribution rather than individual maximizing behavior have predominated. According to Polanyi, with the advent of the Industrial Revolution at the beginning of the nineteenth century and the emergence of economic and political liberalism, the market paradigm revealed itself as completely insensitive to the social cost to communities and individuals of traumatic economic change and dislocation. Moreover, he maintained that the market paradigm commodifies aspects of human and physical nature that are essentially noneconomic and which in premarket societies have been treated as noneconomic, such as land, which Polanyi equated with physical nature, and labor, which he equated with human nature itself. In premarket societies, the rights of individuals to dispose or otherwise deal with either land or labor were heavily constrained by convention, custom, or centrally or collectively imposed formal legal constraints.

Much more recently, Margaret Jane Radin has argued[37] that appropriately rich theories of personhood raise serious questions about whether, for example, the sale of human organs should be permitted; whether a market for newborns should replace the adoption system; whether prostitution should be permitted; whether commercial surrogacy contracts should be allowed; whether the employment relationship should be tightly regulated; and whether residential tenancy agreements should similarly be subject to regulation to protect locational and communal ties. In justifying her position on a number of these issues, she weighs the so-called double bind effect against the so-called domino effect. The problem of the double bind arises because in many contexts prohibiting commodification or exchange may make the plight of the individual whose welfare is central to the commodification objection actually worse. Balancing the double bind effect is the domino effect, where permitting transactions (e.g., prostitution or commercial surrogacy), along with the market rhetoric and manifestations that accompany them, may change and pervert the terms of discourse in which members of the community in general engage with one another about their personal or social relations. Similarly, Titmuss in his book *The Gift Relationship: From Human Blood to Social Policy*[38] argued for a system of voluntary blood donations as opposed to commercial payments for blood transfusions, on the grounds that a voluntary system was likely to outperform the commercial system in terms of the quantity and quality of blood supplied, the avoidance of severe shortages or surpluses, and the fostering of a sense of altruism, reciprocity, and community—important noneconomic values which he claimed the donation system reinforces and which the commercial system undermines.

This is not the place to take positions on any of these problematic issues. It is sufficient to make the point that an internal critique of nineteenth-century contract doctrine as reflected in the case law barely begins to confront the issue of the legitimate domain of markets and private ordering. Yet this external critique of laissez-faire philosophy has proved an enduring and influential one that is not easily resolved by simple appeals to values of personal autonomy or straightforward utilitarian calculi.

V Paternalism

In his essay *On Liberty* John Stuart Mill appeared to take the position that the right of self-government is close to absolute and is an end in itself. For example, according to Mill,

> His own good, either physical or moral, is not a sufficient warrant [for invading his liberty]. He cannot be rightfully compelled to do or forbear because it will be better for him to do so, because it will make him happier, because in the opinion of others, to do so would be wise, or even right. These are good reasons for demonstrating with him or reasoning with him, or persuading him, or entreating him, but not for compelling him or visiting him with any evil in case he do otherwise. To justify that, the conduct from which it is desired to deter him, must be calculated to produce evil to someone else. The only part of the conduct of anyone, for which he is amenable to society, is that which concerns others. In the part which merely concerns himself, his independence is, of right, absolute. Over himself, over his own body and mind, the individual is sovereign.[39]

Later in the essay, Mill states that there is no room for entertaining any interference with a person's conduct "when that conduct affects the conduct of no persons beside himself or need not affect them unless they like (all the persons concerned being of full age, and the ordinary amount of understanding). In all such cases there should be perfect freedom, legal and social, to do the action and stand the consequences."[40]

However, despite the absolute terms in which Mill states this doctrine of antipaternalism, he acknowledges early in his essay that "it is, perhaps, hardly necessary to say that this doctrine is meant to apply only to human beings in the maturity of their faculties."[41] In the second passage quoted above, he confines the proposition to persons of full age and the ordinary amount of understanding. Further, in his famous example of slavery contracts, Mill equivocated in his opposition to paternalism in apparently taking the view that voluntary contracts of enslavement were inconsistent with basic notions of individual self-fulfillment—an individual should not be free to agree not to be free.[42]

Already, rather like his harm principle, we see the seeds of serious ambiguity in Mill's antipaternalism principle. In the case of minors and mental incompetents, long-standing legal doctrines of contractual capacity reflect Mill's qualifications on his antipaternalism principle. However, the legal categories of minors and mental incompetents are quite arbitrary. While the legal system, for pragmatic reasons, may choose a particular age of capacity, maturity of judgment is not a discontinuous or binary state, being completely absent at one moment of time and fully realized in the next. Thus the legal category of minors is both grossly over and under-inclusive. Similarly, mental incompetence, which for pragmatic reasons may be confined to the certifiably insane, is equally not a discontinuous or binary state. Individuals have different degrees of mental competence in relation to different kinds of interactions with others. In extreme cases of infancy or mental incompetence, it may be that individuals lack the capacity to form any stable or coherent preference structure at all (their wills are unformed or paralyzed), but many other cases will not be nearly so clear.

Even assuming that an individual has a stable and coherent set of preferences, in particular circumstances it may be arguable that his or her choices are not consistent with this preference structure. Coercion or information failure may be two such cases. Here an individual's existing preferences remain the basic reference point. However, others would argue for defining the scope of paternalism much more broadly. For example, Sunstein argues for a substantial role for legal paternalism, reflecting a majority's preferences about preferences, or second-order preferences at the expense of first-order preferences, by way of analogy with the story of Ulysses and the Sirens. Examples that Sunstein gives include addiction, habit, and myopia.[43]

Yet others argue that many preferences are endogenous or contingent and reflect adaptive preferences that are at variance with the kinds of choices such individuals would make in the absence of social, economic, legal, ideological, or other influences that have shaped these preferences. This view is potentially highly subversive of traditional autonomy values. As Sunstein acknowledges, "If the ideas of endogenous preferences and cognitive distortions are carried sufficiently far, it may be impossible to describe a truly autonomous preference."[44]

In order to avoid this implication, Sunstein argues that "there is a substantial difference between a preference that results from the absence of available opportunities, or a lack of information about alternatives, and a preference that is formed in the face of numerous opportunities and all relevant information."[45] While this qualification perhaps puts some constraints on the scope of a principle of paternalism, when a preference is formed in the face of numerous "opportunities" and "all relevant" information raises far from axiomatic issues, and moreover it does not directly address the mental or emotional capacity of given individuals to evaluate available opportunities, even if numerous, or all relevant information, even if available to them.

Milton Friedman in *Capitalism and Freedom*[46] appropriately acknowledges the unavoidable anguish that economic and philosophical liberals confront on the issue of paternalism:

> The paternalistic ground for governmental activity is in many ways the most troublesome to a liberal; for it involves the acceptance of a principle— that some shall decide for others—which he finds objectionable in most applications and which he rightly regards as a hallmark of his chief intellectual opponents, the proponents of collectivism in one or another of its guises, whether it be communism, socialism, or a welfare state. Yet there is no use pretending that problems are simpler than in fact they are. There is no avoiding the need for some measure of paternalism. As Dicey wrote in 1914 about an Act for the protection of mental defectives, 'The Mental Deficiency Act is the first step along a path on which no sane man can decline to enter, but which, if too far pursued, will bring statesmen across difficulties hard to meet without considerable interference with individual liberty.' There is no formula that can tell us where to stop. We must rely on our fallible judgment and, having reached a judgment, on our ability to persuade our fellow men that it is a correct judgment, or their ability to persuade us to modify our views. We must put our faith, here as elsewhere, in a consensus reached by imperfect and biased men though free discussion and trial and error.

This seems a long way removed from the ostensibly absolute principle asserted by Mill, and frankly and appropriately acknowledges the inherent political nature of collective decisions about the scope of the principle of paternalism. Of course, this also renders the terrain highly contestable, in a way that simple laissez-faire values are unlikely much to illuminate, at least at the level of generalization or abstraction to which Mill, and apparently Epstein, seem committed.

Conclusion

Like Epstein, I see many virtues in "simple rules for a complex world"[47] in order to temper excessive demands on institutional competence and capacity. Like Epstein, I also favor a limited role for government for similar reasons. As the World Bank states, in a recent report, "The principal message from experience is not that the state should manage less, but manage better."[48] But I seriously doubt that in a complex world this role is a minimalist one. Markets cannot function without effective government, and moreover markets cannot do everything. To pretend otherwise is to define complex problems out of existence. Perhaps simple theories may more readily generate simple rules, but the larger and more daunting challenge is to generate simple rules for a complex world from unavoidably complex normative theories. In this respect, Epstein's essay leaves too much uncontested terrain to external critiques of laissez-faire. Meeting these critiques, unfortunately, is likely to involve more than simply exchanging ideological predispositions at high levels of generality, but rather debating and contesting issues both normatively and empirically, category by category and case by case.[49]

However, it needs to be said in conclusion that, whatever Epstein's polemical or rhetorical excesses on one side of the grander debate, these do not begin to compare with those of some of the critics with whom he joins issue on the other side. As the titles imply, *The Rise and Fall of Freedom of Contract*[50] (Atiyah) and *The Death of Contract*[51] (Gilmore) were always absurdly pretentious forms of overclaiming, particularly given their narrow internal perspective, and rendered more so by the subsequent collapse and transformation of most economies previously committed to a minimal role for private ordering. But one set of rhetorical excesses does not justify another. I do not make any comparably sweeping claims on either side of these internal normative disputes. Nevertheless, I am confident that I have defined more precisely the continuing and genuine theaters of external normative conflict over the role of private ordering in societies committed, as a general predisposition, to market economies and democratic polities.

In Defense of the Old Order

TIMOTHY J. MURIS

In early 1970, Grant Gilmore delivered his famous lectures, proclaiming contract's death.[1] Although his work did not command widespread public attention, his message that classical economics and its accompanying legal structure had failed was hardly isolated. As he spoke, the relationship of government to society was fundamentally changing. The entitlement programs that threaten to bankrupt our nation early in the next century were either created (as were Medicare and Medicaid) or greatly expanded (as was Social Security). The Great Society's transformation of welfare programs accelerated the growth of dependency and the rise of widespread social problems. The modern regulatory state began in far-reaching environmental and health and safety legislation. Closer to the specifics of Gilmore's topic, the consumer protection movement led to numerous changes in statutory and case law designed to correct an alleged imbalance of power between businesses and consumers. Gilmore's brilliant polemic was thus part of a vast change.

Analyzing the intellectual underpinnings of this transformation and its impact on our economy and society is a lifetime task for a university of scholars. This volume, based on a series of conferences at George Mason University School of Law sponsored by the Donner Foundation, attempts to aid the assessment of this era. My own contribution will discuss the failure of the economic theory underlying Gilmore and his fellow critics of classical contract law. By equating classical contract theory with laissez-faire economics, and by finding both wanting, they provided justification for much of the expansion of government discussed in the previous paragraph. After noting the theoretical flaws, I discuss two examples of the new policies: the regulation of franchises and of health claims in advertising. In both, flawed analysis produced flawed public policy.

Throughout, it should come as no surprise that a professor at George Mason University relies on economic analysis. Economics provides a superior method to study law in general, and contract law in particular. Parties desire efficient rules, i.e., rules that maximize the joint value of their enterprise. Inefficient rules simply force them to chose methods other than relying on contract law to facilitate exchange.[2]

I   Economics and the Critics of Classical Contract Law

As Epstein notes, Friedman, Gilmore, and others equated classical contract theory with classical economic (or laissez-faire) theory. Just as classical economic theory was outdated and inadequate for the modern world, so was classical contract theory. Neither theory deserves such easy and sweeping rejection. For many born in the first third of the twentieth century,[3] the rejection of laissez-faire economics was widespread and probably deeply felt. After all, the Great Depression had a deep physical and emotional impact. Initial historical treatment of that depression was harshly critical of the failure of laissez-faire, justifying the need for more activist government. A leading historian of this generation, Arthur Schlesinger Jr., called his first book on "the Age of Roosevelt" *The Crisis of the Old Order*. In his second book, *The Coming of the New Deal*, published in 1959, he noted approvingly a view he ascribed to John Maynard Keynes, that "depression, by everywhere compelling government action, had underlined the obsolescence of laissez-faire."[4]

We now know this simple view of the causes of the Great Depression is wrong. Rather than the result of the failure of an unregulated economy, a major cause of the Great Depression was mismanagement of the Federal Reserve Board. Ironically, the Fed was itself a government institution created under the activist impulses of President Woodrow Wilson to provide superior performance to that of the relatively unrestricted economy that preceded it.[5]

The critics of both classical contract theory and laissez-faire were correct to note that the world in which they lived did not meet the conditions of simple models. But the problem was in the models, particularly the terminology and assumptions used. Critics of laissez-faire frequently noted that the economic model underlying this philosophy assumed conditions that did not exist, such as so-called perfect competition in which price equals marginal cost, a vast number of sellers are present, and information is costless. I agree with Professor Epstein that Aaron Director's view of laissez-faire, with its presumption in favor of the market, provides a better understanding of the appropriate role of classical economic theory than the assumptions of the abstract models.

The focus on the failures of economic theory, however, helps us understand just how flawed the arguments of Gilmore, Friedman, and their associates are. As Armen Alcian and William Allen argue, "if markets in the real world operate in ways that are not accounted for by theory that assumes costless information, then the theory itself is imperfect."[6] Yet the critics, living in a world that did not meet the simple model, too easily prescribed an activist government to remedy deviations from the theoretical world of perfect markets. The logical fallacy in this argument is apparent. We cannot measure the real world against a world in which transaction costs are zero, for that world is unattainable. As Carl Dahlman has noted: "externalties and market failures are not what is the matter with the world, nor is it externalties and market failure that prevent us from re-establishing the Garden of Eden here on earth—our sad state of affairs is rather due to positive transaction costs and imperfect information."[7]

A related problem, now also well known, is that the critics often failed to understand that they needed to compare an imperfect government to an imperfect market. Far from meeting the prerequisites of the perfect competition model, government itself is a monopolist. The government lacks perfect information as well. Besides having information to understand problems, the government must also devise solutions. Implementation of such solutions is hardly omniscient, however. Instead, government has become notorious for pursuing inconsistent policies. For example, government tries to reduce agriculture production through marketing orders and other policies while increasing production through subsidies to farmers. It will mandate weight-adding safety equipment for cars, while insisting on lighter—and hence more dangerous—vehicles to conserve fuel. Moreover, some parts of government promote open markets and free trade, while others work hard at restricting the flow of lower-priced goods to the United States.[8]

The rational attitude of voters provides an additional problem. Most policies affect voters in only a minor way, leaving them to ignore the fact that concentrated groups use government to obtain favors. Thus, so-called special interests are the beneficiaries of much of modern government. These facts do not call for despair. Instead, as Harold Demsetz has noted, "they call for the alternative system approach."[9] Rather than justify activist government by noting that the world is imperfect, in choosing what policies to implement, we need explicitly to compare alternative institutional systems.

Nevertheless, both contract theory and public policy were significantly influenced in the 1960s and 1970s by the belief that market conditions did not fit simple economic models and that activist government was accordingly appropriate. Antitrust provides an example particularly relevant for contract law. Alleged lack of competition was one of the major reasons critics of classical contract law used to reject it. Thus Friedrich Kessler, who would later author a leading contracts casebook with Gilmore, wrote in his famous article "Contracts of Adhesion": "With the decline of the free enterprise system due to the innate trend of competitive capitalism toward monopoly, the meaning of contract has changed radically."[10] The prevalence of competition (or lack thereof) had become a major issue in antitrust at the time critics like Friedman and Gilmore wrote. Because the resolution of the competition issue in antitrust is directly relevant to the critics' complaints about contract law, let me briefly review it here.

The movement to deconcentrate American business brought the competition issue to the forefront of antitrust. Corporations were felt to have too much power in a wide range of industries, including automobiles, computers, many aspects of grocery manufacturing (such as cereals, detergents, and soft drinks), steel, petroleum refining, and many others. This attack on concentration suffered from both theoretical and empirical flaws. Theoretically, in the naïve view of many legal proponents of deconcentration, competition was held to be a function of the number of firms in an industry. After all, the perfect competition model was said to be based on this proposition.

Strictly speaking, this argument is incorrect. In the perfect competition model, a firm that restricts output will not raise the price that consumers pay for the industry's goods. The correct reason, however, is not merely because there are many firms. If consumer demand for the good is normal, and thus varies inversely with price, then a reduction of even one unit *must* raise price, albeit by a tiny amount if the total market is large enough. The reason that price remains at the "competitive" level is not the mere existence of many competitors. Instead those competitors must *act* by increasing output, "returning" price (in the "wink of an eye") to its previous level. This *action*, not merely the presence of a large number of firms, creates competition. Although it is obviously easy to envision that a large number of competitors would be conducive to such action, focusing on behavior, rather than numbers, provides a fundamentally different emphasis. We need to understand the whole range of variables that influence this competitive behavior: numbers may or may not be one of the more significant variables, depending on the circumstances.[11]

A second theoretical flaw of the attack on concentration involves the nature of demand facing an individual firm. In the perfect competition model, firms are price takers. They have flat demand curves, such that if they raise prices they lose all of their sales. In the real world, this is not the case. When firms raise prices, they retain some sales. Thus some economists and lawyers in the deconcentration era focused on firms that advertised heavily, claiming that they produced differentiated products with downward sloping demand curves, and hence with significant market power. But the mere fact of downward sloping demand tells us very little. Virtually all firms face a downward sloping demand curve.

Consider hot dog vendors on the street corners in many major cities. *Any* vendor who raised his price would be unlikely to lose all of his sales. In other words, the demand curve is sloped, not flat. But no one would claim this represents market power in any meaningful sense. An individual vendor could not influence the overall market by itself. The demand curve is sloped because of positive transaction costs. When purchasing a hot dog, most consumers will not find it worthwhile to first survey prices. As is now understood, such transaction costs have profound implications for contract law.

II   Consequences of Abandoning the Classical Theory

Because the market was felt to be so flawed—and with it classical contract theory—courts, legislatures, and government agencies departed from traditional contract law in their effort to protect those felt to be weak from those felt to be strong. Many of the most misguided steps were taken in the 1960s and 1970s, with impacts that remain today. Let me give two of countless examples, illustrating the extremes to which the departures from classical theory went.

FRANCHISING

Franchising has become a major form of business. Because franchisors and franchisees jointly produce a product or service, either party may disagree over their relative contributions to the success or failure of the joint enterprise. In a society as litigious as ours, franchisor-franchisee disputes sometimes end in court. After initial hesitation, courts enforced franchise contracts, even if they could be terminated at will.[12] A desire to "protect" franchisees led courts and legislatures to abandon traditional contract law to favor franchisees. Thus some judges, often relying on legislative pronouncements voiding "unconscionable" contracts or requiring contracts to be performed in "good faith," have aided franchisees, particularly in termination disputes.[13] As in many areas of consumer protection, proponents of franchisee protection have used an alleged disparity in bargaining power between the franchisee and franchisor to justify their actions. For example, one court stated: "Because of the vast disparity in bargaining power between the parties, the franchise relationship frequently amounted to a contract of adhesion unilaterally imposed on reluctant dealers by an all-powerful distributor."[14]

That the disparity of bargaining power argument would be used with franchisees shows just how divorced from reality the critics of traditional contract law became. The facts about actual and potential franchisees are sharply at odds with the picture of helpless individuals forced to accept a "take it or leave it" proposition. Table 1 presents data collected by the Federal Trade Commission in 1984 about the characteristics of actual franchisees. A strong majority obtained outside assistance before signing the contract, mostly from lawyers. Similarly, most thought they had received enough information prior to the contract that they did not desire any additional information. Most had relevant business experience, either working for the franchisor or other directly relevant experience. Moreover, most franchisees had sought other opportunities, frequently meeting with one or more other franchisors. Finally, the overwhelming majority of franchisees were content with their relationship.

The franchisees' personal backgrounds hardly indicate helplessness. Eighty-two percent had attended or graduated college. Moreover, the modal annual income in 1984 was $25,000–$50,000. (In 1984, median family income in the United States in current dollars was $22,415.)[15] The data for potential investors is similar. Sixty percent had comparison shopped, visiting more than four other franchises. The age, experience, education, and income level of potential investors were similar to that of actual franchisees.

Thus the bargaining power model appears dubious. Franchisors and potential franchisees meet in a market in which franchisees are hired. Franchisees can choose from competing alternatives, and franchisors have incentives to compete for the most capable and most skilled franchisees. Moreover, potential franchisees have alternatives, not just among franchisors, but among different lines of business.

A skeptic might reject this conclusion. After all, table 1 reveals that a substantial minority of franchise owners do not search for their franchise, lack informa-

Table 1   Personal and Bargaining Profile of Franchisees
(in percentages, unless otherwise indicated)

Franchise owners who obtained outside assistance before signing franchise contract	69
Franchise owners who consulted an attorney before signing franchise contract	49
Franchise owners who had relevant business experience[a]	60
Franchise owners who sought other opportunities[b]	59
Franchise owners who had personal meetings with one or more other franchisors	34
Franchise owners who believed they had received sufficient information prior to their signing franchise contract.[c]	81
Franchise owners who were content[d] with relationship with franchisor	80
Franchise owners who had attended or graduated from college	82
Modal Income: $25,000–$50,000	
Modal Age: 35–39	

Source: Audits and Surveys, Inc. (1984 survey done for and released by the FTC).
a. I.e., experience either working for the franchisor or other directly relevant experience.
b. The average number of other opportunities considered by franchisees was four.
c. I.e., they did not desire any additional information.
d. Fifty-five percent described themselves as very satisfied, and 25 percent described themselves as somewhat satisfied.

tion, or are not content with their relationship with the franchisor. Although the bargaining power argument hardly seems consistent with a majority of franchisors being such sophisticated consumers, what of the minority? Because franchise contracts are standardized across franchisees,[16] knowledgeable parties are likely to have more influence on the terms than are the less sophisticated. Standardization thus protects, not harms, the minority.[17]

In any event, the mere existence of standard form contracts does not reveal a lack of bargaining power. Such contracts are widely used in all aspects of business. Standard forms are a way to reduce transaction costs; forms avoid the formidable cost of starting each negotiation from scratch. Standardization reflects the high economic cost of individualized negotiations. Moreover, in competing for dealers or customers, businesses have incentives to offer contract terms that the other party will find attractive. The result is standardization, but it is also competitive, reflecting the cost and benefits to both parties of the contract.

Further, for any business that needs to deal with a large number of consumers, standardization is beneficial. These benefits would be lost if a franchisor allowed each franchisee to use a unique set of procedures. For example, Dairy Queen's difficulty in having its franchisees follow a standardized approach has become notorious. As Ray Kroc, the man who built McDonald's, once said, his secret of success in franchising was to avoid doing everything Dairy Queen did.[18]

If the bargaining power argument is transparently inappropriate for franchise contracts, then what explains the movement to protect them? Indeed, as the protection effort blossomed, tens of thousands of individuals sought to enter franchising, a fact hardly indicative of a bargaining problem. At least with legislatures, the source of much of franchise protection, another old-fashioned argument appears justified: political power. Franchisees are numerous; they and their employees vote, and, more important, contribute time and funds. This public choice explanation, rather than a public interest explanation, has more power to explain franchise regulation. Nevertheless, the proponents of such regulation have made easy and convenient use of the arguments that traditional contract law provided inadequate protection.

HEALTH CLAIMS IN ADVERTISING

For at least thirty years, a growing number of scientific studies have demonstrated the link between diet and disease. Studies warned, for example, of the dangers of cholesterol and saturated fats, as well as the benefits of fiber. As this evidence mounted, food manufacturers began to note the content of the foods on labels and in advertising (e.g., "no cholesterol"). Reflecting the belief that markets did not adequately protect consumers, the Food and Drug Administration (FDA) reviewed health claims in advertising. If a food is promoted as aiding in disease prevention, the FDA can classify it as a drug. Because drugs cannot be sold without FDA approval, which requires conducting clinical trials, in the 1960s the FDA successfully prohibited health claims on labels. This undoubtedly discouraged such claims in advertising. (The FTC, not the FDA, has jurisdiction over advertising.) Furthermore, the FDA was willing to infer disease claims from content claims. Thus it effectively prohibited claims that merely mentioned the lack of saturated fat or cholesterol.

In 1973, the FDA reversed its position on content claims, but it still did not allow reference to specific diseases.[19] The situation changed in 1984, when the National Cancer Institute (NCI) began a campaign to broaden the dissemination of information about the role of dietary fiber in preventing cancer. The NCI cooperated with Kellogg in designing All-Bran labels and ads, and the FTC's staff endorsed the campaign. Although the FDA considered seizing the product as a drug, it ultimately backed down and began to draft regulations to allow some health claims.

A trade-off between health or safety benefits and economic costs is common in consumer protection regulations. Economists (and others) who have studied such rules have long argued that, even when some regulation is justified, we should not incur excessive economic costs in pursuit of limited health benefits.[20] This trade-off is present in health messages as well, but there it is reversed—overregulation may produce significant public health costs in pursuit of relatively minor economic benefits.

Sound regulation of health messages for foods must proceed from a recognition that foods are not drugs in fact, even if certain claims arguably make them drugs under some federal and state regulations. The dietary modifications that have been suggested or promoted do not appear to pose any appreciable public health risk. The potential risks from introducing a new drug, however thoroughly tested, are surely orders of magnitude greater. Indeed, the underlying rationale for the statutory distinction between the regulatory standards for foods and the more stringent controls on drugs is the intuitive notion that the immediate consequences of errors in deciding what to eat are far less than the costs of erroneous decisions about drugs.

Conceptually, several regulatory approaches to health claims are possible. A market-oriented strategy, the policy implicit in both classical economic and contract theory, would rely on the power of truthful information to guide markets in the directions that consumers most prefer. Like classical contract law, it would police claims for fraud and deception. Thus it would preserve the benefits of current health claims and allow the possibility of similar benefits in other areas. In contrast, in the 1980s several states recommended the prohibitionist approach that the FDA followed before 1973—just say no. This approach, however, abandons entirely the important benefits that health claims can offer consumers.

A third approach, which the FDA eventually advocated and Congress adopted for food labels,[21] is a nutrition regulation strategy. The basis for this approach is an initial decision about the kind of dietary changes that consumers "should" make. Given this conception of the "true" relationship between diet and health, the nutrition regulation strategy seeks to control the flow of information to manipulate consumer choices. Although it relies on market mechanisms to bring about the desired product changes, the nutrition regulation strategy is based on an essentially paternalistic judgment: if certain choices are nutritionally sound, then consumers should make them.

A study by the FTC's Bureau of Economics demonstrates the benefits of the first approach for health claims.[22] The study examined the changes in the market for high-fiber cereals since Kellogg began advertising for All-Bran. The ad referenced the National Cancer Institute's recommendation that diets high in fiber may reduce the risk of some kinds of cancer. The Bureau of Economics analyzed two periods. In the first, prior to 1985, only government and noncommercial sources provided information about fiber consumption and cancer. In the second period, beginning in 1985, commercial advertising and labeling began. Scientific evidence of the link between fiber consumption and cancer developed rapidly through the 1970s and 1980s; but between 1978 and 1984, before commercial promotion, the study found no significant shift in consumption of higher-fiber cereals. Once commercial promotion began, however, a significant increase did occur.[23]

The manner in which both manufacturers and consumers responded to commercial promotion is revealing. Cereal manufacturers developed new products. Although many new fiber cereals were introduced after 1978, the study found that cereals introduced between 1979 and 1984 contained an average of 1.7 grams of fiber per ounce while those introduced between 1985 and 1987 averaged 2.6 grams of fiber per ounce. Regarding the impact on consumers, the study found significant differences in female choices of cereals across demographic groups before commercial promotion. (Consumption data were available only for women.) Women who either had less education, smoked, lived in households without a male head, or were not white chose low-fiber cereals at a greater rate than other women. After commercial promotion of health claims began, with the exception of difference by education level, all the differences were reduced. In short, health claims in advertising and on labels encouraged consumption changes, especially among those least likely to know of the NCI's recommendation from other sources.

Finally, and of great importance, the study found no evidence that consumers overreacted to health claims. There was no tendency for individuals to consume unusually large amounts of fiber cereals, nor did any of the groups that increased their fiber consumption following health claims achieve the level of consumption of the most educated consumers.[24]

The franchising and health claims examples are hardly isolated. Consumer protection regulation in advertising and other areas is replete with examples in which consumers have been harmed in the name of protecting them, protection that often begins with the premise that markets and the common law of contracts are inadequate.[25] This is not to deny that the government should enforce the basic rules of classical contract theory. The traditional government branch for articulating and implementing the basic rules of the market has been the courts. For transactions among businesses when large amounts are at stake, private lawsuits work well. When problems involve small losses for a large number of consumers, however, problems arise. Litigation is usually too expensive to be worth the effort, and the barriers to class actions are often formidable. Thus government consumer protection agencies, such as the Federal Trade Commission, have a theoretical basis for existence. In practice, of course, they have often failed to justify their potential.

Conclusion

Gilmore and his fellow critics of classical contract law were guilty of both bad economics and bad law. Contrary to the critics, monopoly was not becoming pervasive in the modern American economy. Nor did increasing reliance on standard form contracts signal a decline in consumer welfare. Although opportunistic behavior and information asymmetries may cause problems, standardization has produced tremendous benefits. Franchising, for example, has become immensely popular, benefiting consumers, franchisees, and franchisors. Moreover, restrictions on freedom of contract by courts, legislatures, and government agencies have often harmed all parties.

The Limits of Freedom of Contract in the Age of Laissez-Faire Constitutionalism

GREGORY S. ALEXANDER

It should come as no surprise that, as Professor Epstein's essay details, the internal doctrines of contract law show little influence of laissez-faire ideology. Too many of those doctrines originated long before the appearance of laissez-faire ideas to make it at all plausible to suppose that contract law first popped into the heads of late-nineteenth-century defenders of freedom of contract.

The logical place to look for a strong causal connection between laissez-faire and contract lies at the level of constitutional contract law, not private contract law. It is in the late-nineteenth-century debates over the constitutional limits of private ordering that laissez-faire ideas would be most apt to have appeared in any recognizably modern form or to have exerted a systematic influence on legal doctrine. Examining the Supreme Court's constitutional contracts jurisprudence during the *Lochner* era, this comment argues that even in that context laissez-faire ideology did not reign supreme.

This comment's thesis runs counter to the conventional wisdom about freedom of contract as a constitutional principle during the *Lochner* era. The standard account of judicial protection of economic interests during the late nineteenth century defines that period as the era of "laissez-faire constitutionalism."[1] According to this orthodox historiography, constitutional doctrine protected the twin pillars of laissez-faire, freedom of contract, and private property, above all else. Judges struck down an ever-wider array of regulatory measures that interfered with freedom of the marketplace, the story goes. Using the doctrine of substantive due process, they enshrined laissez-faire as a, if not *the*, central constitutional principle of the age. Liberty of contract, first introduced as a constitutional doctrine into the case law in 1886,[2] the story continues, reached its apogee in 1905 when the Supreme Court in *Lochner v. New York*[3] struck down a state law regulating working conditions in bakeries.

This story about the rise of laissez-faire constitutionalism reflects the residual influence of the old Progressive synthesis. It was not a commitment, however ill-founded, to a legitimate principle that led to the constitutionalization of laissez-faire. Rather, during this period, historians have argued, American judges were little more than pawns of the dominant economic class—wealthy industrialists. Spearheading the defense of the capitalist class's economic interests against legislative depredations was the Supreme Court of the United States.

This interpretation originated in the broader story that the Progressive historians and their latter-day disciples have told about the nineteenth century.[4] According to the Progressives' story,[5] with its crudely Marxist overtones, a continual struggle between "the people" and "the interests" has dominated American history. The late-nineteenth-century legal variant of this story describes how American judges after the Civil War initially rejected the idea of substantive due process but later adopted it during the 1880s and 1890s when grass-roots interests opposed to big business threatened to gain control of state legislatures. To protect the interests of large corporations and wealthy industrialists, the courts, particularly the Supreme Court, eventually read the ideology of laissez-faire economics into the Constitution through the Fourteenth Amendment's due process clause.[6] In the great battle between "the interests" and "the people," the People lost until Big Business was finally vanquished in the 1930s, when a reconstituted Supreme Court sustained the New Deal. Until that final victory of democracy, laissez-faire constitutionalism reigned supreme.

Old stories, like old habits, die hard, and the story of constitutional liberty of contract is no exception. Despite the efforts of some recent historians, notably Howard Gillman, Michael Les Benedict, Charles McCurdy, and Alan Jones,[7] one version or another of the old interest-group story is still told. Lawrence Friedman, for example, argues that what caused what he calls the "outburst of judicial review" in the *Lochner* era was purely and simply a response by courts, as representatives of the business class, to labor's capture of state legislatures. "When a power bloc was thwarted in one branch of government," he writes, "it naturally turned to another. If the legislatures were populist or Granger, there was always one last hope for a railroad or a mining company: the courts."[8]

In this comment, I hope to put this interest-group account of the constitutional liberty-of-contract doctrine to bed once and for all. Without doubting that the late nineteenth century *was* the high water mark of substantive due process or that the Supreme Court did protect economic interests to a greater extent than it does today, I want to offer two propositions that conflict with the traditional account of laissez-faire constitutionalism, one descriptive, the other explanatory. The descriptive proposition is that the Supreme Court never consistently applied liberty of contract as a constitutional doctrine in the late nineteenth century. It was only in the area of employment that the Court actively opposed state regulation of contractual relations, and even there the results were mixed. The interesting question, then, is why the Court selected the instances of contract regulation that it did as constitutionally offensive.

The explanatory thesis is that it was primarily ideas, not interests alone, that led the Court to protect liberty of contract in employment relations. Specifically, what motivated the judges who seemed most solicitous of freedom of contract was not base class interest alone but the residual influence of an intellectual tradition that is largely unknown to us today, a tradition that we can term "proprietarian."[9] The proprietarian tradition, whose roots can be traced back to Aristotle, takes seriously the idea of the commonweal. The common-law maxim *salus populi suprema lex*—the welfare of the people is the supreme law—has real meaning within this tradition.[10] It presumes that not all forms of social order are normatively equal but that some are superior to others. Just what the proper social order is has been an enormously controversial issue throughout American history. Different iterations of proprietarian thought have been based on very different, indeed sometimes contradictory, conceptions of the proper social order. The Puritans' "Shining City on a Hill," for example, was quite unlike the quasi-feudal social order of the antebellum South, yet both were proprietarian. More strikingly, the recent communitarian movement is based on the same proprietarian premise that was the intellectual foundation for the Southern slave system, a social order which modern communitarians otherwise totally repudiate.

What all of the different versions of proprietarian thought shared in common is the belief that the market order is not necessarily the normatively proper social order. Proprietarians do not understand the public good to be whatever the market yields. They regard the market as a realm in which individuals are too vulnerable to the temptation to act out of narrow self-interest rather than, as proprietarian principles required, for the purpose of maintaining the properly ordered society.

This is not to say that the proprietarian tradition is fundamentally antimarket. Many versions of proprietarian thought sought to reconcile propriety with the existence of the market. (The antebellum South again furnishes an example.) What characterizes proprietarian thought is commitment to a conception of the social good that is prior to the market. Proprietarian regimes are not necessarily nonmarket regimes, but neither are they laissez-faire regimes. The commitment to propriety requires that the market, to the extent that it is deemed to conflict with or to threaten the social good, be subordinated to the latter. The proprietarian tradition rejected the presumption that the scope of the market should be unlimited, and it did not resort to the familiar market-failure problems of monopoly or externalities to justify collective restrictions on market freedom.

One hardly expects to find remnants of this sort of intellectual tradition during the late nineteenth century, yet they were there. The residual influence of the old proprietarian tradition, which had been dominant in American legal thought a century earlier, was manifested chiefly in the form of protectionist legislation and in the struggles to define the constitutionally appropriate scope of such legislation. Contrary to conventional wisdom, the United States Supreme Court did not strike down all instances of protectionist legislation between 1870 and 1920. Various measures that it sustained cannot be considered as anything other than protectionist. The protectionist legislation affecting contractual relations that the Court was most likely to strike down was legislation that it considered to be motivated by a legislative desire to correct an imbalance of political power. The Court's concern with legislation favoring one side in contractual relations did not begin with the *Lochner*-era cases. Signs that it was ready to strike down such protectionist legislation appeared shortly after the Fourteenth Amendment was enacted. To the extent, then, that there *was* a constitutional liberty of contract doctrine, its roots in American legal thought extend much earlier than 1886 and trace back to a different ideology than either a simple probusiness mentality or the free market per se.

The upshot of these propositions is that we ought to take the so-called *Lochner* jurisprudence far more seriously than we usually do, without necessarily agreeing with it. We need to get rid of the caricatures of that era that still dominate legal scholarship and recognize the constitutional liberty-of-contract doctrine as a serious, however ill-conceived, attempt to maintain the core commitments of a liberal democracy at a time of unprecedented economic change and social upheaval.

I The Uneven Configuration of Liberty of Contract

Lochnerism neither began with nor defined the *Lochner* era. Courts protected economic interests in contractual relations prior to 1886, and after 1886, they protected contractual freedom only unevenly. Both of these points contradict conventional wisdom and require a bit of explanation.

It is true that the first decision to invoke the phrase "liberty of contract" as a basis for decision did not occur until 1886. It is also true that the great majority of decisions striking down legislation that regulated some aspect of contractual relations occurred after the mid-1880s. But the substance, if not the rhetoric of liberty of contract was evident earlier. Looking to state court decisions, we are apt to focus on the famous cases like *In re Jacobs*,[11] in which the New York Court of Appeals struck down a state law that prohibited cigar-making in tenement houses, or the series of Illinois Supreme Court decisions that ended with the infamous *Ritchie v. People*,[12] where the court voided a statute limiting the working hours of women in factories. Those were only the most spectacular cases, however.

At least as early as 1853, state courts were well aware of the idea of liberty of contract. In that year, a Pennsylvania court upheld a contractual provision that achieved expressly what the fellow-servant rule later achieved impliedly.[13] The Pennsylvania Railroad Company had required all of its employees to sign a standard contract providing that "the regular compensation will cover all risk or liability, from any cause whatever, in the service of the company." The court held that this waiver provision was valid, relying explicitly and heavily on the principle of liberty of contract. The issue in the case was not as straightforward as this makes it seem. The Georgia legislature had previously enacted a statute designed to abrogate partially the common-law fellow servant rule. The statute, applicable only to railroads, reinstated employer liability in cases of employee injuries sustained in the course of employment. The contract in *Bishop* sought to reverse the new statutory allocation of risk by providing, as a condition of employment, that the railroad's employees waived their statutory right. The Georgia court had little problem sustaining the waiver. "[I]t would be a dangerous interference with private rights," the court said, "to undertake to fix by law the terms upon which the employer and employee shall contract." In rhetoric that would repeatedly be echoed later, the court went on to state: "[I] know of no right more precious, and one which laboring men ought to guard with more vigilance, than the right to fix by contract the terms upon which their labor shall be engaged. It looks very specious to say that the law will protect them from the consequences of their own folly, and make a contract for them wiser and better than their own."

When we turn to what happened in the United States Supreme Court, the story is much the same. In substance if not in rhetoric, the principle of liberty of contract was evident before the *Lochner* era. While it was not until 1897 that the Supreme Court first fully relied on a substantive interpretation of the Fourteenth Amendment to strike down a state law regulating contractual activity,[14] the roots of substantive due process extend much earlier in the Court's jurisprudence. Chief Justice Roger Taney had relied in part on a substantive interpretation of the Fifth Amendment's due process clause in *Dred Scott*. Earlier still, the vested rights doctrine, which acted as a substantive check on legislative power over economic interests during the antebellum period, provided the foundation for the substantive due process idea as it later developed. Cases like *Fletcher v. Peck*,[15] *Dartmouth College*,[16] and *Ogden v. Saunders*,[17] all of which protected economic interests on the basis of the contract clause, would have been decided a generation later on the basis of substantive due process. While the Court never invoked the phrase "liberty of contract," the germ of that principle was very much at work. Moreover, we need to recall that in antebellum legal discourse, contract-based economic interests were more likely to be discussed as "property" interests because *property* was then used as a generic term, a genus of private interests of which contract rights were one species.

Turning to the other half of the descriptive thesis, even during the period between 1885 and 1930, the supposed height of laissez-faire constitutionalism, the courts, federal and state, did not uniformly sustain the liberty of contract principle. Legislative regulation of contract increased significantly after 1850, and most statutes, if they were challenged at all, were upheld. Lawrence Friedman has observed that "[i]f one looks, not to treatises, but to the actual business of the courts, it could be argued that the law of contract, after 1850, was beginning a long slide into triviality."[18] While this exaggerates the point, it underscores the fact that large parts of the law of contract, such as the law of common carriers and of insurance, were subject to regulation without any serious challenge, even after 1885. These restrictions cannot be described as anything other than protectionist.

Putting all of this together, when one carefully traces the actual lines of postbellum state and federal decisions invalidating legislation that regulated contract, what clearly emerges is that the liberty-of-contract principle was regularly used in an activist fashion in only one context: the labor contract. It was there, if anywhere, that "Lochnerism" reigned supreme. Every one of the litany of the famous Supreme Court liberty-of-contract decisions—*Allgeyer v. Louisiana*,[19] *Adair v. United States*,[20] *Muller v. Oregon*,[21] *Coppage v. Kansas*,[22] *Adkins v. Children's Hospital*,[23] and, of course, *Lochner* itself—involved a labor contract. Charles McCurdy has accurately summarized the pattern of decisions, stating that in the late nineteenth and early twentieth centuries what was operating was "a largely unarticulated assumption that contracts of employment were somehow special and therefore distinguishable from commercial contracts where the presumption of constitutionality concept applied when legislatures intervened."[24]

The important historical question is why labor contracts were singled out for special treatment under the liberty-of-contract doctrine. The reigning historical explanation is that of the Progressives: economic interest, combined with class bias, made courts particularly anxious about legislative intervention in the employer-employee relationship. Lawrence Friedman's explanation typifies the conventional wisdom: "Forced to choose sides, legal institutions necessarily reflected the wants of their basic constituencies. This meant that legislatures swung back and forth, depending on the strength of interests, blocs, parties and lobbies, or compromised. The courts were more independent of short-run swings of opinion. Partly for this reason, courts could afford to indulge in principles and ideologies. These were usually on the conservative side, because judges were solid, independent men of middle class."[25]

The problem with this interest-focused explanation is that it completely fails to take the idea of liberty of contract seriously on its own terms. One does not have to swing from one extreme to the other, from pure materialism to pure idealism, to credit *Lochner*-era judges with taking principles seriously. If one does so, the question that still remains is why they took liberty of contract more seriously in the employment context than in others.

II   The Social and Economic Context of Liberty of Contract: The Postbellum Problem of Power

In the years following the Civil War, the nation's economy went through enormous changes that transformed the character not only of the economy but of American society as well. The centers of power in the economy shifted from farms and small towns to cities, from small-scale entrepreneurs to large industrial firms. As early as 1868, Henry Adams could express astonishment at the changed conditions of American life. Of his family, which was returning to the United States after ten years in England, he said: "Had they been Tyrian traders of the year B.C. 1000, landing from a galley fresh from Gibraltar, they could hardly have been stranger on the shore of a world, so changed from what it had been ten years before."[26]

The tremendous growth of corporate power during this period prompted concern in several quarters.[27] Small entrepreneurs, labor leaders, farmers, and small-town businessmen all worried about the effects of urban corporate concentration on their futures in the unfamiliar economic order that was emerging. Compounding their anxiety, the postwar era was a time of tremendous cyclical swings in the nation's economy. Three serious economic downturns occurred between 1873 and 1900, including the deep depression that followed the Panic of 1873. Repeated and serious labor unrest added to the sense of the individual's loss of control over his economic circumstances. The railroad strike of 1877 made the Paris Commune of 1871 appear much closer to home than most Americans would have previously imagined possible.

Anxiety about social relations accompanied economic anxiety. Robert Wiebe has elegantly described how, after the strike, Americans felt a of loss of control over their daily lives, as their world of local island communities broke down and was replaced by a new bureaucratic order.[28] The change in the nature of enterprise was very much a part of this social disintegration. In addition to scrambling the hierarchy of power among social groups, the rise of the large industrial corporation created an even deeper ideological problem. The changing structure of the economy seemed to belie the ideal of free labor. While the image of the wage earner as economically independent (or at least potentially so) may have had some reality in the decades before the Civil War, it seemed increasingly unreal in a society where wage earning increasingly meant working in a factory twelve hours a day, six or even seven days a week. Many in the North began to agree with what Southern whites had said all along, that there was no meaningful difference between wage labor and slavery. The comparison was an exaggeration, of course, but it seemed apt to many opinion makers. A *New York Times* writer contended that Northern wage laborers' loss of independence signaled the onset of "a system of slavery as absolute if not as degrading as that which lately prevailed in the South."[29]

The response to this threat was legislation aimed at protecting workers in the employment relationship. Laws aimed at regulating the employment relations of women and children were not the only incursions on liberty of contract that were based on legal paternalism. Measures like the eight-hour workday laws were typically defended on explicitly protectionist grounds. Even statutes requiring companies to pay their employees in cash rather than company script could be seen as protectionist, given the premise of the wage earner's lack of independence.

The world of work was not the only area of social life in which protectionism might be observed in the late nineteenth century. Protectionism was seen by many as a general social phenomenon that, depending on the viewer, either properly responded to the unprecedented social and economic changes of the postbellum era or threatened the moral sociology upon which American democracy depended. It was this broader social debate over protectionism that provided the context for the liberty of contract doctrine. We need, then, briefly to examine that debate before turning to the constitutional reaction.

III "A Crime against Self": Antipaternalism and Personal Responsibility in Late-Nineteenth-Century Thought

Historians[30] have debated the prevalence of Social Darwinist ideas in late-nineteenth-century American thought. Revising the conventional account, usually attributed to Richard Hofstadter,[31] that depicted Social Darwinist ideas as running rampant during the Age of Enterprise, some historians have asserted, as one put it, that "Social Darwinism can now claim a dubious honor: that it has been shown not to have existed in more places than any other movement in the history of social theory."[32] But, as Dean Aviam Soifer has pointed out, antipaternalism "was an appealing surrogate for more explicit Social Darwinist rhetoric."[33] Legal writings between 1880 and 1920 were filled with attacks on paternalism. If Social Darwinism was not a major theme in the social theory of the period, antipaternalism was ubiquitous in the legal discourse of the time.

The most obvious target of these attacks were legislative measures aimed at protecting some seemingly vulnerable group. Legal writers tended to lump all such legislation together and tar it with the label of "socialism" or "communism" or both. Christopher G. Tiedeman's alarmist diatribe against class legislation was typical:

> Socialism, Communism, and Anarchism are rampant throughout the civilized world. The State is called on to protect the weak against the shrewdness of the stronger, to determine what wages a workman shall receive for his labor, and how many hours daily he shall labor. Many trades and occupations are being prohibited because some are damaged incidentally by their prosecution, and many ordinary pursuits are made government monopolies. The demands of the Socialists and Communists vary in degree and in detail, and the most extreme of them insist upon the assumption by government of the paternal character altogether, abolishing all private property in land, and making the State the sole possessor of the working capital of the nation.[34]

In part, the attack on legislative paternalism was a vestige of the Jacksonian ideology of individual equality. That was especially true of commentators, like Tiedeman, who attacked any and all legislative action that was not perceptibly and exquisitely evenhanded. Other critics of legislative paternalism (or at least what they viewed as paternalistic legislation) perverted the Jacksonian message by attacking legislation that was "populistic" and linking such a message with the brooding threat of communism. Joseph Choate's argument against the progressive income tax in *Pollock v. Farmers' Loan & Trust Co.*[35] illustrates this sort of hysterical assault on such legislation. "I believe," Choate told the Supreme Court, "there are private rights of property here to be protected. . . . The act of Congress which we are impugning before you is communistic in its purposes and tendencies, and is defended here upon principles as communistic, socialistic—what shall I call them—populistic as ever have been addressed to any political assembly in the world."[36] Another lawyer echoed the same theme that dependency breeds collectivism, stating, "Losing gradually their independent manhood, as they learn to rely upon the government to do for them what they should do themselves, the people drift more and more into socialistic practices."[37]

Legislative protection of vulnerable groups was not the only form of paternalism that commentators found objectionable. Many social critics considered paternalism no less offensive if it came at the hands of private individuals or groups rather than the government. Some critics carried the attack even further, treating any form of philanthropy as private paternalism. These arguments were especially revealing because what they indicated was that late-nineteenth-century critics found paternalistic acts objectionable not because they sacrificed the beneficiaries' personal autonomy but because paternalism made the beneficiaries weaker. From the perspective of strengthening moral character, it does not matter whether the beneficiary consents or not to the beneficial action. Private charity weakens individual character every bit as much as government restrictions on work hours. One writer went so far as to attack New York soup kitchens, which, in his view, threatened the republican form of government because they bred dependence and weakened the moral character of workers:

> Are we not establishing a debasing and dangerous practice in teaching these hitherto useful laborers, mechanics and clerks, that it is possible for them to live in enforced idleness upon the bounty of benevolent individuals, or the State? And are we not in a sense responsible for the *chronic* pauperism that this *surface* charity is breeding among this vast and rapidly augmenting army of mendicants?
>
> I am entirely satisfied that we are, through this soup house system, degrading and pauperizing the industrial classes, to an extent that will become a positive danger to the whole community, and threatening even the stability of republican Institutions. If you teach an army of industrial workers to live in easy idleness, will they not soon begin to demand support as a right? And when that support is withdrawn, will not society be confronted with a clamorous army of the now "dangerous classes"?[38]

It is easy for us today to laugh at this as the mindless outburts of extreme Social Darwinists, but the fact is that many legal and nonlegal commentators in the last decades of the nineteenth century took these views very seriously. They did so because the assault on paternalistic legislation and private property arrangements was not simply about economics; more importantly, it was based on a political-moral-social vision, a vision that was a vestige of the eighteenth-century civic republican sociology of virtue.[39]

The vision emphasized personal responsibility above all else. Unless your status placed you in one of the categories of persons who were deemed to be incapable of looking out for themselves—categories that included Indians and African Americans, along with children and "idiots"[40]—you were responsible for the material conditions of your own life. No one owed you a duty, legal or moral, to protect you against economic misfortune or to bail you out of economic distress. If people were entitled to be protected against their own ill-considered actions or against the actions of the invisible hand, they would lack incentives to de-

velop the personal qualities necessary for the proper moral and political person-
ality—carefulness, determination, honesty, and above all, energy.

Some commentators additionally urged that those who were wealthy should
not consume their wealth ostentatiously, echoing eighteenth-century republican assaults on "luxury."[41] For the most part, however, frugality was not part of
the late-nineteenth-century image of virtue. Rather, the virtuous citizen was
one who earned his wealth (though not necessarily all of it), paid his own way,
satisfied his debts, was honest and fair in all his dealings, commercial and otherwise, and responded to adversity by exerting himself with renewed vigor. He
was, in short, the self-sufficient, productive man of integrity.[42]

IV   Defining the Scope of Protectionism in Contracts
of Employment: Proprietarian Social Order in the Market Economy

In view of pervasive antipaternalist sentiment, the *Lochner*-era Supreme
Court's commitment to liberty of contract seems less than total. While the
Court used the liberty-of-contract doctrine to strike down the ten-hour workday
for bakers in *Lochner*, it refused to apply it against the eight-hour law for miners
in *Holden v. Hardy*.[43] More surprising perhaps is the fact that Justice David
Brewer, the very paragon of laissez-faire constitutionalism, voted against both
of these protectionist measures but voted in favor of an overtly protectionist
labor statute in *Muller v. Oregon*.[44] How can we explain these apparent paradoxes?

In the remainder of this comment I shall argue that while the Court did take
the idea of liberty of contract seriously, it took equally seriously the task of defining the appropriate scope of that doctrine within the unprecedented labor
conditions of the late nineteenth century. The Court permitted those instances
of protective labor legislation that could legitimately be said to protect vulnerable workers from potentially dangerous working conditions. Women wage earners were, at least from the perspective of American men at the time, the most
obvious such group, but they were not the only workers to whom legal protection could legitimately be given. The pattern of the Court's liberty-of-contract
decisions, then, reflects not only the residual influence of the "separate sphere"
ideology that first made its mark in American consciousness in the first half of
the nineteenth century but also the acceptability of a wider protectionist out-
look during the age of laissez-faire constitutionalism.

That the Supreme Court was prepared to accept protectionist labor legislation
directed at women is clear. For all of its rhetoric about the constitutional imper-
ative that regulatory legislation be "neutral," the Court in *Muller v. Oregon*
(1908) gave its imprimatur to a labor statute that explicitly singled out working
women for special attention. At issue in *Muller* was an Oregon statute declaring

that "no female (shall) be employed in any mechanical establishment, or factory, or laundry in this State more than ten hours during any one day."[45] Predictably, the statute was challenged as a form of "class legislation," void under the due process clause of the Fourteenth Amendment precisely insofar as it singled out women workers. In an opinion written, incredibly enough, by Justice Brewer,[46] the Court held otherwise. Expressly rejecting the analogy made to the New York statute struck down just three years earlier in *Lochner*, Justice Brewer stated that "the difference between the sexes does . . . justify a different rule respecting a restriction of the hours of labor."[47] "That woman's physical structure and the performance of maternal functions," said Justice Brewer, "place her at a disadvantage in the struggle for subsistence is obvious."[48] Women's status as the weaker sex made all the difference, constitutionally, for the statute in question. Delimiting the working conditions of women was a legitimate form of legal protectionism, Justice Brewer openly declared: "Differentiated by these matters from the other sex, she is properly placed in a class by herself, and legislation designed for her protection may be sustained, even when like legislation is not necessary for men and could not be sustained."[49]

The Court's singling out of women as a class in need of protective labor legislation was, in many respects, unsurprising. After all, a unanimous Court (with Justice Brewer again writing for the Court) in 1895 had sustained a criminal conviction of a lawyer who charged a woman client more than the statutory maximum fee for processing her pension under the Dependent Pension Act of 1890.[50] Justice Brewer announced there that "[i]t is within the undoubted power [of Congress] to restrain some individuals from some contracts."[51] Women, along with other social groups regarded as needful of protection, such as Indians[52] and sailors,[53] were an obvious target of legal protectionism, particularly in the employment context. But the Court's approval of protectionist labor legislation did not stop with these obvious categories of workers.

The Court had first signaled its willingness to accept certain instances of protectionist labor legislation in *Holden v. Hardy* (1898). That case involved a challenge to a Utah statute prescribing a maximum eight-hour workday for underground miners and workers in smelters. In the Court's first opportunity to review a state labor law under the Fourteenth Amendment, the Court simultaneously recognized the liberty of contract doctrine and the constitutional validity of certain instances of protective legislation under the state's police power. Calling law "a progressive science,"[54] the Court stated that the state's police power "has doubtless been greatly expanded in its application during the past century, owing to an enormous increase in the number of occupations which are dangerous, or so far detrimental to the health of employés as to demand special precautions for their well-being and protection, or the safety of adjacent property."[55] Coal miners and iron smelters, the Court found, were peculiarly vulnerable to the sort of safety and health risks that are the proper target of police power protection. That these workers may have freely entered into the bargains they did was no response, the Court said. It was not simply a matter of unequal bargaining power; the state has a legitimate and independent interest in protecting peculiarly vulnerable workers: "[T]he fact that both parties are of full age and competent to contract does not necessarily deprive the State of the power to interfere where the parties do not stand upon an equality, *or where the public health demands that one party to the contract shall be protected against himself.*"[56]

Safety and health legislation was one thing. State regulation of other terms of employment contracts was, arguably, another. Nevertheless, the Court's approval of protectionism aimed at discrete groups of workers thought to be particularly likely to act against their self-interest did not stop with safety and health legislation. In *Patterson v. Bark Eudora,*[57] the Court sustained against a due process challenge a federal statute forbidding the advance payment of wages to sailors. The Court made short shrift of the liberty of contract argument. Sailors' contracts were different because, as everyone knows, sailors are a particularly vulnerable class of workers. In a wonderfully paternalistic opinion, Justice Brewer (again!) stated:

> The story of the wrongs done to sailors in the larger ports, not merely of this nation but of the world [the sailors in question were working on an English bark], is an oft-told tale, and many have been the efforts to protect them against such wrongs. One of the most common means of doing these wrongs is the advancement of wages. Bad men lure them into haunts of vice, advance a little money to continue their dissipation, and, having thus acquired a partial control and by liquor dulled their faculties, place them on board the vessel just ready to sail and most ready to return the advances. When once on shipboard and the ship at sea the sailor is powerless and no relief is availing. It was in order to stop this evil, to protect the sailor, and not to restrict him of his liberty, that this statute was passed.[58]

The upshot of these cases is that neither the principle of contractual freedom nor the principle of class neutrality was ever generally applied. States *could* restrict the contractual liberty of certain types of contracts, and legislation *could* be aimed at protecting particular social groups.

V Vestiges of Propriety

What, then, are we to make of the great bugaboo, *Lochner,* and its ilk? After all, the ten-hour workday statute at issue in *Lochner* was, like the statute in *Holden v. Hardy,* seemingly a safety and health measure; why, then, was its protectionist foundation any less secure than the Utah statute's? The immediate answer is the very real possibility that the protectionist ideology could easily get out of hand if not cabined to discrete categories of workers. The vulnerability of workers depended on the nature of their work. Bakeries are not underground mines. The safety and health risk to miners is obvious, so the police power basis for the Utah statute did not appear to the *Holden* Court to be pretextual. The risk posed by long working hours in bakeries is not apparent, or at least it was not so to the Court. There is, the Court said,[59] no sense in which either the workers' or the public's safety or health is at stake in longer working hours.

At a deeper level, the Court's objective in *Lochner* was to define the boundary between those spheres of work where legal protectionism is proper and those in which self-reliance and personal autonomy must remain unchecked. The social vision underlying this enterprise of boundary-definition was not strictly market driven. It was an attempt to accommodate the increasingly market-oriented society with an older social vision that I have called "proprietarian." What characterizes proprietarian thought is the belief in the existence of some substantive social ordering that is normatively proper in the very nature of things. That is, the substantive idea of the proper social order preexists the market. The social order that is proper is one that may (or may not) coincidentally resemble that which the market would produce, but it is not proper by virtue of its being the product of the market.

This tradition has faded considerably in the twentieth century, but historically it exerted a powerful influence on American legal thought. Proprietarian assumptions dominated legal thinking during the eighteenth century and continued to exert a profound influence on American ideas about law and society well into the first half of the nineteenth century. While its influence waned in the second half of the nineteenth and early twentieth centuries, it did not disappear.

It is somewhat misleading to speak of "the" proprietarian tradition. Throughout its history in American legal thought, proprietarian thinking has been neither static nor monolithic. It has developed both diachronically and synchronically. That is, multiple versions of the proprietarian vision have appeared, both over time and within particular periods. In the late nineteenth and early twentieth centuries, lawyers and judges disagreed on the particulars of what constituted the good society, but most of them shared the conviction that the central challenge then facing American law was to preserve the inherited social order, in its basic outline, in the face of the enormous economic and social changes then occurring.

The social ideal that Americans of the late nineteenth century inherited from their forebears possessed two closely related characteristics. It viewed the range of social roles that were appropriate to various social groups as limited, and it conceived of the proper social order as inherently hierarchical. These two characteristics are in tension with the contractarian foundation of laissez-faire ideology, and they provided the bases for the Court's definition of the limits of the liberty-of-contract doctrine.

The proper society minimally required that limits be placed on what roles various social groups held. For all of the popularity of Horatio Alger and other tales of unlimited opportunity and social mobility at the time, many, perhaps most, Americans at the time still believed there were natural limits to social mobility and the fluidity of social roles. This was especially true of specific social groups, among them children, women, blacks, and Indians. Late-nineteenth-century Americans, like their eighteenth-century forebears, regarded these groups as unsuited for certain roles in the natural order. While slavery had been abolished, for example, white America overwhelmingly believed that black Americans should not hold positions of leadership, either in the public or the private sector.

From the perspective of those who clung to this social vision, the demographics of the new wage-earning class posed a dilemma. The rapidly growing cohort of industrial workers included greater numbers of women and children than ever before. There was nothing novel about women and children occupying working roles, of course. Domestic work was considered entirely natural for them, as were some forms of nondomestic labor. But industrialization placed them in positions of work that were largely unprecedented. Many of them now performed, as wage-earning workers, tasks that were indistinguishable from those performed by adult men, violating deeply ingrained perceptions about God-given abilities and natural roles. Women and children were considered inherently weaker than men, more vulnerable to both physical injury and abusive exercises of power.

In one sense, there was nothing surprising or disquieting about vulnerable social groups being left unprotected. All wage-earning workers were considered inferior and more vulnerable than employers, yet few would seriously argue that vulnerability alone imposed obligations on the state to protect all workers regardless of age or gender. The social ideal that dominated late-nineteenth-century thought was hierarchical, and wage earners were lower in the hierarchy in the natural order of things. Taken to its logical extreme, the idea that vulnerability alone created collective obligations to protect those who were weaker would mean virtually all instances of legislation aimed at protecting wage earners against all work-related risks had to be sustained. That would include legislation regulating the wages agreed to in the labor contract, since economic exploitation was as much a risk created by vulnerability as any other condition of wage-earning work. Such a conclusion, however, would deny the very fact that social hierarchy *was* natural and proper. Clearly it could not be contemplated.

The task, then, was to find some means of identifying which instances of vulnerability in the employment relationship warranted collective protection in the interest of the proper social order.

The Supreme Court's response to this dilemma was to focus not solely on the vulnerable status of the worker but also on the identity of the protected class of workers. What distinguished the Oregon maximum hours statute sustained in *Muller v. Oregon* from the New York statute struck down in *Lochner*, for example, was the gender difference of the protected classes in the two cases. Concluding that *Lochner* was not decisive of the question before it, the *Muller* Court squarely rejected the argument that "the difference between the sexes does not justify a different rule respecting a restriction of the hours of labor."[60] Which contractual terms were regulated could also be decisive, as could the type of industry which was affected. For example, in *Muller* the statute did not regulate working hours for women in all occupations but only in a "mechanical establishment, or factory, or laundry."[61] It was "common knowledge"[62] that such occupations were dangerous to health and safety.

Conclusion

By limiting interference with contractual freedom to discrete instances of vulnerability that posed risks for the proper social order, the Court sought to accommodate the new ethic of liberty of contract with vestiges of the inherited proprietarian tradition. While the effect of the Court's approach was to reinforce the extant configuration of economic power, its immediate concern was less with entrenching the interests of the economically dominant class than it was with preserving a particular social vision. The social ordering upon which the Supreme Court's liberty-of-contract decisions were premised was one in which the market was the primary mechanism of social ordering, but it was not the only one. The idea of propriety was still viable, and it was used to carve out discrete categories of society that could and should be insulated from market forces. Liberty of contract might dominate, but it had its proper limits, limits that could not be defined by the logic of the market alone.

Courts and the Tort-Contract Boundary in Product Liability

PAUL H. RUBIN

In this essay I address the appropriate source of liability in cases of injury between parties with a preinjury contractual relationship. This would include, for example, product liability (for direct purchasers, not for injured third parties), and medical malpractice.[1] Since the parties had a preinjury relationship, they could have contracted ex ante for damages and liability standards through warranties and disclaimers. Had they done so, they would probably have chosen standards that would have reduced litigation levels. The current legal system, behaving consistently with arguments made by Atiyah and Gilmore,[2] instead treats these injuries as torts and handles them through product liability, leading to many additional cases. This means that consumers and producers are forced to accept the terms imposed by the courts, and there is no room for variation. The literature arguing for contractual treatments of such injuries is voluminous,[3] as is the literature arguing for the now traditional treatment as a tort, a very small sample of which is discussed below.

I first address the importance of the issue: Why does it matter if product injuries are treated as torts or contractual violations? In order to understand the issue, I speculate about the form of tort recovery that consumers would choose in a world of free contract. I then show how this is related to decisions consumers make about contracts and to court decisions in the event of injury. Under sufficiently Coasian assumptions about bargaining, the way in which we treat product injuries does not matter. Whether we treat product liability as a contract or a tort issue matters only if some standard assumptions regarding rationality and decision making are violated, either by consumers in entering contracts or by juries in deciding cases. Thus the issue of the importance of the legal regime turns on the nature of the situations in which rationality assumptions of various sorts are satisfied or violated.

The existing literature has looked at one side of this issue: the extent to which consumers as parties to contracts violate rationality assumptions and make agreements that are not in their true interests. This literature has applied some of the experimental findings on cognitive decision making to consumer choice, and purports to show that consumers will make erroneous decisions, or can be manipulated into making such decisions, and thus will enter into contracts that do not provide sufficient net benefits. I show that this set of arguments is flawed, and that the conclusions reached (that intervention into contractual freedom is warranted) are indefensible, at least on this basis. Second, and more importantly, I show that this literature itself commits a version of the "Nirvana" fallacy. This is the fallacy of comparing the *actual* operation of one decision system with the *ideal* operation of another. Traditionally, the error is comparing actual markets with ideal regulation. Here, it is comparing actual contracts with hypothetical ideal tort liability. I show to the contrary that the cognitive error literature that purports to justify interference with consumer choice in contracts actually cuts the other way. Even if consumers make errors in contracting, courts and juries in product liability cases can be expected to make even greater errors. If we believe in the importance of cognitive errors, therefore, we should prefer a contractual to a tortious regime even more strongly.[4]

I What Law Would Consumers Want?

If parties in a contractual relationship[5] could bargain for liability and damages standards, producers and consumers would be able to devise an efficient system, as happens in any other free market. Thus any attempt here to define an efficient system is in one sense redundant and at a minimum speculative. However, it is possible to conjecture about the terms that might evolve in such a market, as long as we remember that we are speculating. If the system were allowed to develop freely, then the terms that would actually arise would be the desirable terms, and if these terms differ from those that I hypothesize to be efficient, this merely means that my speculation is incorrect. The problems with the current tort system stem from the willingness of outsiders to impose terms on bargainers that the outsiders believe are optimal; I have no such goals.

Since parties are in a preaccident contractual relationship with each other, the potential victim is paying money to the potential injurer. If tort law imposes costs on the injurer, then these costs will ultimately be borne by victims through higher prices. Once parties to contracts learn that the courts will impose payments in the form of accident compensation, then the expected cost of this compensation will be included in the price of the product. It is this payment that creates the incentive for consumers (who are also potential victims) to desire efficient tort standards.

Tort law is commonly viewed as performing two functions. Plaintiff tort lawyers in arguing before juries commonly stress the compensation function: Injurers should pay to compensate their victims. (This view is commonly rejected by economists.) The other function, generally accepted by economists, is deterrence. Requiring injurers to pay for the cost of injuries they cause will deter them from causing inefficient future harms.

But while tort law may perform these functions, so do other institutions in society. Tort law need not bear the entire burden of either compensation or of deterrence. Consider, first, insurance as a form of compensation. Most consumers have direct medical insurance and loss-of-wages insurance to compensate for the cost of injuries, and life insurance to compensate heirs for lost contributions to the family. Thus tort law does not provide any needed insurance. Moreover, tortious events, even in today's litigious world, are rare. Most deaths and injuries occur in ways that do not generate tort liability. Therefore, consumers desiring life, health, disability, or accident insurance would not be well advised to forgo first-party insurance and rely on the chance that they could collect in court for any injury suffered. Additionally, the cost of operating the tort system is about 50 percent; that is, of every dollar that passes through the system $.50 is taken by transactions costs, including legal fees (for both plaintiffs and defendants, as they are both ultimately paid by consumers) and court costs. This is an extraordinary level of costs—much higher than the operating cost of any other form of insurance. Indeed, it is so high that a consumer would have to be exceedingly risk averse to find insurance with this level of load worth purchasing. Thus, tort law is a highly inefficient method of compensating victims of accidents. For this reason, most students of law and economics (including Landes and Posner[6] and Shavell,[7] who are more favorable to the current tort system than many others) believe that the compensation function of tort law is relatively unimportant.

Tort law provides a deterrent, but so do other forces. The most important such force is reputation. Firms invest large sums in establishing and protecting reputations, and many institutions in the marketplace police and provide information about reputations.[8] There is a downside to reputation as well: a firm which injures consumers suffers a large loss in the value of its reputation.[9] When a firm's product causes an injury or is judged unsafe, the company suffers substantial losses in stock value, indicating that the stock market anticipates that consumers will be reluctant to purchase the products of that firm.[10] Firms are aware of these costs, and therefore have very strong incentives, independently of tort law, to provide safe products.

An additional source for safety in the contemporary U.S. economy is regulation. Virtually all products that might be involved in injuries are regulated by the federal government, through such agencies as the FDA, the CPSC, NHTSA, and others. I am not claiming that such regulation is desirable or efficient, but it does exist. Moreover, when regulation errs, it is often on the side of excessive safety (as shown in the large literature on new drug approvals by the FDA). If there were less regulation, then we would expect new institutions to evolve to provide additional information about product safety to consumers. Indeed, an important function of safety regulation may be the provision of information, as when the market reacts to a recall or other regulatory event indicating insufficient attention to safety by a firm.

Thus, in evaluating tort law, we must remember that it operates in concert with other forces to provide safety and to compensate injured parties. Economic analyses such as those of Shavell and Landes and Posner that assume that the tort system is the only factor leading to safety therefore overstate the importance of this system, and the conditions they derive for efficient levels of safety are stronger than needed. Indeed, an alternative model to theirs would assume that consumers are fully informed about product safety, so that the tort system would have no role in increasing safety. The truth is somewhere in between.

One caveat is in order. It is not possible or useful to go back to 1960 and observe the standards of liability in place then, before the great expansion in liability, to infer what would occur now. From 1959 to 1996, per capita real disposable personal income more than doubled (from $8,638 to $19,242 in 1992 dollars[11]) and, as Aaron Wildavsky[12] has told us, "richer is safer." Thus consumers today might demand greater safety than in the past, and this would imply different liability rules. Ramseyer describes a voluntary, contractual, and apparently successful products liability system that existed until recently in Japan.[13]

In considering the likely outcome of a regime of free contract, it is important to keep in mind the role of competition. For any product, there will be numerous sellers, and sellers will be able to compete in offering different contractual terms. In analyzing contractual "failures," opponents of free contract often appear to believe that there is only one seller offering one contract, and that consumers are at a disadvantage because they cannot bargain with sellers over the forms of contracts, but are faced with a "take-it-or-leave-it" choice. But if they were allowed to, different sellers would offer different contracts, and consumers would then have a choice. Just as sellers compete on price and other terms of sale, so they can be expected to compete in offering different contractual terms and warranties as well. Just as the seller who offers the combination of product quality and price that the consumer most values will succeed, so the seller who offers the most valuable contractual terms will also succeed. The "power" of consumers comes not from face-to-face bargaining but from competition in the market. Since lawyers are professionally involved in the former but not the latter, they tend to underestimate its strength. As we will see below, this competition is lacking when courts write identical contracts for everyone.

With these issues in mind, it will be useful to speculate about the efficient form of law. It is helpful to separate the standard of liability from the level of damages. I discuss each.

One issue in analyzing liability much stressed by economists is the distinction between strict liability and negligence.[14] Under strict liability, the injurer is liable for any harms, no matter what efforts he has made to prevent the harms. Under negligence, the injurer is liable only if he did not take the proper amount of care to prevent the accident. Standards may also differ with respect to the obligation of the victim. In a regime of contributory negligence, any contribution made by the victim to causing the accident (for example, by product misuse) will release the injurer from liability. In a regime of comparative negligence (which is common in the United States today[15]) the victim is compensated in proportion to the fraction of the accident caused by the injurer.

Tort analysts find it useful to distinguish between manufacturing defects and design defects. A manufacturing defect occurs when a particular product does not meet its own advertised specifications. If, for example, the steering wheel in a new car should break during normal driving, this is a manufacturing defect. Many analysts agree that strict liability for manufacturing defects may be appropriate. Under a strict liability standard, the manufacturer is liable for harm associated with the defect. Such defects are relatively rare and therefore do not lead to great costs. They are also independent—finding one defect does not generally mean that an entire product line is flawed. (If a manufacturing defect is common, a product recall can often provide a fix.) There is nothing a consumer can do to avoid these defects since they occur in the manufacturing process and manufacturers decide how much to spend on inspection and quality control. The costs of determining that a fault has occurred are relatively small. Thus a strict liability standard for this class of error might evolve in a free market. Indeed, there is evidence that the original proponents of strict liability for injuries caused by products had exactly this class of defects in mind.[16]

Design defects are quite different. These are said to occur when the courts rule that it would have been possible for the manufacturer to design the product differently and so make it safer. For example, a court may decide that an automobile manufacturer should have put the gas tank in a different location. If there is a design defect, then all units of some product are defective, since all share the same design. Viscusi has shown that part of the great expansion in product liability occurred when the courts extended strict liability from manufacturing defects to design defects.[17] This theory of liability requires courts and juries to second-guess product designers and determine if there was a safer alternative available when the product was manufactured. Plaintiffs claim that such an alternative was available; defendants claim not. This leads to complex debates involving engineering and other experts on both sides. Such second-guessing is difficult or impossible, so litigation of such issues is very expensive. Many of the major problems identified with the current tort system are due to the extension of strict liability to design defects. It is likely that a contractual solution would lead to little or no liability for design defects, and thus fewer cases filed. Moreover, the cases that would not be filed are the most expensive and difficult, so there would be a great saving from eliminating them.

Another major class of modern liability cases involves a "failure to warn." Originally it was thought that product warnings would insulate manufacturers from liability. However, the opposite has occurred: manufacturers are often found liable for failure to warn, sometimes in circumstances where consumers misused the product in dangerous and unpredictable ways.[18] Viscusi indicates that this expansion in liability for failure to warn is the second major cause of the growth in tort liability in the contemporary U.S. legal system. I would suspect that some liability for failure to warn would remain, but only for risks that were reasonably predictable but not obvious in normal uses of the product. Liability might also attach to failure to indicate precautions that would avoid injury in such normal use. Again, the result would be fewer cases.

DAMAGE PAYMENTS

It is useful to divide damage payments into three classes. Pecuniary damages compensate consumers for actual out-of-pocket expenses. The major categories are medical expenses and lost wages. Nonpecuniary damages compensate consumers for other, nonmonetary losses. The most important class of nonpecuniary payments is for pain and suffering. Payments for hedonic losses, or lost pleasure of life, a relatively new and controversial class of payments in the tort system, are also nonpecuniary payments.[19] Punitive damages should be reserved for extremely reckless or grossly negligent behavior, where the goal, in addition to compensating the injured consumer, is to punish the injurer. Today they are used for other purposes, sometimes in bizarre ways.[20]

If we keep in mind that consumers are paying through higher prices for goods and services for whatever damage payments they ultimately receive, then some principles are apparent. Damage payments are like insurance: consumers pay "premiums" as higher prices for products, and receive a payment if injured. Since consumers do find it worthwhile to purchase insurance against medical costs and lost wages, it is appropriate that injurers should also compensate for this class of losses, although some coordination between payments from injurers and payments from direct insurers may be useful.[21] Moreover, it would also be desirable for payments for medical costs to be related to the level of medical insurance that consumers themselves choose, so that the moral hazard associated with unlimited medical reimbursement could be avoided. Even if some cases would be filed for pecuniary damages, calculation of these damages is relatively straightforward, and most such cases would be settled; there would be relatively little litigation over this class of damages.

If given a choice, consumers never buy insurance against pain and suffering.[22] There are sound theoretical explanations for this fact, involving declining marginal utility functions and the fact that death or injury reduces the marginal utility of wealth.[23] Briefly, we would not expect consumers to wish to pay to shift wealth to future states where it provides less utility. Moreover, consumers do not purchase such insurance when given a choice. This means that the value of such insurance is below its cost (including the costs of operating the system) and, since the cost of operating the tort system is higher than the cost of operating any other insurance system, consumers would be even less willing to pay for compensation for pain and suffering through the tort system than in other forms of insurance. For example, moral hazard and adverse selection problems are probably greater when tort law is used to provide the insurance.[24] Thus it is likely that a voluntary contractual system would not provide compensation for nonpecuniary losses. Since many cases are worth bringing only if there is a chance of collecting nonpecuniary damages, this reform would again reduce the number of product liability cases filed. Moreover, since the level of nonpecuniary damages is highly uncertain, litigation is more likely when this class of damages is requested, so that the reduction in cases that go to litigation (which is more expensive) from elimination of nonpecuniary damages would be substantial.

Punitive damages are a more difficult issue. Normal compensatory damages will not adequately deter all firm misbehavior, particularly that which is criminal. Moreover, firms will sometimes try to hide their behavior, and will sometimes be successful. Thus normal penalties will sometimes be insufficient to provide optimal deterrence.[25] Therefore, in some limited circumstances, punitive damages might be in the interest of consumers. A reasonable approach might be to require a higher standard of proof of blameworthiness for punitive than for other damages. For example, the standard might be the same as that in criminal law, proof "beyond a reasonable doubt." This would allow some punitive damages, but only in limited circumstances. This standard would eliminate many of the extreme cases observed today. Again, since some matters are worth bringing only if there is a chance of punitive damages, reducing their scope would reduce the number of cases filed, and, since punitive damages are also uncertain, this would reduce litigation as well.

In sum, if contracts were allowed, consumers would probably want strict liability for manufacturing defects and negligence (perhaps with payments based on comparative negligence) for design defects. Consumers would probably want to be compensated for pecuniary damages, but not for nonpecuniary damages. In certain limited circumstances they might also want punitive damages. If warranties were allowed and disclaimers enforced, then these are the terms that would likely be agreed upon by buyers and sellers. The result would be many fewer filed cases.

Manufacturers would have the option of specifying different terms, and advertising them. For example, a manufacturer stressing the safety of its product might agree to pay nonpecuniary damages, and perhaps advertise, "Our product is so safe that if a court ever rules that we have negligently caused a death, we will provide a $1,000,000 additional insurance payment to survivors."

On the other hand, George Priest has noted that in practice consumer product warranties seldom permit recovery for consequential damages (including injury).[26] This is because the inefficiencies of tort law are so great that buyers and sellers will seldom want to rely on it for compensatory purposes. The tradeoff is between extra costs of insurance (since first-party insurance is much less expensive than third-party insurance through the tort system) and extra safety through the incentives created by the tort system. If Priest is correct and warranties would disclaim consequential damages, this would imply that consumers would not be willing to pay the costs of the liability system for whatever additional safety the use of this system would provide. The issue is (or would be) empirical; as I indicated above, the actual market solution, if the market were allowed to function, would be the one we should rely on. If Priest is correct, there would be even fewer filed cases.

II   Contract and Tort in a Coasean World

Now consider a regime where the tort regime cannot be specified by contract, but where juries are perfect agents for consumers. This model would be consistent with fully informed rational jury self-interest. Since jurors are also consumers and might be involved as plaintiffs in future cases, and since they will pay as consumers for any price increases caused by their decisions, rational behavior might lead them to be such perfect agents. Let us begin with a world of Coasean perfect markets: No one makes errors and the legal system is able to adapt to whatever property rights and decision rules are in place.[27]

How would the courts behave if liability were tortious and not contractual? In a perfect Coasean world, the nature of liability should not matter. A jury faced with an injured party would act as an agent for others likely to be in a similar situation in the future, and would apply liability rules and award exactly that level and form of damages that the party would have wanted to contract for ex ante. Such a jury would not be concerned with the particular injured party involved in the case because the cost of these injuries is sunk. Rather, the jury would reach a decision that would establish an efficient precedent for future parties. Thus, in a products liability decision, a jury should award exactly the amount that the injured party would have contracted to receive in the event of injury ex ante if such contracts were enforceable. Juries would act as if instructions were: "The imposition of any damage payments will increase prices paid by all consumers for goods and services in the future. Thus you should consider the extent to which individuals might prefer to pay lower prices for products instead of receiving compensation for actual losses or for pain and suffering." Then the product price would reflect this level of damage awards, and would be the same as if liability had been assigned through contract.

Either a negligence-contributory negligence or a comparative negligence standard might be efficient.[28] In both cases, the definition of negligence would be that based on the Hand formula, a cost-benefit measure.[29] But the current regime of "strict liability" decided according to ambiguous negligence principles would probably never be chosen. If liability standards were set in this way, potential litigants would realize that they would have greatly reduced chances of collecting, and would not file cases. Thus the results would be equivalent to those under a pure contractual regime.

Before discussing juries, however, I will review arguments that utility maximization is not the appropriate standard for the law. I also consider some literature that claims that consumers often sign contracts that are not in their interest because they suffer from information processing or cognitive deficits that lead to systematic errors.

III   Should Consumers Negotiate Efficient Contracts? Can They?

The literature discussed here[30] is part of a second generation of criticism of contractual freedom. This criticism is part of a new set of defenses of the current regime in which courts refuse to enforce many contracts. Initially, those opposed to freedom of contract made appeals to "unconscionability," "unfairness," the evils of "contracts of adhesion," and "unequal bargaining power."[31] Economic analysis of these arguments has shown their deep flaws[32] so defenders have turned to new arguments.

Two major policy conclusions have emerged from the economic analysis of product liability: buyers and sellers should be permitted to choose the terms that will govern in the case of accident; and consumers would prefer not to be compensated for nonpecuniary damages, including hedonic damages and pain and suffering, if they had a choice. Many legal scholars, wedded to the current system, resist these conclusions.[33] These scholars rely on a new class of arguments,[34] which dispute the economist's assumptions of rational, utility-maximizing consumers. I discuss these assumptions in turn.

SHOULD LAW AIM AT UTILITY MAXIMIZATION?

Some scholars, particularly Croley and Hanson,[35] reject the goal of utility maximization or preference satisfaction. The simplest form of the Croley-Hanson argument is that accidents and other reductions in wealth might in theory in-crease the marginal utility of wealth instead of reducing it, so that it is theoreti-cally possible that nonpecuniary damages would be justified. This is unobjec-tionable, and, as they recognize, not novel. (Although it is unlikely that accidents would in fact have this effect on utility functions.) But they also pres-ent a more complicated argument consistent with nonutility maximizing be-havior. They argue that individuals might contemplate alternate utilities in dif-ferent states of the world and decide to shift wealth (and thus utility) to states where the "baseline" utility is lower. This decision might be made even if it is inconsistent with rational maximizing behavior (that is, with shifting wealth to higher marginal utility states). They call individuals who have such preferences "equimaxers" to distinguish them from "maximizers." This argument, how-ever, rests on explicit nonmaximizing behavior, and thus at best is problematic.

In an unusual article, Pryor rejects the standard utility analysis of risk and argues that risks should be valued from the perspective of the injured person rather from that of the uninjured decision maker.[36] She claims that uninjured persons cannot understand the utility function of those who are injured or dis-abled, and so ex ante judgments of ex post marginal utility should not count. Such a theory is fundamentally inconsistent with expected utility maximiza-tion, or indeed, with rational decision making. Any experience might change ex post utility relative to ex ante anticipation, but we do not on this basis prescribe consumer choices. Most specifically, her theory would seem to imply that all insurance policies should have a mandatory "pain and suffering" component, since those purchasing insurance would undervalue this category.

Feldman believes that there should be compensation for nonpecuniary losses, but she reaches this conclusion by rejecting economic analysis and by arguing that "preferences should not determine tort awards."[37] Rather, she would allow some measure of paternalism in deciding on optimal tort policy. But again, an argument rejecting preferences is a peculiar argument, at least from the perspec-tive of maximization of welfare, the starting point of economic analysis.

In a sense, it might be argued that these articles indicate the correctness of the economic approach. If the only arguments against this approach are based on achieving something other than maximization of consumer welfare, then the arguments must be unconvincing for those who value human satisfaction as a goal.

IRRATIONALITY

The second objection to the economic approach is that those who enter into transactions are not sufficiently rational to do so correctly. These arguments are based on alleged errors in human decision making, as reported by both econo-mists and psychologists in experimental laboratory situations.

Before discussing particular examples of this analysis, a caveat is needed. There is no doubt that in experimental situations, subjects commit predictable errors, of the sort discussed below and elsewhere in the literature. But there is a real debate regarding the extent to which these errors affect actual market behavior. For example, experimental markets seem to give efficient outcomes, even though individual participants may behave inefficiently.[38] It may be that, even if individuals make errors, market forces are sufficiently powerful to override these errors, as Becker argued long ago,[39] and that major policy outcomes should not be based on a preliminary and contested literature. In addition, I do not believe that the policy claims are justified by the literature. In what follows I critique arguments for restrictions on free bargaining that have been made by Richard Hasen, Howard Latin, and Melvin Eisenberg.

Richard Hasen[40] uses psychological analyses of decision making under uncertainty to attempt to shed light on contract and tort issues. He argues that, since there are known biases in consumer processing of information, the legal system should take these into account. In the context of my analysis, this argument would indicate that reliance on contracts would be inefficient because people would agree to inappropriate contracts. In particular, Hasen is concerned with "framing" effects, in which laboratory choices depend on whether payoffs are expressed ("framed") as losses or gains. For example, subjects are apparently more willing to try an experimental medicine if they are told that "80 percent of the people taking this medicine will survive" than if they are told "20 percent of the people taking this medicine will die." (Experienced physicians are subject to the same bias.) Hasen claims that, in many contexts, manufacturers take advantage of this bias in providing contractual terms and that the legal system should adjust.

There are two problems with this analysis. First, it proves too much: the issues raised by Hasen apply to many aspects of seller behavior, not just to contract terms. Second, the same biases would be exhibited by other legal decision makers. In particular, as discussed below, courts would be subject to the same biases, and therefore the legal system might be unable to correct the problems Hasen identifies.

As an example of overgenerality, Hasen discusses the credit terms made famous in *Williams v. Walker-Thomas Furniture Co.*,[41] the well-known Washington, D.C., case in which the terms of a credit contract were overturned as being unconscionable. The provision can be expressed in either the form of a gain or a loss:

> Term G (Gain frame): The buyer may retain all of the goods purchased from the seller provided that all payments are made on time to the seller. If all payments are not made on time the buyer may not retain the goods.
>
> Term L (Loss frame): The seller will not repossess all the goods purchased

by the buyer provided that all payments are made on time to the seller. If all payments are not made on time the seller will repossess the goods.[42]

Hasen claims that expressing the contract in the Gain frame will be perceived as more desirable by potential buyers and will lead to larger sales and profits than expressions in the Loss frame. He therefore suggests that legal definitions of unconscionability be expanded to include framing effects, so that contracts framed in the "gain" mode would be unconscionable.

But the same effects exist, if they exist at all, with respect to all product characteristics. Advertisers generally provide information in Gain frames. Automobile manufacturers advertise that "Our car will get twenty miles per gallon" not "Our car will get no more than twenty miles per gallon." Macy's advertises a "one-day sale" not "364 days of higher prices." Portable computers advertise "four-hour battery life" not "If you leave our computer on for more than four hours, you will lose your data." If advertisers provided this sort of adverse information, consumers would view them as demented. Moreover, the fact that all advertisers provide claims in gain frames means that consumers are used to interpreting commercial information in this way, and presumably are able to discount any framing effects. Like many legal scholars writing about contracts, Hasen treats contract terms as if they were different from other product characteristics. However, arguments that apply to contractual terms also apply to other aspects of products, and there is no reason to treat terms as different.

Next, Howard A. Latin[43] has argued that people make systematic errors in interpreting warnings, and that the use of warnings to eliminate liability is therefore bad policy.[44] That is, he would eliminate any defense in a product liability action based on the existence of an adequate warning. It is difficult to know exactly what to make of this argument. It does not take a deep knowledge of modern cognitive theory—or graduate training in law or economics—to know that consumers sometimes do not follow all warnings meticulously. But what does this simple fact (expanded into 100 law review pages with 439 footnotes) tell us? Virtually nothing. The goal is the solution to some maximization or minimization problem. For the answer to such a problem, more than qualitative information is needed; we must have some way of determining the optimal level of care and warnings, and simply demonstrating that there are complex ways in which warnings may fail does not help us make the necessary calculations.

Latin virtually admits as much. When he discusses policy, he agrees that all actual tests will be suboptimal, and that the factors he discusses are difficult to factor into a legal decision. However, he prefers to err on the side of "too much" safety even though he understands that this will impose costs on society. In fact, it appears that his entire analysis of cognitive errors is simply aimed at his goal of arguing for stricter liability whenever possible. Indeed, although he does pay lip-service to cost benefit analysis, he discusses the amount of safety which is "feasible" as a goal throughout the paper, and argues that firms should make products safer rather than relying on warnings.

There are other difficulties in Latin's analysis; I discuss one. A key point in the analysis is the distinction Latin draws between the "Rational Risk Calculator" (RRC) and the "Mistake and Momentary Inattention" (MMI) models. The first, of course, is the basic law and economics model, which assumes that consumers rationally calculate risk-benefit tradeoffs and make product purchases accordingly. The latter is his preferred model, and assumes that accidents are due to the named factors. But the inconsistency between these models is more imagined than real. One dimension on which products may be safer is exactly their ability to counter momentary inattention. Antilock brakes, to take a relatively familiar example, are particularly beneficial if a driver suddenly observes (as the result of a moment of carelessness or inattention, perhaps) that unless he jams the brakes immediately, he will have an accident. If the brakes still do not do the job, seat belts, air bags, or merely driving a heavier car will still minimize the impacts of the carelessness. Warnings can allow consumers to make appropriate decisions regarding the likely effects of expected levels of inattention, where one decision may be buying the appropriate product.

Finally, Melvin Eisenberg[45] uses arguments from the theory of cognitive errors to explain the courts' unwillingness to enforce contractual terms in several contexts. Here we consider his discussion of "standard form contracts," where Eisenberg takes the standard analysis of "contracts of adhesion" and dresses it up in modern psychological terminology. The devils in Eisenberg's analysis are "bounded rationality, optimistic disposition, systematic underestimation of risks, and undue weight on the present as compared with the future." But the chief devil, and the one discussed most, is "rational ignorance." Sellers know things about contracts that buyers do not know because it does not pay buyers to know them, and sellers use this knowledge to "slant things in favor of the form givers."[46]

There are three major errors in Eisenberg's analysis (and in the analysis of adhesion contracts in general). These are: treating contract terms as being different from other elements of the product; assuming that contract terms are the main determinant of firm behavior; and ignoring price effects.

Perhaps because lawyers (including academic lawyers) study how contracts are formed but not how real goods are manufactured, they seem to believe that contract terms are different from other product characteristics. Let me quote from Eisenberg at some length:

> First, a form contract often contains a large number of legal terms. Form insurance contracts, for example, typically contain thirty, forty, or more terms. Moreover, the meaning and effect of the preprinted provisions will

often be inaccessible to lay persons. In part, this is because the terms are often written in exceedingly technical prose. Even if the terms are clearly written, however, the form taker will usually be unable to fully understand their effects, because preprinted terms characteristically vary the form taker's baseline legal rights, and most consumers do not know their baseline rights.[47]

Now consider a slightly (but not misleadingly) altered version of this paragraph:

First, a *computer* often contains a large number of *parts*. *Laptops*, for example, typically contain thirty, forty, or more *parts*. Moreover, the *purpose and use* of the *parts* will often be inaccessible to lay persons. In part, this is because the *parts* often *perform* exceedingly technical *functions*. Even if the *functions* are clearly *explained*, however, the *computer buyer* will usually be unable to fully understand their effects, because *parts* characteristically vary the *chip's* baseline *performance*, and most consumers do not know their *chip's* baseline *performance*.

Conclusion? Because of asymmetric information and the fact that many of the parts of my computer or software will not be used often (or at all, for any one user) we must still all be using 1960s IBM mainframes, and the machine on which I think I am writing this is an illusion.

Silly? Perhaps. Unfair? I don't think so. The world is full of highly complex products made of numerous obscure parts, and of chemicals with unpronounceable names performing highly technical and unintelligible functions. We rationally don't know much about any of these things—no more, and perhaps less, then we know about contract terms. But that does not mean that the manufacturers "slant" the products toward themselves. On the contrary, manufacturers, driven by forces of competition, are constantly changing products to improve them, even though we may not understand why or how. It is difficult to understand how contract terms are different.

The other two points have already been addressed. Eisenberg overweighs the importance of contract terms in determining firm behavior and performance. Contract terms are only a part—a small part—of what motivates firms. Firms produce products and honor agreements because reputations are valuable, and lowering the value of reputations has severe consequences for the firm.

Finally, price. As Atiyah has recently noted, "[E]conomists are now trying to remind lawyers (though here with, so far, little success) that interfering with some of the terms of a contract probably only affects the price of the bargain, and so may be idle or positively harmful to those who it is sought to help."[48] Like Hasen, Eisenberg spends much of his analysis on *Williams v. Walker-Thomas Furniture*. What Eisenberg does not address is the effect of this decision in increasing the costs of credit to consumers in Washington—the "price of the bargain."

This critique of "contracts of adhesion" has the analysis exactly backwards. In private markets, there is a chance for competition, and if buyers do not like the terms offered by one seller and are willing to pay the costs of more favorable terms, other sellers can be expected to compete and offer better terms. But if the courts order all sellers to offer the same terms, then buyers are forced to buy on those terms or go without. There is no possibility for alternative contract terms, no matter how much the consumer may dislike the court-imposed terms. Thus the true contracts of adhesion with take-it-or-leave-it terms are those written by the courts; it is these contracts that are inescapable, and these terms that cannot be avoided. Moreover, these terms have been written by self-interested parties, interested in their own incomes, just as Eisenberg alleges happens in standard form contracts. The difference is that, in the former case, the parties are attorneys rather than manufacturers, and that there is no possibility of competition or change as long as the courts refuse to enforce contractually specified terms.

IV Will Juries Get It Right?

Since contractual waivers of liability are not enforced, cases are tried as tort rather than contract claims. In addition, many more cases are filed, since the parties would often bargain around tortious liability if permitted to do so. As argued above, if courts were perfect agents for parties to future transactions (which they are not), then this change should not matter. I first present some evidence showing that juries do not even attempt to choose efficient rules, and in fact resent attempts to inform them of such terms or to induce them to accept them. I then discuss the applicability of the literature on cognitive errors to juries, and show that we would expect the results of this literature to apply to court decisions even more than to consumers engaging in transactions. Finally I show that this literature suggests that juries should be expected to make poor decisions.

PINTO

Juries seldom have a chance to consider explicit cost-benefit analysis, for reasons that will be clear. There was one famous case where a jury was confronted with exactly such evidence, and the result was a public policy disaster. This was the *Ford Pinto* case.[49] Schwartz[50] persuasively shows that juries are totally unwilling to accept any hint of an analysis explicitly measuring the cost of lives saved. This is true even when the law expressly requires such balancing. It was the fact that Ford had undertaken such calculations that induced the jury to award large punitive damages in this case. Moreover, the jury's ire was so strong that virtually no defense lawyer is willing to make arguments relating to cost. Schwartz's distillation of conversations with several defense lawyers contains the following statement: "However, one argument that you should almost never make is that the manufacturer deliberately included a dangerous feature in the product's design because of the high monetary cost that the manufacturer would have incurred in choosing another design. If you do argue this, you're almost certain to lose on liability, and you can expose yourself to punitive damages as well."[51]

Nevertheless, the cost of safety improvements goes to the heart of the efficiency of care decisions.[52] If the jury cannot hear arguments about safety costs, it is unlikely to be able to act as an efficient agent for consumers or to arrive at the correct outcome. Indeed, because of the results of *Pinto* and the ability of plaintiffs to obtain documents through discovery, many firms are probably unwilling even to undertake a cost benefit analysis for internal planning purposes, let alone to make such arguments before a jury. In this sense, *Pinto* has probably led to excess harm and injury in the economy.

IS EXPERIMENTAL EVIDENCE RELEVANT FOR JURIES?

I mentioned above that experimental evidence on cognitive errors might not be relevant in analyzing market behavior. That is, market decisions might overcome the judgment biases reported in experimental tests. But these biases are less likely to be overcome in the case of juries. Instead, jurors are almost in the same situation as experimental subjects. If anything, the probability of an erroneous or irrational decision is greatest in the jury box.

Experimental evidence of decision-making errors was first provided by psychologists. Economists were skeptical of these results, and attempted to replicate the experiments in order to correct for what they perceived as misspecifications. Camerer indicates[53] that the main differences are that "psychologists use natural stimuli, do not pay subjects, and do not repeat tasks. Economists pay subjects, prefer blandly labeled random devices as stimuli, and insist on repeating tasks."

Consider now a jury. It makes a decision about an accident that has already (really) occurred, the essence of a natural stimulus, and moreover often one with a substantial emotional load. Jurors are not paid for correct decisions. Finally, cases and juries are unique, so there is no chance of a juror repeating the situation and learning of correct answers. To the extent that the institutions governing juries are like those used by psychologists and unlike those used by economists in experiments, then these institutions are more likely to lead to relatively less rational decisions and to more cognitive errors.

Many of the scholars discussed above (Hasen, Latin, Eisenberg) argued that cognitive effects would lead to biases in decision making, so that consumers would likely make errors in signing contracts. They used this argument to justify interference with contractual freedom, and judicial intervention in private transactions. But interfering with free contracting means that more contractual disputes will go to juries. Juries are more likely to be subject to bias than are consumers. Consumers sign many contracts and buy many products. Consumers pay directly whatever costs are associated with errors, and so receive feedback from erroneous decisions. Thus consumers have a chance to learn. Juries have no such chance. Jurors (as consumers) may end up paying higher prices for goods and services because of their decisions as jurors, but the link is neither obvious nor immediate. As a teacher of law and economics, I can say that it is not intuitively obvious either. Thus, if we believe that cognitive biases are important in decision making (and I am personally ambivalent on this issue), then we must believe that they are more severe with respect to jurors than with respect to individuals engaging in exchange for their own benefit.

EXPECTED JURY BIASES

What does the cognitive literature tell us about particular biases we might expect from jurors in product liability matters?[54] In general, the predictions all point in the same direction: juries are likely to award damages more often and award higher damage payments than consumers would desire ex ante. This additional level of payments will arise partially through a greater likelihood of finding liability and partially through an award of greater damages than would be desired ex ante. Since the errors are systematic, there is no presumption that awards would be random, and a finding of predictability in pain and suffering awards would not be inconsistent with the theory proposed here.[55] Awards will be predictable and might be internally consistent, but will be biased upward relative to efficient levels.

Consider first liability. In a negligence system (and in the odd version of "strict liability" that governs our current product liability system) a firm is negligent if it does not take all cost-justified precautions. But whether a precaution is cost justified depends in part on the probability of the harmful event occurring. A jury observes the product after an accident has happened and must then attempt to infer what level of precautions would have been efficient when the product was made and sold. There are reasons to expect that juries will form incorrect estimates of the relevant probability.

One common cognitive error is "hindsight bias."[56] Once an event has occurred, then subjects view the probability of that event as being greater than before the event occurred. Thus a jury, faced with an already existing accident, will believe that the probability of the accident ex ante was greater than may be objectively true. Therefore, even if a firm behaved non-negligently and took all cost-justified precautions, a jury may find negligence because of its overesti-mate of the probability of the accident. There is both actual[57] and experimental[58] evidence of the importance of hindsight bias in a litigation context, leading to excessive liability.

A similar result follows from what has sometimes been called the "law of small numbers."[59] This is the tendency of experimental subjects to overgenera-lize from small samples. Thus, if the major relationship jurors have with some product is observation of the effects of a mishap regarding this product, then the jurors might well view the product as being more dangerous than it is, again giving rise to overestimates of the risk associated with the product.

Two other effects identified in the cognitive literature will reinforce this over-estimate of probabilities of harm. First, there is evidence that low probability events (approximately, events with probabilities less than .2) are overweighed in decision making,[60] and product injuries are very low probability events. Second, subjects tend to be overconfident of the accuracy of their assessments of proba-bilities[61] so that there is no obvious mechanism that would lead to correction of these erroneous estimates. Jurors would be expected to be overly confident of their estimates of proper damage levels, so there is no reason to expect juror doubt or uncertainty to reduce the level of damages. Subjects also have a biased tendency to interpret new evidence as consistent with their initial hypothesis, so that if jurors start with a belief that the defendant firm is probably negligent, then they will confirm this belief too often.[62]

Finally, there is evidence that individuals greatly undervalue "probabilistic insurance," defined as "an action that reduces but does not eliminate the proba-bility of a loss."[63] Many products involved in products liability are exactly of this sort. Medical care and pharmaceuticals reduce but do not eliminate risks, and much litigation is in fact over the remaining risk.[64] To the extent that jurors undervalue the risk reduction that has occurred, they will undervalue the bene-fits of the product, and will be excessively likely to find liability. The cost of excess liability for such risk-reducing products is particularly high, since it can lead to increased prices and reduced demand for risk-reducing products, such as vaccines.[65]

As for damages, it is very likely that juries will find greater levels of damage payments when viewing an accident ex post than consumers would have wanted to contract for ex ante. One of the major results of cognitive experiments is that losses are overweighed relative to gains. Before an accident, both the acci-dent and the payment for the accident may be viewed as losses ("If you are in-jured, you will lose $10,000 in wages and medical payments." "If you are covered for these injuries, you will pay $10 more for this product.") Thus it may be that consumers will weight gains and losses approximately correctly. Moreover, consumers ex ante are accustomed to making exactly these calculations routinely in markets. But after the accident the actual suffered loss will have excess weight.

One important element discovered by cognitive scientists is the "endowment effect." "Individuals evaluate choices based on absolute changes in value, from a baseline that is typically the status quo, attaching more disutility to losses than utility to gains, and being highly subject to purely formal or semantic manipulation, as in the specification of the status quo, throughout."[66] One implication is that losses are overvalued relative to gains. But once the accident has occurred, then all that is salient are losses. Losses, not product benefits or money saving from reduced prices, are the entire focus of the trial. Indeed, the evidence from *Pinto* suggests that jurors are unwilling to consider the ex ante perspective (that is, the perspective of the cost of additional precautions). Therefore, cognitive theory indicates that juries will systematically place more weight on the actual accident and award more in damages than consumers would desire ex ante.

There is experimental evidence demonstrating this. Calfee and Winston have shown that ex ante consumers are unwilling to pay much for compensation for pain and suffering, as the theory would predict.[67] On the other hand, experimental studies of ex post compensation for pain and suffering report, consistent with cognitive theory, that the "frame" in which the problem is set determines the outcome. McCaffery et al. test an additional implication of the endowment effect, the difference between "willingness to pay" and "willingness to accept."[68] There is strong experimental evidence that consumers will demand more to sell something that they own than they would be willing to pay to buy the same item. In an injury context, this implies that if jurors are asked to award compensation based on the ex ante (selling price) perspective, values should be larger than if the award is framed in terms of the ex post (making whole) perspective; and this is what they find. Of course, both amounts provide more insurance and compensation than the true ex ante amount that theory would predict consumers would be willing to pay for, and more than is consistent with the experimental evidence provided by Calfee and Winston.

This argument is especially relevant for Hasen's analysis. Assume that Hasen is correct and there are framing effects, so that a return expressed as a loss is viewed as less desirable than the value of the same return expressed as a gain. Now consider a jury. In a products liability case, the jury is faced with an actual rather than a potential loss. Thus the jury begins with a loss frame. If framing effects lead to a bias, then juries should be especially susceptible to this bias. If we accept Hasen's arguments regarding framing effects, then we should be more willing to enforce contractual waivers of tortious liability.

Two other factors identified in the cognitive literature cut in the same direction, toward increased damage awards. First, after an accident, the victim is identifiable; indeed, he (or his heirs) is in court. Before the accident, the chance of harm is to a "statistical" or unidentified individual. Since people tend to overweigh harms to identifiable individuals relative to harms to statistical individuals,[69] increased awards may be anticipated. Second, awards may be inflated through "anchoring"—the failure to fully adjust initial estimates of values using Bayes's theorem to reflect new information.[70] Anchoring problems will likely inflate damages awards, since the jury begins with a loss and a claim for damages, rather than with a neutral expected value calculation.

Note that most of the experimental literature discussed above deals with individuals (or with individuals bargaining or trading with each other). A jury is a collective decision maker, and so might behave somewhat differently. However, if each individual is subject to some bias, then a group of individuals should also be subject to bias. Indeed, in the experimental simulations of juries mentioned above,[71] decisions were made by individuals who were told to behave as jurors; no experimental aggregation was performed.

V   Would Judges Do Better than Juries?

It might appear that one factor determining the outcome of litigation is whether the case is decided by a judge or by a jury. If a particular question is determined to be a matter of law, it is decided by a judge; if it is treated as a matter of fact, it goes to a jury. A common theme from the nineteenth century to today is the effort to keep issues out of the hands of juries. Atiyah, for example, states that "[j]uries were not only unpredictable; they were slow."[72] Gilmore discusses the "uneasy, inarticulate distrust of the role of the civil jury."[73] It is generally thought that the purpose is to prevent the natural sympathetic or redistributive impulses of jurors from leading to inefficient or otherwise undesirable outcomes. Others believe that this effort was and continues to be a class-based effort aimed at preserving the status quo in society.[74] The argument here is that juries will make systematic errors that will harm consumers.

However, it is quite possible that judges are almost as subject to the sort of cognitive errors discussed above as are jurors. Judges do see many cases, and so it would appear that they would have a chance to learn. Nonetheless, to the extent that decisions have effects in markets, judges do not actually observe the results of their decisions, since judges do not study markets, and would therefore not receive the feedback needed to be able to improve their decision making. As Cammerer notes, when "experts" are given the same tasks as students in experiments, then they do about the same as students in settings where there is little feedback, although they do better where there is more feedback (e.g., in weather forecasting).[75]

The experimental literature may thus be seen to support an extension of free bargaining principles in tort law. If an injury is treated as a tort, then judges or jurors will be asked to assign appropriate damages. But if tortious liability could be waived by contract, then care levels would be set in consumer markets, where judgment biases are plausibly weaker.

Conclusion

Economic analysis indicates that free bargaining over liability and damages standards in product liability cases, where there is scope for competition to craft efficient rules and remedies, serves efficiency goals. This of course is contrary to the current practice, where tortious standards cannot be waived by contract. Recently, some supporters of this tort-based product liability jurisprudence have argued for this preference because they have claimed that utility maximization is incorrect as a goal for law; this is a puzzling argument. Others claim that modern findings about peoples' cognitive abilities suggest that individuals cannot rationally enter into contracts. But if tort replaces contract, then courts will make decisions for individuals, and there is no reason to expect courts to be exempt from the cognitive errors attributed to consumers. Indeed, there are reasons to expect juries and perhaps judges to do even worse.

Defenders of the current tort system sometimes argue in terms of empowerment of consumers. They argue that consumers should retain their right to trials in product liability matters. Moving from tort to contract does not reduce consumers' rights. Rather, it gives them an additional right, the power to sign contracts and agree not to pay to have their cases heard by a court. Since there are reasons for expecting courts to make systematic mistakes that cost consumers money and reduce social wealth, the right to waive trials through binding contracts is valuable and should be returned to consumers.

Commodifying Liability

ROBERT COOTER

A contingent claim is a right to receive money or goods in the event that a possible event actually occurs. Different people place different values on the risks represented by contingent claims. These differences create potential gains from trade that an efficient market exhausts. Beginning in the 1950s, general equilibrium theorists produced increasingly robust proofs that a complete set of competitive markets for contingent claims allocates risks efficiently.[1] General equilibrium theorists apparently had in mind such contingent claims as stock options, insurance, commodity futures. Their arguments, however, also apply in principle to legal liability for some kinds of harm.

A liability right is conventionally defined as a right of the victim to receive money compensation from the injurer in the event that possible harm actually occurs.[2] A liability right thus combines the victim's right and the injurer's liability. A liability right is contingent upon conditions stipulated in law.[3] When the contingencies occur, a liability right matures into a legal right of action. The contingencies include actual harm to the victim caused by the injurer or, possibly, caused by the injurer's negligence. Legal systems typically do not allow a suit for exposure to risk, as opposed to materialized risk.

In principle, the victim could transfer his right to receive damages to someone else, and the injurer could pay someone else to assume his obligation to pay damages. The transfers could occur before or after the liability right matures. To illustrate the transfer of an unmatured liability right, a person who purchases medical insurance typically assigns to the insurer any legal rights to compensation for medical costs arising from accidents through a subrogation clause. Similarly, a company that purchases liability insurance pays the insurer to assume liability. To illustrate the transfer of matured liability rights, an accident victim who sues the injurer in the United States typically retains an attorney on a contingent fee, which assigns approximately one-third of any court judgment to the plaintiff's attorney.

In some American jurisdictions, companies of nonlawyers buy awards on appeal. To illustrate, the Judgment Purchase Corporation will buy 50 percent of judgments awarded at trial for cases pending appeal, provided the judgment exceeds $300,000 and satisfies certain other conditions.[4] In a piquant example of what the future may hold, a plaintiff recently issued a prospectus acceptable to the Securities Exchange Commission offering to sell 100,000 shares at $5 per share for the claims of John Designer in his lawsuit against Tip Top Toys, Inc.[5]

Different people place different values on the risks that trigger liability, and these different valuations create potential gains from trade. To realize these gains, a potential victim should sell the right to receive damages to someone who values it more, and a potential injurer should pay someone else to bear liability if the latter can do so at less cost. If perfect markets for liability rights existed, they would reach equilibrium when every right to receive damages is owned by the party who values it most, and every duty to pay damages is held by the party who can bear it at least cost. Such an equilibrium is Pareto efficient with respect to the allocation of matured and unmatured liability rights. Exchange in a complete set of perfectly competitive markets allocates liability rights efficiently, regardless of the initial allocation by law.

Law often impedes or forbids the exchange of liability rights, especially liability arising from accidents. For example, consumers and manufacturers usually cannot contract to modify the rights of consumers to receive compensation for injuries caused by defective products. Courts disallow so many contracts to waive, disclaim, modify, or transfer liability for accidental harm that tort scholarship proclaims the decline or death of contracts for liability rights.[6] While the law typically prohibits consumers from selling unmature liability rights to potential injurers, these transactions are permitted once the liability right matures. Specifically, the injurer can purchase all the victim's mature liability rights simply by settling the case out of court. A settlement transfers the liability right from the plaintiff to the defendant.

In common law countries, the old doctrine of champerty prohibits one person from asserting another's legal right.[7] The doctrine has eroded in America to the point that an attorney can purchase a fraction, but not all, of a future judgment through the contingent fee. Many countries outside the United States, including continental Europe, forbid contingent fees for lawyers. Everywhere, professionals with the most expert knowledge about the value of liability rights are restricted or prohibited by law from buying them.

The law may not recognize liability rights as security for a debt.[8] Some specific liability rights, such as the right to recover in medical malpractice, are not assignable in some jurisdictions.[9] Although injurers can purchase liability insurance, some restrictions exist. To illustrate, many American states prohibit liability insurance for punitive damages, even though people especially want to insure against large, unpredictable losses.

What would happen if the legal impediments to markets for liability rights were removed? No one can accurately predict such market developments. Presumably some markets would flourish and others would fail, depending upon the kind of liability right. Inefficiencies in liability law impose high costs on society.[10] Scholars disagree about whether markets for liability rights might reduce inefficiencies and improve the law.[11] I believe that many of the historical abuses of contracts for liability rights resulted from the absence of competition, not exchange itself. Competitive exchange holds promise as a remedy for inefficient tort laws.

Instead of impeding exchange, the law should facilitate competition in markets for liability rights. When legal impediments block exchange, people with different valuations cannot realize gains from trade. I will examine the main causes of different valuations, describe the legal impediments, and speculate on how markets might emerge if the legal impediments were removed. Perfect competition reduces a good to a standardized commodity with a high volume of sales. My subject, consequently, is commodifying liability.

I Deterrence versus Insurance

Potential victims of accidents desire deterrence and insurance. I will explain how this desire creates a strong incentive to exchange liability rights. In simple tort models, optimal deterrence requires injurers to internalize the external benefit of avoiding accidents. In these simple models, injurers internalize the external benefits of precaution when they are liable for perfectly compensatory damages.[12] Damages are perfectly compensatory when they restore the victim to the same level of utility as he would have enjoyed without the injury. In other words, the victim is indifferent between no injury or an injury with perfectly compensatory damages.

Courts distinguish between economic and noneconomic losses caused by accidents. The economic losses include property damage, lost wages, and medical costs. The noneconomic losses include pain, suffering, emotional distress, and lost companionship. Optimal deterrence requires perfect compensation, and perfect compensation requires damages for economic and noneconomic losses. To illustrate concretely, assume an accident causes losses of 20 for hospitalization, 50 for lost wages, and 30 for pain and suffering.[13] Perfect compensation requires damages equal to 100. Assume the injurer can take precautions that reduce the probability of an accident. When the injurer decides how much precaution to take, liability of 100 causes the injurer to internalize the full gain that more precaution conveys upon the potential victim. Consequently, the injurer balances his own costs of precaution against its benefit to the victim.

The right to receive perfectly compensatory damages fully insures potential victims against the destruction of value in accidents where the injurer is liable. Full insurance, however, may not be optimal. People buy insurance in order to shift money from a state of the world in which money is needed less to a state of the world in which money is needed more. In other words, people buy insurance against accidents that increase the marginal utility of money. In the typical case, economic losses cause the marginal utility of money to rise, so people will buy insurance against economic losses. In the typical case, however, noneconomic losses do not cause the marginal utility of money to rise, so people will not buy insurance against noneconomic losses.[14]

The economic waste from compulsory overinsurance has been estimated for some aspects of tort liability. To illustrate, the annual deadweight loss from overinsurance in automobile-related pain and suffering liability judgments in the U.S. was estimated to exceed $1 billion for each of several types of injuries, leading to a total annual loss from all injuries equal to some multiple of $7 billion.[15]

I have explained why people will pay to reduce the probability of economic and noneconomic losses, and why people will only pay to insure against economic losses. Law that pursues the ideal of perfect compensation or the goal of optimal deterrence awards damages for economic and noneconomic losses, thus overinsuring. Law that purses the goal of optimal insurance does not award damages for noneconomic losses, thus underdeterring.

For a concrete illustration, return to the example of an accident that imposes economic losses of 70 and noneconomic losses of 30. A tort system similar to the US, which provides large awards for pain and suffering, will set liability approximately at 100, thus achieving optimal deterrence of the injurer. The victim, however, probably has no desire to insure against pain and suffering, in which case a tort system that sets liability at 100 overinsures the victim. A tort system similar to Germany's, which provides little compensation for pain and suffering, will set liability closer to 70, thus underdeterring the injurer and supplying the efficient amount of insurance to the victim.

An accident that results in a child's death provides a more dramatic example. A typical parent will pay a relatively high amount to reduce the risk of his child's accidental death, so the law should extract relatively large damages from an injurer for the sake of deterrence. The death of a child, however, typically reduces a parent's need for money, so a typical parent does not insure against his child's death. The law should extract relatively small damages from an injurer for the sake of insurance.

Combining optimal deterrence and optimal insurance requires the potential injurer to pay relatively high damages and the potential victim to receive relatively low damages. In private law, the injurer's obligation to pay damages usually *equals* the victim's right to receive damages. This equality creates a trade-off between the two goals, and different legal systems respond differently to this trade-off. To achieve both goals, law must decouple payments to the injurer and victim. Specifically, law can require the injurer to pay a relatively high fine to the state and relatively low damages to the victim.[16]

To illustrate decoupling in the preceding example: law can require the injurer to pay 70 to the victim as compensation and 30 to the state as a fine. Decoupling by law, however, gives injurers and victims an incentive to settle privately to avoid paying a fine to the state. In this example, the private parties might settle for 85 without notifying the state. By avoiding the fine, the victim receives 15 more than the court would award at trial, and the injurer pays 15 less than he would owe after a trial.

To circumvent this problem, decoupling can occur through markets rather than laws. When the liability system provides the potential accident victim with unwanted insurance, a market for liability rights permits him to sell it. If the buyer is anyone other than the potential injurer, the sale reduces insurance without reducing deterrence. For example, a potential victim with liability rights equal to 100, who wants insurance equal to 70, can sell the right to recover damages equal to 30. The buyer might be a law firm specializing in accidents. After completing the sale, the victim of an injury recovers 70 in damages as required for optimal insurance, and the injurer pays a total of 100—70 to the victim and 30 to the law firm—as required for optimal deterrence. Thus sales of unmatured tort claims by potential victims to third parties eliminates unwanted insurance without reducing the injurer's incentives for precaution.

Instead of restricting sales to third parties, suppose the potential victim can sell a liability right to the potential injurer. The sale eliminates a legal cause of action and thus reduces the injurer's potential liability. For example, the manufacturer of a product might lower the price to any buyer who agrees to assume the risk that a defect will cause an accident resulting in pain and suffering. What is the effect on deterrence? In simple tort models, a reduction in liability reduces the injurer's incentives for precaution. To illustrate by the preceding example: an injurer who buys the victim's right to receive damages of 30 reduces his liability from 100 to 70. After the transaction, the injurer internalizes only 70 percent of the benefit of avoiding an accident, so the injurer may reduce his precaution and the number of accidents may increase.

Competition tends to prevent this erosion of incentives. The market price of liability rights responds to the frequency and magnitude of damages. To be more precise, the price of an unmatured liability right in competitive equilibrium roughly equals the expected judgment in the event of an accident, discounted by the probability of an accident.[17] By reducing precaution and increasing the number of accidents, an injurer causes the price of liability rights to rise. The rise in price reduces the profitability of the injurer's strategy of buying liability rights in order to reduce precaution.

For example, assume that an injurer planned to purchase liability rights from potential victims and then reduce his precaution. Firms that understand the injurer's strategy will buy liability rights in anticipation of a rise in their price. The rise in the price of liability rights increases the cost to the injurer of pursuing his strategy. As an alternative strategy, the injurer could commit to taking efficient precaution, thus reducing the market price that the injurer must pay to buy liability rights from victims.

As a concrete example, assume that you buy a used Volvo and assume that the Volvo company is liable to you for accidental pain and suffering caused by a manufacturing defect. The cost of this liability to Volvo may exceed its value to you. Someone can profit from brokering a transaction between Volvo and you. Your auto insurer is the obvious broker. So you might get a reduction in your auto insurance premium in exchange for transferring to the insurer your liability right against Volvo. Your insurer would then resell such liability rights in bulk to Volvo, thus extinguishing such suits. If Volvo gets too careless, a law firm specializing in liability rights might outbid Volvo and purchase a block of liability rights from your insurer.

As another illustration, consider how a market for liability rights might cause a motorist to repackage liability rights and insurance pertaining to automobile accidents. Under existing law, the innocent victim of an accident caused by someone else usually has the right to recover collision damage to the car, hospitalization, lost wages, and pain and suffering. Many motorists purchase insurance against collision and hospitalization. Such insurance contracts usually transfer the insured's right to damages to the insurer. As for pain and suffering, the motorist might not want insurance. Given markets for unmatured liability rights, the potential victim might sell his right to compensation for pain and suffering, and law firms might bid to purchase these unmatured liability rights. Finally, the motorist might choose to retain his right to recover lost wages from an injurer. In this example, the potential victim repackages his unmatured liability rights into elements subrogated to an insurer, sold to a law firm, and retained for himself.

Consider how a market might apply to liability rights for punitive damages. Some punitive damages are a disguised form of compensation, which is awarded when the actual damage is difficult to compute or the law precludes full compensation.[18] More typically, however, punitive damages supplement compensation, resulting in awards that overcompensate relative to the actual harm. In either case, the unpredictability of punitive damages imposes significant costs on risk-averse injurers. Many potential injurers would, consequently, buy the unmatured rights of potential victims to punitive damages at a higher price than potential injurers would charge to part with these rights.[19]

II First- or Third-Party Insurance?

I have explained how liability law provides unwanted insurance and creates an incentive to sell liability rights. The preceding discussion assumed that insurance is unwanted because the harm does not increase the marginal utility of money. Another reason why the victim may not want the injurer to provide insurance is that the victim can buy it cheaper.

Consider a manufacturer who sells a product to a retailer, who resells the product to a consumer. If the manufacturer is strictly liable for consumer product injuries, then the manufacturer in effect sells a joint product consisting in a manufactured good and an insurance policy. In contrast, a rule of no liability exposes the consumer to the risk of injury, thus providing an incentive for the consumer to purchase his own insurance. No-liability induces first-party insurance, and strict liability induces third-party insurance. If third-party insurance is cheaper than first-party insurance, then a rule of strict liability is more efficient than a rule of no liability in simple tort models. Conversely, if first-party insurance is cheaper than third-party insurance, then a rule of no liability is more efficient than a rule of strict liability in simple tort models.

George Priest argues that the legal doctrine of enterprise liability replaced relatively cheap first-party insurance with relatively expensive third-party insurance.[20] If Priest is right, lawmakers created the wrong rule, which imposes excessive insurance costs upon consumers. A market for liability rights can correct this mistake. By assumption, the consumer can insure at less cost than the manufacturer, so a rule of law assigning liability to the manufacturer creates a surplus from exchange. The manufacturer can profitably buy the consumer's liability right at a price exceeding the consumer's cost of insurance. A consumer who sells a liability right and buys insurance converts third-party insurance into first-party insurance.

First-party insurance is often cheaper because of economies of scope. To illustrate, a motorist involved in an automobile accident needs the same amount of insurance regardless of whether the accident was his fault, the fault of another driver, or no one's fault. In general, the need for insurance depends upon the harm, whereas liability depends upon the cause. A comprehensive insurance policy can provide protection against a particular harm, regardless of its cause.

On the other hand, third-party insurance can be cheaper for reasons of deterrence. The manufacturer can often reduce the frequency and magnitude of accidents caused by defective products at less cost than the consumer. Strict liability for consumer product injuries provides a strong incentive for the manufacturer to take precautions against defective products. If the manufacturer purchases liability insurance, the insurance company monitors claims to assure that the manufacturer takes precautions. Monitoring of the manufacturer, however, would be difficult or impossible for the consumer's insurance company.

I have explained why first-party insurance may be cheaper than third party insurance in some circumstances, and the opposite may be true in other circumstances. Markets for liability rights would allow the parties to adjust insurance to circumstances.

III Transaction Costs

Gary Schwartz has found that the plaintiffs' legal costs in the typical American tort suit equal between 29 percent and 44 percent of the damages awarded.[21] Assuming defendants' legal costs are similar in magnitude, total legal costs exceed 60 percent of the damages awarded. Are legal processes worth their cost? Academic literature on dispute resolution contradicts itself on this question. Merchant associations that set their own rules typically resolve disputes by cheap mechanisms.[22] When associations of merchants create mechanisms for resolving disputes, they typically dispense with most procedural protections found in courts. For example, the Visa arbitration committee decides all payments disputes among banks based on written documents alone without appeal.[23] Similarly, arbitration before the International Chamber of Commerce in Paris prohibits appeals and allows the arbitrators great flexibility in choosing a process to resolve the dispute. In contrast, psychological studies report that peoples' satisfaction with dispute resolution depends upon process even more than outcomes.[24] In brief, business studies suggest low values for process rights, whereas psychological studies suggest high values.

In any case, reducing the costs of resolving disputes motivates many proposals for tort reform, such as proposals for no-fault rules.[25] Instead of changing the legal process, markets for liability rights could reduce the transaction costs of resolving disputes. The potential injurer who buys an unmatured liability right extinguishes the potential plaintiff's claim before an accident occurs. In the event of an accident, no one will incur the high cost of asserting a legal claim and resolving a legal dispute. Thus the sale of liability rights can convert the effective regime from fault to no-fault without actually changing the law.

In general, the ability of someone to lower the cost of resolving disputes increases the value they place upon a liability right, so exchange tends to move liability rights to people who can resolve disputes at low transaction costs. Aggregating unmature claims can save transaction costs by realizing economies of scale. To illustrate, many drivers purchase collision and liability insurance. When such drivers collide in an accident, each driver receives compensation from his insurer. Questions of liability are resolved by the two insurance companies. Insurance companies in repeat transaction with each other seldom go to trial. By engaging in wholesale transactions, insurance companies can streamline the processes for resolving disputes with each other.

This same process does not work for personal injuries caused by automobile accidents or consumer product injuries. In these cases, the tort system provides damages exceeding the private insurance of the parties. Consequently, after the parties file claims with their insurance companies, tort claims exceeding their insurance remain to be resolved. For example, the tort system gives damages for pain and suffering, but the parties typically do not buy insurance for pain and suffering. To obtain compensation for pain and suffering, the tort victim must assert the legal claim against the injurer, rather than filing a claim with his insurance company.

A market for liability rights could change these facts. If the tort victim sold his unmature claims to pain and suffering damages, his remaining claims from an accident might be covered by insurance. When victim and injurer have private insurance for the full amount of the legal claim, the parties can deal with their insurance companies and their insurance companies can resolve liability with each other.

Like dispute resolution, the transaction costs of markets for liability rights are large. Reducing the transaction costs of market exchange requires aggregating unmatured liability rights for bulk sales. To illustrate by an earlier example, many drivers purchase collision and liability insurance. When such drivers collide in an accident, each driver receives compensation from his insurer, and questions of liability are resolved by the two insurance companies. By engaging in wholesale transactions, insurance companies can streamline the processes for resolving disputes with each other.

Markets in liability rights could extend these practices of aggregating to reduce transaction costs. For example, insurers could offer lower premiums to drivers who transferred all their liability rights to the insurance company, including the right to damages for pain and suffering. In the event of an accident involving two drivers with such insurance, the drivers would make claims against their insurance companies and the insurance companies would resolve liability with each other, including damages for pain and suffering. Insurance companies might contract to pre-settle such claims, thus eliminating court proceedings.

The same kind of exchange might occur for the right to recover damages from injuries caused by medical malpractice. Specifically, the patient could transfer his right to recover damages for medical malpractice to his insurance company in exchange for lower premiums, and the insurance company could resell the right to the patient's doctors or their insurers. Similarly, a consumer who purchases insurance could transfer to the insurance company his right to recover damages from injuries caused by defective products, and the consumer's insurance company could then deal with the manufacturer's insurance company.

Will markets for liability rights increase or decrease litigation in aggregate? The sale of liability rights to law firms and other specialists should lower the cost of asserting legal claims, thus tending to produce more litigation. Another force, however, works in the opposite direction and reduces litigation. Recall that the purchase of liability rights by injurers extinguishes legal claims before they arise. Similarly, the purchase of liability rights by insurance companies results in more settlements and fewer trials. On balance, markets for liability rights could increase or decrease litigation. My guess is that bulk transactions in liability rights will reduce litigation on balance, and small transactions might have the opposite effect. In either case, the change should favor efficiency by moving liability rights to the parties who value them the most.

Juries can cause inefficiencies in the legal process. In his essay in this volume, Paul Ruben shows that juries are subjected to cognitive biases when thinking about risks that result in excessive awards.[26] Strong evidence exists that juries treat novel risks far more harshly than familiar risks, thus creating a bias against innovation.[27] Thus markets for liability rights could usefully remove disputes from the purview of juries. To illustrate, since consumers do not study their medical insurance contracts, the courts sometimes withhold enforcement of clauses stipulating compulsory arbitration of medical malpractice claims, even though arbitration reduces transaction costs. A competitive market could solve the problem of voluntarily arbitrating disputes. Specifically, companies such as law firms might compete to buy the unmature medical malpractice claims of consumers. In exchange for a fee paid by the health maintenance organization, sophisticated lawyers who own the liability rights might agree to submit any claims that mature to compulsory arbitration, with the courts enforcing such agreements.

The high cost of asserting and defending claims also provides a reason why attorneys may value liability rights more than potential plaintiffs do. One example is class action suits, where transaction costs often loom large. Macey and Miller have advocated that judges auction the rights to pursue class actions, with lawyers bidding against each other in open competition.[28] This process would create a market for mature class action rights.

A vigorous market for liability rights requires the full participation of lawyers, who know best how to value legal claims. Champerty rules inhibit or prevent such participation, thus removing a powerful means of monitoring risks created by manufacturers. For example, suppose that a law firm identifies an obscure product that causes a small injury to many people. Under existing law, the law firm cannot purchase the liability rights from potential victims. Instead, the only remedy is the class action, which protects individuals according to the court's sense of justice.

The prohibition on champerty allegedly protects the ignorant public against swindles by knowledgeable lawyers. In fact, the prohibition on champerty also restricts the ways that lawyers can compete with each other.[29] For example, the prohibition prevents an accident victim from auctioning his liability rights to the lawyer who bids the most. A very different set of regulations from those that we observe would be developed if the aim were to lubricate the market for liability rights and increase competition among lawyers.

IV Consent

Why do modern courts prohibit or restrict contracts to waive, disclaim, or modify liability of producers to consumers? Unequal bargaining power supplies one rationale. Game theory, however, contains no support for the proposition that refusing to enforce a bargain generally benefits the weaker party to it. Furthermore, competition can cure the problem of unequal bargaining power by eliminating everyone's bargaining power. If the real problem were bargaining power, the first solution is increasing competition.

Adhesion contracts supply another rationale for these prohibitions and restrictions. In light of modern economics, however, the phrase "adhesion contract" seems far too broad and misleading to provide a useful guide to the law.[30] A modern legal discussion analyzes form contracts as one aspect of markets with asymmetrical information.[31] The economics of information recognizes that form contracts often benefit both parties by reducing transactions costs.

The best rationale for disallowing contracts for liability rights concerns asymmetrical information. A person who does not know the quality of a product cannot value it correctly. Similarly, a person who does not know the probability and magnitude of a loss cannot value it correctly. Cognitive psychology has supplied new evidence demonstrating large errors in perceiving and thinking about risk. An ignorant person may sell a claim at less than its value, and an ignorant person may pay more than the cost of liability for someone else to assume it. So asymmetrical information can cause markets for liability rights to fail.

If competition drives the price of liability rights to their value, however, ignorant individuals can transact in these markets without making mistakes. An ignorant person who sells a liability right at competitive prices receives full value, and a person who pays a competitive price for someone to assume liability gets insurance at its true cost.

To illustrate by analogy, consider a competitive market for fire insurance. Most homeowners know little about the probability of a fire. Competition among insurers, however, equates the insurance premium with the expected value of claims plus administrative costs. Consequently, every consumer can be ignorant of probabilities and magnitudes of losses, and yet all consumers who pay the competitive price for insurance receive it at cost. Instead of concentrating on collecting information about probabilities, consumers can concentrate on collecting information about prices. This proposition about fire insurance also applies to insurance against illness, disability, or lost wages.

A competitive market for liability rights would work the same way. To illustrate, assume that a consumer wishes to sell unmatured liability claims for pain and suffering. A competitive market would price the claims roughly at the expected judgment discounted by the probability of an accident. Thus an ignorant consumer, who knows nothing about the probability or magnitude of accidents, would receive full value for unmatured claims. Instead of trying to learn about probabilities, most rational individuals would focus on learning about the prices of liability rights.

Consider how this argument applies to the assumption of risk by consumers of potentially defective products. Costly consumer products such as automobiles are very complex. A rational consumer knows little or nothing about the probability that, say, an accident will cause the gas tank to explode. Assume that the consumer, who buys comprehensive insurance against economic losses, wants to sell his right to recover in tort from the injurer. The law blocks such a transaction on the rationale that the consumer is ignorant about the transaction's value. If the market is competitive, however, all the consumer needs to know is the market price. One participant in the market might be the automobile manufacturer, who seeks to extinguish liability by purchasing unmatured liability rights. Another participant in the market might be law firms that specialize in torts. If the manufacturer offered to pay less than the value of the liability right, the law firm would outbid the manufacturer. So competition between the manufacturer and law firms would help the consumer to receive full value for selling the unmatured claim.

To illustrate the power of competition to convey information, assume that a manufacturer offers two cars, each with the gas tank in a different place. For one car, the seller offers $50 off the price for waiving all rights to recover in pain and suffering; for the other car the manufacturer offers $100 off the price for waiving these rights. The consumer correctly infers that the second car is more dangerous. The difference in price reduces complex technical information about a serious risk to terms easily understood.

V   Goals of Liability Law

Objectives conventionally attributed to liability law by courts include deterrence, insurance, low transaction costs, compensation, and fairness. I have explained how markets for liability rights can produce optimal deterrence, optimal insurance, and low transaction costs. Now I briefly discuss the goals of compensation and fairness.

As explained above, a liability rule requiring perfect compensation causes the injurer to insure the victim fully. Potential victims who sell liability rights cannot obtain compensation from the injurer. Some potential victims will sell liability rights and buy insurance, thus substituting an insurance claim for a court judgment. Substituting insurance for a court judgment seems unobjectionable. Some potential victims, however, will sell liability rights and buy little or no insurance. The resulting exposure to risk may seem objectionable. Courts may try to undo the sale of liability rights out of sympathy for the victim.

Sometimes this sympathy is misplaced. To illustrate, assume that a potential victim believes that pain does not increase the marginal utility of money. Since he does not want insurance against pain, he sells his liability right to damages for pain. After he suffers a painful accident caused by someone else, a sympathetic court may want to unravel the sale of his liability right and compensate him. If the court kept in mind that pain does not increase the need for money, the court might recognize that this impulse to compensate is misplaced.

In other circumstances, however, sympathy with the victim has a firmer foundation. For example, assume that a potential victim sells his right to recover damages for hospitalization and then fails to obtain medical insurance due to imprudence. After he suffers high medical costs due to an accident caused by someone else, a sympathetic court may want to unravel the sale of his liability right and compensate him.

An obvious remedy comes to mind: Courts might allow sales of unmatured liability rights by people with insurance, and disallow such sales by people without insurance. Such a rule would cause the buyers of unmatured liability rights to demand proof of insurance as a condition for purchase. Without such proof, the purchaser would risk having the court unwind the transaction.

In any case, compulsory insurance through the liability system is not a good way to address medical needs. People need medical insurance regardless of the cause of hospitalization. Obstructing markets for liability rights provides compulsory medical insurance for harms whose cause triggers liability, but not for harms with other causes. People who want accident victims assured of medical treatment should work toward a more comprehensive solution than closing markets for liability rights.

Now I turn to the issue of fair exchange. Fair exchange can be defined as exchanging items of equal value.[32] Unfair exchange typically occurs because one party does not know the value of an item being traded. In perfectly competitive markets, everyone is a price taker, so competitive exchange is always fair. Courts are troubled by the potential unfairness of selling liability rights when one party is relatively ignorant. By reducing the scope of bargaining, competition would assure fair prices in markets for liability rights.

Conclusion

According to the Coase Theorem, exchange at zero transactions costs allocates liability rights efficiently, regardless of the initial allocation by law. According to general equilibrium theory, exchange in a complete set of perfectly competitive markets allocates liability rights efficiently, regardless of the initial allocation by law. The Coase Theorem and the model of perfect competition disagree concerning the cause of efficient exchange. In the Coase Theorem, bargaining produces efficient resource allocation, whereas transaction costs cause inefficiency. In the model of perfect competition, however, competition produces efficient resource allocation by eliminating bargaining and turning everyone into a price-taker. (Game theory, fortunately, raises the disagreement over market power and transaction costs to another level of sophistication.)[33]

Law and economics scholars usually use the Coase Theorem in studying contracts and property law, and they often use competitive models in studying antitrust law and regulated industries. In the case of liability rights, however, I find the perspective of competitive markets especially useful. I believe that the absence of a competitive market for liability rights causes many of the problems of the tort system, and commodifying liability is the solution.

Regarding liability rights as contingent claims invites an extension of general equilibrium theory to liability law, which could change law in theory and practice. The extension could replace intuition in legal theory with rigor and bring a new perspective to regulating risks. Besides justifying competition on grounds of efficiency, the model of perfect competition diagnoses failed markets. Markets fail when their actual structure diverges too far from the ideal of perfect competition.[34]

Understanding regulation requires a theory of the state. Economists developed theories of the state that could be applied to regulation.[35] According to the economic theory of the state, a good regulation withstands the corrosive influence of self-seeking politicians and bureaucrats.

Taken together, the model of perfect competition and economic theories of the state supply an abstract framework for analyzing regulations. According to this framework, a market that approximates perfect competition should remain unregulated. This principle discredits many regulations that restrict competition for political ends. To make the case for regulation, proof of market failure is necessary, but not sufficient. A complete case also requires proving that a regulatory remedy can succeed against the self-serving strategies of politicians and state officials.[36]

Since law typically prohibits markets for liability rights, no one knows how they would work. Nevertheless, I try to imagine the consequences of marketing liability rights. If liability rights could be unbundled and repackaged, perhaps the volume of sales would sustain competition. Competitive sales would help solve the problems of combining deterrence and insurance, moving liability to the lowest cost insurer, lowering transaction costs of dispute resolution, and improving the quality of consent to disclaimers and waivers of liability. The success of such markets would depend upon the ability of entrepreneurs to develop new contingent commodities. Large, unrealized surpluses from such exchanges, if they exist, will create pressures to liberalize markets for liability rights.

To lubricate competition, lawmakers or courts could adopt the presumption that a contract to transfer a liability right is enforceable when exchange occurs in a competitive market. For example, a contract to waive, disclaim, or assume risk would be enforceable whenever several buyers or sellers bid for it in an arms-length transaction. If market solutions were permitted, the emergence of competition would depend upon the creativity of entrepreneurs, who would need to create new commodities by unbundling, packaging, and reselling liability rights. Effective competition requires reducing liability rights to commodities in wholesale transactions. The first step is a new understanding and attitude in the courts that frees entrepreneurs to create new markets for contingent claims.

The market for unmatured liability rights may seem impractical and visionary. Until recently, however, proposals by economists for a market in pollution rights seemed impractical and visionary. The initial hostility of environmentalists and industry to pollution rights eroded as environmentalists saw an opportunity to obtain a cleaner environment by reducing the cost of abatement, and industries saw an opportunity to obtain valuable rights while reducing the burden of regulation.

Liability rights might repeat the history of pollution rights. Trial lawyers might see the purchase of liability rights from consumers as a profitable extension of contingent fee litigation. Consumer advocates might see consumer sales of liability rights to lawyers as a way to improve consumer protection by policing industry more vigorously. Manufacturers might see the purchase of liability rights as an effective means of limiting their liability and reducing the burden of suits. Insurance companies might see the exchange of liability rights as an opportunity to save transaction costs and reduce their exposure by pre-settling claims. Because exchange creates a surplus, each of these groups may be right.

Appendix: Pricing Liability

In this appendix, I will compute the competitive price of a mature liability right first, and then I will compute the price of an unmatured liability right. I defined a liability right as the right of a victim to receive damages from the injurer in the event that possible harm actually occurs. Let j denote possible damages awarded at judgment after trial of a mature liability right. Let $p(j)$ denote the probability that a trial results in j. Thus the expected judgment, denoted EJ, is given by the equation

$$EJ = \int p(j) j \, dj$$

Given rational expectations, the plaintiff expects to gain EJ at judgment after trial and the defendant expects to lose EJ. Furthermore, the plaintiff and defendant expect to bear trial costs denoted t_p and t_d, respectively.

Instead of proceeding to trial, the parties might settle their dispute for an amount S, in which case the plaintiff receives S and the defendant pays S. In addition, the plaintiff and defendant must bear transaction costs of settling, denoted s_p and s_d, respectively.

Let q denote the probability that the parties settle the dispute, so $1 - q$ indicates the probability of a trial. Thus the value of the plaintiff's legal claim equals the probability-weighted value of settlement and trial, and likewise for the defendant:

value of plaintiff's claim $= q(S - s_p) + (1 - q)(EJ - t_p)$

value of defendant's liability $= q(-S - s_d) + (1 - q)(-EJ - t_d)$

I assume no legal impediments to the plaintiff selling his claim or to the defendant paying someone to assume liability. Thus I assume that entrepreneurs can freely unbundle and repackage liability rights. In a perfectly competitive market, competition would bid the price of a plaintiff's mature claim to its value, and competition would bid the cost of assuming the defendant's liability to its value. Thus the preceding equations characterize the competitive equilibrium prices for the plaintiff's mature claim and the defendant's mature liability. (For the sake of simplicity, these formulae omit some elements required for a complete account, such as the cost of filing a legal complaint and the cost of discovery.[37])

Now I turn to the competitive price of *unmature* liability rights. Let r denote the probability of an accident that triggers the injurer's liability to the victim. To obtain the competitive price of the unmature claim, the value of the mature claim must be discounted by the probability r that it matures:

competitive price of plaintiff's unmature claim =
$$r[q(S - s_p) + (1 - q)(EJ - t_p)] \tag{1}$$

competitive price of defendant's unmature liability =
$$r[q(-S - s_d) + (1 - q)(-EJ - t_d)] \tag{2}$$

To obtain more precise and revealing equations, I will use the Nash bargaining solution to solve for S in equations (1) and (2). The Nash bargaining solution requires specifying the threat values of the parties, the cooperative value of the game, and the cooperative value of the game.

In settlement bargaining, the plaintiff's threat value equals the amount he expects to gain on his own without defendant's cooperation:

$$p\text{'s threat value} = EJ - t_p$$

Similarly, in settlement bargaining, the defendant's threat value equals the amount he expects to lose without plaintiff's cooperation:

$$d\text{'s threat value} = -EJ - t_d$$

The game's noncooperative value equals the sum of the threat values:

$$\text{noncooperative value of game} = EJ - EJ - t_p - t_d = -t_p - t_d$$

Thus the noncooperative value of the settlement game equals the sum of the trial costs.

Now I turn from noncooperation to cooperation. The game's cooperative value equals the value of the settlement to the parties minus the settlement costs to the plaintiff s_p and defendant s_d:

$$\text{cooperative value of game} = +S - S - s_p - s_d = -s_p - s_d$$

Thus the cooperative value of the settlement game equals the sum of the settlement costs.

Finally, the surplus from cooperation equals the difference between the game's cooperative value and its noncooperative value, which reduces to the savings in transaction cost from avoiding a trial:

cooperative surplus from settlement $= (t_p + t_d) - (s_p + s_d)$

The Nash bargaining solution gives each party its threat value plus half of the surplus from cooperation:[38]

Nash payoff for plaintiff $= S - s_p = EJ - t_p + .5[(t_p + t_d) - (s_p + s_d)]$

Nash payoff for defendant $= -S - s_d = -EJ - t_d + .5[(t_p + t_d) - (s_p + s_d)]$

An important consequence of this formula is that parties with symmetrical transaction costs will settle for the expected judgment:

$t_p = t_d$ and $s_p = s_d \Rightarrow S = EJ$

Consequently, symmetry between plaintiff and defendant results in the following competitive prices for liability rights:

symmetrical transaction costs $\Rightarrow$

competitive price of plaintiff's unmature claim $=$
$$r[EJ - qs_p + (1 - q)(t_p)] \tag{3}$$

competitive price of defendant's unmature liability $=$
$$r[-EJ - qs_d + (1 - q)(t_d)] \tag{4}$$

According to equations (3) and (4), the price of an unmature claim equals the difference between the expected value of the judgment and transaction costs, discounted by the probability of an accident. Thus equations (3) and (4) provide a useful benchmark for thinking about markets for liability rights. In the simplest case where settlement approaches certainty (q approaches 1) and settlement costs approach zero (s_p and s_d approach 0), the prices approach rEJ and $-rEJ$, respectively. The simplest case has attractive features of cost-internalization that I discuss elsewhere.[39]

III Contracting for Land Use Law

Zoning by Private Contract

ROBERT H. NELSON

The uses of land, unlike most consumptive acts, are often highly interdependent. If my dog barks all night, it is a disturbance not only to me but also to my neighbors. If I fail to mow my lawn, both my views and those of my neighbors will be spoiled. If I build an apartment house on my suburban lot, my neighbors suffer—even as I make a nice profit—as the quality of the whole neighborhood declines.

In the first half of the twentieth century the rise of cities whose spatial patterns were shaped by the automobile exposed wealthier neighborhoods in particular to novel threats of this kind. In a typical nineteenth-century city, rich and poor lived in neighborhoods of similar densities. Even today, in Manhattan the densities of posh Fifth Avenue apartments are not so different from housing densities in Harlem. In a fancy suburb of the automotive age, however, it is very different. In a well-off neighborhood of five-acre homes, one homeowner might sell to an enterprising land developer if there are no controls on land use. It might well be that the developer could maximize the value of a single lot by building condominiums for middle-income residents. The seller of the lot and the developer would do well financially, but the rest of the neighbors, still residing on their five-acre lots, would see the quality of their neighborhood decline.

Thus a prestigious suburban neighborhood presents a classic example of a problem of the commons.[1] Each lot owner in the neighborhood faces an incentive to sell out for higher density development. However, if all the lot owners follow their individual incentives, the ultimate outcome will be the "overgrazing" of the neighborhood and a deterioration of neighborhood quality, matching the deterioration experienced in open range lands, fisheries, and other commons situations.

A commons problem can be resolved in one of two general ways. One option, the approach typically adopted in the twentieth century in the United States, is government regulation. Indeed, following its first use in New York City in 1916, zoning spread rapidly across the United States. Zoning would become the principal means by which a well-off suburban neighborhood could establish collective controls over the interdependencies that characterize the relationships among nearby property owners. The spread of zoning closely corresponds to the emergence of the metropolitan land development patterns in the United States that were a product of the new mobility introduced by the automobile. Los Angeles would become the prototypical city of twentieth-century America.

However, government regulation is not the only possible answer; a commons situation can also be resolved by creating private property rights. One private alternative to zoning is to establish collective controls over neighborhood land use through the inclusion in each deed of a restrictive convenant. This approach has in fact been adopted in many neighborhoods. Alone among large cities in the United States, Houston has never adopted zoning. Yet the well-to-do neighborhoods of Houston differ little from corresponding neighborhoods in other cities around the United States. These neighborhoods accomplish entirely through private covenants what other neighborhoods accomplish through zoning regulations.[2]

Private covenants can work well but they present several difficulties. First, the enforcement of the covenants creates a free rider problem. Legal action against a violator of the covenants can be expensive for one neighbor who would be providing a free service for all the others in the neighborhood. Second, covenants, as written contracts, are difficult to apply to matters that involve subjective judgments such as aesthetic matters. Third, convenants must be fixed in place at the time of original development and may become outdated over time. And fourth, in neighborhoods that have already been developed without covenants, there is no easy way to write them into the deeds for the whole neighborhood after the fact.

Most homeowners in the United States have therefore looked to zoning to give them collective control over uses of properties in their immediate neighborhood. However, zoning created its own difficulties. Perhaps the most serious was that zoning was administered at the municipal level, thus leaving neighborhood residents potentially subject to the political manipulations of others outside the neighborhood. Zoning was also an inflexible method of land use control that could inhibit adoption of the most attractive neighborhood designs.

Since the 1960s, Americans have increasingly been turning to yet another private property approach to achieving controls over neighborhood land use interdependencies. Indeed, two researchers recently announced a "quiet revolution in the structure of community organization, local government, land-use control, and neighbor relations" in the United States.[3] They were referring to the spread of homeowners associations, condominium ownership of property, and other forms of collective private ownership of residential property. In describing these forms of ownership, different commentators have used terms such as "residential community association," "common interest community," "residential private government," "gated community," and others. All these types of arrangements have in common that they internalize neighborhood interdependencies under a collective form of private ownership. In this essay I will use the term *neighborhood association* to refer to such arrangements.

I The Rise of the Neighborhood Association

In 1998 in the United States, there were about 200,000 neighborhood associations in which more than 40 million people were living—about 15 percent of Americans.[4] In the largest metropolitan areas, according to the estimate of the Community Associations Institute, more than 50 percent of new housing is now being built in neighborhood associations.[5] In the Los Angeles and San Diego metropolitan areas, this figure is in excess of 70 percent. If current trends continue, it will not be many years before 25 percent of the American population will be living in a neighborhood association. California, along with Texas and Florida, has had the greatest concentrations of neighborhood associations. Other places where they are common include New York, Illinois, and the suburbs of Washington, D.C.

The average neighborhood association serves a population of about two hundred people. In 1990 about 42 percent of the units in neighborhood associations consisted of townhouses. Single family homes represented 18 percent of the units. The majority of the associations extended beyond individual buildings to include territorial responsibilities of some sort. The typical operating budget of a neighborhood association is $100,000 to $200,000 per year, but 5 percent of the associations belonging to the Community Association Institute (about 10,000) had budgets greater than $1.5 million per year.

In 1962, there were fewer than five hundred neighborhood associations in the United States.[6] By 1970, this figure had risen sharply to ten thousand associations, but they still contained only 1 percent of U.S. housing units. As of 1970, 12 percent of the then existing neighborhood associations were governed under the terms of condominium ownership. Condominium ownership was 31 percent of all neighborhood associations in 1998, one of the factors giving impetus to the rapid growth of collective private ownership of American housing.[7]

Neighborhood associations typically enforce covenants that were written by the developer and designed to maintain the character of the neighborhood, as it has attracted residents. Neighborhood covenants are generally much more detailed than zoning rules, controlling not only types of land uses but also matters of aesthetics for which local government would not have the legal authority in the typical zoning ordinance. Such matters can include the color of the house paint, the placement of trees and shrubbery, the size and location of fences, the construction of decks and other housing extensions, the parking of automobiles in streets and driveways, the use and placement of television antennas. In the typical neighborhood association, these matters are regulated by the "conditions, covenants, and restrictions" (cc&rs), and overseen by an architectural review committee.

A neighborhood association usually also provides a range of services to its residents, such as garbage collection, street maintenance, snow removal, lawn mowing, gardening, and maintenance of swimming pools, tennis courts, golf courses, and other common recreational facilities. In order to cover the costs of these activities, the neighborhood association levies an assessment on each member. The typical fee—which must be paid by everyone as a condition of owning property in the neighborhood—is about $100 to $150 per month.

Neighborhood associations are governed by a board of directors elected by the membership of the association. Generally, only property owners are allowed to vote. The assignment of voting shares in neighborhood associations can be made according to a number of formulas, commonly per residential housing unit or per square footage. Neighborhood associations often impose tight requirements for residency. Associations of senior citizens may require that each property owner must be at least fifty-five years old. Exclusions or tight restrictions on ownership of pets are also a common feature of neighborhood association rules.

A BRIEF HISTORY

As London expanded in the eighteenth century, private parks were often created for the benefit of neighboring lot owners. This idea was carried over to the United States in Gramercy Park in New York City.[8] A land developer, Samuel Ruggles, had set aside a common private area, and in 1831 assigned it to a set of trustees, with the neighboring lot owners as the collective beneficiaries.

The first true homeowners association was established to provide for the upkeep of Louisberg Square in Boston. A central common area had been established when the development was built in 1826, but no special arrangements had been made for its maintenance. In 1844, the twenty-eight nearby lot owners resolved this problem by signing a mutual agreement to establish the Committee of the Proprietors of Louisberg Square, binding themselves and their successors to keep up the park. This was one of the rare instances in which a neighborhood association has been formed after the fact of separate ownership of individual homes or other properties.

Beginning in the late nineteenth century, housing developers in the United States began to build large private communities in growing numbers. In order to protect the character of the community environment, the developers included extensive private covenants. However, as urban historian David Beito comments, "covenants generally suffered from the lack of an effective enforcement mechanism."[9] In order to deal with this and other needs, a leading early American community builder, James Nichols, established the first community association in 1914 at the Mission Hills development near Kansas City, Missouri.

By the 1920s, many other communities were following a similar practice. The famous Radburn new town in New Jersey, designed in the 1920s by progressive reformers seeking to demonstrate the advantages of comprehensive social and physical planning, included an association whose responsibilities, among others, was to enforce an extensive set of covenants. The growing use of covenants and homeowners associations was, interestingly enough, almost coincident with the rapid spread of zoning. However, they were initially put in place in much different ways, zoning done typically by government fiat after the fact, and the homeowners association created through a developer before the first residents had arrived in a new neighborhood.

Some new neighborhoods relied on private covenants for less savory reasons. In 1917, the Supreme Court found racial zoning to be unconstitutional. However, the Court did not declare racially exclusive covenants to be unconstitutional until 1948. A policy of racial segregation, maintained legally by covenants, was a common feature for large development projects in both the north and south in the period between the wars.

Following World War II, individual home ownership shot upward in the United States. The Urban Land Institute (which had been formed in 1936) and other builder organizations promoted the use of mandatory homeowner associations. The Federal Housing Administration (FHA) also actively encouraged builders to make comprehensive use of deed restrictions and demanded that they be rigorously enforced—helping to ensure that the FHA would not be called upon to bail out problem developments. Following the creation of a mortgage guarantee program in the Veterans Administration in 1944, this agency followed similar policies.

In the 1960s, the growth of neighborhood associations increased dramatically. Like many important developments in land law, it was not a matter of practice following social and economic theory. Rather, the key roles were played by practitioners in the real estate industry and by career officials in the housing agencies of the federal government, who responded to perceived home builder needs that could be met by improving instruments of collective private ownership of residential property.

The major legal innovation of the 1960s was the development of the condominium as a new form of collective private ownership. Although homeowners associations dated back to the nineteenth century, the first condominiums in the United States were found in Puerto Rico, based on a rudimentary condominium law enacted in 1951. The Puerto Rican law had been adopted from Latin

American precedents. Condominium ownership had spread rapidly in South America, following its introduction in Brazil in 1928. Tracing matters back even further, France had had a "horizontal property" law as early as 1804. The earliest known antecedents of condominium ownership are found in the Middle Ages in Germany, where "story property"—the separate ownership of different stories within the same structure—existed in the 1100s.[10]

In 1960, however, the condominium concept was still essentially unknown in the continental United States. At the request of Puerto Rican representatives, hearings were held in the House and Senate. Following these hearings, Congress provided in the National Housing Act of 1961 for the FHA to make its mortgage insurance available to condominium units. FHA promptly took steps to follow up on this authority, including the publication of a model state condominium statute.[11]

In 1963, FHA published technical assistance for homeowners associations in a widely distributed document titled *Planned-Unit Development with a Homes Association*. Working collaboratively with FHA, the Urban Land Institute in 1964 published the Homes Association Handbook, destined in this and subsequent editions to become the bible of neighborhood association management. Byron Hanke, the head of land planning at FHA, was also the principal author of the ULI *Handbook*. By 1967, almost every state had adopted some kind of legislation setting ground rules for condominium ownership, in most cases based on FHA models. All these efforts served to stir wide interest within the building industry in collective ownership forms as a tool of large project development.

In a homeowners association, each person owns his or her unit individually. The homeowners association is a separate legal entity that holds the streets, parks, and other "common areas," and enforces the neighborhood covenants. In a condominium, however, all the individual owners both have title to their own personal units and, as "tenants in common," share a percentage interest in the "common elements." These common elements include things like dividing walls, stairways, hallways, roofs, yards, parks, and other parts of the project outside the individually occupied units.[12]

The development in the 1960s of condominium ownership coincided with the emergence of new pressures for higher housing densities, helping to meet rising demands for home ownership of baby boom families. A slowing of highway construction, tighter suburban limits on land use availability, and greater demands to limit growth for environmental reasons also contributed to a new tightness in metropolitan land supplies and rapid escalation in some places, of the price of land. Neighborhood associations allowed for the realization of land economies of higher densities, including collective provision of parks, green spaces, and other common areas, without sacrificing the advantages of individual ownership of housing units. As Marc Weiss and John Watts observe, condominiums and homeowners associations "continued to enforce deed restrictions but their essential purposes increasingly reflected other priorities: the provision of attractive services and the economical maintenance of common property."[13]

By the late 1960s, neighborhood associations were seen to exhibit significant growing pains. The process of transition from developer to resident control was often troublesome. Many associations experienced difficulties in holding required meetings, keeping adequate records, and enforcing effectively the covenants and other rules of the association. In 1973, a survey of 1,760 condominium residents found that most were satisfied with their overall condominium experience, but that 61 percent were dissatisfied with the operation of the association management. In that same year, key leaders in the real estate industry joined together to form the Community Associations Institute. Its purpose was to promote collective ownership of residential property and to provide technical assistance in the design and managing of neighborhood associations.

In the late 1970s the National Conference of Commissioners on Uniform State Laws (NCCUSL) developed a series of model laws. NCCUSL released a model condominium law in 1980 and a planned community law in 1981. These model laws provided for full disclosure to purchasers of association restrictions and assessments, and tightened enforcement procedures for association rules. In California, the Davis-Stirling Act provides similar rules for governance and assessments.[14]

Since the 1970s, fewer of the very large private communities such as Reston, Virginia, and Columbia, Maryland, have been started, but subdivision-scale neighborhood associations have proliferated. The fiscal crisis of local governments in the 1970s and 1980s meant that governments were often unwilling to accept new responsibilities for building and maintaining streets, collecting garbage, and providing other services. Providing these services privately through a neighborhood association diminished the fiscal burden, and often became a condition of municipal approval.[15] By the 1990s, students of neighborhood associations reported that their widespread use was "transforming the urban and suburban landscape, not just physically but also politically."[16]

As Uriel Reichman has noted, neighborhood associations "possess much of the power and trappings of local municipal government but arise out of private relationships."[17] Indeed, Reichman chose to describe them as "residential private governments." The rise of private neighborhoods was not initially conceived in such socially significant terms. As noted above, collective ownership of neighborhood property met certain practical real estate needs that neither individual covenants nor zoning could satisfy.

As the wider significance of the institution of the neighborhood association has become more apparent, its workings have received much wider attention.[18] A neighborhood association is, on the one hand, a private contractual arrangement much like any other private contract between consenting parties. On the other hand, it also is a new type of government, exercising many functions that are similar to those of a small municipality—and thus, as some have been arguing, potentially subject to an altogether different legal framework. As Dan Tarlock has commented, "American law has [traditionally] drawn a distinction between public and private associations to decide how power should be allocated between the state and individual," but neighborhood associations "strain this distinction."[19]

For example, in what forms of discrimination among potential residents should a neighborhood association be permitted to engage? There is no doubt about the social and legal unacceptability of racial discrimination. But what about age discrimination, which is often illegal in private contracts and in government programs? Following an adverse court ruling, California had to provide specific legislative authorization for associations to sustain the minimum age limits in its many existing neighborhoods for the elderly.

What about an association that is limited to single people, or even more narrowly to divorced single people? What about an association that limits its residents to the members of a particular church, or to a particular ethnic group? What about a gay-person neighborhood or a nudist association? Such possible restrictions in a public municipal context would clearly be an infringement on constitutional principles of equal protection, or of separation of church and state. Yet private individuals are normally allowed to choose their own friends and other associates. Should this principle be extended fully to the choice of close neighbors?

Neighborhood associations pose important new issues of other kinds. Voting rules in neighborhood associations conflict with the one-person, one-vote requirement of the Constitution, as interpreted by the Supreme Court. As private entities, the associations are not subject to this requirement, but some critics argue that, as the social role of neighborhood associations grows, private governments should be held to the same voting standards as the small local municipalities that they so closely resemble. Members of neighborhood associations also complain that they are double taxed. They have to pay assessments for their own association services such as trash collection while the very same services are provided free of charge to municipal residents—even as the association residents continue to pay a full share of municipal taxes.

What about a neighborhood association that, on formation, included no provision for amending its restrictive rules on the use of property, but whose covenants have now become outdated? Under the traditional common law of covenants and other servitudes, it would not be difficult for the courts to vacate inappropriate restrictions on use of property. Under zoning, all that would be required is a municipal change in the zoning ordinance. However, some legal commentators argue that if a set of neighborhood restrictions was entered into voluntarily, with no provision for amendment, the only way to change the restrictions thereafter should be the negotiation of a unanimous private consent among all association members.[20]

For the most part, such issues have not been resolved by statute but rather by judicial construction and private negotiation among property owners and users. For example, a particular neighborhood association might seek a property tax abatement from the local municipality. A person denied entry to a particular neighborhood association might then assert that the association's discriminatory practices violate constitutional or statutory limitations. As more of these specific cases are resolved, there will be a further refinement of the evolving common law of neighborhood associations.

A SOCIAL REVOLUTION

Looking back on the twentieth century, the development of the private neighborhood association may well prove to have as much social significance as the spread of the corporate form of collective ownership of private business property in the second half of the nineteenth century. At that time a new ease of transportation, economies of scale in mass production, improved management techniques of business coordination, and other business innovations led American industry to operate at a whole new scale, and the corporate form of ownership proved to have major financial and other advantages. Although there were few business corporations before the Civil War, by 1900 almost two-thirds of U.S. manufacturing output was produced by corporations, a figure that would reach 95 percent in the 1960s. In 1932, Adolf Berle and Gardiner Means would announce that the rise of private corporate ownership had transformed the basic relationship between private ownership of property in the United States and the managerial control over the means of production.[21]

In the second half of the twentieth century, economic and social changes, such as higher densities of development, the desire for more precise control over neighborhood character, more economical private provision of common neighborhood services, and the increased demand for common recreational and other facilities, have made private neighborhood associations the residential ownership vehicle of choice for millions of Americans. If private neighborhoods continue to spread at the pace of recent years, the long-run result may be that most private property—residential and business alike—in the United States will be collectively owned. It would be a remarkable transition from the general expectation of individual ownership of property that long prevailed in American political and economic thought.[22]

The spread of neighborhood associations has potentially revolutionary implications not only for the forms of residential property ownership but also for the conduct of local government in the United States. Neighborhood associations already represent the leading vehicle for the privatization of government services in this country. They have the potential to assume even wider government functions, such as elementary education. Virtually the entire set of functions of existing small local governments might end up being served in a private rather than public context.

To date, almost all neighborhood associations have been created as part of the development of a brand new neighborhood. The developer assembles the raw land and builds the neighborhood from its initial stages, including the establishment of the neighborhood association. Purchasers of new housing units are required to accept membership in the association as part of the original terms of ownership. By contrast, if a neighborhood has already been developed with individual ownership of the land and structures, there is little prospect that a neighborhood association will be formed. To do so would require that the individual members of the neighborhood voluntarily agree to surrender part of their individual rights and accept collective private control of exterior uses of their property. Obtaining such voluntary consent from several hundred or more property owners would be time consuming and would almost certainly involve major problems with holdouts and other high transactions costs. Few existing neighborhoods have even considered making such an effort.

In section II I propose that legislation be enacted to facilitate the establishment of neighborhood associations in existing neighborhoods. The establishment of a new legal mechanism for this purpose would extend to existing neighborhoods the significant advantages of collective private control over the neighborhood environment, as well as the private provision of common services that new neighborhoods have been realizing in such large numbers. If this approach were widely adopted, private neighborhood associations would largely replace zoning. As compared with a private property right regime, the governmental exercise of zoning powers has had a number of major defects pointed out in a large literature.[23]

II   Privatizing the Neighborhood

Zoning is one of many forms of government regulation established in the progressive era at the end of the nineteenth and early part of the twentieth century. At the federal level, the first regulatory agency was the Interstate Commerce Commission, created in 1887. Others would follow, including the Food and

Drug Administration (1906), the Federal Reserve System (1913), and the Federal Trade Commission (1914). Over the course of the twentieth century, the web of government regulation, largely based on progressive concepts, would extend far into American life.

Since the 1970s, however, the great debates about economic regulation have concerned the possible dismantling of key elements of the progressive apparatus. Congress voted in 1978 to abolish the Civil Aeronautics Board, and in 1980 the Staggers Act largely abolished the regulatory authority over trucking and railroads of the Interstate Commerce Commission. In the 1980s and 1990s, federal regulatory authority over the communications, banking, and energy industries, along with a number of others, has been significantly curtailed. Deregulation in the United States has mirrored a broader process of privatization that has been taking place worldwide.

Of all the forms of such government regulation, the average American citizen probably has the most direct contact with zoning. In the case of existing zoning, to be sure, there has been little overt deregulation or privatization. Yet in brand new housing developments the private neighborhood association has rendered zoning irrelevant. For its residents, private property rights have now become the legal instrument of choice to protect neighborhood quality.

In existing neighborhoods with separately owned homes, however, zoning has continued to play the basic role in controlling land use. As noted above, the extension of principles of private contracts into these neighborhoods is constrained by the severe practical difficulty of assembling a common neighborhood property agreement. Nevertheless, as I will propose below, there may be ways in which government could adopt policies to lower these obstacles, to promote private property regimes in place of zoning, with its many liabilities.

ORIGINS OF ZONING

After being introduced in New York City in 1916, zoning was widely adopted by communities throughout the United States.[24] In 1926, the Supreme Court upheld zoning, resolving widespread doubts that its new limits on the use of private property were constitutional.[25] Among other arguments, the Court was influenced by the contention that zoning was a necessary instrument of municipal planning.[26] Hopes were high at the time that scientific management could be applied in all areas of American society, thus improving the efficiency and effectiveness of American business and government alike. Thus, instead of the disorderly and haphazard patterns of land development of the past, American cities in the future would be planned according to a rational design. They would promote efficiency goals and be visually more attractive—at least this was the great hope of progressive land planners.[27]

Progressives expected that, as comprehensive planning was put into practice, a city planning staff would study housing, transportation, the job market, and other economic and social trends to project future housing needs. These housing needs would then be allocated among parts of the city, say garden apartments in one district, houses on quarter-acre lots in another district, and houses on two-acre lots in yet another district. The function of zoning, as conceived by its early advocates, would be to provide the practical legal instrument to enforce this city design. Zoning would require that new housing be located and built according to the rational specifications of the city's comprehensive plan.[28]

In practice, however, these grand schemes proved to be utopian.[29] Like the plans for scientific management of society in other fields, they presumed a pre-dictability of economic events and capacity for central scientific understanding and management that real-world planners were seldom if ever able to realize. Moreover, although progressive theory assumed that politicians would concede power to expert professionals in matters of scientific expertise, the politicians had other ideas—especially when the scientific skills of the experts often seemed in doubt, as was certainly the case in city planning.[30] Indeed, as Dennis Coyle has commented, "beneath the arcane language and technicalities, dis-putes about property rights [to land] reveal fundamental clashes between oppos-ing perspectives on the proper society"—matters that could hardly be left to any set of progressive expert technicians to resolve.[31]

Instead, land development occurred opportunistically, as housing or other facilities were proposed for particular locations. The city then had to decide whether it wanted that particular development at that particular time in that particular place. In making these decisions, cities typically found that they could not rely on existing plans to guide them. Rather, they had to do a whole new assessment and make a decision based on other grounds. Overall, the pro-cess was that of a business negotiation between the city and the developer, either making or not making a deal with respect to a particular proposed project, according to the specific benefits to each party.

Thus formal plans often gathered dust on shelves, while development pro-ceeded through a process of identifying projects that would be mutually benefi-cial to individual builders and cities. Yet, because the law of zoning continued to require a comprehensive plan, a new profession of land use planners contin-ued to turn out numerous, costly planning documents. They acted out a fiction that had little bearing on land development but was required by the rituals of the law.

A PROPERTY RIGHT TO THE NEIGHBORHOOD ENVIRONMENT

Whereas zoning was proving ineffectual in guiding new development, it was ef-fective in maintaining the character of existing neighborhoods. For example, small lots were excluded as inconsistent with the "ambiance" or "quality" of one-acre lots. Zoning ensured that only people of sufficient economic means, those able to afford large lots, could enter the neighborhood. If the defining feature of a property right is the power to exclude others, zoning gave this power to neighborhoods. Zoning in this respect amounted to a de facto collective property right, giving the whole neighborhood, exercising its political influence over the municipal administrators of zoning, the collective power to exclude unwanted uses.[32]

As with any ordinary property right, an important social consequence of zoning was to segregate residential neighborhoods according to economic means. Poor people drive old Chevrolets and eat at McDonalds; rich people drive new Mercedes Benzes and eat at fancy French restaurants. Zoning made sure that in the purchase of neighborhood environmental quality this same pattern would hold; poor people would live in older, higher density, and less desirable neighborhoods, while rich people would live in fancy homes built on two- to five-acre lots in the best suburban locations. With zoning, a poor person could no more move into such a neighborhood than he could drive off with a rich person's Mercedes Benz. However, in the absence of zoning, by building apartments or other higher density facilities, it would have been economically feasible for housing developers to locate new moderate-income facilities in upper-income, low-density suburban neighborhoods.

Although this kind of wide-ranging, protective function for neighborhood quality was never part of the early official legal justification for zoning, the purposes that zoning served in practice were well understood by at least the 1960s. In 1968, the National Commission on Urban Problems would observe:

> Zoning . . . very effectively keeps the poor and those with low incomes out of suburban areas by stipulating lot sizes way beyond their economic reach. Many suburbs prohibit or severely limit the construction of apartments, townhouses, or planned unit developments which could accommodate more people in less space at potential savings.[33]
>
> [Zoning] regulations still do their best job when they deal with the type of situation for which many of them were first intended; when the objective is to protect established character and when that established character is uniformly residential. It is in the "nice" neighborhoods, where the regulatory job is easiest, that regulations do their best job.[34]

If the practical consequence of zoning was to provide a new form of de facto collective private property right, why not simply provide this property right directly through a more traditional private means? As discussed in section 1, this is in fact what has been happening, as the creation of neighborhood associations has become standard operating procedure for new development in many parts of the United States.

Although neighborhood associations were just beginning to come into wide use in the 1960s, the National Commission of Urban Problems recognized the similarity of function and the potential for substituting private contractual regimes for existing zoning. Indeed, for existing neighborhoods the commission report in 1968 suggested:

> Another [reform] approach would be to create forms of land tenure which would recognize the interest of owners in what their neighbors do. Such tenure forms, which do not exist but which might resemble condominium tenure, might more effectively reconcile the conflicting interests of neighboring property owners than do conventional regulations. The objective of such tenure would be to leave the small-scale relationships among neighbors for resolution entirely within the private sector, while public regulation would continue to apply to the neighborhood as a whole. In addition to giving neighborhood residents greater control over minor land-use changes within their neighborhood, such tenure could include provision for cooperative maintenance of properties where owners desire their services.[35]

THE PROBLEM OF HIGH TRANSITIONAL COSTS

The commission did not suggest how this proposal might be implemented. While brand new neighborhoods frequently adopted the types of tenure it proposed, few existing neighborhoods did so.[36] Instead, they continued to rely on zoning, since the transactions costs of forming a new private land tenure would be prohibitive. By contrast, zoners did not have to overcome the bargaining problem, because zoning could be imposed by fiat.

In existing neighborhoods when zoning was first imposed, government simply used its sovereign authority to redistribute property rights coercively, canceling individual rights and imposing a de facto collective property right regime. This resembled an exercise in eminent domain; the municipality took certain important rights from the neighborhood residents, but it then provided compensation for this taking by giving the residents other new and valued collective rights. In most cases, the compensation was sufficient that the majority of neighborhood residents saw themselves as better off in the end, and supported the new zoning for the neighborhood. To be sure, inevitably there were some objectors; under zoning, the preferences of holdouts were sacrificed by government action to the wishes of the dominant neighborhood group.

There was nothing in American legal and policy traditions to justify such a coercive government redistribution of property rights within neighborhoods. The closest analogy may have been the urban renewal programs of the 1950s and 1960s—although here the government paid cash to owners of condemned property rights that were being assembled into a new property regime, rather than providing compensation through an assignment of new rights in the overall project. If zoning had been described for what it really was, it might well have been declared unconstitutional in the legal environment of the 1920s. At a minimum, governments would have been required to enact legislation spelling out the true purposes of the rights assembly process provided by zoning, and the way in which new compensating collective rights were effectively being provided in place of the individual rights being taken.[37] Instead, zoning operated under various myths and fictions, perhaps because it would have been more difficult politically to obtain acceptance for zoning if its real workings had been made explicit.

Thus, in retrospect, the traditional nuisance law and planning justifications for zoning have served their most important practical functions by securing legal acceptance for property right change. They provided the necessary legal camouflage to permit a fundamental land law innovation that was much more radical than the early advocates of zoning cared to admit. Zoning was nothing less than the redistribution of neighborhood property rights to create a new private collective right to the neighborhood environment, decades in advance of the collective rights that today are created through neighborhood associations.

By now, of course, zoning is a long established fact, and the collective property rights created by zoning have been protecting the quality of tens of thousands of American neighborhoods for many years. Given this history, it would be a less radical step today to recognize formally the real workings of zoning by acting to privatize its land use control functions in these neighborhoods.

A PROPOSAL

In order to expand the advantages of private property ownership, I propose a method by which neighborhood associations might be formed in existing neighborhoods. While I recognize that many approaches are possible, I propose the following five-step process.

First, a group of individual property owners in an existing neighborhood could petition the state (or in a large city, perhaps the municipal government) to form a private neighborhood association. The petition would describe the boundaries of the proposed private neighborhood and the instruments of collective governance intended for it. The petition would state the services expected to be performed by the neighborhood association and an estimate of the monthly assessment required. The petition would have to come from owners cumulatively possessing more than 60 percent of the total value of neighborhood property.

Second, the state would determine whether the proposed neighborhood meets certain standards of reasonableness, including having a contiguous area, boundaries of a regular shape, an appropriate relationship to major streets, streams, valleys, and other geographic features. The state would also certify whether the governance instruments of the neighborhood association meet state standards.

Third, if the application met state requirements, a neighborhood committee would be authorized to negotiate a service transfer agreement with the municipal government in which the neighborhood was located. The agreement would specify the future possible transfer of ownership of municipal streets, parks, swimming pools, tennis courts, and other existing public lands and facilities located within the newly proposed private neighborhood (possibly including some compensation to the city). It would specify the future assumption of garbage collection, snow removal, policing, and fire protection, to the degree that the private neighborhood would assume responsibilities for such services. The transfer agreement would also specify future tax arrangements, including any property or other tax credits that the members of the new neighborhood association might receive in compensation for assuming existing municipal burdens. The state government would serve as an overseer and mediator in this negotiation process, and would have ultimate authority to resolve disputes.

Fourth, a neighborhood election would be called. The election would occur at least one year after the submission of a complete description of the neighborhood proposal, including the articles of neighborhood incorporation, the municipal transfer agreement, estimates of assessment burdens, a comprehensive appraisal of individual neighborhood properties, and other relevant information. During the one-year waiting period, the state would supervise a process to inform property owners and residents of the neighborhood of the details of the proposal and to facilitate public discussion and debate.

Fifth, the state would supervise the conduct of the election. In the election, approval of the neighborhood association would require both of the following: (1) an affirmative vote of property owners cumulatively representing 90 percent or more of the total value of the proposed neighborhood; and (2) an affirmative vote by 75 percent or more of the individual unit owners in the neighborhood. If these conditions were met, all property owners in the neighborhood would be required to join the neighborhood association and would be subject to the full terms and conditions laid out in the neighborhood association charter.

Zoning already regulates many of the details of housing design, such as the size of the lot, the amount of floor space, and the setback from the street. Why, then, some may ask, go to the trouble of devising a whole new property right regime for neighborhoods that are already adequately protected by zoning? While zoning and neighborhood associations do in fact overlap in key respects, a full private neighborhood status offers four major advantages over zoning.

First, except where a historic or other special district can be justified, zoning does not provide for control over the fine details of neighborhood architecture, trees and shrubbery, yard maintenance, and other aesthetic matters that may have a major impact on the character of the neighborhood.

Second, the administration of zoning takes place at the municipal level, where the politics typically includes many people who are not residents of the neighborhood. Yet, in matters such as the control of fine details of neighborhood architecture, there is no need or justification for broader municipal involvement. Indeed, under zoning the substantial influence on such matters by outsiders leaves the neighborhood exposed to unwanted regulatory actions. This lack of secure control over the details of zoning administration is a main reason why neighborhoods are reluctant to accept more precise and comprehensive zoning controls over aesthetic matters relating to neighborhood land use.

Third, because zoning is regarded as a form of public regulation, the direct sale of zoning is prohibited. However, if the acceptance or exclusion of a use were considered an ordinary exercise of a private property right, as in a private neighborhood, neighborhoods could sell rights of entry (say for a new neighborhood convenience store) into the neighborhood. They might also sell rights to make certain broader changes in land use within the neighborhood, or even sell off all the neighborhood property in one package for comprehensive redevelopment in a brand new (and much more valuable) type of land use. The ability to sell entry rights directly would introduce a much needed flexibility to accommodate new use demands in metropolitan land markets, significantly improving the overall efficiency of their operation.[38]

Lastly, the advantages of neighborhood associations are not limited to improvements on zoning. Neighborhood associations can serve as a vehicle for more efficient and effective provision of common local services. The establishment of a neighborhood association can be a way of sustaining a strong spirit of community, supporting an identity that would be lacking if the neighborhood had no formal status. In a time when many churches, women's organizations, fraternal groups, and other traditional parts of civic society have been declining, it may be important to provide strong institutional support for neighborhood allegiances.

SHOULD CONSENT BE UNANIMOUS?

As proposed here, a new private neighborhood association could be established by some high percentage vote (ultimately to be decided by the legislature) but less than unanimous consent. Thus at least some property owners might vote against forming a private neighborhood association but nevertheless be compelled to join.

Several factors justify such an approach that, considered in isolation, is admittedly objectionable. First, in most existing neighborhoods zoning already has redistributed property rights in a compulsory manner. Creation of a private neighborhood is not so much the establishment of a new collective authority to manage the neighborhood environment as the transfer of management authority to a new holder of this authority, operating under new rules. Instead of the municipal government, neighborhood land use would now be controlled by the residents themselves, as an exercise of a private property right.[39]

Consider a proposed change to allow a new type of use in a neighborhood. Under zoning, this would require either a change in the zoning ordinance (which would require an act of the city council) or a zoning variance. In a neighborhood association, there would be a wider range of ways of dealing with such a proposed use change. It might in some instances be precluded altogether by the rules of the neighborhood association (impossible under zoning, because future municipal legislative actions cannot be so constrained). Acceptance of the proposed new use might require a majority vote of the neighborhood association board of directors. If the use change is major, it might require approval by a supermajority of the neighborhood association property owners. Because it would be a private property right transaction, the approval might also be conditioned on making a money payment by the proposed new use to the neighborhood—something that would probably be classified as bribery under zoning, and thus would be illegal.

The formal declaration documents of a neighborhood association amount to a type of neighborhood constitution. Thus in an existing neighborhood the establishment of a new neighborhood association might involve what could be described as a constitutional convention. When the U.S. Constitution was approved in the 1780s and 1790s, each state held a convention wherein the requirement for state approval of the new constitution was a simple majority vote of the previously elected delegates. The ratification procedure required that nine of the thirteen colonies vote to join before the Constitution would take effect. Each state voting negatively thereby maintained the option to stay out of the Union.

Reflecting on a wide variety of such constitutional experiences around the world, one can imagine a range of alternative rules for forming a new neighborhood association. In some circumstances, the geography of the neighborhood might easily allow dissenting property owners to opt out of the neighborhood association. Another possibility would be to bring into the neighborhood association only those residents who vote affirmatively, but to leave minority property owners subject to the continued operation of existing municipal zoning. A third alternative would be to require that new neighborhood associations offer to buy out objecting property owners for fair market value (plus perhaps some generous premium for the troubles of having to move). Finally, if voting procedures were appropriately designed (e.g., a secret ballot), it might still be possible to require a 100 percent vote of approval, which would be less difficult to achieve in this way than an unstructured process of negotiating separate agreements with each individual property owner in the neighborhood.

Whatever the degree of coercion, the restriction on choice would have to be weighed against the advantages of a new private property regime for protecting neighborhood environments, as compared with continuance of the existing zoning system. The liabilities of zoning are so great that there should be a strong presumption in favor of opening up new private options under transitional arrangements that make them a real possibility in practice.

ABOLISH ZONING OF UNDEVELOPED LAND

Zoning has been applied not only for existing residential neighborhoods but also for undeveloped land. It is important to make a fundamental distinction between the two circumstances of an existing neighborhood and undeveloped land. When zoning is applied to undeveloped land on the fringes of metropolitan areas, it is more objectionable. For undeveloped land, zoning results in major inequities to land owners and large social inefficiencies in the use of the land.

In an existing neighborhood, the initial imposition of zoning may be criticized for the coercive element but, as discussed, each property owner receives compensation in the form of a new collective property right. However, there is no such compensation provided in the typical suburban zoning of large tracts of farm or other undeveloped land. The zoning simply reduces the value of the land while benefitting the rest of the municipality—a classic example of rent seeking by one politically powerful group at the expense of the rights of weaker parties.

The beneficiaries are typically the more densely settled and thus more numerous recent arrivals in the area. Indeed, over the past few decades this "doorslammer" or "last-to-get-in" phenomenon has been widely noted. Large areas of metropolitan land in the United States are being held out of development, at large cost to the rest of society, but providing substantial environmental benefits to the locally dominant political groups of homeowners. As William Fischel has explained:

> [Through zoning] communities *can* have a substantial impact on the overall density of population. The major reason is that courts of law are willing to sustain zoning laws (or, more frequently, amendments to zoning laws) that substantially reduce the value of undeveloped land. This allows the community to reap the benefits of restrictive zoning (to current homeowners and other voters) without having to confront the cost that these regulations impose on developers and prospective residents. . . . Communities do not have to do anything approximating benefit-cost analysis before imposing land use regulation. This leads to overregulation and residential densities that are too low.[40]

Considered from a metropolitan-wide perspective, the zoning system has typically provided an inadequate supply of undeveloped land for many kinds of new housing, especially housing suitable for lower- and moderate-income groups.[41]

In California, the courts have been particularly tolerant of municipal restrictions, essentially giving municipalities carte blanche to do almost anything they want with their zoning (or other types of growth controls). According to one study, the California Supreme Court has been "more hostile to development than any other high court in the nation."[42]

Combined with the strong preference for open spaces and environmental amenities of many California residents, the result has been a severe degree of restriction on the amounts of land available for less expensive housing in most metropolitan regions. In 1970, before the growth control enthusiasm had spread to municipalities throughout the state, the price of California housing on average was 35 percent higher than the rest of the nation. By 1980, it was 79 percent higher, and by 1990 it was 147 percent higher. Adjusted for quality, one estimate in 1978 showed that California housing was 57 percent higher than in other parts of the United States.

Although the state of California represents an extreme case, in general there is no sound justification for the existing municipal practices across the United States of zoning of undeveloped land areas of significant size. This form of zoning, I propose, should simply be abolished. In the long run, if zoning of existing neighborhoods were also ended, by substituting private contracts through neighborhood associations as proposed above, it would be possible to abolish zoning altogether. The prospect of the abolition of zoning in all its forms—and thus curtailing the abundant rent seeking temptations that zoning inevitably offers—provides yet another reason for substituting private contractual arrangements for zoning regulation in existing neighborhoods.

If zoning of undeveloped land were abolished, another important innovation would be to encourage the formation of new neighborhood associations of undeveloped land owners. The resulting encouragement to private planning of land use might result in much greater coordination of uses over wider areas than has ever been achieved in practice under zoning. Moreover, in private neighborhoods the doorslammer phenomenon is prevented by rules keeping land use controls in the hands of the developer until the overall project is substantially complete.

Conclusion

My proposal for the move from zoning to private collective rights in existing neighborhoods is consistent with longstanding patterns of property rights evolution.[43] Except in times of revolutionary turmoil, new property rights are seldom created by legislatures from whole cloth. Rather, they typically emerge gradually and informally, often at odds with the received economic and property right theories of the day. As experience accumulates, however, the informal practice comes to be better understood and the merits to be better appreciated. At a still later point, the informal practice is fully accepted, and may be codified.[44]

In describing the long history of British land law, Sir Frederick Pollock wrote that "the history of our land laws, it cannot be too often repeated, is a history of legal fictions and evasions, with which the Legislature vainly endeavoured to keep pace until their results . . . were perforce acquiesced in as a settled part of the law itself."[45] Indeed, although the substantive workings changed greatly, the outward form of English land tenure was not greatly altered from the thirteenth to the nineteenth centuries. Pollock described the manner of property rights evolution in Britain up to the late nineteenth century: "[Over this period] the system underwent a series of grave modifications. Grave as these were, however, the main lines of the feudal theory were always ostensibly preserved. And to this day, though the really characteristic incidents of the feudal tenures have disappeared or left only the faintest of traces, the scheme of our land laws can, as to its form, be described only as a modified feudalism."[46]

In the twentieth century we like to think that the world is more rational, and that we can do without legal fictions. Whole professions, such as that of public administration, depend on the assumption that societal goals can be stated directly and realized by a process of rational deliberation. However, the twentieth-century history of zoning suggests otherwise, for it closely resembles the process described by Pollock. In zoning, the legal myth of scientific planning continues to obscure its real purposes. We should now dispense with the myth, and focus upon the real benefits of land use controls.

Society should find better means—best accomplished through private contract—to protect neighborhood quality. Replacing zoning with private contracts would recognize the failure of yet another of the legacies of the progressive-era aspirations for the scientific management of American society.[47]

Dealing with the NIMBY Problem

WILLIAM A. FISCHEL

American land use controls present a problem for efficient utilization of land in metropolitan areas. As a rural community is transformed into an exurban and then suburban community by development, new residents eventually take over the political machinery.[1] Unlike the original residents, they are not much interested in local economic development for jobs or business-related reasons. They typically commute to jobs elsewhere in the metropolitan area. What they are interested in is the value of their major asset, their homes.

Owner-occupied housing is, for the vast majority of residents, the largest asset that they will ever own. Homeowners believe that the value of this huge asset will be affected by deterioration of neighborhood and municipal-wide conditions. Scores of economic capitalization studies show that they are rational in this belief.[2] As a result, homeowners are exquisitely interested in any neighborhood change or changes in municipal taxes and services that will affect the value of their homes. This may explain why homeowners are far more apt to vote in municipal elections than renters.[3]

It also accounts for the NIMBY ("not in my back yard") homeowner. NIMBYS are mostly nearby homeowners who object to further development within their community. The development may be homes just like the ones in which they live, but the neighbors are opposed because they fear that greater density will adversely affect local road congestion, neighborhood character, crime, taxes, and public services.

NIMBYS appear at the zoning and planning board reviews to which almost all developers of more-than-minor subdivisions must submit. If NIMBYS fail to reduce the scale and density of the project at that stage, they will often deploy alternative regulatory rationales at other local, state, and federal government forums, including courts of law. For example, they might raise concerns about environmental impact statements, historic districts, aboriginal burial sites, agricultural preservation, wetlands, flood plains, access for the disabled, and the protection of (often unidentified) endangered species. I have heard all of these arguments—and others too elaborately bizarre to list—in my ten years as a member of the Hanover, New Hampshire, zoning board. And if NIMBYS fail in these efforts, they will seek, often by direct democratic initiatives, to have the local zoning and planning regulations changed to make sure it does not happen again.

The larger problem with NIMBYism is that its cumulative impact causes metropolitan areas to develop at excessively low densities.[4] By zoning large tracts of developable land off-limits to development, NIMBYism compels developers to look elsewhere. Although in principle the "elsewheres" could be in the central city, the more likely direction for new development is to rural areas. For most cities, the problem of metropolitan sprawl can thus be attributed to pressure from hundreds of small NIMBY groups.

Bob Nelson's answer to the NIMBY problem is to collectivize and privatize the potential profits of development, disfranchising the nascent NIMBYS in the process.[5] Nelson envisions an exurban community dominated by landowning farmers who are largely in favor of development. The obvious reason they like development is that each farmer has an asset—extensive land holdings—that might be sold for development at considerable profit. However, rather than allow the first few farmers to develop as they please, which would result in the newcomer-NIMBYs preventing the hindmost farmers from developing, Nelson proposes that the owners of developable land form an entrepreneurial neighborhood association. This private association would overcome the NIMBY problem at the crucial, initial development stage, by adopting the voting rules that prevail in most newly developing, privately planned communities.[6] The developers (in Nelson's case, the collective of original farmer-landowners) would hold a majority of votes in the neighborhood association until the development was nearly completed. After completion, voting control over the neighborhood association would pass to the residents.

As a historical aside, the tension between original proprietors and early settlers appeared immediately in the development of seventeenth-century New England towns.[7] The initial proprietors, who advanced the capital for town development, adopted a solution much like Nelson's, by carefully limiting who could vote. With subsequent development in the early 1700s of independent town meetings, which offered a more liberal franchise, settlers were able to transfer much of the proprietors' remaining common holdings to themselves. It is not clear, however, whether this outcome retarded or promoted town development, since settlers were eager for more company in those days.

For suburban communities that have already gone part way down the NIMBY path but have not completely locked up their open land, Nelson suggests that state legislation enable a subset of owners of developable land to form neighborhood associations. Nelson's proposal avoids deciding what configuration of residential development is efficient by leaving this entirely up to the proprietors of his neighborhood association. The proprietors have every incentive to develop their neighborhood efficiently. They will not leave excessive amounts of open space, because doing so would leave some profits untapped. But they will not overdo the density in their plans, because they would repel potential residents. As long as the developers must be true to their plans, they have every incentive to develop their property efficiently.

The evidence in support of this behavioral view comes from existing communities that were laid out and regulated (at least through their development period) by a single private developer. Although Reston, Virginia, and Columbia, Maryland, are among the better-known recent examples of this phenomenon, the most sophisticated economic study of a planned community was of Foster City, California.

Foster City was literally created from the muck of San Francisco Bay in the 1960s by one T. Jack Foster.[8] Mr. Foster and his company did all of the planning; San Mateo County, the only local jurisdiction with land use control authority, stood on the sidelines. The result is a high-density, high-income community of about seven thousand persons per square mile. ("Urbanized Areas," the census designation of central city and suburban built-up area, average about three thousand persons per square mile.) Despite the high average income of residents, the city is not homogeneous in style. Mr. Foster built single-family homes and apartments and a commercial area, and his original plan was in fact carried out almost exactly, even after he sold it to a consortium.

Foster City was the subject of a Berkeley doctoral dissertation by Theodore Crone.[9] Crone examined the city to see if its configuration of land uses in fact maximized net land values. The issue that Crone was interested in was not whether apartments might devalue nearby land devoted to single-family homes (they did, a little), but whether such proximity lowered the value of homes more than they raised the value of land for apartments. Crone found that this did not happen; the land uses dictated by Foster appeared in fact to maximize the joint value of land for apartments and single-family homes.

Crone took the results of his fine study to what I thought was an odd conclusion. He said that it proved that municipal zoning, which supposedly tries its best to segregate land uses, was not justified. He inferred this from the fact that Foster City actually was efficiently laid out, even though apartments were often in close proximity to single-family homes. I wrote a note pointing out that what Crone had actually proven was that single-developer private zoning—the type that Bob Nelson now commends to us—was actually efficient.[10] Crone had implicitly assumed that Foster City, because it was privately developed, had no zoning. As I gathered from visits to the city, a local history volume, and a chat with T. Jack Foster Jr. (the founder's son and partner), Foster City was arguably the most exquisitely planned and zoned community in the United States. What distinguished it from publicly zoned communities was that all of the land was owned by the planner, and he quite consciously internalized spillover effects that might in other areas have become externalities.

Nelson's proposal to facilitate Foster City-style developments thus deserves a serious hearing. Even if the proprietors of his neighborhood associations are not experienced developers, they can easily hire planners or sell to someone with the experience of a T. Jack Foster, James Rouse (of Columbia), or Robert Simon (of Reston). The division of labor in land development is extensive. From a contractarian viewpoint, Nelson's proposal has one substantial drawback. In order to consolidate rural parcels to create a neighborhood association, some landowners must be coerced to commit themselves to an association that they might not voluntarily join. Yet we should not dismiss out of hand a proposal simply because it may involve some coercion. It may be that alternatives that are most likely to be adopted would involve still more coercion and be less effective in dealing with metropolitan sprawl. I shall describe the government-oriented reform that is most often offered as a solution for the excesses of NIMBYism.

The source of excessive NIMBYism is that suburban homeowners do not accurately perceive the opportunity costs of their preferences. As Nelson has pointed out in previous work,[11] one way of making residents aware of the cost of excluding subsequent development is to cut them in on the deal. His current proposal —to form neighborhood associations to exploit the profits of development— arises from his conviction that most development has only neighborhood effects. Allowing the existing municipality to sell zoning or, to put it more gently, to accept voluntary exactions from developers who seek to change zoning laws, cuts too many people in on the deal. I had at one time endorsed "zoning for sale,"[12] but I now advocate it only within the context of a movement to compensate landowners subjected to excessive restrictions.[13]

But there is another market that may make existing homeowners more aware of the opportunity costs of NIMBYism. The political market's failure in NIMBYism is that those who would benefit from the project are either absent from the jurisdiction or present in such small numbers that they are politically ineffective. If land use controls were solely the province of a metropolitan or regional political body, the "outsiders" discriminated against by NIMBYs would in fact be "insiders" to the polity.[14] The prospective beneficiaries need not directly exercise their powers in a larger-government forum. Groups that "represent" potential residents of a vacant tract in a residential area could be homebuilders, construction unions, and advocates for low-income housing. While all of these groups may attempt to pressure municipal officials in the present fragmented governance structure, the force of their words is dissipated when they can muster few votes in local elections. Moreover, in most small local governments where NIMBYism is strongest, even campaign money for prodevelopment officials does little. Most suburban elections are on issues that are transparent to voters. Even where direct democracy does not have to approve zoning changes (as it does in New England towns), convincing econometric evidence supports the supposition that in small towns the preferences of the median voter—usually a homeowner—prevail in local political decisions.[15]

Anthony Downs has long advocated metropolitan governance as the solution to NIMBYism.[16] Downs, like Nelson, seeks to undermine local voters' authority. But where Nelson seeks to devolve zoning authority down to the neighborhood, Downs seeks to move it up to the metropolitan level. Downs's metropolitan commissions would not eliminate local government, but would override local instances of exclusionary zoning. There is indeed empirical evidence that larger-area political bodies are more prodevelopment than smaller ones. The perennial attempts by state governments to promote employment growth with tax breaks and other policies are one example.[17] Smaller units of government seldom pay much attention to employment issues because most of the benefits of success would be enjoyed by people outside their political borders. Most pro-industry local governments, with the exception of depressed central cities, have their eyes trained on fiscal benefits.

Another manifestation of the inclusionary effect of size is that big cities tend to be less exclusionary in their zoning than their suburbs.[18] It is not a coincidence, I submit, that the largest (and virtually only) city in the United States not to have zoning, Houston, is one of the few whose municipal boundaries encompass almost all of its metropolitan population. Judging from the analyses of several plebiscites, Houston would probably have adopted zoning if its suburbs were separate from its downtown so that more homogenous groups could be formed. Opinion polls in Houston found that low-income voters and Hispanics generally opposed zoning in part because of their anxiety of being dominated by middle-class suburban interests.[19] Thus there is reason to believe that shifting land use controls to metropolitan government would make zoning more sensitive to the demands of potential homeowners.

The problem with metropolitan zoning is that it is more likely to be captured by special interests and less likely to respond to legitimate local concerns. Special interests are apt to go too far in either direction. On the one hand, special-interest politics can result in excessive development: not enough NIMBYism. At the state level, where job creation often dominates political concerns, there are numerous examples of seemingly excessive fiscal giveaways to potential employers.[20] Large central cities whose politics are dominated by construction firms and their unions may sometimes discount objections that the megadevelopment stadium or convention center will disrupt traditional neighborhoods.[21]

On the other hand, the experience of statewide land use controls in places like Hawaii and Vermont suggests that state-appointed commissions, rather than represent the demands of potential residents and would-be consumers, act as yet another constraint on development in response to local environmental groups.[22] I have observed that Vermont's Act-250 commissions provide a powerful lever for entrenched businesses to exclude potential competitors.[23] In the instance I cited, the Vermont Motel Owners Association intervened to oppose a proposal by Motel 6 to build in an area zoned for motels and eagerly sought by the local government. The motel association raised specious issues about soil conditions to wear down the developer, who finally quit the project. There is also some evidence that larger units of local government in metropolitan areas can function (perhaps inadvertently) as cartel organizers to keep housing prices artificially high.[24]

Portland, Oregon, is an interesting (and rare) example of a metropolitan government that has taken over a great deal of land use control.[25] It is one of the few cities that is willing to override local zoning to promote infill development.[26] The problem is that Portland shows signs of behaving like an exclusionary suburb with respect to the rest of the world.[27] Its original plan, implemented in the early 1970s, had urban growth boundaries that were intended to contain urban sprawl.[28] This did little harm and perhaps some good as long as growth was moderate and there was plenty of land within the boundaries.

Portland's recent decision not to expand the growth boundary in the face of more rapid immigration to the city, however, seems to account for its sudden and rapid rise in housing prices.[29] Portland planners have responded to this with plans to require housing development at high densities within the city. Such housing plans are in principle admirably inclusionary, but for immigrants to Portland who want to live in moderate-density suburban houses, the existing stock is what they must bid for. In a sense, the unrealistically high-density development plans are as exclusionary as unrealistically low-density development. Both extremes make accessible but undeveloped land off limits to normal suburban development. Similar situations of metropolitan governance causing housing price inflation by excessively limiting suburban development are Seoul, Korea,[30] Kuala Lumpur, Malaysia,[31] and Reading, England.[32]

The efficiency evaluation of metropolitan governance is problematical on both counts. In terms of achieving the efficient density of development, metropolitan governments may address the problem of excessively low densities. But this strategy has a high variance. It seems almost as likely that outcomes could be excessively high-density in some situations and too low in others. The risk of error seems especially high where the metropolitan governance structure would end up with a double-veto system, in which the metropolitan body can override only the "yes" votes of local governments. Most of the state and regional plans adopted since the 1970s (Portland excepted) seem only to add a layer of regulation, and thus give the NIMBYs another bite at the apple.[33] Developers would be left with another layer of review, which could end up vetoing projects that some local governments favor, without the offsetting advantage of being able to override parochial antidevelopment decisions.

This brief survey should give pause to those who would dismiss Nelson's proposal because it is inconsistent with freedom of contract. I do not dispute that in this comment. I wish to show only that the alternative to dealing with the problems that Nelson addresses may involve even more extensive infringements on property rights, not to mention much larger government entities whose actions may be more antideveloper than those of the entities they replaced.

Devolutionary Proposals and Contractarian Principles

STEVEN J. EAGLE

Land uses are coordinated through private contracts and governmental regulations. Almost all cities in the United States have comprehensive zoning laws, typically enacted in the 1920s. These regulate the residential and commercial uses permitted in different localities and the physical characteristics and placement of buildings on individual parcels. In suburban subdivisions, on the other hand, private agreements largely substitute for zoning regulations.

In these subdivisions, many important aspects of land use are controlled by covenants (i.e., contracts that bind their successors as well as the original home-buyers). These covenants set forth the principal restrictions on homeowners and establish residential community associations (RCAS), which are empowered to enforce these rules and to establish additional regulations. Suburban covenants, and the role of RCAS, have been the subject of an ongoing debate between those who admire their contractarian bases and those who fear that governmental regulations are needed to protect residents from oppressive RCAS and the broader society from elite and exclusionary private communities.[1] Regardless of such criticisms, RCAS have flourished in recent decades.

Municipal zoning regulations often are overly rigid and yet arguably insufficiently detailed. They are not very responsive to dynamic changes, especially at the neighborhood level. Yet traditional zoning long has been accepted without much question as the preeminent basis for urban land regulation.[2] This is largely a function of the reliance interests that landowners have formed in existing regulations, and of the presumption that the transaction costs entailed in replacing the regulatory regime with a contractarian one are prohibitive.

In his essay,[3] Robert H. Nelson proposes that collective property rights largely substitute for urban zoning. He argues that the exercise of such collective rights to exclude inferior uses from neighborhoods has been the unarticulated purpose of residential zoning all along. To accomplish this task, Nelson would devolve many state regulatory powers upon neighborhood associations (NAS), along with the effective transfer to them of rights long deemed the property of individual owners. Neighborhood supermajorities would have to approve, but there would be no unanimity requirement.

Nelson's response is an attempt to finesse the contract issue with devolutionary change. The proposal's principal justification must be a pragmatic assumption that only such a strategy could cut the Gordian knot of unresponsive regulations and insurmountable barriers to bargaining. From the perspectives of contract theory and economic efficiency, however, the result is only partially satisfactory. I believe that contract is more robust than Nelson gives it credit for, and that the new NAS would excessively regulate nonconsenting owners.

I An Overview of Neighborhood Privatization

Suburban RCAs have flourished in recent decades. By 1992, the residences of almost 32 million people, some 11 percent of Americans, were encompassed within some 150,000 assocations.[4] In some metropolitan areas, such as Los Angeles and San Diego, this figure exceeds 70 percent.[5] RCAs generally are established in the documents creating individual subdivisions. The law conclusively presumes that home buyers and their successors will have read these documents and have consented to their terms. RCAs own common areas within the subdivision and regulate many aspects of neighborhood life, ranging from the design and color of homes and the landscaping through the hours during which portable basketball hoops might be set up in driveways. RCAs rarely have been introduced in established neighborhoods, on the theory that disparate existing uses, reliance upon fairly inflexible zoning laws, and collective action problems could be surmounted only at such high transaction costs as to make their creation in existing neighborhoods prohibitive. Thus owners would not form RCAs even where they would confer a significant collective benefit.[6]

Nelson proposes that states solve this collective action problem through legislation. Landowners whose cumulative holdings in an area they specify comprise a substantial supermajority of the owners and value of the private property in that area would be permitted to apply for the creation of an NA. The state would have to certify that the proposed boundaries were reasonable with respect to compactness, geographical features, infrastructure, and other considerations. If the application were approved, a neighborhood committee would be authorized to negotiate a service transfer agreement with the municipal government. The agreement would specify the ownership of public facilities in the neighborhood, including streets and parks, and would allocate the responsibility for future provision of services like fire and police protection and trash collection. It also would specify future tax arrangements. After approval, all owners would be required to join the NA, and would be subject to its terms.

Once in place, the NA could regulate the fine details of neighborhood aesthetics. It also would be able to provide services more efficiently to residents. Since the gain from NA activities would inure to residents, they would no longer resist almost all land use changes as they typically now do. The association's powers would be so extensive as to permit the most profound changes, ranging from the sale of entry rights into the residential area to convenience stores, for example, through the sale of the entire neighborhood for comprehensive redevelopment in an entirely different use.

II The Conflation of Property Rights and Zoning into "Collective Property"

Building upon Nelson's earlier work, Professor Fischel has argued that "zoning should be thought of as a collective property right," albeit one that "evolved without any conscious decision to reassign ownership of property."[7] However, while property is an attribute of the autonomous individual, zoning is a manifestation of the state's power to intervene in citizens' lives for the protection of the public health, safety, and welfare. Thus zoning has a different conceptual basis and is not easily transmutable into property. While remnants of feudal property obligations lingered in Europe, purchasers of land in America have since colonial times obtained absolute title.[8] Although government subjects their land to direct regulation, owners never have been forced to participate in private collective arrangements for coordination of land uses.

Nelson describes the original public welfare justification of zoning as a necessary camouflage for a widespread redistribution of rights to downtown merchants and emerging suburbs. This argument is supported by the Supreme Court's casual and sweeping endorsement of comprehensive land use regulation in its 1926 *Euclid* decision.[9] Nelson acknowledges that zoning proponents did not intend to create de facto property rights, but asserts that this inevitable consequence of their efforts has become increasingly clear as attempts to engage in scientific land use planning have proven to be utopian dreams. It is not useful, however, to view zoning in Manichean terms, since some regulations are intended to increase wealth and others to redistribute it.

Certainly, Nelson's view has some basis in fact. It is easy to see comprehensive zoning legislation as a classic public choice story,[10] with local officials enacting ordinances favored by interest groups offering the highest rewards.[11] Suburban homeowners have contrived to utilize land use regulations to maximize their wealth at the expense of owners of undeveloped land and newcomers.[12] On the other hand, Justice George Sutherland, who wrote the *Euclid* opinion, was a social conservative as well as a believer in markets.[13] He also supported some social welfare legislation, and his record "defies facile ideological categorization."[14] Sutherland's principal biographers have interpreted *Euclid* as based not on economics but on a fear that overpopulation and urban congestion might lead to an increase in tuberculosis and other diseases.[15] Thus the opinion reflected his "moral inclination . . . to presume in favor of local regulations that . . . seemed to bear an obvious connection to the public health."[16] Similarly, more recent policies such as "inclusionary zoning," which requires developers to include moderate-income housing in expensive subdivisions, do not have as their goal wealth maximization and indeed might be wealth reducing.[17]

In sum, zoning is more than "collective property," and is not as readily transmutable into contract rights as Nelson avers.

III Is Compulsory "Privatization" Really Contractarian?

There is a certain irony in Nelson's privatization proposal: at the behest of interested parties, state law would impose a contractarian regime upon those who prefer a regulatory one.

The role of contract in determining the use of land is immense. Adjoining owners often coordinate land uses through a sale to a single owner or through mutual covenants. In either case, the result is Pareto efficient since the parties have internalized both costs and benefits. It is not necessary that the state appraise the bargain, since their unanimity demonstrates that none of the parties has lost in the exchange.[18] Each party prefers the agreement to its alternatives and thereby has maximized value and minimized costs.[19]

Nelson's principal justification for binding nonconsenting owners is that NAs would enhance the value of neighborhood land. This seems consistent with the mainstream contractarian view that "private ordering through contract is presumptively legitimate because it best serves their efficiency objective."[20] Yet, as Professor Bainbridge notes, "For conservative contractarians, this is precisely backwards: we regard efficiency as a presumptively legitimate norm precisely because it best serves our preference for private ordering through contract."[21] For market conservatives, then, the issue is whether privatization of land use controls in existing neighborhoods maximizes value. For social conservatives, the question is whether it maximizes liberty.[22] Bainbridge's concern mirrors that of Justice Sutherland, who was perturbed not about whether an enactment would maximize wealth, but with whether its "determinism" would relegate persons to status roles in which they would be regulated without regard to the moral significance of their acts.[23] Only if wealth maximization trumps these contrasting values do the advantages of nonunanimity seem enticing.

Another recurring leitmotif in Nelson's proposal is that cities should defer to neighborhood wishes. Nonresidents would not understand local needs as well, and their actions might reflect an agenda adverse to neighborhood interests. Residents also might custom-tailor their own rules and monitor compliance more readily. This theme reflects the Catholic Church's "principle of subsidiarity," which declares that "it is an injustice, a grave evil and a disturbance of right order for a larger and higher organization to arrogate to itself functions that can be performed efficiently by smaller and lower bodies."[24]

In many respects, however, the proposal would relegate decisions to larger and higher bodies. An agency of the state would serve as an overseer and mediator in the negotiation process among owners. The state planning agency would decide if the "neighborhood's" boundaries were appropriate, if the proposed allocations of existing assets and tax revenues between the locality and NA were fair, and if land use powers permitted the association were reasonable. Furthermore, the state agency might well have to arbitrate not only the claims of the city and the original group of landowners, but also those of other landowner groups wanting to include some parcels in competing NAS. The state agency would have to supervise the discussion process and ensuing election. If a plan were approved, inevitably the state would have to deal with charges of collusive malfeasance involving association and municipal officials.

In effect, the state agency would likely become an administrative tribunal adjudicating not only traditional land use regulations but also the equivalent of lawsuits on covenants and shareholder derivative actions. The encroachment of intense state supervision in what have hitherto been local matters would benefit interest groups most able to organize on a statewide level.[25] Equally important, state regulation would reduce the incentive for similar jurisdictions to compete for residents through better services and lower taxes.[26] Such competition also serves as an important check on governmental exactions from landowners.[27]

Even if Nelson correctly asserts that neighborhood privatization brings governance closer to home, NAS are not necessarily less oppressive than broader-based entities. Examples of "grassroots tyranny" by both local governments[28] and RCAS[29] abound. As James Madison noted in the *Federalist Papers*, small societies are apt to contain fewer counterbalancing interests, and local majorities find them convenient locations in which to "concert and execute their plans of oppression."[30] The nonconsensual nature of NAS exacerbates the risk that they will disregard the interests of dissenting owners.

It is important to consider as well Nelson's assumption that NAS are value enhancing. Bargains based on unanimous consent self-evidently make each party better off. Bargains achieving only supermajority consent may make unwilling participants worse off. Given Nelson's crucial assumption that the cost of obtaining unanimous consent is prohibitive, neighborhood privatization requires elimination of the need to obtain owner consent to changes in use. Prior to the establishment of the NA, a dissenter would be entitled to a court order prohibiting interference with his lawful use of his parcel. Afterwards, he would be entitled only to compensation for significant losses caused by the mandated restrictions.[31]

Nelson would permit NAS to change land uses or even to sell all of the neighborhood land for comprehensive redevelopment. In effect, the state would delegate to NAS its inherent right to "take" private property for public use (i.e., its "power of eminent domain").[32] Under the United States Constitution, the exercise of this power is conditioned upon the payment of "just compensation" (i.e., fair market value).[33] However, "just compensation" rarely is full compensation. Aspects of the property that are of personal value to the present owner are disregarded, including sentimental attachment, special suitability for particular needs, and avoidance of relocation costs.[34]

The NA might assert that the nonconsenting landowner would benefit from the increase in fair market value created by its ability to redevelop the neighborhood. But a high sales price is not necessarily adequate compensation to an owner who has a different subjective definition of value. "Cost is that which the decision-maker sacrifices or gives up when he selects one alternative rather than another. Cost consists therefore in his own evaluation of the enjoyment or utility that he anticipates having to forgo as a result of choice itself."[35]

This problem with aggregating individual utility functions is a serious obstacle to ascertaining the utility of a group or the welfare of society as a whole.[36] It has been my view that the systematic destruction of subjective value is an important reason why the Fifth Amendment conditions eminent domain on "public use" as well as on "just compensation."[37] The harm resulting from the Supreme Court's evisceration of the "public use" requirement likely would be greater were the proposal enacted.[38]

IV   The Lingering Threat of Excessive Regulation

The "privatization" of neighborhood land use controls does not ensure freedom from excessive regulation. Indeed, Nelson's proposals might result in new governmental intrusions and in NA regulations exceeding those that might result from consensual agreements.

"Neighborhoods" do not own property; individuals do, and they might or might not consider themselves "neighbors." Proposals for privatization would be made by groups of individual owners and the state would certify whether their proposed neighborhoods had the requisite geographical integrity to quality for NA status. It is unclear whether the neighborhood would have to be purely residential, or whether it could be mixed or heavily commercial. While some might associate neighborhood with social solidarity, others would be motivated by opportunism. Some groups will maneuver to include bordering nonconsenting parcels so long as the control group profits and the necessary supermajorities for ratification are not jeopardized. Potential "victims" might seek to form their own defensive NAs, or to align with other organizing groups. Dissatisfied landowners might mount secession movements. Ultimately the state must decide, which is a daunting prospect.[39]

Nelson crucially assumes that the transaction costs of establishing completely consensual NAs would be prohibitive. Yet contract might prove far more robust than he believes. The proposed extended period between the submission of the privatization application and the vote by owners, during which the state would supervise an elaborate information campaign, might with similar effort yield sufficient owners of contiguous land to agree to a viable redevelopment plan. They then could apply for a zoning change. Early candidates for such voluntary NAs would be small groups of adjoining owners with similar interests and large potential gains from NA status. Their success might encourage somewhat larger and more heterogeneous groups. Problems with holdouts might be averted through such devices as secret ballots that would reveal the lack of unanimity but not the identity of dissenters.

It is true that, in some cases, high transaction costs might present insuperable barriers to bargaining. This would preclude some land from being placed in an NA even where that status would add to its market value.[40] Even with respect to these parcels, however, it might be argued that sometimes "transaction costs" might better be considered as long-term investments in sound development. Just as opportunity costs are subjective, transaction costs are subjective, too.[41]

Were Nelsonian NAs established, their intensely local nature would make them prone toward excessive regulation and compliance monitoring. At the same time, their nonconsensual nature would tempt control group insiders to benefit themselves at the expense of their conscripted members. Even in suburban RCAs, complaints about extensive regulations on building appearance, landscaping, and personal activities are common. Yet the houses in recently constructed subdivisions are apt to be more homogeneous than those in long-established urban areas, and their owners are more apt to have similar tastes. Thus RCA officers might need to impose fewer regulations in order to maximize the property values and personal satisfaction of members.

NA officials, on the other hand, must deal with parcels and owners that vary more considerably, even within the same urban neighborhood. In the absence of a unanimity requirement, this problem might be exacerbated substantially. The owners of border parcels and other lands that might have been incorporated into the NA against their wishes would be particularly affected. They might be subjected to stringent requirements necessitating expensive structural changes and unwelcome aesthetic values.

Furthermore, Nelson's proposal might lead entrepreneurs to form NAs largely for the purpose of exacting wealth from unwilling members, an example of the process known as "rent seeking."[42] The proposal gives the impression that NA leadership would arise from neighborhood barbecues and bake sales. More realistically, groups of sophisticated owners or investors might conceptualize neighborhoods with commercial development potential, in which they have or could obtain control over key parcels. With no unified opposition, they could submit privatization proposals and heavily influence their consideration. Once they gain the approval of the requisite supermajorities of owners and market value, they could engage in self-dealing ranging from selling services to the association through affiliates to selling the neighborhood to affiliates. While Gordon Tullock explained that "there are only transitional gains to be made when the government establishes privileges for a group of people,"[43] those gains might be large indeed. As the experience of trying to deal with developers overreaching through several generations of condominium statutes informs us,[44] eliminating abuse is difficult.

Landowners who resist the formation of NAS might be termed "illogical holdouts," and those who resist stringent redevelopment regulations might be accused of "idiosyncratic behavior." However, an entirely different dynamic might be at work. Friedrich Hayek described experts' delusions that they could amass sufficient information to direct an economy or a sphere of life as the "fatal conceit."[45] Whether the experts are city planners motivated by communitarianism, or economists motivated by efficiency, they ignore the uncanny ability of the free market to produce order by organizing "chaotic" information into coherent patterns.[46] The imposition of their own values on nonconsenting owners short-circuits this spontaneous process and thus deprives planners of all stripes of the very information that they need to plan effectively.[47]

While nonconsensual NAS may impose excessive regulations on landowners, they do not necessarily alleviate governmental regulations and might actually increase them. Government cannot sell the police power and, were the Nelson proposal enacted, government still would regulate NAS.[48] Many attempts by NAS to maximize the value of their holdings will significantly affect adjoining areas. Plans to build stadiums, shopping malls, or office complexes might create regional infrastructure or environmental problems. Efforts at gentrification might raise welfare issues involving the poor. There is every reason to believe that local and state governments will intervene in such situations.

Finally, an RCA is accorded substantial autonomy largely because its members unanimously consent to the provisions in the association's original documents."[49] In an important decision upholding association rulemaking, the California Supreme Court recently noted that those who buy with knowledge of RCA powers "accept 'the risk that the power may be used in a way that benefits the commonality but harms the individual.'"[50] If their establishment is to require only supermajority consent, NAS should not expect the judicial deference accorded RCAS and predicated on unanimity.

Already RCAS are being subjected to the criticism that land use decisions affect the community too much for them to be left to contractual agreements.[51] Some critics would cut back their prerogatives on the grounds that membership is not truly "voluntary."[52] The introduction of nonconsensual NAS with powers to redevelop neighborhoods would lend strength to opponents of all market-based land use coordination mechanisms. This is one more reason why those who value the contractarian principles that sustain both economic freedom and individual responsibility should favor a clear demarcation between rules based on governmental regulation and those based upon contracts arrived at by unanimous consent.

The (Limited) Ability of Urban Neighbors to Contract for the Provision of Local Public Goods

ROBERT C. ELLICKSON

In his contribution to this volume, Robert H. Nelson makes two central normative arguments.[1] First, Nelson asserts that an association controlled by property owners tends to be more capable than a municipality at the task of governing land uses within a small neighborhood. This initial proposition is consistent with the libertarian spirit of many of the essays included here. Nelson's second contention, by contrast, is apt to raise the hackles of a staunch contractarian. He urges enactment of state legislation that would authorize a supermajority of property owners in a city subarea to coerce dissenters into forming a compulsory-membership association that would have significant powers over the affected territory.

I agree with both of Nelson's central arguments. Because municipal zoning gives rise to an excessive centralization of power in City Hall, the fostering of new forms of formal association among neighbors is a promising land use policy.[2] However, like both Nelson and George Liebmann, two pioneers in designing new micro-institutions for old neighborhoods,[3] I am convinced that landowners in a previously subdivided urban territory would have great difficulty negotiating a contract agreeable to all of them.[4] Because this volume is devoted to the potential of free contracting, in this essay I explain my willingness to entitle a supermajority to coerce a minority into joining the supermajority's venture. The essence of the argument is that a legal innovation that newly enables the many to structure a voluntary arrangement can advance the cause of freedom of contract—*broadly understood*—even though the many would gain at the expense of the few.

In another article I develop in more detail a concrete proposal for experimentation with entitling property owners to create mandatory-membership Block Improvement Districts (BLIDs).[5] The basic idea is to enable the retrofitting of the residential community association (RCA), an institution commonly found in new housing developments, to a previously subdivided block. The proposal would require passage of a state-enabling act governing the formation, structure, and powers of these institutions. Like one of Nelson's proposed neighborhood associations, a BLID's property owners would elect a board of directors, which would be empowered to levy assessments, finance public goods, and perhaps even waive city zoning restrictions. As demonstrated below, there are many precedents for entitling a supermajority to compel a minority to create a submunicipal institution. A notable recent example is the Business Improvement District (BID).[6] BIDs have succeeded in revitalizing many central business districts.[7] A Block Improvement District similarly might be able to rejuvenate an inner-city residential area, accomplishing results that landowners would not be able to achieve if each were entitled to veto a collective endeavor that most of them favored.

I   The Niche for Block-Level Institutions

BLOCK-LEVEL PUBLIC GOODS

Local public goods are services or physical improvements that enhance the appeal of a particular territory. Some local public goods, such as a mosquito abatement program, sewer system, or tourism office, can benefit an entire *metropolitan area*. Others, like a softball diamond or branch of a public library, benefit a *neighborhood*, that is, a submunicipal territory with a population typically in the range from two thousand to fifty thousand. This essay focuses, however, on the problem of providing public goods that primarily benefit a yet smaller territory, the *block*. In most contexts a block should be taken to denote a handful of face-blocks, that is, the lots that front on both sides of a common street (or streets) in a small, contiguous area.[8] In a residential neighborhood a block typically contains a resident population that numbers from a few dozen to a few hundred households.

The block is the optimal level for the provision of many public goods.[9] For example, the "broken windows" theory of crime developed by James Q. Wilson and George Kelling underscores the significance of highly localized collective action.[10] According to Wilson and Kelling, graffiti, litter, abandoned buildings, and other low-level disorders signal an absence of social control. If disorder persists, pedestrians become fearful and miscreants are tempted to misbehave. There is mounting evidence that city residents, including residents of low-income and minority neighborhoods, care greatly about the appearance and orderliness of their blocks.[11] Mayor Rudolph Giuliani's efforts to attack quality-of-life crimes in New York City are widely regarded as having contributed to the decline in felony rates.[12] Healthy daffodils in a sidewalk planter, it appears, may help deter armed robbery.

According to standard economic theory, market forces fail to provide an adequate supply of public goods. The basic problem is that either a provider of a public good cannot practicably exclude free riders from consuming its benefits, or it is good policy to provide the good to additional users at a price of zero because consumption of the good is nonrival. Restated in simpler terms, the supply of a public good generates positive externalities for which a provider either cannot or should not charge. If so, the provision of a public good somehow must be collectively financed, preferably by those who benefit from it. Because economic theory assumes that all actors are self-interested, the theory of public goods supposes that voluntary contributions to finance the provision of a public good tend to be inadequate because some beneficiaries are apt to succumb to the temptation to free-ride on the contributions of others. Thus a dose of coercion, namely mandatory taxes on beneficiaries, is said to be justified to overcome this free-riding dynamic.[13]

THE SUCCESS OF MANDATORY-MEMBERSHIP COMMUNITY ASSOCIATIONS IN NEW DEVELOPMENTS

Is there any evidence that block-level public goods are currently undersupplied in old neighborhoods? The strongest evidence is indirect. In a new residential development, where the transaction costs of creating a residential community association are lowest, a developer is highly likely to form one. This fact suggests (but hardly proves) that transaction-cost barriers alone are inhibiting the emergence of efficient micro-institutions in already subdivided territories.[14]

It is indisputable that RCAs have met with resounding market acceptance in new real estate developments.[15] The number of RCAs in the United States increased from fewer than 1,000 in 1960 to 150,000 in 1992. By 1992 some 32 million Americans were living within the jurisdiction of a residential community association.

Today a developer of a large subdivision routinely organizes an RCA before selling the first unit and publicizes the RCA during the marketing period. This business strategy would be sound only if most home buyers anticipated that the value of an RCA's services would exceed the costs of assessments and other burdens it would engender. The prevalence of RCAs in new developments demonstrates that most home buyers sense that these micro-institutions are effective providers of localized public goods. Because members rarely vote to terminate an RCA, their initial expectations apparently tend to be fulfilled. Indeed, residents of RCAs generally report a high level of satisfaction with the operation of their associations.[16]

The favorable track record of RCAs suggests not only the potential utility but also the optimal scale of a micro-institution retrofitted onto an already subdivided urban territory. The typical RCA includes from 40 to 160 dwelling units.[17] This implies that micro-territorial institutions are best scaled to the level of the block, not the neighborhood.[18]

THE INADEQUACIES OF CITIES AND SPONTANEOUS ORDER

Formal block-level organizations would have no useful role to play, of course, if other mechanisms could better provide localized public goods. This section briefly identifies the shortcomings of two other prime candidates: municipal governments and informal social arrangements. If either of these institutions were superior, landowners would see no need for a BLID in an old neighborhood or, for that matter, an RCA in a new one.

How a City Is Handicapped by Excessive Size. The primary function of a municipality is to provide public goods to its residents. An efficient city would provide a service as long as the marginal benefits of the service exceed the marginal costs of providing it. If cities in fact could achieve that level of competence, there would be little or no case for establishing institutions at the subcity level. It is hardly news, however, that many cities are inept. After a blizzard in 1996, for example, the District of Columbia was notoriously incapable of plowing the city's streets.[19]

Why might a city be less competent than a block-level institution? The basic reason is that increasing size weakens a constituent's incentives and ability to monitor the organization. A city therefore is more vulnerable to being captured by rent-seeking groups such as political machines, municipal unions, public-works lobbies, and downtown business interests. Members of these groups favor city policies that deliver largesse to them. To disguise this largesse from voters, these interest groups push for cumbersomely indirect systems for the delivery of favors. Vulnerability to rent-seeking thus leads to substantive city policies that are inherently wasteful.[20] In addition, state law and a city's charter may dictate complex procedures for such matters as public hiring, bidding for public contracts, and the sale of public assets, possibly for the purpose of reducing the city's vulnerability to capture by rent-seekers. While these procedural safeguards may stem corruption, they also make municipal bureaucracies relatively sluggish.

Small institutions can outperform larger ones for a number of reasons. First, micro-institutions seem to be optimally scaled for the efficient production of the most localized varieties of public goods.[21] RCAs in suburban developments commonly engage in refuse removal, landscaping of public spaces, management of recreation facilities such as swimming pools, and the administration of regulations such as architectural controls. Similarly, in an inner city, a BLID might maintain sidewalk planters and tot-lots, remove litter and abandoned vehicles, conduct block-watch programs, and provide other highly localized benefits.

Second, as just noted, because a small organization generally is easier to monitor than a large one, a block association is less vulnerable than a city to capture by an interest group. Who can doubt that a BLID in Washington, D.C., would have been more responsive than that city to demands for street plowing? Relatedly, because block-level organizations are relatively invulnerable to rent-seekers, they can be freed from most of the substantive and procedural shackles that state statutes and city charters place on cities. For example, a BLID could be exempt from civil service rules, public bidding requirements, and the Davis-Bacon Act regulations that require cities to pay the equivalent of union wages in certain contexts.

Third, a block-level institution is better able than a larger one to cater to micro-variations in individuals' tastes for public goods. For example, if artists were to concentrate their studios on a particular city block, their BLID could make unusually heavy expenditures on street sculptures. Indeed, the prospect of forming a Block Improvement District might encourage artists to cluster together in the first instance.[22]

Fourth and finally, block-level institutions are well scaled to strengthen members' involvements and skills in collective governance. The proceedings of a block organization provide members easy opportunities for engaging in meaningful debate, voting, office seeking, and other forms of community participation.[23] Candidates for office are few; there is little or no wait to speak at a meeting; participants are unlikely to be intimidated by the setting because the turf is familiar and most faces are known.[24] On many issues of block welfare, an ordinary owner or resident has little reason to be cowed by the views of experts. Many commentators seek to revitalize civic life in the United States.[25] They should welcome block organizations that might serve as incubators of local social capital.[26]

The Limited Effectiveness of Social Norms. If a city refused to provide block-level public goods, to what extent could block residents generate those goods informally through some mechanism of spontaneous order? Neighbors commonly do succeed in coordinating in the absence of a formal institution.[27] For example, informally enforced social norms may induce landowners to paint facades or trim shrubbery. An important variable in this context is the amount of social capital present on a block.[28] A person who knows his neighbors, for example, is more likely to maintain a property's appearance, refrain from littering, and provide what Jane Jacobs calls "eyes upon the street"—the informal vigilance that enhances pedestrians' sense of security.[29]

A high level of informal solidarity generally is easier to maintain in a small group than in a large one. Smallness enhances the quality of internal gossip and the frequency of chance encounters.[30] As a result, within a block's social circles, pressures to pull one's oar tend to be stronger than they are at the neighborhood—and certainly the city—level.[31] Homogeneity of membership also facilitates informal order because individuals who have thickly stranded relationships can more readily administer informal rewards and punishments on one another.[32]

Households in a closely knit town or urban enclave therefore might find a formal block association unnecessary. In those settings, land use coordination might be better achieved through social norms than through either city zoning or the regulations of a formal block-level institution such as a BLID. The pro-liferation of RCAs in the suburbs, however, suggests that that degree of close-knittedness is relatively rare. Informal social forces seem to succumb quickly to free-riding dynamics as the number (and heterogeneity) of a group's members rises. Spontaneous order is likely to be particularly ineffectual in old central-city neighborhoods with small lots and diverse populations. The presence of a more formal institution might help.

II Alternative Methods of Forming a Block-Level Organization

In a new neighborhood a developer can create a residential community associa-tion unilaterally by recording appropriate covenants prior to selling the first lot. In an already subdivided neighborhood, this low-transaction-cost option is no longer feasible. How might a block association be retrofitted onto an existing urban block?

VOLUNTARY ASSOCIATIONS OF NEIGHBORS

Following the traditions of civic participation that Tocqueville famously praised, Americans frequently establish voluntary neighborhood organizations to achieve common ends.[33] Compared to spontaneous order, a voluntary civic group offers the advantages of a formal structure—namely, legitimatized lead-ers, bureaucratic specialization, and explicit procedures for pooling resources and taking collective action. For example, voluntary civic associations fre-quently lobby city hall on local issues, such as a school closing or zoning amend-ment. While voluntary associations may be effective in these limited en-deavors,[34] their efforts to raise funds and mobilize volunteer labor inevitably are beset by free-riding. As a result, the resources of voluntary block associations tend to be puny compared to those of RCAs that have the power to levy manda-tory assessments.

A UNANIMOUSLY RATIFIED CONTRACT AMONG NEIGHBORS

In selected circumstances, property owners in a particular district may be able to contract unanimously for mechanisms to provide localized public goods. For example, the owners of several adjoining buildings may agree to apportion the costs of hiring a security firm. This method of coordination is especially appeal-ing to libertarian observers who are wary of authorizing supermajority coercion.

Nevertheless, as the number and heterogeneity of owners increases, the risk of free riders increasingly thwarts the possibility of universally endorsed con-tracts. It is plausible to suppose, for example, that the per-member net benefits produced by a block association increase slowly (at best) with the number of members, but that the per-member transaction costs of obtaining unanimous consent rise much more rapidly. If so, as the number of parties involved rises, the transactions costs of overcoming holdouts tends either to obviate the creation of an otherwise cost-justified block association, or to make the costs of its creation higher than they would be if an antiholdout mechanism were in place.

AUTHORIZING A SUPERMAJORITY OF PROPERTY OWNERS
TO CREATE A MANDATORY-MEMBERSHIP INSTITUTION

The Case for Coercion of Holdouts. The utilitarian case for authorizing super-majority coercion is straightforward. The success of RCAS suggests that the creation of a BLID or other mandatory-membership block association would lead to the provision of block-level public goods that are now undersupplied in old neighborhoods. These gains in coordination are the *allocative benefits* of creating of a BLID. Nelson, Liebmann, I, and others who regard the holdout dynamic as serious anticipate that these benefits would be significant in many settings. From these benefits a utilitarian would deduct the *transaction costs* of creating and running the BLID and the *coercion costs* (disutilities) that members of the minority would suffer as a result of being forced to join. To a utilitarian, the rules for creating a BLID should be designed to maximize expected net benefits, namely: (1) allocative benefits, less (2) the sum of transaction costs and coercion costs.[35] In a situation where formation of a BLID would be cost-justified overall, this calculus implies that coercion by a supermajority is justified as long as the transactions costs saved on account of the coercion exceed the coercion costs incurred.[36]

Many commentators reject utilitarianism on the ground that it accords insufficient respect to individuals who lose as a result of collective endeavor.[37] In response, I urge observers—especially libertarians—to make a sober assessment of the actual institutions that operate in urban areas. Cities and other governments are mandatory-membership institutions. These governments wield extensive coercive powers. Because these institutions have many constituents and are territorially large, an individual cannot readily use voice or exit to check their abuse of power. As a general matter, block-level associations promise to be more accountable than municipalities. The upshot is that libertarians should welcome mildly coercive micro-institutions whose advent promises to diminish the future role of more coercive cities.

Historical Precedents for Supermajority Coercion. Long before economists developed the theory of public goods, legislators intuitively recognized the problem of free-riding. Numerous statutes have authorized majorities to coerce would-be holdouts to join collective endeavors. Procedures for the incorporation of a new municipality, for example, never require all property owners (or residents) to agree to the creation of the new entity.[38] There also are many examples at the submunicipal level. For example, prior to the American Revolution colonial governments permitted landowners to conscript reluctant neighbors into participating in the draining of meadows and marshes.[39] Some states have enacted unitization statutes that authorize a supermajority of landowners to compel the minority to participate in joint exploitation of a common field of oil and gas.[40] As noted at the outset, beginning in the 1980s many states began authorizing landowners to petition to create a Business Improvement District (BID).[41] There also is some precedent for the compulsory unitization of residential neighborhoods in cities.[42] In the early twentieth century, before the Supreme Court had upheld the constitutionality of ordinary zoning, a few states authorized a majority of homeowners in a neighborhood to prohibit uses other than single-family housing, provided that the majority compensated the property owners damaged by the restrictions.[43] These precedents should hearten supporters of state experiments with BLIDs.

The Most Fertile Soil for Experimentation with Block Improvement Districts.
If authorized, on what sorts of blocks would BLIDs be most likely to sprout? The wide diversity of RCAs suggests that block-level institutions can thrive in a wide variety of settings. Studies have found that homeowners are far more likely than tenants to become block-level leaders, in part because their stakes are greater and time horizons longer.[44] Grassroots leaders also tend to have more wealth and years of education than their neighbors do.[45] This evidence suggests that the most promising soil for a BLID would be a gentrified (or gentrifying) block located in a city particularly inept at delivering cost-justified local public goods. Indeed, the possibility of later establishing a BLID might prompt a developer to assemble parcels on a block that was prime for gentrification. A BLID also promises to facilitate "incumbent upgrading"[46] on any relatively stable and homogeneous block, for example, one where working-class homeowners predominate.[47] It is far from certain, however, that a BLID would prove to be a useful institution on a declining block inhabited mostly by poor tenants of absentee landlords. Nevertheless, in these distressed environments the potential gains from institutional innovation might be particularly large.[48] If state enabling legislation authorizing BLIDs were to be adopted, a charitable foundation concerned with the problems of central cities would be wise to fund experiments in poor neighborhoods with diverse populations.

Conclusion

Many wealthy people in the United States live in a managed residential environment that largely insulates them from the poverty and disorder of the inner city. Robert Reich and other commentators have lamented this "secession of the successful" and worried about its effects on the nation's social fabric.[49] Some hyper-egalitarians have sought to reverse the trend by attacking the legality and legitimacy of the residential community association. This strategy is exactly backwards. The resounding success of RCAs in new housing developments indicates the merits of enabling the stakeholders of inner-city neighborhoods to mimic—at the block level—the micro-institutions commonly found in the suburbs.

My proposal for experiments with block improvement districts assumes that the benefits of these institutions are potentially large, and that the transaction costs of overcoming holdouts has prevented their emergence by voluntary contract. Both assumptions may prove to be false. Nevertheless, it is worth recalling that the passage of state enabling acts sparked the rapid proliferation of business improvement districts after 1990. That precedent demonstrates that freedom of contract and spontaneous order both have their limits.

IV Free Bargaining in Family Law

A Contract Theory of Marriage

ELIZABETH S. SCOTT AND ROBERT E. SCOTT

The evolution of marriage from a relationship based on status to one that is regulated by contractual norms achieved a milestone with the enactment of the Louisiana Covenant Marriage Act.[1] Under this statute, couples entering marriage can choose to have the relationship regulated under conventional no-fault divorce rules, or they can voluntarily undertake a greater marital commitment. For couples who select covenant marriage, either party can terminate the relationship on fault grounds, but unilateral termination of the marriage is available only after a substantial waiting period.

The Louisiana statute reflects a widespread dissatisfaction with the current social and legal landscape of marriage and divorce. Although Louisiana lawmakers have embraced a contractual solution to the problem of marital instability, many critics have identified the move from status to contract as the underlying source of the problems with modern no-fault divorce law. Communitarians see abolition of fault and the use of "market discourse" in conceptualizing marriage as destructive of the values of caring and commitment that contributed to the stability of traditional marriage.[2] Emblematic of the communitarian concerns is the model of marriage as contract, under which the state enforces the bargains of autonomous self-interested parties. These critics contend that such a limited conception of marriage leaves women vulnerable, harms the interests of children, and undermines social welfare. Their prescription is to resurrect notions of fault, create rules for marital termination that protect the interests of wives and children, and recover (insofar as possible) a world in which marriage is a privileged status, albeit without the patriarchal trappings.

Other critics, using law-and-economics methodology, are comfortable with the model of marriage as contract, but argue that no-fault divorce has transformed marriage into an "illusory contract," which provides no remedy for breach of the marriage vows.[3] From this perspective, the availability of unilateral no-fault divorce encourages opportunistic behavior by the husband, which destabilizes the relationship and threatens the marital investment of traditional wives. The predictable result is a reduced investment in the risky venture of marriage.[4] Thus both communitarian and law-and-economics critics argue that the no-fault regime has caused a decline in the importance of marriage and a loss of its valuable social functions.

In our view both of these critiques miss the mark. As Louisiana has recognized, the claim that a contract-based conception of marriage lacks norms of commitment is based on a misinterpretion of the nature of contractual relationships. The claim that, without fault, a marital contract is illusory is based on an underestimation of the multifaceted dynamics of relational contracting. Both of these concerns evaporate if contemporary marriage is analyzed as a long-term relational contract.[5] Like relational contracts in commercial contexts, a marital contract contemplates a long-term commitment to pursue shared goals, the fulfillment of which will enhance the joint welfare of the parties. There are various mechanisms for enforcing this commitment that do not require reintroducing notions of fault. As in other contexts, a complex network of social and relational norms will reinforce the parties' efforts to achieve their mutual goals.

But if marriage is to be understood as a relational contract, how is one to explain the peculiar patterns of legal enforcement and nonenforcement? Under the no-fault regime, the law declines to enforce the explicit promises of the marriage partners (the wedding vows); neither does it enforce promises about conduct during the marriage. On the other hand, when the relationship terminates, the law purports to enforce the implicit understandings of the couple regarding investment in the joint venture, understandings that often have never been expressly articulated.

Relational contract theory largely resolves this puzzle. The marriage vows express the couple's emotional commitment and use hortatory language to emphasize the seriousness of the undertaking. But emotional commitments are difficult to translate into quantifiable standards of performance, and assessing responsibility for breach is vexingly difficult. Thus the law relies on social and relational norms to promote cooperation and to enforce intramarital promises. Indeed, formal legal enforcement of all the terms of a "marital bargain" is inadvisable, because legal intervention risks undermining the parties' cooperative equilibrium, and ultimately subverting their efforts to sustain a lasting relationship. Legal enforcement is properly limited to policing massive defections from cooperative norms and to resolving economic and parental claims upon termination of the marriage (when the extralegal incentives to cooperate are greatly diminished). Law's domain is the area beyond the boundaries of social and relational norms. In that sphere, rights and obligations can be specified either by agreement or by a scheme of default rules that protects investment, reduces opportunism, and reinforces evolving patterns of cooperation.[6]

In many respects, the current legal regime conforms to the patterns of legal and extralegal enforcement that regulate relational contracts in other settings. Given the high rate of marital breakdowns, however, and the evidence that the interests of women and children are systematically discounted at divorce, the contemporary legal regime does not yet seem to have generated the optimal set of legal rules necessary to sustain a cooperative equilibrium.[7] The abolition of fault per se is not, however, a significant cause of these instabilities. Rather, the problem stems from two distinct sources that together reflect the incomplete evolution from status to contract. The first is the failure of contemporary legal rules governing divorce adequately to protect marital investment and to discourage opportunistic defection. The second is the failure to afford couples the opportunity to undertake a legally binding commitment to marriage.

A key source of the instability of contemporary marriages is the assumption embedded in the reform law that individual freedom is antithetical to commitment. A contractual framework, to the contrary, assumes explicitly that autonomous individuals frequently will pursue their own ends by voluntarily restricting their future freedom through enforceable legal commitments to others; indeed, it will often be impossible to pursue individual ends in any other way. A legal regime that constrains the freedom to commit actually limits individual freedom. Thus, properly conceived, a contractual lens challenges not only the excessive constraints on marital contracting found in traditional law, but also modern legal reforms that discourage precommitments to marital cooperation.

I Rethinking the Progression from Status to Contract

Under the trend that has been called the privatization of family law, marriage is a relationship the terms of which are largely determined by the parties themselves rather than by the state.[8] Carl Schneider sees the law's recent disinclination to dictate the terms of marriage and its termination as evidence of moral neutrality in family law.[9] Others emphasize the social trend toward gender equality as central to the legal developments.[10] In any event, the legal reforms are part of a broader trend in family law under which the family as an organic unit is less privileged than was once true and its members are increasingly treated as autonomous individuals. This progression is greeted by some observers with equanimity and by others with distress. While its extent may be debated, there is little controversy about the general direction of movement.

THE TREND TOWARD PRIVATE ORDERING

The trend from state control to private ordering within marriage is pervasive. There are few state-prescribed obligations associated with marriage, and fewer still that cannot be altered by the parties. The contractual paradigm is most evident in marital dissolution proceedings, specifically in the judicial response to the enforcement of separation and premarital agreements. Divorce courts have historically exercised far-reaching, paternalistic control over the termination of marriage. Couples generally were not free to agree to divorce, and their agreements about the terms of the dissolution were subject to judicial oversight. Today, the choice to end the marriage is a private one. While courts retain the authority in some states to reject the divorcing couple's agreement about property, spousal support, and (particularly) custody, judicial review is typically perfunctory and its scope has narrowed.[11] For example, under the Uniform Marriage and Divorce Act (the model for many state statutes), the parties' agreement is binding on the court, except for those provisions dealing with custody and child support.[12] Even as to custody arrangements, observers have argued, and most courts generally seem to agree, that parents are better able than courts to make these sorts of decisions.[13]

The abandonment of fault as a mandatory requirement for release from marital obligations is the hallmark of the law's retreat from regulating marriage. Today, all states permit spouses to divorce without proving fault and most allow either party to unilaterally terminate the relationship. In many states, fault is also excluded from consideration in the determination of alimony and property division.[14] Some states retain fault as an alternative grounds for divorce, but having fault as just one option in a no-fault regime dramatically reduces its significance.

The increasingly routine enforcement of premarital agreements is another clear representation of a changed attitude toward private ordering. Courts traditionally declined to enforce premarital agreements on the grounds that such arrangements encouraged parties to divorce. Today, the formerly hostile judicial response has been replaced by a presumption of enforceability. Twenty states have adopted a version of the Uniform Premarital Agreement Act, which directs the enforcement of premarital agreements (except for provisions affecting children) according to general contract principles.[15] The law regulating premarital contracting increasingly reflects a straightforward contractual perspective, one in which couples are encouraged to reach an ex ante agreement about the terms of their relationship and its dissolution.[16]

The contractual paradigm for marriage has been reinforced by its extension to long-term nonmarital intimate relationships. Since *Marvin v. Marvin*,[17] courts increasingly have been receptive to enforcing the agreements of cohabiting parties regarding division of assets and support upon termination of the relationship. This development signals an acceptance of the primacy of private choice in an area of social life once subject to strict regulation, and is a broad endorsement of the contractual ordering of intimate relationships. Judicial willingness to enforce cohabitation agreements signifies as well the law's neutrality toward the choice between marriage and nonmarital options.

Marriage as Contract and the Character of Marriage. The trend toward private ordering is much regretted by communitarian scholars and others who believe that the conception of marriage as contract distorts and undermines the meaning of this unique relationship. On this view, the vision of marriage as a cooperative, altruistic relationship characterized by long-term commitment has been replaced by a model of two self-interested persons (usually described as atomistic) entering into a limited agreement in which both are likely to behave opportunistically.[18] When such a marriage no longer serves the individual self-interest of either party, the relationship is discarded in favor of a more desirable alternative, at great cost to the discarded spouse and children. In contrast to the world in which marriage was a permanent and stable commitment, a contractual model is seen on this view as inviting the couple to "unite temporarily for their mutual convenience."[19]

The law's embrace of private ordering in marriage is part of a broader policy of maximizing the freedom of individuals to pursue personal ends in intimate relationships.[20] Those who dislike the underlying individualistic norm tend to view its various expressions in divorce law as all of a piece. Thus many communitarian critics see the trend toward private ordering as seamlessly linked with limited commitment motivated by selfish interest, with a unilateral right of termination, and with policies promoting a clean break without regret when marriage ends. These separate strands are conceptually linked, however, only in the unlikely event that the latter policies express (either implicitly or explicitly) the parties' ex ante understandings regarding the terms for dissolving the relationship.

The Role of Law (and Fault) Under a Contractual Regime. The law's ability to affect the marriage relationship is more limited under a contractual regime than under traditional law. The law's principal role in such a regime is to provide the background rules for enforcing marital contracts. It is often assumed that this requires formal passivity about the substance of the agreements that couples make. A further implication of taking private ordering seriously, on this view, is that the law becomes indifferent to choices about intimate arrangements and neutral as between cohabitation and marriage. The upshot is that a contractual model of marriage negates the ability of the state to promote marital stability, a key focus of traditional law.

Many critics target the abolition of fault grounds for divorce as exemplifying the deficiencies of the new legal regime. The criticism takes different forms. Communitarian scholars view fault grounds for divorce as expressing a societal consensus about the moral obligation of spouses to each other. A breach that constitutes a fault ground is a serious moral violation, causing injury to the innocent spouse and to society, and should be punished.[21] It follows that the abolition of fault is emblematic of a regrettably amoral stance toward marital obligation and an endorsement of party autonomy. The no-fault "reform" is thus seen as inextricably linked to the modern conception of marriage as contract. With the removal of fault, marriage is more like a commercial venture. The couple is free to set the terms that serve their interests and to terminate the relationship when it is no longer useful to them. Under the no-fault regime, the notion of condemning a moral wrong is as out of place as it would be in a commercial contract.

Law-and-economics critics also regret the removal of fault, but on contractual rather than moral grounds.[22] They treat the marriage vows as essential terms of the marital contract. A spouse who is guilty of a fault ground commits a breach of the marriage contract and should be liable for damages. The removal of fault grounds and the ability of spouses unilaterally to abandon the marriage under modern divorce law eliminates any remedy for breach and makes the contract illusory and unenforceable. In turn, the absence of an effective sanction for breach encourages opportunistic behavior. In such a regime, traditional wives, whose most valuable investment occurs in the early childbearing and rearing years, are vulnerable to strategic behavior by husbands whose investment tends to increase over time as earning power increases. Husbands are motivated to appropriate the benefits of their wives' prior investments and thereafter either leave the marriage or defect from the shared marital norms. For this reason, wives are deterred from undertaking optimal marriage-specific investments. These critics argue that, by resurrecting fault as a criterion for property settlement and support determinations, breach of the marriage vows could (and would) be compensable upon divorce. With the abolition of fault, the current scheme of legal regulation has contributed to the instability of marriage and undermined the welfare of wives and children.

Private Ordering and the Welfare of Women and Children. The view that women fare poorly under the modern regime extends beyond a critique of the abolition of fault grounds for divorce. Divorce has a destructive impact for women who undertake the traditional homemaker's role, regardless of which party bears the responsibility for ending the marriage. The wife's homemaking and child-rearing roles are a marriage-specific investment in that they are not readily transferable to the employment market if the marriage ends. The breadwinner husband, in contrast, develops his human capital in the workplace; thus divorce has little or no impact on his ability to earn income. Many critics have argued that the no-fault regime contributes to an expectation that marriage is a short-term commitment that each can set aside unilaterally. This expectation leaves women vulnerable to financial hardship when the relationship ends, a burden that is even greater if the wife has custody of the children of the marriage.[23] The costly impact of divorce on women and children is seen as inherent in the specialization of marital roles in a world in which marriage is unstable and exit is easy. This criticism is supported by empirical research which demonstrates that custodial mothers and children bear a disproportionate share of the financial burden of divorce.[24]

The conception of marriage as a means of self-realization under the no-fault regime also contributes to the problem for women. This conception supports the inclination to make a clean break and deemphasizes ongoing responsibility. Long-term alimony, grounded in a conception of marriage as a lifelong obligation, is thus very much the exception.[25] Until recently, enforcement of child support obligations has been sporadic, a reaction that has been linked to the emphasis on personal freedom.[26] Relational feminists, translating these concerns into more abstract terms, conclude that much of the problem derives from the primacy of individual autonomy, on which the legal model of marriage as contract is built. They argue instead for a legal regime shaped by relational (feminine) values of care, commitment, and responsibility.[27]

Feminists have also drawn on game theory to challenge the contractual paradigm, arguing that women are socially and biologically disabled in negotiating the marriage contract in ways that will systematically result in their getting a smaller share of the benefits of marriage. Amy Wax has argued that women's bargaining position is systematically disadvantaged because the value of women in the remarriage market declines relative to that of their husbands. This leads women to accept a smaller share of the marital surplus.[28] Beyond this, many feminists have argued that women are poorer negotiators than men because of a power imbalance deriving from women's historically subordinated status.[29] Thus a contractual model of marriage may systematically disfavor women because they are disabled from asserting their self-interest in pursuit of individual ends.

Critics argue that the trend toward private ordering threatens the welfare of children even beyond its financial impact on the family unit. The freedom of parents to quit the marriage can impose substantial costs on children, who are excluded from decisions to marry and divorce.[30] Moreover, in bargaining over divorce, parents are free to decide their children's future through negotiations in which custody and support are the currency of exchange. The withdrawal of the state from its historic role in setting the terms of marriage and supervising the decisions of parents for their children thus further harms the welfare of children.[31]

RETHINKING THE MEANING OF MARRIAGE AS CONTRACT

The conventional wisdom about how modern family law contributes to the instability of marriage and the decline in social welfare rests on fundamentally flawed assumptions. One assumption is that contractual obligations are inherently limited and inconsistent with deep commitment. Beyond this, some critics assume that individual freedom and binding commitment are irreconcilable, and that a legal regime that values autonomy must allow the freedom to renege on the marriage contract. Finally, the critics assume that the marital bargain can only be enforced (and the investment of homemakers and children protected) by reintroducing fault to provide a legal remedy for breach.

Communitarian critics associate contract with limited, narrowly self-interested arrangements in which each party negotiates for a short-term commitment that best serves her or his personal ends, one that can be readily set aside if breach is efficient. Contrasted with this model is the deep, lasting relationship that represents marriage at its best—a relationship which is characterized by an internalized sense of involvement and obligation that cannot easily be set aside. To these critics, the contractual model expresses a destructive vision of marriage, a vision that influences couples to think about their relationship in terms of self-interest, necessarily undermining the caring and commitment that are central to the value of marriage. It is not surprising that, from this perspective, the trends toward contractual ordering and toward maximizing individual freedom which characterize contemporary divorce law are merged together as contributing in an undifferentiated way to marital instability. Both elevate the value of autonomy and posit individuals making choices to further their personal ends.

This description caricatures the contractual model of marriage, in large part by misperceiving the core meaning of contract as commitment. To the extent that society has an interest in the stability of marriage, and individuals view lasting marriage as part of a life plan, contract can serve very well as a basis for an enduring, committed relationship. Only a modest assumption is required: that many individuals entering marriage are motivated to undertake a long-term commitment and wish to secure reciprocal commitments from their partners. Substantial empirical research supports this account of the intentions of many individuals entering marriage, and there is little support for the notion that prospective spouses view the undertaking as limited or short-term.[32] To be sure, the view that individual freedom is antithetical to commitment does find expression in the rules permitting unilateral termination of marriage. But this view is quite inconsistent with the premise of contract, which holds that individuals can often fulfill their purposes only by voluntarily undertaking legally enforceable commitments that limit their freedom in the future. Both parties to a contract believe that by binding themselves and thereby being able to rely on the commitment of the other, they are better able to achieve their goals than if they were to act without so restricting their freedom.

The premises of contract and the premises that underlie the current right of unilateral divorce rest upon very different conceptions of individual autonomy. To the extent that modern divorce law exalts unilateral termination and declines to enforce promises to stay married, it elevates the freedom to renege on a promise (what we might call "ex post autonomy"). But the freedom to renege necessarily forecloses the freedom to make binding commitments (what we might call "ex ante autonomy"). Since the freedom to commit includes the freedom to choose not to commit, ex ante autonomy is a more robust conception of personal freedom. This is illustrated by the rules governing the contracts of infants. Much like divorcing couples today, infants (who are seen as lacking moral imagination) are free to renege on their promises at any time, even after they have promised to perform and have enjoyed the fruits of the other's performance.[33] It is well understood that such a "freedom" is actually a limitation on the autonomy of minors, who are unable to make legally binding commitments and thus are disabled from securing the commitments of others. In short, the very essence of contract—the notion that the law will coercively enforce a promise that is voluntarily undertaken even after the promisor has come to regret the promise—is inconsistent with the freedom to renege.

Applying principles of contract theory to marriage produces a more optimistic picture of the capacity of private ordering to ameliorate the impact of divorce on homemaker wives and children. Using a hypothetical bargain heuristic to analyze the negotiations between homemaker and breadwinner spouses suggests that parties bargaining ex ante would devise terms to deal with role specialization and asymmetric investment. To the extent that the investments of wives are not protected under current rules regulating financial distribution on divorce, these rules depart from those that would be predicted by contract theory. Moreover, nothing in contract law or theory gives contracting parties the authority to devise terms that harm third parties, and thus contract law offers no support for marital provisions that harm children. Again, many of these harmful effects may be attributed to notions of ex post autonomy that are inconsistent with the norms of contract.

Law-and-economics critics of modern marriage law employ a contractual model and understand well that contract and commitment are quite compatible. But at least some of their critiques also rest on suspect assumptions. In this instance, a key assumption is that law is the sole (or at least the primary) mechanism for enforcing marital promises.[34] Much of the contractual analysis of marriage thus implicitly posits a contractual relationship in which the parties are presumed capable of allocating and assessing responsibility for failures to fulfill the terms of the marital agreement. In such a world, contract terms are clearly specified, legal enforcement is ubiquitous and straightforward, and expected performance is clear. Marriage does not fit this model well.

But many commercial contracts also do not easily fit the presuppositions of this classical contractual analysis. In relational contexts, where the future contingencies are complex and uncertain, the classical model of contract fails to capture the dynamic and interrelated functions of norms and legal rules, and of informal and formal methods of contract enforcement. Parties to such relational contracts are incapable of reducing important terms of the arrangement to well-defined obligations. Definitive, legally binding commitments may be impractical because the parties are unable to identify in advance uncertain future conditions and specify the complex adaptations required of each or because they are unable to verify violations of the contractual obligation to third parties. Relational contracts thus create unique, interdependent relationships in which unknown contingencies, the intricacy of the required responses, and the inability to verify nonperformance prevent the specification and enforcement of legal standards of performance.[35]

A typical response to this problem of complexity and uncertainty is to define the legal obligation in unusually general terms and to rely upon social and relational norms to specify and enforce most of the "terms" of the bargain. The contractual relationships of principals and agents, including the fiduciary obligation that attaches to corporate officers and trustees (and parents), and the relationships between parties to long-term commercial contracts are only a few examples of how legal and extralegal obligations are interwoven in relational contracts. Because the terms of these relationships are general and flexible, they require more creative enforcement mechanisms than do conventional contracts. We will argue that marriage fits *this* model of contract quite well, indeed.

Challenging the twin assumptions of short-term commitment and contingent contracting also leads to the conclusion that the role of fault in marriage law is misunderstood by both communitarian and law-and-economics critics. Contrary to the communitarian view, marriage vows of fidelity and loyalty are not rendered meaningless under a contract model. To the contrary, marital vows play an important role (albeit a more informal role than is understood by the law-and-economics analysts). The higher level of aspiration in terms of fidelity and commitment that each spouse assumes upon marriage substitutes for more commonly observed "terms" in commercial contracts. While these terms are enforced through social and relational norms and not by legal action, they remain key features of the network of behavioral controls that cement the marital relationship. In short, the elimination of fault under marriage law does not mean that marital bargains are unenforceable, nor would the reintroduction of fault grounds for divorce predictably lead to more stable and enduring marriages.

Characterizing marriage as a relational contract offers a promising perspective from which to understand and evaluate the contemporary trend toward private ordering. In many regards, as in the removal of fault, this framework provides an account of contemporary legal regulation of marriage and divorce which responds to critics' concerns. Modern no-fault divorce law may well promote a shallow commitment to marriage and impose disproportionate costs on women and children. But these deficits cannot be attributed in any significant measure to the law's contractual nature, unless shallow commitment and unprotected investment represent the ex ante choices of prospective spouses. Rather, as we have suggested, the deficiencies result largely from policies that are inconsistent with contractual commitment. In section II we turn to the question of precisely how a legal regime fully grounded in the principles of relational contract would function.

II A Relational Contract Model of Marriage

BASIC ASSUMPTIONS

Most people contemplating marriage do not bargain explicitly, or choose terms to govern the performance of their marital obligations, or consciously select among different enforcement options to ensure that each will behave in the future in ways that advance their shared goals. It is tempting to conclude, therefore, that the idea of a "marital bargain" is entirely hypothetical. But the fact that people seldom bargain explicitly over marriage is, in large part, a function of the relative harmony between their preferences and the societal norms and legal rules that form the common understandings about marital behavior and of the relative immaturity of tailor-made alternatives to the standard marital regime.[36] Parties will bargain for a tailor-made marital agreement only when their preferences diverge from the baseline of default rules and they are legally free to supplement or trump those rules with well-established alternatives.[37]

Thus the explanatory and prescriptive force of a contractual paradigm cannot be determined from observations of the behavior of couples contemplating marriage. An alternative approach is to undertake a mind experiment using the familiar heuristic of the hypothetical ex ante bargain. This analytic technique begins by assuming that the prospective marital partners are rational actors who seek to maximize their own individual well-being or satisfaction. The model does not imply completely selfish, atomistic actors. Each party can be motivated by altruism, love, and concern for the other. But there is a divergence to some extent between self-interest and collective interests. Under these conditions, we can then ask how two prototypical parties who possess these basic endowments might design legal rules to govern a marital relationship.[38]

Assume that two rational utility maximizers, Elizabeth and Robert, contemplate entering into a contract to secure the benefits that inhere in an intimate relationship. E and R face several discrete choices. They must first select between the option of formal marriage and the more informal contractual alternatives available in a cohabitation relationship. In making this choice, E and R are required to accept without modification the mandatory legal rules that define the legal categories of marriage and cohabitation. Beyond that, E and R are free to bargain over the "terms" of their marital contract. Both contemplate a relationship of extended duration, but they are also aware of the fact that both external circumstances and their own reactions to them will change over time. Thus their challenge is to design a contractual relationship that will be capable of adapting to future contingencies as well as accommodating to the endowments and preferences each brings to the bargain at the outset. In short, E and R wish to form a contract that will maximize the expected benefits from a successful relationship and minimize the expected risks of relational failure.[39]

Assume further that, if E and R choose the option of a formal marriage, they are required to supplement any state-imposed mandatory rules by bargaining in advance for any additional contract terms that they wish to govern their marital relationship. In undertaking this task, they have the option of selecting any set of terms (including sanctions for breach) that would be enforceable in a simple contract between two informed and competent parties. Assume that both bring to the bargain a fully internalized sense of the set of societal norms that are attached to marriage and the marital relationship. Assume finally that they are equally informed about the consequences of any strategies for adjusting the relationship over time or any patterns of cooperation (or noncooperation) that might evolve from repeated interactions within the relationship. Under these assumptions, we ask: *if* E and R choose to marry, what marital bargain might they negotiate?

WHY MARRY?

Parties such as E and R decide to form intimate relationships in which they share emotional, intellectual, and economic assets because they believe that this relationship will produce "value" greater than the sum of their individual investments. By exchanging contractual commitments, the parties can enhance both the quantity and the quality of this relational value or surplus. This value is not cost-free, however. The more formal the contractual commitment, the more difficulty the parties will experience in exiting from their relationship should the relational surplus fall below either party's "go-it-alone" alternatives. Thus E and R confront initially the foundational choice between marriage and nonmarital alternatives.

The Goals and Expectations for Marriage. In contemporary society, couples can live together in intimate relationships without social sanction. Cohabitation relationships are undertaken and discarded with far less cost than marriage, and each cohabiting partner retains a greater measure of personal freedom.[40] At first glance, it would seem that most of the functions and purposes of marriage could be achieved through an informal cohabitation relationship. No formal status or commitment is needed for a relationship that includes the production and rearing of children, sexual intimacy, mutual companionship, the sharing of assets and income, and the provision of care and support (both emotional and financial) in times of need. Despite the fact that all of these benefits can be obtained in an informal union, however, the evidence is clear that most people believe that their goals can be more fully realized through marriage. Indeed, for most people, an enduring and successful marriage is an integral part of a life plan.[41] Why do people conclude that they can better realize their personal ends through marriage than through a more informal cohabitation relationship?

People marry because they expect to benefit from undertaking a greater commitment than is possible through other, informal options.[42] The essence of this commitment is constraint. To be sure, many friendships and cohabitation relationships involve a sense of commitment. Marriage, however, adds an overlay of legal and social sanctions that further restrict the freedom to renege and thus enhance the potency of each partner's commitment.

To a large extent, therefore, what distinguishes marriage from informal unions is what distinguishes contracts from informal cooperation in other settings. Both parties believe that, by formally restricting their own freedom and by being able to rely on a reciprocal commitment from the other, they will be able to achieve their goals better than if both were able at less cost to renege on the commitment—as would be true in a cohabitation relationship. Parties such as E and R derive two primary benefits from this constraint: (1) the ability through precommitment (or self command) to pursue long-term rather than short-term goals; and (2) the ability to secure a reciprocal commitment from the other party.

These constraints on the parties' freedom work together to promote their mutual goals for a lasting relationship. The precommitment function of marriage is a self-generating constraint. Each spouse will benefit because her or his own behavior will be constrained. Marriage promises to discourage the individual from acting in ways that reflect transitory preferences that are inconsistent with the long-term goal of a lasting relationship.[43] A further benefit of marriage to each spouse is that the other is bound. A part of the anticipated advantage of marriage over an informal relationship is that each spouse can more confidently rely on the other's commitment, and have greater assurance that her or his own investment in the relationship will not be lost because the other spouse defects. This assurance has substantial value. A relationship that serves the many functions of marriage requires significant investments on the part of each spouse. Each party's willingness to make that investment understandably depends on trust that the partner generally can be relied upon to fulfill her or his end of the bargain. That trust is facilitated and reinforced by the mutual commitment of marriage.

A cohabitation relationship, in contrast, is understood to be a more limited undertaking.[44] Each party, knowing that the other is free to terminate unilaterally, has a choice of either risking the loss of a substantial investment or investing more modestly to protect against future disappointment. Not surprisingly, many parties conclude that the goal of a long-term, mutually reinforcing intimate relationship can best be achieved by elevating the level of mutual commitment through marriage.

The relative strength of any commitment derives from its enforceability. As we explore in detail below, the potency of the marital commitment is a product of three distinct sources: social expectations about marriage embodied in widely shared societal norms that are enforced through social sanctions; relationship-specific expectations derived from patterns of cooperation that generate self-enforcing "relational norms"; and, should the relationship break down, legal expectations that are enforceable by state-sanctioned coercion. Each of these forces function interactively. Together, these extralegal and legal mechanisms underwrite the marital commitment to a greater extent than analogous but weaker constraints that enforce commitment in cohabitation relationships.[45] Thus, in general, couples such as E and R will enter marriage with a greater commitment to the relationship than do those who choose cohabitation. They then have available an array of mechanisms that more effectively constrain their actions and thus reinforce their commitment.

The Mandatory Terms of the Marital Contract. E and R face some key trade-offs in choosing marriage over nonmarital alternatives. The need to preserve the integrity of this foundational choice provides the justification for the mandatory rules that limit the choices of parties who might wish to select the marriage option. Often lost in the autonomy norms that undergird the law of contract is the fact that contract routinely embraces arguments for limiting itself.[46] These arguments are of three general types. One class focuses on defects in the bargaining process. Preserving the key elements of a free, informed, and rational choice requires rules that prohibit contractual enforcement where individual promises were the product of duress or unconscionable information deficits or where the parties lacked the capacity and judgment to evaluate the risks being exchanged. A second class of mandatory rules focuses more directly on the bad outcomes of certain bargains. Some bargains—such as contracts of enslavement—are faulty regardless of whether the bargaining process was rational. These first two classes of arguments for mandatory rules explain the relatively uncontroversial rules of marriage law that police the capacity of the parties who undertake marital commitments; grant relief from duress, undue influence, fraud, and unconscionable marital bargains; and limit the terms, including the methods of enforcement, that parties can select.[47] A much more significant issue, however, is whether parties who marry should be limited in their freedom to choose whether to divorce (or not to divorce). This issue can only be understood in terms of a third class of arguments for mandatory rules, one that rests on an independent state interest in preserving the signaling function of contractual obligation. Rules as seemingly diverse as the Statute of Frauds and the doctrine of consideration can be understood as enabling parties to select among clearly identifiable contractual forms that carry prescribed consequences.[48] This signaling function implies that the legal system should maintain a meaningful categorical distinction between the options of marriage and nonmarital cohabitation.

Mandatory rules governing binding commitments not to divorce. Assume that E and R declare their intent voluntarily to enter into a binding commitment to make legally enforceable the marriage vow "till death do us part." Two separate contract-based arguments might be invoked to support a prohibition against enforcement of such a promise never to divorce. The first is grounded in the paternalist claim that the parties are not competent to make rational decisions in the premarital setting, or that even thoughtful decisions may turn out to be mistaken.[49] If the process of marital decision making is peculiarly susceptible to systemic errors of judgment, then the bargaining process can no longer be trusted to generate socially desirable results. Consider, for example, the now-familiar anchoring phenomenon which suggests that the way choices are framed affects individuals' assessments of the gains and losses of exercising any particular option. Prospective marital partners may suffer from such a cognitive bias if the benefits of the marriage commitment are anchored to the prospect of a long and happy life together and not to the prospect of discord and strife—a prospect that may seem remote when the bargain is struck.[50]

The biasing effects of framing are, by themselves, a slim reed on which to hang prohibitions on inflexible commitment terms. The existence and effects of cognitive biases continue to be the subject of serious dispute among psychologists.[51] Moreover, there are means of correcting for the biasing effects of framing that do not involve prohibition. Enhanced disclosure and cooling-off periods are the obvious (and familiar) examples from the law of consumer transactions. A prohibition of "no divorce" contracts finds additional support, however, in the long-standing rules against contracts of enslavement. To the extent that contracts of enslavement are grounded in the idea that people should not be permitted to bargain away too much of their liberty, then lifetime marital commitments are similarly suspect. The argument cannot be used, however, to condemn all efforts to undertake a meaningful and binding marital commitment. It is important to remember that the commitment here is not to live together in disharmony and strife, but rather to forgo the right to divorce and to marry again. While the law may well forbid agreements never to divorce, such a prohibition does not condemn enforcing voluntary commitments not to divorce within a clearly prescribed (and limited) period of time. After all, appropriately limited, but temporally binding, commitments are the essence of contractual constraint in other settings.

The signaling justification for a mandatory commitment period. The question remains, however, whether such limited commitments should be prescribed by the state or open to individual choice by the contracting parties, perhaps with the specification of a state-supplied default rule. The justification for a mandatory rule that fixes the extent and nature of marital commitments ultimately must be grounded in the signaling argument. As Lon Fuller observed in a classic article on the law of consideration, mandatory rules that prescribe both the form and the essential character of obligation serve to increase deliberation (and thus enhance bargaining process values), enhance the verifiability of commitments, and, most importantly, facilitate the matching of parties who share similar preferences for commitment.[52] Thus contracting parties remain disabled from transforming certain oral agreements into enforceable contracts or from making gratuitous, nonreciprocal promises legally enforceable. Only the state can solve the collective action problem that would otherwise lead individual bargainers to dilute the potency of the signal "contract" by opting out of these "categorical" rules.

The signaling function of marriage (as distinct from a cohabitation agreement) serves to reveal a person's preferences toward sexual and social relationships in which he or she may wish to become involved.[53] Preferences about long-term relationships are likely to vary widely. Parties can be expected to differ on the desired length of the term of the relationship, the degree of sexual loyalty expected from their principal partner, and generally on the expected level of commitment to the relationship. Given this diversity of preference, the legal category of marriage conveys a signal to prospective partners of the signalers' preferences as to the nature of the relationship. Permitting individual parties the freedom of choosing many varied forms of commitment will inevitably dilute the informational value of the signal.

On the other hand, if the choices are too few in number, the result may be an inefficient pooling equilibrium—one where partners choose (or do not choose) marriage as the best available choice even though they would prefer a different relationship. The efficient number of commitment choices needed to create an efficient separating equilibrium cannot be specified a priori. But it seems clear that, at a minimum, there needs to be a meaningful choice between a relationship without effective binding commitments (cohabitation) and a relationship with a minimum commitment (marriage). Just as gratuitous promises without consideration are unenforceable regardless of the desires of the promisor, a cohabitation agreement permits termination at any time regardless of the desires of the parties. Similarly, an exchange of promises binds each party to a contractual obligation regardless of subsequent regret. So too, an option to marry would ideally result in a minimum commitment that would permit termination only following an appropriately defined period. In sum, preserving the signal of the core category of marriage calls for a minimum commitment period (say, for example, two or three years) prior to divorce and remarriage.

The signaling function of marriage argues not only for a categorical minimum, but for a categorical maximum as well. If marriage is to be a clear signal that promotes better choices among options and thus better matches, then parties should be similarly precluded from opting for fixed period commitments longer than any state-imposed maximum. Unlimited freedom to create customized fixed period commitments will dilute the quality of the signal established by the mandatory minimum period. (It is an independent question whether the state should create a limited menu of options within the marriage category, say, for example, a category-one marriage with a five-year commitment and a category-two marriage with a two-year commitment, etc.) A ban on opting into more extended commitments beyond a designated maximum is supported by the expected costs of designing alternatives to the state-created choices. Experience teaches us, in any case, that unlike the parties to many commercial contracts, E and R lack the ability to predict the optimal duration of a relationship that depends upon extended investments and emotional maturation. Whether and when the parties have children, the value of the emotional bonds that are generated by the marriage and the value of alternative relationships are only a few of the numerous factors that will affect the durability of the relationship. Under these circumstances, although E and R may aspire to a lifelong relationship, they are properly precluded from making a lifetime contract (or any other "excessive" commitment term) that does not preserve the possibility of escaping the commitment in the future should the returns from the relationship fall below the nonmarital alternatives.

The problem E and R face is one shared by all potential marital partners: each wishes the benefits of a long-term commitment, but each is unwilling to obtain those benefits at the risk of a lifetime trapped in a relationship that is suboptimal. Under these conditions, no single commitment term is likely to satisfy the preferences of a broadly representative group of bargainers. It is possible to imagine an infinite array of marriage commitments, each ideal for any particular set of marital partners. Thus the choices for policy makers in fixing the prescribed minimum (and maximum) are clear: Any reduction in the minimum commitment period requires parties to trade off some of the upside returns from long-term commitment so as to minimize the risk of regret. An increase in the minimum period has the opposite effect. On a different dimension, an increase in the number of options dilutes the signaling effects of marriage but increases the prospects of efficient separation of preferences. Quite obviously, these choices turn on a number of complex variables, including the diversity of preferences and the calculation of ex ante probabilities of success and failure in marriage.

NEGOTIATING THE DEFAULT TERMS OF THE MARITAL CONTRACT

Specifying the Objective: A Long-Term Relationship of Indefinite Duration. By electing marriage over the alternative of nonmarital cohabitation, E and R have chosen to negotiate the terms of their relationship within the parameters of the legal category of marriage. The choice of marriage also signals their shared belief that, through mutual investments, their relationship can produce an expected "value" greater than the sum of their individual investments. Thus we might expect the parties to assign each other specific and precise responsibilities according to relative advantages and preferences in order to maximize the expected relational value. But how can E and R agree to undertake these optimal investments in a world of uncertainty where future circumstances and their relative capacities to adapt to them are known only probabilistically?

When the future contingencies cannot be calculated in advance, E and R cannot reduce their obligations to precise statements. In these circumstances, they are motivated to consider alternative means to achieve their goals. One option that they have discarded by choosing marriage over cohabitation is to undertake a commitment that is terminable at will or otherwise explicitly limited. A short-term commitment has a number of disadvantages, but such an arrangement would permit E and R more readily to reach agreement on specific marital obligations. But even without a mandatory commitment period, most parties choosing marriage would still not prefer a commitment that is terminable at will. Under a regime of unilateral termination at will, both parties will be reluctant to invest in the relationship to any level beyond that which they can recoup within its expected duration. Intimate personal relationships, even more than commercial relationships, require long-term, relation-specific investments if the full value from the combined efforts of the couple is to be realized. Moreover, marital investments are often asymmetric. Thus, for example, R may elect to stay in a career-limiting job in order to finance E's law school education, on the expectation of sharing in the financial and emotional rewards of her professional career. If the commitment is subject to continual renegotiation, E might thereafter be tempted to seek a larger share of the relational surplus as a condition for remaining in the relationship.

Whether such a temptation would ever be acted upon is less important than the fact that the risk of such vulnerability will cause R to reduce his investment in the relationship, thus reducing the value of the joint benefits to the parties. Quite obviously, the roles can be reversed several years later when E decides to take a few years off from her job as an attorney to stay home with their children. Thus specialization makes each party more vulnerable to strategic demands by the other. This problem is only exacerbated when specialized investments yield deferred returns, because this creates asymmetrical vulnerability for one partner or the other to the threats of dissolution or other strategic behavior at different times during the life of the relationship.[54]

There are, of course, specific contractual mechanisms that E and R might devise to help cope with problems of asymmetric investment and opportunism. Their choices are constrained, of course, by any state-prescribed mandatory rule that limits agreements not to divorce. A viable option is a commitment to an exclusive relationship for an extended but indefinite duration. This choice is framed by any state-prescribed restrictions on divorce, but permits termination thereafter under specified conditions. Subject to termination, the relationship would continue potentially for a lifetime. Such indefinite duration contracts, even those lasting potentially "until death do us part," do increase the risk of strategic threats of termination, with which the parties must cope in other ways.

The Mutual Obligation of Best Efforts. A long-term commitment, even one that might be terminable after a prescribed period, introduces the relational dilemmas caused by uncertainty and complexity.[55] E and R, by agreeing to a relationship of mutual dependence and vulnerability, will seek assurances from the other that the expected level of investment will be made. But since the relationship has an extended horizon, the parties cannot specify those investments in terms of fixed and determinate obligations. In such a setting, each party is motivated to promise the other to use his or her "best efforts" to invest optimally in the relationship. A mutual exchange of best efforts will ensure that the goal of full development of the potential relationship can be achieved. Each would agree to reciprocate in return for the other's promise of best efforts, and thus each "compensates" the other for undertaking the optimal level of the respective activity.

Notwithstanding the frequency with which best-efforts terms are used in commercial contracts, the precise legal meaning of a best-efforts requirement is not completely clear. Nevertheless, there is a relatively straightforward definition that emerges from the problem faced by parties who are attempting to set a contractual output in which they have joint interests. As one of us has argued elsewhere, the best-efforts obligation is most sensibly understood as the duty of each party to invest sufficiently to produce the maximum joint value from the relationship. This interpretation directs the result that best reflects the ideal collective outcome that E and R could hope to achieve from their relationship. In addition, the optimal relationship definition of best efforts is consistent with fairness principles. Each party is required to treat the marital partner "fairly," giving the other's interests equal weight with his or her own when investment decisions are made. Such special consideration during the relationship presumably has been "paid for" at the time of contracting through the reciprocal undertaking of the other party or through some other compensatory concession.[56]

A best-efforts obligation provides the framework for assigning individual responsibilities to provide the emotional, intellectual, and economic inputs necessary for the relationship to develop optimally. The flexibility and generality of the best-efforts obligation makes it an attractive option for achieving the parties' purposes but also substantially complicates the problem of assigning individual responsibility for the inevitable failures to perform as promised. By choosing a long-term relationship in which they do the best they can to maximize the joint returns, E and R are trading off their ability to make clear and verifiable assignments of individual responsibility. It is tempting to suggest, therefore, that the high cost of monitoring individual efforts might override the theoretical attractiveness of the best-efforts option. The wisdom of the best-efforts standard of performance is confirmed, however, once E and R consider the associated problem of assigning the risks of regret.

Distributing the Risks of Regret. Contracts exist to ensure performance (or its equivalent value) in circumstances where one party or the other experiences some regret owing to an intervening contingency. Thus parties entering marriage contracts will also agree to distribute the risks of uncertain future events in some fashion. E and R will anticipate and plan for the possibility that future contingencies may arise—e.g., financial reversals, poor health, a reduction in the emotional returns from the relationship—that either reduce the benefits from the marriage or make performance of the marital bargain more costly. This element of risk allocation is powerfully expressed in the traditional exchange of marriage vows: "for richer or poorer, in sickness and in health."

In general, E and R will be motivated to allocate risks in ways that reduce the anticipated burden of the risk, either by reducing its incidence or its impact. In broad terms, E and R face a choice between two alternative risk-bearing strategies. A strategy of *risk control* assigns the entire risk to the party who can exercise some control over the incidence of the risk or the impact of the risk or both. Under a *risk sharing* arrangement, by contrast, each party accepts responsibility for a portion of a set of risks that are unchanged by their individual actions. Unlike risk control, this strategy does not look to reducing risk per se but rather seeks to reduce the burdens of risk bearing. If the contingencies are uncertain and both parties are risk averse, a risk-sharing scheme reduces the amount of uncertainty and thereby the cost of the risk for each party. Thus parties benefit from a risk-sharing arrangement because it reduces the variance in risk; each has a *higher* probability of incurring a *smaller* future loss.[57]

In many contractual settings, a risk-control strategy—one that allocates entire risks to one party or the other—will be preferable to a risk-sharing arrangement. This is because the costs of subsequently monitoring and enforcing the agreement as conditions change and contingencies materialize tend to be lower under risk control. It is much easier, for example, to identify and to sanction a failure to perform when one party is entirely responsible for the performance in question. The task of assigning individual responsibility for nonperformance is complicated when parties share obligations and adjust their respective efforts over time.

The benefits of a risk-control strategy decline sharply, however, in contexts such as a marital relationship where key risks depend on interactive or interdependent contingencies. The core of the marital relationship is an emotional commitment that manifests itself in bonds of intimacy, love, nurturing, and sharing that require reciprocal efforts to stimulate and sustain. Both the inputs and the outputs of this emotional core of the relationship are uniquely incapable of being separated. Consider, for example, the risk that E may no longer find in R the companionship, support, and intimacy that make the relationship more valuable than her "go it alone" alternative. This risk is a function of E's efforts and R's efforts as well as a function of the value that E places on the outputs from the relationship. E may have a superior ability to bear the risk of the contingency that her "later self"[58] might not gain the same returns from the relationship as well as the risk that her own efforts may be inadequate, but R is better able to guard against the inadequacy of his own efforts that may have contributed to the changes in E's emotional response. In these circumstances, a risk-control strategy simply will not work because E and R are unable effectively to separate the contingencies, and thus neither can take cost-effective precautions independently.

Some of the contingencies that influence the relationship will not have these interdependencies. Thus, for example, E and R might be able to separate the risks of the income-producing efforts that provide the material support for the relationship. But any attempt to separate these responsibilities in order to encourage optimal precautions necessarily undermines the shared emotional value that is a central motivation for entering into the marriage agreement. It is implausible, for example, that the parties would require R to borrow to fulfill his obligation to provide economic support should his income decline. In addition to interdependence, other forces propel the parties toward a risk-sharing contract. A strong social norm of sharing ("for better or worse") governs the relationship and contributes to the production of a relational surplus that is largely indivisible. Moreover, the dynamics of a long-term relationship will argue for continuous adjustment in the parties' efforts. Inevitably, some contingencies become more (or less) probable, while others that were beyond calculation materialize. Both parties stand to gain, therefore, if they agree in advance to adjust efforts in response to changed conditions so as enhance relational benefits and reduce anticipated future costs.

In sum, the interactive and ever changing character of the contingencies that affect the emotional "value" of the marital relationship, and the common ownership of the relational surplus, will lead E and R to adopt a broad strategy of shared responsibility and cooperative adjustment. The resulting risk-sharing agreement will require each spouse to adjust their individual efforts in the future in order to minimize the *joint* costs of maintaining the relationship.

Profound implications follow from the decision to share risks as well as to pool efforts. Most fundamentally, the parties are selecting a peculiarly interactive and interconnected form of obligation that they must police themselves during the life of the marriage. While the parties can expect over time to develop finely tuned norms to monitor individual behaviors, they recognize that responsibility for individual failures to perform as promised often cannot be established with sufficient clarity to permit a sanction to be imposed by a court or other third-party decision maker. Thus they must accept the fact that they are uniquely dependent on each other to monitor and enforce the terms of the contract, and that third-party enforcement will be problematic so long as the relationship continues.

Distribution of the Marital Surplus. One particularly vexing issue facing E and R in their negotiations concerns the appropriate baseline rules for dividing the anticipated surplus from the marital bargain. While the specific distribution of relational assets will vary in any particular case, the shape of the agreement the parties have negotiated does suggest some broad distributional principles that would command widespread support.

The concurrent ownership principle. E and R confront two separate distributional challenges. First, they must agree upon a principle for sharing the marital surplus during the marriage. Here the nature of their relationship and the absence of a pricing mechanism argue strongly for a concurrent ownership rule. Under such a rule, E and R would each have an equal right to an undivided interest in the entire surplus generated during the marriage. Much as husband and wife own real property as tenants by the entirety, E and R would own the surplus "by the whole and not by the part."[59] Moreover, since neither would own an individual interest in the surplus, neither would be able unilaterally to transfer rights in the surplus to a third party or to compel a partition of the assets during the life of the relationship.

A concurrent ownership rule is the only practical method by which E and R can distribute the intangible and emotional products of the marriage. Love, friendship, intimacy, mutual support, and the fulfillment of raising children are indivisible and incommensurable assets. They are "owned" together or not at all. The rule may seem more problematic, however, in the case of tangible economic assets, particularly where those assets are generated by only one spouse in a relationship with role specialization. However, a concurrent ownership rule has the merit of saliency and coherence with the distribution of other assets in the relationship. It is also consistent with the norms of marriage and offers the parties the alternative to a cohabitation agreement where the default rule of no-sharing of economic assets is available. Starting with a presumption of common ownership is thus a simple and obvious coordination solution even for parties who wish to bargain out of the standard defaults.

Property distribution and alimony upon divorce. The distribution agreement becomes more complicated when E and R contemplate the possible termination of the marriage. Upon termination, much of the relational surplus evaporates. The net benefits gained from intimacy, love, and other shared emotional experiences are relation-specific and, in general, will not survive the dissolution of the relationship. Typically, therefore, the assets remaining to be divided upon termination are rights in the economic assets and in the children produced by the marriage. In the case of tangible marital property, the predivorce sharing principle leads as well to a presumption of equal distribution of marital property rights upon divorce (including, for example, the value of business interests and of the good will of a professional practice). Equal sharing of any tangible property upon divorce is the only principle that will not distort the parties' incentives in choosing between remaining in the marriage or deciding to quit.

To be sure, equal division of existing assets does not address the most difficult issue of all: how do the parties distribute ownership rights in future assets that are produced by individual human capital where that capital was developed through joint efforts? Here the parties are again motivated by the underlying objective of promoting best-efforts investment of both spouses. They recognize that a key to realizing their goal will be to provide security to protect individual human capital investments during the marriage. A failure to do so could lead to underinvestment and opportunistic defection. This principle can be used to derive relatively clear rules governing alimony, spousal support, and compensation for financial or other investments by one spouse in the education or other human capital of the other. The challenge is to motivate investments by one spouse that may not have economic equivalents outside the marriage or for which the "compensation" is deferred. In such instances, the different character of each party's investments precludes an equal-sharing/equal-division solution, one in which each party walks away from the marriage with his or her individual human capital intact.

Assume, for example, that E's optimal investment is as a homemaker, a capital asset that is marriage-specific and has little independent economic value. In this case, she cannot realize significant benefits from her investment once the relationship dissolves, and would not agree ex ante to an equal-sharing/equal-distribution rule. In order to induce E to invest optimally, the parties must provide her upon divorce with a predetermined economic equivalent for her efforts within the home. E will require insurance against the risk of divorce in order to protect her investment in assets that will have little economic value outside the marriage. E and R can solve the problem by agreeing upon an appropriate method of self-insurance. For example, R can promise to provide E alimony upon divorce to be paid from R's future earnings. An optimal amount of insurance would require alimony payments in an amount equal to the opportunity cost of her decision to forgo developing independent skills that have economic value outside the marriage.[60] Under this contract term, E will know that if the marriage succeeds she will share fully in the expected surplus. If the marriage is terminated, she will be at least as well off as she would have been had she elected not to pursue the homemaker's role.

A related problem arises if the specialized investments of the parties are asymmetric. It is commonly assumed, for example, that the homemaker's investments are disproportionally greater early in the marriage when children are raised, the family unit is established, and the breadwinner's career is launched. On the other hand, the breadwinner's income is a function of seniority and experience and will generally increase over time. Thus, during the early years of the marriage, the breadwinner will be "borrowing" against his future earning capacity in order to reap the benefits of the homemaker's investment in the family unit. The homemaker, in turn, will have made marriage-specific investments that yield deferred returns over a lifetime. If these assumptions hold for E and R, a decision to pursue specialized roles means that E will be vulnerable to a strategic termination unless the parties agree that she is entitled to a payment upon divorce that reflects the present value of her proportionately greater investment in the relationship. Any lesser payment would give R a perverse incentive to walk away from the marriage after E has produced children and sacrificed her youth and alternative prospects to invest in the marriage. The requirement that the parties' reciprocal investments in the marriage "net out" upon divorce assures the parties that any decision by R to terminate the marriage would be based on a nonstrategic assessment that the nonmarital alternative had more value than the fully paid for returns from the marriage.

Child custody. The parties face a different set of issues when they bargain over the rights to custody of children of the marriage. During marriage, there is a presumption of equal sharing of undivided rights and responsibilities, and both parents would have an equal right to share custody and to make parental decisions together. This presumption has salience because of the equal sharing norms that ground the relationship while the marriage is intact.[61] The difficult issue, however, is how to distribute *future* rights to custody of the children upon divorce. In providing for divorce, the parents will pursue two compatible goals; they will want to both maintain an ongoing relationship with their children and to protect human capital investment in child rearing. Thus the optimal division of custody rights is proportional to each party's investment in the relationship with the children prior to divorce, and each party is presumed to continue to invest at that level afterward.

Assume, for example, that E has invested far more energy and effort in child rearing than R. E should be entitled to future custody in the same proportion that her greater investment in child rearing signaled a larger interest in parenting during the marriage. Such an "approximation" approach encourages optimal investment, because each parent's investment will be protected on termination. It also balances the incentives for both spouses to remain in the marriage.[62] For example, if the parties adopt a plan for traditional role division, R, who has invested principally in income-producing human capital, will anticipate losing some portion of the shared custody that he enjoyed during marriage if the marriage ends. In contrast, an equal division of custody on divorce would create incentives for him to defect. He would be able to escape the marriage with the ownership of his human capital, subject, of course, to E's claim for alimony, and lose none of his shared custody rights.

Terminating the Marriage: The Right to Divorce. No more important issue confronts E and R than to specify the conditions under which either can terminate the relationship. The parties must develop their understandings about the conditions for termination within the constraints of any state-prescribed mandatory commitment terms. As our earlier analysis suggested, by choosing to marry E and R will (in an ideal world) face a mandatory period of commitment that specifies both the minimum (and maximum) fixed marital term. However, a mandatory commitment term leaves significant room for negotiation over the conditions under which the parties are entitled otherwise to terminate the relationship and the conditions for any notification prior to termination.

The termination question is particularly difficult because the marital partners may be motivated to terminate the marriage in three distinct circumstances, each of which raises different concerns. First, the parties can imagine a *retaliatory* termination by one spouse in response to a substantial failure by the other to perform as promised. As is the case with most bilateral contracts, E and

R both understand that the best-efforts promise of each spouse is dependent on the reciprocal performance by the other. Thus, if E defects significantly from the cooperative norm by having an extramarital affair or otherwise substantially neglects the relationship, R is entitled to quit his efforts as well. In addition, granting the injured spouse the unilateral right to terminate the marriage is a self-enforcing contract term that can effectively bond the promisor to faithful performance of the marital obligations. At least in theory, both parties would be motivated to offer the strongest possible bonds to reassure the other. Thus the most potent right of retaliatory termination would be one that is exercisable unilaterally by the injured spouse without requiring prior notice or an extended waiting period. The threat of a prompt sanction for a major breach of the contract will reduce the temptation to cheat on the agreement and encourage mutual investment in the relationship.

The question is more complicated, however, when the parties must accommodate the trade-offs generated by the risk of a *strategic* termination. This second motivation to terminate is a perverse incentive that results from asymmetric investments undertaken by one party or the other at different points in the life of the relationship. Thus R may be tempted to terminate after E has invested many years in child rearing and nurturing and prior to the time when his investment obligations require more efforts than hers. Even though the parties have agreed upon contract terms that are designed to reduce these incentives, the threat cannot be eliminated in a world of costly enforcement. Strategic terminations have, by definition, no social utility to the parties and, if unchecked, the threat of such behavior leads to underinvestment by the vulnerable party. If the parties were able to verify a strategic termination to a third party, therefore, the simple solution would be to punish all strategic terminations (perhaps by the forfeit of a stipulated penalty upon divorce). Unhappily, although the conditions that distinguish a retaliatory termination from a strategic termination are observable to the parties, they are peculiarly incapable of verification to a third party. The bona fides of the spouse who is seeking to terminate will depend upon privately held motivations that are a product of complex interactions and easily malleable behaviors.

The problem of sorting out the motivations that underlie a decision to terminate the marriage is even more difficult once the parties acknowledge that the relationship may fail to provide either or both spouses the anticipated surpluses that exceed their "go it alone" alternatives. This could happen because either or both spouses change over time, or because the initial marriage decision was a mistake, perhaps because one or both spouses lacked sufficient information about the other. Thus both E and R will wish to reserve a right to terminate for *relational failure* whenever the returns from the marriage for either spouse are less than those anticipated from other options. However, since the costs and benefits of marriage and of the alternatives to marriage may fluctuate over time, E and R are also motivated to guard against both short-term miscalculations and strategic behavior. Thus, if E and R could be assured of perfect accuracy in adjudication, they would prohibit strategic terminations, permit retaliatory termination at the unilateral option of the aggrieved spouse, and authorize termination for relational failure following an agreed-upon notice period. Unhappily, E and R will be motivated to abandon this first-best solution once they consider the difficult challenge of enforcing the termination provisions of their agreement. A third-party adjudicator is simply incapable of reliably distinguishing strategic termination from either retaliatory or relational failure terminations. This problem of nonverifiability threatens the integrity of any scheme that permits termination without notification as well as any purported waiver or claim of good faith modification.

E and R can respond to these concerns by agreeing to a unilateral right of termination (following any mandatory period of commitment), subject to a notification requirement—such as a two-year waiting period from the time of notification before divorce. By raising the barriers to exit, an extended notification period increases the costs of termination and encourages long-term investments that may not pay off in the short term. In the same vein, a precommitment to delay divorce sorts out cases where the desire to divorce reflects a transitory preference from those in which changes in preferences have permanently reduced the value of the relationship (or increased the value of alternatives) to the terminating party.[63] Finally, a notification requirement reduces the risk of asymmetric investment and encourages each party to invest optimally in the relationship even though the spouse's reciprocal investment is deferred. As a matter of theory, an ex ante agreement to prohibit modification or waiver of the waiting period serves to transform the notification rule into a binding precommitment that, once selected, ties both parties' hands so as to eliminate the temptation to act strategically thereafter.[64]

An extended waiting period does, however, generate some associated problems. The parties must be alert to the risk of strategic or spiteful behavior, such as dissipation of economic assets and refusals to provide continuing economic support. E and R thus must establish terms governing their relationship during the period prior to divorce. These terms would specify *pendant lite* rights to custody, support, and preservation of the parties' economic assets.

Enforcing the Contract. At the time of contracting, E and R will share the same goal: to structure the contract so as to promote cooperation and reduce conflicts of interest (situations that compromise fidelity and loyalty) at the least cost. The parties recognize that selfish considerations will affect each party's behavior from time to time, and that one or the other party may regret a contractual obligation, and be tempted to "chisel" or otherwise defect from the shared objectives. In other long-term relationships, parties devise bonding and monitoring mechanisms (both informal and formal) to encourage each party to act in the interests of the other as well as her own. Similar enforcement mechanisms are available to R and E as well. Bonding arrangements are precommitments that align the interest of each spouse with that of the other through self-limiting constraints. Such arrangements promote trust as they broadcast each spouse's cooperative intentions. Monitoring arrangements assist each spouse to detect and sanction selfish spousal conduct in the partner.

E and R can utilize both extralegal and legal mechanisms to encourage faithful performance and enforce contractual understandings. Extralegal enforcement mechanisms include endogenous relational norms (the understandings about marital obligations that emerge through the couple's interaction over time), together with prescribed conventions, traditions, and exogenous societal norms that define acceptable behavior and attitudes in marriage. In seeking to design efficient arrangements, E and R know that extralegal enforcement mechanisms are substitutes for more costly legal mechanisms. Thus their strategy is to anticipate the evolution of relationship-specific norms, assess the potency of existing social norms, and, thereafter, specify legal enforcement only where legal rules are more efficient substitutes for the existing and evolving normative framework.

The evolution of relational norms. While the problems of monitoring individual performance may seem daunting, the parties can anticipate developing a finely tuned set of relational norms that will enable them to detect and sanction failures by either spouse to perform as promised. The intimate character of the relationship and the iterated nature of the interactions will influence the spouses to develop reciprocal patterns of cooperation over time. The pervasive social norm of reciprocity is particularly relevant to long-term interactions, offering a particularly stable foundation for an evolving pattern of conditional cooperation. Such a strategy seems credible to the parties because it relies upon behavioral responses that "go without saying."[65]

Of critical importance to the stability of the relationship are the patterns of interaction for resolving disputes and restoring a cooperative equilibrium. Although these are largely a function of the personalities of the individuals and the interpersonal dynamics of the particular relationship, certain patterns are predictable in ongoing relationships such as a marriage. The fact that the married couple anticipates continuing interaction in the future will assist them to establish patterns of cooperative interaction. Either E or R may be tempted on a given occasion to act selfishly, as some short-term preference (to work late, to invest excessively in leisure activities, to spend excessively) overwhelms the long-term benefits of a cooperative relationship. However, because E and R have bound themselves to a long-term relationship, the prospect of future interaction will influence their behavior in responding to conflict situations. Because both parties retain the ability to evade responsibility or to cooperate in the future, each must consider the effect of his or her choice not only on the immediate conflict but also on later conflict situations.

The dynamics of repeated interactions of indefinite duration suggest, therefore, that a pattern of cooperative conflict adjustment frequently will emerge. If one party begins by adjusting cooperatively and the other responds, mutual cooperation is introduced and then reinforced by a "lock-in" effect.[66] Indeed, at least in theory, E and R can promote a cooperative equilibrium at the outset by announcing their mutual commitment to conditional cooperation upon any conflict situation. The marriage vows implicitly serve this precommitment function. By the expedient of punishing defection and rewarding cooperative adjustment, each party can "bring out the best" in the other and thereby reinforce the cooperative equilibrium.[67] In this way, E and R will, over time, develop detailed and precise "rules" governing the daily interactions that form the core of the marriage relationship. Through a trial and error process those rules will become appropriately calibrated to mete out proportional punishment for defection and equivalent rewards for cooperation. Unlike broad commitments to pool efforts and share risks, these relational norms are highly contextualized and precise. As long as the relationship continues, relational norms are the dominant instruments for enforcing the parties' reciprocal commitments.

Despite a precommitment to conditional cooperation, however, marital breakdowns can occur. A single retaliatory response of equal consequences will not always deter noncooperation, and over time, therefore, a retaliatory pattern of noncooperation and defection can emerge. This pattern is also subject to "lock-in" effects. A series of mutual recriminations erodes the initial commitment to cooperation, and eventually leads to relationship breakdown. The "lock-in" effect, therefore, tends to push the parties either toward a stable pattern of cooperation or the trap of mutual conflict.

Can E and R in their marriage contract create an environment that discourages defection and thus promotes a long-term cooperative equilibrium? The major threat to a cooperative equilibrium is the variance in the payoffs between cooperation and defection. The parties realize that temptations to defect may sometimes outweigh the rewards from cooperation embedded in the relational norms. Contemplating this possibility, R and E must turn to supplemental enforcement systems in order to maintain the relative advantages of long-term cooperation over short-term defection. To be effective, however, these additional deterrents must be both carefully calibrated and credible. Credibility, in turn, requires both ex ante commitment and ex post sanctions.

The function of societal norms. In long-term commercial and social relationships, informal social norms play an important role in promoting cooperation that reinforces and often supplants legal enforcement mechanisms.[68] For several reasons, social norms can be expected to play a large role in shaping the marital contract between E and R. First, marriage is subject to many tangible social conventions that announce and reinforce the parties' commitment. Beyond this, behavior in marriage is subject to longstanding societal expectations that will tend to constrain the parties' freedom and influence them toward trustworthiness, fidelity, honesty, and altruism. The threat of social censure discourages conduct inconsistent with the announced norms.[69] Moreover, social norms that are internalized by each party are self-enforcing in the sense that the behavior "goes without saying." Both E and R expect to be constrained by their social roles as married persons and each has the assurance that the other is similarly constrained.

Many social customs and traditions surrounding marriage serve a bonding function, reinforcing the parties' commitment to maximize relational value. These conventions signal to the community the serious and exclusive character of the relationship that the couple is undertaking, and through their established social meaning assure broad community recognition of the commitment. The community, in turn, responds with certain behavioral expectations of the married couple. Engagement periods announce the impending change of status. Engagement and (particularly) wedding rings symbolize the couple's bond, announcing to the world that the married individual is not available for an intimate relationship and is subject to the social norms that define spousal roles. The wedding ceremony and celebratory reception signal the importance of the couple's commitment and change of status in the community. The marital vows represent a public declaration of the parties' intentions, accompanied by hortatory language that expresses the seriousness of the obligation that each spouse is undertaking. Finally, the celebration of wedding anniversaries reminds the couple of the seriousness and importance of their commitment.

Aside from these tangible ways of providing a bond for faithful performance, internalized societal norms define optimal and unacceptable behavior in marriage, reinforcing the couple's commitment to use their best efforts to develop fully a relationship that serves their collective welfare. Norms of trustworthiness, solidarity, openness, honesty, harmony, and fulfillment of obligation between spouses and toward children are widely accepted and frequently serve both bonding and monitoring functions. Take, for example, the norm of marital fidelity. Acts of infidelity are costly to transact, because they must be kept secret not only from the spouse but from others as well. The prospect of guilt generated by the internalization of the norm and of societal disapproval serves a bonding function.[70] In addition, friends and acquaintances are likely to be observant monitors, disapproving of conduct that is inconsistent with marital fidelity; thus the risk of detection may loom large, deterring the tempted spouse.

In the same vein, norms of truth telling and open communication in marriage serve both bonding and monitoring purposes. These norms encourage interdependence and trust, which makes extrication from the relationship costly, and they promote mutual oversight by each spouse of the other's activities through disclosure and information sharing. For example, the sharing of secret and intimate personal information serves a bonding function. Because such information is subject to disclosure, each spouse holds the secret as a hostage that can be used if the other defects from the relational objective.[71] Marital behavior is also constrained and cooperation promoted by norms of harmony and solidarity that deter serious spousal conflict (particularly if it affects children or involves violence). Further, married couples are subject to social expectations that each spouse expend considerable efforts to resolve problems, accept shared responsibility for problems, and not defect in difficult times. This norm of mutual effort may be simply a recognition that the personal commitment undertaken by the parties to a marriage contract derives from a social context that supports and endorses it. Finally, norms defining family obligations of financial and emotional support discourage selfish conduct that destabilizes the relationship.

The effect of norms on marital conduct cannot be predicted precisely, but two distinct effects can be identified. First, each spouse may anticipate social approval or disapproval depending on whether he or she conforms to social expectations. Social sanctions can include reputational harms from gossip, reduced social acceptance, and ostracism. The social costs of violating norms about marital conduct will vary in their severity, depending on the nature of the violation and the social context. In addition to the obvious psychological costs, violating social norms can also have financial consequences, to the extent that conforming to norms about marriage has salience to business or professional advancement. Social norms and a sense of acceptable boundaries of the marital roles are also likely to be internalized, constraining individual behavior through habit and the anticipation of anxiety or guilt for misconduct.[72]

The power of societal norms effectively to enforce compliance with marital obligations rests on the extent to which they are internalized by the parties, and on whether serious social sanctions for violation are anticipated. If norms that support stability in marriage are strong, E and R will be motivated to undertake cooperative adjustments, resolve disputes within the framework of the relationship, and expend efforts (beyond that which individual self-interest may direct) to promote their collective welfare. If societal norms only weakly endorse roles and conduct in marriage that support the stability of the relationship, then social expectations will be less effective in reinforcing the couple's cooperative purposes. If E and R look around their social world and observe infidelity and opportunistic behavior as common among other married couples, their original cooperative intentions may be undermined.[73]

Broad societal norms are mediated through smaller social groups, and norms supporting marriage are likely to vary in their impact on individual behavior depending on whether they are amplified or ignored in this setting. In general, norms function most effectively to regulate behavior in close-knit social communities, in which members interact on an ongoing basis.[74] Under these circumstances, monitoring of violations is facilitated, and the sanctions of disapproval or ostracism carry a high cost. The couple's community could be of several types—extended family, social group, religious group, or geographical community—and different communities can overlap in enforcing norms about marital behavior. Predictably, amplification will be powerful if the couple belongs to several close-knit groups that strongly endorse marital commitment. On the other hand, if the couple's social affiliations are attenuated or if marital obligation is not reinforced in their social context, the broader societal norms are likely to have a much more modest impact on behavior.

Legal enforcement of the marital bargain. E and R will not rely exclusively on either relational or social norms to ensure a cooperative equilibrium. They will also consider the extent to which legal enforcement mechanisms are needed to buttress the stability of the relationship and encourage optimal investment in the marriage.

E and R will not agree to legal enforcement of the terms of the marital bargain unless third-party adjudication would provide a more efficient substitute for or a complement to informal normative sanctions. There are a number of reasons to believe that this criterion would preclude legal enforcement of almost all intramarital promises. The marital relationship is peculiarly interdependent because of the parties' commitment to pooling efforts and to sharing burdens and benefits. The interactions that frame any particular marital conflict are thus highly relation-specific and interactive. There are no plausible grounds for believing that the complex web of behaviors known to and observable by the parties alone can be verified to a court or other third-party adjudicator. Not only would legal enforcement of intramarital promises—such as the parties' wedding vows—impose substantial direct costs on the parties, but the risk of error would be impermissibly high. The parties risk a court incorrectly identifying the sequence of defection and retaliation and thus permanently disrupting the delicate patterns of reciprocity necessary for a cooperative equilibrium. The law's tools are simply too crude to adjust conflicts in intimate ongoing relationships that are shaped by subtle and delicate dynamics. Rather than stabilizing a cooperative equilibrium, legal enforcement of intramarital performance is as likely to undermine the relational norms that stimulate mutual efforts and adjustment.[75]

Moreover, legal enforcement during the marriage of the terms of the marital bargain will threaten the efficacy of the social norms that otherwise discipline marital behavior. Legal adjudication is structured as a single iteration zero-sum game, setting the parties against each other as adversaries. The adversarial system implicitly presumes that the contestants deal at arm's length, or at least that they will not resume an intimate relationship. Legal enforcement effectively trumps the social norms of harmony, reciprocity, and solidarity, and thus a credible commitment to litigate conflict is fundamentally incompatible with many of the social norms that surround marriage. In sum, at least in ongoing intimate relationships, legal mechanisms are imperialistic and do not function effectively in concert with extralegal forces. Given their goal of promoting stability in an ongoing intimate relationship and of resolving conflicts at least cost, E and R would choose not to adjust intramarital conflicts through formal adjudication.

E and R must decide whether to seek legal resolution upon divorce of serious disputes that arise during the marriage. The marriage ceremony includes explicit promises and implicit agreement about the limits of appropriate behavior in marriage. The understanding that adultery, physical and mental cruelty, and desertion are unacceptable spousal behavior was captured under traditional law in fault grounds for divorce which gave a right to terminate the marriage to the "innocent and injured" spouse. Clearly, E and R would agree that such prohibited behavior (e.g., adultery, desertion, cruelty) would constitute a breach of the marriage contract, excusing the other from performance of her marital duties. Moreover, serious misbehavior could be the subject of criminal or tort sanction. The important question here is whether, under a modern marriage contract, these agreements about bad marital behavior would be subject to formal legal enforcement as contract terms upon divorce.

At first blush, there seems to be a strong case for legal enforcement of fault provisions on divorce. Legal enforcement of contractual provisions prohibiting conduct that is likely to undermine or destroy the relationship can deter major defections and promote marital stability. Moreover, the divisive effects of formal adjudication are less important upon termination of the relationship. Nevertheless, E and R will be motivated to reject the legal enforcement of fault provisions, because incorporating fault is likely to generate more costs than benefits. The "fact finding" problems of isolating and evaluating spousal defection are simply too formidable. Disputes in marriage are embedded in a complex framework of multiple expectations and understandings, which makes assigning responsibility and providing an appropriate remedy extremely difficult. In the subtle continuous interactions of an ongoing marriage, implicit assent or dissent from questionable spousal conduct will be hard to discern, and protest may be genuine, jocular, or strategic. Moreover, sorting out for a neutral third party a defection that is a straightforward breach from one that is a retaliatory response to an evasion by the other spouse (which itself may be a retaliatory act) will often be impossible. Conflicts that arise in this most intimate relationship will be peculiarly hard to untangle. The bright-line rules that are embodied in traditional law fail to capture the complexity of what is often shared responsibility for marital failure. To be sure, some failed marriages may involve the stark example of one defecting spouse and one fully performing partner, but the process of sorting these cases from those in which the behavioral strands are intertwined will be extremely difficult and error prone.

Given the difficulty in accurately assessing responsibility for behavioral defections, E and R would perceive a substantial risk that fault claims would be used strategically. If alimony and property distribution claims were affected by a fault determination, both parties would be vulnerable to strategic claims by the other. In practice, however, these risks would be more acutely felt by the homemaker spouse, because of her economic vulnerability. Those critics who argue for a return to fault determinations in making financial settlement awards fail to recognize that fault claims are a two-edged sword.

In rejecting legal enforcement of fault grounds, E and R will weigh the relative advantages of alternative methods of enforcement. Bad behavior certainly justifies retaliation in the context of the parties' relational norms. Thus, for example, E can consider separation and termination of reciprocal efforts as a retaliatory response to R's adultery. Moreover, social norms prescribe acceptable marital behavior and proscribe spousal abuse, desertion, and adultery.[76] Although divorce has far greater social acceptance than was true a generation ago, there is no evidence that standards for behavior in marriage have declined. Indeed, some behaviors such as spousal and child abuse and desertion are subject to greater social disapproval today than in an earlier era. Moreover, noncontractual remedies such as criminal penalties for abuse and nonsupport and social service intervention are more effective than formerly. Indeed, there may be less tolerance of marital misbehavior in an era in which divorce is more readily available. Given the high costs of sorting bad behavior from merely inadequate efforts, therefore, E and R are motivated to rely instead on the established framework of extralegal mechanisms to sanction a spousal fault.

Legal enforcement of the marriage contract will play a modest but important role when the marital relationship terminates. The parties' foundational understandings have produced agreement on the terms for divorce, property settlement, alimony, ownership of economic assets, and child custody and support. Unlike the intramarital obligations that function to maintain the relationship and are governed largely by social and relational norms, the obligations that are triggered by a termination of the marriage are efficiently enforced by legal coercion. The requirements of prior notice, division of economic assets, and even child custody and support focus on assignments of individual rights and responsibilities and turn on facts that can be verified by a court. Thus the parties will agree to live under two sets of rules: a more flexible set of rules for social and relational enforcement during the marriage and a stricter set of rules for legal enforcement upon divorce.

Legal enforcement plays an important role ex ante. Introduction of formal legal enforcement upon termination of the relationship provides a powerful signal that the relationship has broken down and creates a threshold across which the parties will be hesitant to cross. Without such a "large strike" capability, each party would be subject to the other's defection whenever the short-term gains from defection exceed the present discounted value of future cooperation. Thus E and R are motivated to develop a supplemental system to enforce their foundational understandings regarding distribution of economic assets, alimony and support, and custody of children. Social and relational norms are unsatisfactory safeguards to protect these individual "paid in" investments in the relationship.

Consider a familiar example. Assume that E and R agree that R will work to support the family while E attends medical school. Thereafter, E and R can share the lifestyle made possible by a physician's income. Should the marriage falter shortly after E completes her medical training, she may be tempted to leave the relationship and retain the entire benefit of her accumulated human capital without compensating R for the value of his investment. A legally enforced termination rule that requires E to wait two years after notification before securing a divorce coupled with a rule that permits R to claim a portion of the outputs of E's human capital will deter E from strategic defection. R in turn will be motivated by the protection of the law's umbrella to use his best efforts to invest in E's career development. Without legal enforcement, the risk of E's uncompensated default will lead R to underperform and the parties will suffer a loss of relational surplus.

Legal enforcement mechanisms are also important ex post. E and R appreciate that the social and relational norms that promote cooperation in marriage will exert little influence on their behavior upon divorce. Moreover, the relational dynamics that create incentives to cooperate in ongoing relationships will have deteriorated. Each party, looking toward the end of the relationship, is no longer motivated to consider the interest of the spouse or their mutual benefit. Thus, in the example, E, as the newly minted physician, is no longer inclined by either relational or social norms to credit or to compensate R for his investment in her career. Once again, legal enforcement in this setting substitutes for inadequate normative constraints and ensures a clear and predictable termination process.

We conclude the discussion in this section with a word of caution. The contract that the model predicts E and R are most likely to conclude does not reflect the terms of a marriage contract that any particular couple would agree upon. A hypothetical bargain between two rational utility-maximizers provides instead a template for the specification of default rules that would suit the purposes of a broad number of couples entering into marriage. Central to any system of contractual default rules is the invitation to individual parties to opt out of any majoritarian default rule that ill-suits their goals and to design their own more tailored alternative. Majoritarian default rules are efficient, therefore, if they save most (or at least many) bargainers the time, effort, and error of replicating the process that E and R have engaged in. As a first step in specifying optimal default rules for marriage, the model developed above suggests a series of foundational terms that address the nature and duration of the marital commitment, the mechanisms to facilitate cooperation, the means by which each party can protect his or her investment in the relationship, and the conditions for termination. We turn, in section III, to an analysis of the descriptive and prescriptive implications of the relational model for the contemporary law of marriage and divorce.

III Marriage as Contract under No-fault Divorce Law

In this section, we apply the model of marriage as relational contract to contemporary family law. To a considerable degree, the model explains the deep structure of the law as well as many of the features of the legal regulation of marriage and divorce. The relational paradigm offers, in addition, a coherent normative criterion for evaluating the legal doctrines regulating divorce. A central normative implication of the analysis is that important default rules governing divorce fail adequately to protect marital investments. The analysis also reveals the relative immaturity of the contractual regime. Couples today are unable to undertake a substantial legal commitment to marriage. This restriction on commitment, coupled with the erosion of societal norms promoting cooperation in marriage, provides a powerful explanation for why so many marriages fail despite the ex ante intentions of the spouses.

THE GENERAL CONTOURS OF MARRIAGE AS RELATIONAL CONTRACT

The strongest evidence of a contractual regime is the freedom of parties to opt out of the state-provided legal rules. On that basis, the contractual nature of the modern law of marriage is indisputable. It is simply inaccurate to describe the legal regulation of marriage today as a "basket of immutable obligations."[77] Although there are mandatory rules governing who can marry and on what basis, such constraints are fundamental to all contractual regimes. In fact, most of the rules governing marriage today are default rules. Under the Uniform Premarital Agreement Act, for example, parties have broad freedom to contract before marriage about a wide range of issues, and courts routinely enforce these agreements under contract principles.[78] Moreover, divorcing couples today have the freedom to opt out of virtually all of the legal rules surrounding divorce. They can (and do) set their own terms for distribution of property, alimony, and (in practice) even child support and custody.

As the relational model predicts, the default terms of modern marriage law are enforceable through a combination of extralegal and legal mechanisms. Thus extralegal mechanisms are used to ensure performance in the intact marriage, and legal enforcement is seldom available.[79] Courts may chastise the miserly husband who refuses to provide adequately for his homemaker wife despite ample financial means, but they view judicial intervention to enforce his support obligations as destructive of the harmony of marriage.[80] Even under the Uniform Premarital Agreement Act, which permits contracting over intramarital affairs, there is little evidence that courts are prepared to resolve any resulting disputes. Implicitly, this policy endorses reliance on extralegal enforcement and acknowledges that adversarial adjudication would undermine the informal mechanisms that generally promote cooperation in intact relationships.[81]

Legal enforcement of the marriage contract is focused, as the model predicts, on the termination of the relationship. Substantive legal issues surrounding divorce include distribution of financial assets and provision for the future care of the children of the marriage. The legal duty to provide for family financial needs is formally enforced through alimony and child support orders upon divorce. The state's interest in the welfare of children generally results in explicit supervision of parenting decisions on the grounds that divorcing parents can no longer be presumed to cooperate regarding child-rearing decisions.

The trend toward the abolition of fault grounds for divorce and the removal of fault as a factor in support and property distribution is also explained by the relational framework. No-fault reform was justified, in part, by the formidable enforcement problems associated with judicial efforts to verify bad behavior under traditional law. The perception that fault determinations carry substantial enforcement costs supports the contention that the exclusion of fault is not the fatal flaw that makes a marriage contract "illusory."

While the deep structure of the legal regulation of marriage and divorce is predicted by the model, the contemporary regime deviates from the ideal in several notable respects. Societal norms supporting marriage are less potent forces for ensuring performance than the model assumes and that was true in an era in which strong religious and moral prescriptions dictated marital behavior. In general, divorce, including unilateral termination, is more acceptable today, and normative sanctions for defection from a relationship are relatively modest. This point should not be exaggerated, however. Within some close-knit religious, ethnic, and geographical communities, social norms continue to function effectively to promote marital stability. Even in the broader society, marital infidelity, disloyalty, and cruelty are still met with disapproval. Indeed, a heightened awareness of the costly impact of divorce on children has generated disapproval of parental selfishness, complicating the tolerant social attitudes of the 1970s and 1980s. Nonetheless, it is surely true that an important part of the regulatory scheme for enforcing the marital contract does not function today with optimal effectiveness. Moreover, the parties' inability to undertake legally binding commitments further contributes to the attenuation of social norms supporting marriage and also limits couples' ability to create substitute enforcement mechanisms.

DESIGNING DEFAULT RULES FOR MARRIAGE AND DIVORCE

In the absence of a premarital agreement, the legal terms of the marriage contract will be the regime of legal rules dealing with the termination of marriage. Contract theory would direct lawmakers to formulate legal rules regulating marriage and divorce that embody the terms that plausibly would be agreed to by the broadest number of informed, rational actors in the premarital context.[82] In the absence of overriding public policy considerations that justify restricting the parties' contractual freedom, these default rules function to save many (if not most) parties the time, expense, and error of crafting in a premarital agreement all of the terms for dissolving their marriage. The substantive legal rules defining the conditions for divorce, alimony, and, to a lesser extent, child custody, are thus usefully analyzed as contract default rules. From this perspective, the contract terms generated by the relational model can function as the basis for both an explanatory theory and a normative critique.

Analyzing contemporary legal regulation as default rules within a contractual framework offers a normative justification that responds to the feminist challenge that the interests of wives are harmed under a no-fault regime. Each party to a hypothetical bargain is presumed to be rational, informed, and self-interested. The parties voluntarily agree to terms (which then constitute the default rules) that further their mutual objectives for the relationship. Each party stands to gain more from the resulting contract than he or she could achieve under a "go it alone" alternative. Subject to these constraints, default rules regulating divorce are likely to satisfy the minimum interests of both husbands and wives, because otherwise the conditions for (hypothetical) agreement could not be achieved. These baseline conditions reduce the risk that the resulting legal rules will impose a disproportionate burden on a particular group or gender.

To be sure, the contractual paradigm does not promise distributional equality of the marital surplus for both parties, especially since background social conditions may result in a disparity in bargaining positions. The hypothetical bargain framework does reduce, however, the impact of cultural and historical gender-linked traits that could make women less effective bargainers. If women are less assertive and less likely to pursue self-interest single-mindedly (or more likely than men to identify with the welfare of others), then they may be disadvantaged in negotiating a marital contract.[83] However, these differences will be excluded from negotiation in the ex ante hypothetical bargain, and thus will not be reflected in the legal default rules, which, once generated, create presumptive entitlements establishing a baseline for subsequent negotiations.

In designing optimal default rules for property division, alimony, and child custody, the challenge is to translate theoretically ideal terms into workable and cost-effective legal rules. Thus, in each case, lawmakers are led to consider the use of crude but clear proxies to accommodate difficult measurement and valuation dilemmas.

Distribution of Property and Alimony. The rules relating to property ownership and division are broadly congruent with the predictions of the relational model. In general, although courts have considerable discretion, the norm upon divorce is a roughly equal division of property acquired during the marriage.[84] Upon divorce, spouses retain ownership of their individual human capital, even though future earning capacity and related assets are acquired during the marriage, often with the support of the other spouse. In some regards, contemporary alimony doctrine also functions as the relational model predicts. As was true under traditional law, alimony generally is not a vested claim by one spouse against another. Courts retain jurisdiction to modify and terminate alimony orders, and payments are contingent on continued financial need. The most important contingency, of course, is the former homemaker's employability. Alimony also ends upon remarriage of the payee spouse, and upon the death of either spouse. In many jurisdictions, fault is excluded from consideration in awarding alimony. The removal of fault is a predicate to legal recognition of the essential function of alimony as financial protection if the marriage ends for the spouse who undertakes substantial marriage-specific investments.

In significant respects, however, contemporary alimony law does not reflect the default rules that would be adopted in an explicitly contractual regime. Parties who conclude that it is mutually beneficial for one spouse to undertake a role that involves substantial marriage-specific investment would predictably agree to greater protection against financial loss should the marriage fail than the law currently awards.

Crafting optimal alimony rules requires balancing costs and benefits so that neither party is motivated to initiate divorce for strategic reasons. A default rule that uses a reliance measure as the basis of spousal support serves this purpose well. Since the homemaker's reliance interest is never greater and generally less than her expectancy, the expected payout will not tempt the homemaker to leave the marriage. At the same time, once her expectancy is frustrated—for example, when the value of the relationship declines below her "go it alone" alternative—she will not be deterred from leaving the now-unfulfilling relationship. A greater challenge is to deter the breadwinner from opportunistic defection. Because of the asymmetric character of their investments, the breadwinner may be tempted to leave after receiving substantial benefits from the homemaker's contributions to the marriage and before his own obligations have fully matured. Without an obligation to pay alimony, his temptation to defect increases as his own income increases and the marginal value of the homemaker's performance declines. Thus the optimal alimony obligation also increases in direct proportion to the declining value of the homemaker's marital contribution. This causes the breadwinner to internalize the homemaker's past contributions to the relationship.

Current alimony law distorts these incentives by imposing on the homemaker a disproportionate share of the financial costs of divorce. She is overdeterred from leaving an unfulfilling marriage by the prospect of an undercompensatory alimony award. On the other hand, the breadwinner has a positive financial incentive to initiate divorce, having captured the benefits of the homemaker's prior investment and knowing that his future earning capacity is subject to an undercompensatory alimony claim.

Child Custody. Although the law historically recognized parental investment in child rearing as the basis of child custody allocation on divorce, that factor has been obscured under the modern decision rule. The tender-years presumption awarded custody to mothers in recognition of the traditional maternal role of primary caretaker. As more egalitarian norms began to dominate family law generally, the preference for mothers was replaced by the gender-neutral best-interest-of-the-child standard, although mothers continued to assume primary responsibility for child care. The modern standard is notoriously indeterminate, allowing the court to base the child's future custody on any factors that are deemed relevant to the child's future welfare.[85]

The debate about reform of child custody law in recent years has focused in part on whether parental investment in child rearing should receive substantial protection, and, if so, how this protection can best be achieved. Thus feminist support for the primary caretaker preference is grounded in the belief that the mother's role as principal caretaker is discounted under the best-interest standard.[86] Advocates for a rule favoring joint custody, on the other hand, argue that such an arrangement is the only means of assuring that two parents who have shared child rearing responsibilities can continue to do so after divorce.[87]

The relational contract perspective suggests that the joint custody and primary caretaker alternatives represent an advance over the best-interest standard in focusing on the factor of parental investment, but that neither is an optimal rule in a world in which families vary greatly in their child-rearing arrangements during marriage. An approximation rule that allocates future custody on the basis of parental investment is likely to be preferred by most parties ex ante, because it maximizes beneficial investments and minimizes the incentives for strategic defection. As in the case of attempts to measure human capital investments in other contexts, courts employing an approximation standard can be expected to develop proxies to reduce the inherent problems of measurement and valuation.[88]

NO-FAULT DIVORCE LAW AS AN IMMATURE CONTRACTUAL REGIME

Although the law regulating divorce conforms in many respects to the relational contract model, contractual principles are not fully realized under the no-fault regime. In an ironic contrast to the constraints faced by parties under traditional law, where lifelong commitment was mandatory, contemporary divorce law permits unilateral termination at any time regardless of the commitment promises that have been exchanged.[89] The relational model suggests that legal limitations on parties' freedom to commit have significant effects on the marriage relationship, as well as feedback effects on already stressed social norms promoting cooperative behavior in marriage.

Legal Restrictions on the Freedom to Commit. Conventional wisdom holds that contemporary regulation of marriage is shaped by principles of private ordering. In fact, the options available to couples who are interested in substantial commitment are limited in several ways. First, in most states couples are not free to specify a duration to their marriage that restricts their freedom to exit. Under the unilateral no-fault rule, all marriages are functionally terminable at will. Most courts today are unlikely to enforce a term in a premarital agreement that provides for a waiting period prior to divorce.[90] Moreover, the limits on parties' freedom to undertake contractual commitment extends beyond durational provisions. Parties are unable generally to opt out of no-fault provisions by imposing a monetary penalty enforceable against either party for serious defection or by conditioning divorce on fault. Even a contractual provision to undertake marital counseling before leaving the marriage is probably not enforceable in most jurisdictions. Thus the foundational rules that prescribe duration, conditions of termination, and penalties for breach collectively define marriage as a relationship without legal commitment.

These restrictions on contractual freedom to commit are puzzling. One explanation is that the no-fault reformers, reacting to the oppressive restraints on individual freedom under the fault regime, presumed erroneously that commitment is antithetical to personal autonomy. Put differently, the architects of contemporary divorce law have confused ex ante autonomy, which includes the right to restrict one's future freedom, with ex post autonomy, the freedom to renege on promises. Another rationale for restricting the freedom of parties to commit to marriage is that the parties are not "competent" to make rational decisions in the premarital setting, or that even thoughtful decisions may turn out to be mistaken. Such mistakes could be costly if the relationship fails and the marriage provides less value to one or both spouses than the alternative of going it alone. In this situation, a commitment term that makes divorce extremely difficult (a ten-year waiting period or a large fine, for example) could bind the parties to a relationship with little social value. Such concerns form the basis of a claim that restrictions on divorce, even when they are voluntarily assumed by the parties, violate public policy and should be prohibited.

As our previous analysis suggests, the concern that some parties will be bound to unhappy marriages may justify a public policy prohibition of extremely inflexible commitment terms, such as a term which forbids divorce altogether.[91] Restrictions on more tempered commitments, however, cannot be explained on these grounds. The potential for regret exists in every contract; otherwise, legally enforceable commitment would be unnecessary. As long as the conditions of contract formation are free from impediments that impair rational and voluntary choice, contract theory argues for the freedom to commit notwithstanding the risk that either party may later come to regret the commitment. Moreover, concerns about cognitive impairments evaporate should the state elect to define the category of marriage in terms of mandatory commitment periods. As we suggested in section II, the signaling function of marriage strongly argues for state-specified commitment parameters within which customized commitment options would be enforceable.

The Effects of Restrictions on Commitment. The legal constraints on the freedom to commit to marriage have substantial effects. To be sure, any legal prohibition on contracting limits the parties' range of choice in deciding how best to maximize their joint utility. These constraints, however, undermine the parties' foundational choice voluntarily to bind themselves through contractual commitment. The relational model argues for granting parties the right to signal their desire to constrain their future freedom by choosing to marry. Thus the law's hostility toward legally binding marital commitment undermines the ability of parties to find partners with matching preferences and, thereafter, to achieve their basic purposes for the relationship.

The relational model suggests that these restrictions will have significant feedback effects on marital relationships. Parties who seek a stable, lasting marriage can make a long-term commitment and rely on extralegal enforcement mechanisms, but are limited in their ability to use legally enforceable substantive terms to assist them in achieving their goal. It is commonly assumed that the societal norms surrounding marriage function less effectively to enforce cooperative behavior in contemporary social life than was true a generation ago. To the extent that this is true, legal enforcement of long-term commitments is a particularly valuable method of bolstering extralegal norms. The background threat of legal enforcement can have a stabilizing effect on the cooperative interactions in marriage. Retaliatory patterns of noncooperation are less likely to develop, and parties are less motivated to defect from the relationship.

Restrictions on legally enforceable commitments also have an indirect effect on the enforcement of a marriage contract. The law's hostility toward marital commitment reduces the potency of societal norms promoting fidelity, loyalty, and cooperation in marriage. The unilateral exit option sends the signal that commitment in marriage is not distinguishable from commitment in cohabitation relationships. There is thus a disconnection between the formality and seriousness with which many people undertake the commitment to marriage and the ease with which the bond can be legally severed. In short, the legal account of marriage describes a relationship of limited investment. The impact of these messages on the social norms surrounding marriage may have contributed to the instability of marriage as reflected in the current divorce rate.

There is some evidence that the law is moving in the direction of permitting couples to legally commit to marriage. Some courts have enforced the premarital agreements of couples who have decided that legal enforcement of behavioral promises (regarding fidelity and sobriety, for example) was an important condition of their marital commitment.[92] Further, and most significant, the Louisiana Covenant Marriage Act invites parties to choose between alternative commitment options. The statute does not impose a requirement that fault be established before divorce is granted, as do the recently rejected Michigan bill and other proposals for reform of no-fault divorce law. Under the Louisiana statute, couples are presented with two options for the termination of their relationship that involve different levels of commitment. One is the standard no-fault rule, while the other allows divorce only on fault grounds or after a two-year separation. Couples are free to choose the commitment option which best corresponds with their mutual goals for the relationship.

The statute is a first step toward a more mature contractual model of marriage. It is revolutionary among the reform proposals directed at no-fault divorce law in that the parties can opt for a legally binding commitment. To be sure, the commitment option provided by the statute may not be optimal if, as the model predicts, many couples would choose the termination term but not the fault grounds. Nonetheless, the progression to a broader menu of options could allow couples greater capacity to customize their marriage contract to their particular needs.

Conclusion

The preceding analysis goes far toward resolving a troublesome puzzle about modern divorce law: why are marriages, which share so many features with relational contracts in other settings, so peculiarly prone to fail? The structure of the law governing marriage and divorce conforms in large part to the regulation of relational contracts in other settings both in the reliance on nonlegal enforcement mechanisms and in the function of legal default rules governing the terms for separation and divorce. It is clear, however, that the combination of extralegal and legal enforcement mechanisms functions less effectively to promote cooperative equilibrium in marriage than they do in other relational contexts.

Several factors undermine the effectiveness of the various mechanisms that reinforce commitment to marriage. First, the societal norms promoting cooperative behavior in marriage have weakened in the past generation, in part because of the signaling effects of no-fault divorce. Spousal defection and marital failure are far less stigmatic today than they once were. This effect is magnified, of course, if dissatisfied spouses observe others leaving their marriages with ease. Thus one clear implication is that an important impediment to successful enforcement of the marriage contract is exogenous to the relationship itself, inhering in the social and cultural environment.

The dilution of social norms has a particularly costly impact because couples are not free to substitute legal mechanisms to reinforce their commitment. The law's preference for ex post autonomy over ex ante autonomy has particularly acute costs in an environment in which extralegal mechanisms function suboptimally. This tendency is captured most forcefully in the mandatory unilateral termination rule. Finally, this rule (and the default rules for alimony and child custody) fails to respond to the ubiquitous problem of asymmetric investments. By providing inadequate protection for the spouse whose investment has marriage-specific value, or who invests heavily in the marriage at the outset of the relationship, the law discourages what may be optimal investment for some couples, and tempts the spouse who benefits from the early investment to defect.

A contractual framework both clarifies the structure of the marriage relationship and illuminates key deficiencies in the current regulatory regime. It also provides a guide for designing legal default rules that would better reinforce marital stability. A mature contractual regime does not correct structural social inequality. It does offer the couple that desires a long-term committed relationship a means to pursue their self-defined goals.

Marriage as a Signal

MICHAEL J. TREBILCOCK

I   Marriage as Status or Contract?

In their superb essay, "Marriage as Relational Contract," Elizabeth and Robert Scott argue persuasively that viewing a marriage as contract—specifically, as relational contract—rather than as status (historically the prevailing perspective), is not inconsistent with caring, sharing, loving, and long-term commitments. A critical element in their analysis is the default rules that should govern intramarital and postmarital rights and obligations. I accept their view that the law has a minimal role to play in directly enforcing intramarital commitments, which for the most part depend, and should depend, on relationship-specific and social norms. The adversarial character of legal enforcement means that once the law is called upon to enforce commitments in a marriage, the relationship is or shortly will be at an end, although this may not preclude precommitment to less adversarial forms of mediation or arbitration of conflicts in ongoing relationships, invoking the aid of trusted friends, family members, pastors, or marriage counselors (much as disputes between members of trade associations are often resolved). However, the authors recognize that once a relationship is at an end, relationship-specific and social norms lose much of their force in ensuring compliance with mutual commitments, and legal enforcement must necessarily play a much more central role. Moreover, the terms prescribed by the legal system for governing postmarital rights and obligations will clearly, as they recognize, indirectly significantly influence intramarital relations by specifying the costs and benefits of exit.

In developing a set of default rules governing rights and obligations following marital termination, the authors adopt a hypothetical contract framework in which prospective spouses, as rational actors, at the time they enter into marriage attempt to specify complete contingent claims contracts, containing at least presumptive rules that will govern the contingency of marital failure. This is a framework that I and my co-author Rosemin Keshvani have ourselves employed in previous writing, especially with respect to the entitlements of an economically dependent spouse (typically the wife) in a traditional marriage with respect to alimony or support following marriage breakdown.[1] In such a case, where there is a sharp division of labor with the wife devoting most of her time and energies to household production and the husband devoting most of his time and energies to market production, the wife bears an asymmetric risk, in the event of marriage breakdown, that her labor-market human capital will have depreciated substantially as a result of the marriage, while his will have been unaffected, and in many cases enhanced. In such marriages, it would be rational for the parties at the time of entering into the marriage for the wife to demand an insurance policy from the husband insuring her against the asymmetric risks that she is bearing from her relationship-specific investments in the event of marriage breakdown. The Scotts adopt a similar framework of analysis, but extend it beyond issues of alimony or support to the allocation of the benefits of professional degrees acquired during the course of marriage by one spouse and facilitated by the other; to the grounds for divorce; and to child custody and maintenance arrangements.

Most features of the hypothetical complete-contingent-claims contract that they develop I find compelling. In particular, I am persuaded by their arguments that the return to either a fault-based divorce regime or a fault-based alimony regime, while superficially attractive as a means of deterring opportunistic behavior by one or other spouse or egregious breaches of the marriage compact, is unlikely to prove operational in practice for the same reasons that the traditional divorce and alimony regime proved unsatisfactory—it is next to impossible for a third-party adjudicator to figure out cause and effect relationships in performing postmortems on failed intimate relationships to which they are not directly privy. Moreover, at least in the case of a fault-based divorce regime, it would, if mandatory, re-create all the previous incentives to manipulate the system through perjury, collusive arrangements, and the like, by parties choosing to extricate themselves from a failed marriage. However, this rejection of fault, either as a determinant of grounds for divorce or entitlements to alimony, places a substantial burden on the Scotts' proposals for compensating economically dependent spouses for opportunity costs incurred following marriage breakdown as a result of the marriage. Here, they would essentially compensate the economically dependent spouse (assumed in most cases to be the wife) for her reliance costs incurred as a result of a marriage in forgoing the development of her labor-market human capital insofar as these translate into reduced economic prospects in the labor market following marriage breakdown. I myself remain to be convinced that a reliance cost measure, as opposed to an expectation measure, is sufficiently compensatory, or sufficiently discourages opportunistic behavior by husbands where wives are the first movers in a relationship in terms of contributions to child rearing and homemaking, against an expectation of the provision of economic well-being and security in the later years of the marriage. For example, the nineteen-year-old waitress who marries, stays home and nurtures four children, and takes care of her husband may be able to demonstrate few opportunity costs of marriage if her husband leaves her at age fifty, but nevertheless she can reasonably argue that he has denied her the expectation of economic security in her later years. However, I acknowledge that a full expectation measure of compensation creates significant moral hazard problems where a wife would, in theory, be rendered indifferent between preserving the marriage and leaving it, suggesting, following commonly observed insurance principles, some sharing of risks (co-insurance) and perhaps some measure of alimony or support between the reliance and expectation measures. In this respect, the Scotts are not entirely consistent, in that, while they favor the reliance measure as a general principle in compensating the economically dependent spouse for the asymmetric risks of relationship-specific investments, in the case of professional degrees they argue for a form of profit sharing, or expectation measure, rather than a reliance measure.

One objection that might be directed at either a reliance or (a fortiori) an expectation measure of compensation is that it is likely to encourage traditional, economically dependent marital relationships and hence endorses a highly problematic normative conception of marriage. I see little force in this objection. First, there is the problem of legal transitions—many marriages were concluded in the past on a very different set of understandings than are many contemporary marriages, and the legal system cannot responsibly ignore the realities of these relationships when they fail. Second, even with respect to contemporary or future marriages, it can reasonably be argued that by making economically dependent relationships much more expensive for men in the event of their termination, this may discourage many such relationships where these are driven by considerations of exploitation or subordination rather than by genuine considerations of mutual advantage.

Given the centrality of the Scotts' alimony proposals to the hypothetical complete-contingent-claims contract that they sketch, let me note other general reservations that need to be confronted in this model. The Scotts hypothesize that while their model set of default rules is unlikely to be appropriate to all marital relationships, in choosing default rules one should choose majoritarian default rules that are appropriate to a broad range of cases, while leaving the parties free to tailor default rules for themselves in other cases. This framework of analysis raises two very large issues, neither of which is satisfactorily dealt with by the authors. The first issue relates to the circumstances and conditions under which prospective or existing marital partners are able to contract out of these default rules. This is a sufficiently important issue that I devote the next section of my comments to it. The second issue is whether the authors can be confident that their proposed default rules are in fact majoritarian default rules. I should add that this criticism has also been directed at my own insurance-based proposals for evolving rules relating to alimony and support. In an increasingly secular age, marriage encompasses almost an infinite range of relationships, and any taxonomy—necessarily required in order to generate a set of default rules— is vulnerable to the criticism that it grossly oversimplifies the range and variety of relationships to which it purports to apply. For example, the default rules that the Scotts propose with respect to alimony (much like mine) assume a marriage in which there is a fairly sharp division of labor, with the wife devoting most of her time to household production and the husband most of his time to labor-market production. Presumably, many modern marriages do not entail nearly as sharp a division of labor, especially in the case of dual career families. Yet this scarcely warrants a simple or crude binary classification of marriages as either "traditional" or "modern." Large numbers of marriages will fall between these two extremes, with the wife devoting a larger proportion of her time and energy to household production than her husband, but pursuing a part-time or lower intensity career that may pay less and offer fewer promotional or career development possibilities but provide more flexible time, or provide flexibility to the wife in accommodating relocational career decisions by the husband and so forth. My own casual intuition is that perhaps a majority of contemporary marriages fall somewhere between these extremes of complete specialization and no relationship-specific specialization. This substantially complicates the task of designing majoritarian default rules in the first place, or at least applying them to particular marital relationships subsequently. Yet because the Scotts eschew any reliance on fault-based divorce or alimony rules to discourage opportunism or misconduct, their proposed default rules relating to alimony carry most of the weight in performing this role—arguably more weight than they can reasonably be asked to bear.

One possible line of response to this concern is that, whether the authors' proposed default rules are truly majoritarian default rules or not, they are only default rules, leaving open to parties to particular marital relationships the option of contracting out of these default rules and fashioning a set of rules that are specifically adopted to their own relationships. However, the question of under what circumstances and conditions and at which junctures parties would be free to contract out of the proposed default rules, and the related question of whether all of them are optional or whether some of them are mandatory, receives little attention in their essay. However, this is a crucial issue in designing a default regime, and I devote the next section of my comments to it.

II Marriage as a Signal

Much of the recent literature that analyzes or debates recent or proposed family law reforms has focused on their impact on intramarital relations and postmarital consequences, and infirmities or inequalities in bargaining processes surrounding these two phases in a marriage.[2] A good deal less attention has been paid to how the choice of family law regime may affect the premarital context, in particular the search process for a partner. Here, I believe that an undernoticed paper by William Bishop provides a number of important insights which are relevant to the initial choice of default rules, to the question of whether all default rules should be optional or some should be mandatory, and to how the choice to opt out of optional rules should be structured.[3]

Bishop points out that Gary Becker's original economic theory of marriage focused centrally on specialization as the economic foundation of, and motivation for, household formation. However, according to Bishop, this may explain the formation of households but does not explain the institution of marriage. Law-and-economics scholars, beginning with Elizabeth Landes,[4] have relied less on a specialization theory of marriage and more on an investment theory of marriage. To the extent that marriage requires relationship-specific investments, these investments are unlikely to be made unless there is an assurance of a return on the investment. Thus the marriage contract provides this guarantee. If either party wishes to withdraw from the arrangement he or she must be prepared to compensate the other for the lost prospective return, if any. Marriage is thus seen as an implicit contract that requires a default clause (alimony rights) to protect relationship-specific investments.

However, according to Bishop, while specialization in itself only explains households and is consistent with informal unions of any duration that might or might not unite two persons, even the expanded theory of protecting relationship-specific investments is not an entirely satisfactory explanation of marriage. Nonspecialization is very common in the modern family. Very often people marry intending to have no children, or often intending that both continue to pursue independent careers and share in household responsibilities. On either a specialization or investment conception of marriage, in such cases a discharge of the contract by mutual agreement would be instantly and completely effective to end the marriage, as with other contracts. Marriage for a limited period would be recognized. Indeed, there would be no special law of marriage in an obligatory standard form that the individual can only take or leave but not modify. Rather, there would only be the general law of contract.

For Bishop, the most compelling characterization of marriage is not as status or contract but as a signal about a person's preferences toward sexual and social relationships in which he or she may wish to become involved. These preferences are likely to differ widely. Bishop argues that four objectives commonly influence a person's preferences. First, the individual wants a social/sexual partner. Second, he wants the power to decide the length of the term of the relationship, because being dropped by a principal partner of the moment is costly. Third, most people (but by no means all) want sexual loyalty from their principal partner. Fourth, some may want freedom to pursue subsidiary relationships. This list could probably be substantially extended. Some individuals may want to realize economies of scale from operating a common household. Other individuals may want to realize the benefits of specialization of labor (as in Becker's model). Other individuals may want to establish a long-term family environment for the purpose of providing a stable and nurturing upbringing for children.

Bishop refers also to the Omar Sharif utility function, quoting the actor as saying that the reason why he would like to get married was to stop the incessant and intrusive attentions of female admirers. Clearly, individuals' relational preferences vary enormously.

In the market for partners, in theory at least a willingness or unwillingness to marry conveys a signal to prospective partners of the signaler's preferences as to what kind of relationship he or she is seeking. To the extent that marriage as a legal and social institution implies a reasonably well-understood set of commitments, it serves an efficient signaling (information economizing) function in the search, sorting, and matching process for partners (relative to cohabitational or other forms of relationships).

Viewing marriage as performing an important signaling function in the premarital search and sorting market for partners, the question then arises as to why several different types of marriage might not be recognized by the law (for example as Louisiana does with its Covenant Marriage law, although one could easily imagine a much wider menu of options). According to Bishop, one difficulty with such laws is that they attenuate the informational value of marriage. Where there is one marriage law for all, the signal is clear and simple; but with several kinds of marriage the information that must be conveyed to others and assessed by them is more complex. However, Bishop does not acknowledge that a single marriage regime has clear offsetting costs, in that it may induce an inefficient pooling rather than separating equilibrium. For example, if the only marriage regime available is a relatively stringent, mandatory fault-based regime, on a netting out of expected costs and benefits of marriage, many partners may choose to marry, even though they would prefer not to bear the risk of being trapped in an unfulfilling relationship which cannot readily be terminated simply on the grounds that it has broken down. On the other hand, a relatively permissive mandatory marriage regime, like many current no-fault regimes, may also result in an inefficient pooling equilibrium, in that they are likely to embrace both individuals who wish only to make a qualified commitment to their partners and other individuals who are seeking long-term exclusive relationships. Thus the difficult question is posed as to how many marriage regimes are optimal in order to achieve, through their signaling function, efficient separating equilibria. It is important to note at this juncture that a signaling perspective on marriage is entirely agnostic as to what kinds of relationships are socially desirable: it seeks simply to improve the search and sorting process in the market for partners, taking their private preferences as given. Thus it does not depend on broader and contestable normative claims about the centrality of "family values" (whatever these may be taken to embrace) to the social well-being of the community. Whatever kind of relationship makes two people happy, relative to alternative relationships, is the benchmark, and the goal of the legal system is to enhance the matching process by making it easier for individuals with convergent preferences to find each other.

We are, nevertheless, still left with the difficult question of how many signaling mechanisms the legal system should make available to individuals seeking partners, given that, on the one hand, multiple signaling mechanisms may in theory achieve more efficient separating equilibria, but may in fact complicate and obfuscate the informational content of a given signal, and on the other hand that too few signaling mechanisms may result in inefficient pooling equilibria. My own judgment is that the recent wave of family law reforms beginning in the 1960s in most industrialized countries has erred in the latter direction. They have done this in two ways: first, through the adoption of no-fault divorce and alimony regimes, they have attenuated the commitments entailed in marriage; second, cohabitational arrangements outside of marriage of any significant duration have increasingly been assimilated to marriage in terms of the legal commitments entailed, for example, with respect to division of joint assets and support obligations. In short, in terms of legal properties, marital and cohabitational relationships have become closely assimilated to one another.

My own admittedly casual instincts are that, not as a matter of broader social policy about the value of families as a social institution but rather from the narrower perspective of efficient signaling mechanisms in the market for partners, the legal system would facilitate this signaling function better by more sharply differentiating marriage from other forms of cohabitational relationships. This would entail, on the one hand, removing most of the marriagelike legal properties of purely cohabitational relationships, and on the other hand moving to a single and more stringent legally ordained marriage regime, perhaps analogous to the Louisiana Covenant Marriage law. If my proposals were to stop there, this would entail largely a return to the prereform family law era.

However, I do not advocate this, because the binary choice that would be entailed for individuals seeking partners between a relatively stringent marriage regime and a highly permissive cohabitational regime is almost surely poorly adapted to the myriad of preferences of individuals that lie somewhere in between these two alternatives. If we were then to contemplate an additional intermediate option, such as marriage at will (which would largely resemble the current no-fault regime in many jurisdictions), we would then need also to contemplate whether such a regime should carry with it the kind of alimony obligations that the Scotts and I favor at least for traditional marriages with a sharp division of labor, or whether the marriage-at-will option should embrace a "clean break" approach to postmarital financial commitments by one partner to the other. However, such a regime, while still labeled "marriage," would be closely assimilated to nonmarital cohabitational relationships, and insufficient partitioning (as at present) is likely to attenuate the value of marriage as a signal.

Even with respect to the more stringent marriage option, decisions would have to be made as to whether fault should play any role in grounds for divorce or in the award of alimony, or whether the stringency of the regime would largely rest on a lengthy waiting period between marriage breakdown and the availability of divorce and the ability to remarry. However, once we go down this path, it will quickly be appreciated that there are likely to be as many optimal marital and cohabitational regimes as there are individuals with distinctive preferences as to the kinds of relationships they are seeking. Thus the value of marriage as a signal would quickly be lost in the sea of "off the rack" options that the law would make available to parties to choose from.

Hence, I am attracted by the idea of the legal system making available to prospective partners a quite limited set of ex ante options, in order to maximize the signaling value of these options, but subject to a major caveat which the Scotts do not explore in their essay—that is, individualized ex ante and ex post contractual modifications of these regimes. This entails careful analysis of the scope that the legal system should provide for both premarital contracts and postmarital separation agreements. I believe that according a broad scope to individuals to fashion ex ante or ex post contractual modifications to these legally recognized regimes is consistent with the signaling function that marriage serves, in that, particularly in the case of ex ante contractual modifications, the process of contracting itself serves a valuable informational function in conveying information by one prospective partner to another of preferences as to the nature of the relationship each is seeking. Here optional (penalty) default rules serve an important information-forcing function (by way of analogy with the *Hadley v. Baxendale* remoteness rule in contract law). Historically, the law adopted a hostile attitude to the enforceability of premarital contracts, including premarital contracts that purported to stipulate the consequences for the parties on marriage breakdown, and was equally reluctant to become involved in direct enforcement of intramarital obligations provided for in such agreements. Recently, as reflected in the U.S. Uniform Premarital Agreement Act, the law has become much more willing to enforce premarital agreements at least with respect to the consequences of marital breakdown, with the possible exception of custody arrangements pertaining to children. Premarital contracting, while confronting forseeability and excessive optimism problems, exhibits the countervailing virtue of entailing greater equality of bargaining power than either intramarital or postmarital bargaining. The concept of premarital contracts could obviously also be adapted to nonmarital cohabitational arrangements.

The question then becomes whether the scope for contractual modifications of the legally ordained marriage or nonmarriage regimes should be entirely unconstrained. In the case of cohabitational arrangements, which under my proposals would presumptively carry few of the legal characteristics of marriage, I can see no reason why parties to such arrangements should not be able to negotiate ex ante contracts to stipulate for some of the legal incidents of marriage if they so wish (for example, with respect to sharing in joint assets, financial support in the event of termination of the relationship). In the case of modifications to the relatively stringent marriage regime that the legal system might offer as an alternative, suppose that we were to adopt the Scotts' proposed default rules and exclude fault as a relevant element in grounds for divorce or the award of alimony, adopt a substantial stand-down period following marriage breakdown before an individual can obtain a divorce or remarry, and adopt their compensatory alimony proposals. Are there any legitimate objections to allowing parties to premarital contracts to vary features of these default rules? For example, could individuals who are parties to such agreements specify various fault-based grounds for divorce (for example, cruelty, adultery, desertion)? Could they modify the proposed compensatory alimony rules? Could they, conversely, stipulate in effect for a no-fault regime with a "clean break" principle governing postmarital financial commitments by one to the other? In principle, I can see no grounds for objection to permitting any of these kinds of ex ante contractual modifications (and others). These are fully consistent with the signaling theory of marriage, in that the very process of negotiating these modifications conveys valuable information by one prospective partner to the other as to their preferences regarding the relationship in question. Obviously, this information is conveyed at greater cost than simply opting into one of the legally ordained options available to the parties, but nevertheless one must assume that parties to such agreements would not be prepared to incur the transaction and related costs of negotiating such arrangements unless they felt that the benefits of tailoring an arrangement to their particular preferences outweighed the costs.

One might reasonably ask why the legal system should not attempt to reduce these transaction costs for the parties seeking more specifically tailored regimes by offering a whole menu of off-the-rack marriage or cohabitational options. My response to this is that the range of options that would have to be offered in order to meet the myriad of preferences that individuals have as to desired relationships are likely to be such that the legal system is unlikely to achieve any significant savings in transaction costs for the parties in choosing among a comprehensive array of options. Second—and here I introduce for the first time a social perspective on marriage—to the extent that one believes that stable, long-term marriages have any public goods properties, that is, with respect to the welfare of children or the welfare of communities, it seems to me appropriate that the legal system should put a light thumb on the scales by imposing on the parties the transaction and related costs of contracting away from the basic relational options made available by the legal system. In this respect the law can play a modest symbolic or aspirational role in reinforcing or shaping social norms.

A somewhat similar set of issues arise with respect to ex post contractual modifications of the legally recognized marriage regime (under my proposals a single and more stringent marriage regime than the current legal system offers) or premarital contracts that may have been concluded. Suppose, for example, that two partners have initially opted into the legally ordained marriage regime, the marriage fails, and both are now confronted with a substantial stand-down period before they can obtain a divorce or remarry. However, one of the ex-partners has found a new partner and would like to abbreviate this period. Alternatively, the other ex-partner, rather than obtaining a compensatory alimony payment, would prefer to obtain the entire family home (rather than merely a half share in it). Again, in principle, I cannot see any grounds for objections to these kinds of mutually agreed ex post modifications to the marriage bargain. Obviously, because mutual agreement will be required before the ex ante bargain can be modified ex post, the party agreeing to make concessions with respect to features of the ex ante bargain will demand offsetting concessions. Such bargaining will occur in the "shadow of the law"[5]—either the legally ordained marriage option chosen or the premarital contract governing the relationship—and these background default entitlements will clearly shape the ex post contract modification process.

With relatively simple and stark relational options made available by the legal system, complemented by a broad scope for ex ante and ex post contractual modifications of these regimes, I believe that the signaling function of marriage in the search and sorting process in the market for partners is likely to be enhanced.

An important subsidiary issue that the legal system would need to address with respect to this expansive scope for ex ante and ex post contractual modifications of the legally recognized relational regimes is what procedural or substantive protections, if any, should be mandated to protect the integrity of the bargaining processes entailed.[6] Bargaining over premarital contracts may be afflicted by unreflective love, even infatuation. Bargaining over separation agreements may be afflicted by guilt, remorse, anger, or emotional turmoil. With respect to the negotiation of separation agreements, I and my co-author Rosemin Keshvani have previously argued that there may well be a case for mandatory independent legal or other counseling before such agreements are entered into and perhaps a short subsequent cooling off period (for example, sixty days) before they become legally enforceable. Presumably, a similar set of requirements could be imposed on premarital contracts. Perhaps further requirements would need to be considered relating to misrepresentation or nondisclosure of material facts and so forth. In the case of separation agreements, these might be rendered subject to ex post judicial review if an aggrieved party is able to demonstrate that the agreement prima facie generates significantly inferior net benefits to the background entitlements, creating a presumption of unfairness which the other party would bear the burden of rebutting by demonstrating the absence of any of these factors. While I do not offer a fully elaborated set of proposed procedural protections here, it would be folly to assume that a family law regime that accords broad scope to ex ante and ex post contractual modifications of the legally recognized relational options is likely to be legally or politically sustainable without careful attention being paid to the procedural prerequisites of valid relational contracting.

III Conclusion

In focusing, as I have done, on possible mechanisms for improving the search and sorting process in the market for partners, the question might legitimately be asked whether, even if my proposals were effective in this respect, they are likely to mitigate substantially any of the major social pathologies (if that is what they are) of current relationships, such as high divorce rates, many single-parent families, and an increase in the number of children born out of wedlock. I doubt it. It seems to me unlikely that recent family law reforms have been a major contributing factor to these trends or that counter-reforms of the kind that I have proposed—which after all mostly entail a limited extension of the stand-down period—are likely to substantially mitigate them. It is always tempting (and indeed self-aggrandizing) for lawyers to exaggerate the importance of law (or marginal changes in it) in shaping basic patterns of human conduct. Obviously, however, these trends are mostly driven by a broader set of economic, social, psychological, and philosophical changes which recent law reforms in large part reflect rather than motivate. Among these various forces, applying Becker's original insight, the dramatic increase in women's participation in external labor markets, with the concomitant reduction in the returns from specialization of labor within the family (relationship-specific investments), has surely been a significant factor (for better or worse) in reducing the relational surplus and hence the value of marriage as a social institution, reflected in both a lower incidence of marriage in the first place and then a higher rate of exit from unsatisfactory marriages, given lower exit costs. The law, in this respect, is thus working on a very narrow ledge. To the extent that it attempts to prescribe more stringent mandatory commitments as part of the marriage bargain, it will simply induce substitution effects (of indeterminate magnitude) toward other kinds of nonmarital or cohabitational relationships, which the law has never attempted, nor realistically could attempt, to regulate closely (inducing an inefficient separating equilibrium). Thus setting appropriately modest but attainable objectives for this body of law is an implicit premise in my proposals. Facilitating the search and sorting process in the market for prospective partners should play a prominent role in this more modest set of objectives.

Family Law and Social Norms

ERIC A. POSNER

Most of the benefits of marriage can be obtained only in long-term, exclusive relationships, but such relationships are subject to so many contingencies that the marital obligations that would maximize the benefits cannot be specified in advance. If a dispute arises, the complexity of marital relations would overwhelm any effort by a court to determine fault and apply a proper punishment. Yet if people believed that opportunistic behavior during marriages would never be deterred, they would not make the marriage-specific investments necessary to maximize the marital benefits in the first place. Fortunately, "social and relational norms" deter spouses from succumbing to the day-to-day temptations to cheat. The role of the law is limited to enabling potential mates to signal their commitment to each other, and it does this by making termination of the marriage costly to both parties and by supplying default rules that describe the termination arrangements that most parties would choose.

So argue Elizabeth and Robert Scott in their sophisticated and interesting essay "Marriage as a Relational Contract." They further argue that the current system of family law is consistent with their relational theory. But this claim must give one pause. For all the talk of the increasing "privatization" of family law, we are far from a system in which parties are free to contract for any marital arrangement that they want. Aside from the restrictions on termination provisions in prenuptial agreements, potential mates cannot bind themselves legally to marriages in which spouses' domestic, financial, and sharing obligations are specified by contract. Polygamous and same-sex marriages are prohibited. These laws are not default rules, but restrictions on freedom of marital contract, and they strikingly distinguish family law from contract law. A satisfactory theory of family law must account for them.

The Scotts' main theoretical contribution is to emphasize, within an economic framework, the importance of social norms in family relationships and the sensitivity of the law to the existence of these norms. Their use of the concept of the "relational contract" to bring out these themes is useful. But their argument contains many difficulties that require close examination. In particular, although the concepts of the "social norm" and "relational norm" play central roles in the Scotts' argument, they do not use the term "norm" consistently, invoking the concept at different times for different purposes; relatedly, they do not develop a theory of norms; and their assertions about the "power" of norms and the likelihood of judicial error are based on hunches, not evidence. The first problem is correctable, the third problem is unavoidable, but the second problem is serious. Without a fleshed-out theory of norms, an account of the law that relies on norms is likely to be incomplete.

This comment analyzes the Scotts' reliance on theories of social norms. To do so, it draws on a model of marital relationships that I have described elsewhere,[1] but my focus on the Scotts' argument and space limitations will preclude a full defense of my model. Accordingly, the arguments that I present as alternatives to the Scotts' should be considered speculative and suggestive only, as possible approaches to filling the gaps in their discussion.

I   The Role of "Social Norms" in the Scotts' Argument

The concept of the "social norm" has received increasing attention among legal scholars.[2] One reason for this development is that although the importance of social norms for legal issues has long been understood, advances in economics and game theory have enabled a more systematic approach to this difficult topic than had been possible before. But the proper role of economics in understanding law and social norms is controversial, and the scholarship in this area has been confused.

A close reading of the literature reveals two conflicting approaches. The first approach is to treat social norms as exogenous. Followers of this approach sometimes argue, for example, that the reason that parties in a prisoner's dilemma might not cheat is that a social norm deters them from cheating. Social norms are seen as the solutions to the pathologies that would arise when people act in their rational self-interest. This approach, however, does not explain why social norms deter people from cheating. The usual response to this question is that when people violate social norms they feel guilty and they are shamed by the other members of the closely knit groups to which they belong, like families, unions, and religious organizations. No one explains why people feel guilty, or why other people would sanction those who deviate. If the parties in the prisoner's dilemma would not cooperate in the absence of social norms, but the social norms are supplied by the group, who produces and enforces the social norms that enable the group to cooperate in producing social norms? Although the idea that sanctions are more powerful in close-knit groups gives one some analytic purchase, enabling one to argue that behavior changes over time as groups break apart and come together, the idea is too imprecise to provide much insight into the interaction between law and social norms.

The second approach is to treat social norms as endogenous. In a true prisoner's dilemma people do not cooperate, but we observe a great deal of cooperation in the world because the prisoner's dilemma is a poor model of social interaction. Cooperation occurs because people find themselves in repeated prisoner's dilemmas, or in signaling games, or in coordination games, where in equilibrium the payoff from cooperation exceeds the payoff from defection. When we observe the patterns of behavior that emerge in these games, we might say that social norms determine this behavior, but this is not because social norms can adequately be treated as exogenous in analysis. This is just a figure of speech. To say that the seller did not cheat on the contract with the buyer because a social norm deterred him from cheating is just to say, for example, that the seller feared that if he cheated, the buyer or other buyers would refuse to do business with him in the future, resulting in greater discounted long-term losses than the short-term gain from cheating.

The main problem with the second approach is that it relies on theories of strategic behavior that are in their infancy and which, as far as anyone knows, may never emerge from infancy. Even very simple models produce multiple equilibria, and the literature on equilibrium refinements has produced little agreement on how to deal with this problem. Nevertheless, the second approach, carefully handled, enables greater analytic precision than does the first.

Although a few articles consistently follow one approach or the other, most blur them, and the Scotts' essay belongs to this latter category. Their discussion of "relational norms" assumes that such norms arise endogenously from spouses' incentives to cooperate over the long term. Their discussion of "social norms" assumes that social norms are imposed on spouses by outsiders, and does not explain the incentives that outsiders have to develop and enforce these social norms. The different analyses have different implications for understanding the power of norms to coerce individuals, and for understanding whether, and when, norms are desirable. To clear up these difficulties, one needs a clearer understanding of the role of social norms in marital behavior than the Scotts provide.

II   A Model of the Influence of Social Norms on Marital Behavior

One can achieve what the Scotts describe as "the production and rearing of children, sexual intimacy, emotional fulfillment, mutual companionship, the sharing of assets and income, and the provision of care and support (both emotional and financial) in times of need" outside of a legal marriage, indeed in a series of short- or long-term relationships with different people, depending on one's tastes and abilities. Until recently many marriages focused on the production of children and mutual support, while each spouse obtained emotional fulfillment and companionship, and sometimes sexual intimacy, in relationships outside the marriage. Many people today seek companionship in celibate extramarital relationships, sexual intimacy and emotional fulfillment in multiple short-term relationships, care and support from kin and community, even child production on their own or with the assistance of service providers found in the market—whether or not they are at the same time committed to a legal marital relationship. Still, I will assume with the Scotts that the cluster of benefits they identify is a goal of most people at the current time in the United States and that these benefits can be obtained only through a long-term relationship with a single person. Although I will call these benefits the "marital surplus," I assume that the long-term relationship necessary to produce them can be achieved either though a legally sanctioned marriage or through an unsanctioned "informal marriage" or long-term cohabitation.

The marital surplus is the difference between the gains that two people can achieve through a marriage and what they could achieve without having a long-term intimate relationship or by having such a relationship with the next best person. Because the marital goods are collective goods, actions that maximize the marital goods will not be in the self-interest of the spouse who should perform them unless he or she faces sanctions for failing to engage in these actions. I will say that each spouse has an "obligation" to perform these actions, but they face an incentive to violate their obligations. The marital surplus will be generated only if the spouses can be deterred from this kind of shirking. Parties can reduce the chance of marital breakdown by choosing their mates carefully, and sending signals about the kind of partner they would be.

More formally, to obtain the marital surplus, parties must overcome two groups of strategic problems. The first group of problems arises in what can be called the search or courtship stage when men and women choose mates from the relevant population. The second group of problems arises during the relationship stage when each party must cooperate in order to create the marital surplus.

Notice that the obligations that would maximize the value of a marital relationship will vary from couple to couple, and from culture to culture. Different people have different attitudes, for example, over whether a fertile man or woman is obliged to remain married to a sterile partner. Different people and cultures have different expectations about extramarital sexual relationships. "Cheating," then, is defined with reference to the expectations of the parties, as is the case in ordinary contracts; it does not, for example, refer to an extramarital affair if the parties agree that the marriage will be "open." Notice also that "cheating" is not necessarily improper or immoral behavior, as when one party violates a marital obligation in retaliation for the other party's earlier opportunism.

The argument proceeds as follows. The courtship stage is modeled as a signaling game. The relationship stage is modeled as repeat games, involving (a) husband and wife, and (b) the parents (or families) of each spouse, and as a signaling game involving (c) the community. Finally, legal implications are discussed.

To simplify, imagine a society in which men specialize in market activity and women specialize in raising children and in household production. Unmarried people play a signaling game, in which the woman wants to show that she will bear high-quality children and take care of them well, and the man wants to show that he can produce high-quality children and support the household. Both parties want to show that they are generally "cooperative" types, that is, that they have low discount rates; that they are physically and psychologically healthy; and, in addition, the man wants to show that he has good market skills or opportunities. They also want to show each other that they are generally agreeable people. (The model can be straightforwardly extended to interactions in which women also engage in market activity and men also take care of children.)

Signals are actions that distinguish the "good types" from the "bad types." Good types are those with better physical and psychological endowments, with greater wealth, and with lower discount rates. The low discount rate is crucial. As the Scotts argue, and as I discuss in the next section, the marital relationship is best modeled as a repeat game. Repeat games are most likely to produce cooperative gains if both parties care about future payoffs relative to current payoffs. Thus a good marriage partner is a person who has a low discount rate.[3]

During the courtship stage people signal in an effort to show that they are good types and not bad types.[4] Some actions will separate the good types from the bad, because only the good types can afford to engage in them. But because of uncertainty and exogenous changes, actions that once created separation might no longer, yet everyone will continue to engage in them, for fear that failing to engage in an action will cause others to infer that one is a bad type. This "pooling," in which people engage in costly actions that do not distinguish anyone from anyone else, causes the good types to search for new actions that will enable them to distinguish themselves from the bad types.

It is useful to discuss quickly some of the typical signals of courtship. One of the salient features of courtship is the long period during which the two people must confine their attentions to each other and ignore everybody else. This period of exclusivity is a straightforward signal that (1) a person has a low discount rate and (2) the person is committed to the proclaimed object of desire, rather than to someone else.

Another important feature of courtship is gift giving, culminating (in some times and places) in an expensive engagement ring. Gifts also serve as signals of commitment.[5] They signal that (1) the donor has a low discount rate, and so will sacrifice assets for the sake of long-term opportunities; (2) the donor has invested time and effort to learn the tastes of the donee; and (3) the donor is wealthy, and thus will be able to support the donee. However, the latter point must be understood carefully: if a donor is sufficiently wealthy, an expensive gift does not commit him as much as an identical gift from a poorer donor. A millionaire can afford to give diamond rings to a dozen paramours; a poor person can afford to give a diamond ring only to one person, so that if this gift is a necessary condition of marriage, only that poor person effectively binds himself to the donee. An expensive gift, then, is a credible signal of commitment only if the donee knows that the donor is not rich. This is not a problem only if the donor's wealth is known.

Related to gift giving is conspicuous consumption. Conspicuous consumption allows the suitor to show his or her wealth and taste. Wealth is valued because it means that the suitor will be able to support the household. Taste is valued because a person with good taste is a person who is perceptive about community norms (see below).

Suitors cannot show in advance that they are fertile. They can, however, signal that they are healthy, which is a good in itself, and which may be evidence that the suitor is fertile. Men and women signal their healthiness by engaging in sports and other vigorous pursuits.

Celibacy can be a signal of commitment, but so can sex. A man's lengthy and celibate courtship of a woman may be a signal of his interest in a long-term relationship; however, a woman's willingness to engage in premarital sex can be a signal of her commitment to the man if she thereby risks becoming pregnant and dependent. (Unprotected sex is an even more reliable signal.) Premarital sex is also a way for partners to show that they are healthy and able to engage in sex, and that they find each other mutually attractive. But how can the man signal his commitment by remaining celibate with a woman who signals her commitment by engaging in sex? Sex would have to occur after a delay but before a binding commitment.[6]

These signals, then, are typical of courtship. As noted, they are not necessarily successful. Pooling can arise in which the signals fail to distinguish the cooperators from the cheaters. Don Juans and Casanovas succeed not just by being sexually attractive, but by deceiving their victims through the manipulation of signals. Lavish gifts and exclusive attention persuade the victim that they seek a long-term relationship.

Signaling is important because when it succeeds, it establishes that future mates share similar interests, resulting in relatively little conflict during the marriage; and it establishes that the future mates have low discount rates: they care enough about the future that they are unlikely to cheat early in the relationship for the sake of short-term gains. The second point bears emphasis: both parties expect to enter a repeat game after they are married; repetition can solve prisoner's dilemmas only if both parties care enough about the future; so a reliable signal of a partner's low discount rate is an important indication that marriage is worthwhile.

I go on at such length because the best interpretation of the marriage vow is as a signal of one's long-term commitment, that is, one's low discount rate and one's sharing of interests with the potential mate. A vow to remain in a long-term intimate relationship does not serve as a signal if it is costless: what makes it costly is (a) that violation of the vow might destroy one's reputation as a reliable person, leading to ostracism from the community; and (b) that violation of the vow will lead to legal penalties if a legal regime exists. Neither of these costs is necessarily higher than the other, and neither is necessarily higher than the loss of time, effort, and wealth that results from the other forms of signaling: an expensive gift, for example, might more effectively bind the donor to the recipient than a legally or socially enforceable wedding vow. In determining the optimal marriage law, one must take account of all the substitute forms of signaling, because a change in the legal penalty for violation of the marriage vow will not make it easier or harder for parties to capture the marital surplus if near substitutes are available.

NONLEGAL ENFORCEMENT BY HUSBAND AND WIFE

A variety of nonlegal mechanisms deter shirking during the relationship stage. One form of sanctioning comes directly from husband and wife. As the Scotts argue, the marital relationship can be modeled as a repeat prisoner's dilemma, in which each spouse deters the other from cheating by threatening to punish any transgression of the marital obligations. One strategy might be tit-for-tat: each spouse "cheats" in response to cheating by the other spouse in an earlier round. The husband fails to come home on time; the wife refuses to agree to the vacation he wants. The wife withholds some of her income from the household; the husband starts staying out late with friends. To avoid retaliation, spouses do not cheat. Information problems complicate the interaction, however. Parties may disagree about what counts as cheating, or whether an instance of cheating really occurred. Discussions, arguments, and threats may resolve these issues prior to any real punishments. From these interactions the marital obligations emerge (recall that they cannot be specified in advance), always subject to change in light of new circumstances. "Relational norms" are best understood as these marital obligations, although the Scotts use the term in different ways (for example, to refer to reciprocity, which is just a feature of the tit-for-tat strategy and similar strategies that might emerge in equilibrium.)

Nothing in the theory of repeat games would lead one to believe that this form of sanctioning is inevitably successful or even likely to be successful at enabling the parties to capture the potential marital surplus. There are many problems.

First, as the Scotts recognize, when outside opportunities change in certain ways no strategy can maintain the relationship. For example, one spouse acquires an advanced degree, which greatly increases his or her future income, and abandons the other spouse. Everything that the abandoned spouse could withhold from the relationship is less valuable to the cheater than the opportunities afforded by the new relationship he or she enters.

Second, even when outside opportunities are low, strategic failures to coordinate will prevent the parties from obtaining the full potential marital surplus. The Scotts recommend tit-for-tat, and, indeed, if both parties choose tit-for-tat, they will create the full marital surplus; but if one party chooses tit-for-tat and the other party chooses tit-for-tat-except-cheat-on-the-first-move, they will obtain nothing. Theory and common experience teach that people do not always choose the same strategies: some people forgive easily, others never forgive; some people cheat every once in a while, some cheat as often as they can, some never cheat. The Scotts assert that the tit-for-tat strategies in a repeat game will cause "lock-in," leading to pure cooperation or complete breakdown. This assertion allows the Scotts to claim that any relationship that survives is going to do extremely well, so legal intervention is not necessary for any marriage that survives. But the Scotts do not explain how lock-in works, and in the absence of such an explanation one must assume that most (all?) marriages suffer from varying but always suboptimal levels of cooperation. Whether the law can improve on this is another question, but the question should be kept separate.

Third, in the absence of perfect information the possibility of suboptimal cooperation becomes significant. When noise causes interpretive mistakes, tit-for-tat is dominated by more generous strategies, but these strategies also create new opportunities for exploitation.[7] Parties might respond to information problems by sending each other signals. Such a strategy is more complex than generous tit-for-tat, requiring parties to engage in actions that are individually costly as a way of signaling to their partners that they remain committed to the relationship. An example is the exchange of gifts at holidays and anniversaries even though the parties share their assets.[8] Because neither party knows what the other party would most prefer to a portion of the existing stock of household cash, each inevitably buys the other a gift that fails to optimize the joint value of the relationship. In addition, as mentioned earlier, signaling can lead to pooling, in which the parties spend resources without revealing additional information about their degree of commitment, and this is an additional cost to the relationship.

Another way for spouses to mitigate information problems is by dividing obligations and rewards in certain ways. Suppose a husband and wife jointly work and jointly take care of the child in shifts. The problem is that each partner cannot observe and evaluate the actions of the other. One spouse does not know whether the other works hard enough in the market and cares for the child with adequate attention. If the husband is fired, he can blame the firing on his boss's unreasonableness when in fact it was his own shirking on the job. He did not work hard because he knew that he could rely on his wife's wages in case he were caught shirking and fired. If the husband watches television with his child rather than taking care of the child in a more active way, the wife may not observe the effects of this inattentiveness for years. This moral hazard problem affects both parties: each may shirk both in household and in market production because he or she shares the residual with the other spouse.

The traditional family may be considered a solution to this joint moral hazard problem, as the Scotts suggest.[9] The wife specializes in household production, and the husband specializes in market production. The wife does not shirk because she bears the full consequences of bad parenting: if the child is in a bad mood the next day because she put it to bed late, then she, not her husband, bears the consequences. The husband does not shirk at work because if he is fired, he cannot rely on his wife's wages. These considerations might account for the relative stability of the traditional family over time and its appearance in different cultures (but not the usual assignment of household obligations to women), and also the current failure of the ideal of perfect equality between the sexes, where both participate equally in the market and in household production.

But the traditional family is highly unsatisfactory in the modern era, and one can detect new responses to the moral hazard problems that do not condemn spouses to traditional roles but that also do not conform with the ideal of perfect equality. The armchair anthropologist of the mating rituals of American middle-class young adults will detect three trends: the rise of the "sensitive male," the increasing respectability of part-time or low-intensity careers for educated women, and the gradual decline of the stigma against the "house husband." The last two trends suggest a return to the division of labor in the household, but less extreme than before and perhaps less dependent on traditional sex roles; thus spouses recapture the advantages of the traditional marriage, where each has more or less exclusive authority over one aspect of the household and both incur the costs and enjoy the residual benefits that are associated with their spheres of authority. The first trend suggests that men are promising in return to take more child care responsibility and have a closer relationship to their children. Women are demanding more altruistic men than they did in the past; because women have higher opportunity costs of staying home, they want men to commit to some child care, and altruism commits men to engage in some child care. Naturally altruistic men, who had to suppress their altruism under the old system, profess their sensitivity and no doubt demonstrate it during the courtship; and now less altruistic men must mimic the more altruistic men during the courtship stage in order to avoid rejection. Having committed themselves to be sensitive males ex ante, even nonaltruists may suffer reputational sanctions if they fail to be sensitive ex post. It is not clear whether this new arrangement will be stable: there are advantages to both sides and disadvantages.[10]

So information problems and strategic opportunities within a relationship, and the high-value opportunities outside a relationship, all pose a threat to the stability of marriages. To protect themselves, men and women engage in signaling at the courtship stage; and husband and wife take on roles that minimize information problems while allowing each to deter opportunism through the threat of retaliation. However, there are additional nonlegal sanctions, beyond those in the power of husband and wife, that help deter opportunistic behavior.

NONLEGAL ENFORCEMENT BY THE HUSBAND'S AND WIFE'S FAMILIES

Historically, the parents of husband and wife have played a larger role in deterring opportunistic behavior than they do in modern American society. This was true both at the search stage, in which the families might arrange marriages or at least cull respectable mates from the pool, and at the relationship stage, in which the parents of one spouse would provide protection for him or her and would retaliate against the other spouse when that person engaged in opportunistic behavior. Most significantly, parents can influence the behavior of their children and their spouses by distributing wealth to the household or withholding it. It remains true today that parents sometimes threaten to refuse to pay their children's college tuition if the children do not break off relationships they do not like (often on religious grounds). Striking examples of parental influence can be found today in India.

At first sight, one might wonder what is added through the parents' participation. It might appear that instead of having a repeat game between the relatively poor husband and wife, one has a repeat game between the relatively wealthier parents of each. But increasing the endowments of two players in a repeat prisoner's dilemma does not, by itself, increase the chances of cooperation and may reduce them.

One advantage of parental involvement is that parents have better information than their children about potential mates, including their wealth, their skills, the advantages of their family connections, and their reliability. Parents usually have better judgment, as a result of age, and it is not clouded by emotion. They might foresee future conflicts, for example, over the rearing of the grandchildren, that their besotted children do not anticipate.

Another advantage of parental involvement arises when the spouses have unequal endowments: the parents of the poorer spouse can provide leverage in household disputes. If one spouse has greater outside opportunities, the other spouse might not be able to deter cheating through tit-for-tat and similar strategies; but if the latter spouse's parents can bring pressure on the first spouse, the relationship can be maintained. A person might be deterred from cheating by the prospect of gifts and, eventually, a bequest from the spouse's parents.

A more interesting advantage of parental involvement is that parents have longer time horizons than their children do when the children are at a marriageable age. Most adults invest in a reputation as responsible members of the community. The "family name" becomes a kind of trademark associated with reliability. They might want to transfer this reputational advantage to their children for several reasons: because they care about their children, because they want their children to be wealthy enough to support them when they are old, and because they want their children to maintain the family name. Indeed, the "family," like a corporation, might be considered an immortal (or at least, indefinitely long-lived) institution that solves the end-game problem by giving every member an incentive to maintain the family reputation. Parents try to restrain their children's romantic and sexual impulses, and encourage them to make marriage choices based on the wealth and status of the potential partner.

The disadvantages of parental involvement are numerous. History, theory, and common experience contradict the Scotts' assumption that parents' and children's interests are aligned. Parents care about themselves and about their children. Otherwise, few parents would maintain leverage over their children by retaining wealth until their deaths, and would instead purchase an annuity and give their children, while still young adults, the excess over what the parents will need for the remainder of their lives. Parents might be more concerned about the way the family name supports their interests than their children's relationships. By promising bribes or threatening punishment, they might force their child to marry someone who is not a good partner but would be a good ally for the parents. The tension between parents and children in this respect culminated in the frequent practice in early modern Europe of clandestine marriages, and, since then, elopement.

Parents frequently try to educate or prepare their children so that they do well at the search stage, without taking account of how well they do during the relationship. This may be due to the fact that parents obtain payoffs from their children's relationship at an earlier stage in that relationship than the children do. A "good marriage" redounds immediately to the benefit of the family name, leaving the children to bear the consequences of a loveless relationship. For example, parents have frequently kept information about sex from their daughters in order to suppress their curiosity and deter experimentation prior to marriage. This allows the daughters to enjoy a reputation as a "good type" during the courtship stage, but leaves them ill-prepared for the sexual demands of the relationship.

Another form of nonlegal enforcement comes from "strangers," by which I mean people who are not related by birth or marriage to the husband and wife in question, but who do have some information about them (through direct observation or gossip), and have the option of socializing or doing business with them, on the one hand, or ostracizing them, on the other. Thus strangers are likely to belong to the same community, except to the extent that the behavior of the husband and wife are publicized more broadly. For example, an unfaithful husband who is later appointed to an important government position might be sanctioned by the press and opposed by the public when his behavior comes to light.

Nonlegal enforcement by the community is, historically, of considerable importance. The most striking examples come from "charivari," where gangs of local youths and young adults would harass people whose behavior violated community norms, including norms against marriages between people of different ages or status, against wife beating and husband beating, and against adultery. Authorities generally tolerated this behavior before powerful governments came into existence.[11]

Efforts to model community enforcement as an n-person prisoner's dilemma have produced little success. A more promising approach is to model it as an n-person game in which people signal their loyalty to each other by engaging in costly, observable actions. Just as potential mates signal to each other their reliability as cooperative partners, so do members of the community signal to other members their reliability as cooperative partners. Signaling is a way of establishing a reputation: if I do those things that reliable people do (go to school, join the right church, work hard all day, support the local establishment), and unreliable people find these activities too costly, I will be sought out as a cooperative partner and I earn returns covering my costs over the long term. One signal of reliability is participation in (costly) nonlegal punishment of deviants who threaten or appear to threaten the community. The problem of free-riding is partly overcome by everyone's desire to reveal that he is a cooperative type.[12] Notice that people will also marry in order to signal to the community (not just to each other) that they are reliable types.

If formal marriage serves to deflect suspicions about one's reliability as a member of a community, then in equilibrium people might believe that those who marry by a certain age are good types and those who do not marry by a certain age are bad types. Their attitudes will be revealed in many ways, some subtle, some not. The unmarried might be less sought after as business or social partners; they might be considered "defective" in a vague sort of way. To avoid these inferences about themselves, everyone or almost everyone might marry even if they expect the marital surplus (as defined earlier) to be negligible. It is also possible, however, that in equilibrium many people will not get married, and marriage will not be a signal of type.

Community enforcement can be more or less effective. It can be effective because communities, like families and corporations, have longer time horizons than individuals do. People in the community care about how well parents raise their children, because they have to deal with the consequences over a longer time period than the parents do. A child of an illegitimate relationship may become a burden on the community. In addition, community enforcement can be effective because members of the community may have good information about the behavior of married couples.

Community enforcement becomes less effective when people can easily exit the community, or it is difficult to observe people's behavior, or to communicate detected transgressions. It becomes less effective when members of the community have heterogeneous values. All of this is familiar. More seriously, the signaling analysis suggests that individuals interested in showing their loyalty to the community will punish anyone who can plausibly, or even just momentarily, be thought to be a threat to the community. Gossip and ostracism are directed against anyone who behaves in an unusual way, and through feedback effects, people who are not guilty of any harm may be severely punished. Signaling can lead to spiraling violence and can be exploited by bad types out for private gain,[13] including those who feel resentment at good marriages. One way to draw attention to one's attack on an alleged deviant is to do so in an entertaining way, for if other people do not observe one's punishment of a deviant, this action does not serve as a signal of one's loyalty to the community. This is why charivari involved mockery, parody, music, gaming, and other festive elements associated with carnival. These elements draw observers and participants, overcoming the problem of collective action. But if punishment is fun, it may be initiated for its own sake, not because the victim deserves to be punished.

Communities have less control today over the family relationships of its members than in the past, but they still have much control. Politicians pay a heavy price when they violate ordinary family norms, and no doubt less visible people do as well. In academia, the obloquy heaped on academics who propose unconventional theories, or who violate the current standards of personal and professional conduct, stands in striking contrast to academics' self-image as rational and tolerant truth-seekers. But informal systems of social control always exhibit such pathologies.

III   The Law

The discussion so far can be thought of as a way of unpacking the Scotts' claims about the role of nonlegal sanctions, or "social and relational norms." It shows that (1) there are many sources of nonlegal constraint on marital opportunism;

(2) each source follows a different logic and therefore may respond to legal interventions in a different way; and (3) each source produces pathologies as well as advantages. Notice that social norms are endogenous to games in which people maximize their interests through cooperation. I have avoided discussion of internalization not because it does not exist, but because it would not add anything useful to the analysis. The question now is whether the analysis of social norms helps one understand divorce law.

The Scotts argue that the hypothetical marital bargain would restrict divorce. For a traditional family, where H works and W raises the children and takes care of the home, a termination rule might require a two-year waiting period after which H must pay alimony to W. The two-year waiting period deters W from opportunistically suing for divorce, as does the limitation of alimony to, say, support. The alimony requirement deters H from opportunistically suing for divorce. By making the divorce costly, the law gives each party a powerful weapon for retaliating when the other acts opportunistically. For a dual-earner family, an alimony rule makes little sense, but the two-year waiting period could deter some opportunistic divorces. Notice that the law does not itself punish the opportunist, for the Scotts assume that courts cannot verify fault.

The Scotts' argument here recalls the signaling model. H commits himself to W by marrying her, because if he subsequently divorces her, he incurs significant costs. If H were not interested in W or had a high discount rate, he would not send this signal. But if H and W anticipate a dual-earner family, the two-year termination provision would hardly seem to impose much of a cost on either party. H and W can both pursue intimate relationships with other people during the termination period; they can even have, with these other people, children no longer stung by the stigma of illegitimacy as in the past; they are only restricted from a subsequent formal marriage within those two years. Yet it is quite possible that H and W face as deep a commitment problem ex ante as they would in a traditional household. So the signal is too cheap, and ineffective.

The Scotts' response to this argument is that the law should make available a menu of options to the parties. If a two-year waiting period is insufficient, then the parties can choose a five- or ten-year waiting period. The logic of their argument carries the Scotts further than they want to go, however. Why shouldn't the parties be able to choose a no-termination rule? The Scotts respond that parties are not competent enough to choose such a rule, but this argument explains too much. Lacking any principle for distinguishing terms only incompetent people would choose from those that competent people would choose, one could justify any restriction on the marital contract or none. But competency to choose terms is not the issue anyway. Competent parties could agree to a contract that said that upon divorce each party had to pay half his or her future lifetime wages to the government or to a charity. They could no doubt agree to stranger contracts: marriages in which, say, only spousal abuse but not extramarital affairs are grounds for termination; or marriages in which one spouse is permitted two illegitimate children and the other spouse is permitted none. They could agree to a marriage contract anticipating a traditional household in which the woman must pay the man if he decides to divorce her. Any of these contracts could be chosen by competent parties who seek to overcome commitment problems.

Rather than supplying default rules and allowing parties to contract around them, marriage law offers a basket of immutable obligations and forbids almost any deviation from it. The long history of restrictions on marital contracts includes restrictions on sex before marriage and outside of existing marriages (including laws against fornication, adultery, and bigamy, and penalties inflicted on illegitimate children); mandatory rules governing divorce, distribution of property, and authority over children; and rules governing the authority within marriage over property. What is crucial is not the content of the rules, which the Scotts would presumably treat (and reject) as possible default rules, but the fact that they are not default rules, but, for the most part, mandatory. Enough of these rules linger in modern times, and the sentiment behind them remains strong enough, that any satisfactory theory of marriage law must confront them.

I do not have a complete explanation for these phenomena, but let me suggest a few possibilities, all of which require further work.

(1) The restrictions on freedom of marital contract make the formal marriage contract focal, facilitating community enforcement. Imagine that there were no restrictions, and I could have four "marriages" with four women, who perhaps are also married with other people, and I could have children with all four women; or in a single marriage my spouse and I could agree that she may have two extramarital affairs and I may neglect the children. Put aside the interests of the children for the moment, and suppose that one can credibly commit to any one of the relationships in the first place only if community enforcement deters opportunism. The problem is that the existence of multiple or idiosyncratic relationships might be so confusing to the members of the community that community enforcement becomes impossible. Whereas an extramarital affair counts as opportunism in a traditional household, and quickly and easily calls for community sanctions, it does not count as opportunism in my household if my spouse and I have permitted a certain number of affairs in our contract. The members of the community cannot be expected to know enough about our marriage agreement to be able to determine whether any particular action violates the agreement. They need a standard form marriage against which to measure mine, so that it knows what counts as opportunism. Marriage can serve as a signal of commitment only if community members deter opportunism, but community members can deter opportunism only if the actions that count as opportunistic are common to all marriages.[14]

(2) The restrictions on freedom of marital contract, by making the formal mar-

riage contract focal, facilitates legal intervention. This argument presupposes that the Scotts' assumption of nonverifiability is false. On the contrary, the purpose of requiring a marriage license and standardizing the marriage contract is to establish certain verifiable actions as a violation of the marriage contract. Under the old fault system, adultery but not emotional coldness constituted grounds for divorce. In a real marriage it is quite possible that an instance of adultery would be forgivable but emotional coldness over the long term would not. Still, one might argue that on average adultery constitutes a violation of the marital bargain whereas emotional coldness does not; or that adultery usually cannot be deterred by the victim through retaliation whereas emotional coldness usually can. If so, legal punishment of adultery but not of emotional coldness would deter opportunism more effectively than legal deference to all forms of marital opportunism.[15]

(3) The restrictions on freedom of marital contract prevent parents from abandoning or neglecting their children. The problem with extramarital and premarital affairs, and with divorce, is that they result in children whose parents (one or both) prefer starting a new household to taking care of them. Restrictions on the marriage contract do not, on this theory, necessarily serve the interests of the parents; they serve the interests of children or authorities who are responsible for supporting unwanted children.[16]

(4) The restrictions on freedom of marital contract promote equality in the marriage market—either between men and women or between high-status and low-status people of the same sex. The restrictions, for example, forbid formal polygamous marriages and discourage de facto polygamy (for example, men keeping mistresses). In polygynous relationships women must share the marital surplus with each other and with the man, resulting in great inequality. Polygynous relationships also deprive low-status men of wives. Some historical evidence suggests that restrictions on such relationships arose in part at the behest of civil and religious authorities that were trying to win the support of ordinary people. The latter resented the powerful aristocrats who took concubines from the pool of marriageable lower-class women. The Scotts' assumption that the purpose of family law is to enable parties to maximize the marital surplus prevents them from accounting for laws that are designed to equalize shares of the marital surplus rather than to maximize them.[17]

(5) Strict divorce laws might have been justified at a time when parents had great control over who their children married. Suppose that children at marriageable age have poor judgment and lack the self-control needed to overcome sexual passion and to evaluate a potential partner soberly. If divorce and cohabitation laws are strict, people will make and be unable to leave bad marriages. But if parents control their children's marriages—perhaps through a legal consent requirement or through their control over the children's future wealth—then they may ensure that children make desirable marriages. Strict divorce and re-

strictions on extramarital relationships, then, might serve as a commitment mechanism after the parents' influence wanes. An analogy can be found in the restrictions on loans to expectant heirs, who are tempted to use their expectancies as collateral for loans that finance their youthful dissipation. However, marital restrictions might also have reflected nonaltruistic efforts by parents to maintain control over their children.[18]

Notice that each of these five theories justifies a strict divorce law but also requires restrictions on near substitutes for legal marriage. If the termination rules are too severe, people will not marry but cohabit and have illegitimate children,[19] or they will have adulterous relationships. Each theory therefore justifies laws against premarital fornication, adultery, bigamy, and polygamy, and also laws punishing illegitimate children as a means of deterring extramarital sex. In addition, the first two theories explain the refusal of the law to enforce idiosyncratic sharing arrangements and obligations within marriages. The third theory may explain restrictions on inheritance and gift giving.

The Louisiana covenant statute will probably not have a substantial effect on marital arrangements, nor would a more aggressive statute that provided a menu of options, as advocated by the Scotts. Unless the legislature also decides to crack down on adultery and illegitimacy, "covenant marriages" will not be significantly more costly than ordinary marriages, because parties can substitute informal marriages (that is, adulterous relationships) if their covenant marriage becomes unsatisfactory.[20] One might argue that the community will punish people who violate covenant marriages, but community enforcement depends on clear signals. Even if the community were willing to punish people who violate marriage covenants, it could do so only if it knows whether a particular marriage was a covenant marriage or not. But people with casual knowledge of the marriage will not know what kind of marriage it is, and there is no opportunity for a courtlike proceeding in which the victimized spouse proves to the community that the marriage was a covenant marriage. For community enforcement, there would have to be different kinds of wedding ceremonies establishing different levels of commitment, with each ceremony being different enough to make an impression on observers and to allow them to remember the level of commitment. But one suspects that simply knowing whether a couple is married or not exhausts the recollective capacities of the public. Because covenant marriage will be no more binding than ordinary marriage, they will not be more effective signals of commitment than ordinary marriages.

IV Conclusion

The Scotts properly emphasize social norms in their discussion of family law, but further progress in understanding family law requires greater precision in the analysis of these complex phenomena. I have provided a rough sketch of the directions that such an analysis might take, focusing on the Scotts' arguments about divorce law. As an aside, it should be noted that the theory of social norms that I have described casts doubts on other elements of the Scotts' discussion, especially their conclusion that the law should not intervene in intramarital disputes.[21] Let me conclude with some speculation about the positive and normative implications of my arguments.

Positive. What is striking about trends in marital behavior is their discontinuity: the sudden change in attitudes over the last thirty years, attitudes that had been relatively constant for decades and even centuries earlier. The rapidity of the change suggests the existence of feedback mechanisms. When beliefs and behavior are self-reinforcing, they will be stable over time; but a severe exogenous shock (or an accumulation of exogenous shocks) may cause them to collapse. Thus, to understand family behavior and family law, one must look at such things as (1) how an increase in earning power affects a woman's strategies in a marital relationship with a man, and the effect of those strategies on the equilibrium. If this has made marriage less attractive for men or for women, then, as marriage became less popular, it may have become a less effective signal of reliability as a partner, resulting in the collapse of a separating equilibrium. One must also look at (2) why parents exert less control over their adult children than they used to, and the interaction of this trend and the marital equilibrium. Parents are increasingly bequeathing wealth to their children in the form of education while the children are still young rather than in the form of assets upon the parents' death. There may be many reasons for this, and one possible consequence is decreasing parental control of children, with the result that children may more likely enter ill-advised, unsustainable marriages than in the past. And one must look at (3) whether (and why) the community exerts less control over members than it used to, and whether changes in community participation influence the marital equilibrium. The standard story is that increasing market opportunities draw people away from the communities into which they were born; but does this mean that new communities have less control over people because the latter are newcomers or transients, or that they have more, because people have a stronger incentive to signal their reliability when dealing with relative strangers?

Normative. The "privatization of family law" is said to consist of the increasing replacement of status with contract (ignoring the fact that medieval marriages were far more contractual than modern marriages). Let me suggest a more literalistic interpretation, namely, the increasing exclusion of the crowd from participation in the regulation of the family. There are two issues here: (a) whether people should be able to enter and have enforced idiosyncratic marriages; and (b) who should enforce those marriages. We might condemn the historic involvement of the community and even of parents in their children's marital choices, on the ground that essentially arbitrary and sometimes dysfunctional mechanisms for promoting the solidarity of the community result in hardship for people with idiosyncratic tastes and needs, and even for complete innocents, such as illegitimate children. Fear of the crowd has always induced conformity and although the prospect of shame and ostracism has discouraged some obvious breaches of marital relationships, such as desertion and abuse, there is no reason to believe that it maximizes the marital surplus. The gradual replacement of social and parental sanctions with legal sanctions may have reflected a preference for the order and precision of the judicial bureaucracy, to the pathologies of the crowd. The law might reflect the values and interests of the crowd, but legal enforcement is fundamentally different from (and, I would argue in this context, better than) social enforcement. And if courts cannot identify marital opportunism very well, perhaps because the distance that enables them to be objective also disables them from understanding the facts of particular marital disputes, then the decreasing strength of the marital bond might be thought a reasonable price for the increase in privacy, autonomy, and individual welfare.

If enhancing the effectiveness of community enforcement of marriages is undesirable, then one might think that the only alternative is to increase the strictness of divorce laws. But making divorce law stricter, whether or not at the option of the parties, will not by itself increase marital surpluses. Stricter divorce laws will not necessarily cause people to engage in more careful search and more binding commitment; instead, such laws would likely cause people (ex ante) to delay marriage, cohabit, and produce illegitimate children, or (ex post), having married, to enter adulterous relationships and produce illegitimate children. To change behavior substantially, the state would have to launch a full-scale assault against all the near substitutes of marriage, and this would mean bringing back archaic penalties on fornication, adultery, illegitimacy, serial polygamy. Given the popular indifference to these behaviors, and the powerful interests that support them, a successful legal intervention—one that encouraged marriage, deterred cohabitation and illegitimacy, discouraged divorce, and maximized the marital surpluses—would have to be dramatic and highly coercive. This would be neither desirable nor possible.

Contracting around No-Fault Divorce

MARGARET F. BRINIG

The growing feeling that no-fault divorce has spawned substantial social problems set the stage for the movement toward what Louisiana has recently enacted as covenant marriage.[1] Attacks on no-fault have been mounted before, and have always been unsuccessful. Advocates of free contracting can learn at least two things from these earlier trials. Expanding free contracting in marriage will require legislation protecting helpless members of society and will pose particular challenges for conflicts of law.

The Louisiana legislation does not revoke no-fault divorce laws. For couples who elect an easy exit, unilateral divorce will still be possible after six months. However, for those who wish to enter into a covenant marriage after counseling and an explicit waiver of no-fault, barriers to divorce are strengthened. Divorce will be permitted only on the traditional fault grounds for divorce: adultery, physical or sexual cruelty to the other spouse or the child of either or both, and imprisonment at hard labor for a felony, plus separation for eighteen months. For less serious marital problems, permanent separation (called a bed and board separation) remains available.[2] The covenant marriage is also available for Louisiana couples who are already married.

Even though the divorce rules for Louisiana covenant marriages are not dramatically different from the existing no-fault rules, the idea of precommitment to a more stringent regime has sparked enormous interest. Like the Scotts, I support covenant marriages. But I might give greater weight to the moral forces at work in family law. I would not allow free contracting in the direction away from responsibility to dependents, whether homemaker spouses, aged relatives, or children.

Covenant marriage will lead to greater investment in the sorts of things that make marriages better but that are bad investments in the less permanent world of no-fault. It should promote more marital autonomy (freedom from state regulation while marriage continues), while permitting enforcement of whatever contracts the couple wishes to make.[3] As a bonding device, covenant marriages would help the parties to commit to better marital behavior.[4] A precommitment to a more lasting marriage frees each spouse to participate fully for the common good. As William Murchison has written, "Here is commitment in the fullest sense: It frees in the instant it binds. If the marriage vow forecloses quick escape from the relationship, so it affords freedom from gnawing anxiety, gained from the knowledge that one's partner is similarly bound. In such an environment mutual trust can grow: We are in this together."[5]

Covenant marriage should foster the kind of permanence that would allow more specific investments in the marriage.[6] This would include not only children but also investments in childless marriages, such as "human capital" investments in advanced degrees. In 1994 Steven Crafton and I noted that the divorce revolution had also produced considerable litigation involving investments in the other spouse's education that were not realized before the marriage dissolved.[7] We posited that the tremendous increase in litigation involving professional degrees was not coincidental but resulted from no-fault divorce. A spouse whose education has been subsidized by his partner has an incentive to seek a divorce on graduation, unless his opportunism is sanctioned by a penalty. Covenant marriages would bind the spouses together more closely and give them stronger incentives to invest in the marriage. This will strengthen the marriage and reduce the temptation to divorce.

Covenant marriage also makes law coextensive with emotional realities. Elsewhere I have argued that law occasionally pretends to cut off relationships that are destined, for biological or emotional reasons even more than financial ones, to be lifetime commitments.[8] Where children are involved, parents carry a shared interest in their offspring regardless of their legal status. Even when coparenting is no longer the issue, lives may become so intertwined (through what Gary Becker would call specific investments in the marriage)[9] that a "clean break" divorce is not really possible. Covenant marriage officially recognizes that marriages are lifetime commitments.

Against this, it is sometimes objected that informational handicaps will prevent couples from making wise choices over divorce options. Lynn Baker and Robert Emery[10] have shown that most couples, even those seeking marriage licenses, do not know much about marriage and divorce law, and are overly optimistic about the chances for their own marriage. Baker and Emery found, however, that the engaged couples did know the statistics on divorce. The couples' confidence is characteristic not only of marriage agreements, but of the many long-term relational contracts that courts enforce every day, and therefore it should not be a barrier to marriage precommitment contracts.

Another type of information problem is described in the important article by Becker, Landes, and Michael.[11] These economists note that marriages entered into when the parties could not complete an optimal search for a new partner are often unstable. Such hasty marriages, which tend to break up within the first couple of years, often include those in which the woman is already pregnant or has one or more minor children from a previous relationship, or those in which the couple has religious or racial differences. But since the Louisiana couples are required to have counseling before covenanting to marry, much of the problem should diminish, especially for couples past college age.

A related objection, discussed at length in Michael Trebilcock's comment, is that couples might be stampeded into covenant marriages because they would otherwise signal that they were not really serious about marriage. However, the experience thus far with the new law suggests this may not be a concern, since relatively few couples elect for covenant marriages. Through November 1998, only 2.5 percent of Louisiana couples elected covenant marriage.

The major feminist objection to covenant marriage is that more difficult divorces will enhance the power imbalances of marriages.[12] Women who are deeply troubled in their relationships and who would otherwise obtain no-fault divorces might not be able to prove fault or might be afraid to seek a divorce based upon fault grounds, particularly cruelty. Because they generally have less secure financial positions than their husbands, they might not be able to get as good legal assistance prior to divorce, including the expert witnesses they could need to prove cruelty or intoxication, for example. They therefore might have to "trade" property or other financial resources in order to simply escape. Or they might have to endure increasing amounts of abuse at their husbands' hands. A related feminist question is whether covenant marriages favor traditional marriages in which the man works in the paid labor force while his wife becomes a domestic specialist. Less equal marriages imply less economic power for women.[13]

How great a concern these wealth transfer effects might be depends on who is seeking the divorce. If it is the man who wants out, then he would be called on to pay for it through a one-sided property division. Since wives are generally more committed to the marriage, and more dependent on the relationship financially and psychologically,[14] the move to restrict divorce options would on average benefit women. In addition, I have found that making divorce more costly decreases abuse.[15] Fault grounds impose a "penalty" for marital misbehavior, and this gives the parties stronger incentives to invest in the marriage.

Any costs to covenant marriages are plausibly exceeded by the gains of covenant marriage, particularly for men. Married men live longer, are healthier, and earn far more than do their single counterparts.[16] But even more than their parents, it is children who would benefit from a tightening of divorce grounds. A great deal of research suggests that children of parents who divorce will be worse off in the vast majority of cases. Children may lose out for a number of reasons. They will be poorer than those of intact families, and will in all probability suffer a variety of psychological and social problems. They have lower academic achievement, more behavioral problems, poorer psychological adjustment, more negative self-concepts, more social difficulties, and more problematic relationships with both mothers and fathers.[17] In the first few years following divorce, children in divorced families show more antisocial, impulsive acting-out disorders, more aggression and noncompliance, more dependency, anxiety, and depression, more difficulties in social relationships, and more problem behavior in school.[18]

The majority of academics and professionals who deal with children conclude that a two-parent home is best.[19] Fathers and mothers may perform complementary roles, by balancing each other's power and by acting as examples the children can emulate as they mature.[20] Unless the children experience serious conflicts between their parents, divorce has more costs than benefits for children.[21] In high-conflict families, where there is a history of physical aggression, children consistently exhibit emotional, behavioral, and social problems regardless of what happened to their parents' marriage.[22]

Two features of the Louisiana covenant marriage proposal seem to benefit the offspring of a marriage. The first is that fewer couples will likely divorce, and, since divorce almost always harms children, children will benefit. The other interesting feature of the legislation is the inclusion of abuse directed against a child as a ground both for absolute (fault) divorce and for a mensa divorce (or separation from bed and board).[23] At present, the only other state that allows fault divorces where it is not the spouse but the child who is physically or sexually injured is West Virginia.[24]

Some of the opposition to the Louisiana legislation is fueled by the specter of a return to the hypocrisy of the pre-no-fault era, a fear that divorce lawyers, whose status has arguably improved since the mid-1960s, might once again counsel their clients to perjure themselves or contrive situations from which the other can sue for adultery. But the Louisiana legislation's bilateral release provision, in which divorce is permitted after a lengthy separation, makes it less likely that we shall see a return to wholesale deception.

There is another reason why fraudulent pleadings are unlikely, and why the costs and benefits of covenant marriages are smaller than have been thought. A party seeking a divorce after a covenant marriage might avoid its strictures by moving, permanently or temporarily, to another state which does not recognize covenant marriages.

Before no-fault laws were generally available in every state, spouses who wanted to escape their marriages often left temporarily for states with easier divorce rules. They were able to obtain divorces after meeting relatively short standards for domicile. The spouses left behind sought to maintain that the home states (or states of matrimonial domicile) should be able to govern the prevailing divorce rules for the marriages in question. Not so, declared the Supreme Court in the famous case of *Williams v. North Carolina*.[25] Divorce jurisdiction is based upon domicile of either or both of the spouses, since it affects the marital status of husband and wife. The marriage, the *res* giving the forum subject matter jurisdiction, follows either spouse to a new domicile. As long as the migrating spouse meets the divorce state's residence requirements and intends to establish a new domicile, it matters not that the matrimonial domicile's policy against easy divorce is thwarted. The full faith and credit clause of the constitution requires that a court honor a sister state's valid divorce decree, however painful this might be to the marital domicile's public policy, fisc, or the abandoned spouse.

The migratory divorce is a much less costly alternative than it was in the 1940s and 1950s. Average earnings have greatly increased, and real travel expenses are far lower. We are also a much more mobile society. As such, we can expect even greater reliance on this option than in the past, where a spouse has elected a covenant marriage and now wants to escape it.

In sum, the right to a covenant marriage represents an expansion in bargaining freedom, since the parties are permitted to waive the no-fault divorce regime that would otherwise be mandated. The protections and burdens offered by the new Louisiana law are more limited than have been thought, since the law is nuanced in its remedies, and since no-fault divorce will remain a possibility for spouses who seek to escape a covenant marriage through an out-of-state divorce. Nevertheless, the initiative is worthwhile, since the right to fetter divorce rights permits the spouses to invest more heavily in their marriages. This will benefit them, their children, and society at large.

V Bargaining around Bankruptcy Reorganization Law

Contracting for Bankruptcy Systems

ALAN SCHWARTZ

This essay will argue that parties to lending agreements should be permitted to contract for the bankruptcy system that will govern their affairs if the borrower becomes insolvent, just as parties to ordinary agreements can contract for the dispute resolution system that will govern their affairs should they later disagree. "Bankruptcy contracts" are desirable because the optimality of a bankruptcy system partly depends on the circumstances that obtain when the borrower becomes insolvent. As an example, liquidation—the Chapter 7 system—may be suboptimal if a firm becomes insolvent when its industry is in a down cycle. Liquidation entails selling the insolvent firm or parts of the firm to the market. When the industry is depressed, demand may be low and asset sales hard to finance. It may then be efficient to "sell" the firm to current claimants. To do this is to use the Chapter 11 reorganization system. In contrast, it may be optimal to liquidate the firm when demand is high because a liquidation is less costly to administer than a reorganization.

If the creditors could act jointly ex post, they would choose the optimal bankruptcy system because this would maximize their insolvency state payoffs, but creditors have high coalition costs.[1] These commonly prevent creditors from agreeing on the system that will control agreements. The firm's incentive to raise money will induce it to offer these agreements.

To argue for the legalization of bankruptcy contracts is implicitly to assume that bankruptcy systems exist only to increase efficiency. This is because contracts that maximize creditors' expected returns may slight the interests of other constituencies. Many American commentators argue that bankruptcy systems also should protect persons or entities that do not have current claims against the insolvent firm. In the literature, protected classes include workers with an interest in continued employment and local communities that benefit from the firm's continued presence. These commentators are willing to sacrifice bankruptcy value to advance the interests of workers and communities. This essay's second claim, however, is that bankruptcy law should function only to facilitate the access of firms to debt capital. Bankruptcy systems cannot protect employees or communities effectively.[2]

Scholars have debated bankruptcy goals[3] and questioned the current United States system's monopoly on insolvency adjudication.[4] This essay therefore covers some familiar ground. In addition, it shows how banning bankruptcy contracts adversely affects a firm's ability to raise money, and how parties could solve their coordination problem at the contracting stage and thus would write bankruptcy contracts if permitted to do so. The essay also adds some institutional arguments to the literature about bankruptcy law's proper function.

Section I argues that bankruptcy should protect only those holding current claims against the insolvent firm; section II analyzes the problem of contracting for preferred bankruptcy systems; and section III concludes. Scholars have come increasingly to treat business law issues as contracting problems. Defining the corporation as a nexus of contracts between the various inputs to production is perhaps the most famous example.[5] The ultimate claim made here is that bankruptcy law is business law; it is not special.[6] To accept this view is to believe that the freedom to contract should prima facie be taken to be as desirable in the bankruptcy context as it is elsewhere.

I Bankruptcy Goals

THE CURRENT DEBATE

In the debate about the goals of bankruptcy systems, we may distinguish between "free marketers" and "traditionalists." Free marketers argue that a bankruptcy system should maximize the ex post value of the insolvent firm[7] and distribute firm value to current claimants according to the absolute priority rule.[8] To follow absolute priority is to pay debts in the order that the firm's contracts with investors direct. Under the rule lenders are paid before shareholders and lenders with mortgages are paid before lenders without. The goal of maximizing ex post firm value follows directly from the pursuit of Kaldor Hicks efficiency. The goal of following absolute priority also is Kaldor Hicks efficient. If the Bankruptcy Code deviated from absolute priority in systematic ways, then the firm and its creditors sometimes would have incentives to use or avoid bankruptcy strategically. For example, unsecured creditors would prefer bankruptcy to state law if bankruptcy shifted wealth from senior secured creditors to junior creditors, while the secured creditors would prefer the reverse. Legal disputes between these parties would waste resources and so not maximize the ex post value of the firm.[9]

Traditionalists agree that the efficiency norm is relevant to bankruptcy issues. In the traditionalist view, however, the Bankruptcy Code is a loss allocation mechanism that divides the losses from business failure among affected parties according to particular goals. These goals include but are not exhausted by economic efficiency.[10] Thus, while traditionalists also prefer bankruptcy systems to maximize the ex post value of the firm and to discourage strategic behavior, the traditionalists additionally want these systems to protect the interests of persons or entities that do not hold current contract-based claims against the insolvent firm.[11] The principal such persons and entities are employees, who have an interest in future employment,[12] as well as the congeries of interests summarized by the phrase "the community."[13] The community includes potential customers and suppliers of the firm, taxing authorities, and perhaps others. Two justifications are offered for protecting employees and communities. The first is loss spreading.[14] Traditionalists argue that a bankruptcy system should award part of the insolvent firm's value to employees (independent of the employees' contract rights) because creditors are more able than workers to protect themselves against losses from business failure in the ex ante contracts they write with the firm, or to spread those losses over the universe of borrowers. Protecting the community is argued to be desirable because it promotes distributional justice and because it allegedly internalizes the costs of business failure.[15] For example, the costs of a bankruptcy fall on local suppliers as well as on creditors. If firms are reorganized at some value loss to creditors, the creditors, anticipating this loss, presumably will make wiser lending decisions.

Traditionalists have not developed criteria to help a court or legislature decide how much of an insolvent firm's value should be devoted to protecting parties without current claims. Nor have traditionalists strongly urged particular reforms to make this protection more effective.[16] Rather, traditionalists show that sections of the current Bankruptcy Code protect parties who are not creditors,[17] and the traditionalists assert, in direct response to the free marketers, that bankruptcy should not be a one-value scheme.

All participants in this debate about the appropriate goals of a bankruptcy system recognize that bankruptcy law affects the ability of a firm to borrow money. Thus everyone acknowledges that secured creditors should have a high bankruptcy priority (though how high is now in dispute) because otherwise some firms could not borrow.[18] Also, traditionalists acknowledge that a highly inefficient bankruptcy system will discourage entrepreneurial behavior. The current debate, however, primarily takes an after-the-fall focus, in which the emphasis is on how best to resolve the problems that arise after insolvency has occurred. This focus perhaps exists because many commentators believe that to consider contractual alternatives to current bankruptcy systems would waste time: in the conventional view, if parties were legally free to contract about bankruptcy, creditor conflict and transaction costs would preclude efficient contracting.[19]

Protecting Community Interests. It is unnecessary for bankruptcy law to protect communities when thick markets exist. In a thick market, there are many substitutes for the firm's performance. New York City does not suffer when a boutique clothing store closes. Therefore, the issue of community protection is important only when an insolvent firm would be difficult for a community to replace. Bankruptcy law should not attempt to protect communities even in this case, however, because the effort actually will hurt communities.

To see why, realize first that it is customary to define the value of a firm as the discounted present value of the firm's expected income. This definition is too narrow: the true value of a firm is the present value of the firm's income (its private value) plus the present value of the gains the firm enables suppliers, customers, landlords, and taxing authorities to make (its social value). Communities want to attract firms with high social values.

To put a community's problem precisely, let a cash-constrained firm consider whether to locate in a community that would value its presence. If the firm enters, it will earn an expected profit that is its expected revenue less operating and fixed costs and less financing costs. To write down a simple equation, let the firm's profit be π, its expected revenues be r, its nonfinancing costs be c and its financing costs be d (all of these are in present values). Assume also that the bankruptcy system seeks only to maximize the expected value of firms that become insolvent; none of that value will be devoted to community protection. On these assumptions, the firm will expect to make a profit of $E(\pi) = r - c - d$. The firm will not enter if $E(\pi)$ is negative: in English, the firm will stay out if it expects to take losses.

A welfare maximizing community will compare these losses to the firm's social value. If the firm's social value would exceed its private loss, the community should subsidize firm entry. Such subsidies are common today and usually take the form of reducing the firm's nonfinancial costs. Communities create tax-free enterprise zones, build factories for firms, and create local infrastructure. In the equation above, a sufficiently large decline in c, the firm's nonfinancial costs, can turn a negative expected profit into a positive one.

Next consider the case when a firm would enter without a subsidy $(E(\pi) > 0)$ but let the bankruptcy system now attempt to protect communities by reorganizing—that is, continuing—some firms that should be liquidated. The system would take value from creditors in these cases because it is saving firms whose liquidation values exceed their going concern values.

Creditors have rational expectations, and thus will anticipate lower bankruptcy returns. A creditor's expected gain from a loan is a weighted average of its solvency and insolvency state payoffs: that is, the creditor expects to earn the sum the firm promises to repay times the probability that the firm will be solvent enough to repay it plus the value of the creditor's bankruptcy payoff times the probability of bankruptcy. In a competitive credit market, the creditor's expected gain will be zero: the creditor expects to make a competitive return on the capital it invests but not to make pure profits. Therefore, when the bankruptcy system reduces creditors' bankruptcy payoffs, and a creditor functions in a competitive market, the creditor can avoid losses only by requiring the firm to increase the sum it will pay if the firm remains solvent. Because American credit markets are workably competitive, the face value of loans thus will rise when the bankruptcy system shifts value away from creditors to communities. The variable d in the firm's profit equation above that reflected the firm's financing costs thus should now be replaced with the higher variable d' $(d' > d)$. The result will be that in some cases a firm that would have entered to serve the community without a subsidy will not enter. This firm would expect to make losses under the value shifting bankruptcy system (bankruptcy law would have converted the firm's expected profit into an expected loss).

The public policy error that is made when a bankruptcy system attempts to protect community interests is to *tax* an activity whose social return exceeds its private return rather than to subsidize that activity. The activity in question is the efficient location of firms. When the bankruptcy system shifts value from creditors to communities ex post, it necessarily creates a tax on entry into those communities. The tax takes the form of an increased cost of debt capital, and the tax falls on all firms that may enter because creditors do not know who will fail and thus raise rates to all. The result is to deter entry.

The best bankruptcy response to the problem that too few firms may locate in particular communities is to minimize the costs of collecting debts. These costs are minimized when creditor returns are maximized. Local communities have the expertise and the incentive to decide whether to subsidize the entry of firms that would go elsewhere under a cost-minimizing bankruptcy system. Therefore, bankruptcy law should not attempt to protect the congeries of interests (such as suppliers and landlords) that constitute "the community."[20]

Protecting Employee Interests. The mistake in attempting to protect community interests with bankruptcy law is to pursue a salutary goal in the wrong way—to tax an activity that should be subsidized. To use bankruptcy to protect jobs is to make the same category of mistake, which here is to tax job creation rather than subsidize it. To see why, realize first that employees lose jobs because of technological change; because of increased competition, which puts pressure on firms to control costs; and because of managerial incompetence, which can cause firms to shrink or fail. These causes sometimes are related.

Thus well-run firms may survive the entry of new competitors while badly run firms will not.

American society partly insures workers against job loss, by paying unemployment benefits, and it also attempts to facilitate employment. There are, broadly speaking, two methods of facilitating employment: to preserve jobs at particular firms and to help workers who lose jobs get new ones. The latter method is pursued through subsidizing the creation of new human capital with education and job retraining, and subsidizing the worker's search for new employment with unemployment insurance and by providing workers with labor market information and providing firms with information about available workers.

American society generally protects employment by helping displaced workers get new jobs. This method is preferable to preserving jobs at particular firms for four reasons. First, encouraging worker mobility increases the probability that a worker will locate at the firm with the highest valuation for the worker's services. Second, encouraging mobility improves the responses firms can make to technological change or increased competition: firms can shift resources from capital to labor conveniently if workers are mobile, and firms can shift resources from labor to capital conveniently if they are free to dismiss redundant workers. Third, preserving jobs at a firm implies keeping the firm afloat at some minimum scale, and thus retards the process of weeding out weak firms. Fourth, and referring to reason one, if workers must be kept when hard times arrive, then the expected cost of hiring workers rises, and fewer workers will be hired. Preserving jobs at particular firms thus may reduce the total number of jobs.

A bankruptcy system can protect employment only by helping workers to stay at the same (insolvent) firms. This strategy retards the elimination of weak firms and creates a tax on jobs. As regards the "tax issue," to reorganize firms that have higher liquidation values will transfer wealth from creditors to employees ex post. Creditors will anticipate that the reorganization probability has increased and so raise interest rates. At the entrepreneurial stage, this will distort a firm's choice between labor and capital. Because firms that have more workers will have higher borrowing costs, firms will have an incentive to propose projects to lenders that use as few workers as possible.[21] Therefore, when firms whose liquidation values exceed their going concern values are reorganized to save jobs, the bankruptcy system is pursuing the right goal in the wrong way.

FREEDOM OF CONTRACT AND BANKRUPTCY

Bankruptcy systems not only should restrict themselves to maximizing ex post firm value; they also should not prevent parties from contracting about bankruptcy. In understanding why, it is helpful to contrast bankruptcy with commercial law generally, where the concern is with ex ante rather than ex post efficiency. Commercial law has this concern because parties ordinarily can achieve ex post efficiency through renegotiation. To see how, realize that parties commonly write sales contracts before the state of the world in which they plan to transact is known. For example, a seller sometimes will agree to produce a product before the seller knows its actual production cost. That cost is a function of variables the seller can affect (wages) and variables the seller cannot affect (the later market price of various inputs). Similarly, a buyer sometimes will agree to purchase before the buyer knows the valuation it will place on performance. That valuation is a function of variables the buyer can control (the amount the buyer invests in the contract) and variables the buyer cannot affect (the state of demand in the buyer's resale market). An efficient sales contract thus maximizes the parties' ex ante (or expected) utility.

This contract may turn out to be inefficient when the true state of the world is realized. As an illustration, the parties may have agreed to trade twenty units at a price p, only to find that, given the actual state of demand in the buyer's market, it would be efficient to trade only ten units at p, or perhaps twenty units at a lower price than p. The seller in this illustration has a legal right to have the buyer take twenty units at p (or pay damages for not doing so), but the location of this entitlement is irrelevant because transaction costs are low. The parties will modify the contract—that is, engage in renegotiation—to permit the buyer to take fewer units or to pay less, because the parties can split the surplus created by switching to the ex post efficient deal. Therefore, it is unnecessary for commercial law to focus on ex post efficiency: the parties have, in effect, chosen their own mechanism to achieve it, that mechanism being renegotiation if later events outmode the contract. Commercial law instead provides parties with default rules that, in theory anyway, direct the ex ante efficient result in standard cases.

Bankruptcy law differs from other areas of commercial law because renegotiation after insolvency is difficult. Creditors cannot conveniently coordinate their collection efforts or positions respecting the appropriate disposition of the insolvent firm because there commonly are many creditors, and their interests may diverge. The firm also has no power to compel creditors to agree. A bankruptcy system is necessary to facilitate the parties' ability to renegotiate to ex post efficient outcomes.

That bankruptcy law must be concerned with ex post efficiency cannot of itself imply the irrelevance of ex ante efficiency as a policy goal. For example, assume that different feasible bankruptcy systems would yield different renegotiation outcomes for a particular firm and its creditors. Bankruptcy law apparently then should facilitate the ability of these parties to choose the bankruptcy system, and thus the renegotiation outcome, that they prefer. This raises the question whether the conventional view is correct that parties would be no better at coordinating ex ante bankruptcy bargains than they are at coordinating ex post renegotiations.

II   Contracting for Bankruptcy Systems

METHODOLOGICAL INTRODUCTION

Three obstacles to the making of bankruptcy contracts have been identified: a firm may have numerous creditors; these creditors commonly lend at different times; and they may have different preferences about bankruptcy systems. The analysis begins by assuming that all of a firm's creditors lend at the same time and have the same preferences respecting bankruptcy. On these assumptions, the obstacle of numerous creditors dissolves because the firm can offer the same contract to everyone. I initially take up the questions of whether parties would contract about bankruptcy systems under the assumed conditions, and what would be the effect of banning the contracts that parties might write. Later, I argue that the conclusions reached initially do not change when sequential credit extensions and heterogenous creditor preferences are taken into account.

The question of what an optimal bankruptcy contract would contain is an economic contract theory question, so it is worth introducing readers to the problems that this theory attempts to solve. The theory applies when either of two market imperfections obtains: hidden information or hidden action. There is hidden information when a party does not know the "types" of its potential contract partners. For example, a seller who is considering whether to make a warranty does not know whether any particular buyer will be an intense user (and thus likely to make warranty claims) or a less intense user. The contract theory task is to identify the contract that parties will make when one side of the market does not know the types—in this example, the different buyers' use patterns—of the other side.

This essay analyzes a variant of the other market imperfection, hidden action. A party may take an action after a contract is made that disadvantages its contract partner. Thus a firm may raise money from investors to pursue a business project but divert part of the money to perks such as plush offices. This diversion will harm the investors if the probability that the project succeeds is a function of how much money is invested in it. If investors could observe the firm's ex post actions and prove in court that investing in offices rather than machines would reduce the success probability, then the contract theory problem is trivial: the optimal contract will prohibit the firm from using funds for new offices.

In life, the contract theory problem is not trivial, for two reasons. First, the investors may be unable to observe at reasonable cost how the firm is spending their money (there is hidden action). Second, it may be very costly to write contracts that proscribe certain ex post actions and require others. To continue with the example, a firm can shirk in other ways than by building nice offices. The firm's managers might instead work less hard than they should, arrange the firm's project so that it will earn certain but low returns relative to a more risky but optimal version, or structure the project so that it is easy to manage rather than difficult but more profitable. Prescribing the optimal and proscribing every suboptimal set of managerial actions in an investment contract would be very costly. In addition, proving in court that an action is suboptimal—that the firm should have invested in Venezuela rather than the United States—would be difficult and costly. When the investment contract cannot expressly require the firm to behave optimally, the contract theory problem is to identify the contract, if any, that will induce optimal actions.

This essay asks whether parties can contract to use the bankruptcy system that is optimal in their situation. A contracting problem exists because an insolvent firm and its creditors may disagree ex post about which bankruptcy system to use. The firm will prefer the bankruptcy system that is more likely to permit it to survive or to enjoy control privileges for a longer time if it ultimately fails. The creditors will prefer the system that maximizes the firm's net expected insolvency return because creditors can only recover monetary returns.

If parties have a choice of bankruptcy systems, and a particular firm and its creditors expect a certain system always to be optimal for them, then the contract theory problem is trivial. These parties would write a contract requiring the firm to use the efficient bankruptcy system upon insolvency.[22] However, the contract theory problem is serious, even given our assumptions about identical creditor preferences and lending times, because in many cases which bankruptcy system is optimal can only be known ex post. For example, the parties may not know at the time the money is lent whether the firm should be reorganized or liquidated in the event of failure. Thus a lending agreement which required the firm to use a bankruptcy system that commonly chooses reorganization might turn out to yield a suboptimal choice. A relatively simple contract apparently could require the firm to use the "reorganization system" when certain circumstances materialize but to use another system under different circumstances. The difficulty here, as in the investment example above, is describing the circumstances. Litigation over whether firms should be reorganized or liquidated suggests that the decision is fact specific: describing all of the possible facts and their implications in the lending agreement thus would be a costly enterprise.

Bankruptcy contracting therefore poses a difficult contract theory problem. In consequence, the model described below assumes that parties can contract over bankruptcy systems but cannot write contracts of the form: "Choose system A in the following circumstances; otherwise, choose system B." This argument will make two claims. First, a set of contracts that will induce optimal bankruptcy choices exists. Second, prohibiting parties from writing these contracts produces "underinvestment": firms could finance more projects if they had more freedom to contract.

THE MODEL

A firm has a project to pursue.[23] At a time denoted t^0, the firm attempts to borrow the project's cost in a competitive capital market. The project will begin at t^1 and the firm will repay its creditors at t^2 if the project is successful. If the firm is insolvent at t^2, it will choose a bankruptcy system to use at t^3. The project continues to run during the course of the system the firm chooses, and creditors are paid their bankruptcy return at t^4. Two bankruptcy systems are assumed to exist. One is denoted "R", and is the current Chapter 11 reorganization regime with two exceptions: unlike the current regime, system R strictly follows absolute priority; also, parties are free to contract in the lending agreement for system R or the other system. This system is denoted "L", and auctions insolvent firms, or the assets of those firms, to the market, distributing the proceeds strictly according to absolute priority.[24]

The monetary return the firm earns during bankruptcy is a function of the bankruptcy system the firm chose and the circumstances obtaining when the firm made the choice. Under some circumstances, it will be optimal for the firm to use the system R and under other circumstances L will be best. Creditors can prove in court how much money the firm earned while in whatever bankruptcy system it chose (bankruptcy returns are "verifiable"), and everyone can observe the circumstances that exist ex post. Thus everyone knows after insolvency which of the two bankruptcy systems would be optimal. As in the illustrations above, however, the ex post circumstances and their relation to what an optimal bankruptcy choice would be are too costly to describe in a contract. Thus contracts of the form "Choose R if certain facts obtain but otherwise choose L" are excluded. The parties, however, can observe a "signal" that correlates (sometimes well and sometimes badly) with the return the firm would earn under either system. The signal may be the performance of a relevant economic index. For example, the firm's returns may correlate positively with the Consumer Price Index. Hence, if the firm becomes insolvent when the CPI is rising, the firm perhaps should be reorganized; while if the firm becomes insolvent when the CPI is falling perhaps it should be liquidated. Parties are assumed able to prove the content of the signal in court (the CPI's performance for the most recent quarter, say), and so may condition a contract on it. Such a contract may pay the firm a percent of the bankruptcy return to use system R if a certain value of the signal is observed but otherwise pay the firm nothing.[25]

The parties also may choose not to contract about bankruptcy in the lending agreement. In this event, the firm will either choose the system it prefers given the circumstances obtaining when it becomes insolvent, or the parties may renegotiate after insolvency. The firm is assumed to have all the bargaining power in a renegotiation because creditors have difficulty coordinating strategies after insolvency. Thus renegotiation involves the firm's making an offer to creditors to use one or the other system in return for the entire marginal gain that using the optimal system would create.[26]

To understand when parties will write contracts about bankruptcy, rely on renegotiation to induce an optimal bankruptcy choice, or let the firm choose unimpeded, it is necessary to make the conflict between an insolvent firm and its creditors more precise. Firms generate monetary returns, and their owners or managers (here the two are assumed to be the same) can consume private benefits. These benefits are the pleasure or status derived from running the firm, the excess consumption of leisure while employed, and the opportunity to continue to be paid a salary. Creditors cannot observe the consumption of some forms of private benefits (there is hidden action), and are assumed unable to prove in court that the firm consumed excessively. Thus lending agreements, just as in the introductory investment example, cannot regulate private benefits (or perks), and they are the source of conflict between the firm and its creditors. In particular, because creditors are legally entitled to the monetary return when the firm becomes insolvent, creditors want the firm to choose the bankruptcy system that maximizes monetary returns. In contrast, since after insolvency the firm legally has no claim to monetary returns, the firm prefers the bankruptcy system that permits it to consume the most private benefits. The firm makes an optimal bankruptcy choice when it picks the system that maximizes the sum of monetary returns and private benefits.[27]

When a certain state of the world obtains ex post that is denoted θ_L, it is assumed to be optimal for the parties to use the bankruptcy system L; this system would maximize the sum of monetary returns and private benefits for these parties. When the second possible state of the world obtains ex post, denoted θ_R, it will be optimal to use system R. Thus a firm that makes optimal bankruptcy choices will choose system L when state θ_L obtains, and will choose system R when state θ_R obtains. The parties know the probability that one or the other of these ex post states will materialize.

The private benefits that the firm can obtain derive from continuing to operate the firm's project. These benefits are likely to be greater under bankruptcy system R because this system prefers reorganization, and thus permits the firm to survive intact for a longer period. Thus it is assumed that the firm derives greater private benefits from system R whatever state of the world obtains ex post; that is, the firm always will choose system R unless it is constrained by ex ante contract or by ex post renegotiation.

Recall that choosing system L when state θ_L obtains maximizes the sum of monetary returns and private benefits. If the firm nevertheless obtains greater private benefits from choosing system R even when the circumstances summarized by θ_L obtain, it must follow that monetary returns are maximized by system L given θ_L. As a consequence, when state θ_L does obtain ex post, the insolvent firm and its creditors will be in conflict; the firm will prefer system R—want to reorganize—but the creditors will prefer system L—want to liquidate. Moreover, if the firm is unconstrained, it will inefficiently choose system R. In contrast, the parties' preferences are in harmony when state θ_R obtains. The firm will prefer to choose system R then, and because R in this case generates greater monetary returns than L, the creditors will prefer R as well. The parties' contracting problem thus is to induce the firm to choose bankruptcy system L when the ex post state of the world θ_L obtains.

Before seeing how this problem can be solved, the general description of the parties' incentives and circumstances should be completed. All of the parties are assumed to be risk neutral. Creditors care only about monetary returns, but the firm cares about these and private benefits because the two are substitutes: creditors can bribe the firm with money to forgo private benefits. As shown above, the creditors' expected return under any lending agreement is zero because credit markets are assumed to be competitive.

In this model, firms bear the consequences of choosing inefficient bankruptcy systems. Creditors plausibly expect firms to choose suboptimally some of the time. This expectation lowers the creditors' anticipated insolvency return, and because creditors earn zero profits, they must then require firms to repay higher sums when projects succeed. Firms thus have an incentive to offer lending agreements to creditors that minimize this moral hazard risk. A firm, however, cannot simply promise to use the efficient bankruptcy system (to choose system L when ex post state θ_L obtains) because the circumstances that make a system optimal cannot be described in a contract. Can the firm otherwise make a credible commitment to choose optimally?[28]

BANKRUPTCY CONTRACTS

A firm has three contractual choices in the situation modeled here. First, it can offer creditors a "renegotiation proof" contract that will induce the firm to choose the optimal bankruptcy system in the event of insolvency. The contract is called renegotiation proof because no party will have an incentive to propose changes in it in light of later events. Second, the firm can offer creditors a contract that does not deal with bankruptcy. In this case, the parties rely on renegotiation to induce the optimal bankruptcy choice. Third, the firm can offer a contract that conditions the bankruptcy choice on a signal that correlates with the firm's ex post circumstances. Parties will have an incentive to renegotiate this contract when the signal inaccurately indicates that state θ_R will obtain, but state θ_L turns out to exist instead, so this contract is called "partially renegotiation proof." The firm will offer creditors the contract that maximizes the creditors' expected insolvency return because this will maximize the sum the firm can borrow.

Renegotiating Proof Contracts. A contract that cannot require the firm to choose optimally must bribe it to choose optimally. Under a renegotiation proof contract, creditors after default will pay the firm s percent of the insolvency monetary return no matter which bankruptcy system the firm chooses. The firm thus does better monetarily if it chooses the system that maximizes monetary returns, but the firm also wants to consume private benefits. Thus the percent return s must be high enough so that the firm will do better all in all when it chooses optimally.

To see how the percentage s is set, recall that the object is to induce the firm to choose bankruptcy system L when insolvency state θ_L obtains. Denote the firm's monetary return when it does choose L in this case as $y_{L,L}$ and the firm's monetary return when it inefficiently chooses system R as $y_{L,R}$.[29] Also, denote the firm's private benefits when it chooses system L in state θ_L as $b_{L,L}$, and its private benefits when it inefficiently chooses system R as $b_{L,R}$. If the firm must do better all in all choosing system L when θ_L obtains, the following inequality must be satisfied:

$$sy_{L,L} + b_{L,L} \geq sy_{L,R} + b_{L,R}$$

Recall that s is the percentage share of the insolvency monetary return that the firm is permitted by the contract to keep. The first term on the left hand side of this inequality thus is the firm's monetary payoff for choosing the optimal bankruptcy system L in state θ_L, and the first term on the right hand side is the firm's monetary payoff if it chooses suboptimally. The second term on the left-hand side represents the private benefits the firm realizes if it chooses the efficient system L in state θ_L, and the second term on the right-hand side represents the larger private benefits the firm would obtain from choosing the suboptimal system. The left-hand side of the inequality will exceed the right-hand side if the firm's share of the relatively high monetary return from choosing optimally makes up for the lower private benefits of accepting liquidation.

Solving this inequality for $s^\star$, the optimal bribe, yields

$$s^\star = \frac{b_{L,R} - b_{L,L}}{y_{L,L} - y_{L,R}}$$

This equation shows that the optimal bribe is lower when the firm cannot realize significantly greater private benefits from choosing wrongly ($b_{L,R} - b_{L,L}$ is small), and when the marginal monetary return from choosing correctly is large

$(y_{L,L} - y_{L,R}$ is big). The former result should be obvious. As for the latter, when the marginal return from choosing optimally is large, the firm needs to be given a smaller share of it to induce good behavior.

This analysis implies that the firm's preference for private benefits over efficiency causes underinvestment. If the firm must be given a share of the bankruptcy return to induce optimal behavior, the firm can credibly promise to repay less money when insolvent than if the firm always would behave optimally. The lower the creditors' insolvency payoff, the less they will lend. Thus some positive value projects that would be funded if creditors could directly control the firm will not be funded when the firm instead must be bribed to behave optimally. The extent of underinvestment and the contribution of bankruptcy contracts to reducing it is best shown by example.

The examples that follow assume that the firm has available to it a project that will return $260 if it succeeds. If the project fails, and if reorganization would be optimal, the monetary reorganization return would be $180; if liquidation would be optimal upon project failure, the liquidation return would be $120. The probability that the project succeeds is .8. In the event of failure, the probability that reorganization will be optimal is .3. The reorganization probability is chosen to be relatively low because it often is efficient to liquidate failed firms. If the firm would always voluntarily choose the optimal bankruptcy procedure without being bribed, the project would have an expected value of

$$E(R) = .8 \times 260 + .2[.3 \times 180 + .7 \times 120] = \$235.60$$

The first term on the right-hand side of this equation is the expected value of the firm's solvency return; the second term is the expected value of the insolvency return if the firm were to efficiently choose system R in θ_R and system L in θ_L. The project's expected return would then be $235.60, and the project would have a positive net present value if it cost less than this to do. However, in this model the firm sometimes will make a suboptimal choice of a bankruptcy system (it will choose system R when L would be efficient), and this will cause the project's expected return to fall below $235.60.

To see how a bankruptcy contract could respond to this problem, let the firm obtain private benefits of $40 if state θ_L were to obtain and the firm would then choose bankruptcy system L; but the firm would obtain private benefits of $70 if it chose system R instead. The firm thus would choose R unless it were paid not to do so. Also, if the firm inefficiently chose system R when θ_L obtained, the monetary return from reorganization would fall to $30. Using the equation for s^* set out above, on these values for the parameters, the firm would have to be paid one-third of the bankruptcy return in order to induce an optimal bankruptcy choice. This bribe reduces the amount available to creditors in the insolvency state, with the result that the firm can promise to repay creditors at most $226.49.[30] Hence, if the firm's project would cost between $226.50 and $235.59, the project could not be financed, even though the project would have positive expected value.

This example teaches two lessons. First, a renegotiation proof contract exists that will induce the firm to choose the efficient bankruptcy system. The contract is renegotiation proof because the firm does better choosing efficiently and being bribed than choosing inefficiently; because the contract always induces the firm to choose optimally, the creditors' return is maximized. Thus no one has an incentive to renegotiate. The second lesson is that there can be underinvestment even with free contracting: because creditors must bribe the firm to choose optimally ex post, creditors will lend the firm less money ex ante; consequently, the firm may be unable to finance a positive value project.[31]

Renegotiation Contracts. The firm also could offer creditors a contract that does not deal with bankruptcy. Such a contract would not pay the firm a bribe to choose the optimal bankruptcy system $(s^* = 0)$. If state θ_R obtained upon insolvency, the firm would choose system R voluntarily for the reasons given. Because the bribe then is zero, creditors could keep the full monetary return that using the optimal system would generate. On the other hand, if state θ_L were to obtain, the firm also would choose system R unless the creditors bribed it to choose the optimal system L. It is assumed here that the firm has all the bargaining power in a renegotiation, and so could capture the entire marginal return from making an efficient bankruptcy choice. In the example here, that would be the difference between the optimal state θ_L monetary return and suboptimal state θ_R monetary return $(120 - 30 = \$90)$. On the values for the parameters here, such a renegotiation contract would produce an expected gain for creditors of

$$E(R) = .8 \times 260 + .2[.3 \times 180 + .7 \times 30] = \$223.00$$

The first term within the brackets indicates that creditors keep the entire monetary return when state θ_R materializes and the firm voluntarily chooses system R; the second term reflects the firm's ability to keep the entire renegotiation rent (the $90) should state θ_L occur.

Partially Renegotiation Proof Contracts. A partially renegotiation proof contract would be conditioned on a signal that correlates with the firm's insolvency state circumstances. Denote this signal v and assume that a high value for v signals an increasing probability that the firm is in state θ_R, in which the firm would choose the optimal bankruptcy system voluntarily, while a low value for v signals an increasing probability that the firm is in θ_L, in which it would have to be bribed to choose optimally. A partially renegotiation proof contract would pay a bribe of zero if a high value for v is observed when the firm becomes insolvent and a bribe of $sv^* > 0$ if a low value for v is observed then. The parties will renegotiate this contract only if a high value for v is observed but θ_L surprisingly occurs. In this case, because the contract pays no bribe the creditors must renegotiate to induce the firm to choose the efficient bankruptcy system.

Partially renegotiation proof contracts do best when the signal is highly informative. In this event, the parties will seldom have to renegotiate in the state (θ_L) when renegotiation would maximally disadvantage creditors. To see how such a contract would work, retain all of the values set out above, and let ζ_R be the probability that the firm is in state θ_R when v_{high} is observed, and ζ_L be the probability that the firm is in state θ_R when v_{low} is observed. Assume that the signal is highly informative: $\zeta_R = .9$ and $\zeta_L = .1$. Then using the values in the examples above the creditors' return under a partially renegotiation proof contract is $235.30.[32] This contract almost replicates the full information result: under the contract, the firm would only be unable to finance projects that would cost between $235.31 and $235.60.

THE EFFECT OF PREVENTING PARTIES
FROM WRITING BANKRUPTCY CONTRACTS

The legal prohibition on contracting for bankruptcy systems is inefficient because the ban restricts the parties to "renegotiation contracts," even when other contracts would generate higher expected values for creditors and permit more positive value projects to be funded.[33] A table illustrates the maximum value that the firm could promise to creditors were it voluntarily to choose optimally and under the three contracts considered above.

Voluntary Optimal Choice	$235.60
Partially Renegotiation Proof Contract	$235.30
Renegotiation Proof Contract	$226.49
Renegotiation Contract	$223.00

Current law will not enforce the first two contracts, which pay bribes to induce firms to make optimal bankruptcy choices. The law thus forces parties to use the renegotiation contract, which is silent about bankruptcy, relying instead on ex post renegotiation to achieve efficient choice. The table above shows that parties sometimes would eschew renegotiation contracts in favor of one or the other bankruptcy contract. The legal ban thus exacerbates the underinvestment problem: firms today cannot finance projects that they would be able to finance if the ban were repealed.

THE CHOICE BETWEEN RENEGOTIATION AND CONTRACT

Despite the comparison above, parties will sometimes prefer the renegotiation contract. This preference exists when the expected value of choosing reorganization—system R—in the "reorganization state"—θ_R—is high. To see why, recall that under the renegotiation proof contract, the creditors may pay an unnecessary bribe: the contract always awards the firm s^* of the monetary return, but the firm would choose the optimal system voluntarily if state θ_R turned out to occur. This contract nevertheless can maximize the creditors' insolvency return because it ensures creditors a positive payoff when state θ_L obtains: as shown, without a bribe, the firm appropriates the entire rent from choosing the optimal system in θ_L. The strategy of always paying a bribe is unlikely to be maximizing, however, when the probability that the firm will voluntarily choose optimally is high or when the creditors' payoff from optimal voluntary choice would be high. Thus, when the expected value of choosing system R in state θ_R is high, the creditors' expected insolvency return could be maximized under the renegotiation contract.

BARRIERS TO BANKRUPTCY CONTRACTS

The conclusion that it is inefficient to ban contracting for bankruptcy systems would have only theoretical interest if practical obstacles were to prevent parties from writing bankruptcy contracts. One possible obstacle to writing these contracts is that a firm may have many creditors. This obstacle is not serious, however, because the firm can offer contracts to creditors, and it would offer the efficient contract (respecting bankruptcy) to all. A possibly more serious obstacle is that creditors sometimes lend at different times, whereas the parameters that determine which contract would be optimal can be time variant. Thus bankruptcy contracting poses an intertemporal coordination problem. Another possibly serious obstacle is that a firm's creditors may have inconsistent preferences over bankruptcy systems. If so, there is no contract that everyone will take. Here I argue that parties could overcome these barriers with some help from the law. Because bankruptcy contracts today are illegal, there is no data about real contracts that could support the argument. The goal, rather, is to render plausible the view that bankruptcy contracting would occur if it were permitted.

Intertemporal Coordination. There exists a set of contracts that will achieve the results described above although creditors lend at different times. To describe these contracts, let a firm have two creditors with the first arriving at t^0 as in the model above. Assume that it is optimal at t^0 to use a renegotiation proof contract that would pay the firm s^* of the bankruptcy return to choose the optimal bankruptcy system. The initial creditor and the firm would sign this renegotiation proof contract though the variables that determine the optimal bribe may vary over time: in an efficient market, the best estimate of the value that s^* will take at a future time is the value for s^* when estimated as of t^0.[34] Now let a second creditor arrive at t^1. If the factors that determine the optimal bribe have changed, the fraction s in the second contract could vary from the original s^*. The initial contract could resolve this problem by providing that the bribe would change to the bribe in the later contract. The initial lender would agree to this because, as just said, for it the optimal bribe would not vary in expectation.

There apparently would be cause for concern if the lending agreement that turned out to be optimal at t^1 differed from the contract that initially was optimal. For example, suppose that the expected values for the t^2 parameters as of t^1 imply a renegotiation contract rather than the renegotiation proof contract that the first creditor signed. The firm wants to offer its second creditor the currently optimal contract, but the firm's set of contracts respecting bankruptcy must be consistent. Consistency can be achieved if the contract between the initial creditor and the firm has a conversion feature which provides that this creditor's contract will convert (only as regards bankruptcy) to the contract that is currently optimal for the firm. Thus, if it becomes optimal for the firm to offer the second creditor a renegotiation contract, the initial creditor's contract will convert to a renegotiation contract as well. The initial creditor would agree to a contract with a conversion feature because the firm would switch contracts only if the new contract would give creditors a greater expected return than the old, and the firm would offer the conversion feature because the firm benefits from the flexibility to switch contracts as economic conditions change.

Therefore, that a firm may have numerous creditors, and that these may lend at different times, would not preclude bankruptcy contracting. The large-number coordination barrier falls because the firm deals with everyone and so can coordinate bankruptcy contracting. The intertemporal coordination barrier falls because a set of sequentially efficient contracts (respecting bankruptcy) exists.

Creditor Conflict. Creditors care only about monetary returns, and so apparently could agree upon contracts that induce firms to choose bankruptcy systems that maximize monetary returns. Such agreement seldom could be achieved today, however, because the current U.S. bankruptcy system does not respect absolute priority. Rather, the liquidation system (Chapter 7) respects absolute priority much more than the reorganization system (Chapter 11) does. As a consequence, senior creditors today commonly prefer that firms use Chapter 7, whether liquidation would be efficient or not, while junior creditors commonly prefer that firms use Chapter 11, whether reorganization would be efficient or not. The creditors in the model here would have similar conflicting preferences over systems L and R if they expected the two systems to vary in the order in which they paid claims, and this conflict would make bankruptcy contracts hard to write. The model assumes this conflict away by supposing that systems R and L both pay claims strictly in order of priority. There is, therefore, an additional normative reason to prefer bankruptcy systems to respect absolute priority: if every system in the choice set does this, a large barrier to writing bankruptcy contracts would be removed.

There may be two other sources of creditor conflict. To understand the first of these, it is helpful to begin by assuming that all creditors would be paid pro rata. Under this distributional rule, each creditor receives a sum that is determined by multiplying the firm's bankruptcy return by a fraction that is the ratio of the particular creditor's claim to the firm's total indebtedness. The amount the creditor lent and the firm's total debt are fixed when bankruptcy occurs, and so the ratio that determines what the creditor receives also is fixed then. Given a fixed payout ratio, the variable that is relevant to the creditor is the firm's monetary return during the bankruptcy procedure. This analysis implies that when creditors are paid pro rata, there is no creditor conflict: every creditor wants the firm to choose the bankruptcy system that maximizes the monetary return.

This preference would continue to exist in most cases if the firm's creditors ranked unequally. If absolute priority is respected, junior creditors would prefer that the firm choose the system that maximizes the monetary return because they are paid nothing until claims senior to theirs are paid in full. A senior claimant also would prefer the firm to choose the optimal procedure if it would be paid less than in full under either system (L or R) or under one of these. A senior claimant would be indifferent to the firm's bankruptcy choice if it would be paid in full under both procedures. Such a creditor would be unwilling to incur the cost of a bankruptcy bribe to induce the firm to choose optimally. However, a senior creditor who expected to be paid in full regardless of the bankruptcy system the insolvent firm chose would hold riskless debt, and this is unusual. On the analysis so far, then, if systems L and R both respect absolute priority, creditor conflict would seldom exist: every creditor would be willing to bribe the firm to choose the optimal system except senior creditors who held riskless debt.

Trade creditors, however, sometimes would share the firm's preference for system R, even when R is inefficient, because the firm can operate for a longer time under a reorganization system. A trade creditor may prefer R if the firm would be liquidated piecemeal under system L and the firm would be hard for the creditor to replace.[35] Then the creditor perhaps could earn more in new transactions with the firm during the pendency of a wasteful reorganization attempt than it would lose by having its prebankruptcy debt collected under an inefficient system. Trade creditors who anticipated preferring system R in all cases would be unwilling to bribe the firm to choose system L when L turned out to be optimal for creditors as a group. Too many such holdouts could preclude bankruptcy contracting.

The current Bankruptcy Code binds minority dissenters in a reorganization proceeding to the deal a majority prefers in order to avoid inefficient holdout behavior.[36] A trade creditor who preferred an inefficient bankruptcy contract also should be bound to the bankruptcy bargain that the ex ante majority preferred. The freedom to contract should not be used to prevent efficient contracting. And in sum, if the ban on contracting for bankruptcy systems is repealed, absolute priority is respected, and majority rule were to govern the contracting process, the current U.S. system would encourage investment more than it now does.

III Conclusion

Bankruptcy issues traditionally have been analyzed in the insolvency context. Scholars agree that a major task of a bankruptcy system is to maximize the value of the insolvent estate for the benefit of creditors. High coalition costs prevent creditors from performing this task themselves by coordinating on jointly maximizing debt collection strategies. Scholars disagree on whether a bankruptcy system should pursue additional goals, such as distributing value to employees or local communities. Most participants in bankruptcy debates also agree that the problems that prevent creditors from coordinating strategies after insolvency also would be present ex ante, when the firm borrows money. Apparently because contracting about bankruptcy is thought to be impractical, few scholars have analyzed the mandatory nature of Western bankruptcy systems. Parties are required to use the bankruptcy system the state supplies, and cannot contract out of many of the rules in the monopoly system.

This essay has argued that bankruptcy systems should attempt only to maximize the value of the bankrupt estate. A system's pursuit of other goals would be either ineffectual or counterproductive. The essay makes two positive showings: preventing parties from inducing the choice of an optimal bankruptcy system in the lending agreements produces underinvestment; and parties probably would contract over bankruptcy systems were they free to do so.

There are three normative implications. First, the state should permit parties to contract for the bankruptcy system that they prefer. Second, to prevent holdout problems, the state should bind a creditor minority to the contract a majority prefer (just as it now binds a dissenting creditor minority to the reorganization plan a majority prefer). Respecting the third normative implication, bankruptcy systems are sufficiently complex that creating them is likely beyond the resources of parties to typical credit extensions: that is, a bankruptcy system is largely a public good. Thus the state should supply parties with a set of default bankruptcy systems, just as state business laws today supply parties with a set of default business forms, such as the close corporation, the public corporation, and the like.[37] These proposals would make bankruptcy a part of business law generally, which is where bankruptcy belongs.

Free Contracting in Bankruptcy

F. H. BUCKLEY

A defense of freedom of contract may take one of two forms. First, it might be argued that every bargain freely entered into by the parties affected by its terms should be enforceable. This might be called a *procedural* defense, since it focuses on contractual inputs rather than outputs. The second defense of freedom of contract is *substantive*, and identifies a value-increasing bargaining outcome which barriers to free contracting would deny to the parties.

A procedural defense of freedom of contract in bankruptcy law would assert that debtors and creditors are capable of bargaining in their own best interests. Such claims are uncontroversial when the debtor is a business and are quite persuasive when the debtor is a consumer.[1] Professor Schwartz's defense of free bargaining in bankruptcy law is instead substantive. He describes a bargaining gain which the parties are not permitted to exploit under Chapter 11. Denial of this gain imposes a cost on debtors, for whom Chapter 11 is ostensibly designed to benefit, and this argues for a relaxation of contractual waivers of Chapter 11.

I An Incentive Theory of Bankruptcy

The bargaining gains Schwartz identifies result from a reduction in *underinvestment* costs.[2] On default, firm managers may either liquidate under Chapter 7 or reorganize under Chapter 11 of the Bankruptcy Code. They will choose strategically, so as to maximize private gains, and may thus adopt a value-decreasing procedure. For example, the managers might inefficiently reorganize even though firm value would be maximized through liquidation. Creditors will anticipate management's opportunistic behavior, and will discount the firm's promise of repayment. Because of this, the firm will not be able to finance some profitable opportunities. The resulting underinvestment costs are born by the firm's shareholders.

The firm may reduce underinvestment costs through risk-sharing features in the loan agreement. Schwartz shows how the firm can credibly commit ex ante to make the efficient bankruptcy decision ex post through a loan agreement in which creditors share a portion of their reorganization gains with managers. Of course, the parties may also agree ex post to make the efficient reorganization decision, through a side payment by creditors. However, Schwartz shows that underinvestment costs are sometimes lower when the risk-sharing agreement is made ex ante.

Firm managers have a greater ability ex ante to cure the underinvestment problem than Schwartz gives them credit for. To see this, recall that, in Schwartz's model, the probability of default is exogenous, as is the probability on default that reorganization (liquidation) will be more efficient than liquidation (reorganization). Schwartz also assumes that the management misbehavior problem arises only when firm value is maximized in liquidation and management has a private incentive to reorganize.

$$y_{L,L} + b_{L,L} > y_{L,R} + b_{L,R} \tag{1}$$

$$b_{L,R} > b_{L,L} \tag{2}$$

where:

y	=	firm value (all of which is paid to creditors on default)
b	=	private benefits available to management
$y_{L,L}, b_{L,L}$	=	firm value y or private benefits b when liquidation is efficient and firm liquidates
$y_{L,R}, b_{L,R}$	=	firm value y or private benefits b when liquidation is efficient and firm reorganizes

Because management is better off in reorganization (inequality (2)), the firm might not liquidate, even though this is the efficient bankruptcy decision (inequality (1)). But this is an unstable equilibrium, for the gains from liquidation represent an unexploited bargain opportunity. In an ex post renegotiation, assume that creditors will agree to give up their entire liquidation gains $(y_{L,L} - y_{L,R})$ to managers, who will then take the firm into liquidation.

Schwartz next shows how the prospect of ex post renegotiation will affect the price which creditors will pay for their claims ex ante. Under Schwartz's renegotiation contract, the creditors anticipate the loss of the liquidation surplus, and value their claims as follows:

$$C_{REN} = qy_g + (1 - q)[p_R y_{R,R} + p_L y_{L,R}] \tag{3}$$

where

C_{REN}	=	value of debt claims when management is expected to extract renegotiation concessions by threatening an inefficient reorganization
q	=	probability of solvency
y_g	=	face amount of debt claim (maximum payout to creditors on solvency)
p_R	=	probability that reorganization is efficient
$y_{R,R}$	=	firm value when reorganization is efficient and firm reorganizes
p_L	=	probability that liquidation is efficient

$y_{L,R}$ = firm value when liquidation is efficient and firm reorganizes

This is less than creditors would receive if management could credibly pledge to liquidate whenever it is efficient to do so. In that event, creditors would receive:

$$C_{MAX} = qy_g + (1 - q)[p_R y_{R,R} + p_L y_{L,L}] \qquad (4)$$

The difference between (4) and (3) is $(1 - q)p_L[y_{L,L} - y_{L,R}]$, and represents the expected wealth transfer from creditors to management through renegotiation after default. Given this shortfall, the firm will underinvest, passing up profitable opportunities with a project cost between C_{REN} and C_{MAX}.

Schwartz then shows how the firm may reduce underinvestment costs through ex ante incentive features in the loan agreement. However, incentive strategies are more robust than Schwartz credits them to be.

To induce management to make the efficient bankruptcy decision, Schwartz suggests that the loan agreement might offer managers a share s of the liquidation gains of $y_{L,L} - y_{L,R}$. Management then will liquidate rather than reorganize, provided that:

$$b_{L,L} + s(y_{L,L} - y_{L,R}) \geq b_{L,R} \qquad (5)$$

To reduce underinvestment costs, the firm will set s at the lowest possible value which satisfies (5), where:

$$s = (b_{L,R} - b_{L,L}) / (y_{L,L} - y_{L,R}). \qquad\qquad 0 \leq s \leq 1$$

The value of the debt claim will then be:

$$C_{CON} = qy_g + (1 - q)\{p_R y_{R,R} + p_L[y_{L,L} - s(y_{L,L} - y_{L,R})]\} \qquad (6)$$

Using Schwartz's numerical examples, $C_{CON} = 231.40$. This exceeds both C_{REN} and the value Schwartz ascribes to a renegotiation-proof debt claim. C_{CON} will always exceed C_{REN} by $(1 - q)p_L(1 - s)(y_{L,L} - y_{L,R})$. Given the assumptions that $y_{L,L} \geq y_{L,R}$, that s is bounded by 0 and 1, and that $(1 - q)p_L$ is positive, the difference between C_{CON} and C_{REN} can never be negative.

In sum, the parties can always agree ex ante to incentive features which (1) give managers adequate incentives to liquidate the firm when this is efficient, and (2) result in debt claims worth more than they would be if managers were able to capture the entire liquidation surplus of $y_{L,L} - y_{L,R}$ through an ex post renegotiation.[3]

II A Governance Theory of Bankruptcy

There is a second way in which managers might credibly forswear value-decreasing reorganizations. In the above, we assume that the right to elect whether to liquidate or reorganize has been given to management. With free bargaining, however, the parties may opt out of Chapter 11 and assign the bankruptcy decision to creditors.

Let us again assume, with Schwartz, that the only agency cost problem is that of misbehavior by managers who take the firm into an inefficient reorganization. This agency problem disappears when the decision whether to liquidate or reorganize is made by creditors. In that case, the firm will always be liquidated when this maximizes its value, and the debt claims will be worth C_{MAX}. Underinvestment costs may therefore be eliminated through a governance strategy in which management control passes to creditors upon default.

Assigning the bankruptcy decision to creditors addresses a second agency cost problem. When a firm's debt claims have a positive probability of default, mean-preserving investments which increase the firm's risk effect a wealth transfer from creditors to shareholders. To exploit these distributional gains, shareholders and their management allies will adopt value-decreasing investments. The resulting *overinvestment* costs, like underinvestment costs, will be born by shareholders.[4]

Schwartz's ex ante incentive contracts might reduce overinvestment as well as underinvestment costs. As Thomas Jackson and Robert Scott have noted, firm managers have reduced incentives to adopt inefficient risky projects when they are given a share of the debt claims.[5] This is what happens on a shift from absolute to relative priority standards on a bankruptcy distribution, and Jackson and Scott therefore suggested that relative priority rules might usefully address agency cost concerns.

Nevertheless, overinvestment and underinvestment costs are better policed through governance strategies than through the incentive strategies suggested by Jackson-Scott and Schwartz. Relative priority schemes do not address the extreme misincentives of managers at end-period. At that point, it is far more effective to permit creditors to assume control of the firm, as governance strategies would do. Underinvestment costs are also better addressed through governance strategies. As we have noted, assigning the bankruptcy decision to creditors raises the value of debt claims to C_{MAX} and eliminates the underinvestment problem. In addition, incentive strategies will unwind as the firm approaches default. This does not happen in Schwartz's examples because the probability of default and expected values are assumed to be exogenous. However, the probability of default is a function of leverage ratios, because of the overinvestment problem. At any particular leverage ratio, shareholders have an incentive to increase the risk of default q. When default becomes more likely, the overinvestment misincentives are exacerbated. In end-period, shortly before default, misincentive costs are greatest, and incentive strategies are least likely to be successful. Upon default, therefore, incentive strategies should yield to governance strategies that transfer control of the firm from shareholders to creditors.

Governance strategies impose their own set of agency costs. When the bankruptcy decision is made by management, the agency cost problem arises where liquidation is efficient but reorganization is privately optimal for managers.

$$y_{L,L} + b_{L,L} > y_{L,R} + b_{L,R} \qquad (1)$$

$$b_{L,R} > b_{L,L} \qquad (2)$$

When the bankruptcy decision is made by creditors, on the other hand, the agency cost problem arises where reorganization is efficient but liquidation is privately optimal for creditors.

$$y_{R,R} + b_{R,R} > y_{R,L} + b_{R,L}$$

$$y_{R,L} > y_{R,R}$$

To see how this may happen, assume that the values for the variables are as follows:

$$y_g = 150$$

$$y_{R,R} = .5(240) + .5(0) = 120$$

$$b_{R,R} = 100$$

$$y_{R,L} = 110$$

$$b_{R,L} = 50$$

Reorganization will then produce a joint value of 220, as against a joint value of 160 on liquidation. However, creditors are better off on liquidation, where they receive 110, than on reorganization. This is because the loan amount of 150 places an upper limit on payouts to creditors.[6] The reorganization lottery gives them a .5 probability of 150 and a .5 probability of zero, and has an expected value of 75.

An efficient governance policy will therefore seek to minimize the total costs of management and creditor misbehavior. Giving creditors veto powers will be most costly when the firm is highly solvent, while the costs of management misbehavior will be highest when the firm nears default. This argues for a turnover of management responsibilities to the creditors at some point near default.[7] This might occur through the appointment of a private receiver by a repossessing secured lender, or of a bankruptcy trustee by a petitioning creditor.

The possibility of creditor misbehavior does not justify restrictions on free contracting. The costs of premature creditor termination will be born primarily by managers, who have every incentive to resist a broad grant of termination rights to creditors. Where the firm has unambiguously granted termination rights to creditors, therefore, there is little reason to impeach free contracting on procedural grounds.[8]

Schwartz dismisses governance strategies because of the possibility of creditor misbehavior and because he thinks that creditor termination rights would be impracticable. If this were correct, Canadian debtors and secured lenders would never have bargained as they did for receivership remedies. The theoretical problems that Schwartz and other commentators have identified are clearly of great interest. But sometimes an ounce of comparative law is worth a pound of theory.

Since American bankruptcy law is among the most restrictive in the First World, it is odd that bankruptcy scholars have paid so little attention to other regimes that offer a broader scope for free bargaining. The most obvious comparison is with Canadian law. No other set of business laws so closely resembles American law.[9] But the differences stop with bankruptcy law. Canadian bankruptcy law favors the secured lender much more than American bankruptcy law does. Until recently, a Canadian bankruptcy did not affect the property rights of secured lenders. Secured lender repossessory rights therefore survived a Canadian petition.[10] On default, a Canadian secured bank would usually appoint a private receiver to take charge of the debtor's assets and manage his business.[11] The private receiver assumed control of the business, either to manage or to sell it, and his appointment suspended the powers of the debtor's officers and directors. The receiver took his instructions from the appointing secured lender, and even owed primary fiduciary responsibilities to him.

By contrast, a Chapter 11 bankruptcy petition stays the secured lender's hand by the most effective of poison pills. Bankruptcy Code § 362 provides for an automatic stay of secured lender repossessory remedies, including the right to appoint a receiver over the assets.[12] Moreover, Chapter 11, and a compliant bankruptcy bench, ensure that management will control the reorganization proceedings even though they might take many years.[13]

The comparison with Canada permits a better understanding of why American governance structures turned out as they did. While Canadian and American business laws are very similar, there are sharp differences in their banking and bankruptcy laws. Apart from bankruptcy reorganization law, Canada's Chartered Banks were never barred from operating across provincial borders, or prevented from operating branch banks. These differences explain why the Canadian economy is concentrated relative to the United States.[14]

Canada's five major Chartered Banks stand at the apex of the country's economy. The banks have historically been able to insist that their clients deal exclusively with a single bank,[15] and both banker and client typically share the services of the same lawyers, investment dealers, accountants, and trust companies, often within a few blocks of the corner of King and Bay streets in Toronto. The result is a private intelligence network centered upon the bank.[16] These ties are formalized through a web of interlocking directorships on common boards, with a far greater banker presence in the corporate boardroom than in the United States.[17]

The relationships among the parties developed into a stable Canadian keiretsu. A firm within the hierarchy found it easy to do business with fellow members who shared the same professional and investment advisers. At the individual level, these ties were cemented by long-standing personal acquaintances among members, who saw each other over deals, frequented the same clubs, lived in the same neighborhood, and often attended the same schools as youths. Ascending up the hierarchy, one became acquainted with fellow members of the business group in other Canadian cities, and developed the similar ties with them.

Canadian-American differences in banker dominance cannot be attributed to the borrower's needs for external financing or to leverage ratios, since these are about the same in the two countries.[18] Nor did banker dominance arise from direct equity investments, since Canadian banks are prohibited from holding more than 10 percent of the voting stock of a Canadian corporation.[19] Canadian banks are also restricted to low-risk "legal for life" investment policies. In addition, a bank that takes an active role in the affairs of a solvent firm might be found to have engaged in trade or business, as prohibited by Bank Act § 410(2).[20] As a consequence, less than 2 percent of the Cdn$846 billion of domestic bank assets are equity investments in nongovernmental enterprises.[21] Moreover, regulatory barriers do not channel firms toward banks, as Japanese laws are said to do.[22] Like the United States, Canada has a healthy public securities market, and firms were not restricted to bank financing. Canadian firms could also raise capital through private placements with nonbank investment intermediaries.

Canadian corporate and securities laws were adopted from American precedents. Differences in the role of the board of directors and in tender offer rules and proxy regulations are slight. And while Canadian banks are relatively larger than American ones, it is unlikely that this difference by itself can account for differences in economic concentration. Though American banking is relatively fragmented, American banks are still large as compared to their clients.

If these were the only cross-border legal differences, then, Canada and the United States should have ended up in the same place. But they did not, and the most plausible difference is bankruptcy law. Canadian concentration may in large measure be attributed to the threat advantage Canadian secured lenders had on default. Had American secured lenders enjoyed the same advantages as Canadian lenders in this respect, the American economy would have been much more concentrated. And that is just what happened during the money trust era, when creditors dominated the reorganization process.[23]

It is important to note that the banker's threat advantage in Canada was not limited to firms in financial distress. On distress, bankers had the unfettered right to fire or retain managers. But even if solvent, a Canadian manager would not know the day or hour of distress, and had far greater reason to defer to his banker than an American manager.

This helps to explain why creditor control is so much stronger in Canada. To be sure, American debtors are not immunized from creditor clout. On financial distress, management turnover rates are significantly higher and creditors are able to shape corporate policies.[24] Creditors may also bargain for a strong management voice through Highly Levered Transactions.[25] But this is not to say that American creditors have the same bargaining leverage that Canadian banks possessed. If the private receivership did not advantage creditors, why should prodebtor American scholars resist it? And why is the Canadian economy so much more concentrated than the American one?

IV Free Contracting and Relational Lending

Legal barriers to corporate concentration in the United States impose costs, but the fragmentation that results from broad equity markets has compensating advantages. Since German and Japanese financial regulations are said to inhibit broad equity markets, many commentators are agnostic about which system is better.[26] That is why the comparison with Canada is so useful. The Canadian regime affords the best example of what a corporate governance regime would look like under free bargaining and enforceable property rights. The fact that the American regime is fragmented is not evidence that a fragmented regime is superior, since concentration was not an available option. But the fact that the Canadian regime is concentrated is evidence that such a regime is superior, since Canadians had choices. Had a fragmented regime the advantages which Americans claim, Canadians could have emulated it. They could have sold overpriced concentrated claims and bought underpriced fragmented ones.

American lenders do not have the right to opt out of Chapter 11's mandatory stay. But Canadian lenders could have barred repossessory remedies and crafted a private stay in their loan agreements had they wished.[27] The fact that they never did so must be embarrassing to the apologist for the American regime. If the American regime is as efficient as it is said to be, why did Canadian bankers never bargain for it? As Joe Biden used to ask, were they simply thick?

The reason why Canadian bankers bargained for receivership remedies, and why debtors conceded them, is that they served efficiency goals. The private receivership permitted a crisis-ridden firm to redeploy its assets far more quickly than a Chapter 11 reorganization.[28] The receivership remedy was also asserted at a time when the overinvestment costs described in section 2 were at their highest.

Moreover, banker dominance in Canada offers firms many of the advantages that come from belonging to a Japanese keiretsu. Membership in a keiretsu increases access to credit, since more information production is shared with lenders.[29] Because keiretsu members have a long-term stake in each other's fortunes, they also have stronger incentives to monitor each other. This benefits claim holders throughout the keiretsu, including public shareholders. In addition, long-term relational lending gives the parties stronger incentives to invest in a reputation for nonopportunistic behavior.[30] These benefits are self-reinforcing. Since they increase the benefits of membership in the keiretsu, they reduce the likelihood that a firm will leave it. A Canadian firm can always switch its accounts to another bank. However, this will impose substantial costs for little benefit, since there is relatively little competition in the provision of banking services.

Reliance on a main bank, rather than on several sources of financing, introduces the possibility of creditor misbehavior. For example, a bank might seek to exploit a situational monopoly by extracting concessions from debtors when they are in no position to refuse them, or by vetoing value-increasing but risky investment opportunities.[31] But this does not supply a justification for a mandatory stay of creditor remedies, since debtors are free to bargain for a private stay in nonmandatory regimes. Since Canadian debtors failed to do so, one may infer that the costs of creditor misbehavior under the private receivership are exceeded by the costs of managerial misbehavior under the American stay. In addition, Canadian lenders bonded themselves against misbehavior in several novel and interesting ways.

First, Canadian banks bond themselves against opportunism through bank governance policies. Bank boards are large, and the directors are chosen from keiretsu members. Major loan decisions are made at the board level,[32] and banker opportunism would be quickly known throughout the Canadian financial establishment.

Second, the Canadian banker, benignly neglected by the American theorist, solved the common pool problem which the theorist thought justified the bankruptcy stay.[33] Were it not for the stay, the theorist argued, creditors would divide up the debtor's firm-specific assets. But even without a stay, Canadian bankers preserved firm-specific assets through the private receivership. They required their debtors to deal with a single bank, and to pledge all their assets to it. On default, then, the bank simply asserted its priority over other creditors to keep the assets together.

Third, the Canadian keiretsu reduced the costs of creditor misincentives that arise because creditors do not share in the debtor's residual earnings.[34] By not competing for clients, Canadian banks took an implicit residual claim in their long-term clients. The banks grew with them, and shared in their fortunes.

Finally, Canadian debtors police creditor misbehavior through concentrated shareholder blocks. Voting control is much more likely to rest in the hands of a single or small group of shareholders in Canada than in the United States.[35] This is plausibly a consequence of the greater clout Canadian creditors possess, with shareholder blocks serving as a counterpoise to the weight of a dominant creditor. Under free contracting, concentration begets concentration.

An expansion in bargaining rights might remove any lingering doubts about the superiority of the Canadian regime. The fact that secured lending is prevalent in regimes which permit it does not prove that chattel security is efficient, as debtors may pledge their assets to effect wealth transfers.[36] Nor is the gradual acceptance of chattel security by common law courts evidence of its efficiency. To be sure, a rich academic literature describes the possible benefits of secured lending. Nevertheless, some authors have suggested, as a theoretical matter, that it might be inefficient.[37] These doubts would largely be answered if debtors could bind themselves by charter not to issue secured debt. As they would then bear the costs of an inefficient grant of security, they would have an incentive to forswear its use were it value-decreasing.[38]

The Canadian secured lender's repossessory remedies were weakened by the 1992 Bankruptcy and Insolvency Act, which stays repossessory remedies.[39] However, the new Canadian Act is considerably more pro-creditor than Chapter 11. The initial stay is for only thirty days, and while it can be extended for successive forty-five-day periods, the total period cannot exceed five months.[40] In addition, financial deregulation over the last ten years has considerably strengthened Canadian banks.[41]

V Conclusion

Professor Schwartz has offered a theoretical defense of bargaining around mandatory American bankruptcy rules. If anything, the defense of free contracting in bankruptcy law is stronger than Schwartz credits it to be. The common pool problem, which is said to justify the mandatory stay of secured lender repossessory remedies, may be effectively addressed through free contracting and enforceable property rights. The underinvestment costs Schwartz identifies may always be better reduced by ex ante bargaining than by ex post renegotiation around mandatory terms. Finally, underinvestment and overinvestment inefficiencies are better addressed by bargaining around the mandatory bankruptcy stay than by adjusting management payoffs.

A theoretical defense of free bargaining, such as Schwartz offers, may be very useful. But as the dispute is ultimately an empirical matter, it is more valuable still to see how creditor and debtor bargain where they are permitted to do so. For Americans, the most obvious comparison is to Canadian bankruptcy law, which is less restrictive than American law, and which until recently did not stay repossessing secured lenders. Given the right to bargain for their bankruptcy regimes, Canadians opted for the strongest possible repossessory rights, rather than for private stays.

The comparison with Canada is also useful in showing how free bargaining may result in profound changes. Much more than the American economy, the Canadian economy is centralized, and this has permitted Canadian investors to share in the benefits of relational lending. If one asks what legal difference between the two countries best explains the different paths their economies followed, the most obvious answer is secured lender repossessory remedies. The costs of mandatory rules in bankruptcy might thus be far greater than has been realized.

Free Contracting in Bankruptcy at Home and Abroad

ROBERT K. RASMUSSEN

Alan Schwartz's essay makes an important contribution to the question of what constitutes an efficient bankruptcy system. It crafts a persuasive argument that party choice, which is the core concept of free contracting, can produce gains in overall social welfare in bankruptcy, just as it can in commercial law generally. Schwartz begins with the tacit assumption that the overriding normative goal of bankruptcy is efficiency. It is an assumption that I (and I think the rest of the commentators on the paper) share.[1] Moreover, it is an assumption that has long been part of our bankruptcy law. Bankruptcy law as it is written may contain multiple goals, but few would gainsay that at least one major purpose of bankruptcy law is to promote efficiency. Indeed, it has long been accepted that bankruptcy law was needed to prevent an inefficient race to the failing debtor's assets. That bankruptcy law should be concerned with efficiency is thus beyond dispute. What remains is specifying the contours of an efficient bankruptcy law.

Traditionally those endorsing the proposition that bankruptcy should be efficient have also endorsed the notion that it is the role of government to prescribe mandatory bankruptcy rules. Creditors, left to their own devices, created a common pool problem in which too many claims were chasing too few assets. The government, by imposing a mandated proceeding that sorted out the affairs of the debtor, could reduce or even eliminate this problem. As Alan Schwartz's paper nicely demonstrates, this conventional wisdom can no longer be accepted.[2] The attack launched by Schwartz is compelling. It demonstrates that the current mandatory rule that assigns the choice of bankruptcy procedure—reorganization or liquidation—to the firm's managers does not maximize firm value. Schwartz also shows that private parties at times can generate more efficient outcomes through private contract. Schwartz thus takes the general economic argument in favor of free contracting and shows that it has equal force in the bankruptcy setting.

This comment supplements Schwartz's work along two lines. First, it responds to arguments that the defenders of contractual prohibition in bankruptcy could mount in favor of governmental regulation. They might attack Schwartz's conclusion by pointing to what they perceive as practical impediments to implementing a regime of unfettered contractual choice. I suggest that a menu of bankruptcy regimes from which a firm can select at the time of incorporation comports with Schwartz's theoretical point while addressing these practical concerns of those leery of contractual freedom in the bankruptcy context.

Second, this comment expressly broadens the debate to include transnational firms. To be sure, nothing in Schwartz's work suggests that it is limited to domestic concerns. The force of Schwartz's arguments is not constrained by territorial borders. Yet on a pragmatic level, the existence of multiple jurisdictions creates additional impediments to law reform. It is one thing to convince the United States Congress to enact optimal bankruptcy reform; it is another to convince every country in the world to follow suit. This would seem to suggest that domestic bankruptcy reform should fare better than transnational bankruptcy reform. Surprisingly, however, this may not be the case. American law grants firms greater contractual freedom in international transactions than it does in domestic ones. Contractual provisions that would not be enforced if both parties resided in the United States may be enforced when one of the parties resides abroad. This differing treatment creates an opportunity for transnational firms to contract out of domestic bankruptcy law in favor of another country's law. Although such freedom does not offer the benefits of full contractual free choice, it does promise efficiency gains by expanding the number of options available to the insolvent firm.

I A Bankruptcy Menu

Schwartz's case for the efficiency of free contracting in bankruptcy runs as follows. The value of an insolvent firm differs according to whether it undergoes liquidation or reorganization. For some firms, the liquidation value is higher; for others, the reorganization value is higher. Creditors receive a higher payout when the firm ends up in the procedure that maximizes its value. It is impossible, however, to ascertain in advance which procedure will be better for any given firm. Under current bankruptcy law, the managers of a firm decide which bankruptcy procedure is used. The managers always do better in reorganization than liquidation because they receive personal benefits from operating the firm. The creditors and the managers can, however, always negotiate over which procedure will be used. If the gains to the creditors from choosing liquidation over reorganization exceed the private benefits that the managers receive from running the firm in reorganization, the creditors can in effect bribe the managers to file for liquidation. Thus it will always be the case that, ex post, the firm will end up in the efficient procedure.[3]

The problem with this arrangement is that the cost of inducing the managers to choose liquidation when it increases net social welfare can be quite high. If lenders know that they will have to pay a lot to managers on the back end to induce them to put the firm in liquidation when that is the efficient course of action, they are less likely to lend money on the front end. In the language of Schwartz's model, the bank's participation constraint increases. This leads to the heart of Schwartz's paper. Schwartz's model demonstrates that in some situations creditors may, at the time they lend money, expect a higher payout from an insolvent debtor if the debtor at the time the loan is made precommits to file for liquidation when certain verifiable events occur. Of course, such a commitment on the part of managers is a commitment to forgo the private benefits they receive in reorganization. Thus the contract promises the managers that they will, under certain circumstances, receive a portion of the firm's value. The mangers thus receive part of the gains of liquidation over reorganization, and the creditors receive the rest. In short, whereas current law results in an ex post bribe to managers to place the firm in liquidation, Schwartz's proposal is for an ex ante bribe set in the contract. To the extent that this contract allows debtors to credibly commit to higher payouts in states of financial distress, they can fund more projects that have a positive net expected value. Thus, by allowing debtors to commit to future action via contract, societal efficiency is increased because more projects that have a positive expected value will be undertaken.

Schwartz anticipates a major objection to his call for contractual choice of bankruptcy procedure. Different creditors may have different preferences for bankruptcy procedures. Trade creditors who sell goods to the firm may prefer reorganization to liquidation because of the return that they can earn on the goods that they sell while the firm is attempting to reorganize. Unsecured creditors may prefer a procedure under which the payout deviates from strict contractual priority. Moreover, the debtor cannot mediate these disputes at a given time. The debtor's pool of creditors changes over time. Old creditors get paid; new creditors extend credit. The new creditors do not know the terms of the other contracts that the debtor has already made. Thus it may well be the case that in a regime of free contracting a debtor will have outstanding contracts that contain different bankruptcy terms. The existence of conflicting contractual terms raises the question of what course of action the managers are legally bound to take once the firm becomes insolvent.

Schwartz's response to this objection is that, first, if all creditors have the same preferences regarding bankruptcy procedures, they will insist on the same value-maximizing contract regardless of when they contract with the firm, and there will thus not be a problem. The problem arises only when creditors have different preferences. Here Schwartz offers two responses. The first is that, to the extent that the conflict of creditor preferences is over whether seniority of claims is recognized, all contracts should be required to respect seniority. As to conflicts based on which procedure is to be used, Schwartz proposes to bind all creditors to the bankruptcy contract to which a majority of the debt (in amount) agreed.

The problem, however, is not so simple. Schwartz's model posits contracting over a binary choice—liquidate or reorganize. Moreover, Schwartz assumes that all parties agree on what contract sets forth the optimal bribe for managers. This is because he assumes that all of the relevant values in his model—the probability of bankruptcy, the returns to the managers and creditors in both liquidation and reorganization, and the value of the firm if it is successful—are all common knowledge. Thus we only have two possible contracts: one which provides the optimal bribe;[4] and one which contains no bribe.

Yet in the more complex world in which we live, there are many more potential contracts. First, contracts concerning bankruptcy procedure could focus on isolated provisions of the Bankruptcy Code rather than on simply the choice of reorganization or liquidation. For example, one could imagine a firm and a creditor attempting to reverse via contract the Bankruptcy Code's provision which bars the enforcement of contract terms that provide for automatic termination immediately upon the filing of a bankruptcy petition. Other parties may prefer a contract which modifies the Bankruptcy Code's automatic stay on collection efforts so that it does not apply to the firm's major financing creditor.[5] Still others might wish to enter into a contract which transfers the equity position to the most junior debt holders if there is a default.[6] Second, even if we were to limit arbitrarily the parties to simple decisions about whether the managers should file for liquidation or reorganization, the optimal bribe to managers may differ in each contract that the firm signs. Not only may different creditors have differing perceptions of the value of the relevant variables, but these values will change as the firm continues its operations. What is optimal when the first creditor enters its contract may not be optimal when the second creditor enters its contract.

A world that allows firms to commit to multiple and possibly inconsistent bankruptcy procedures threatens to dissipate the gains from free contracting. To see this, consider the case of a single creditor deciding whether or not to lend money to the firm. Assume further that, given the relevant values, contracting over bankruptcy procedures is preferable to negotiation with the managers after default. To the extent that this optimal contract supports additional investment, it will only do so to the extent that the creditor believes it will be enforced. Once there is a positive probability that this contract will not be enforced but that some other one will, the creditor's expected return is affected by its lower return on these other contracts.[7] Thus, even if a creditor is offered a contract with what it believes is the optimal bankruptcy clauses, its expected return will be lower than it would be if it were assured that this term would be enforced. This lower expected return under the optimal contract makes it less likely that the creditor will loan money in the first instance. In the language of Schwartz's model, the creditor's participation constraint increases.

The problem here is that the debtor has no method by which it can credibly commit to a single contract. Schwartz apparently recognizes this problem. When he turns to actual legal reform, Schwartz leaves his model behind. Schwartz does not propose, as his model suggests, that Congress amend the Bankruptcy Code so as to allow firms to enter into contracts regulating whether the firm should file for liquidation or reorganization. Rather, he suggests that the government should create a small number of alternate bankruptcy procedures.[8] A procedure would be included so long as it is likely that a number of firms would be likely to use that procedure. Presumably Schwartz envisions firms writing contracts which either unambiguously commit the firm to select a certain procedure or state the conditions which determine which procedure will be chosen by the managers once the firm encounters financial distress.

Schwartz does not justify the move from the choice set in his model to this broader choice set. Presumably, the justification would run along the following lines. The model demonstrates that if there are two potential bankruptcy procedures and neither is optimal for all firms, social welfare is increased by allowing the firm and its creditors to contract over these two choices. Scholars have suggested a number of potential bankruptcy procedures as improvements over the current choices of liquidation or reorganization. To the extent that these alternative procedures are more efficient for some firms, these firms should be allowed to contract for them. Finally, it is better to have these procedures enacted as positive law rather than simply allowing private firms to specify them in individual contracts because this method reduces transaction costs.

This last point deserves some amplification. Schwartz has shown that welfare is increased by allowing firms to contract for bankruptcy procedures. But why not simply allow firms to contract out of extant bankruptcy law into a regime of their own design? Under traditional economic analysis of contract law, the virtue of allowing parties to contract around legal rules is that the parties can decide whether the legal rule in place maximizes the value of the contract, and if it does not, the parties can choose a better rule at a relatively low cost. Thus legal rules should be "defaults": they apply unless the parties contract around them.

Recent work borrowing from the economic literature on network externalities has questioned this simple proposition. A network externality in a product area exists where the value of the product depends upon the number of persons using the product.[9] For example, part of the value of having an IBM-compatible PC is that many other people own them, thus creating a market for software and hardware. Michael Klausner has applied this learning to the choices that a firm must make in setting up its internal affairs.[10] Firms are generally allowed great latitude in this area; states normally provide a default rule, and firms are free to depart if they so choose. Klausner demonstrates that when the value of a default rule to a firm turns on how many other firms have adopted it, the choice made by a single firm whether to adopt or depart from that rule may not be socially optimal. At times, all firms may adopt the default rule, even if social welfare would be improved by having a diversity of rules. At other times, all firms may opt out of the default rule, and select their own customized rule, even if there is a single rule which, if adopted by all firms, would increase social welfare. In such situations, efficiency can be improved by having a menu of options from which firms can select rather than by having a single default rule.[11]

While a detailed analysis of the network externalities problem in the bankruptcy contracting context is beyond the scope of this comment, it does appear that such externalities exist, thus lending support for the menu approach. Almost all recognize that a single set of insolvency rules would not be optimal for every firm. Yet if there were a single default rule, it may be that network effects would lead to a "lock-in" effect where all firms adopted this single rule. The sources of these network externalities include legal service externalities and marketing externalities.

Legal service externalities exist where lawyers are familiar with the default rule, and this familiarity creates an incentive for the client to adhere to that rule.[12] Once lawyers are familiar with particular contractual terms, it costs the client more in legal fees to have the lawyers draft a new contract with new language and new terms than it would to simply go with the familiar ones. In the bankruptcy context, there are a number of potentially complicated issues whose resolution both requires elaborate drafting and permits many alternative terms, as the current morass that is international bankruptcy law illustrates. Given a default rule of private contract enforcement, there will be a cost advantage for the firm on the front end in choosing the existing terms rather than attempting to customize a set of bankruptcy rules for the firm. The savings in fees could lead a firm to adopt the default rule even though a different rule would maximize firm value.

A similar externality exists in the marketing area. Firms need investors, both at the stage when they first form, and when they first go public. The investors have to evaluate the product that they are buying. To the extent that there is a well-used default rule, the investors will be familiar with the costs and benefits of this rule.[13] If the firm decides to adopt a customized set of bankruptcy rules, however, the investors will have to spend resources in trying to ascertain the costs and benefits of this unfamiliar term. The same holds true for all subsequent creditors deciding whether or not to extend credit to the firm. They will price the cost of having to learn any unfamiliar term. Once again, there are cost savings for the firm adopting the existing default rule instead of attempting to craft a rule that better suits the needs of the firm.

These costs are ameliorated by having a menu of options from which firms can select. By having a number of publicly disseminated insolvency rules, lawyers will gain expertise with each of the rules.[14] Thus, as among the rules on the menu, there will be few or no legal service externalities. A lawyer will be conversant with the various choices available to the firm, and thus should charge roughly the same amount for each of the available choices and have no biases toward any particular choice. Only if the firm decides to craft a set of insolvency rules that departs from the choices on the menu will there be legal service externalities. Thus, to the extent that a well-crafted set of options can cover the needs of a large majority of firms, the problems associated with legal services externalities would be greatly reduced.

Adopting a menu of insolvency options would also decrease marketing externalities. Those deciding to invest money in the firm, either by taking an equity stake or by extending credit, would be familiar with the various options on the menu. To be sure, these investors will charge differing rates depending on how they are treated under the differing options. Yet, because they are already familiar with these options, there will be no charge for the added cost of having to learn an entirely new set of insolvency rules. By shifting from a single default rule to a menu of options, the marketing externalities should be reduced significantly.

Once it is decided that a menu of options would be superior to a single default rule, one must face the question of whether the market can provide such a menu through the creation of standard forms or whether it should be enacted by the government. As a general matter, I endorse market solutions to bankruptcy problems. Yet in the area of producing a menu of bankruptcy options, it is probably the case that the government can do a better job. The network externalities that exist under a single default rule would prevent the market from forming the standard forms necessary to create a well-functioning menu regime. Even if one law firm decided to invest resources to create a set of standard forms, it is unlikely that a firm would choose one of these forms rather than the default rule.

The default rule has an installed base of interpretation; other lawyers know how courts have interpreted the rule. Such a base of interpretation does not exist with respect to the privately generated forms. Also, those who invest money in the firm already know the contours of the default rule; they would have to spend additional resources to determine the contours of the insolvency rules drafted by the firm. It is these very problems which doom the default-rule approach. Only if the law firm were able to draft a set of insolvency rules whose efficiency gains exceeded these network externalities would a firm have an incentive to deviate from the default rule. It is the government's comparative advantage in publicizing its menu that leads to the conclusion that the government, rather than the market, should craft the menu of bankruptcy options.

Schwartz is thus correct that the government should adopt a menu of bankruptcy options. Yet Schwartz's proposal still does not solve the problem of a single firm having conflicting debt contracts. The solution here is to adopt a mechanism by which the firm can publicly select a single contract term which all creditors can then rely on. Rather than having individual loan contracts specify which procedure will apply if the firm becomes insolvent, the firm should publicly state in its corporate charter which procedure it selects.[15] To be sure, this proposal removes the creditors from the negotiation over bankruptcy procedure. Yet the firm has the incentive to select the optimal charter provision. It gains the benefit of such provision through the ability to fund additional projects that have a positive net present value. Such charters have the advantage over contracts of being publicly available to all creditors. In a world where corporate charters contain provisions that describe the mechanism by which a firm can be taken over, it is not difficult to imagine such charters describing the mechanism by which a firm deals with financial distress.

Proposing that free contracting over bankruptcy procedures take place at the level of the corporate charter rather than individual debt contracts raises a new problem. The basic characteristics of a firm change over time. A bankruptcy procedure that was optimal when the firm was privately held may not be optimal once the firm becomes a public corporation. Presumably this evolution is accounted for in Schwartz's proposal by the fact that new debt contracts will specify the optimal bankruptcy choice for that time. As the needs of the firm change, the debt contracts will change. Once debt contracts which specify the new optimal choice amount to over half of the firm's outstanding debt, the firm will have moved from the old procedure to the new, more efficient procedure.

No such natural evolution takes place when the bankruptcy choice is enshrined in the corporate charter. What is needed is a procedure that allows charter amendments so that the choice of bankruptcy procedure can change as necessary, but which also guards against opportunistic changes forced through by the managers. A similar mechanism is needed to move from the current regime, which is essentially the same as having a mandatory charter provision giving the choice of bankruptcy procedure to the firm's managers, to one in which firms have a choice of bankruptcy procedure. A menu approach needs to accommodate both the fact that the optimal procedures vary as a firm changes (the "midterm amendment" problem) and the fact that there is a large number of extant firms which have to be integrated into any new legal regime (the "transition amendment" problem).

There are two ways to guard against managers using a menu approach opportunistically. Firms would be allowed to change the bankruptcy provisions of their charters (or include a new provision if one does not already exist) subject to two constraints. The first is that there be a lag between the time a firm announces that it intends to change its bankruptcy selection and when that change is effective. This lag would give the creditors the opportunity to examine the proposed change. If they ascertained that the change was an attempt to enrich the managers at their expense, they could declare a default, demand repayment, and, if no repayment was forthcoming, initiate an insolvency proceeding prior to the change taking effect.

The second constraint, which applies only to the mid-term amendment problem, is the market. Creditors can anticipate that managers may behave opportunistically. Managers have to make credible commitments that they will not do so or risk losing financing. Thus creditors in their lending agreements could limit the ability of the firm to change its bankruptcy procedure. The contract could specify that the firm would not alter its charter without the creditor's consent. Such a contract assures the creditor that any change will not transfer money from it to the managers.[16]

Schwartz's paper represents a major contribution to the bankruptcy literature. It provides the first formal confirmation of the intuition that firms, acting prior to the onset of financial distress, are better able to select the appropriate bankruptcy procedure than is a mandatory rule that grants to managers an unfettered choice between reorganization and liquidation. Moving from the abstraction of the economic model to the complexity of bankruptcy procedure is a matter of judgment: which method captures the gains from free contracting with the lowest possible transaction costs. Credible ex ante commitments tend to perform better than commitments the validity of which can only be determined ex post.

II   Choosing Bankruptcy Law by Contract

Implicit in Schwartz's essay is a focus on domestic American bankruptcy law. The essay examines the choice that the managers of American firms have under the United States Bankruptcy Code of filing for either liquidation or reorganization. Such a focus is not surprising. All of the law-and-economics analysis of bankruptcy law to date has focused on domestic bankruptcy law. Most of this scholarship has focused on American bankruptcy law, with some attention paid to the domestic law of other countries. What is missing is the economic analysis of the bankruptcy law that applies when a multinational firm encounters financial distress.[17]

A multinational firm has assets in at least two different countries. Historically, insolvency courts have ignored the multinational aspect of such firms. The courts of each country by and large administer the firm's assets within its borders according to the country's laws without any regard to the other assets of the insolvent firm. This approach to transnational bankruptcies has come to be known as the "territorial approach," or, more derisively, as the "grab rule."

I do not here want to discuss the grab rule, or the extant suggestions for a set of rules to determine which nation's bankruptcy laws should apply when a multinational firm files for bankruptcy. Both extant law and all proposed changes assume that it is the role of the various governments involved to specify the bankruptcy procedures that will apply to the multinational firm. In this context, I simply want to note that Schwartz's generic arguments apply with equal force in the transnational as well as domestic context. While Schwartz situates his model in the choice faced by the managers of American firms, the argument driving Schwartz's result applies to all firms in a market economy. The heart of the model is the assumption that there is not a single bankruptcy procedure which is optimal for all firms at all times, and that efficiency can be increased by allowing the firm and its creditors to contract over the procedure that will govern this particular firm. All creditors, whether they be in the United States or Japan, prefer more money to less money. Similarly, the managers of all firms, be they Canadian or French, stand to receive benefits by continued operation of the firms. Thus there is little reason to suspect that, as a normative matter, Schwartz's proposal should be addressed only to American lawmakers. Free contracting over bankruptcy procedures should be extended to all firms worldwide.

While such an approach has great normative appeal, there is little hope that it will soon be adopted. There is virtually no chance that the Bankruptcy Commission currently studying American bankruptcy law will propose increasing contractual freedom over bankruptcy matters. On top of this, the United States has yet to complete successfully any international treaty on bankruptcy. In this situation, it would be fanciful to suggest that we would soon see the United States entering into a treaty which allowed multinational firms to contract about bankruptcy procedures. Yet there exists in current law a method by which firms may be able to both gain some flexibility in choosing bankruptcy procedures and induce countries to craft more efficient bankruptcy rules. This approach emerges from the conflict of law rules that apply in international disputes.

Outside of the bankruptcy context, the problem of which sovereign's law to apply is a familiar one. For centuries parties have refused to confine their business dealings to territorial borders. Inevitably, these dealings would lead to disputes. In such situations, there were often at least two jurisdictions that were affected by the transaction. From one perspective, the rules that developed for sorting out which jurisdiction should provide the forum to resolve the dispute and which law should apply are quite complex. For example, the Restatement (Second) of Conflict of Laws provides a seven-factor balancing test to ascertain which law should apply.[18] These factors include such elusive concepts as the policies of the various states, the policies of the area of law at issue, and the protection of justified expectations. It is hard to imagine courts applying such an amorphous test consistently. It is thus not surprising that Dean Prosser concluded that "[t]he realm of conflict of law is a dismal swamp, filled with quaking quagmires. . . . The ordinary court . . . is quite lost when engulfed and entangled in it."[19]

Yet from another view, the rule governing conflict of law problems is quite straightforward. Within broad limits, the parties can decide, at the time they enter into a transaction, which country should provide the forum and which country's law should govern. As a general matter, both forum selection clauses (contractual provisions designating the host forum) and choice-of-law clauses (contractual provisions identifying the law that will resolve the dispute) are enforced by the courts.[20] Indeed, courts will often enforce such provisions even when they are certain that such enforcement will lead to a different substantive outcome than would obtain if the court decided the matter itself according to its own law. A court will decline to enforce such provisions only when following the law of the other jurisdiction would be contrary to the fundamental policy of the court's own state.[21]

The justification for the general rule of party choice is one that tracks the general argument for freedom of contract: it fulfills the expectations of the parties and allows them to ascertain with relative certainty what their rights will be under the contract.[22] The only concern in following this reasoning is that one of the jurisdictions involved has barred enforcement of the provision in question. Yet this objection carries little force. When two parties sign a contract that contains a provision that would be enforceable in the jurisdiction in which one party is located but not in the jurisdiction where the other party finds itself, there is no ex ante reason to favor the policy judgment of one jurisdiction over the other. Given this indecision, the sensible solution is to allow the parties to choose which jurisdiction's law is to apply.

The United States Supreme Court has endorsed this reasoning. In *The Bremen v. Zapata Co.*,[23] a United States shipper entered into a contract with a German carrier to ship one of its drilling rigs. The contract contained a forum selection clause which directed that any disputes arising out of the shipment be litigated in London. The contract contained an exculpatory clause which protected the carrier from any claims arising out of damage to the shipped drilling rig.[24] The U.S. shipper brought suit in the United States. American courts would not enforce the exculpatory clause, but English courts would.[25] The Supreme Court held that the forum selection clause should be enforced. It noted that "[t]he choice of the [English] forum was made in an arm's-length negotiation by experienced and sophisticated businessmen, and absent some compelling and countervailing reason it should be honored by the parties and enforced by the courts."[26]

The rule articulated in *The Bremen* should be extended to allow a firm to select which forum should adjudicate its bankruptcy. Countries differ in their insolvency laws. Some laws, like that of the United States, are viewed as being relatively soft on a firm's managers, while others, such as that of Great Britain, are not. American law generally does not auction off insolvent firms; German law does. Thus, if one views each country in which a multinational firm has significant contacts as offering one choice on the menu, allowing the firm to precommit to having its insolvency administered by one country has the effect of creating a menu of options. While this menu may not be as exhaustive as one crafted by an efficiency-seeking legislature, it does offer firms a meaningful choice.

Two modifications of the rule of *The Bremen* are needed to translate that decision to the bankruptcy context. Conflicts of law principles generally distinguish choice of forum from choice of law. Parties can specify both the forum that will adjudicate a dispute and the law that the forum will apply. In the bankruptcy context it makes sense to combine these principles. Bankruptcy rules are notoriously complex. It is fanciful to expect a court to apply the bankruptcy law of a foreign country with anything approaching an acceptable degree of accuracy. Thus, for pragmatic reasons, a forum should generally apply its own bankruptcy law. A firm should not be allowed to select one country as the forum for the dispute but then specify that it should apply another country's bankruptcy law.

A second modification of the rule of *The Bremen* tracks the difference between an insolvency proceeding and a standard two-party contract. The two-party contract only binds the immediate parties; other parties are usually unaffected by its provisions. In the bankruptcy context, however, the choice of a bankruptcy regime affects all of the firm's creditors. Thus, if a firm borrowed money from a bank and the lending agreement included a clause which stated that if the firm encountered financial distress it would file for bankruptcy in England, the enforcement of this clause would affect all of the firm's creditors. These creditors may have no reason to expect the bankruptcy to be held in England.

This in effect is the same problem with Schwartz's proposal about having bankruptcy clauses in loan contracts and, as shown above, can be easily overcome. Rather than having the bankruptcy selection in a single contract between the firm and one of its creditors, to be enforceable the clause should be in the corporate charter. This would give notice to all creditors as to where the bankruptcy of the firm would be heard.[27]

One possible objection to bargaining over choice of bankruptcy clauses is that it might lead to a "race to the bottom." The managers of firms would have an incentive to select the country's law that provided the greatest protection for themselves. They would eschew laws, regardless of their efficiency, that turned them out on their ears. Since creditors could not write individual contracts over bankruptcy procedures, they would be stuck with the bankruptcy term that the managers placed in the charter. Rather than increasing efficiency, extending the rule of *The Bremen* to bankruptcy law would ensure that all firms chose the law which best aided managers. Indeed, to the extent that jurisdictions desire that their law be selected as the controlling one, they would have an incentive to amend their law so as to be even more solicitous of managerial interests.

This argument runs parallel to a familiar one in corporate law. Corporations are generally free to choose the state of their incorporation. This freedom initially led some scholars to suggest that the managers of firms, who control the incorporation decision, would select a state whose corporate laws protected them at the expense of the firm's shareholders.[28] As states competed for the income raised by issuing corporate charters, they would have an incentive to amend their laws in ways that firm managers would find attractive.

The race-to-the-bottom argument fails to persuade in either the general corporate or the bankruptcy context. The now standard response in the corporate context is that market forces check managerial aggrandizement. Managers are concerned about the share price of their firm's stock. The share price reflects the value of the governance apparatus of the firm. To the extent that managers select a state of incorporation which allows them to capture firm benefits at the expense of the shareholders, this will decrease the value of the firm and the price of its shares. To the extent that a firm's managers have an incentive to maximize share price, they will have an incentive to choose the state of incorporation which maximizes firm value. Since states do compete for charter income, under this understanding of the competitive process, states now have an incentive to provide rules that maximize shareholder wealth. The race to the bottom has been replaced with a race to the top.

This same analysis carries over to the bankruptcy context.[29] Firms must induce consensual creditors to deal with it. To the extent that a firm commits to filing for bankruptcy in the country which offers the more efficient bankruptcy law, it will increase the number of projects that it can fund. Selecting a bankruptcy law that transfers value from the debt holders to the managers will result in a cost which is borne by the firm, not by the debt holders. To the extent that countries would compete for bankruptcy business, this competition would induce them to enact more efficient bankruptcy regimes.

Conclusion

Schwartz's essay attacks one of the few remaining bastions of government-mandated rules in the commercial law context. It shows that the general argument in favor of free contracting extends to contracting over bankruptcy procedure. Implementing this insight would best be accomplished by allowing firms to select at the time of their incorporation the appropriate bankruptcy procedure from a menu of options. This approach provides the best avenue by which the theoretical gains from contracting identified by Schwartz can be realized in practice.

The potential for efficiency gains exists in the transnational as well as the domestic context. To be sure, it is unlikely that the world's countries would agree via treaty to a worldwide menu approach. However, current law would allow firms to choose which country's law applies in the case of financial distress. Indeed, such law provides us both with an opportunity to ascertain whether firms are interested in contracting over bankruptcy procedures and, if they are, with the possibility that countries may begin to innovate in an attempt to produce more efficient bankruptcy laws.

Contract and Jurisdictional Freedom

BRUCE H. KOBAYASHI AND LARRY E. RIBSTEIN

Bargaining freedom is typically described in terms of the law of a single jurisdiction. Parties bargain by adding to or varying the terms that the jurisdiction would imply in the contract. But the parties also can determine presumptive and mandatory terms by specifying the state whose law will govern the contract, through a choice-of-law clause. They may also bargain over where the dispute will be litigated, through a choice-of-forum clause. This ability to bargain over the applicable law and the courts importantly expands freedom of contract.

An important effect of permitting free choice of law is to improve state rules and regulations by reducing interest group incentives to promote inefficient laws. Lawmakers may be able to impose costs on, or may provide suboptimal benefits for, those who have little influence on the lawmaking process because they reside outside of the jurisdiction or belong to interest groups that are relatively weak in particular jurisdictions.[1] We refer to these costs as *spillovers*. On the other hand, potential *competition* between lawmaking bodies limits the extent to which they can impose costs.[2] The greater the effect of competition in constraining cost-externalization, the more the legal system will be efficient and the more it should facilitate competition. Permitting the parties to bargain for the law to govern their contract promotes jurisdictional competition. Enforcing contractual choice significantly lowers exit costs and increases jurisdictional competition as compared with a rule that forces parties physically to relocate to a particular jurisdiction in order to be subject to its laws. However, the same public choice considerations that might cause jurisdictions to impose the costs of their laws on nonresidents seem to suggest that these jurisdictions will seek to block easy exit by contract. Indeed, legal constraints on the enforceability of choice-of-law contracts appear to support this intuition.

We examine these competing hypotheses concerning spillovers and jurisdictional competition in light of the availability of contractual choice of law, focusing on the specific context of the United States federal system.[3] We show that, despite lawmakers' incentives and legal rules that are hostile to contractual choice of law, contracting parties have significant power to choose the law applicable to their contract. This implies that laws may have less impact on contractual relationships than might appear if one does not consider the potential for choosing the applicable law. We support this conclusion by analyzing the effects of competition on contractual choice of law. Theory and data indicating that law is inefficient may be incomplete because they examine only jurisdictions' initial attempts to externalize costs rather than the ultimate outcome of jurisdictional competition. In addition to its general implications for jurisdictional competition, our analysis has specific implications for the appropriate mode of analyzing the efficiency of state law and of a federal system.

I Contractual Choice and Jurisdictional Competition

Legislators can gain benefits such as money and votes, often referred to as "rents," by engineering wealth transfers among interest groups that have differing costs of organizing to promote or defeat laws.[4] These laws may be inefficient in the Kaldor-Hicks sense in that the benefits to the strong winners may outweigh the costs to the organizationally weak losers. Such disparity of strength may exist between those who are influential in the enacting jurisdiction through residence or their ability to organize and those who reside or whose political influence is concentrated in other jurisdictions. In the U.S. federal system, reliance on state law may enable minority interest groups to gain from wealth transfers in particular states even if they could not obtain such legislation at the federal level. A classic example is state product liability law that benefits local consumers and trial lawyers and imposes costs on out-of-state manufacturers and consumers.[5] By dividing rulemaking power among separate jurisdictions, a federal system promotes these spillovers of lawmaking.[6] We refer to this as the *spillover* hypothesis of federalism.

A federal system like that in the United States can ameliorate the problems it creates by helping affected parties to avoid laws that impose costs.[7] This induces competition among the states for residents and resources that can constrain interest groups' ability to effect wealth transfers.[8] We refer to this as the *competition* hypothesis. Under it, the degree to which states compete, and therefore the extent of potential spillovers from state laws, depends critically on exit costs.

Exit is facilitated by variation among the states combined with comity. Comity helps actors avoid state laws they do not like by preventing states from imposing their laws on anyone they can subject to legal process. Without comity, actors can avoid a state's law only by avoiding all contact with the state. With comity, parties may be able to avoid a state's law simply by avoiding the more substantial contacts with the state that are required by the choice-of-law rule, such as residence in the state or conduct or contacts that give rise to litigation.[9]

Moreover, the parties are not constrained by the need to choose a regime in which assets are located because comity ensures enforcement of the judgment in any state in which there are assets.[10]

Actors may be able to exit state regulation inexpensively by contracting ex ante for the application of a particular law rather than physically avoiding regulating states. The wider the choice of possible laws, and the lower the cost of exit under a contractual choice-of-law regime, the less the parties are subject to potential cost externalization. At the limit, state regulation of contracts would be "trivial" in the sense of having no effect on resource allocation.

Exit costs under contractual choice of law may depend to some extent on the parties' contracting costs. Statutory standard forms may significantly reduce contracting costs, particularly in complex, long-term contracts.[11] This means that exit costs under a contractual choice-of-law regime may depend on the availability of alternative forms across jurisdictions. This availability depends partly on state legislators' incentives to supply alternative forms.[12] Also, new forms may be slow to evolve because of the importance of cases, customs, and privately developed form contracts that have been generated by existing statutes.[13]

This essay focuses on the role played in the spillover/competition debate by contractual choice of law. In other words, taking the basic characteristics of a federal system, including both potential spillovers and competition, should contracting parties be able to bargain freely over the applicable law? In general, we show that choice-of-law clauses in contracts can constrain potentially inefficient regulation by reducing lawmakers' ability to transfer wealth between contracting parties or from the contracting to third parties. Although contracting parties could attempt to avoid the regulation by adopting alternative arrangements or by pricing the offending term, such techniques alone may not be fully effective.[14] Among other things, contractual arrangements are not fungible, and it may be uncertain which terms the jurisdiction will enforce.[15] To be sure, choice-of-law clauses cannot fully reverse any wealth transfers resulting from the effect of the law on existing contracts. However, such wealth transfers can be lessened by the parties' ability to bargain for stable regimes and to rely on the Contracts Clause of the Constitution.[16] Moreover, the incentives of interest groups to sponsor inefficient legislation are reduced when their effects are dissipated by choice-of-law clauses.

II Mechanisms of Enforcing Contractual Choice of Law

As just shown, contractual choice of law promotes competition and thereby erodes legislators' rents from engineering wealth transfers. One might therefore expect legislators and their judicial agents to protect these rents by resisting enforcement of choice-of-law contracts. As discussed below, this initial impression is supported in the United States by the Restatement (Second) of Conflicts. However, there are strong pressures on courts and legislators to enforce contractual choice of law. Although state lawmakers have strong incentives to try to prevent affected parties from avoiding their laws, they are constrained in their ability to do so by the parties' ability to employ counterstrategies such as choosing an alternative forum or avoiding all contact with the jurisdiction.

The original Restatement of Conflicts was hostile to choice-of-law clauses.[17] However, section 188 of the Restatement (Second) of Conflicts makes enforcement of such clauses the basic conflicts rule except in the "absence of effective choice by the parties." However, section 187(2) provides that the contract will not be enforced as to issues such as validity (when the choice of law matters most) if there is no "substantial relationship" between the chosen law and the parties or transaction or other "reasonable basis" for the parties' choice, or application of the chosen law would contravene a "fundamental policy" of a state with a materially greater interest whose law would apply in the absence of contract.

It is not immediately apparent why contracting parties need a "reasonable basis" for selecting this or any other contract term.[18] Alternatively, the reasonable basis might be provided by the state's interest in attracting business in the form of franchise fees or litigation, particularly if this competition results in a race to the top to provide efficient laws, as suggested by the competition thesis. The real function of this barrier to contract may be to raise the cost of exit by limiting contracting parties' range of choices to where they are bound by residence or other factors.

The second ground of nonenforcement, which invalidates choice-of-law clauses that interfere with a "fundamental policy" of a state's law, invites courts to determine and effectuate the underlying goal of the interest groups that promoted the law. Of course, courts that are so inclined might enforce choice-of-law clauses by narrowly interpreting the purpose of the avoided law.

These grounds accommodate the courts' incentives not to enforce contractual choice of law. As discussed in section 1, choice-of-law clauses are designed to limit legislators' ability to engineer wealth transfers. Legislators, in turn, control judges' power, salary, and tenure.[19] Thus judges can be expected typically to resist enforcement of contractual choice of law to the extent that it interferes with enforcement of local regulatory law (i.e., where the clause chooses a law other than that of the forum). Moreover, judges may have their own incentives not to enforce contractual choice of law. They may want to expand their budgets and powers by competing for litigation business. They also may want to promote application of forum *law*, including their own past and future decisions, even if this reduces the total amount of their business, in order to enhance their power, prestige, job satisfaction, and the value of their human capital.[20] Enforcing choice-of-law clauses may deprive judges of the power not only to make the choice-of-law determination, but also possibly to make new law on the relevant issue.[21] These incentives may lead state courts not to enforce contractual choice of law, particularly if enforcement would deter plaintiffs from suing in the state.

The parties may be able to exit inefficient rules despite these legal rules and incentives that would lead courts to block exit. Most importantly, the parties can exploit adjudicators' varying incentives to block exit. In the U.S., arbitrators and federal courts are more likely than state courts to enforce contractual choice of law. To be sure, federal judges must apply state conflicts rules[22] and arbitrators may do so. However, adjudicators who are so inclined have substantial room to trivialize the vague Restatement exceptions to enforcement of contractual choice of law. Arbitrators and federal courts have little incentive to uphold state legislation because their tenure, salary, and perks are not controlled by state legislatures. Arbitrators normally make no law at all because they do not write opinions.[23] They therefore have no personal reason to want to add to their prestige by setting precedent[24] and are more likely to compete for adjudication business through efficient dispute resolution.[25] Similarly, federal courts deciding state law issues in diversity or federal question litigation must apply existing state decisions rather than make new law. They too may gain from enforcement of contractual choice of law that attracts litigation business.

Because of adjudicators' varying incentives to enforce contractual choice of law, it matters whether the party who favors the choice-of-law clause chooses who decides the case. Parties may choose a forum at the time a matter is litigated simply by choosing to file the claim in a particular court. In the United States, the plaintiff can choose from among the various states as well as whether to litigate federal question or diversity cases in federal court. Moreover, *defendants* in federal cases can seek removal from state to federal court. A party's control over the forum may depend on its costs and benefits from litigating the issue. A litigant or its attorney who is involved in many cases of the same type over time may be willing to incur risk-adjusted costs that exceed its risk-adjusted benefits in a given case but that are less than benefits over many cases in terms of precedents that might be generated.[26] For example, franchisors may be more likely than franchisees to sue to enforce contractual choice of law if they are the repeat players.[27] This may not only spur legal change of antifranchisor rules, but may also give litigation-maximizing courts an incentive to slant their rules toward franchisors.

Contracting parties also can choose the adjudicator ex ante, in advance of litigation, through contract clauses that (1) require disputes to be tried in a designated court;[28] (2) provide that the parties consent to the jurisdiction of a designated court, such as one conducive to enforcement of contractual choice; or

(3) require that the parties agree to submit disputes to arbitration. By selecting the forum in the contract, the party who favors contractual choice of law can help ensure that the case will be tried in an enforcing jurisdiction even if that party does not have the litigation initiative.

Courts may have stronger reasons to enforce choice of forum than they have to enforce choice of law. First, the law may give stronger support to choice of forum. U.S. Supreme Court cases decided on constitutional or admiralty law grounds have recognized the enforceability of consent to jurisdiction[29] and forum-selection.[30] Although these precedents do not directly apply in most state cases, they support decisions to enforce contractual choice of forum or law by state courts that are inclined for other reasons to do so. Second, judges face lower costs in enforcing choice-of-forum clauses as opposed to choice-of-law clauses. If the court enforces a contract that chooses the law of a different jurisdiction it may have to go to the trouble of hearing the case without the benefit of making law. While courts may respond to this problem by not enforcing either clause, they have strong incentives to enforce contracts and thereby attract procontract litigants. By enforcing a choice-of-forum clause a court can enforce the contract while at the same time avoid contravening legislative policy or establishing a potentially troublesome precedent on contractual choice of law. Indeed, enforcing the forum-selection clause resembles what some courts would do without the clause—dismiss the suit on *forum non conveniens* grounds or transfer it to the state whose law is chosen. Though commentators have sharply criticized enforcement of contractual forum selection in consumer form contracts on the ground that no "real" contract is involved in these cases,[31] courts *do* enforce these clauses even against parties who arguably need protection.[32]

Contracting parties may also contractually compel arbitration which, as discussed above, is conducive to enforcement of contractual choice of law. Section 2 of the U.S. Federal Arbitration Act mandates enforcement of arbitration agreements involving transactions in interstate commerce.[33]

Even if contracting parties cannot be sure that courts will enforce their contractual choice of law, they can avoid a jurisdiction's regulation by exiting the jurisdiction and thereby the state's predicate for imposing its law on the contract. Thus the price of a jurisdiction's enforcing its own law may be its loss of benefits from the business transaction. This hurts interest groups that would gain from the business and politicians and interest groups that would gain from taxing and regulating it. As a result, lawmakers have incentives to provide for contractual choice of law even if they might incur some costs from the erosion of local regulation.

Finally, legislators can trump the common law exceptions to enforcement of contractual choice by clarifying enforcement in certain situations. They have done so through provisions for foreign corporations and other business associations discussed below, as well as through choice-of-law statutes that apply outside the business associations context.[34] This may happen where a strong interest group in the jurisdiction, such as lawyers, favors enforcement or legislators and groups within the jurisdiction have little to gain from nonenforcement because of actors' ability easily to avoid contacts with the jurisdiction. In this situation legislators may act more quickly than courts because they do not gain from adjudicating cases under local law.

III   Effect of Contractual Choice of Law on Efficiency of State Legislation

This essay has discussed two hypotheses concerning the efficiency of law, focusing on efficiency within a federal system. Under the spillover hypothesis, state law is more likely to be inefficient than federal law because state legislators have a greater opportunity than federal legislators to transfer wealth from interest groups that are based outside the political boundaries. Under the competition hypothesis, a system divided into component jurisdictions may be more efficient than the comparable unitary system because of competition between the components. Whether this is the case depends significantly on the parties' cost of exit from a given state. Choice of law and forum clauses are techniques for reducing costs associated with the inefficiency hypothesis and promoting gains associated with the competition hypothesis.

Given the importance of exit costs, the efficiency of the system depends on whether contracting parties can exit a regime by contracting for the applicable law without physically locating in a particular jurisdiction. The parties' ability to do so may reduce the incentives to maintain the law by interest groups that formerly benefited from it, thereby increasing the relative strength of the groups that oppose the law. As a result, the laws themselves eventually may be weakened to the point that they are trivial (i.e., have little or no effect on resource allocation) or eliminated. The history discussed here supports these assertions.

In general, we show how competition can trivialize state law through a multistage process. In the first stage, the state imposes wealth-transferring legislation at the behest of locally strong interest groups. In the second stage, the losers attempt to escape the regulation by exiting the regulation, possibly through contracts to apply the law of a nonregulating state.[35] Lawmakers may resist exit up to the point that the cost of resistance exceeds the benefits because of actors' ability to gain enforcement of their choice, by choosing the adjudicator or exiting as discussed above. In the third stage, the states enforce contractual choice through judicial decisions or legislation. Finally, in the fourth stage, enforcement of contractual choice trivializes the initial regulation, and works backwards to reduce the incentive of states to enact wealth-transferring legislation in the first place. The examples discussed below show the process in various stages, from corporations in which the process is complete, through unincorporated firms in which the law has recently progressed rapidly through most stages, and finally in franchise laws in which the process is currently unresolved.

CORPORATIONS

Corporate law is one of the clearest examples of the use of contractual choice of law to break down mandatory state laws.[36] The first stage was characterized by blatant rent-seeking in the form of legislators' sale of the incorporation "privilege" for private gain. In the second stage firms shopped for advantageous state incorporation rules without regard to where they did business. Legislators in first-mover states were motivated to offer lenient and cheap charters because of the additional revenues from new formations and the advantages to constituents such as lawyers. However, lawmakers in other states had incentives not to recognize foreign incorporations in order to protect their own and the state's revenues and other benefits associated with issuance of domestic corporate charters. In the third stage, firms' choice of incorporation state was generally recognized by all states. State corporation law is now so easily avoided that it has little bite and state legislators have little opportunity to externalize costs by regulating corporate governance.[37]

Corporations have so overcome state regulation that they seem to be an exceptional case rather than an illustration of the general effects of contractual choice of law. The "internal affairs" rule in corporate law provides that rules regarding the internal governance of a corporation are usually determined by the law of the state in which the parties chose to incorporate.[38] Except for a few exceptional cases involving firms that are closely connected with a single state but incorporate elsewhere,[39] courts apply the law of a nonincorporating state only to issues relating to a firm's torts or other "external" acts in the forum. By contrast, choice-of-law clauses receive only a qualified enforcement outside of corporate law, as we have seen. General choice-of-law criteria even apply to such entities as business trusts[40] and limited partnerships.[41]

There are several plausible but incomplete explanations for why a special choice-of-law rule has been applied to corporations. First, courts have been almost entirely preempted by corporate statutes that provide explicitly for registration and recognition of foreign corporations and for application of incorporation-state law.[42] If courts had been left in charge, this issue might have been resolved differently. But the statutes must themselves be explained. Why not such a law for other types of contracts, and why in this country but not in many other industrialized countries?

Second, one might argue that corporations are inherently distinguishable from other types of contracts or firms. They are traditionally characterized as legal entities created by the incorporating state rather than by contract.[43] But the entity doctrine itself must be explained. Corporations do not clearly differ from other contracts in terms of the policies underlying choice of law.[44] The parties' decision to choose the corporate form of contract is driven by the same types of transaction cost considerations that drive selection of other organizational forms.[45] As indicated by the extensive literature on franchising,[46] the decision whether to organize transactions within a firm or between separate firms may be a close one. In their need for the ex ante predictability of a single rule, corporations resemble national franchisors with hundreds of outlets located in many states.[47]

Third, some commentators have suggested that constitutional provisions, such as the commerce and privileges and immunities clauses, have bolstered interstate competition for corporate governance.[48] But the Constitution has played a smaller role in facilitating this competition than these commentators suppose.[49] If corporations are artificial persons, they are *not* protected by the privileges and immunities clause.[50] Even if states can bar or restrict corporations that were incorporated outside the state from doing business locally, they are almost certainly not constitutionally required to apply the incorporating state's law on matters such as limited liability.

The real reasons for the special treatment of corporations may have more to do with the role of interstate competition in giving legislators incentives to enforce firms' contractual choice of law than with the special nature of corporations.[51] This competition ensured that legislators stood to gain more by encouraging corporate contacts with the state than by using these contacts to trigger application of local law. The Commerce Clause, the states' common language and culture,[52] and the principle of comity that requires states to apply other states' laws all encourage the development of interstate firms by letting firms easily do business in several states. The interstate nature of corporate enterprise led to the development of constituencies in each state that would gain from giving the firms local access. These include lawyers who gain from promoting use of the state's courts and of their own expertise as corporate planners.[53] Though legislators might have required additional contacts to a state before applying its law, this would have discouraged some firms from establishing such contacts in states that applied the rule. Moreover, the rules create enough uncertainty that marginal firms might have avoided all contacts with the state, particularly if they could do so without much cost because their operations were based elsewhere. Legislators in some states therefore would stand to gain more from welcoming interstate firms and offering them friendly terms than by appeasing groups that would gain from the application of local law.

In short, the erosion of state regulation of corporations is best explained by corporations' ability to avoid state regulation in a federal system rather than by any peculiar characteristics of corporations compared to other contracts. This avoidance ability forces states into competition despite their incentives to impose their regulation and to block exit. As shown below, this kind of competitive pressure can be, and has been, replicated with respect to other types of contracts with similar results.

UNINCORPORATED FIRMS

Recent developments in the law of unincorporated business firms provide a good opportunity to test the competing inefficiency and efficiency hypotheses. As noted above, unincorporated firms are treated differently than are corporations under the common law of choice of law. However, as with corporations, state legislatures have increasingly provided for application of formation state law for partnerships, LLCs, and other unincorporated firms.[54] This development has provided a wealth of recent data that demonstrate firms' power to provoke state competition and the effect of this competition on the underlying law. It also provides a basis for studying assertions that transaction cost and interest group pressures impede interstate competition for business formation.

The law of unincorporated firms has gone through stages similar to those relating to corporate law discussed above. In the first stage, spillovers prevailed as state courts and legislators made corporate advantages, notably including limited liability, available only to corporations. Legislators thereby protected benefits they received from controlling and being able to charge for access to corporate privileges,[55] including raising revenues from corporate taxes[56] that legislators can spend on their constituencies. Courts, too, have an interest in blocking exit from mandatory corporate rules to the extent that these rules effectuate legislators' interests. Firms attempted exit through customized contract terms, selection of alternative forms, or organization under the law of another state. But unincorporated limited liability business forms such as the limited partnership were initially restrictive and costly. For example, in order to obtain full limited liability the general partner had to bear the costs of incorporation, and limited partners incurred personal liability if they participated in control.[57] Also, firms could not organize under a liberal state's law and operate locally with any assurance that their liability shields would be recognized outside the state of organization.[58]

During the second stage, restrictions on unincorporated business forms were eroded. As with the corporate developments discussed above, legislators in first-mover states had incentives to loosen restrictions on unincorporated business forms in order to capture some revenue from new formations, and legislators in follower states had incentives to recognize contracts organized under foreign law in order to prevent firms from avoiding contacts with the state.

States are now moving toward, but have not yet reached, the third stage in this development, in which parties have full bargaining freedom in their choice of law. In this stage, the parties are free to adopt any business association available under any state's law and have this contract enforced in any state where they do business.

Several significant impediments to this stage have now been overcome. Most important were federal corporate tax constraints on unincorporated business forms. The federal income taxes on corporations were initially rationalized by the existence of corporations as separate, and therefore taxable, entities, and by the supposed special privileges of incorporation, including limited liability.[59] The government could not initially justify on similar grounds a separate tax on *all* business entities, and doing so now obviously would involve political problems. The problem for the federal government was to ensure that firms could not avoid the corporate tax by the simple expedient of organizing other than under state corporation laws. This gave rise to federal tax rules that subjected unincorporated firms to the corporate tax if they had too many "corporate" features, including limited liability.[60] These rules inhibited demand for statutory standard forms for unincorporated firms, and thereby "protected" states from rent and revenue-reducing competition.

Even apart from federal tax constraints, there were at least theoretical impediments to competition at the state level. Legislators' incentives to make new forms available depend on their costs and benefits of doing so. Costs include legislators' own time and energy, the revenues states would lose from permitting fully contractual alternatives to incorporation, and rents legislators would lose from interest groups that favored restrictions on organizational form. For example, lawyers, a potent interest group in this context,[61] would prefer clear tax-oriented restrictions on form in order to protect themselves from potential malpractice liability for drafting mistakes that led to corporate tax classification.[62]

Legislators' benefits depend on the demand for new limited liability forms[63] and on whether first-mover legislators can capture enough of the gains from innovation to offset the costs, given that state legislation can easily be copied by other states.[64] Demand for a new business form theoretically might have been limited by several factors. There was initial uncertainty concerning the tax treatment of LLCs,[65] and their ability to operate outside their formation states.[66] Moreover, the parties to partnerships and corporations incur significant transition costs in making the move to a new business form. The parties may have to incur tax on gain realized as a result of cashing out of the old form, change existing agreements to accommodate the new statutory default rules, and risk discontinuity in their relations with third parties. The advantages of statutory business forms include their ability to attract a large enough network of users to justify production of a stock of published transaction forms and case law.[67] Adopting a new type of business association would force the parties to draft documents from scratch until the network of users of the new form was large enough to justify production of a comparable supply of forms. These costs might lock firms into existing statutes.[68] Finally, legislators arguably have little incentive to innovate where this would simply cause changes in business associations that have already been formed in the state rather than attracting new firms. Because closely held businesses normally do business in a single state, they must incur extra costs in order to avoid their home state's law. There is therefore little nationwide market for revenues in which legislators can compete for foreign formations.[69]

Despite these considerations, there were strong reasons at this point to believe that competition eventually would develop. Even if legislators alone have little incentive to compete for formation revenues, lawyers can earn enough rents from new statutes to have an incentive to compete.[70] Lawyers have an interest in attracting and retaining transactional and litigation business by having state-of-the-art business association statutes in their state. Moreover, regardless of the share of the national market a state can earn by legislating, lawyers can prevent existing clients from moving elsewhere to avoid a restrictive law, and can capture a larger share of their in-state market through reputational benefits and client referrals.[71] In addition to drafting and lobbying for new statutes, lawyers can compete for business by drafting forms that can be used in connection with new types of business associations.

Recent developments have shown the extent to which state competition has been able to break down potential impediments to full enforcement of contracts, including those imposed by federal law. In other words, actual events have disproven arguments that the law of unincorporated firms was locked into inefficiency. To begin with, liberalization of limited partnership law, including the recognition of the incorporated general partner and the erosion of the control rule, gradually reduced the benefits of basing federal tax classification on limited liability. As bureaucrats came increasingly to bear the costs of maintaining the system in a time of declining budgets, they no longer had an incentive to maintain the system through repeated rulings and adjustments.[72] As a result, in 1988 the IRS approved partnership tax treatment of LLCs, which initially resembled limited partnerships except that they had complete limited liability and no control rule.[73] This triggered the rapid spread of LLC statutes[74] and later the development of the limited liability partnership (LLP).[75]

Once the federal tax impediment was gone, other potential impediments to state competition turned out not to be important. At first, some of the larger states resisted permitting LLCs because of concerns about revenue loss.[76] However, within eight years of the 1988 tax ruling that paved the way for LLCs, all states had adopted LLC statutes that provided for recognition of foreign LLCs.[77] Because of the flexibility of the LLC form, almost any kind of provision for closely held firms is available under some state's law and enforceable everywhere else. This competition, in turn, has led to gradual elimination from LLC statutes of mandatory cost-externalizing rules.[78]

The reason for the rapid passage of LLC statutes is apparent from state-by-state data on new formations of LLCs.[79] This data demonstrates sufficient demand for new business forms to give legislators and lawyers an incentive to supply these forms. The number of LLCs in each of the states that provided data increased rapidly beginning in the early 1990s. Firms embraced the LLC form instead of business forms with well-entrenched statutes and interpretive networks of case law, customs, and expertise. This tends to refute the hypothesis that competition among these business forms is inherently limited by "lock-in" to existing forms.[80] Thus lawyers and legislators in laggard states saw that they risked flight of capital and revenue if they delayed enacting an LLC statute. There is significant anecdotal evidence that lawyers pushed hard for LLC statutes in their states.[81]

The history of LLPs similarly demonstrates both the absence of a lock-in phenomenon and the parties' ability to avoid state taxation and regulation through state competition. The LLP was first invented in Texas in 1991, primarily to help lawyers to escape sudden tort and regulatory liability arising out of savings and loan cases.[82] The LLP has two theoretical advantages over the LLC. First, it enables firms—particularly professional firms—to avoid taxation and regulation that some states apply to LLCs. In particular, since the LLP is explicitly defined as a partnership, it may be able to avoid entity-level tax applied to nonpartnerships in some states, including both LLCs and corporations.[83] Professional firms that must be partnerships under local licensing and ethical rules also can use the LLP form. Second, the LLP can be used to overcome the "lock-in" problem of firms' adhering to existing standard forms. Since an LLP is defined as a partnership, partnership law and forms developed for partnerships apply. Thus a general partnership does not lose the advantages of its existing "network" by becoming an LLP, as it might if it became an LLC.[84]

Despite these theoretical advantages of the LLP form, in most states LLP formations are only a small fraction of LLC formations.[85] Only in Texas, where LLPs were invented, are they a significant fraction of LLC formations. LLPs' invention and popularity in Texas may be at least partly attributable to the fact that Texas taxes LLCs, but not LLPs, like corporations.[86] Thus, while the acceptance of the LLP illustrates how state competition can erode tax and regulatory barriers, comparisons between LLP and LLC formations suggest that "lock-in" is not an inherent impediment to development of new statutory business forms.[87]

While unincorporated firms have rapidly moved toward the third stage of bargaining freedom over choice of law, they have not fully arrived. Rather, they have moved into an intermediate stage, in which competition is eroding but has not eradicated remaining restrictions. The data show that LLCs have replaced general partnerships rather than other limited liability business forms. While LLC formations were increasing, the numbers of new limited partnership and corporate formations generally remained relatively constant and the total number of corporations in virtually every state increased.[88] This suggests that the rise of the LLC occurred as a result of firms switching from the general partnership form to obtain limited liability.[89] Since new formations of limited partnerships and corporations have remained steady, it seems unlikely that existing firms were converting from these forms in large numbers.[90] The move from vicarious liability to a tax-friendly form of limited liability is apparently worth the transition costs discussed above, while the move from another form of limited liability is not. For example, many existing closely held firms have not moved to the LLC form because they can obtain flow-through taxation and limited liability by organizing as Subchapter S corporations, or even as standard Subchapter C corporations by eliminating most taxable income through deductions. Though these firms may incur some costs because of the tax constraints and unsuitable default rules of the corporate structure, the costs are not high enough to justify the transition costs of moving to the LLC form.[91] As a result, legislators can exact fees or rents up to the firms' exit costs.

There is no reason why state competition for LLC formation business should end at this stage. States have continued to liberalize their LLC statutes,[92] thereby increasing the benefits and reducing corporations' and limited partnerships' moving to the LLC form. Most importantly, state variations produced federal rulings that gradually expanded and clarified the extent to which LLCs would be treated as tax partnerships. These rules, in turn, reduced the revenue benefits and increased the administrative costs, already under pressure from declining budgets, of maintaining restrictions on the form of closely held firms that would be entitled to flow-through taxation. This led ultimately to the recent federal rule permitting virtually all unincorporated closely held firms to choose their form of taxation.[93]

As a result of the new federal rule, the tax restrictions on flow-through incorporated firms are now significantly more stringent than those for unincorporated firms.[94] This further increases firms' demand for the LLC form, as well as legislators' incentives to meet this demand. Legislators have recently responded in several ways. Perhaps most notably, many states have taken advantage of the elimination of the corporate resemblance tax classification rule by providing for corporate-type continuity of the firm rather than dissociation of a member.[95] Several states have passed conversion provisions that permit both foreign and domestic corporations or limited partnerships to become LLCs with a simple filing that is not a taxable event.[96] These provisions preserve the underlying business entity and reduce doubt about the status of the entity's debts, contracts, and title to property.[97] Moreover, several states have moved to reduce judges' discretion to impose vicarious liability, which is a particular hazard for closely held firms,[98] by enacting provisions that restrict the grounds for veil-piercing in LLCs.[99] Finally, the states have taken advantage of the new tax classification rule, which clarifies the tax status of one-member LLCs, by sharply reversing course and permitting one-member firms.[100]

In sum, the recent history of the law of unincorporated firms demonstrates the power of state competition to break down barriers to contracting. State competition not only eroded mandatory provisions in state law, but also helped bring down the federal tax classification rules. Once limitations on free contracting were reduced, the competition proceeded quickly despite theoretical constraints on the supply of and demand for new business forms.

FRANCHISEE PROTECTION STATUTES

Franchising is a fruitful area for examining the interplay of competing efficiency and competition hypotheses of state law. On the one hand, the potential for inefficient spillovers seems significant. While franchisors can effectively coordinate on the national level because of lower organizing costs,[101] franchisees within a given state may be more influential than the national franchisor organization.[102] Thus state laws may benefit local franchisees at the expense of national franchisors or consumers.[103] On the other hand, franchise contracts also lend themselves to contractual choice of law: They are complex and standardized, so that the marginal costs of inserting the clause are low; they are complex enough to afford ample opportunities for the franchisor to gain the initiative in litigation; and they involve enough money that federal diversity jurisdiction is often available.

As a result of these countervailing forces, the state regulation of franchise contracts illustrates the ongoing struggle between the passage of statutes that would increase externalization costs and contractual and organizational evasion of these statutes. In the first stage, franchisees lobbied home state legislators to secure passage of franchisee termination statutes.[104] Franchisors responded in the second stage by seeking enforcement of choice-of-law and choice-of-forum clauses in franchise contracts. Franchisees, in turn, opposed this enforcement in court and lobbied state legislators to enact statutory end-runs around contractual choice-of-law. Franchisors have also increased their efforts to influence the legislative process at the state level, resulting in favorable amendments to existing legislation and preventing the passage of new legislation.[105] The process has continued in this way without a clear resolution.

In the first stage, consistent with the inefficiency hypothesis, states passed franchise regulation statutes that regulate the relationship between the franchisor and franchisee. Sixteen regulate, among other things, nonrenewal and termination-at-will of franchisees.[106] Ten states also mandate that the franchisor allow a franchisee a limited or reasonable period to "cure" any defects.[107] These statutes may be costly for franchisors because state regulation of termination and nonrenewal of franchisee limit a franchisor's primary means of deterring shirking or free-riding on the franchisor's trademark by franchisees.[108] Absent a mechanism to control shirking and free-riding, a franchisee that largely serves nonrepeat customers has an incentive to reduce quality below that desired by the franchisor. While such actions may inefficiently reduce the profitability of the *chain* because it damages the brand name, it may be privately optimal for the shirking *store*. Nonrenewal or termination of a shirking franchisee causes the franchisee to lose the remaining quasi-rents to its franchise-specific investments. The potential loss of these remaining quasi-rents reduces the franchisee's incentive to shirk and free-ride. It follows that franchisee protection laws increase shirking and free-riding by franchisees by reducing franchisors' ability to penalize franchisees. Though franchisors may be able to reduce the future impact of the statutes by pricing or changing the terms of their franchises, they may be particularly harmed by statutes that change the terms of existing contracts.[109] Franchisors affected by such statutes will attempt to limit shirking by increasing monitoring and franchisees' quasi-rents.[110] Even statutes that apply only prospectively harm franchisors by affecting renewals and forcing franchisors to substitute owned for franchised outlets.[111]

Under the spillover hypothesis, the magnitude of the statutes' long-run effect on brand-name owners as a general class depends on franchisors' relative costs of switching to a different organizational form. This, in turn, depends significantly on how important the incentives generated by termination and nonrenewal are to preventing franchisee shirking. Operators who rely on local repeat business are less able to free-ride off the franchisor's brand name, and thus require less monitoring and fewer incentives than those who rely on transient business.[112] More established brand-name owners are likely to have more company-owned stores than less-established owners because the more established firms have better credit than potential franchisees and have had an opportunity to observe which locations are most profitable.[113]

Consistent with these observations, Brickley et al.'s study of franchisee termination statutes[114] showed that the number of franchises dropped in states with franchisee termination laws. This drop was statistically significant in industries characterized by nonrepeat business, in which the deterrence of shirking and free-riding by franchisees through the power to terminate is most important. However, the drop was not statistically significant when applied to the entire sample of franchised businesses. Muris and Beales examined the effect of specific provisions of the state franchise laws on the own-or-franchise decision,[115] and, like Brickley et al., found the largest negative effects in nonrepeat industries. However, their results suggest that these effects are concentrated in states where the statute mandated a franchisee right to cure.[116] Further, this effect is seen in both repeat and nonrepeat industries.

The Brickley et al. study also showed that share returns of franchisors around the adoption of the California law indicated large wealth losses for shareholders of those companies.[117] This evidence suggests that organizational forms are not fungible, and forcing a switch to a form that is not suited to the particular firm can impose costs.[118] Such legislation can impose costs on franchisors by affecting existing contracts.[119] Also, it may be costly for franchisors to avoid the laws by switching organizational form or physically exiting jurisdictions with franchise laws.

On the other hand, the competition hypothesis suggests that firms can adapt to enactment of the restrictive state laws in less costly ways. Rather than physically leaving the regulating state by eliminating franchise outlets or incurring costly changes in their organizational form by substituting company ownership for franchised outlets, firms have attempted to avoid franchise laws by contracting for the application of the law of a nonregulating state. Under this hypothesis, once the parties develop an efficient mechanism for contractual choice of law, the effect of the current state's regulation on organizational form, the focus of prior economic analyses of this issue, and therefore its effect on brandname owners generally should drop or disappear.

Consistent with this hypothesis, the parties started litigating choice-of-law and choice-of-forum clauses in their franchise contracts, primarily in federal court soon after the passage of the first set of franchise regulation statutes.[120] In *Burger King v. Rudzewicz*,[121] the U.S. Supreme Court held that a terminated Michigan franchisee had established "minimum contacts" with and could be subject to jurisdiction in Florida. The court held that the franchisee had knowingly agreed to a contract that had "substantial connections with the forum state," including a provision that provided for application of Florida law.[122] The court therefore rejected the franchisee's arguments that the Michigan Franchise Investment Law governed the relationship and thus precluded Florida from asserting jurisdiction.[123]

The Supreme Court specifically refused to make a bright-line rule on choice-of-law rules and minimum contacts, and has not addressed specifically the issue of whether or not application of choice-of-law rules would allow Burger King to avoid the Michigan Franchise Investment Law. Although one writer asserted in 1989 that "[m]ost courts . . . have held that the parties to a franchise agreement cannot avoid the franchise law of the state in which the franchisee is located by providing in their agreement that the laws of another state will govern,"[124] two important cases decided in the Sixth and Eighth Circuits in the late 1980s allowed avoidance of state regulation through the enforcement of choice-of-law clauses.[125] In *Tele-Save*, the court upheld a contractual choice-of-law provision choosing New Jersey Law despite the prohibition in the Ohio statute of waivers of franchisee rights.[126] And in *Modern Computer Systems*, the Eighth Circuit held that a choice-of-forum clause requiring "exclusive venue in Douglas County Nebraska in any litigation between them concerning this contract" precluded application of the Minnesota Franchise Act in spite of the existence of an antiwaiver provision in the statute.[127]

Under these holdings, parties would have had an effective, though certainly not foolproof, mechanism for exiting oppressive state laws. A franchisor who wished to avoid oppressive state regulation of franchising would move to a non-regulating state and specify in his contracts that its law is to govern, and this would satisfy the two prongs of the Restatement conflicts rule for contracts.[128] In particular, the first prong (existence of a "substantial relationship" to the chosen forum) would have been satisfied by the franchisor's move to the forum state. The possibility that franchisors would move their home offices to nonregulating states gave all states an incentive to liberalize their conflicts rules to attract franchisors to relocate in their state.

To escape the second prong of the Restatement test, the franchisor would avoid those states where choice-of-law clauses are contrary to a fundamental policy of a state. Under *Tele-Save* and *Modern Computer Systems*, the franchisor might even settle in one of the fourteen states which prohibit waivers of franchisee rights but which respect free bargaining over choice of law.

Enforcement of choice-of-law clauses over general antiwaiver statutes has not, however, been uniform. Some courts have voided contractual choice-of-law clauses based on nonspecific nonwaiver provisions.[129] The Seventh Circuit in *Wright-Moore v. Ricoh*[130] applied the provisions of the Indiana Franchise Law over a clause choosing New York law. *Wright-Moore* would cover three franchise statutes and would create conflicts and uncertainty with the other circuits' holdings if not distinguished from the holdings of the Eighth and Sixth Circuits. In distinguishing *Wright-Moore* from *Modern Computer Systems*, the court failed to find a substantial relationship to the forum state, noting that although Ricoh was incorporated in New York, its principal place of business was New Jersey. Second, in contrast to the *Modern Computer Systems* court's findings that the franchisee's domicile (Minnesota) had expressed a strong preference for upholding contractual choice of law, the court in *Wright-Moore* did not find such an expression by Indiana.

More importantly, state legislators reacted swiftly to attempts to negate the federal decisions. Soon after the Eighth Circuit's decision in *Modern Computer Systems*, the Minnesota legislature passed a provision explicitly voiding choice-of-law provisions in franchise contracts by adding the phrase "including any choice of law provision" to the section voiding waivers. Since 1988, six states have explicitly voided choice-of-law and choice-of-forum clauses. Only two, Washington and Iowa, void both types of provisions. The California, Illinois, and Michigan statutes have provisions voiding choice-of-forum provisions but not choice-of-law provisions. The Minnesota statute explicitly voids choice-of-law provisions but does not explicitly void choice-of-forum provisions.

The legislative response leaves room for enforcement of contractual choice-of-law clauses even in the states that have enacted specific antichoice provisions because the application of these statutes depends on the places of business of the franchisee and franchisor. For example, in *JRT v. TCBY Yogurt*,[131] the Eighth Circuit also held valid the contractual choice of Arkansas law, and affirmed the dismissal or summary judgment of plaintiff's claims based on the Michigan Franchise Investment Law. Both the Arkansas Franchise Law and the Michigan Franchise Investment Law require cause for termination and allow the franchisee the right to cure, and the Arkansas law additionally requires cause for nonrenewal. While the Arkansas Franchise Law is even stricter than Michigan's, it can be used only by a franchisee that maintains a place of business in Arkansas. Thus, *neither* the Arkansas nor the Michigan franchise statute applied to the franchisee in *JRT*.[132] Similar clauses are contained in the franchise statutes of many of the regulatory states.

By limiting the application of their statutes to in-state franchisees, the majority of states with franchise protection statutes have eliminated the incentive for franchisors to move away from regulating states.[133] Consider the case of an Iowa franchisor contemplating a move to a nonregulating state. Under the Sixth and Eighth Circuits' holdings in *Tele-Save* and *Modern Computer Systems*, the specific anti–choice-of-law provisions in statutes such as Iowa's does not allow the franchisor to avoid the franchise laws of Iowa by locating in a nonregulating state. At the same time, because the Iowa statute only applies to in-state franchisees, out-of-state franchisees cannot use the Iowa statute when a court upholds a franchisor's contractual choice of Iowa law. Thus, despite having the most invasive franchise regulation in the country, a franchisor currently located in Iowa would not gain any advantage from moving its headquarters and its choice of law to another state. This suggests that state legislators are aware of the potential for exit to avoid onerous regulation and that they design their statutes to minimize it.

The above analysis illustrates that consideration of choice of law and the legal landscape suggest a more complex response to regulation than previously noted in the economic literature. Growing franchisors can minimize the impact of state franchise regulations by locating *either* in nonregulating states *or* in regulating states that effectively limit contractual escape from their laws and prevent application of these laws to out-of-state franchisees. Franchisors would not want to choose the law of states that regulate nonrenewal and termination at will and fail, either via statute or through judicial rulings, to limit application of their strict franchise regulation to in-state franchisees.

Some insight into the competition hypothesis can be gained by examining franchisors' choice of their principal place of business. Based on a survey conducted by *Entrepreneur Magazine*,[134] firms in our sample of 226 franchisors have avoided two of the jurisdictions that do not limit the application of their franchise protection laws to in-state franchisees (the District of Columbia and Hawaii). More generally, while 22 of 226 franchisors in the sample (9.7 percent) have located in states that regulate the franchisor/franchisee relationship and do not limit application of the statute to in-state franchisees, 144 (63 percent) have located in states that do not regulate the franchisor/franchisee relationship, and 60 (26.5 percent) have located in states that limit application of their franchise protection statutes to in-state franchisees.

As noted above, the magnitude of the statutes' effect depends on the extent to which a franchisor must rely upon the incentives generated by nonrenewal or termination at will.[135] If a franchisor does not highly value these incentives, the passage of a franchise protection statute will not cause it either to change organizational form or to relocate its headquarters to a nonregulating state. In contrast, choice of a favorable jurisdiction, its law,[136] and the substitution of company operation for franchising will be in the interest of franchisors that must rely on such incentives to discipline franchisees.

Our analysis predicts that franchisors that rely on termination-at-will clauses to discipline franchisees and that are located in jurisdictions that apply their franchise statutes to out-of-state franchisees are more likely to move from a franchise to a nonfranchise organizational form. We were unable to verify this prediction, since such firms are unlikely to be observed in our dataset, which is based on large, growing franchise operations. However, we were able to test the further hypothesis that franchisors are more likely to remain in such jurisdictions when they are less likely to rely on termination-at-will clauses, as where the agency costs of franchisee misbehavior are small. We would therefore expect the likelihood that a franchisor will locate in such a state to be positively correlated with other indicia of low agency costs, such as the absence of selective company ownership, which is also used by franchisors to control agency costs. The evidence is consistent with this prediction. States that apply their franchise regulations to out-of state franchisees are unattractive places in which to locate headquarters for all but a small number of franchisors where company ownership is rare.[137]

Our analysis suggests that changes in organizational form, particularly including the percentages of owned and franchised outlets, are likely to be observed only in those regulating states that have effectively preempted escape through contractual choice of law, such as Iowa, Washington, and Minnesota.

Previous economic analyses of state regulation of franchise contracts do not differentiate regulating states based upon whether the state has effectively prevented exit via contractual choice of law. Failure to account for the availability of exit via choice of law causes an estimation of an average effect that understates the effect in states that block exit via contractual choice of law and overstates the effect where states have not blocked such exit.

To the extent that franchisees' efforts to externalize costs through legislation are blunted by competition, they can move to restrict jurisdictional competition. Franchise contracts have been addressed by the National Conference of Commissioners for Uniform State Laws (NCCUSL),[138] federal regulators and Congress. The Uniform Franchise and Business Opportunities Act of 1987, which has not been adopted by any state, requires a general duty of good faith between the franchisor and franchisee and regulates offers and sales. Article 3 of this uniform act sought to supplement voluntary compliance on disclosure under a 1979 FTC Rule.[139] Though there have been frequent attempts to pass general federal legislation that would regulate the franchisor-franchisee relationship,[140] these attempts have not been successful. Specific federal regulation of automobile franchises under the Federal Automotive Dealer Franchise Act (FADFA)[141] and gasoline franchises under the Petroleum Marketing Practices Act (PMPA),[142] as well as the most recent proposed federal franchise regulation,[143] are weaker than many state regulations, particularly in not mandating a right to cure.[144] This may reflect the franchisors' relative lobbying strength at the federal level. While a uniform federal law would force regulation even in states that choose not to regulate franchises, such regulation may be beneficial to franchisors to the extent that it preempts more onerous state regulation. However, states have been able to enact significant regulations beyond those contained in the federal statutes. For example, state regulation of automobile dealerships is far more extensive than those contained in the FADFA or the state's general regulation of franchises.[145] The PMPA did not preempt a preexisting law in Maryland that prohibits refiner control of retail gasoline stations,[146] and has not and would not prevent the enactment of similar laws in other states.[147] And the proposed federal law to make uniform the regulation of franchises would *not* preempt state franchise law.[148]

In general, franchise regulation, like the regulation of business association governance, illustrates a continuing "dialectic" of regulation and exit. As a result, studying the regulation itself without reference to exit opportunities misses an important part of the picture. That enforcement of contractual choice of law in this area has so far not achieved the clarity that it has in the business associations context may be because those who favor regulation—i.e., franchisees—comprise a much stronger interest group than those who favor regulation of business association governance. It also may result from the application in this context of general contractual choice-of-law rules, which are less favorable to contractual choice than are corporate rules. Though these rules themselves are vulnerable to erosion, as illustrated by the case of unincorporated firms, the initial rule can be a marginal impediment to jurisdictional competition.

EFFICIENCY CONSIDERATIONS

The above discussion shows that state regulation may have little effect with regard to contracts since the parties can escape regulation by contracting for choice of law. It does not follow, however, that escape is efficient. Though ample theory and evidence show that corporate charter competition leads to efficient results,[149] noncorporate choice-of-law and choice-of-forum clauses still are viewed suspiciously.[150] Nevertheless, it is important to keep in mind that markets discipline choice of law. Although a state might try to become a haven for miscreants, contracts that chose the state's law would be priced accordingly. Despite apparent disparities of information or bargaining power that seem to enable contracting parties to avoid some of this discipline, the facts may come to light if there are enough sophisticated consumers or analysts in the market.[151] Moreover, the fact that the parties must choose a law that applies to many of those who reside in the enacting jurisdiction provides a political constraint on inefficient contractual choice.

Two types of choice-of-law contracts present potential problems. First, the contract may be tainted with a common law barrier to enforcement, such as fraud. For example, nondisclosure bordering on fraud may be a problem in contracts that choose a "proprietary" jurisdiction whose laws are not subject to a significant political constraint. But these special cases should be handled by the law of fraud or by specific regulation rather than by a general rule that also catches efficient transactions.[152] Second, the contract may present an externalities problem, as with rules governing marriages discussed below.

Even apart from contract enforcement problems, the rules that result from enforcing contractual choice are not necessarily those that would exist in a perfect world because of inefficiencies in the supply of law. Lawyers may produce too many or the wrong kinds of laws because they get the benefits from new laws of increased reputational capital and additional drafting business without incurring the costs.[153] Some contracts, such as limited tort liability, impose costs on third parties who cannot easily avoid the harm by contract or otherwise. Perhaps most importantly, states may cause wealth transfers by changing the terms of existing contracts.[154]

Even if there are potential problems with enforcing contractual choice of law, it is important to keep in mind that lawyers and other interest groups undoubtedly would influence any federal law that replaces state regulation. This regulation would be locked in place until interest group dynamics change. On the other hand, state law inefficiency may be only the first stage of a competitive process that leads to efficient laws. Even if federal law produces better law at the first stage, it may be inferior to the ultimate product of state competition.

IV Extensions of the Analysis

This essay has focused on the more conventional uses of contractual choice of law, beginning with the paradigmatic corporate setting, and extending only slightly into other business associations and long-term contracts. Yet contractual choice of law and the general principles underlying ex ante choice of legal regime have potential applications in many other consensual settings, including bankruptcy,[155] securities regulation,[156] and marriage.

The marriage context illustrates the potential problems with extending our analysis. Under the inefficiency hypothesis, state legislators responding to strong local interest groups would pass cost-externalizing legislation. For example, the move to no-fault divorce effected wealth transfers from women whose high initial investments make them vulnerable to opportunism if divorce laws are loosened.[157] On the other hand, under the competition hypothesis, states would compete for residents on the basis of the rules they offer for marriage and divorce. For example, states may try to attract residents and tourists by authorizing single-sex marriage.[158] If the parties could select rules by which they would be mutually bound, the rules would be more likely to match the parties' mutual preferences and therefore to be more efficient, assuming the parties' choice has no external effects. The problem with the contractual choice solution for marriage is that marriages have effects beyond the married couple, on children and others.[159] Thus a simple rule mandating enforcement of marriages would not necessarily maximize social welfare. The problem is finding a general principle that takes these externalities into account while facilitating exit and competition as constraints on excessive regulation.

Another unconventional use of the principles of contractual choice of law would involve extending contractual choice of law beyond consensual relationships—for example, to torts.[160] If competition solves spillover problems in contractual settings, perhaps it would do the same in noncontractual settings. This suggests that parties ought to be able to choose the applicable law by moving to or traveling in a particular state before engaging in or being subject to the relevant conduct, rather than having this law determined by the forum, as often happens under existing choice-of-law rules.[161]

We have discussed only contractual choice within the U.S. federal system. The general principles discussed in this essay are equally applicable to competition between nations generally, and within other types of federal systems such as the European Economic Community. However, it is important to emphasize the differences among these various settings. Contractual choice may be even more important internationally than within the U.S. federal system because of the greater differences among legal regimes and among nations regarding their willingness to make durable commitments.[162] On the other hand, those very differences may make jurisdictions that relate differently than do states in the U.S.—particularly those that do not share constitutional rights and a tradition of comity—less willing to enforce contractual choice.[163] For example, without a full faith and credit rule,[164] contractual choice of law in the international context may be limited by the need to choose the law of a jurisdiction in which assets are located. Contractual solutions to this problem may entail transaction costs that parties do not incur in choosing among jurisdictions within the United States.

V   Conclusions and Implications

The efficiency of a jurisdiction's law depends *both* on the jurisdiction's ability to externalize costs *and* on the ability of those who are excluded from the political system to redress the harm by contracting for the applicable law. This article shows that these contracts can and do negate the potential harm from such spillovers. This analysis and data have several policy implications. First, the efficiency of contractual choice of law and the effect of contractual choice in eroding inefficient barriers to contracting suggest that these contracts *should* be widely enforced, at least within the U.S. federal system, which has been the focus of our study.

Second, given the fact that choice-of-law contracts *are* widely enforced and the existence of robust state competition in the U.S., state law is more likely to be efficient than critics of federalism have argued. Though a state law may externalize costs at first, firms can adjust by physical and contractual exit, and states can respond by adjusting their regulation. Thus the state law that emerges in the final stage is likely to be efficient. A corollary of this point is that tests of the efficiency of state law, such as those in the large literature on franchising,[165] may not yield accurate results because they take a static rather than dynamic view of the efficiency of state law.

Third, federal law or the Constitution should be used sparingly to correct supposed problems of state law. Since our analysis shows that inefficient state laws are unstable, Constitutional or other legal protection of contractual choice of law may be unnecessary in the long run. Moreover, it is important to keep in mind that federal laws are subject to the same interest-group pressure that infects state laws. Federal legislators may refrain from acting precisely in those situations where state legislators and interest-groups derive significant rents from the state law regime.[166] Thus, while federal law may be better than comparable *initial* state laws, they are likely to be worse than the *ultimate* state rule that emerges in a later stage as a result of state competition.

We have suggested some possible avenues of additional inquiry. The discussions of noncontractual settings and of potential inefficiencies of competition even in contractual settings suggest boundaries for the competition principle where externalities inhere in the relationship being regulated. However, even in these contexts, preservation of state competition would prevent externalities from excessive regulation. In short, the solution to the supposed problems of state regulation may be less, rather than more, federal law. Our analysis and data focus on the U.S. federal system. Both the costs and the benefits of contractual choice may be higher outside this context. Accordingly, the international setting and other types of federal systems offer fruitful contexts for additional study of the theories presented in this essay.

A Comment on Contract and Jurisdictional Competition

MICHAEL KLAUSNER

In "Contract and Jurisdictional Competition," Bruce Kobayashi and Larry Ribstein argue that if choice of law were fully contractable, then market forces would neutralize the attempt of any state to enact either inefficient laws or laws that redistribute wealth among parties to the contract. In this comment, I raise three questions regarding the robustness of their claim. First, I question the extent to which their analysis applies to wealth transfers, as opposed to inefficient laws. Second, I suggest that increasing returns may lead to suboptimal equilibria in the choice of law. Third, I pursue the logic of their argument that state legislators will experience pressure to allow contractual choice of law, and ask why choice of law is not even more expansive in the area of business associations.

I   The Limited Applicability of the Kobayashi-Ribstein Framework to Wealth-Transferring Laws

The crux of Kobayashi and Ribstein's analysis is the dynamic that they argue will "trivialize" state laws that regulate contractual relationships. In a nutshell, it goes as follows. First, a state enacts legislation that favors one party to a contract (an in-state, politically powerful party) and disfavors another (an out-of-state party or an in-state politically weak party). Second, the party that the legislation disfavors escapes the law's impact by opting into the law of another state, ideally by a contractual choice-of-law clause.[1] Third, states enforce the contractual choice of law. The result is that the initial attempt to regulate the contract is rendered useless because the contracting parties have exited the jurisdiction.

The Kobayashi-Ribstein dynamic applies most directly to laws that render a contractual relationship inefficient. In the familiar case of corporate law, where free choice of law is available by incorporation and reincorporation, a state law that imposes an inefficient governance structure on corporations tends to induce corporations to reincorporate elsewhere. In combination with the states' interest in revenues associated with incorporation, this dynamic creates a race at least toward the top.[2] The same would occur if, as Kobayashi and Ribstein explain, an inefficient relationship were imposed on the franchisor-franchisee relationship or on other contractual relationships if free choice of law were permitted, and if a state (or important state constituents) reap some benefit from having parties choose its law.

Kobayashi and Ribstein argue, however, that this dynamic applies as well to laws that transfer wealth between contracting parties—for example, from franchisor to franchisee—and it is here that their claim has limitations.

For a law to transfer wealth from one party to a contract to another in the first place, two conditions must be present. First, there must be rents or quasi-rents to transfer between contracting parties. That is, it must be the case that if the contract is terminated, one or both parties cannot redeploy their efforts and resources to obtain equivalent value. Rents arise from monopoly power or some lesser degree of market power; and quasi-rents arise from fixed investments that cannot be redeployed. The value of these rents places an upper limit on the amount of wealth that can be transferred between contracting parties. If the state imposed costs greater than this value, the parties would simply decline to contract with one another. Second, the terms of the law must prevent the contracting parties from reinstating their initial allocation of rents by either opting out of the law or by making compensating changes in other contract terms (such as the price term, to name the most obvious).[3] Kobayashi and Ribstein state that, even without such a legal prohibition, such compensating adjustments may be unworkable because contractual arrangements are not fungible. Here, however, they have in mind a situation in which the regulation imposes inefficient terms on the parties to a contract, not one in which the regulation simply transfers wealth between them. More specifically, their example of the regulation of franchise contracts is not redistributative but inefficient regulation. Of course, state regulation can both transfer wealth and cause inefficiency. The point, however, is that absent inefficiency, the dynamic that Kobayashi and Ribstein describe will have limited applicability.

In short, if a state law prohibits contractual reallocation of wealth and if there are rents or quasi-rents associated with a contractual relationship, then a state may be able to transfer some amount of wealth from one contracting party to another and to have the transfer stick. The role of contractual choice of law in this context, however, is limited. Parties to regulated contracts defined by these two limits will choose to exit a state's legal regime only if the party disfavored by the regulation has the bargaining power to have the favored party return the rents that the law extracted from him. The dynamic here is not one of the "losers" escaping the burden of a state's law, as Kobayashi and Ribstein contend. It is a dynamic of both contracting parties agreeing to reallocate rents in a manner different from that which the law imposes. The role of choice of law here is simply to do what could not be done by explicit contract within a state's regulatory regime—to reverse (fully or partially) the transfer of rents that the law effected. Thus, choice of law will be relevant in the context of wealth-transferring laws only where (a) the party disadvantaged by the law has the bargaining power to reallocate rents, (b) direct contractual reallocation, by simply opting out of the law, is prohibited, and (c) reallocation by contractual choice of law is permitted.[4]

The choice-of-law dynamic that Kobayashi and Ribstein describe can thus "trivialize" laws that impose inefficiencies on contractual relationships and, to a limited extent, laws that transfer wealth between contracting parties. In some contexts, however, it can also trivialize possibly efficient laws that protect third parties from the actions of contracting parties. This would occur where a law protects third parties by regulating the contracts of others, rather than protecting the third parties directly through tort or similar structures.

Kobayashi and Ribstein's example of unincorporated business laws is best conceptualized as this type of situation. States initially required owners of unincorporated businesses to be responsible for their debts to third parties, most importantly their debts to involuntary creditors such as tort victims. The absence of a limited liability law protected third parties. Business people lobbied for relief from this tort obligation in the form of limited liability, and legislators complied in exchange for fees. After one state enacted an LLC statute (and the IRS clarified its tax treatment), competition drove other states to follow suit and to recognize each others' rules. The direct winners from this legislation were managers and investors in unincorporated businesses, and the losers were their tort victims and other involuntary creditors. There may have been other winners as well, and the gains to the winners may outweigh the losses to the losers, but the dynamic is one in which the parties to the unincorporated business contract prompted states to compete to produce a law that imposed losses on third parties. There is no a priori reason to believe that choice of law and state competition are efficient in cases like this, where third-party spillover effects are present.

II   Increasing Returns in Forms of Business

In tracing the evolution of unincorporated businesses, Kobayashi and Ribstein discuss the possible role of network externalities, and observe that firms' rapid move to the LLP and LLC forms revealed that firms were not "locked in" to the traditional business forms (i.e., the corporation, the general partnership, and the limited partnership). Since this is an issue on which I have written in the past, I will revisit the issue in light of their discussion, and extend and refine some of my prior thoughts.[5]

As Kobayashi and Ribstein recognize, state-created business forms perform a standardizing function in the specification of legal relationships among a firm's managers and investors.[6] The Delaware corporate form, for example, is in effect a standard form contract specifying certain legal relationships among managers and investors in a firm. The contract terms are provided by Delaware law. A group of managers and investors can adopt this contract by simply incorporating in Delaware. Or, depending on the nature of the relationships they want to establish, they can instead adopt a California LLC, a Texas LLP, a Pennsylvania corporation, a Florida general partnership, or any of a wide range of business forms available through the fifty states, each of which is a standard form contract used by some number of other firms.[7]

SOURCES OF INCREASING RETURNS

Standardization of legal relationships within a firm is privately valuable and can be socially valuable because contracts that define those terms offer "increasing returns" as more parties use a particular contract. That is, the more firms there are that have used or that are expected to use a particular business form, the more valuable that form will be.[8] These increasing returns take two forms. First, firms that adopted a business form in the past created certain benefits for firms that adopt the form today: They litigated issues of general relevance to firms that currently use the form; they drafted documents that others can now copy; they provided experience to lawyers that can be valuable to firms today; and they educated other third parties such as investment analysts on the general nature of the business form. These remnants of the past use of a business form enhance its value for firms considering adopting it today. Marcel Kahan and I have referred to these benefits of past use as "learning benefits."[9]

In addition, even if a business form has not been widely used in the past, the prospect that it will become widely used can enhance its value. So, for instance, when the LLC was first introduced, it had not been used in the past and hence offered no learning benefits, but it may have been expected to be widely used in the future. The sources of value in the future are much the same as those that create learning benefits, but the nature of the value is slightly different. It stems from an anticipation that a business form will be used *contemporaneously* with many other firms in the future. That anticipation may stem from the fact that many firms already use the form, or from a judgment that many firms will begin using it in the future. By adopting a business form that many firms contemporaneously use in the future, a firm can reasonably expect to benefit—for instance, from judicial precedents that resolve issues that arise along the way as the business environment changes and details of the form are worked out in a variety of contexts. At least up to some limit, the greater the number of firms expected to adopt a particular business form, the more valuable these future benefits will be. Their present value enhances the value of the business form at the time of adoption.

These benefits are analogous to the value an early computer user expected when he bought the first personal computer. Although applications software was limited, so many people were buying PCs that new applications were expected in the not-too-distant future. In addition, the existing stock of applications provided a market for future upgrades. The expectation of future applications and upgrades contributed to the attraction of the early PCs. The reverse occurred in the case of the Beta VCR. Once it became clear that VHS was gaining dominance, Beta users faced the prospect of being unable to rent a movie in the Beta format, and the value of the machines plummeted to reflect the expected shortage of movies in the future.[10]

The examples of the PC and the VCR are familiar cases of "network products"—products whose value depends on the availability and price of complementary products.[11] Kahan and I have argued that business forms (as well as long-term contracts and other social institutions) have network characteristics as well. A business form's complementary "products" include legal precedents that resolve uncertainty as the business environment changes, higher quality, and lower-cost legal services as lawyers accrue experience by responding to questions or disputes regarding elements of the business form. For publicly traded firms, the availability of a large number of investors and securities analysts who can price a firm's securities is another complementary product.

Kobayashi and Ribstein's discussion of LLPs reflects the increasing returns associated with business forms. As they explain, the LLP is defined as a partnership, which means the preexisting partnership law, document forms, and legal expertise applied to LLPs beginning at the time of their inception. This "backward compatibility" is analogous to that of new versions of software such as the Windows operating system. Each new version can run preexisting software while at the same time offering additional benefits to users.

LOCK-IN

When increasing returns are present in a product, the theoretical link between competitive equilibrium and social optimality is severed and market forces can yield suboptimal outcomes. One type of suboptimal outcome that can occur is that an existing product can become "locked-in"—it may remain widely used despite the fact that better products have been developed, or its presence may deter the development of better products.[12] Although the merits of the particular claims are subject to debate, the QWETY keyboard and the Beta VCR are often cited as examples of lock-in.[13] This can occur in the case of business forms and other social institutions as well. Whether it does or not and how often it happens are empirical questions to which I have no answers at this point.

In a recent series of articles, S. J. Liebowitz and Stephen Margolis have argued, in the context of competing technologies, that lock-in is highly unlikely to occur.[14] They argue that if there are gains to be reaped from having users switch from old Technology A to a superior Technology B, the owner of Technology B will internalize network externalities by subsidizing early users to switch, thereby building up network externalities in the new technology that eventually will attract users of Technology A.

Liebowitz and Margolis's point is a good one with respect to some technologies, but it has little applicability to the context of contracts, business forms, or other social institutions. No one can acquire an ownership interest in a new social institution the way one can in a new technology. Hence, no one can internalize the externalities created by a transition from an old institution to a new one. If the Delaware corporate form is locked-in, for example, it is difficult to imagine a party owning an alternative form such as the LLP and thereby internalizing the learning and network externalities created by the early users of the form. A competing state could do this in principle, paying firms cash to use its business form, but the practical difficulties would be immense.[15]

Kobayashi and Ribstein cite the experience with LLCs as evidence that lock-in is not a problem in the context of business forms. The move from traditional business forms to the LLC entailed the sacrifice of learning and network benefits associated with the traditional forms. Lock-in, therefore, was a theoretical possibility. Kobayashi and Ribstein contend, however, that the rapid growth in the use of LLCs indicates that lock-in did not occur. They may be correct, but it is still possible that there are suboptimally few LLCs. In fact, based on what Kobayashi and Ribstein report, there is reason to investigate further. They report that the growth in the use of LLCs has come at the expense of general partnerships. That is, firms that otherwise would have formed general partnerships instead formed LLCs once the LLC became available. But if this is really what is happening, there is something odd going on. Firms that, in the past, would have chosen the general partnership form, thereby giving up limited liability in exchange for managerial flexibility and single-layer taxation, are now getting the best of both worlds with the LLC. Yet firms that in the past would have chosen the corporate form are continuing to do so. At least some of those firms must be paying corporate tax unnecessarily or incurring transaction costs to maintain their status as

S Corporations in order to avoid doing so. For at least some, the LLC must be inherently superior. Kobayashi and Ribstein do not purport to analyze precisely where the LLC growth came from, and indeed some LLCs might have been corporations in the past. But if in fact the corporation is still equally attractive, relative to the alternatives, as it was before the LLC became available, then some potentially suboptimal stickiness seems to be present.[16]

Lock-in in the context of business forms has some precedent. Beginning in the 1960s, Delaware and other states enacted close corporation statutes tailored to the specific nature of close corporations, which had previously operated along with public corporations under the general corporation laws. As it turned out, however, only a small fraction of close corporations opted into these special statutes. The vast majority chose to be governed by the general corporation statutes. Commentators at the time expressed dismay at the failure of firms to use these statutes. An entirely plausible answer, however, is that the inherent benefits of the close corporation statutes, combined with firms' expectations regarding how many firms would ultimately use these statutes, failed to exceed the then current value of the general corporation statute given the learning benefits that had accrued to the general corporation and the network externalities expected to be created by the large number of close corporations expected to continue using that statute. What seems to have occurred is that close corporations' use of the general corporation statutes was locked in for close corporations, and the inherently superior close corporation statutes went nearly unused. This seems to be a case in which choice of law and state competition did not yield the expected result.[17]

IMPLICATIONS FOR CHOICE OF LAW

So what does this mean for contracts, business forms, choice of law, and state competition? It means that competition will not necessarily yield the optimal arrangement if increasing returns are substantial. A suboptimal regime may become locked in. How often does this occur, if at all? Perhaps not very often, or at least not too severely. Historical research is needed to answer this question.[18]

As a threshold matter, lock-in would occur only if a state's law became the law of choice for a large number of contracts of a particular type. The choice of Delaware for corporations is a candidate, as is Massachusetts for mutual funds. But these may be exceptions rather than the rule.[19] In addition, a state's law can become locked in only if learning or network externalities are significant, which means that the law would have to be either complex or characterized by open-ended standards as opposed to specific rules. If the law is complex, legal expertise will be important and a large number of contracts choosing a state's law will produce a high volume of legal work for that state's lawyers, which will enhance their quality relative to lawyers in other states. If the law is dominated by standards, judicial precedents will be valuable, and a large number of contracts will increase the volume of those precedents. Finally, even if increasing returns are significant, the inherent quality of the law is still important and limits the extent to which increasing returns can produce lock-in. If a state's law is sufficiently poor, lock-in will not occur.

III   Why Don't States Allow More Choice of Law for Business Associations?

Kobayashi and Ribstein argue that state legislatures will feel pressure to allow contractual choice of law. If a party wants to avoid a state's law it can exit the state by contract, or it can avoid contact with the state. For instance, a firm can avoid setting up headquarters in a state that will use that contact to apply an onerous law. Such avoidance is costly to in-state constituencies that would benefit from the establishment of business headquarters. Kobayashi and Ribstein argue that this sort of pressure led states to adopt the internal affairs doctrine, under which the law of the incorporating state applies to the internal affairs of a corporation. They also report that states are moving toward this rule for unincorporated businesses as well.

The internal affairs doctrine allows a firm to choose a state law by incorporating in that state. As Kobayashi and Ribstein explain, this simple choice-of-law rule unleashes state competition. States could go further, however, in allowing choice-of-law. Nevada, for example, could allow a firm to incorporate there but to include in its charter a choice-of-law provision that elects the law of another state—Delaware, for instance. By doing so, Nevada would get franchise fees, Nevada lawyers would get more corporate law business,[20] Nevada courts would get litigation business, and the firm would get Delaware law. Nevada could compete further by beating the competition on franchise fees. In fact, Nevada could go yet another step further by allowing a firm to make different choices of law with respect to different rules of corporate law. A firm could, for example, choose Delaware law for the duty of care and Wisconsin law for the corporate opportunity doctrine.[21]

From Nevada's point of view, this seems to be a more effective means of competing with Delaware than writing a new corporate code, although it could do that as well and let firms choose it if they so desire. To be sure, a Nevada court choosing Delaware law would not get everything a Delaware corporation gets. It would not get the Delaware courts or Delaware lawyers, but no other competitive strategy would get those benefits for Nevada corporations either. Enactment of a corporation code identical to Delaware's would be an inferior option because it would not incorporate Delaware case law. The Nevada statute could adopt existing case law, but that would still omit future case law, which as described in section 2 is valuable in the initial incorporation decision. The statute could adopt future case law along with past case law and the statute itself, in which case the state would replicate what I have proposed here, but only with respect to Delaware. Firms could not choose the law of another state, and Nevada could not experiment itself with trying to offer improvements in its own corporate law statute.

This choice-of-law strategy has two counterparts in the product market. It is similar to the commitment some stores make to meet the price of any competitor. This commitment allows a store to compete on price without actively monitoring the prices other stores are charging. The choice-of-law strategy allows a state to compete without monitoring other states' laws and without incurring the expense of drafting and enacting a new law. This strategy also has an analog in network product markets. When a network technology is dominant, producers of other technologies attempt to make their products compatible with the dominant technology. By doing so they allow users of their products to reap network externalities associated with the dominant product. Making Macintosh computers capable of running Windows software is an example of this. The choice-of-law strategy that I have suggested is similar in that it would make the Nevada charter compatible with the Delaware charter. A Nevada corporation that chooses Delaware law would be able to reap existing learning benefits associated with Delaware such as past precedents and general knowledge and expertise regarding Delaware law. It would also acquire network benefits such as future court decisions interpreting Delaware law.

Having suggested this as a strategy by which states can compete, I must add that as a policy matter it is troubling in that it would tend to reduce the incentives of state legislatures to enact statutory improvements. The result could be analogous to price fixing. Moreover, if increasing returns are indeed significant in business forms, this strategy would make lock-in more likely to occur. I describe the strategy here simply to raise the question of why states have not adopted it.

Choice of Law as a Precommitment Device

GEOFFREY P. MILLER

Bruce Kobayashi and Larry Ribstein's essay provides an interesting and valuable contribution to the literature on interstate economic relations and the interaction between public and private incentives. The authors propose the optimistic theory that effective party choice of applicable law and/or applicable forum will substantially counteract the problem of in-state interests expropriating wealth from out-of-state counter-parties in a federal system.[1] Thus the ability of the parties to select the governing law and forum can effectively "trivialize" state law. Kobayashi and Ribstein envisage a "multistage" process in which (a) in-state interests obtain favorable legislation, (b) out-of-state interests exit by means of choice-of-law/choice-of-forum clauses, (c) states allow enforcement of these clauses, and (d) the original legislation is effectively nullified.[2]

In proposing this theory, Kobayashi and Ribstein present two "competing" hypotheses in the economic debate over the efficiency of a federal system: first, that a state can impose costs on (or provide inadequate benefits to) out-of-state interests because such interests lack influence in the state's political process relative to the influence of in-state interests; and second, that states are limited in their ability to impose such costs because of interstate competition: if a given state attempted to impose excessive costs on an out-of-state interest, that interest could simply flee to a more congenial location at minimal cost.

In this comment, I attempt to expand on some of the efficiency considerations set forth in the Kobayashi and Ribstein essay by framing the analysis in terms of the elasticity of demand for a state's legal services, and by considering in detail some efficiency implications of respecting or not respecting privately negotiated choice-of-law or choice-of-forum clauses. I will then address a potential problem with the essay identified by Michael Klausner,[3] namely that choice of law and forum works only when the parties have the ability to set the terms of their relationship by contract, and since the parties can contract, they can simply adjust the payment terms of their contract to reflect the possibility of expropriation by in-state interests. I will try to connect this observation with another difficulty in the Kobayashi-Ribstein essay: the problem of explaining why state legislatures would allow parties to select the law of another state to govern their affairs, given that doing so reduces the ability of politicians in the state to provide valuable benefits to their constituents. I will suggest that state recognition of contractual choice-of-law and choice-of-forum clauses represents a form of precommitment by the state and the affected interest groups, to tie their hands against the temptation to engage in ex post opportunism that is wealth reducing ex ante.[4] Finally, I will suggest some ways in which the Kobayashi-Ribstein theory might be applied in the international context.

I Elasticities of Demand for State Law and State Forum

Kobayashi and Ribstein propose that state cost imposition and free choice of law and forum are "competing" hypotheses, since the second tends to counteract the first. It would probably be more accurate to say that these hypotheses are not competing so much as complementary. States clearly do have an incentive to expropriate wealth from out-of-state interests, but their ability to do so is constrained by the ability of out-of-state interests to move elsewhere and avoid the state's yoke. One does not have to choose between the hypotheses. Both are correct. The problem is not to pick a winner but to assess the strengths of the relative effects.

One can predict that a given state will attempt to maximize its revenues from out-of-state firms subject to the elasticity of demand that such firms have for use of the state's legal system. If a firm can easily escape (either by exiting a state where it is currently organized, or by electing to be organized initially in another state), then its elasticity of demand is high. The state cannot impose more than a transitory or slight "price" increase—in the form of imposing extra costs or providing reduced benefits—on an out-of-state firm without losing the firm's business. On the other hand, if demand of out-of-state firms for the state's legal regime is inelastic, then the state can impose relatively large costs or reduce benefits substantially without losing the business.

As Ribstein and Kobayashi cogently observe, the values given to these variables affect the choice of optimal policies. If demand is highly elastic, then the market can be relied on to act as a check against wealth-reducing state regulations that provide benefits to local interests but do so at the expense of outside interests. On the other hand, if demand is highly inelastic, then interstate competition will not be an efficacious remedy. Federal preemption of state law then becomes a more attractive solution to the problem, although a federal solution carries with it dangers of its own (if the federal regulation becomes captured by special interests, there will be no ready avenue of escape to the states).

II Efficiency Implications of Party Autonomy
in the Choice of Law and Forum

As a matter of policy, there appears to be little reason to disregard a choice-of-law clause freely and voluntarily agreed to by the parties unless (a) that provision is subject to the type of defense which would operate against any other general agreement in a contract, (b) that provision fails to take account of negative externalities on third parties; or (c) applying the law chosen by the parties would be unduly difficult or burdensome to the courts of the forum state.

As to the first justification for not enforcing a choice-of-law provision, it is evident that contractual defenses ought to be as good here as for any other term of the contract. For example, suppose the parties contracted to apply the law of a particular state (let's call it "Athens") to any disputes arising under their contract, Athens being at the time a jurisdiction subject to a rule of law and a democratically elected legislature. Subsequently, after the contract is negotiated but before a dispute arises, a political revolution occurs in Athens and the country is taken over by religious fundamentalists who impose a rigid and doctrinaire system under which the supplier of goods is considered to be obligated to provide the goods free of any interest charges, despite the fact that interest is called for in the contract and was perfectly valid under the law of Athens at the time the contract was drafted. The supervening and unforeseeable change in Athens law might operate, under standard contract principles, to release the parties from the agreement to apply Athenian law when a dispute arises, since the intent of the parties was not to subject themselves to a legal regime of the sort now in effect in Athens. A similar situation might arise if the country whose law is chosen ceases to exist during the life of the contract. One might imagine, for example, a contract written to apply the law of the former federal state of Yugoslavia; it seems unlikely that a court would interpret the contract under the now-applicable law in the present state of Yugoslavia, which is comprised only of Serbia and Montenegro.

Similarly, one can imagine that choice-of-law clauses might be declared unenforceable because of mistake (the parties agree that the law of Athens applies to their transaction in the erroneous, material, mutual belief that Athens law permits contracts for barter, when in fact it does not), fraud (one party fraudulently induces the other to accept application of a particular state's law by means of false representation as to the content of that law), or even unclean hands (the parties agree to apply the law of Athens, but then one party improperly obtains a change in Athens law in order to obtain an advantage under the contract). Some of these examples may sound far-fetched, but there is no reason in principle why standard contract defenses should not also apply to disputes over choice-of-law clauses.

The much more difficult situation is the choice-of-law clause that imposes negative externalities. In the contract setting, it is rather difficult to think of cases in which the election of a law to govern the relationship of the parties inter se would in fact impose negative externalities. Regardless of any choice-of-law clauses, the state where the contract is to be performed certainly maintains regulatory jurisdiction to protect against externalities. For example, if the parties contracted to operate a factory in Athens in such a way as to impose pollution costs on the residents of that state, Athens would have regulatory jurisdiction to prevent the pollution even if the contract calls for its interpretation and enforcement by another state, Sparta, which would permit the operation of the factory under similar circumstances.

Because contracts relate to the relationships among the parties, they rarely involve significant external interests. Accordingly, there appears to be little reason in public policy for a court to refuse to enforce a contractual choice-of-law provision. If, however, an externality could be shown in a given case, this would provide a theoretical justification for a state's refusing to enforce a choice-of-law rule. For example, a contract of marriage arguably involves not only the interest of the spouses but also that of children (born or unborn). The state might reasonably refuse to apply the law of another state to a contract of marriage over which the state has jurisdiction if the state whose law is chosen imposes substantive regulation of the marriage contract which in the view of the forum state is harmful to the interests of nonparties to the contract (such as children).

A third situation in which a forum might properly refuse to respect a choice-of-law clause freely agreed to by the parties is when doing so would be unduly difficult or burdensome for the forum state court. For example, suppose the parties agreed that their contract is to be interpreted according to the oral law of the Gypsies. Such a law does exist, and, perhaps with some effort, it could be researched and the relevant principles revealed.[5] But it might nevertheless be the case that the forum court would refuse to apply Gypsy law to the contract simply because the court is so unfamiliar with the rules of an oral, customary law that it can have no assurance that it will be applying the law correctly. In such a case, the court might elect to defer to some other jurisdiction with greater expertise in the area, but deference may be too costly in a given case, or it may be, as in the case of Gypsy law, that no reasonably available forum offers greater expertise. In such a situation it would appear consistent with economic efficiency for the court to trump the agreement of the parties and apply some other body of law to resolve a dispute.

Even if a court had the expertise to apply the law of a foreign jurisdiction, it might prove excessively costly in a given case to identify and prove that law. Problems of identifying legally binding documents or translating complex terms from unknown languages may prove so daunting that a court might in a given case throw up its hands and simply apply its own law. However, in practice, courts have often been willing to make heroic efforts to identify and apply the law of other jurisdictions, and cases where a court will refuse to apply a foreign law merely because of difficulty of proof or unfamiliarity of use are likely to be uncommon.

In the absence of any of these three conditions—standard contract defenses, negative externalities, or undue burden or unfamiliarity—efficiency considerations counsel for a court to apply whatever body of law the parties voluntarily choose to govern their transaction. We may even go further than this. It is not even necessary that the parties choose a given, existing body of governmentally created law. They could just as easily elect to have their contract governed by principles created through private means, such as trade associations or self-regulatory organizations, or even by usages of trade in an industry. All that is required is that there be a reasonably ascertainable body of rules that can be enlisted to govern the terms of the transaction; it is not necessary that those rules be of governmental origin.

Thus, even omitting consideration of federalism, the economic analysis counsels for a highly deferential approach to choice-of-law clauses in private contracts. The Kobayashi-Ribstein essay provides an additional reason for respecting choice-of-law and choice-of-forum clauses in contracts involving interstate parties: doing so substantially reduces the danger that the states will be able to impose value-decreasing substantive regulations to the bargains which help the in-state party at the expense of the out-of-state party and of society at large.

III   The Problem of the Coasean Bargain

Michael Klausner, in his comment, suggests an important objection to the Kobayashi-Ribstein essay. The parties need not adopt a choice-of-law provision to avoid costly state regulation. To see this, assume that there are two contracting parties, A (a resident of Athens) and B (a resident of Sparta). First, take the case where Athens, the state for performance of the contract, has in effect Regulation X that benefits its resident, A, at the expense of the out-of-state party, B. In the absence of Regulation X, the contract is worth $1,000 to B in expected profits, but with Regulation X in effect, the contract is worth only $100 to B. A receives the $900 that B loses. Assume further that B is unwilling to enter the contract unless its profit is $1,000.

Kobayashi and Ribstein observe that in this case A and B can mutually agree to a choice-of-law/choice-of-forum clause that avoids Regulation X, thus trivializing Athens's attempt to impose its law on the transaction. As Klausner suggests, however, this is not the only approach to the problem. A and B could keep the contract under the law of Athens, but simply adjust the price term. A can agree to pay B $900 extra in compensation. Other things equal, this would have exactly the same effect as a choice-of-law/choice-of-forum provision, while avoiding the inconvenience of subjecting the arrangement to a foreign court.

A similar situation arises when Regulation X is not in effect in Athens at contract time, but may be obtained by A afterwards at minimal expense (because of A's political power in the state). After the contract is signed, A can go to the state government and change the regulatory regime in such a way that A gains $900 and B loses $900. Assume that there are no externalities. In this circumstance, B will continue to perform the contract, because it is still a profitable (although much less profitable) venture for B; but A has used its political clout in the state to expropriate $900 of B's wealth.

As in the case of legislation already in effect, the contractual choice-of-law or choice-of-forum clauses discussed by Kobayashi and Ribstein can substantially reduce the danger of future measures favoring in-state residents. B, knowing that A is likely to obtain the favorable legislation ex post, may insist on a contractual provision to the effect that the contract is to be interpreted according to the law of some other jurisdiction (or be arbitrated). A does not have the political clout in the chosen jurisdiction to obtain the favorable legislation. Thus B is protected against the possibility of ex post opportunistic behavior by A.

Klausner's observation has cogency in this situation also. The parties need not go to the length of choosing another law or another forum. If B knows that A is likely to go to the Athens government for a $900 favor, B can incorporate that fact in the contract B negotiates with A ex ante—say, by insisting on a profit of $1,900 instead of $1,000. Now when A goes to the government, the relationship between the parties is essentially unchanged. Accordingly, the parties do not need to adopt a choice-of-law or choice-of-forum clause.

Klausner's observation is important because it frames the economic issue clearly. The observation might suggest that the Kobayashi-Ribstein framework is incomplete because it leaves other types of private arrangements out of the equation: a "loser" in the Kobayashi-Ribstein model can neutralize a wealth-transferring law by contract.

Klausner is clearly right that choice of law need not be the only solution to the problem of wealth expropriation. However, there are a number of reasons why private choice of law might be superior to other types of contractual arrangements.

1. Transactions costs. First, choice-of-law/choice-of-forum clauses may reduce transactions costs as compared with alternative options. To bargain around the contractual risk through the use of a price term, for example, would clearly be costly. The parties would need to quantify the contractual risk, which would require an ex ante valuation of the magnitude of the harm to the out-of-state party from Regulation X. In addition, in the situation where Regulation X is not on the books, but might be obtained by A ex post, the parties would need to value both the probability that A will in fact obtain the regulation and the cost of the regulation (not yet drafted) if A does obtain it. These values would be difficult to quantify.

In addition to the costs of quantification, the residual uncertainty will impose costs on both parties if they are risk-averse. A choice-of-law/choice-of-forum term does not involve these costs, because the parties know that if it is effective, they will not have to worry about the costs of legislation in the state.

Another transaction cost, where Regulation X is not yet on the books, is that reliance on the price term essentially commits the in-state party to seek the favorable regulation, since it has been required to pay ex ante for the right to do so. Seeking regulation is costly, and since the in-state party makes itself no better off doing so than it would have been had it agreed ex ante to a choice-of-law/choice-of-forum clause, the party would probably prefer the latter approach.

2. Regulatory inefficiency. A second problem with types of contractual neutralization other than choice-of-law/choice-of-forum clauses is that the regulation that the in-state interest obtains may be inefficient. Assume, for example, that the regulation that A (the in-state party) obtains benefits A by $500, but imposes costs on B of $900. The lost value of $400 is due to the fact that the regulation imposes deadweight social costs. A would prefer to capture the full amount of B's loss, but because of political or legal constraints in the state, A is not able to do so. Now both parties are worse off ex ante even if they agree to contract around the political risk by the use of a price term, because the available surplus from the contract has been reduced. Not only are the parties worse off, but society as a whole loses by the amount of the deadweight loss.

3. Third-party expropriation. A slightly different (but basically similar) problem would arise if A, going into the political process, would have to make concessions to other interest groups in order to obtain the desired legislation. For example, suppose that when A goes to the government to obtain a benefit of $500, powerful consumer groups will insist that B also expend $400 for the benefit of their constituencies. Here, the net result of the political bargaining may not be inefficient socially (society is no worse off, because the contract continues to be performed and the wealth transfer has no efficiency consequences). But A and B would still be worse off under this regime because third parties are able to expropriate $400 of the joint surplus of their deal.

4. Ex post opportunism. A fourth problem with types of contractual neutralization other than choice-of-law/choice-of-forum clauses is that the neutralization may fail because of ex post opportunism. Assume that in the absence of a neutralization agreement A would go to the legislature to obtain a benefit of $900 and impose a cost of $900 on B. The parties attempt to neutralize this problem by providing B with an extra $900 in compensation ex ante. Now, however, A may find it in A's interest to get *more* than $900 from the legislature. Contractual neutralization does not prevent A from doing this.

For these and perhaps for other reasons, neutralization by contract may not work. This leads to a way of characterizing some of the incentives of the contracting parties and the state that is slightly different from the characterization provided by Kobayashi and Ribstein, although basically in line with their thinking. The decision by the parties to adopt choice-of-law/choice-of-forum provisions ex ante can be thought of as a form of precommitment mechanism.

Assume that, for the reasons outlined above, the parties jointly prefer at contract time to avoid an ex post recourse to the legislature by A.[6] However, once the contract is signed, it will be in A's interest to go to the legislature unless the contract contains effective restrictions on A's ability to do so. A will go to the government, ex post, because A can make itself better off by doing so, even though in the process A makes B worse off by an amount larger than A's gain.

Most contractual solutions do not solve this problem because they leave A free, ex post, to engage in opportunistic behavior.

Choice-of-law/choice-of-forum provisions can be understood as mechanisms of precommitment that benefit both parties ex ante. By adopting such a provision, the parties ensure that A will not behave opportunistically ex post, since it will not be in A's interest to do so. A gets no benefit from seeking recourse from the political system because the contract with B will be determined under the law, or by the courts, of another state in which A has no influence. A choice-of-law/choice-of-forum provision functions similarly to a bond posted by A committing it not to engage in opportunistic behavior ex post.

This analysis also provides some further light on the question of why the politicians in A's home state would agree to allow the enforcement of choice-of-law/choice-of-forum clauses. After all, such clauses prevent the in-state party from seeking recourse from the state's legislature, and thus would appear to reduce the power of state politicians as well as their ability to extract campaign contributions for political favors.

In part, states probably have adopted a fairly lenient attitude toward choice-of-law/choice-of-forum clauses because it is difficult for them to prevent such clauses from taking effect. Kobayashi and Ribstein point to a number of difficulties states face in blocking such clauses. For example, the plaintiff has the initial choice of forum, and if the plaintiff elects to bring a lawsuit in another state, the courts of that state are likely to take jurisdiction over the case and to enforce the choice-of-law provisions of the contract. Similarly, if a state refused enforcement of choice-of-law/choice-of-forum clauses, outside interests might cease doing business in the state, at least at the margin. The ultimate effect would be to harm the state's interests rather than help them.[7]

In addition to these constraints, however, there may be another reason why states would recognize choice-of-law/choice-of-forum clauses that select the law or courts of another state to resolve disputes, even though doing so reduces the ability of state politicians to extract rents from in-state interests in exchange for providing favorable regulations. As we have seen, it is in the interest of the contracting parties ex ante for the states to give effect to choice-of-law/forum clauses. The discussion above demonstrates that the conflict between the in-state and out-of-state parties occurs only after contract time. Before the parties enter into a contract, it is very much in their mutual interest to have the option of selecting the law or the forum of another state. Thus it is not only out-of-state interests that benefit from choice clauses. In-state interests benefit just as much as out-of-state firms on an ex ante basis. Although ex ante lobbying in a state is likely to be less effective than ex post lobbying (because parties may not know whether they are going to enter into a contract or not), the universe of in-state parties that stand to benefit from enforceability of choice clauses is also much larger than the universe of parties that would profit by nonenforcement. Overall, the political balance tips in favor of enforcement of choice-of-law/forum clauses.

IV   Some International Considerations

The insights of the Kobayashi-Ribstein essay would appear to apply with even greater force in the international context than in the domestic context. International contacts are often negotiated between citizens of different countries. In the international arena, the disparity of political power between citizen and noncitizen is likely to be far greater than in the domestic arena. Moreover, the choice of law and forum is likely to make much more difference in the international arena than in the domestic context, simply because legal regimes and court systems vary across countries much more than they do across states. Thus one would expect to see widespread use of choice-of-law and choice-of-forum provisions in international contracts. Consistently with the Kobayashi-Ribstein essay, it appears that choice-of-law and choice-of-forum provisions are, indeed, routinely found in international agreements. Usually, the jurisdictions chosen are centers for international business, such as London or New York.

Moreover, the precommitment issue looms even larger in the international arena than in the domestic context. Because parties in the international context face a greater risk of opportunistic action by the citizens of the foreign state—up to and including the risk of complete expropriation of the entire value of the investment—the contracting parties have an interest at contract time in obtaining the strongest possible precommitment against ex post opportunism, both by the domestic counter-party and by the government of the foreign country itself. Further, for the same reason that states may have an interest in respecting choice-of-law/choice-of-forum clauses even when such clauses select the law or courts of another state, nations have a similar interest in respecting the choices of the contracting parties because doing so will be beneficial to their citizens ex ante.

In the case of international agreements, however, there is the additional problem that a given state's commitment to respecting the free contractual choice of the parties may not be durable. While courts in London, New York, and other international centers tend to display a high degree of reliability—in part because the wealth of their own jurisdictions are enhanced if the legal system is reliable—courts in emerging or transitional economies may not enjoy the same level of trust from international contracting parties. How can a country precommit itself to respecting the contractual rights of the parties?

This problem has been dealt with in a number of interesting ways in recent years. One of the most fascinating is the approach of Peru. Until quite recently, Peru was an unstable nation, subject to military coups, guerrilla movements, and periodic hyperinflation, where democratic procedures were shaky at best and the judiciary had a reputation for being both poorly trained and unreliable. When the government of Alberto Fujimori took office in 1991, it made a major drive toward increasing overseas investment. But the government faced serious difficulties in assuring overseas investors that Peru was a safe bet, especially given the activities of the Tupac Amuru and Sendero Luminoso movements in the countryside. To reassure international investors, the government adopted regulations promising investors a highly favorable environment in which to do business, including control over investment, national treatment of foreign firms, automatic authorization for foreign investment, free remittance of profits, dividends, and other forms of income, free reexportation of capital, free currency exchange, unrestricted access to domestic credit, and freedom to contract for insurance against sovereign risk both within Peru and abroad.[8]

These were substantial concessions to foreign investors. But how could these promises be relied on? The Fujimori government could not assure foreign investors that it would be in power forever, or that a subsequent government would not rescind all the promises previously made. Here is where Peru adopted several creative precommitment devices to provide additional assurances to foreign investors who might not have been satisfied with mere promises not backed by legally enforceable rights.

In order to provide additional assurances to major investors, the Peruvian government stands ready to enter into "legal stability agreements" with any foreign investor who either makes a cash investment in excess of $2,000,000 or who makes a cash investment of at least $500,000 coupled with the creation of at least twenty permanent jobs in Peru or at least $2,000,000 annual export revenues in the first three years of operation. These legal stability agreements have the force of law—that is, they are binding contracts between the government of Peru and the international investor. Under Peruvian law, the contracts have a civil (as opposed to an administrative) nature, so that they can only be modified, amended, or terminated by the agreement of both parties. The agreements are enforceable in court like any contract. Moreover, they are recognized in a provision of the Peruvian constitution.

Legal stability agreements guarantee the following: (1) stability of the income tax system in effect at the time of the signing of the agreement; (2) stability of the system of freely disposable foreign income; (3) stability of the right to freely remit profits, dividends, capital, and other forms of income; (4) stability of the right to use the most favorable exchange rate available; (5) stability of the right to equal treatment under the law; and (6) stability of the labor hiring system in any of its forms. What the government attempted to do, through these agreements, was to tie not only its own hands but also the hands of any successors with respect to various forms of sovereign risk.

One could still ask whether the government effectively precommitted itself to respecting these agreements, since a successor could repudiate prior agreements, abrogate contracts, and neutralize the courts. But Peru provided further assurances to the international investment community by formally committing itself to agreements both with international agencies for dispute resolution and guarantees and with other nations on a bilateral basis. Peru has an agreement with the Multilateral Investment Guarantee Agency under which the country agrees to cover the following noncommercial risks: currency transfer risk, risk of expropriation or similar measures, breach of contract risk, and risk of war and other civil disturbance. The government entered into a separate agreement with the International Center for the Settlement of Investment Disputes, providing for the arbitration of disputes arising under legal stability agreements. Peru also has an agreement in force with the Overseas Private Insurance Corporation (a U.S. entity) and bilateral investment treaties signed, approved, or in force with twenty-five separate countries.

It would be extremely costly for any subsequent government to abrogate these agreements. Essentially, Peru has done all that it realistically could do to tie its hands and guarantee foreign investors that their wealth will not be expropriated through opportunistic measures ex post—just as the Kobayashi-Ribstein approach would predict. The Peruvian project appears to have worked: as of 1997 there were 184 legal stability agreements in force, covering total foreign investments of $4.7 billion.[9]

An even more creative approach, although one that has not yet been implemented, is the idea of selective incorporation of foreign legal systems to promote emerging nations as international financial centers. Some emerging nations may be well positioned (because of geography, political orientation, or other factors) to act as home country to international financial institutions doing business in a region. However, the legal regime in these countries may not be well developed, and potential investors may not trust that any legal regime that is developed will serve their interests.

One proposal that has been advanced in policy circles is for countries in this position to allow firms that enter to bring their own regulatory laws with them.[10] The host country would identify a limited number of existing, well-developed legal regimes and allow qualified foreign firms to establish international financial operations as long as the firms conduct their operations in the host country in accordance with one of the legal regimes. Under such an approach, a French company establishing an international lending office in an emerging economy could elect to be governed by French law, while a German company entering the same market could elect to be governed by German law. Although the principal objective of this choice-of-law regime is to provide ready-made, sophisticated, and effective regulatory regimes for countries without a developed domestic regulatory structure, another important value is that the emerging economy precommits not to revise its own law so as to expropriate wealth from the foreign entrants—a result which again would seem to flow from the considerations insightfully articulated in the Kobayashi-Ribstein paper.

Conclusion

Kobayashi and Ribstein have proposed that the ability of contracting parties to select the governing law or governing forum is a substantial counterweight to the tendency of in-state interests to expropriate wealth from out-of-state counter-parties. They argue that this exit option essentially trivializes state law by making it a series of optional terms rather than a mandatory regime. In this comment, I have attempted to expand on the Kobayashi and Ribstein essay in several ways. First, I observe that what drives the mechanism posited in the Kobayashi-Ribstein paper is the elasticity of demand for the state's legal regime. Essentially, Kobayashi and Ribstein propose that demand is highly elastic, and therefore that states lack a high degree of power to impose wealth-reducing expropriations on out-of-state contracting parties. Second, I consider the efficiency arguments for respecting choice-of-law and choice-of-forum provisions. Third, I address some implications of Michael Klausner's observation that because we are dealing here in a world of contract, the parties have other means of contracting around the political risk (e.g., through price terms) than by way of choice-of-law/forum clauses. While Klausner's observation is true, the choice-of-law/forum approach offers significant advantages as a way to obtain the in-state party's reliable precommitment not to behave opportunistically ex post by seeking to expropriate the counter-party's wealth through political lobbying. I use the concept of precommitment as a means of explaining why state legislatures actually have an interest in respecting contractual choice of law and forum even when the parties are opting out of the state's legal regime. Finally, I turn to the international setting and suggest that the Kobayashi-Ribstein approach is particularly cogent here, since the disparity of political power among citizens and noncitizens is likely to be even greater than that between citizens of different states, and since differences in legal regimes and court systems make much more of a difference internationally than domestically. I describe a number of interesting initiatives in the international arena that appear grounded in dynamic processes similar to those that Kobayashi and Ribstein have described for domestic contracting.

Corporate Law as the Paradigm for Contractual Choice of Law

ROBERTA ROMANO

Bruce Kobayashi and Larry Ribstein's essay develops this book's broad theme of the importance of freedom of contract through an examination of contractual choice-of-law clauses. Kobayashi and Ribstein's "bottom line" is that, in general, the preferable public policy is to enforce contracting parties' explicit choice-of-law decisions. The distinctive feature of their analysis is that it is based not on the benefits to the contracting parties (i.e., that enforcement maximizes the contracting parties' welfare), but rather, on broader social benefits created by such a policy, that it constrains states from enacting inefficient substantive laws (that is, that choice-of-law clause enforcement minimizes governmental rent-seeking). The mechanism that creates this state of affairs is the ability of private parties to avoid inefficient state laws by choosing an alternative regime through a choice-of-law clause. Their exit (particularly when in large numbers) or threat to exit from a regime signals its inefficiency to the state, providing incentives for legislative reform (as states are motivated to adjust their laws in order to stem departures from their legal domain).

Kobayashi and Ribstein's paradigmatic case for the impact on substantive law of choice-of-law clause enforcement is corporate law. The judicial choice-of-law rule applied in corporate law in all fifty states, referred to as the "internal affairs" doctrine, is the epitome of a choice-of-law clause approach. Under the internal affairs doctrine, the incorporation state's laws govern manager-shareholder relations; the incorporation state is chosen by the parties to the corporation, and can be a purely paper domicile, that is, a state in which the firm has no physical presence. The internal affairs rule is automatically applied in corporate law without examining whether the corporation has the requisite "contacts" with its chosen incorporation state, or whether another state's "interest" is greater than the incorporation state's in regulating the corporation (examinations otherwise commonly undertaken to determine which state's law applies). Moreover, this choice-of-law rule is critical for the effectiveness of state competition for corporate charters because it is the choice-of-law rule with the lowest cost of switching regimes, and thereby it produces the strongest signals to states regarding the efficacy of their laws.

The paradigmatic case of contracting for choice of law, corporate law, is the starting point of my comment. The comment discusses why corporate law is the paradigm, that is, why a contractual choice-of-law approach is uncontroversial in corporate affairs. This entails identifying what characteristics of the corporate setting have enabled courts to affirm unhesitatingly the contracting parties' choice, as well as the integral relation between the internal affairs doctrine and the efficacy of state competition for corporate charters. The effort to explain what makes corporate law paradigmatic is undertaken in order to shed light upon extensions of the contractual conflict-of-law approach to contracts beyond the corporate charter, where the parties' explicit choice is not automatically followed by courts. The first extension considered concerns securities transactions, a field in which I believe the appropriateness of applying an internal affairs approach is compelling, despite courts' failure to do so and its consequent absence from Kobayashi and Ribstein's discussion. The comment then turns to the principal extension that Kobayashi and Ribstein discuss, which is further removed from corporate law than securities transactions, franchise contracts.

I   The Internal Affairs Doctrine and State Competition for Corporate Charters

U.S. corporate law is unique among federal systems in that it is competitively produced by the states. The European Union (EU) and Canada, also federations, have not developed active markets for corporate charters. This section reviews how state competition for charters works in the United States and locates the principal reason for the absence of competition in the EU and Canada as the restriction of firms' choice of their governing legal regime—that is, the failure of those federations to adopt an effective internal affairs approach to corporate governance. It concludes with an effort to identify why the internal affairs doctrine was successfully applied in the U.S. corporate law context.

STATE COMPETITION FOR CHARTERS

In the United States, corporate law—the law governing relations between shareholders and managers—is a matter for the states.[1] Firms choose their state of incorporation, a statutory domicile that can be entirely independent of the firm's physical presence and can be changed with shareholder approval, from among the fifty states and the District of Columbia. Thus the choice of incorporation state for a corporation is analogous to a choice-of-law provision in a contract.

The legislative approach of corporate law is, in the main, enabling: Corporate codes supply standard contract terms for corporate governance that function as default provisions for charters which a corporation can customize to its needs where necessary. Firms can thereby particularize their charters under a state code, as well as seek out the state code which best matches their needs so as to minimize their cost of doing business, and correspondingly increase the value of the firm for its shareholders. Firms choose their incorporation state by reference to the content of the legal regime—substantive statutes, as well as the stock of judicial precedents interpreting the statutes, and the expertise of the judges fashioning those precedents. They typically incorporate locally or in Delaware.

States compete for corporate charters because of financial incentives: states collect franchise tax revenues from locally incorporated firms. Delaware, for example, over the past thirty years obtained an average of 16.5 percent of its total tax revenue from the franchise tax.[2] Moreover, the costs of maintaining its corporate law system—the budget for the office of the Secretary of State which processes corporate charter filings and the courts that handle corporate law cases—are much lower than the tax revenues received.[3] There is a variety of evidence indicating that states compete for charters, despite Delaware's predominance. Corporate law innovations diffuse over the states in an S-shaped curve (the proportion of adopters increases with time) paralleling the diffusion of technological innovations, a pattern interpreted in the economic literature as a sign of powerful competition; state franchise revenues are positively related to the responsiveness of a state's corporate law to corporate preferences (measured as a function of the rate and extent to which legal innovations considered desirable by reincorporating firms are enacted), a relation that holds up even when Delaware is excluded from the statistical analysis; and firms migrate from states with low levels of responsiveness to those with higher levels.[4]

Delaware is the leading incorporation state despite few physically present firms. The explanation of Delaware's success in attracting corporate charters lies in its investment in assets whose value is specific to administering corporate law (assets with no comparable value in an alternative use), and which are related to the aspects of a legal regime that are attractive to reincorporating firms. These assets are a reputation for responsiveness (based on the fact that Delaware is not only a leader in corporate law innovations but also extraordinarily quick to update its code if another state innovates first), judicial expertise in corporate law, and a large stock of legal precedents. By investing heavily in such assets, Delaware provides substantial certainty regarding the corporate law environment. The certainty takes two forms. Not only does its legal capital afford firms ease in business planning but it also enables firms to relocate in Delaware without concern that the desirable features of its corporate law regime will be changed after the firms have invested in the domicile move. This is because Delaware's specialized assets (its legal and reputational capital) commit it to continue its course of corporate-law responsiveness: firms know that if it did not maintain a legal regime that was responsive to firms' preferences as business conditions changed and the firms reincorporated elsewhere, the loss of franchise revenues would be ruinous for Delaware, a small state with no indigenous revenue source to readily replace the franchise tax.

The internal affairs rule plays a crucial role in the success of the system. Delaware's attractiveness to firms depends on the credibility of its commitment to responsiveness, which is a function of its high franchise to total tax revenue ratio, and which is a financial incentive possible only for a small state. A domicile recognition rule that depended on the physical presence of the corporation or its shareholders, rather than a mailing address, would effectively rule out a small state as a domicile.

What guarantees that the laws produced by this competition (that is, by Delaware's responsiveness) benefit shareholders rather than the managers who choose the domicile? As Ralph Winter elaborated in his classic paper on state competition, corporations are embedded in a series of markets—capital, labor, product, and corporate control—that constrain managers' domicile choices.[5] The cost of capital to firms that operate under a legal regime that does not maximize shareholder wealth will be higher than that of firms operating under a legal regime that does maximize value, and the former firms will, accordingly, be outperformed by the latter firms. This will cause their stock prices to drop, subjecting their managers to displacement through hostile takeovers or insolvency. Thus managers have incentives to choose the incorporation state whose regime best matches shareholders' preferences. The many markets identified by Winter to align manager and shareholder interests concerning the choice of legal regime would have to be highly imperfect for managers to be able to exploit shareholders through the domicile choice.[6]

The best available empirical evidence supports Winter's view of the competitive process. There have been six event studies (a statistical technique for measuring the impact of new information on stock prices) investigating stock price reactions to domicile changes to measure the wealth effects of state competition on shareholders. Examining the price effects of a statutory domicile change is equivalent to studying who benefits from state competition, managers or shareholders, because the actions of reincorporators, as the marginal consumers of charters, drive the market (that is, state's competitive responses), and the price change on reincorporation measures the market's response to the new legal regime.

Measured over a variety of time intervals and sample firms, these studies find either a significant positive stock price effect or no significant stock price effect upon reincorporations in general, and reincorporation in Delaware in particular.[7] No study observes a negative stock price effect. To consider whether the price effects were due to confounding events—anticipated changes in the firms' business motivating the domicile change—rather than the change in legal regime, in my study I examined the returns to reincorporating firms subdividing the sample by the anticipated transactions. The differences across the groups were not statistically significant.[8] The event studies therefore provide compelling evidence that shareholders benefit from competition.

State competition is not, however, perfect. In the 1980s when hostile takeovers emerged as a mechanism for changing control and, correlatively, replacing incumbent management, the vast majority of states enacted laws that attempted to lower the probability of a hostile takeover. Because shareholders receive substantial premiums in hostile takeovers, most commentators hypothesized that the objective of these statutes was not to enhance shareholder welfare but to entrench management.[9] Consistent with the view that restricting hostile takeovers harms shareholders, the enactment of antitakeover laws produced negative or statistically insignificant stock price reactions.[10]

Still, the data are not one-sidedly against state competition even in the takeover context. Delaware, with the largest stake in the chartering business, stands out, for instance, as an anomaly in the takeover legislative process. In contrast to its position as an innovator in corporation laws, in the context of takeover statutes, Delaware was a laggard behind other states and its regulation is considerably less restrictive of bids. In addition, the stock price reaction to its statute was not negative.[11] More important, charter competition limits the extent to which states can restrict takeovers: when Pennsylvania enacted what is considered a draconian statute, a majority of firms opted out of its coverage because of demands made by their investors, who raised the prospect of selling their shares and reinvesting in firms incorporated in states with no or less restrictive statutes, such as California and Delaware. Consequently, other states did not adopt the Pennsylvania statute. Here too, the internal affairs rule served as an important constraint on competition's producing laws adverse to shareholder interests. The most effective statutes at preventing hostile bids—"first generation" statutes that required bidders to submit plans to a state agency and obtain approval before proceeding—were struck down by the Supreme Court as unconstitutional burdens on interstate commerce because they permitted multiple states to regulate the transaction, as their legislative jurisdiction depended on the physical location of corporate assets rather than statutory domicile.[12]

In short, the state competition for charters that is facilitated by the application of the internal affairs doctrine produces laws that enhance share value rather than laws that redistribute wealth from outsiders to in-state residents. There is no evidence that changing statutory domicile, and hence state competition, harms shareholders and, in fact, there is substantial evidence that it is a wealth-increasing event. Although, as the experience with state takeover laws indicates, in the short run there will be deviations from the optimum in a federal system, in the longer run competitive pressure is exerted when states make mistakes, as in the example of firms opting out of Pennsylvania's takeover statute.

PRODUCTION OF CORPORATE LAW IN THE
EUROPEAN UNION AND CANADA

In contrast to U.S. states, neither the countries of the EU, nor Canadian provinces, compete for charters.[13] There is a key legal distinction in these two federations, compared to the United States, that explains the absence of competition: the EU and Canadian legal systems have barriers that prevent firms from choosing their legal regime and thereby attenuate the constituent governments' incentives to engage in charter competition.[14]

European Union. The critical legal difference between the EU and the United States is the choice-of-law rule for corporate governance. European nations (with the exception of the Netherlands and the United Kingdom) follow the law of a corporation's real or effective seat, which requires a significant physical presence in the country for the domicile choice to be effective. European firms therefore cannot establish statutory domiciles by a paper filing to take advantage of a particular nation's regime; rather, they must physically relocate their headquarters in the nation with the preferred corporate code. Because of the substantial cost of reincorporation under the real seat rule, EU members have reduced incentives to compete for charters by offering responsive codes: the pool of recruitable corporations is small. Carney provides suggestive supporting evidence: provisions long abandoned as cumbersome in U.S. codes are prominent and mandatory in the EU directives on corporate law.[15]

While the choice-of-law rule explains why charter competition has not emerged within the EU, it does not explain why European nations have not altered the rule in order to foster competition and thereby enhance share values. There are, in fact, political and institutional reasons that prevent important EU members from advocating such a switch. Germany, for instance, has a corporate law regime that furthers objectives other than shareholder-wealth maximization, evidenced most explicitly by its codetermination (two-tier) board system, which requires that half of the supervisory board of large corporations be elected by the firm's employees. Not surprisingly, there is a growing literature that suggests that codetermination boards are unwieldy institutions that make it difficult to advance shareholder interests, and no evidence that such boards positively affect shareholder wealth.[16] Indeed, in countries such as France where codetermination is an available option rather than mandatory, virtually no firms have adopted such a board structure.[17] The codetermination board structure, and hence a system that is not directed at maximizing share value, could not be preserved in a competitive charter system because equity investors will dominate the choice of incorporation state since their capital is the most mobile of the firms' participants. The EU's choice-of-law rule's effect is most graphic in this context. It has produced a form of within-nation competition over organizational forms, by which nations such as Germany have offered certain firms the choice to organize as privately held entities through which they can avoid codetermination and other regulatory requirements imposed on public corporations. Competition over choice of law connected to choice of organizational form is more limited than U.S.-style competition over choice of law because the regime choice entails forgoing access to capital markets. Moreover, the EU organizational options for private firms appear to be constricted compared to those offered under an internal affairs rule, as witnessed by the explosive growth in new business forms across U.S. states that Kobayashi and Ribstein detail.

Canada. The principal reason for the attenuated charter competition across Canadian provinces is the inability of provincial governments to control their corporate law regimes. Provincial security administrators, whose jurisdictions are based on the location of shareholders and not issuer domicile,[18] are able to regulate corporate governance and can override provincial corporate law. In addition, the Supreme Court of Canada can review all provincial appellate court decisions. The overlapping jurisdictions that characterize the Canadian approach weaken provinces' incentives to compete for charters, just as the physical domicile rule does for EU nations, for the necessary investments a province must make to become a Canadian Delaware can be easily devalued without recourse by the decisions of security administrators or the Canadian Supreme Court. The return on any such investment will also be small because a province cannot credibly commit to responsiveness when it can be overruled by other authorities.

Canadian firms correspondingly have less reason to invest in optimizing domicile decisions than U.S firms, which in turn has a feedback effect, further diminishing provincial incentives to compete. The overlapping authority of securities administrators, a national court, and provinces renders a corporation's choice of law—its statutory domicile—not a truly effective choice with respect to its governing rules, despite Canada's application of the same internal affairs doctrine as the United States.

WHY IS CORPORATE LAW PARADIGMATIC?

State competition for corporate charters has been successful in producing laws that maximize shareholder value because a statutory domicile enables firms to choose their legal regime without incurring prohibitive capital costs as entailed by alternative choice-of-law rules, such as head office location. The internal affairs doctrine, in other words, facilitates competition. But the choice-of-law rule is not the sole reason for charter competition's success. It would not be successful without the mobility of financial capital and efficiency of financial markets that are an essential feature of the corporate landscape. These market features enable investors to set the price for their capital conditioned on the corporate law regime and thereby direct managers' choice of domicile toward the regime that most benefits shareholders in order to lower their cost of capital. For as long as investors are informed of the legal regime,[19] they will not invest in a firm or require a higher return on capital in a firm that is operating under an inferior corporate code (a code that does not maximize share value). Efficient markets ensure that investors will be informed of the legal regime, and capital mobility dictates the higher return for investments in firms operating under suboptimal regimes.

The constraints placed on managers by the capital market render the legislative output of state competition created by the internal affairs doctrine efficient (that is, the laws tend to maximize share value). Capital mobility, coupled with market transparency that prices corporate codes, provides incentives for management to seek the code that maximizes share value, and the internal affairs rule reduces management's cost of finding such a code because it entails the lowest reincorporation expense—the cost of legal work entailed by paper filings and a shareholder vote. Because the contracting concerns that motivate courts to reject parties' choice-of-law clauses involving defects in contract formation, such as unconscionability and mistake,[20] are of scant relevance in this context, courts uphold the parties' choice—they apply the internal affairs rule—without hesitation.

The connection between the choice-of-law rule and the efficiency of state laws does not fully explain, however, why courts adopted the internal affairs doctrine for corporate law. State corporation codes do not, for instance, mandate the choice-of-law rule. The rationale most frequently offered for the internal affairs rule—the need for uniform treatment of the many parties to the corporation—suggests another distinctive feature of the corporate contract that helps to explain the rule's longstanding judicial acceptance. This is the fact that corporate contracts are contracts between multiple parties whose identities change over time but whose interests regarding corporate policies are homogeneous (all favor maximizing equity share prices) under standard finance assumptions of competitive capital markets. A firm's shareholders may be located in all fifty states, and the possibility of having fifty different voting or dividend rules would render the corporate form infeasible for engaging in commerce. Courts have recognized that, for operation as a firm to be practical, the contract's law must not vary with the participants but must be tied down (one state's law must be accorded precedence).[21] The one identifiable constant readily identified by the courts is the legal domicile of the firm itself.

The distinctive context, an ever-changing intertemporal multiparty contract, distinguishes corporations from many of the contracts that state legislatures are most actively interested in regulating and to which courts are most resistant to apply internal affairs reasoning, such as marriage contracts. It also may explain why courts did not historically recognize the analogy between the partnership and corporation and extend the internal affairs doctrine: the partnership's members were not in constant flux, for under traditional common law rules the death or departure of a partner dissolved the partnership. The traditional doctrine arguably reflects further distinctions between partnership and corporate shares, that partners' preferences over firm policies may differ, in contrast to those of shareholders, because their equity interests do not trade in liquid capital markets and their liability is unlimited. As the partnership form has evolved from its common law origins to outlive the identities of the founding partners and has increasingly taken on aspects of a corporation, with newer organizational forms such as limited liability partnerships and companies, as Kobayashi and Ribstein trace, modern choice of law has extended the internal affairs doctrine to entities beyond corporations, and states have sought to ensure that result by express provision in the legislation creating the new forms.[22]

II Extensions of the Paradigm

Having reviewed briefly why the internal affairs rule works well in the corporate charter context, we can now consider the desirability of applying this approach in other commercial settings where it is not the norm. Two such settings are examined: securities transactions and franchise contracts. Securities transactions are contracts in which the internal affairs rule can, and should, quite naturally be extended, as the same dynamics regarding the incentives of the contracting parties and states operate in both contexts. The extension of the approach to franchise contracts is less obvious given the apparent differences between the franchise and stock investment contexts.

SECURITIES TRANSACTIONS

The current choice-of-law rule for securities transactions follows the site of the transaction,[23] and thus the applicable state law varies across a firm's shareholders. The problems this poses for uniform treatment across investors have been mitigated because of the mandatory application of the federal securities laws to public firms in conjunction with states' exemption of such firms' shares from state registration requirements and plaintiffs' traditional preference of bringing fraud claims under the federal laws. But the enactment of the Private Securities Litigation Reform Act of 1995[24] has increased the incentive of securities lawsuit plaintiffs to file state law claims in order to avoid the strictures imposed by that act (such as its tightened pleading requirements and limits on pretrial discovery).[25] The legislation thus raised both the specter of inconsistent treatment of a firm's shareholders and a pragmatic issue concerning federalism: Must federal regulation be preemptive, given that the presence of parallel state court claims can circumvent nonpreemptive federal legislation?

Although Congress chose preemption,[26] there is a more preferable solution that would enhance federalism at the same time as it prevents frivolous securities claims. If an internal affairs rule were applied to securities transactions instead of a transaction-situs rule, inconsistent treatment across firm shareholders would not be possible, as one state's law would govern all securities issues, no matter where the shares were purchased or sold. More important, congressional concerns about the diversion of securities lawsuits to state courts from federal courts would be moot because altering the choice-of-law rule would produce competition among the states for securities laws, paralleling the competition for corporate charters, which would result in more efficacious litigation rules, as firms will locate in states whose regimes benefit all shareholders rather than redistribute corporate wealth to the plaintiffs' bar.

The rationale for application of the internal affairs rule to corporate law disputes is equally applicable to the choice of law for securities transactions.[27] Indeed, the substantive issues in securities and corporate law litigation are often indistinguishable, as they typically involve the fiduciary standard of conduct governing an officer's or director's judgment concerning a corporate transaction. There is no reason why a management decision to pay a dividend or undertake a merger should be reviewed under a legal regime different from that used to review a management decision regarding the firm's disclosures in a public document, nor why all of management's actions during a takeover should not be subject to the same legal regime.

Conflict-of-law scholars typically rationalize the disparate choice-of-law approach to securities law that insulates state regulation of transactions in foreign corporations' shares from application of the internal affairs rule by contending that concerns over uniformity are not implicated by individual securities transactions.[28] The explanation advanced for the distinction has two prongs: (1) In stock transactions, the individual purchasers are not yet shareholders (that is, not members of the "corporate community") and therefore the transaction can be characterized as of purely local effect, which is said to give the buyer's domicile state an "interest" in regulation more significant than the issuer's state; and (2) a corporation can avoid a state's regulation by not selling its shares in that state, and thus need not be subject to inconsistent regulations.[29] By analytically fixing on the individual transaction at a single point in time, the transaction is considered distinguishable from the intertemporal multiparty contract of the corporation that calls for application of the internal affairs rule.

The choice-of-law distinction between corporate and securities law is, however, a legerdemain. The flaw in the choice-of-law analysis that distinguishes corporate and securities laws is easy enough to identify. In the anonymity of modern capital markets, the information provided by the issuer is not personalized to the individual investor, and accordingly it is a mistake to ignore the multiparty feature of the contract and differentiate common shares by the state in which they are bought and sold. In modern securities litigation, the multiparty contract is the critical legal factor. The suits are brought as class actions, and common law fraud rules have been adapted accordingly (such as replacing individualized proof of reliance by the "fraud-on-the-market" test of the efficiency of the market for the stock in question[30]) because management's alleged misstatements or omissions are never differentially directed at any individual investor. The composition of the class of affected shareholders is thereby fortuitous (those who entered into transactions in the relevant interval). Hence, neither the prospective feature of the shareholder relation for a buyer of new securities nor the voluntary choice of selling securities in particular states can be plausibly claimed to individualize the multiparty context of the contract so as to override the desirability of regulatory uniformity across transactions.

The conventional conflicts-of-law objection to application of an internal affairs doctrine to securities transactions, which is captured by the public policy exception to choice-of-law clause enforcement and requirements that the chosen state have a reasonable relation to the transaction or parties,[31] is that the investor's domiciliary state has a more important "interest" in a securities dispute than the issuer's domicile. The policy concern that is confusedly asserted as a state's "interest" in this instance is that the issuer's state will not provide an adequate regulatory regime against fraudulent sales practices because the buyers (or a majority of them) are not its citizens. Of course, the same arguments that underlie the securities transactions choice-of-law approach regarding the interests of states other than the issuer's domicile state could have been raised in corporate law. They were correctly rejected in favor of the internal affairs rule, and should also be rejected in the securities setting because the concern is founded on a mistaken premise: the research on state competition for charters indicates that issuers do not choose states that disadvantage investors but rather those that investors prefer, and that states that compete for corporate charters, correspondingly, do not enact regimes that diminish investors' wealth. The same dynamic forces will be at work in the securities context under an internal affairs rule, with the result that competitively produced securities codes will enhance investor wealth.

The greatest benefit of applying the internal affairs approach in securities law would be the development of competition in the production of securities laws, which is currently stymied by the transaction site rule because no single state's law controls all of the securities transactions of one firm.[32] Investors will benefit from an internal affairs rule for securities disputes because investors' preferences will drive the regulatory (substantive law) competition.[33] State competition for securities law would not truly be achievable even under an internal affairs approach, however, unless, of course, the federal securities laws were made optional, serving as one choice among the fifty states and the District of Columbia.

Franchise contracts usually contain choice-of-law clauses. But as Kobayashi and Ribstein discuss, many states have enacted franchise statutes that override the terms in franchise contracts, including, in particular, choice-of-law clauses where enforcement would vitiate the statute's revision of the contract in order to favor franchisees over franchisors. Although Kobayashi and Ribstein indicate that courts have not always rigorously enforced these trumping statutes, the choice-of-law approach used in corporate law is not as transparently transferable to the franchising relation as it is to securities sales contracts. This is because key elements of the corporate law context, such as efficient capital markets, are absent in the franchise contract setting. As a consequence, courts' traditional choice-of-law clause concerns over defects in contract formation that trump the operation of such clauses can be more plausibly advanced in the franchise than charter context. Legislatures, correspondingly, have more actively intervened in these contracts to mandate specific terms.

The case for applying a contract defect theory in the franchise, as opposed to corporate, context is, however, problematic because the differences between franchise and stock contracts that would seem to justify invalidating the parties' choice of law are more apparent than real. But the benefit of competitive federalism that Kobayashi and Ribstein emphasize as a by-product of choice-of-law clause enforcement is more limited in the franchise, as opposed to the chartering, context because the incentives for states to compete to produce efficient laws are far weaker for franchise contracts than they are for corporate charters.

Are Franchise and Stock Contracts Significantly Different for Choice-of-Law Purposes? State franchise laws typically rewrite contractual arrangements that enable a franchisor to terminate a franchisee in order to provide the franchisee with greater rights to retain its unit. There are several notable differences between franchisees and shareholders that on first impression seem important and may help to explain why courts and legislatures do not straightforwardly enforce franchise contract choice-of-law clauses in contrast to the internal affairs approach applied to corporate charters. But rejection of the corporate law choice-of-law approach in the franchising context is misplaced, because the differences are far less significant than they initially seem.

The differences in the investments of franchisees and shareholders are, at first glance, quite striking. First, franchisees make real asset investments in a particular state when they enter into a franchise relationship, which limits the mobility of their capital. Second, there is no capital market for franchise units. In the absence of market prices that provide information on the efficacy of legal regimes, it will be more difficult for a franchisee to value a franchise unit under a specific legal regime than it is for an investor to value a share of stock with a specific domicile. These two differences can provide courts (and legislators) with a plausible presumptive basis for overriding contractual choice of law: the ostensibly weak position of franchisees, in terms of capital mobility and information, compared to the franchisor, can be used to construe the franchise contracts as defectively formed, in contrast to stock contracts (corporate charters).

But this contrast is misleading. Although shareholders' investments are not fixed geographically, as Oliver Williamson has pointed out, once an equity investment is made, shareholders are more vulnerable to management opportunism than other corporate participants because they are the residual claimants, whose return is not specified and whose capital is not guaranteed repayment.[34] Second, many franchisee investments are not highly relation-specific. Rather, upon termination of the franchise, the assets can be reused to provide the same services under another name without significant loss in property value.[35] In addition, the initial fees required to purchase a franchise are frequently quite small and unrelated to the value of the future profits obtained from running the franchise.[36] In short, the rents from a franchise arrangement come from the stream of future profits, and the penalty from termination is the loss of access to that stream and not the loss of a lump-sum initial payment or asset investment.

The distinction between franchise and corporate contracts based on a difference in the relation-specificity of franchisee and stockholder investments does not, then, hold up to scrutiny. Franchisees' capital is fixed in-state, compared to that of shareholders, but it is not immobile (it can typically be employed readily and profitably in other uses). It must be noted, however, that this particular difference between the contracts is of great import on a nondoctrinal dimension: Because franchisees' investments are state-specific, their concerns are of significance to state officeholders, whether or not they enhance organizational value, and they can have an adverse effect on the efficacy of state competition.

The second distinction noted between the franchise and corporate contexts, the more limited information available to the franchisee compared to shareholders given the efficiency of the stock market, offers a slightly different rationale for courts and legislators to ignore contractual choices of law than the distinction regarding the nature of the investment: franchisees who are poorly informed about their investment's value will not understand the significance of choice-of-law clauses for their welfare, and franchisors will be able to choose a regime that facilitates franchisee exploitation, rendering the contracts unconscionable. However, the absence of a liquid secondary market for franchise units does not mean that prospective franchisees are ignorant and vulnerable investors who, unable to recognize the significance of a choice-of-law clause, enter into adhesion contracts. Franchisees are, in fact, "generally well-educated, have relevant experience, explore alternative franchise opportunities and often receive outside help in evaluating franchise contracts."[37] The franchise market, in other words, has devised mechanisms by which franchisees obtain information about prospective ventures to compensate for the illiquidity of the market in which franchise units trade.

Besides these two differences in investment attributes, there is a positional difference between franchisees and shareholders, that is, the relationship among the parties in a franchise arrangement is quite different compared to those in a business corporation. The corporation consists of a set of multiple principals, the stockholders—whose interests can be treated as homogeneous under standard finance assumptions (that is, all investors want the firm to maximize equity share prices)—who contract with manager-agents. A franchise arrangement, in contrast, is difficult to characterize as an agency relationship. It consists of multiple agents, the franchisees, whose interests conflict with each other as well as with the franchisor: that is, there is a free-rider problem in that an individual franchisee does not bear the full costs of skimping on quality and devaluing the franchise. But the franchisor is not a principal analogous to shareholders because there is a two-sided moral hazard in the franchise relationship: the franchisor can also behave opportunistically toward the franchisees, by, for example, modifying the franchise environment or strictly enforcing termination clauses in order to extract the value of the franchisee's investment.[38]

From this two-sided moral hazard perspective, an agency characterization is not particularly useful for this type of market contract because each side can impose agency costs on the other. Although shareholders could conceivably impose costs on managers by opportunistically breaching implicit employment contracts,[39] it is implausible to characterize shareholders as agents since they have no performance obligations (in contrast to franchisors). This difference further complicates the transferability of the corporate law choice-of-law paradigm to franchise contracts by bolstering the rationale implied by the other distinctions between stock and franchise contracts for courts and legislatures to override franchise contracts' choice-of-law clauses (defective contract formation).

The two-sided moral hazard context that distinguishes the franchise and corporate investment contexts, in conjunction with the ostensible difference in investment-specificity, provides another rationale for judicial and legislative restrictions on franchise contract terms, and the consequent overriding of a choice-of-law clause. Franchisees' investments make them vulnerable to franchisors' ex post opportunistic behavior to extract the value of those investments, and laws restricting termination will protect the franchisees from such behavior otherwise permitted under the governing law chosen by their contract. This is an ex post justification for intervention in contract terms—abuse of termination rights—rather than an ex ante justification—defective formation—underlying the prior rationales. Yet while a franchisor might terminate a franchisee for illegitimate reasons (that is, for reasons unrelated to franchisee opportunism) in order to appropriate value from the franchisee, there is in fact little systematic empirical evidence of such franchisor misbehavior.[40] Moreover, franchisees can (and often do) eliminate the problem of franchisor opportunism by owning the franchise themselves.[41] Indeed, the preponderance of economic theories of franchising suggest that laws restricting termination are inefficient. In particular, the franchisor protects the value of the franchise against free-riding most effectively by the threat of termination.[42] Laws restricting termination accordingly will decrease the value of the franchise arrangement. Courts and legislatures considering franchisees' initial investments' susceptibility to franchisor opportunism as a reason to override contract terms as unconscionable are therefore working from an erroneous premise.[43]

Finally, apart from the theoretical distinctions between franchise and corporate contracts, the bilateral feature of individual franchise contracts can obscure the fundamental multiparty character of the franchise relationship and facilitate courts' divergence from an internal affairs approach to franchise contracts, as in the traditional conflicts treatment of securities transactions. The individuation of the franchise relationship blinds courts to the applicability of the internal affairs approach and, accordingly, enables them to disregard both the question whether uniform treatment across franchise units would be desirable and its counterpart, whether franchisee rights' varying with state of residence are undesirable. Yet, as with securities transactions, the factual circumstances of franchise contracts illuminate their essential multiparty nature. Although a franchisor could write customized contracts with each franchisee, including terms specific to the individual features of a unit that are relevant to the moral hazard problem, such as tailoring a termination provision to the likelihood of a unit's successful free-riding (proxied by, for example, a unit's distance from the franchisor's headquarters as an indication of the center's monitoring costs), franchisors use uniform contracts whose terms do not vary across franchisees.[44] Moreover, uniformity—applying one state's law to all of a franchisor's contracts—has a beneficial organizational impact. It may, as Henry Hansmann suggested to me, facilitate the franchise's development of a national reputation, which is likely to be the best mechanism for aligning franchisee and franchisor incentives to reduce opportunism and maximize the value of the franchise.

Taken together, the data suggest that the differences between franchise and stock contracts are more apparent than real, supporting the extension of the corporate law choice-of-law approach to franchise contracts and perhaps explaining Kobayashi and Ribstein's finding that courts have often limited the applicability of franchise statutes and enforced the parties' contracts. The data are most consistent with Kobayashi and Ribstein's characterization of franchise statutes as efforts at rent-seeking by franchisees that should be overturned by choice-of-law clause enforcement, rather than as efforts directed at mitigating franchisor opportunism and unconscionable contracts.

Will States Compete for Franchises If Choice-of-Law Clauses Are Enforced?
The analytical basis for not enforcing the parties' contractual choice of law is dubious; but will enforcement of such clauses result in a competition that produces legislation that tends to be efficient? Franchisors will seek to maximize the value of the franchise, and the choice-of-law clauses they select would further that objective. If such choices are enforced, then statutes restricting termination rights would not be expected to survive in a competitive system. Such laws increase the value of individual franchise units rather than the aggregate franchise value, and franchisors will, accordingly, not choose the law of states with such statutes for their franchise contracts' governing law.

It is plausible that franchisors' preferences will dominate the choice of law because the availability of alternative forms of capital for the franchisor, including internal operation of units, places franchisors in a position analogous to that of shareholders concerning the choice of corporate domicile.[45] This advantage does not mean they can exploit franchisees through the choice of law—competition among franchisors, as well as other business opportunities, provide franchisees with many choices for the use of their capital besides a particular franchise. A franchisor who terminates franchisees opportunistically will have difficulty selling additional units and, similarly, a franchisor who selects a legal regime that facilitates such behavior will not attract many franchisees, given the research indicating that franchisees are informed investors. Thus, when the franchisor can select the regime that maximizes the value of the franchise, it will not be a regime that promotes opportunistic terminations.[46] How the enhanced franchise value due to the choice of an efficient legal regime is shared between the franchisor and franchisees will depend, of course, on the competitiveness of the franchise market, which affects the relative bargaining positions of franchisor and franchisee. It will, furthermore, be more difficult, if not impossible, to change the chosen regime opportunistically midstream to extract value from the franchisee in favor of the franchisor compared to the corporate charter context: to change the governing state law for a franchise contract, the specific contract must be rewritten and thus the franchisee must consent, in contrast to corporate law's majority vote, unless the franchise contracts contain a provision permitting such a change nonconsensually.

But even if the contract's governing law is determined by the party whose objective is to maximize firm value, there is still a question whether enforcement of choice-of-law clauses will produce the efficacious competition that we see in the chartering context. In the franchising context there is little or no adverse economic effect on a state from maintaining an inefficient regime, in contrast to the corporate charter market where state tax revenues follow incorporations.[47] To guarantee that competitive federalism will work to enhance firm value, financial incentives must be devised that motivate the states to compete for franchisors' business. Otherwise, local interests—franchisees—will be able to continue to dominate state policy, and states will, accordingly, have incentives to enact laws that provide one-time windfalls to existing franchisees.[48] As an increasing number of states regulate franchise contracts, it will be difficult for franchisors to circumvent such regulation through choice-of-law clauses, and the efficacy of competition will be diminished. For without a viable exit option, the competitive equilibrium that produces value-maximizing regimes will not be sustainable. To achieve the benefits of state competition that would accompany the enforcement of choice-of-law clauses in the franchising context, it is therefore necessary to craft a mechanism to reward states to compete, such as the institution of franchising taxes based on the number of outstanding units, analogous to the payment of business franchise taxes according to outstanding shares.

Conclusion

This comment has explored Kobayashi and Ribstein's important theme that state competition over legal regimes is, in general, a socially beneficial activity, and that freedom to choose the law applicable to a contractual relationship is an integral component of such competition. Corporate law is the paradigmatic case because the conditions conducive to effective competition are present: both the contracting parties and the states have self-enforcing financial incentives to choose laws that tend to maximize the value of firms. To the extent that similar conditions can be replicated in other contexts, we are all better off. Enforcing choice-of-law clauses in such contexts is a necessary first step in that direction.

Introduction

I should like to thank Eric Posner for his valuable comments.

1   Grant Gilmore, *The Death of Contract* (1995 [1974]).

2   P. S. Atiyah, *The Rise and Fall of Freedom of Contract* (1979).

3   The most prominent neoformalist is Mary Ann Glendon. See Glendon, *A Nation under Lawyers: How the Crisis in the Legal Profession Is Transforming American Society* (1994).

4   Stephen A. Ross, "The Economic Theory of Agency: The Principal's Problem," 63 *Am. Econ. Rev.* (Papers and Proceedings) 134 (1973).

5   For this reason, James Buchanan cautioned against judicial activism in a review of the first edition of Richard Posner's *Economic Analysis of Law*, preferring legislative deliberation, warts and all, to the unbounded lawmaking of unelected judges. See James Buchanan, "Good Economics—Bad Law," 60 *Va. L. Rev.* 483 (1974).

6   Charles Fried, *Contract as Promise* (1981).

7   Ernest Weinrib, *The Idea of Private Law* (1995). Weinrib labels his Kantian vision of private law as "Formalism," and he argues that only through it can one regard the law as an independent discipline. Weinrib, "Legal Formalism: On the Immanent Rationality of Law," 97 *Yale L. J.* 949 (1988).

8   Peter Benson, "Abstract Right and the Possibility of a Nondistributive Conception of Contract: Hegel and Contemporary Contract Theory," 10 *Cardozo L. Rev.* 1077 (1989).

9   On constitutive rules, see John R. Searle, *The Construction of Social Reality* (1995); John R. Searle, *Speech Acts* 33–42 (1970). In "Two Concepts of Rules," 64 *Phil. Rev.* 3 (1965), John Rawls noted that the conventional analysis of promising is consistent with consequentialist theories of ethics. I extend this analysis by arguing that, as a convention, promising can *only* be justified from a consequentialist perspective.

10 I describe such a society—Tonga—in "Paradox Lost," 72 *Minn. L. Rev.* 775 (1988). In Tonga, the word for promise is said to mean something like "I expect to do *x* in the future but don't blame me if I change my mind." Whether Tonganese promises are as I describe them is less important than that they *might* be so.

11 "Of the Original Contract," in David Hume, *Essays: Moral, Political, and Literary* 465 (1987 [1777]).

12 On why theories of gratitude and of fairness, which argue that one ought to support institutions from which one had taken a benefit, cannot support promissory and contractual institutions, see Buckley, supra note 10, at 793–804.

13 On self-control theories, see Thomas Schelling, *Choice and Consequence* 57–112 (1984); Thomas Schelling, "Enforcing Rules on Oneself," 1 *J. L. Econ. & Org.* 357 (1985). There are many noncontractual methods of binding oneself (see Anthony Kronman, "Contract Law in the State of Nature," 1 *J. L. Econ. & Org.* 5 [1985]), but these cannot substitute fully for contract.

14 This is why Goetz and Scott label the benefit of promising as "beneficial reliance."

Charles Goetz and Robert Scott, "Enforcing Promises: An Examination of the Basis of Contract," 89 *Yale L. J.* 1261 (1980).

15 The great exception here is marriage, where the nonwaivable exit option of divorce constitutes a major restriction on bargaining freedom. See part III.

16 Gilmore, supra note 1, at 96.

17 Atiyah also worried about whether a present self could bind a future one. Supra note 2, at 755. He would not have denied expectation claims in contract, but would have granted them in some cases in tort as well. Id. at 762.

18 P. S. Atiyah, *Promises, Morals, and Law* 193–94 (1981).

19 On the content-independency of promises, see H. L. A. Hart, "Legal and Moral Obligation," in A. Melden, ed., *Essays in Moral Philosophy* 82, 102 (1958); Joseph Raz, "Voluntary Obligations and Normative Powers II," 46 *Proceedings of the Aristotelian Soc.* 79, 95–98 (Supp. 1972).

20 P. S. Atiyah, *An Introduction to the Law of Contract* 27–34 (1995).

21 On reputatational theories, trial judges can be expected to resist a return to formalism, since Wetlaw offers them immunity from reversal. The trail judge may get formal rules wrong, but it is far harder to overturn a decision about fairness or good faith. Appellate court review may then be seen as a device to cure the misincentives of trial judges to fuzzy up the law. Alternatively, the move to Wetlaw may have resulted from the expansion of appellate courts.

22 19 Ch. 462, 465 (1875).

23 See George L. Priest, "Contracts Then and Now: An Appreciation of Friedrich Kessler," 104 *Yale L. J.* 2145, 2146 (1995); George L. Priest, "The Invention of Enterprise Liability: A Critical History of the Intellectual Foundations of Modern Tort Law," 14 *J. Legal Stud.* 461, 485, 495 (1985).

24 Alan Schwartz and Louis L. Wilde, "Intervening in Markets on the Basis of Imperfect Information: A Legal and Economic Analysis," 127 *U. Pa. L. Rev.* 630, 630 (1979). On standard form contracts, see generally Alan Schwartz, "A Reexamination of Nonsubstantive Unconscionability," 63 *Va. L. Rev.* 1053 (1977); Michael J. Trebilcock, "The Doctrine of Inequality of Bargaining Power: Post-Benthamite Economics in the House of Lords," 26 *U. Toronto L. J.* 359 (1976).

25 92 Eng. Rep. 270 (1705). See F. H. Buckley, "Three Theories of Substantive Fairness," 19 *Hofstra L. Rev.* 33 (1990).

26 See Vernon L. Smith, "Experimental Economics: Reply," 75 *Am. Econ. Rev.* 265 (1985).

27 See Amos Tversky and Daniel Kahneman, "Judgment under Uncertainty: Heuristics and Biases," 185 *Sc.* 1124, 1128–29 (1974).

28 See Thomas H. Jackson, *The Logic and Limits of Bankruptcy Law* 238–39 (1986). See generally Cass Sunstein, "Interference with Individual Choice," 53 *U. Chi. L. Rev.* 1129 (1986).

29 See F. H. Buckley, "The American Fresh Start," 4 *So. Cal. Interdisciplinary L. J.* 67 (1994).

30 H. L. A. Hart, *Law, Liberty, and Morality* (1962); Patrick Devlin, *The Enforcement of Morals* (1965).

31 Social capital may be defined as the third party benefits of individual human capital. See James S. Coleman, *Foundations of Social Theory* (1990); Gary S. Becker, *Accounting for Tastes* (1996). On human capital theories, a person's propensity to behave morally might depend on his religious sentiments; on social capital theories, the religious sentiments of his neighbors might also affect his behavior, even if he is an atheist.

32 Of course, social conservatism will appeal to few of the academics who today support bargaining restrictions.

33 Ronald H. Coase, "The Problem of Social Cost," 3 *J. L. & Econ.* 1 (1960).

34 Christopher Lasch, *Haven in a Heartless World: The Family Besieged* (1977).

35 For evidence that the introduction of no-fault divorce resulted in increased divorce levels, see Margaret F. Brinig and F. H. Buckley, "No-fault Laws and At-Fault People, 18 Int.," 18 *Rev. L. Econ.* 325 (1998).

Contracts Small and Contract Large

I have benefited from the trenchant comments of Richard Craswell, Richard Helmholz, Daniel Klerman, and Eric Posner. I should like to thank Deborah Healy, Jeffrey Greenblatt, and Rex Sears for their usual cheerful and tenacious research assistance.

1 See, e.g., David Abraham, "Liberty and Property: Lord Bramwell and the Political Economic of Liberal Jurisprudence, Individualism, Freedom, and Utility," 38 *Am. J. of Legal Hist.* 288 (1994); Anita Ramasastry, "The Parameters, Progressions, and Paradoxes of Baron Bramwell," 38 *Am. J. of Legal Hist.* 322 (1994). For my qualified defense of Baron Bramwell, see Richard A. Epstein, "For a Bramwell Revival," 38 *Am. J. of Legal Hist.* 246 (1994).

2 For discussion see, e.g., Francis H. Bohlen, "Voluntary Assumption of Risk," 20 *Harv. L. Rev.* 14 (1906).

3 See, e.g., *Loewe v. Lawlor*, 208 U.S. 274 (1908) (holding labor unions subject to the Sherman antitrust law, at least when boycotted goods were shipped across state lines). See also *Duplex Printing Press v. Deering*, 254 U.S. 443 (1921) (holding unions liable under Clayton antitrust act for secondary boycotts).

4 See, e.g., *Smyth v. Ames*, 169 U.S. 466 (1898).

5 Friedrich Kessler, "Contracts of Adhesion—Some Thoughts about Freedom of Contract," 43 *Colum. L. Rev.* 629 (1943).

6 Grant Gilmore, *The Death of Contract* (1974).

7 Lawrence Friedman, *Contract Law in America* (1965).

8 Patrick S. Atiyah, *The Rise and Fall of Freedom of Contract* (1979).

9 Kessler, supra note 5, at 632–39.

10 For a strong defense of the earlier common law position, see William L. Prosser, "Delay in Acting on an Application for Insurance," 3 *U. Chi. L. Rev.* 39 (1935). Prosser rejected efforts to impose duties to respond to offers under contract law (id. at 45). He also opposed manufacturing new torts out of the failure to respond (id.).

11 Gilmore, *The Death of Contract* 106.

12 Friedman, supra note 7, at 20. The passage was cited favorably in Gilmore, *The Death of Contract* 5–8, and in Atiyah, *Rise and Fall* 402–5.

13 Christopher Columbus Langdell, *A Summary of the Law of Contracts* 18–19 (2d ed. 1880).

14 See, e.g., Bowen L. J.'s remarks in *The Moorcock*, 14 Probate 64, 68 (1889): "I believe if one were to take all the cases, and they are many, of implied warranties or covenants in law, it will be found that in all of them the law is raising an implication from the presumed intention of the parties with the object of giving the transaction such efficacy as both parties must have intended that at all events it should have." 14 P. at 68. As applied in that case, Bowen made the sensible judgment that a defendant wharfinger who operated over public waters was under a duty to warn about risks of which he

had superior knowledge but under no duty to repair the condition of waters over which he had no control.

15 Gilmore, *The Death of Contract* 8–12. Note that Gilmore does not cite or discuss John Joseph Powell, *Essay upon the Law of Contracts and Agreements* (1790), which, heavily influenced by Lockean principles, seeks to develop a general theory of contract law.

16 See, e.g., Lisa Bernstein, "Merchant Law in a Merchant Court: Rethinking the Code's Search for Immanent Business Norms," 144 *U. Pa. L. Rev.* 1765, 1801–02 (1996), noting the industry loyalty to the perfect tender rule. On efficient breach, see infra at section 3.

17 See, e.g., George White, *The Law Respecting Masters and Work People* 5–6 (1824), defending the prohibition on in-kind payments against the delusions of "your theoretical political economists." These restrictions were the subject of the Truck Acts (as in barter and exchange). See, e.g., the opinions in *Archer v. James*, 121 Eng. Rep 998 (Ex. 1861). For discussion, see Richard A. Epstein, "Bramwell," 38 *Am. J. Legal History* at 253–55.

18 See, e.g., David Hume, *A Treatise of Human Nature*, ed. L. A. Selby-Bigge, pt. 2, bk. 2, sec. 5, at 520 (1888): "Besides, the commerce of mankind is not confin'd to the barter of commodities, but may extend to services and actions, which we may exchange to our mutual interest and advantage. Your corn is ripe to-day; mine will be so tomorrow. 'Tis profitable for us both, that I shou'd labour with you to-day, and that you shou'd aid me to-morrow."

19 Thus Jacob Viner writes: "I will carefully avoid using the term laissez faire to mean what only unscrupulous or ignorant opponents of it and never its exponents make it mean, namely, philosophical anarchism, or opposition to any governmental power or activity whatsoever. I will in general use the term to mean what the pioneer systematic exponents of it, the Physiocrats and Adam Smith, argued for, namely, the limitation of governmental activity to the enforcement of peace and of 'justice' in the restricted sense of 'commutative justice,' to the defense against foreign enemies, and to public works regarded as essential and as impossible or highly improbable of establishment by private enterprise or, for special reasons, unsuitable to be left to private operation." Jacob Viner, "An Intellectual History of Laissez-Faire," 3 *J. Law & Econ.* 45, 45 (1960). Such attacks that Viner deplored are legion. See, e.g., Frederick Harrison's claim that the "sticklers for absolute respect for Liberty and Property" should favor the repeal of laws against fraud, monopoly, and infectious diseases, quoted without criticism by Atiyah (who should know better) in *Rise and Fall* 587. See, e.g., Jessel M. R.'s statement of the principle, infra at section 5.

20 "[T]he well being of a community, depends upon a thorough knowledge of social principles, and an entire obedience to them. What, then, do they want a government for? Not to regulate commerce; not to educate the people; not teach religion; not to administer charity; not to make the roads and railways; but simply to defend the natural rights of man—to protect person and property—to prevent the aggressions of the powerful upon the weak—in a word to administer justice. This is the nature, the original, office of a government. It was not intended to do less; it ought not be allowed to do more." Herbert Spencer, *Six Essays on Government, Society, and Freedom*, Letter 1, found in *Man Versus the State* 184, 187 (Liberty Press ed. 1843 [1981]). He makes no allowance for an eminent domain power independent of taxation.

21 Nigel Simmonds, *The Decline of Juridical Reason: Doctrine and Theory in the Legal Order* 54 (1984).

22 "Laissez-faire has never been more than a slogan in defense of the proposition that every extension of state activity should be examined under the presumption of error." Aaron Director, "Parity of The Economic Market Place," 7 *J. Law & Econ.* 1, 2 (1964). Director does not specify what it takes to override the presumption, on which see infra at section 5.

23 "The sort of men who became judges towards the middle of the century were imbued with the creed of 'philosophical Radicals' who drove the chariot of reform, and for whom the authority of the orthodox economists came second only to Bentham's." Frederick Pollock, "A Plea for Historical Interpretation," 39 *Law Quart. Rev.* 163, 165 (1923). The one judge named was Baron Bramwell. Id. at 165. For a guarded assessment of Bramwell's role, which emphasizes his gradual disenchantment with the English politics of his time, see Anita Ramasastry, supra note 1.

24 Id. at 403.

25 Id. For Mill's version of the argument, see John Stuart Mill, *On Liberty* 9 (Hackett 1859 [1978]), which emphasizes the harm, or tort, side of the nineteenth-century liberal position. For my views, see Richard A. Epstein, "The Harm Principle—And How It Grew," 45 *U. Toronto L. J.* 369 (1995).

26 *Lindenau v. Desborough*, 108 Eng. Rep. 1160, 1162 (1828). For similar sentiments, see Lord Mansfield's earlier opinion in *Carter v. Boehm*, 97 Eng. Rep. 1162 (1766); *London Assurance v. Mansel*, 11 Ch.D. 363, 368–69 (1879), holding that an insured must disclose all that is known to him, even if he does not understand why the information is material to the evaluation of the risk.

27 27 Marine Insurance Act, 1906, s. 18(1).

28 *Allnut v. Inglis*, 12 East 525, 104 Eng. Rep. 206 (1810). I discuss this problem at length in Richard A. Epstein, *Principles for a Free Society: Reconciling Individual Liberty with the Common Good*, ch. 10 (1998).

29 Gilmore, *The Death of Contract* 95.

30 Id.

31 For a fuller account of my own views on the interconnections, see Richard A. Epstein, "The Utilitarian Foundations of Natural Law," 12 *Harv. J. of Law & Public Policy* 713 (1989); Richard A. Epstein, "The Ubiquity of the Restitution Principle," 67 *So. Cal. L. Rev.* 1369 (1994).

32 Thomas Hobbes, *Leviathan*, ed. R. Tuck, ch. 15, at 105 (1991), picked up by Atiyah, *Rise and Fall* 71, and just about everyone else. For a perceptive account of how Hobbes could be regarded as both the father of the totalitarian state and the early champion of economic liberty, see Viner, "Laissez-Faire," 3 *J. Law & Econ.* at 57, noting that Hobbes contemplated the virtuous sovereign as using his power largely for national defense. And for Hume's version of the same point see, D. Hume, *Treatise*, supra at note 18.

33 Aristotle's *Ethics* contains a discussion of commutative and distributive justice in his treatment in his ethics, and treats (for reasons that escape me) the first as arithmetical and the second as geometrical. *Nicomachean Ethics*, bk. 5, ch. 4. But Aristotle does offer a defense of private property against common ownership that relies on the superior incentive effects when a single person is placed in charge of a given resource. "Property should be in a certain sense common, but, as a general rule, private; for, when every one has a distinct interest, men will not complain of one another, and they will make more progress, because everyone will be attending to his own business." See Aristotle, *Politics*, 1263a25–29 (Jowett trans. 1943). But his hostility to the retail trade makes him at most a partial forbearer of laissez-faire. See id. at 1256b40–

1258b8, condemning the retail trade as "unnatural, and a mode by which men gain from one another." The gist of the passage is to make Pareto-efficient exchanges immoral, in favor of a regime of self-sufficiency in production—a far cry from laissez-faire.

34 There is a learned dispute as to whether the just price referred to some external standard, typically administered by the state. For the opposite position, see Jacob Viner, "Laissez-Faire," 3 *J. Law & Econ.* 45, 53 (1960), noting that "the standard late-medieval meaning of 'common estimation' was market price under free competition." The text was designed to filter out the short-term perturbations brought on by sudden famine, plague, siege, and the like, which sounds like a far more sensible doctrine.

35 236 U.S. 1 (1914).

36 Id. at 17.

37 Id. at 27.

38 Justinian, Digest, 18.1.1. "Sale originates in barter. For in the early days there was no such thing as money nor were there distinct terms for the merchandise and the price, but according to his occasions and needs a man would barter what was useless to him for what was useful, since it commonly happens that what one man has in superfluity another lacks." The text does not quite get the principle of comparative advantage because it never quite says that you will trade that which you value less for that which you value more. Instead of exploiting the gains from gradation, the passage presupposes the stark but unnecessary contrast between useless and useful.

39 "Trade was a 'commutation of superfluities' in which each gave what he could spare in exchange for what he needed." Atiyah, *Rise and Fall* 72. The enclosed words come from Sir Dudley North, *Discourses on Trade*, which according to Atiyah date from the end of the seventeenth century, about the time of Locke's *Treatise on Government*.

40 See, e.g., *Boston Ice Co. v. Potter*, 123 Mass. 28 (1877).

41 1 Christopher Columbus Langdell, *Cases on Contract* xi–xii (2d ed. 1880).

42 Reproduced, id. at vii–ix.

43 3 B. & S. 825, 122 Eng. Rep. 309 (Q. B. 1863).

44 9 Ex. 341, 156 Eng. Rep. 145 (1854).

45 20 N.Y. 268 (Ct. App. 1859).

46 1 B.& S. 393, 121 Eng. Rep. 762 (Q. B. 1861).

47 6 N. H. 481 (1834).

48 17 N.Y. 173 (Ct. App. 1858).

49 *Printing and Numerical Registering Co. v. Sampson*, L. R. 19 Eq. 462, 465 (1875), quoted inter alia in Kessler, *Contracts of Adhesion*, at 631; Cheshire and Fifoot, *The Law of Contract* 21 (6th ed. 1964), the edition from which I learned contract law when a student at Oxford from 1964 to 1966.

50 Cheshire and Fifoot, *Contract*, at 22. The only portion of the quotation found there reads: "the intent of a man cannot be tried, for the Devil himself knows not the intent of a man."

51 Gilmore, *Death of Contract* 686.

52 The Restatement flip-flop on the issue goes as follows. The first Restatement found no contract when A said he offered his horse for sale, when he meant his cow, even though B knew that cow was meant. Restatement of Contracts § 71, illustration 2. The second Restatement shifts course and concludes that the contract is made, for the sale of the cow (which both parties meant) but not for the horse. Restatement (Second) of Contracts, § 71, illustration 2.

53 See *Hotchkiss v. National City Bank of New York*, 200 F. 287, 293 (1911 S. D. N. Y.), which begins with the proposition that "[a] contract has, strictly speaking, nothing to do with the personal, or individual, intent of the parties." The point of that remark is that a one-sided mistake does not furnish an excuse against performance. But even Learned Hand goes on to create an exception for "some mutual mistake, or something else of the sort." It took the more dogmatic mind of Williston to assert a contract on the terms that neither side accepted. "It is conceivable that contract may be formed which is in accordance with the intention of neither party." 1 Williston § 95. Both passages set out seriatim in Kessler and Gilmore, *Contracts*, at 707. Williston's position, for what it is worth, is that it is conceivable that if A says pig, but thinks horse, while B hears cow, there is a contract for the sale of a pig. So who will sue, and for what?

54 For discussion, see Andrew Kull, "Unilateral Mistake: The Baseball Card Case," 70 *Wash. U. L. Q.* 57 (1992). Kull's example was the real cases where a twelve-year-old card collector purchased a Nolan Ryan/Jerry Koosman rookie card worth about $1,200 for $12. The card had been marked at 1200/, which had been misread by an inexperienced clerk to mean $12.00. For a another example, see the 1961 Cary Grant, Audrey Hepburn classic *Charade*, where irreplaceable stamps were traded by a young boy for a large set of worthless ones. The stamps were returned by the apologetic dealer, who had beheld them with awe.

55 2 Hur & C. 906, 159 Eng. Rep. 375 (Ex. 1864).

56 Gilmore, *Death of Contract* 35–43.

57 A. W. Brian Simpson, "Contracts for Cotton to Arrive: The Case of the Two Ships Peerless," 11 *Cardozo L. Rev.* 287, 288–93 (1989).

58 Where everyone agrees the result is correct. See Gilmore, *Death of Contract*, at 121, n. 91 citing *Kyle v. Kavanagh*, 103 Mass. 356 (1869).

59 For example, see Judah Benjamin, *A Treatise on the Law of Sale of Personal Property; Reference to the American Decisions and to the French Code and the Civil Law* 51 (J. Perkins, first American edition 1875); Frederick Pollock, *Principles of Contract at Law and in Equity* 2 (1876) (opting for a subjective view); William Anson, *Principles of the English Law of Contract* 130 (1879) (subjective view); Oliver Wendell Holmes, *The Common Law*, Lecture 9 (1881) (taking the objective view).

60 Simpson, "Contracts for Cotton to Arrive," 11 *Cardozo L. Rev.* at 324–33.

61 Id. at 315.

62 Lisa Bernstein, "Opting out of the Legal System: Extralegal Contractual Relations in the Diamond Industry," 21 *J. Legal Stud.* 115 (1992).

63 Id. at 312.

64 Simpson, "Contracts for Cotton to Arrive," 11 *Cardozo L. Rev.* at 313.

65 A. W. B. Simpson, "The Origins of Futures Trading in the Liverpool Cotton Market," in Peter Cane and Jane Stapleton, eds., *Essays for Patrick Atiyah*, 179 (1991).

66 Justinian, *Institutes*, 3, 22 (Moyle ed. 1883). The full quotation reads: "Obligations contracted by mere consent are exemplified by sale, hire, partnership and agency, which are called consensual contracts because no writing, nor the presence of the parties, nor any delivery is required to make the obligation actionable, but the consent of the parties is sufficient. Parties who are not present together, therefore, can form these contracts by letter, for instance, or by messenger."

67 *Carlill v. Carbolic Smoke Ball Co.* [1893] 1 Q. B. 256.

68 Restatement (Second) of Contracts, § 32 (Invitation of Promise or Performance). The precedent is not precise because the taking of the corn and grain is not tantamount to

providing the benefit to its owner, as would be the case if the stubble were to be carted away at a price.

69 *Edgington v. Fitzmaurice* 29 Ch. 459, 483 (1885).

70 For a parallel discussion, see Charles Fried, *Contract as Promise: A Theory of Contractual Obligation* 49–54 (1981), inclining toward the mailbox rule.

71 1 B. & Ald. 681, 106 Eng. Rep. 250 (K. B. 1818).

72 Id. at 683, 106 Eng. Rep. at 251.

73 See Langdell, *Summary* at 18–19, criticized in Fried, *Contract as Promise*, at 51, stressing the ability of an offeror to condition an offer on receipt of the acceptance.

74 Langdell, *Summary* at 21.

75 Id. at 21, quoted in Friedrich Kessler and Grant Gilmore, *Cases and Materials on Contracts*, 287–88 (2d ed. 1970).

76 Langdell, *Summary* at 40, 45.

77 6 Ex. 108 (1871).

78 Cheshire and Fifoot, *Contracts*, at 21.

79 *British & American Telegraph*, 6 Ex. at 118.

80 See, e.g., *General Time Corp. v. Eye Encounter, Inc.*, 50 N. C. App. 467, 274 S. E.2d 391 (1981) (contract formed where acceptance faxed); *Entores Ltd. v. Miles Far East Corp.*, [1955] 2 Q. B. 327 (contract formed when fax received).

81 For an exhaustive account of the early history of the doctrine, see A. W. B. Simpson, *A History of the Common Law of Contract: The Rise of the Action of Assumpsit* (1975). His chapter 6 in part 2 traces its evolution from the doctrines of "causa" in the canon law; chapter 7 deals with its evolution of consideration in connection with assumpsit.

82 See, e.g., *Dutton v. Poole*, 84 Eng. Rep. 1168 (1677). The facts revealed a clear bargain between the plaintiff's father and the defendant. The plaintiff's father had agreed to refrain from cutting down certain timbers if the defendant would pay his daughter Grizil £1,000, which he refused to do. "The apparent consideration of natural affection" between father and daughter, allowed her to sue on the promise made to her father, in effect, as a third-party beneficiary. See Simpson, *History*, at 418–21.

83 Simpson, *History*, at 414.

84 See, e.g., Lon L. Fuller, "Consideration and Form," 41 *Colum. L. Rev.* 799 (1941); Melvin Eisenberg, "Donative Promises," 47 *U. Chi. L. Rev.* 1 (1979); Andrew Kull, "Reconsidering Gratuitous Promises," 21 *J. Legal Stud.* 39 (1992).

85 See, Langdell, *Summary*, at 104–5: "Thus, mutual promises will be binding, though the promise on one side be merely to do a thing which the promisee is already bound to a third person to do, and the actual doing of which would not, therefore, be a sufficient consideration."

86 For a summary of the extensive literature on which I have relied, see Richard Bronaugh, "A Secret Paradox of the Common Law," 23 *J. Law & Phil.* 193 (1983).

87 See *Rose & Frank Co. v. Crompton Bros.*, [1923] 2 K. B. 261, aff'd, [1925 A. C. 445 (H. L.), which gave full effect to a gentlemen's agreement, although it enforced specific contracts of sale entered pursuant to its terms. The earlier decision in *Balfour v. Balfour*, [1919] 2 K. B. 751, contains Atkin L. J.'s beautifully written but wrongheaded decision. The informal separation was more akin to a business arrangement than to an invitation of hospitality. The background norm should have been for enforcement. Indeed, the specific result in the case was reversed by the Maintenance Agreements Act, 5, 7 6 Eliz. (1957).

88 See Pollock, *Principles of Contracts* 191 (8th ed.).

89 For some discussion, see the law of conditions infra.

90 Gilmore, *The Death of Contract* 57–76.

91 "There has thus, as we shall see, been a decline in promise-based liabilities and a growth in benefit-based and reliance-based liabilities." Atiyah, *Rise and Fall* 716.

92 See his decisions in *De Cicco v. Schweizer*, 221 N.Y. 431, 117 N.E. 807 (1917); *Allegheny College v. National Chautauqua County Bank*, 246 N.Y. 369, 159 N.E. 173 (1927).

93 "In commercial cases among merchants the want of consideration is not an objection." See, e.g., *Pillans v. Van Mierop*, 3 Bur. 1663, 97 Eng. Rep. 1035 (K.B. 1765).

94 *Rann v. Hughes*, 4 Brown P.C. 27; 7 Times Rep. 350; 101 Eng. Rep. 1014 (1778), taking the view that "the law of nature" required keeping serious engagements, but the law of England required proof of consideration. *Eastwood v. Kenyon* 11 Ad. & El. 438. 113 Eng. Rep. 482 (1840).

95 Kessler and Gilmore, *Contracts* 37.

96 *Stilk v. Myrick*, 6 Esp. 129, 170 Eng. Rep. 851; 2 Camp. 317, 170 Eng. Rep. 1168 (1809). Gilmore relies on both reports (Gilmore, *The Death of Contract* 22–28).

97 *Lingenfelder v. Wainwright Brewing Co.*, 103 Mo. 578, 15 S.W. 844 (1891) (knocking out an extractive promise for want of consideration). The cases are collected in E. Allan Farnsworth, *Contracts* §§ 4.21–4.22 (2d ed. 1990).

98 *Webb v. McGowin*, 27 Ala. App. 82, 168 So. 196 (1935). See also Restatement (Second) of Contracts, § 89A, illustration 7 (1936).

99 Restatement of Contracts, 89A and illus. 7.

100 80 Eng. Rep. 284 (K.B. 1616).

101 For a comprehensive view of the defense, which concludes that it excuses only defendants who have taken extraordinary care, see Stephen Gilles, "Inevitable Accident in Classical English Tort Law," 43 "Emory L.J." 575 (1994); for my views favoring a still more literal reading of "inevitable," see Richard A. Epstein, *Cases and Materials on Torts*, 101–3 (6th ed. 1995).

102 82 Eng. Rep. 897 (K.B. 1647).

103 Id. at 27, 82 Eng. Rep. at 897. The one phrase that is somewhat discordant in this passage is "if he may," which I do not take to undo the basic thought of the section, that impossibility is no defense, but only to stress that specific performance is the preferred remedy, and damages the backstop.

104 In truth the allowable excuses on the public side are still narrower: not only must the defendant not be in default, but he must also have no remedy against third parties. In these cases the English tradition seems to have made it clear that if the defendant has the remedy over, then he can be bound, notwithstanding the fact that practically speaking the remedy is worthless. See "Tithes Case," Y.B. Trin., 21 Hen. 7, f. 26, 27, 28, pl. 5 (1506), and for discussion, Richard A. Epstein, "Holdouts, Externalities, and the Single Owner: Another Tribute to Ronald Coase," 36 *J. Law & Econ.* 553, 579–81 (1993).

105 See Gaius, *Institutes* 3, 97–99. Justinian, *Institutes*, 3, 19, 1, 2.

106 See 1 Powell, *Essay on Contracts*, at 160–62 (1790).

107 Id. See *Flureau v. Thornhill*, 2 W. Bl. 1078, 96 Eng. Rep. 624 (C.P. 1776) (allowing return of deposit, but no expectation damages for "the fancied goodness of the bargain").

108 See *Slater v. Baker*, 2 Wilson 359, 24 Eng. Rep. 860 (K.B. 1767), allowing contract action but using gross negligence standard. For the modern skeptical view on contracts for cure, see *Sullivan v. O'Connor*, 363 Mass. 579, 296 N.E.2d 183 (1973).

109 See Restatement of Contracts, § 459 and illustration 11.

110 As under the contract of mandate, see Gaius, *Institutes*, 3.

111 See supra at note 14.

112 See, e.g., *School Trustees of Trenton v. Bennett*, 27 N.J.L. 513 (1859).

113 See *Stees v. Leonard*, 20 Minn. 448 (1874), which continued: "No hardship, no unforeseen hindrance, no difficulty short of absolute impossibility, will excuse him from doing what he has expressly agreed to do." Id. at 451.

114 120 Eng. Rep. 688 (Q. B. 1858).

115 See his views on the perfect tender rule, infra in this section.

116 See Restatement of Contracts, § 459 and illustration 8. If the inability to marry is the result of voluntary misconduct, the result is otherwise, to control against moral hazard. Id. at illustration 9.

117 3 B & S. 826, 122 Eng. Rep. 310 (Q. B. 1863).

118 See, e.g., *Butterfield v. Byron*, 153 Mass. 517, 27 N. E. 667 (1891).

119 *Hoare v. Rennie*, 5 H & N. 19, 157 Eng. Rep. 1083 (1859).

120 See, e.g., *Norrington v. Wright*, 115 U.S. 188 (1885), upholding the perfect tender rule in a case where the time of shipment did not appear to go to the essence of the agreement. See the account of the case background in Kessler and Gilmore, *Contracts*, at 831. The decision was in conformity with English precedent, see *Hoare v. Rennie* supra and *Bowes v. Shand*, 2 A. C. 455 (HLE 1877).

121 *Filley v. Pope*, 115 U.S. 213 (1885).

122 230 N.Y. 239, 129 N. E. 889 (1921). In understanding this case, there is much to be said for Richard Danzig's suggestion that the specification of Reading pipe was used to ensure that wrought iron pipe, and not inferior pipe (i.e. with steel scrap) was used in construction. So the name was a substitute for a standard that was met. See Richard Danzig, *The Capability Problem in Contract Law* 120–23 (1978). Why not therefore treat the name as the source of latent ambiguity and allow parole evidence in on the point, as was done in *Raffles*?

123 Where replacement cost was allowed in *City School District of the City of Elmira v. McLane Construction Co.*, 85 A.D. 2d 749, 445 N.Y. S. 2d 258 (1981).

124 Varouj A. Aivazian, Michael Trebilcock, and Michael Penny, "The Law of Contract Modifications: The Uncertain Quest for a Benchmark of Enforceability," 22 *Osgoode Hall L. J.* 173 (1984). The trade-off is difficult because enforcing the contract modification usually allows short-term mutual gains from trade. But it also increases the probability that one side will hold up the other. See the good discussion in *Angel v. Murray*, 113 R. I. 482, 322 A.2d 630 (1974), noting the risk of the "hold-up game" but accepting the modification when facts made it clear that it was in line with the increased costs of the promisor for circumstances beyond his control.

125 Oliver Wendell Holmes Jr., *The Common Law* 301 (1881).

126 *Veer v. York*, Y. B. Hen VI (1470) (reproduced in Fifoot, *Sources* at 251).

127 6 N. H. 481 (1834).

128 See, e.g., *Stark v. Parker*, 19 Mass. 267 (1824); *Smith v. Brady*, 17 N.Y. 173 (1859).

129 Gilmore, *The Death of Contract* 81.

130 For a fuller consideration of these cases, see Richard A. Epstein, "The Problem of Forfeiture in the Welfare State," 14 *Soc. Phil. & Pol.* 256 (1997).

131 "Any apprehension that this rule may be abused to the purposes of oppression, by holding out an inducement to the employer, by unkind treatment near the close of a term of service, to drive the laborer from his engagement, to the sacrifice of his wages, is wholly groundless. It is only in cases where the desertion is voluntary and

without cause on the part of the laborer, or fault or consent on the part of the employer, that the principle applies." *Stark v. Parker*, 19 Mass. 267, 275 (1824).

132 Id. at 273–74.

133 "[T]he usages of the country and common opinion upon subjects of this description are especially to be regarded, and we are bound judicially to take notice of which no one is in fact ignorant. It may be safe to affirm that in no case has a contract in the terms of the one under consideration, been construed by practical men to give a right to demand the agreed compensation, before the performance of the labor, and that the employer and the employed alike universally so understand it." *Stark v. Parker* at 274.

134 Id. at 273.

135 Andrew Kull, "Restitution as a Remedy for Breach of Contract," 67 *So. Cal. L. Rev.* 1465 (1994).

136 See for its exposition, Richard A. Posner, *The Economic Analysis of Law* 119–20 (4th ed. 1992). For criticism, Daniel Friedmann, "The Efficient Breach Fallacy," 18 *J. Legal Stud.* 1 (1989).

137 Lisa Bernstein, "Merchant Law in a Merchant Court," 144 *U. Pa. L. Rev.* at 1801–02.

138 Holmes, *The Common Law* at 300–301.

139 See *Lumley v. Gye*, 2 El. & Bl. 216, 118 Eng. Rep. 749 (Ex. 1853) (allowing the tort action); *Lumley v. Wagner*, 1 De G., M. & G. 604, 42 Eng. Rep, 687 (Ch. 1852).

140 *Printing and Numerical Registering Co. v. Sampson* 19 Ch. 462, 465 (1875).

141 Id.

142 Id. at 462.

143 Id. at 464; Christopher Columbus Langdell, "The Northern Securities Case and the Sherman Anti-Trust Act," 16 *Harv. L Rev.* 539, 553 (1903).

144 Id. at 465.

145 *Boston Ice Co. v. Potter*, 123 Mass. 28, 30 (1877); *McDonald v. Massachusetts*, 120 Mass. 432 (1876), making the same point for charitable hospitals. *United States v. Colgate*, 250 U.S. 300, 307 (1919): "In the absence of any purpose to create or maintain a monopoly, the Sherman act does not restrict the long recognized right of a trader or manufacturer . . . freely to exercise his own independent discretion as to the parties with whom he will deal." *Great Atlantic & Pacific Tea Co. v. Cream of Wheat Co.*, 227 F. 46 (2d Cir. 1915) (antitrust laws do not influence general common law rule except in restraint of trade cases).

146 Matthew Hale, De Portibus Mari (Of Carriage at Sea), quoted in *Allnut v. Inglis*, 12 East 525, 538, 104 Eng. Rep. 206, 210–11 (K. B. 1810).

147 *Allnut v. Inglis*, 12 East 525, 538, 104 Eng. Rep. 206 (K. B. 1810).

148 Michael Trebilcock, *The Common Law of Restraint of Trade: A Legal and Economic Analysis* (1986); see also William Letwin, "The English Common Law Concerning Monopolies," 21 *U. Chi. L. Rev.* 355 (1954).

149 Langdell, "The Northern Securities Case" at 539.

150 For a discussion, see Richard A. Epstein, *Principles for a Free Society: Reconciling Individual Liberty with the Common Good*, ch. 2 (1998).

The Decline of Formality in Contract Law

My thanks to the participants at the Donner Conference, and to Matthew Adler, Sally Gordon, Leo Katz, and Stephen Perry.

1 Grant Gilmore, *The Death of Contract* (1974).

2   P. S. Atiyah, *The Rise and Fall of Freedom of Contract* (1979); Lawrence M. Friedman, *Contract Law in America: A Social and Economic Case Study* (1965).

3   "Symposium: Reconsidering Grant Gilmore's *The Death of Contract*," 90 *Nw. U. L. Rev.* 1 (1995).

4   See, e.g., Friedrich Kessler, "Contracts of Adhesion—Some Thoughts about Freedom of Contract," 43 *Colum. L. Rev.* 629 (1943).

5   See, e.g., John P. Dawson, "Economic Duress—An Essay in Perspective," 45 *Mich. L. Rev.* 253 (1947).

6   See Richard A. Epstein, "Contracts Small and Contract Large," in this volume.

7   Holmes was, of course, known as a great enemy of methodological formalism. Methodological formalism must be distinguished from formalistic doctrine; the latter can be derived using the former. Formalistic doctrine is defined in the text; formalistic *method* refers to any axiomatic approach, justified either by the self-evidence of the axioms (as in Langdell's account), or by their plausibility and usefulness (as in modern normative economics). Holmes did not clearly reject methodological formalism until after he had written *The Common Law*, and indeed the methodology used in that book, especially its chapters on contracts, often has a formalistic flavor. On these tensions in Holmes's methodological views, see Robert Gordon, "Holmes' *Common Law* as Social and Legal Science," 10 *Hofstra L. Rev.* 719 (1982); Thomas C. Grey, "Holmes and Legal Pragmatism," 41 *Stan. L. Rev.* 787 (1989); Thomas C. Grey, "Molecular Motions: The Holmesian Judge in Theory and Practice," 37 *William & Mary L. Rev.* 19 (1995); Morton Horwitz, "The Place of Justice Holmes in American Legal Thought," in Robert W. Gordon, ed., *The Legacy of Oliver Wendell Holmes, Jr.* (1992).

8   Classic articles on formality in the law include Lon L. Fuller, "Consideration and Form," 41 *Colum. L. Rev.* 799 (1941); Duncan Kennedy, "Form and Substance in Private Law Adjudication," 89 *Harv. L. Rev.* 1685 (1976); Frederick Schauer, "Formalism," 97 *Yale L. J.* 509 (1988); elements of my discussion will be familiar from this work.

9   Compare Raz's discussion of positivism, according to which a "jurisprudential theory is acceptable only if its tests for identifying the content of the law and determining its existence depend exclusively on facts of human behavior capable of being described in value-neutral terms, and applied without resort to moral argument." Joseph Raz, *The Authority of Law: Essays on Law and Morality* 39–40 (1979).

10 On this, see Mark DeWolfe Howe, "Introduction," in Oliver Wendell Holmes, *The Common Law*, ed. Mark DeWolfe Howe, xxi (1963).

11 Holmes, supra note 10, at 231–32.

12 Id. at 234–35.

13 Id. at 246.

14 By "derivation" I mean conceptual, not historical. See, e.g., *Alaska Packers' Ass'n v. Domenico* 117 Fed. 99 (9th Cir. 1902); cf. Samuel Williston, *Contracts* § 130 (1924). In fact, the preexisting duty rule predates the bargain theory.

15 Cf. Thomas C. Grey, "Langdell's Orthodoxy," 45 *U. Pitt. L. Rev.* 1 (1983); and see sources cited supra in note 7 for discussions of these tensions in Holmes's thought.

16 See Williston, supra note 14, at § 115b.

17 See Melvin Aron Eisenberg, "Third-Party Beneficiaries," 92 *Colum. L. Rev.* 1358 (1992).

18 Holmes, supra note 10, at 241–42.

19 I make these assumptions even with the knowledge that generalization about laissez-faire is extremely hazardous. Its popular and political manifestations have been crude (for descriptions, see Arthur J. Taylor, *Laissez-Faire and State Intervention in*

Nineteenth-Century Britain [1972]), and unfortunately scholars, such as Gilmore, have sometimes succumbed to the temptation to take this popular sense as the only true understanding of laissez-faire. On the other side, sophisticated philosophical defenses of laissez-faire, such as Mill's (see John Stuart Mill, *Principles of Political Economy*, ed. Jonathan Riley 324–67 [1994] are so subtle and full of qualifications and exceptions that it becomes hard to pin down what is meant by the term.

20 Markets can generate value-maximizing terms even when parties do not bargain over them or "intend" them in any meaningful way. E.g., *Carnival Cruise Lines, Inc., v. Shute*, 499 U.S. 585 [1991]. But we can merge the ideas through the back door: if a court strikes down a market-generated term, we can expect parties to bargain around it next time. A problem with all the work in this area—Gilmore's, Atiyah's, Friedman's, Kessler's, and others—is that it assumes that freedom of contract requires actual haggling or a "bargain" and that it necessarily permits the deception and unequal bargaining power often associated with those terms. But to the extent that freedom of contract has a utilitarian or Pareto basis, the extent to which courts should police against deception and unequal bargaining power depends just on their ability to evaluate evidence, on institutional division of labor (i.e., separate antitrust actions) and on similar considerations. Of course, some people's commitment to laissez-faire has rested on other premises—moralistic individualism, for example, which places great value on self-reliance, or Social Darwinism—and they would reject this analysis.

21 Jacob Viner, "The Intellectual History of Laissez-Faire," 3 *J. Law & Econ.* 45 (1960).

22 Daniel A. Farber and John H. Matheson, "Beyond Promissory Estoppel: Contract Law and the 'Invisible Handshake'," 52 *U. Chi. L. Rev.* 903 (1985); Randy E. Barnett and Mary E. Becker, "Beyond Reliance: Promissory Estoppel, Contract Formalities, and Misrepresentations," 15 *Hofstra L. Rev.* 443 (1987); Edward Yorio and Steve Thel, "The Promissory Basis of Section 90," 101 *Yale L. J.* 111 (1991).

23 See Epstein, "Contracts Small and Contract Large," in this volume, section 3.

24 *Wood v. Lucy, Lady Duff-Gordon*, 118 N. E. 214 (NY 1917).

25 See Dawson, supra note 5.

26 Cf. Arthur A. Leff, "Unconscionability and the Code—The Emperor's New Clause," 115 *U. Pa. L. Rev.* 485 (1967).

27 See Duncan Kennedy, "Distributive and Paternalist Motives in Contract and Tort Law, with Special Reference to Compulsory Terms and Unequal Bargaining Power," 41 *Md. L. Rev.* 563 (1982).

28 See Eisenberg, supra note 17.

29 P. S. Atiyah and Robert S. Summers, *Form and Substance in Anglo-American Law: A Comparative Study of Legal Reasoning, Legal Theory, and Legal Institutions* 115–27 (1987).

30 See, e.g., Robert Hale, "Coercion and Distribution in a Supposedly Non-Coercive State," 38 *Pol. Sci. Q.* 470 (1923).

31 See Friedman, supra note 2, at 98–105. Friedman interpreted these cases as inconsistent with the requirements of the market.

32 See, e.g., *Escola v. Coca-Cola Bottling Co.*, 150 P.2d 436 (CA 1944) (concurrence); *Pacific Gas & Elec. Co. v. G. W. Thomas Drayage & Rigging Co.*, 442 P.2d 641 (CA 1968).

33 See Samuel Williston, "Freedom of Contract," 6 *Cornell L. Q.* 465 (1921).

34 See Arthur L. Corbin, "The Interpretation of Words and the Parol Evidence Rule," 50 *Cornell L. Q.* 161 (1965).

35 See Arthur L. Corbin, "Mr. Justice Cardozo and the Law of Contracts," 48 *Yale L. J.*

426 (1939). In all but one or two of the cases Corbin discusses, he praises Cardozo for seeing through form and enforcing the parties' intentions.

36 See Friedrich A. Hayek, *Law, Legislation, and Liberty: Rules of Order*, vol. 1 (1973).

37 Some theories assume that litigants (or their lawyers) drive changes in doctrine; I ignore them for the sake of brevity.

38 This problem is a defect in other theories of legal change, for example, Horwitz's argument that judges adopted increasingly formalistic modes of legal analysis in order to present the law as neutral and apolitical, thus insulating themselves from criticism when their democratic legitimacy was questioned. See Morton J. Horwitz, *The Transformation of American Law, 1870–1960: The Crisis of Legal Orthodoxy* 33–63 (1992). The problem is that even if it served all judges' interest to be thought neutral "discoverers" rather than makers of the law, it was in each judge's individual interest to decide cases in the way that he thought best and that enhanced his (individual, as opposed to the judiciary's) reputation and to hope that the other judges would attend to the problem of legitimacy. A theory of reputation might overcome this problem, but I have not seen one.

39 I rely loosely on the model of conformity in B. Douglas Bernheim, "A Theory of Conformity," 102 *J. Pol. Econ.* 841 (1994), who however does not discuss judicial behavior.

40 There are other approaches to discussing reputational effects on judicial behavior, which come to similar conclusions about judicial conformity to precedent. In one model, judges derive zero reputational utility if they conform to precedent, positive utility if they depart and future judges follow them, and negative utility if they depart and future judges do not follow them. See Thomas J. Miceli and Metin M. Cosgel, "Reputation and Judicial Decision-Making," 23 *J. Econ. Behavior & Org.* 31 (1994). In another model judges derive reputational utility when future judges follow them. See Eric Rasmusen, "Judicial Legitimacy as a Repeated Game," 10 *J. Law, Econ., & Org.* 63 (1994).

41 Compare the argument to Johnston's theory of cycling between rules and standards; it is, however, based on an assumption of judges' trying to implement a moral theory (efficiency) and does not assume that they care about their reputation. See Jason Scott Johnston, "Uncertainty, Chaos, and the Torts Process: An Economic Analysis of Legal Form," 76 *Cornell L. Rev.* 341 (1991).

42 See Johnston, supra note 41, at 388–96. His examples of areas of doctrine that appear to exhibit a trend toward increasing formalism include products liability and landowner liability.

43 350 F.2d 445 (D. C. Cir. 1965).

44 161 A.2d 69 (N.J. 1960).

External Critiques of Laissez-Faire

1 See Richard A. Epstein, "Contracts Small and Contract Large," in this volume (p. 25); see also Epstein, "The Utilitarian Foundations of Natural Law," 12 *Harvard J. L. & Pub. Pol.* 713 (1989).

2 Michael Trebilcock, *The Limits of Freedom of Contract* ch. 10 (1993).

3 See, e.g., Anthony Kronman, "Contact Law and Distributive Justice," 89 *Yale L. J.* 672 (1980).

4 Charles Fried, *Contract as Promise: A Theory of Contractual Obligation* (1981).

5 The most philosophically sophisticated case for the incoherence of nineteenth-

century contract law is developed by James Gordley, *The Philosophical Origins of Contract Doctrine* (1991).

6   See Ronald Dworkin, "What Is Equality?" Part 2: "Equality of Resources," 10 *Philosophy and Public Affairs* 283 (1981).

7   Kronman, supra note 3.

8   Trebilcock, supra note 2, at ch. 3.

9   F. H. Buckley, "Paradox Lost," 72 *Minn. L. Rev.* 775 (1988).

10   S. M. Waddams, *The Law of Contracts* 209 (3d ed. 1993).

11   2 C. P. D. 416, 421 (C. A.) (1877).

12   2 K. B. 394, 403 (1934).

13   See W. David Slawson, *Binding Promises: The Late Twentieth-Century Reformation of Contract Law*, ch. 1 (1996).

14   See, e.g., Friedrich Kessler, "Contracts of Adhesion: Some Thoughts about Freedom of Contract," 43 *Col. L. Rev.* 629 (1943); Todd D. Rakoff, "Contracts of Adhesion: An Essay in Reconstruction," 96 *Harv. L. Rev.* 1172 (1983); David Slawson, "Standard Form Contracts and Democratic Control of Law-Making Power," 86 *Harv. L. Rev.* 529 (1971).

15   Trebilcock, supra note 2, at 119.

16   Id. at 119, 120.

17   *Smith v. Hughes*, L. R. 6 Q. B. 597, 603–4 (1871).

18   *Bell v. Lever Bros.*, A. C. 161 (H. L.) (1932).

19   Id. at 224.

20   See Kim Lane Scheppele, *Legal Secrets: Equality and Efficiency in the Common Law* (1988); Anthony Kronman, "Mistake, Disclosure, Information, and the Law of Contracts," 7 *J. Legal Stud.* 1 (1978); Anthony Duggan, Michael Bryan, and Frances Hanks, *Contractual Non-Disclosure* (1994).

21   See Trebilcock, supra note 2, at ch. 5.

22   *Rylands v. Fletcher*, L. R. 3 H. L. 330 (1868).

23   See *Pearce v. Brooks*, L. R. 1 Ex. 213 (1866).

24   See Richard A. Epstein, "The Harm Principle—And How It Grew," 45 *Univ. of Toronto L. J.* 869 (1995).

25   Trebilcock, supra note 2, at ch. 3.

26   John Stuart Mill, *On Liberty* (1947 [1859]).

27   Joel Feinberg, *Harm to Others* 12 (1984); see also Giudo Calabresi, "The Pointlessness of Pareto: Carrying Coase Further," 100 *Yale L. J.* 1211 (1991).

28   See, e.g., Fred Hirsch, *Social Limits to Growth* (1978).

29   Epstein, *Forbidden Grounds: The Case against Employer Discrimination Laws* 3, 505 (1992); for searching critiques of Epstein's thesis, see J. Hoult Verkerke, "Free to Search," 105 *Harv. L. Rev.* 2080 (1992), and George Rutherglen, "Abolition in a Different Voice," 78 *Va. L. Rev.* 1463 (1992).

30   1 D. L. R. 81 (S. C. Can. (1940).

31   Id. at 82.

32   Id. at 81.

33   Epstein, supra note 24, at 417.

34   Kenneth Arrow, "Gifts and Exchanges," 1 *Philosophy and Public Affairs* 342 (1972).

35   Karl Polanyi, *The Great Transformation* (1944).

36   Freidrich A. von Hayek, *The Road to Serfdom* (1944).

37   See Margaret Jane Radin, "Market Inalienability," 100 *Harv. L. Rev.* 1849 (1989); Radin, *Contestable Commodities* (1996).

38 Richard Titmuss, *The Gift Relationship: From Human Blood to Social Policy* (1970).

39 Mill, supra note 26, at 9, 10.

40 Id. at 76.

41 Id. at 10.

42 Id. at 104.

43 See, e.g., Cass Sunstein, "Legal Interference with Private Preferences," 53 *U. Chi. L. Rev.* 1129 (1986); Sunstein, "Preferences and Politics," 20 *Philosophy and Public Affairs* 3 (1991).

44 Sunstein (1986), supra note 43, at 1170.

45 See Sunstein, "Disrupting Voluntary Transactions," in John Chapman and Roland Pennock, eds., *Markets and Justice* 275 (1989).

46 Milton Friedman, *Capitalism and Freedom* 33–34 (1962).

47 Richard Epstein, *Simple Rules for a Complex World* (1995).

48 World Bank, *The Reform of Public Sector Management: Lessons from Experience* (1991).

49 See Cass Sunstein, *Legal Reasoning and Political Conflict*, chs. 4–5 (1996).

50 Patrick Atiyah, *The Rise and Fall of Freedom of Contract* (1979).

51 Grant Gilmore, *The Death of Contract* (1974).

In Defense of the Old Order

I have benefited from comments from Fred McChesney and participants in the Conference on the Doctrine of Contract and Modern Societal Policy, sponsored by the Donner Foundation, on 15–16 November 1996. Michael Langan provided valuable research assistance. The comments of my colleague Richard Murphy, who moderated the discussion, were especially valuable. Richard's tragic death shocked and saddened us all. We miss him more than words can convey.

1 Grant Gilmore, *The Death of Contract* (1974). Besides this conference, the recent "Symposium: Reconsidering Grant Gilmore's *The Death of Contract*," 90 *Nw. L. Rev.* 1 (1995), reveals the continued interest in Gilmore's work.

2 This view is consistent with that of Professor Epstein, when he argues that efficient rules facilitate the security of exchange. As Alan Schwartz has argued in a recent working paper, "The Law and Economics Approach to Contract Theory," both law and economics and other contract scholars often ask the same question, "How can we make the law consistent with good business practice?" Because the law and economics analyst has better tools for answering that question, law and economics provides a superior approach in analyzing commercial behavior, which, after all, is the mainstay of contract law.

3 Gilmore was born in 1910; Friedman in 1930.

4 As Friedman himself noted, "the activism of government . . . was a judgment that the market was a failure." Lawrence M. Friedman, *Contract Law in America* 198 (1965).

5 The importance of monetary policy in modern economic thought can be seen through the oft-cited example of Paul Samuelson's leading economics text book, *Economics*. In the first edition, published in 1948, monetarism received little attention; in the last edition, published in 1995, monetarism was given the prominent position it now occupies in economics.

6 Armen Alcian and William Allen, *Exchange and Production, Competition, Coordination, and Control* 177 (2d ed. 1977).

7   Carl J. Dahlman, "The Problem of Externality," 22 *J. Law & Econ.* 141, 161 (1979).

8   For a recent discussion of "government policy: ideal and real," see Douglas F. Greer, *Business, Government, and Society,* ch. 3 (1993).

9   "Information and Efficiency: Another Viewpoint," 12 *J. Law & Econ.* 1 (1969). See also Oliver E. Williamson, "Legal Implications of Imperfect Information in Consumer Markets: Comment," 151 *Journal Instit. & Theoretical Econ.* 49, 49–50 (1995) (listing five mitigating factors to the argument that public policy intervention on behalf of consumers is a way to relieve information and power disparities).

10 Friedreich Kessler, "Contracts of Adhesion—Some Thoughts about Freedom of Contract," 43 *Colum. L. Rev.* 629 (1943). To Kessler, the growth of monopoly was apparently self-evident. He offered no evidence to support his statement.

11 The relationship between concentration and competition was much debated by economists. Although most once believed that highly concentrated industries were poorly performing, that consensus no longer exists. The arguments in *Industrial Concentration: The New Learning* (1974), based on a conference the year before, were responsible for shattering the consensus. We now know that concentration is consistent with efficiency, providing maximum benefits to consumers, at least in many industries.

12 The history is recounted along with calls for reform in contract law in Ernest Gelhorn, "Limitations on Contractual Termination Rights—Franchise Cancellation," 1967 *Duke L. J.* 465.

13 This modern trend is surveyed in Michael J. Lockerby, "Franchise Termination Restriction: A Guide for Practitioners and Policy Makers," 30 *Antit. Bull.* 791 (1985).

14 *Munno v. Amoco Oil Co.,* 488 F. Supp. 1114, 1118 (D. Conn. 1980). Alleged disparity of bargaining power was a favorite theme of critics of classical contract law. See, e.g., Kessler, supra note 10.

15 *Statistical Abstract of the United States,* 1993, table 712.

16 Francine Lafontaine, "Agency Theory and Franchising: Some Empirical Results," 23 *Rand J. Econ.* 263 (1992).

17 McAfee and Schwartz make a similar argument. R. McAfee and M. Schwartz, "Opportunism in Multilateral Vertical Contracting: Nondiscrimination, Exclusivity, and Uniformity," 84 *American Economic Review* 210 (1994).

18 See "When Franchisees Go Their Own Way," *Wall Street Journal,* 6 July 1989, at B1. The argument in the text does not deny that asymmetric information can lead to problems in consumer transactions. For excellent law and economics treatments, see Richard Craswell, "Property Rights and Liability Rules in Unconscionability and Related Doctrines," 60 *U. Chi. L. Rev.* 1 (1993); Alan Schwartz, "Liability Rules, Legal Implications, and Imperfect Information in Consumer Markets," 151 *J. Inst. & Theoret. Economics* 31 (1995). Opportunitistic behavior can also cause problems. See generally, Timothy J. Muris, "Opportunistic Behavior and the Law of Contracts," 65 *Minn. L. Rev.* 521 (1981).

19 Perhaps because they were not subject to FDA approval for new products, some food manufacturers resisted FDA policy and in fact advertised their products contrary to FDA rules, even before the early 1970s. See generally Peter Barton Hutt, "Government Regulation of Health Claims in Food Labeling and Advertising," 41 *Food Drug Cosmetic L. J.* 1 (1986).

20 For an overview of the issues, see Timothy J. Muris, "Economics and Consumer Protection," 60 *Antitrust L. J.* 103 (1991).

21 Nutrition Labeling and Education Act of 1990, 104 Stat. 2353.

22 Pauline M. Ippolito and Alan D. Mathios, *Health Claims in Advertising and Labeling: A Study of the Cereal Market* (1989), FTC Bureau of Economics Staff Report.

23 Critics of this study claim that it does not support the market approach to advertising because the ads involved were precleared by government agencies. This claim is incorrect. Although the original Kellogg campaign was a cooperative effort with the NCI, the numerous other health claims ads during the period the study analyzed were not preapproved.

24 Moreover, consumers did not overreact by eating cereal with greater amounts of sodium and fat. The preexisting trend toward lower sodium and fat consumption continued. Id. at 41.

25 For analysis of such regulation, see, e.g., J. Howard Beales and Timothy J. Muris, *State and Federal Regulation of National Advertising* (1993); Kenneth Clarkson and Timothy J. Muris, eds., *The Federal Trade Commission since 1970* (1981).

The Limits of Freedom of Contract in the Age of Laissez-Faire Constitutionalism

Portions of this essay are drawn from my book *Commodity and Propriety: The Competing Visions of Property in American Legal Thought* (1998). I am grateful to all of the participants at the Donner Colloquium for their valuable comments and to the Law and Economics Center for inviting me. I am especially grateful to Frank Buckley for his helpful suggestions in revising the paper. All errors, of course, remain mine alone.

1 The classical expressions of this interpretation include Robert G. McCloskey, *American Conservatism in the Age of Enterprise* (1951); Charles Grove Haines, *The Revival of Natural Law Concepts: A Study of the Establishment and of the Interpretation of Limits on Legislatures* (1930), and Edward S. Corwin, *Liberty against Government: The Rise, Flowering, and Decline of a Famous Judicial Concept* (1948). The "laissez-faire constitutionalism" label still persists in recent historical writing. See, e.g., James W. Ely Jr., *The Guardian of Every Other Right: A Constitutional History of Property Rights* 100 (1992); Arthur S. Miller, "Toward a Definition of 'the' Constitution," 8 *U. Dayton L. Rev.* 633, 647 (1983).

2 The first case usually credited with relying on liberty of contract as a constitutional doctrine is *Godcharles v. Wigeman*, 113 Pa. 431, 6 Atl. 354 (1886).

3 198 U.S. 45 (1905).

4 Progressive history is lucidly explained and analyzed in Ernst A. Breisach, *American Progressive History: An Experiment in Modernization* (1993).

5 For a brief excellent critique of Progressive legal history, see Morton J. Horwitz, "Progressive Legal Historiography," 63 *Ore. L. Rev.* 679 (1984). As Horwitz explains, while Progressive historiography has now been widely repudiated in virtually all other areas of American history, it continues to exert a strong pull in late-nineteenth-century legal history, especially constitutional history. Horwitz's explanation is that constitutional historians continue to focus on "questions that originally arose because of the Supreme Court's attack on and then capitulation to the New Deal. Id. at 680. For examples of the general critique of Progressive historiography, which has been ongoing for the past three decades, see Richard Hofstadter, *The Progressive Historians* (1968); Robert E. Brown, *Charles Beard and the Constitution* (1956).

6 For examples of this historiography, see Arnold Paul, *Conservative Crisis and the Rule of Law: Attitudes of Bar and Bench, 1887–1895* (1960); Clyde E. Jacobs, *Law Writers*

and the Courts: The Influence of Thomas M. Cooley, Christopher G. Tiedemann, and John F. Dillon upon American Constitutional Law (1954); Benjamin R. Twiss, *Lawyers and the Constitution: How Laissez Faire Came to the Supreme Court* (1942).

7 See, e.g., Howard Gillman, *The Constitution Besieged: The Rise and Demise of Lochner Era Police Powers Jurisprudence* (1993); Alan Jones, "Thomas Cooley and 'Laissez-Faire Constitutionalism': A Reconsideration," 53 *J. Am. Hist.* 751 (1967). The work that has contributed most to my understanding of judicial thought during the Gilded Age is Michael Les Benedict, "Laissez-Faire and Liberty: A Reevaluation of the Meaning and Origins of Laissez-Faire Constitutionalism," 3 *Law & Hist. Rev.* 293 (1985); Charles W. McCurdy, "The Roots of 'Liberty of Contract' Reconsidered: Major Premises in the Law of Employment, 1867–1937," 20, in Supreme Court Historical Society, Yearbook (1984); Charles W. McCurdy, "Stephen J. Field and the American Judicial Tradition," in Philip J. Bergan, Owen M. Fiss, and Charles W. McCurdy, eds., *The Fields and the Law* 5 (1986); and Charles W. McCurdy, "Justice Field and the Jurisprudence of Government-Business Relations: Some Parameters of Laissez-Faire Constitutionalism, 1863–1897," 61 *J. Am. Hist.* 970 (1975).

8 Lawrence M. Friedman, *A History of American Law* 361 (2d ed. 1985).

9 In emphasizing the role of proprietarian thought, I do not mean to imply that class distinctions played no role in the Lochner era liberty-of-contract cases. To the contrary, proprietarian thought has often been characterized by the view that the proper social order is hierarchical in one respect or another, and the Gilded Age's version of the proprietarian tradition was no different. My basic point is that courts acted not directly to advance the interest of the ruling capitalist class but to preserve a social ideal, an ideal in which class did play a role but was not the determining factor in what constituted the proper social order.

10 On this maxim and its impact on early-nineteenth-century legal regulation, see William J. Novak, "Public Economy and the Well-Ordered Market: Law and Economic Regulation in Nineteenth-Century America," 18 *Law & Soc. Inq.* 1 (1993).

11 98 N.Y. 98 (1885).

12 155 Ill. 98, 40 N.E. 454 (1895).

13 See McCurdy, supra note 7, at 30–31.

14 *Allgeyer v. Louisiana*, 165 U.S. 578 (1897).

15 10 U.S. (6 Cranch) 87 (1810).

16 *Trustees of Dartmouth College v. Woodward*, 17 U.S. (4 Wheat.) 518 (1819).

17 25 U.S. (12 Wheat.) 213 (1827).

18 Friedman, supra note 8, at 533.

19 165 U.S. 578 (1897).

20 208 U.S. 161 (1908).

21 208 U.S. 412 (1908).

22 236 U.S. 1 (1915).

23 261 U.S. 525 (1923).

24 McCurdy, supra note 7, at 24.

25 Friedman, supra note 8, at 555.

26 Henry Adams, *The Education of Henry Adams* 237 (1961 [1918]).

27 A particularly striking expression of this sense of anxiety is Justice Field's essay "The Centenary of the Supreme Court of the United States," 24 *Am. L. Rev.* 351 (1890). Field there acknowledges that "the enormous aggregation of wealth possessed by some corporations excites uneasiness lest their power should become dominating in

the legislature of the country, and thus encroach upon the rights or crush out the businesses of individuals of small means." Id. at 366–67. Field argued that constitutional protection of property was the antidote to this imbalance of power.

28 Robert H. Wiebe, *The Search for Order, 1877–1920* (1967).

29 Quoted in McCurdy, supra note 7, at 28.

30 The phrase used in the heading, "a crime against self," is drawn from an 1887 essay by W. M. Grosvenor, vehemently denouncing government paternalism as "communism." W. M. Grosvenor, "The Communist and the Railway," 4 *International Rev.* 585, 597 (1877). Grosvenor, the economics editor of the *New York Times* from 1875 to 1900, was an influential journalist who had substantial political contacts. He was an ardent free-trader and frequently assailed trade tariffs. See W. M. Grosvenor, *Does Protectionism Protect? An Examination of the Effect of Different Forms of Tariff upon American Industry* (1871).

31 See Richard Hofstadter, *Social Darwinism in American Thought* (rev. ed. 1955).

32 David A. Hollinger, "Comments on Papers by Sharlin and Wall, in Symposium on Spencer, Scientism, and American Constitutional Law," 33 *Annals of Science* 476 (1976). The leading works reinterpreting Social Darwinism as un-Darwinian are Robert C. Bannister, *Social Darwinism: Science and Myth in Anglo-American Social Thought* (1979); Howard L. Kaye, *The Social Meaning of Modern Biology: From Social Darwinism to Sociobiology* (1984); Peter J. Bowles, *The Eclipse of Darwinism: Anti-Darwinian Evolution Theories in the Decades around 1900* (1983).

33 Aviam Soifer, "The Paradox of Paternalism and Laissez-Faire Constitutionalism: United States Supreme Court, 1888–1921," 5 *Law & Hist. Rev.* 249, 252 (1987).

34 Christopher G. Tiedeman, *A Treatise on the Limitations of Police Power in the United States* vi–vii (1886).

35 157 U.S. 429 (1895).

36 Id. at 532.

37 H. Teichmueller, "Economic Freedom," 29 *Am. L. Rev.* 373, 382 (1895).

38 John H. Keyser, "The Problem of Poverty, and How to Deal with It, Through Immediate Colonization, submitted to the Church of the Strangers, New York City, Feb. 25, 1874." Keyser's preferred solution to the problem of increasing poverty in New York was to create agricultural colonies in the South to which the unemployed would be sent, with or without their consent, to work for their food and shelter. (Nothing like working in a turpentine forest in Georgia to build character!) Keyser himself was hardly a practitioner of Social Darwinist messages. The plumbing and heating contractor in Boss Tweed's famed ring, he bilked the city of New York for huge sums of money. It is estimated that in one year alone he made over $1 million. See Alexander B. Callow Jr., *The Tweed Ring* 202 (1966).

39 This sociology of virtue has retained considerable appeal even in our time. Many people today regard public welfare as a form of "charity," and attack it on the basis of arguments quite similar to those expressed by Choate. The widespread appeal of these arguments is indicated by the enactment of the 1996 welfare reform act.

40 On the discretionary character of late-nineteenth-century antipaternalism, see Soifer, supra note 33.

41 For an example of calls to avoid "astounding consumption" (though not necessarily to avoid acquiring great wealth), see John F. Dillon, Property—Its Rights and Duties in Our Legal and Social System," 29 *Am. L. Rev.* 11, 187 (1895).

42 On the moral dimension of this vision, focusing on the work of one of its exponents,

see David M. Gold, "John Appleton of Maine and Commercial Law: Freedom, Responsibility, and Law in the Nineteenth-Century Marketplace," 4 *Law & Hist. Rev.* 55 (1986).

43 169 U.S. 366 (1898).

44 208 U.S. 412 (1908).

45 Id. at 416.

46 For a revisionist look at Justice Brewer, arguing that he was not the rigid conservative he is usually thought to have been, see John E. Semonche, *Charting the Future: The Supreme Court Responds to a Changing Society* 168–79, 244–45 (1978).

47 208 U.S. at 419.

48 Id. at 421.

49 Id. at 422.

50 *Frisbie v. United States,* 157 U.S. 160 (1895).

51 Id. at 165.

52 See *Choctaw Nation v. United States,* 119 U.S. 1 (1886).

53 See *Robertson v. Baldwin,* 165 U.S. 275 (1897). On the Court's treatment of both groups, see Soifer, supra note 33, at 262–68.

54 169 U.S. at 385.

55 Id. at 391–92.

56 Id. at 397 (emphasis added).

57 190 U.S. 169 (1903).

58 Id. at 175.

59 *Holden v. Hardy,* 198 U.S. 45, 57 (1905).

60 208 U.S. at 419.

61 Id. at 416.

62 Id.

Courts and the Tort-Contract Boundary in Product Liability

1 For notational convenience, I will refer to these as "product liability" cases in what follows. This is the only type of tort law that I address.

2 P. S. Atiyah, *The Rise and Fall of Freedom of Contract* (1969); Grant Gilmore, *The Death of Contract* (1974).

3 For some examples, see John E. Calfee and Paul H. Rubin, "Some Implications of Damage Payments for Nonpecuniary Losses," 21 *J. Legal Stud.* 371 (1992); Richard A. Epstein, "The Legal and Insurance Dynamics of Mass Tort Litigation," 13 *J. Legal Stud.* 475 (1984); Peter W. Huber, *Liability: The Legal Revolution and Its Consequences* (1988); Michael I. Krauss, "Tort Law and Private Ordering," 35 *St. Louis University L. J.* 623 (1991); George L. Priest, "The Current Insurance Crisis and Modern Tort Law," 96 *Yale L. J.* 1521 (1987); Paul H. Rubin, *Tort Reform by Contract* (1993); Alan Schwartz, "Proposals for Products Liability Reform: A Theoretical Synthesis," 97 *Yale L. Rev.* 353 (1988). For an interesting variant, see Robert Cooter, "Commodifying Liability," this volume.

4 The literature on cognitive decision making is immense, and I will neither summarize it nor provide comprehensive references. Many of the articles I cite below provide summaries. I rely most heavily on Colin Cammerer, "Individual Decision Making," ch. 8, in John H. Kagel and Alvin E. Roth, eds., *The Handbook of Experimental Economics* (1995), and, to a lesser extent, on Roger G. Noll and James E. Krier, "Some Implications

of Cognitive Psychology for Risk Regulation," 19 *J. Legal Stud.* 747 (1990). For a discussion of the legal literature involving this research, see Donald C. Langevoort, *Behavioral Theories of Judgment and Decision-Making in Legal Scholarship: A Literature Review*, Vanderbilt L. Rev. Symposium on Human Behavior, Behavioral Economics, and Law (in press 1998).

5 For this section see Paul H. Rubin, "Fundamental Reform of Tort Law," 4 *Regulation* 26–33 (1995).

6 William Landes and Richard Posner, *The Economic Structure of Tort Law* (1987).

7 Steven Shavell, *The Economics of Accident Law* (1987).

8 For a general discussion of reputation, see Daniel B. Klein, ed., *Reputation: Studies in the Voluntary Elicitation of Good Conduct* (1997), and particularly Klein, "Trust for Hire: Voluntary Remedies for Quality and Safety," at 97–133.

9 Indeed, as discussed below, the nature of cognitive decision making is such that the loss in reputation may be greater than would be warranted by the injury, since individuals seem to overweigh losses.

10 Mark L. Mitchell, "The Impact of External Parties on Brand-Name Capital: The 1982 Tylenol Poisonings and Subsequent Cases," 27 *Econ. Inq.* 601 (1989); Mark L. Mitchell and Michael T. Maloney, "Crisis in the Cockpit? The Role of Market Forces in Promoting Air Travel Safety," 32 *J. L. & Econ.* 329 (1989); Sam Peltzman and Gregg Jarrell, "The Impact of Product Recalls on the Wealth of Sellers," 93 *J. Pol. Econ.* 512 (1985); George E. Hoffer, Stephen W. Pruitt, and Robert J. Reilly, "The Impact of Product Recalls on the Wealth of Sellers: A Reexamination," 96 *J. Pol. Econ.* 663 (1988); Paul H. Rubin, R. Dennis Murphy, and Gregg Jarrell, "Risky Products, Risky Stocks," 1 *Regulation* 35 (1988); W. Kip Viscusi and Joni Hersch, "The Market Response to Product Safety Litigation," 2 *J. Reg. Econ.* 215 (1990).

11 *Economic Report of the President*, Washington, 1997, table B-29.

12 Aaron Wildavsky, *Searching for Safety* (1987).

13 J. Mark Ramseyer, "Products Liability through Private Ordering: Notes on a Japanese Experiment," 144 *U. Pa. L. Rev.* 1 (1996).

14 The original analysis is in John P. Brown, "Toward an Economic Theory of Liability," 2 *J. Legal Stud.* 323 (1973).

15 Christopher Curran, "The Spread of Comparative Negligence in the United States," 12 *Int. Rev. L. & Econ.* 317 (1992).

16 George L. Priest, "Strict Products Liability: The Original Intent," 10 *Cardozo L. Rev.* 2301 (1989).

17 W. Kip Viscusi, "The Dimensions of the Product Liability Crisis," 20 *J. Legal Stud.* 147 (1991).

18 James A. Henderson and Aaron D. Twerski, "Doctrinal Collapse in Products Liability: The Empty Shell of Failure to Warn," 65 *N.Y. Univ. L. Rev.* 265 (1990).

19 To be fair to the lawyers, I should point out that this class of damages was invented by an economist. For a history see John O. Ward, ed., *A Hedonic Primer for Economists and Attorneys* (1992).

20 For a discussion of one such case, with some analysis of the economics of punitive damages, see Paul H. Rubin, John E. Calfee, and Mark F. Grady, "BMW v. Gore: Mitigating the Punitive Economics of Punitive Damages," 5 *Supreme Court Econ. Rev.* 179 (1997).

21 These payments are called "subrogation." Subrogation—payment from the injurer to the victim's insurance carrier—seems to be common in automobile accidents, but

not in other accidents. It may be that the transactions costs of determining if such payments are available are too great, given the relatively small number of tortious injuries. Further research on this topic would be useful.

22 Steven P. Croley and Jon D. Hanson, "The Nonpecuniary Cost of Accidents: Pain-and-Suffering Damages in Tort Law," 108 *Harv. L. Rev.* 1785 (1995), claim that consumers do want such insurance, and purport to provide examples, but come up with only a few marginal instances where insurance decisions are difficult to explain. The article is criticized in more detail below and in John E. Calfee and Paul H. Rubin, *Indicting Liability: How the Liability System Has Turned against Itself* (forthcoming 1999).

23 The strongest theoretical argument for such payments is Mark Geistfeld, "Placing a Price on Pain and Suffering: A Method for Helping Juries Determine Tort Damages for Nonmonetary Injuries," 83 *Calif. L. Rev.* 773 (1995). However, this article does not provide a useful way of actually computing the optimal value for such damages, if they are desired, and does not consider risk-reducing products such as medical care and vaccines. See Calfee and Rubin, supra note 3, for a more complete discussion.

24 George Priest, "The Current Insurance Crisis and Modern Tort Law," 96 *Yale L. J. 1521* (1987). Under adverse selection, more insurance will be purchased by those with a higher probability of harm.

25 David D. Haddock, Fred S. McChesney, and Manachem Spiegel, "An Ordinary Economic Rationale for Extraordinary Legal Sanctions," 78 *Calif. L. Rev.* 1 (1990).

26 George Priest, "A Theory of the Consumer Product Warranty," 90 *Yale L. J.* 1297 (1981). Priest's sample of warranties was obtained at a time when courts were already unwilling to enforce such disclaimers, so it is not clear what form warranties would take now if it were worthwhile for firms to spend resources crafting them.

27 These assumptions go beyond those needed for the Coase theorem, but I believe they are in the spirit of such a world. Ronald H. Coase, "The Problem of Social Cost," 3 *J. L. & Econ.* 1 (1960).

28 Christopher Curran and David D. Haddock, "An Economic Theory of Comparative Negligence," 14 *J. Legal Stud.* 49 (1985).

29 Richard A. Posner, *Economic Analysis of Law* 180 (1998).

30 The two major treatises on the economics of torts (Landes and Posner, supra note 6, and Shavell, supra note 7) both argue that contract is not an efficient solution to risks associated with purchased products. The basic argument against contractual solutions for product liability problems is that product-related injuries are rare events and consumers do not have enough information to rationally contract regarding such risks. I have discussed this argument at length in Rubin, supra note 3 and will not repeat that discussion here.

31 George Priest, "The Invention of Enterprise Liability: A Critical History of the Intellectual Foundations of Modern Tort Law," 14 *J. Legal Stud.* 461 (1985).

32 For some examples, see Alan Schwartz and Louis L. Wilde, "Intervening in Markets on the Basis of Imperfect Information: A Legal and Economic Analysis," 127 *U. Pa. L. Rev.* 1979, and "Imperfect Information in Markets for Contract Terms: The Examples of Warranties and Security Interests," 69 *Va. L. Rev.* 1387; Richard A. Epstein, "Unconscionability: A Critical Reappraisal," 18 *J. L. & Econ.* 293 (1971); Sanford Grossman, "The Informational Role of Warranties and Private Disclosure about Product Quality," 24 *J. L. & Econ.* 461 (1981); George Priest, "The Current Insurance Crisis and Modern Tort Law," 96 *Yale L. J.* 1521 (1987).

33 It is noteworthy that this belief is in the economic self-interest of those holding it. See

Paul H. Rubin and Martin Bailey, "The Role of Lawyers in Changing the Law," 23 *J. Legal Stud.* 807 (1994); Richard A. Epstein, "The Political Economy of Product Liability Reform," 78 *Am. Econ. Rev.* 311 (1988).

34 This is not to say that all scholars have abandoned the previous generation of arguments; for example, see W. David Slawson, *Binding Promises: The Late Twentieth-Century Reformation of Contract Law* (1996), or Jean Braucher, "The Afterlife of Contract," 90 *Nw. Univ. L. Rev.* 49 (1995), a symposium issue on *The Death of Contract*.

35 Steven P. Croley and Jon D. Hanson, supra note 22.

36 Ellen Smith Pryor, "The Tort Law Debate, Efficiency, and Kingdom of the Ill: A Critique of the Insurance Theory of Compensation," 79 *Va. L. Rev.* 91 (1993).

37 Heidi Feldman, "Harm and Money: Against the Insurance Theory of Tort Compensation," 75 *Texas L. Rev.* 1567, 1577, 1582 (1997).

38 Cammerer, supra note 4, at 674–75.

39 Gary Becker, "Irrational Behavior and Economic Theory," 70 *J. Pol. Econ.* (1962).

40 Richard L. Hasen, "Comment: Efficiency under Informational Asymmetry: The Effect of Framing on Legal Rules," 38 *UCLA L. Rev.* 391 (1990).

41 350 F.2d 445 (D. C. Cir. 1965).

42 Id. at 431.

43 Howard A. Latin, " 'Good' Warnings, Bad Products, and Cognitive Limitations," 41 *UCLA L. Rev.* 1193 (1994).

44 W. Kip Viscusi, "Individual Rationality, Hazard Warnings, and the Foundations of Tort Law," 48 *Rutgers L. Rev.* 625 (1996), points out that Latin was overly pessimistic regarding the extent to which individuals are unable to respond to warnings, and that they do have a role in the tort system.

45 Melvin Aron Eisenberg, "The Limits of Cognition and the Limits of Contract," 47 *Stanford L. Rev.* 211 (1995).

46 Id. at 243.

47 Id. at 241.

48 P. S. Atiyah, *An Introduction to the Law of Contract* 30 (5th ed. 1995).

49 *Grimshaw v. Ford Motor Co.*, 119 Cal. App. 3d 757, 174 Cal. Rptr. 348 (1981).

50 Gary T. Schwartz, "The Myth of the Ford Pinto Case," 43 *Rutgers L. Rev.* 1013 (1991).

51 Id. at 1038.

52 I have often attempted to convince product liability defense lawyers that economic testimony about cost-benefit analysis of the sort that is routinely performed at the Consumer Product Safety Commission would help their cases. However, all have implicitly agreed with the quoted statement.

53 Camerer, supra note 4, at 680.

54 For a similar analysis, but in a different context, see Cass R. Sunstein, "The Future of Law and Economics: Looking Forward: Behavioral Analysis of Law," 64 *U. Chi. L. Rev.* 1175 (Fall 1997).

55 As found by W. Kip Viscusi, "Pain and Suffering in Product Liability Cases: Systematic Compensation or Capricious Awards?," 8 *Int. Rev. L. & Econ.* 203 (1988).

56 Cammerer, supra note 4, at 613.

57 Hal R. Arkes and Cindy A. Schipani, "Medical Malpractice v. the Business Judgment Rule: Differences in Hindsight Bias," 73 *Oregon L. Rev.* 587 (1994), find that there is significant hindsight bias in actual medical malpractice litigation.

58 Kim A. Kamin and Jeffrey J. Rachlinski, "Ex Post ≠ Ex Ante: Determining Liability in Hindsight," 19 *Law and Human Behavior* 89 (1995), report that experimental subjects

are more likely to find a breach of care standards after an event has occurred than they are before the event. Only 24 percent of the ex ante subjects found taking a precaution worthwhile, while 56 percent of the ex post subjects found negligence for failure to take the same precaution.

59 Cammerer, supra note 4, at 602.

60 See, e.g., id. at 641.

61 Id. at 590–91.

62 Matthew Rabin and Joel Schrag, "First Impressions Matter: A Model of Confirmation Bias," *Quarterly Journal of Economics* (1999).

63 Noll and Krier, supra note 4, at 758–59.

64 Calfee and Rubin, supra note 3.

65 Richard L. Manning, "Changing Rules in Tort Law and the Market for Childhood Vaccines," 37 *J. L. & Econ.* 247 (1994).

66 Edward J. McCaffery, Daniel J. Kahneman, and Matthew L. Spitzer, "Framing the Jury: Cognitive Perspectives on Pain and Suffering Awards," 81 *Va. L. Rev.* 1341, 1353 (1995). For discussion of some legal implications of the endowment effect, see Herbert Hovenkamp, "Legal Policy and the Endowment Effect," 20 *J. Legal Stud.* 225 (1991), and Paul H. Rubin and Christopher Curran, "The Endowment Effect and Income Transfers," *Research in Law and Economics* 225 (1995).

67 John E. Calfee and Clifford Winston, "The Consumer Welfare Effects of Liability for Pain and Suffering: An Explanatory Analysis," Brookings Papers on Economic Activity: Microeconomics 133 (1993).

68 Supra note 66.

69 Noll and Krier, supra note 4, at 749.

70 Id. at 754.

71 Sunstein, supra note 54, McCaffery et al., supra note 66.

72 Atiyah, supra note 1, at 390–91. See also id. at 123, 732.

73 Id. at 99, 42.

74 Howard A. Latin, supra note 43.

75 Cammerer, supra note 4, at 593–94, 611–12.

Commodifying Liability

This essay expands upon Robert Cooter, "Liability Rights as Contingent Claims," in Murray Milgate, John Eatwell, and Peter Newman, eds., *The New Palgrave* (1998), which develops ideas first proposed in Robert D. Cooter, "Towards a Market in Unmatured Tort Claims," 75 *U. Va. L. Rev.* 383 (1989).

1 K. J. Arrow and F. Hahn, *General Competitive Analysis* (1971).

2 Guido Calabresi and Douglas Melamed. "Property Rules, Liability Rules, and Inalienability: One View of the Cathedral," 85 *Harv. L. Rev.* 1089 (1972).

3 Robert Cooter, "Economic Theories of Legal Liability," 5 *J. Econ. Perspectives* 11 (1991).

4 See the Internet advertisement at *http://www.lawfinance.com/lf__paper.cgi.*

5 View the prospectus at *http://www.lawmall.com/files/suit__oc2.html.*

6 P. S. Atiyah, *The Rise and Fall of Freedom of Contract* (1979); Guido Calabresi, "Torts—The Law of the Mixed Society," in B. Schwartz, ed., *American Law: The Third Century* (1976); Grant Gilmore, *The Death of Contract* (1974).

7 Richard W. Painter, "Litigating on a Contingency: A Monopoly of Champions or a Market for Champerty?" 71 *Chicago-Kent L. Rev.* 625 (1996).

8 Harold R. Weinberg, "They Came From 'Beyond the Pale': Security Interests in Tort Claims," 83 *Ky. L. J.* 443 (1994–95).

9 Tom W. Bell, "Limits on the Privity and Assignment of Legal Malpractice Claims," 59 *U. Chi. L. Rev.* 1533 (1992).

10 Peter W. Huber, *Liability: The Legal Revolution and Its Consequences* (1988); W. Kip Viscusi, "Regulating the Regulators," 63 *U. Chi. L. Rev.* 1423 (1996).

11 Some legal theorists favor allowing disclaimers and waivers, or developing new contracts to exchange liability rights. George Priest, "A Theory of Consumer Product Warranty," 90 *Yale L. J.* 1297 (1981); Paul H. Rubin, "Courts and the Tort-Contract Boundary in Product Liability" (this volume); Clark Havighurst, "Private Reform of Tort-law Dogma: Market Opportunities and Legal Obstacles," 49 *Law & Cont. Prob.* 143 (1986); Peter W. Huber, *Liability: The Legal Revolution and Its Consequences* (1988); Robert D. Cooter, "Towards a Market in Unmatured Tort Claims," *U. Va. L. Rev.* 383 (1989); Peter C. Choharis, "A Comprehensive Market Strategy for Tort Reform," 12 *Yale J. Reg.* 435 (1995). Other scholars are more circumspect about contract remedies in torts. Mark Geistfeld, "The Political Economy of Neocontractual Proposals for Products Liability Reform," 72 *Tex. L. Rev.* 803 (1994); Jeffrey O'Connell and Robert H. Joost, "Giving Motorists a Choice between Fault and No-Fault Insurance," 72 *Va. L. Rev.* 61 (1986). Or hostile to them. Peter A. Bell, "Analyzing Tort Law: The Flawed Promise of Neocontract," 74 *Minn. L. Rev.* 1177 (1990). And some scholars favor dramatic noncontractual reforms. Steven P. Croley and Jon D. Hanson, "Rescuing the Revolution: The Revived Case for Enterprise Liability," 91 *Mich. L. Rev.* 683 (1993). Stephen D. Sugarman, "American Law Institute Reporter's Study, Enterprise Responsibility for Personal Injury," 44 *Stan. L. Rev.* 1163 (1992). For a general discussion of possible problems with such market concerns as externalities and interdependencies, see Kenneth Arrow, "The Organization of Economic Activity: Issues Pertinent to the Choice of Market versus Non-Market Allocation," in *The Analysis and Evaluation of Public Expenditures: The PPB System*, Joint Economic Committee U.S. Congress 47 (1969); David Starrett, "Fundamental Non-convexities in the Theory of Externalities," 4 *J. Econ. Th.* 180 (1972); Robert Cooter, "How the Law Circumvents Starrett's Nonconvexity," 22 *J. Econ. Th.* 499 (1980).

12 John Brown, "Toward an Economic Theory of Liability," 2 *J. Legal Stud.* 323 (1973).

13 W. Kip Viscusi writes, "Data collected in 1977 indicated that pain and suffering accounted for some 30–57 percent of the amounts awarded by juries in personal injury suits, with these proportions varying according to the nature of the injury." Quoted in John E. Calfee and Clifford Winston, "The Consumer Welfare Effects of Liability for Pain and Suffering: An Exploratory Analysis," in Martin Neil Baily, Peter C. Reiss, and Clifford Winston, eds., *Brookings Papers on Economic Activity* 133 (1993), citing Viscusi, *Reforming Products Liability* (1991) at 102.

14 W. Kip Viscusi, "Comment on John Calfee and Clifford Winston's 'The Consumer Welfare Effects of Liability for Pain and Suffering: An Exploratory Analysis',," in Baily, Reiss, and Winston, eds., *Brookings Papers on Economic Activity* 181 (1993). Viscusi writes, "Although there is no evidence supporting the desire to ensure pain and suffering compensation in the case of job injuries, for less severe product injuries the evidence is consistent with such compensation. Thus pain and suffering compensation is potentially desirable from the standpoint of optimal insurance in the case of these minor injuries, whereas it is apparently not as desirable in the case of more severe outcomes." See also David Cook and Philip J. Graham, "Demand for Insurance and Protection: The Case of Irreplaceable Commodities," 91 *Q. J. Econ.* 143 (1977). Rare

examples of people buying insurance against pain are found in Steven P. Croley and Jon D. Hanson, "The Nonpecuniary Costs of Accidents: Pain-and-Suffering Damages in Tort Law," 108 *Harv. L. Rev.* 1785 (1995).

15 John E. Calfee, and Clifford Winston, supra note 13, at 152.

16 A. Mitchell Polinsky, and Yeon-Koo Che, "Decoupling Liability: Optimal Incentives for Care and Litigation," 22 *Rand J. Econ.* 562 (1991).

17 Cooter, "Towards a Market in Unmatured Tort Claims," supra note 11.

18 I agree with Craswell that this is a bit of a sham that confuses categories. Richard Craswell, "When Is a Willful Breach 'Willful'? General v. Specific Deterrence in Contract Remedies," paper read at American Law and Economics Association, Chicago (mimeo 1996).

19 A novel theory of punitive damages that would require changes in my argument is found in Andrew F. Daughtey and Jennifer Reinganum, "Settlement, Deterrence, and the Economics of Punitive Damages Reform," paper read at American Law and Economics Association, Toronto (mimeo 1997), which asserts that punitive damages can force a monopolist to represent product safety accurately.

20 George Priest, "The Invention of Enterprise Liability: A Critical History of the Intellectual Foundations of Modern Tort Law," 14 *J. Legal Stud.* 461 (1985); George Priest, "The Modern Expansion of Tort Liability: Its Source, Its Effect, and Its Reform," 5 *J. Econ. Perspectives* 31 (1991).

21 Gary Schwartz, "Directions in Contemporary Products Liability Scholarship," 14 *J. Legal Stud.* 763 (1985).

22 Lisa Bernstein, "Opting Out of the Legal System: Extralegal Contractual Relations in the Diamond Industry," 21 *J. Legal Stud.* 115 (1992).

23 Edward L. Rubin and Robert Cooter, *The Payment System: Cases, Materials, and Issues* (2d ed. 1994).

24 E. Allan Lind and Tom R. Tyler, *The Social Psychology of Procedural Justice: Critical Issues in Social Justice* (1988); Tom R. Tyler, *Why People Obey the Law* (1990).

25 O'Connell and Joost, supra note 11.

26 Rubin, supra note 11.

27 Huber, supra note 11.

28 Jonathan R. Macey and Geoffrey P. Miller, "The Plaintiffs' Attorney's Role in Class Action and Derivative Litigation: Economic Analysis and Recommendations for Reform," 58 *U. Chi. L. Rev.* 333 (1991); Randall S. Thomas and Robert G. Hansen, "Auctioning Class Action and Derivative Lawsuits: A Critical Analysis," 87 *Nw. U. L. Rev.* 423 (1992); Jonathan R. Macey and Geoffrey P. Miller, "Auctioning Class Action and Derivative Suits: A Rejoinder," 97 *Nw. U. L. Rev.* 458 (1993).

29 Painter, supra note 7.

30 The original paper on adhesion contracts seems utterly irrelevant to a modern understanding of markets. Friedrich Kessler, "Contracts of Adhesion—Some Thoughts about Freedom of Contract," 43 *Colum. L. Rev.* 629 (1943).

31 Hein Koetz, "Unfair Terms in Consumer Contracts: Recent Developments in Europe from a Comparative and Economic Perspective" (photocopy 1997).

32 Jim Gordley, "Equality in Exchange," 69 *Cal. L. Rev.* 1587 (1981).

33 Numerous games yield efficiency without competition, thus contradicting the spirit of general equilibrium theory. Numerous games yield inefficiency with low bargaining costs, thus contradicting the spirit of the Coase Theorem. In game theory, strategic behavior bears so little resemblance to other costs that labeling strategy as "transaction costs" obscures more than it clarifies.

34 Bator, "The Anatomy of Market Failure," 82 *Q. J. Econ.* (1958); Stephen Breyer, *Regulation and Its Reform* (1982); Charles L. Schultze, *The Public Use of Private Interest* (1977).

35 Kenneth J. Arrow, *Social Choice and Individual Values* (2d ed. 1963); James M. Buchanan, and Gordon Tullock, *The Calculus of Consent: Logical Foundations of Constitutional Democracy* (1967); Anthony Downs, *An Economic Theory of Democracy* (1957); Robin Farquharson, *Theory of Voting* (1969); Dennis Mueller, *Public Choice* (1st ed. 1979); Mancur Olson, *The Logic of Collective Action: Public Goods and the Theory of Groups* (1965); William Riker, *The Theory of Political Coalitions* (1962); Kenneth A. Shepsle, and Mark S. Bonchek, *Analyzing Politics: Rationality, Behavior, and Institutions* (1997); George Stigler, ed., *Chicago Studies in Political Economy* (1988).

36 William Niskanen, *Bureaucrats and Politicians* (1975); George Stigler, "The Government of the Economy," in R. W. C.a.R. S. Eckaus, ed., *Contemporary Issues in Economics,* (1972); George Stigler, *The Citizen and the State* (1975).

37 The formula is is extended in chapter 10 of Robert D. Cooter and Tom Ulen, *Law and Economics* (2d ed. 1996).

38 Ariel Rubinstein, "Perfect Equilibrium in a Bargaining Game," 50 *Econometrica* 97 (1982); Ariel Rubinstein, "On the Interpretation of Two Theoretical Models of Bargaining," in Kenneth Arrow et al., ed., *Barriers to Conflict Resolution* (1995); John Nash, "The Bargaining Problem," 18 *Econometrica* 155 (1950); R. Duncan Luce and Howard Raiffa, *Games and Decisions: Introduction and Critical Survey* 124 (1967).

39 See Cooter, "Towards a Market in Unmatured Tort Claims," supra note 11, at 383; Robert Cooter and Daniel Rubinfeld, "An Economic Model of Legal Discovery in the U.S.," 23 *J. Legal Stud.* 435 (1994).

Zoning by Private Contract

1   Garrett Hardin, "The Tragedy of the Commons," 162 *Sc.* 1243 (1968).

2   Bernard H. Siegan, *Land Use without Zoning* (1972).

3   Steven E. Barton and Carol J. Silverman, Preface, in Steven E. Barton and Carol J. Silverman, eds., *Common Interest Communities: Private Governments and the Public Interest* (1994).

4   *Community Associations Factbook* 3 (1998).

5   Id. at 19.

6   C. James Dowden, *Community Associations and Local Governments: The Need for Recognition and Reassessment in Residential Community Associations: Private Governments in the Intergovernmental System?* 27 (U.S. Advisory Commission on Intergovernmental Relations, 1989).

7   See *Community Associations Factbook,* supra note 4, at 19.

8   This history draws on Evan McKenzie, *Privatopia: Homeowner Associations and the Rise of Residential Private Government* (1994).

9   David T. Beito, "The Formation of Urban Infrastructure through Nongovernmental Planning: The Private Places of St. Louis, 1869–1920," 16 *J. Urban Hist.* 283 (1990).

10 See Robert G. Natelson, "Comments on the Historiography of Condominium: The Myth of Roman Origin," 12 *Ok. City L. Rev.* 28 (1987).

11 Id. at 31.

12 D. Clurman, F. Jackson, and E. Hebard, *Condominiums and Cooperatives* (1984).

13 Marc A. Weiss and John W. Watts, "Community Builders and Community Associa-

tions: The Role of Real Estate Developers in Private Residential Governance," in *Residential Community Associations*, supra note 6, at 101.

14 Curtis Sproul, "The Many Faces of Community Associations under California Law," in *Residential Community Associations*, supra note 6, at 65–67.

15 Dowden, supra note 6.

16 Barton and Silverman, supra note 3, at 39.

17 Uriel Reichman, "Residential Private Governments: An Introductory Survey," 43 *U. Chi. L. Rev.* 253 (1976).

18 See Barton and Silverman, supra note 3; McKenzie, supra note 8; R. J. Dilger, *Neighborhood Politics: Residential Commmunity Associations in American Governance* (1992); Edward J. Blakely and Mary Gail Snyder, *Fortress America: Gated Communities in the United States* (1997).

19 A. Dan Tarlock, "Residential Community Associations and Land Use Controls," in *Residential Community Associations*, supra note 6, at 76.

20 Richard A. Epstein, "Notice and Freedom of Contract in the Law of Servitudes," 55 *S. Cal. L. Rev.* 1353 (1982).

21 Adolf Berle and Gardner Means, *The Modern Corporation and Private Property* (1932).

22 See J. Harris, *Property and Justice* (1996); Carol M. Rose, *Property and Persuasion: Essays on the History, Theory, and Rhetoric of Ownership* (1994). Of course, the spread of individual ownership was itself a development only a few centuries old. It was part of the evolution of property right institutions by which capitalism supplanted feudalism as the dominant social form.

23 For reviews of this literature, see W. Fishel, *The Economics of Zoning Laws: A Property Right Approach to American Land Use Controls* (1985); W. Fishel, *Regulatory Takings: Law, Economics, and Politics* (1995).

24 See Seymour Toll, *Zoned American* 172–87 (1969); Edward M. Basset, *Zoning: The Laws, Administration, and Court Decisions during the First Twenty Years* (1936).

25 *Village of Euclid v. Ambler Realty Co.*, 272 U.S. 394 (1926).

26 A. Dan Tarlock, "Euclid Revisited," 34 *Land Use L.* 8 (1982).

27 *A City Planning Primer* (Advisory Committee on Zoning, U.S. Department of Commerce, 1928).

28 Charles Haar, "In Accordance with a Comprehensive Plan," 68 *Harv. L. Rev.* 1154 (1955).

29 James Huffman and R. Plantico, "Toward a Theory of Land Use Planning: Lessons from Oregon," 14 *Land & Water L. Rev.* (1979).

30 See Richard Babcock, *The Zoning Game: Municipal Practices and Policies* (1966).

31 Dennis J. Coyle, *Property Rights and the Constitutution: Shaping Society through Land Use Regulation* 18 (1993).

32 See Robert H. Nelson, *Zoning and Property Rights: An Analysis of the American System of Land Use Regulation* (1977); Robert H. Nelson, "Zoning Myth and Practice: From Euclid into the Future," in Charles M. Haar and Jerold S. Kayden, eds., *Zoning and the American Dream: Promises Yet to Keep* (1989); Robert H. Nelson, "The Privatisation of Local Government: From Zoning to RCAs," in *Residential Community Associations*, supra note 6.

33 *Building the American City: Report of the National Commission on Urban Problems* 7 (1969).

34 Id. at 16.

35 Id. at 248.

36 One scholar who did follow up on the commission concept was Dan Tarlock. See A. Dan Tarlock, "Toward a Revised Theory of Zoning," in F. S. Bangs, ed., *Land Use Controls Annual* (American Society of Planning Officials, 1972).

37 In other countries, there have been official "land pooling" programs whereby the government condemns property in an area expected to be redeveloped in a whole new use, and then pays the original property owners by assigning them new rights in the overall collective land holding resulting from the pooling effort. See William A. Doebele, ed., *Land Readjustment: A Different Approach to Financing Urbanization* (1982).

38 See Robert C. Ellickson, "Alternatives to Zoning: Covenants, Nuisance Rules, and Fines as Land Use Controls," 40 *U. Chi. L. Rev.* 681 (1973); Robert C. Ellickson, "Suburban Growth Controls: An Economic and Legal Analysis," 86 *Yale L. J.* 385 (1977).

39 See George W. Liebmann, "Devolution of Power to Community and Block Associations," 25 *Urban Law.* 335 (1993).

40 Fischel, *The Economics of Zoning Laws*, supra note 23, at 65.

41 Sidney Plotkin, *Keep Out: The Struggle for Land Use Control* (1987).

42 Joseph F. DiMento et al., "Land Development and Environmental Control in the California Supreme Court: The Deferential, the Preservationist, and the Preservationist-Erratic Eras," 27 *UCLA L. Rev.* 872 (1980).

43 Robert H. Nelson, "Private Rights to Government Actions: How Modern Property Rights Evolve," 1986 *U. Ill. L. Rev.* 361.

44 Oliver Wendell Holmes, *The Common Law* (1881).

45 Frederick Pollock, *The Land Laws* 62 (1883).

46 Id. at 51–52.

47 See also Robert H. Nelson, *Public Lands and Private Rights: The Failure of Scientific Management* (1995); Robert H. Nelson, *The Making of Federal Coal Policy* (1983).

Dealing With the NIMBY Problem

1 Thomas K. Rudel, *Situations and Strategies in American Land-Use Planning* (1989).

2 William A. Fischel, *Do Growth Controls Matter?* (1990); Mingche M. Li and H. James Brown, "Micro-Neighborhood Externalities and Hedonic Housing Prices," 56 *Land Econ.* 125 (1980).

3 James M. Burns, J. W. Peltason, Thomas E. Cronin, and David B. Magleby, *State and Local Politics: Government by the People* (7th ed. 1993); Peter H. Rossi and Eleanor Weber, "The Social Benefits of Homeownership: Empirical Evidence from National Surveys," 1 *Housing Policy Debate* 7 (1996); Pamela H. Moomau and Rebecca Morton, "Revealed Preferences for Property Taxes: An Empirical Study of Perceived Tax Incidence," 74 *Rev. Econ. Stat.* 176 (1992).

4 William A. Fischel, *The Economics of Zoning Laws* (1985).

5 By *disfranchise* I mean a voting procedure that guarantees that they will not have a majority, not that they cannot vote at all.

6 Uriel Reichman, "Residential Private Governments: An Introductory Survey," 43 *U. Chi. L. Rev.* 253 (1976).

7 J. F. Martin, *Profits in the Wilderness: Entrepreneurship and the Founding of New England Towns in the Seventeenth Century* (1991).

8 Foster City History Project Committee, *A New Town Comes of Age* (1985).

9 Theodore M. Crone, "Elements of an Economic Justification for Municipal Zoning," 14 *J. Urban Econ.* 168 (1983).

10 William A. Fischel, "Zoning, Nonconvexities, and T. Jack Foster's City," 35 *J. Urban Econ.* 175 (1994).

11 Robert H. Nelson, *Zoning and Property Rights* (1977).

12 William A. Fischel, "Equity and Efficiency Aspects of Zoning Reform," 27 *Public Policy* 301 (1979).

13 William A. Fischel, *Regulatory Takings: Law, Economics, and Politics* (1995).

14 Robert C. Ellickson, "Suburban Growth Controls: An Economic and Legal Analysis," 86 *Yale L. J.* 385 (1977).

15 Randall G. Holcombe, "The Median Voter Model in Public Choice Theory," 61 *Public Choice* 115 (1977); Douglas Holtz-Eakin and Harvey S. Rosen, "The 'Rationality' of Municipal Capital Spending: Evidence from New Jersey," 19 *Regional Science and Urban Economics* 517 (1989).

16 Anthony Downs, *Opening Up the Suburbs: An Urban Strategy for America* (1973); Anthony Downs, *New Visions for Metropolitan America* (1994).

17 Timothy J. Bartik, *Who Benefits from State and Local Economic Development Policies?* (1991).

18 James C. Clingemeyer, "Distributive Politics, Ward Representation, and the Spread of Zoning," 77 *Public Choice* 725 (1993); Peter Linneman and Anita A. Summers, "Patterns of Urban Population Decentralization in the United States 1970–1987," Wharton Real Estate Center Working Paper #76, University of Pennsylvania, 1990.

19 John F. McDonald, "Houston Remains Unzoned," 71 *Land Economics* 137 (1995).

20 Robert Tannenwald, "State Business Tax Climate: How Should It Be Measured and How Important Is It?," *New Eng. Econ. Rev.* 23 (January/February 1996).

21 Terry Jill Lassar, ed., *City Deal Making* (1990).

22 William A. Fischel, *The Economics of Zoning Laws* 224 (1985); David L. Callies, *Preserving Paradise: Why Regulation Won't Work* (1994); Robert G. Healy and John S. Rosenberg, *Land Use and the States* (2d ed. 1979).

23 Fischel, supra note 22.

24 Louis A. Rose, "Urban Land Supply: Natural and Contrived Restrictions," 25 *J. Urban Econ.* 325 (1989); James A. Thorson, "An Examination of the Monopoly Zoning Hypothesis," 72 *Land Economics* 43 (1996).

25 Gerrit Knaap and Arthur C. Nelson, *The Regulated Landscape: Lessons on State Land Use Planning from Oregon* (1992).

26 Carl Abbott, "The Portland Region: Where City and Suburbs Talk to Each Other— and Often Agree," 1 *Housing Policy Debate* 11 (1997).

27 William A. Fischel, Comment on Carl Abbott's "The Portland Region: Where City and Suburbs Talk with Each Other—and Often Agree," 1 *Housing Policy Debate* 65 (1997).

28 Gerrit Knaap, "The Price Effects of Urban Growth Boundaries in Metropolitan Portland, Oregon," 61 *Land Econ.* 28 (1985).

29 Gerald C. Mildner, Kenneth J. Dueker, and Anthony M. Rufolo, "Impact of the Urban Growth Boundary on Metropolitan Housing Markets," Portland State University, Center for Urban Studies, 10 May 1996.

30 Lawrence Hannah, Kyung-Hwan Kim, and Edwin S. Mills, "Land Use Controls and Housing Prices in Korea," 30 *Urban Stud.* 147 (1993).

31 Stephen Mayo and Stephen Sheppard, "Housing Supply under Rapid Economic Growth and Varying Regulatory Stringency: An International Comparison," 5 *J. Housing Econ.* 274 (1996).

32   Paul Cheshire and Stephen Sheppard, "British Planning Policy and Access to Hous-
       ing: Some Empirical Estimates," 26 *Urban Stud.* 469 (1989).
33   William A. Fischel, "Centralized Control: Do We Want a Double-Veto System?," 55
       American Planning Asso. Journal 205 (Spring 1989).

Devolutionary Proposals and Contractarian Principles

1   See, e.g., Robert C. Ellickson, "Cities and Homeowners Associations," 130 *U. Pa. L.
      Rev.* 1519 (1982); Gregory Alexander, "Dilemmas of Group Autonomy: Residential As-
      sociations and Community," 75 *Cornell L. Rev.* 1 (1989).
2   Alexander, supra note 1.
3   Robert H. Nelson, "Zoning by Private Contract," this volume. See also Nelson's *Zon-
      ing and Property Rights* (1977) and *The Privatization of Local Government: From Zon-
      ing to RCAs, in Residential Community Associations: Private Governments in the
      Intergovernmental System?* 45 (1989).
4   Clifford J. Treese, ed., *Community Associations Factbook* 13 (1993).
5   Evan McKenzie, *Privatopia: Homeowner Associations and the Rise of Residential Pri-
      vate Government* 120 (1994).
6   See Ronald H. Coase, "The Problem of Social Cost," 3 *J. L. & Econ.* 1 (1960).
7   William A. Fischel, *The Economics of Zoning Laws* 21 (1985) (citing Robert H. Nelson,
      Zoning and Property Rights [1977]).
8   James W. Ely Jr., *The Guardian of Every Other Right: A Constitutional History of Prop-
      erty Rights* 11 (2d ed. 1998).
9   *Village of Euclid v. Ambler Realty Co.*, 272 U.S. 365 (1926). "The ordinance . . . and all
      similar laws . . . must find their justification in some aspect of the police power, as-
      serted for the public welfare. The line which . . . separates the legitimate from the ille-
      gitimate assumption of power is not capable of precise delimitation. . . . A nuisance
      may be merely a right thing in the wrong place, like a pig in the parlor instead of the
      barnyard." Id. at 387–88. Whatever specific dangers might result from the evils touched
      upon in *Euclid* could have been solved by means far less sweeping than comprehensive
      zoning. See Richard A. Epstein, *Takings: Private Property and the Power of Eminent
      Domain* 132–34 (1985).
10   Seminal works include Kenneth Arrow, *Social Choice and Individual Values* (1951);
      Anthony Downs, *An Economic Theory of Democracy* (1957); and James Buchanan
      and Gordon Tullock, *The Calculus of Consent* (1962).
11   See Jonathan R. Macey, "Promoting Public-Regarding Legislation through Statutory
      Interpretation: An Interest Group Model," 86 *Colum. L. Rev.* 223, 229 (1986).
12   See generally Robert C. Ellickson, "Suburban Growth Controls: An Economic and Le-
      gal Analysis," 86 *Yale L. J.* 385 (1977).
13   See, e.g., *Adkins v. Children's Hospital*, 261 U.S. 525, 546 (1923) (invalidating mini-
      mum wage for women in the District of Columbia as violative of freedom of contract
      and due process).
14   Ellen Frankel Paul, "George Sutherland," in *The Oxford Companion to the Supreme
      Court of the United States*, ed. Kermit L. Hall, 848, 849 (1992).
15   Joel Francis Paschal, *Mr. Justice Sutherland: A Man against the State* 126–27, 166,
      242–43 (1951).
16   Hadley Arkes, *The Return of George Sutherland: Restoring a Jurisprudence of Natu-
      ral Rights* 70–71 (1994).

17 See Robert C. Ellickson, "The Irony of 'Inclusionary Zoning'," 54 *S. Cal. L. Rev.* 1167 (1981).

18 See James M. Buchanan, "Rights, Efficiency, and Exchange: The Irrelevance of Transaction Cost," rpt. in Robert D. Tollison and Viktor J. Vanberg, eds., *Economics: Between Predictive Science and Moral Philosophy* 161 (1987), quoted in Todd J. Zywicki, "A Unanimity-Reinforcing Model of Efficiency in the Common Law: An Institutional Comparison of Common Law and Legislative Solutions to Large-Number Externality Problems," 46 *Case W. Res. L. Rev.* 961, 968 n. 23 (1996).

19 See Zywicki, id., at 966 n. 12.

20 David Millon, "Communitarianism in Corporate Law: Foundations and Law Reform Strategies," in Lawrence E. Mitchell, ed., *Progressive Corporate Law*, at 1, 5 (1995).

21 Stephen M. Bainbridge, "Community and Statism: A Conservative Contractarian Critique of Progressive Corporate Law Scholarship," 82 *Cornell L. Rev.* 856, 895 n. 199 (1997).

22 The belief that individual property ownership was vital to a culture of family self-reliance and liberty was most pronounced among the Southern Agrarians. See, e.g., M. E. Bradford, *Remembering Who We Are: Observations of a Southern Conservative* 86 (1985).

23 See *Adkins v. Children's Hospital*, 261 U.S. 525, 556–57 (1923); Arkes, supra note 16, at 75–78.

24 Pope Pius XI, *Quadragesimo Anno* (1939).

25 See generally George J. Stigler, "The Theory of Economic Regulation," 2 *Bell J. Econ. & Mgt. Sci.* 3 (1971).

26 See Charles Tiebout, "A Pure Theory of Local Expenditures," 64 *J. Pol. Econ.* 416 (1956).

27 See Vicki Been, "'Exit' as a Constraint on Land Use Exactions: Rethinking the Unconstitutional Conditions Doctrine," 91 *Colum. L. Rev.* 473 (1991).

28 See Clint Bolick, *Grassroots Tyranny: The Limits of Federalism* (1993).

29 See McKenzie, supra note 5.

30 James Madison, *The Federalist No. 10*, ed. Clinton Rossiter, at 83 (1983).

31 See Guido Calabresi and A. Douglas Melamed, "Property Rules, Liability Rules, and Inalienability: One View of the Cathedral," 85 *Harv. L. Rev.* 1089 (1972).

32 See Patrick J. Rohan, *Powell on Real Property*, ¶ 876.13[1] (rev. ed. 1994); *Kohl v. United States*, 91 U.S. 367 (1875).

33 U.S. Const. amend. V (1791) ("[N]or shall private property be taken for public use, without just compensation"). The NA would be regarded as an agent of the state and hence subject to its constraints. See *Reilly Tar & Chem. Corp. v. St. Louis Park*, 121 N. W.2d 393 (Minn. 1963).

34 See *Coniston Corp. v. Village of Hoffman Estates*, 844 F.2d 461, 464 (7th Cir. 1988).

35 James M. Buchanan, "Introduction: L. S. E. Cost Theory in Retrospect," in *L. S. E. Essays on Cost*, 1, 14–15 (quoted in Zywicki, supra note 18, at 966).

36 See Lawson Gary, "Efficiency and Individualism," 42 *Duke L. J.* 53, 57 (1992) ("to the extent that the term 'efficiency' refers to human satisfaction, it is incoherent or empty whenever a large number of people are involved").

37 Steven J. Eagle, *Regulatory Takings* §3–7(d) (1996). See also Thomas W. Merrill, "The Economics of Public Use," 72 *Cornell L. Rev.* 61 (1986).

38 *Hawaii Housing Authority v. Midkiff*, 467 U.S. 229, 240 (1984) (declaring the public use requirement "coterminous with the scope of a sovereign's police powers").

39 For a discussion of problems in defining groups of market actors, see Robert Pitofsky, "New Definitions of Relevant Market and the Assault on Antitrust," 90 *Colum. L. Rev.* 1805, 1806–7 (1990).

40 See Ronald H. Coase, "The Problem of Social Cost," 3 *J. L. & Econ.* 1 (1960).

41 See Zywicki, supra note 18, at 968.

42 See Gordon Tullock, "The Welfare Costs of Tariffs, Monopolies, and Theft," 5 *Western Econ. J.* 224 (1967), Anne O. Krueger, "The Political Economy of the Rent-Seeking Society," 64 *Amer. Econ. Rev.* 291 (1974).

43 Gordon Tullock, "Rent Seeking," in Charles Rowley, ed., *Property Rights and the Limits of Democracy* 66 (1993).

44 See, e.g., Robert G. Natelson, "Condominiums, Reform, and the Unit Ownership Act," 58 *Mont. L. Rev.* 495 (1997).

45 Friedrich A. Hayek, *The Fatal Conceit* 27 (1988).

46 See Friedrich A. Hayek, *Individualism and Economic Order*, chs. 7–9 (1980 [1948]).

47 See Ludwig von Mises, "Economic Calculation in the Socialist Commonwealth," in Friedrich A. Hayek, ed., *Collectivist Economic Planning* (1935).

48 E.g., *Carlino v. Whitpain Investors*, 453 A.2d 1385, 1388 (Pa. 1982) ("Zoning is an exercise of the police power to serve the common good and general welfare. It is elementary that the legislative function may not be surrendered or curtailed by bargain").

49 Robert C. Ellickson, "Cities and Homeowners' Associations," 130 *U. Pa. L. Rev.* 1519, 1526–27 (1982).

50 *Nahrstedt v. Lakeside Village Condominium Ass'n*, 878 P.2d 1275, 1282 (Cal. 1994) (quoting Robert G. Natelson, "Consent, Coercion, and 'Reasonableness' in Private Law: The Special Case of the Property Owners Association," 51 *Ohio State L. J.* 41, 47 [1990]).

51 See, e.g., Gregory S. Alexander, "Dilemmas of Group Autonomy: Residential Associations and Community," 75 *Cornell L. Rev.* 1 (1989); Harvey Rishikof and Alexander Wohl, "Private Communities or Public Governments: 'The State Will Make the Call'," 30 *Val. U. L. Rev.* 509 (1996). See also Robert Reich, "Secession of the Successful," *N.Y. Times Magazine*, 20 Jan. 1991, at 42.

52 E.g., Richard Thompson Ford, "The Boundaries of Race: Political Geography in Legal Analysis," 107 *Harv. L. Rev.* 1841, 1884 n.131 (1994) ("The fetishism of origins that characterizes the contractarian notion of association is ill-suited to a spatial context in which the original 'contract' affects individuals distant from the agreement in both space and time. . . . It is this feature that makes the association's rules more like a government than a private contract").

The (Limited) Ability of Urban Neighbors to Contract for the Provision of Local Public Goods

I thank Clay Gillette for a comment and Julie Becker for able research assistance.

1 Robert H. Nelson, "Private Zoning by Contract," this volume.

2 I previously have argued in favor of alternatives more decentralized than municipal zoning. See Robert C. Ellickson, "Alternatives to Zoning: Covenants, Nuisance Rules, and Fines as Land Use Controls," 40 *U. Chi. L. Rev.* 683 (1973).

3 See Nelson, supra note 1; George W. Liebmann, "Devolution of Power to Community and Block Associations," 25 *Urb. Law.* 335, 381 (1993).

4 Nelson, Liebmann, and I differ, however, on many details. These differences are explored in Robert C. Ellickson, "New Institutions for Old Neighborhoods," 47 *Duke L. J.* 75 (1998).

5 Id.

6 See, e.g., Cal. Sts. & High. Code §§ 36600–36651 (West Supp. 1997) (first enacted in 1994); N.Y. Gen. Mun. Law § 980 (McKinney Supp. 1997) (first enacted in 1989); David J. Kennedy, "Restraining the Power of Business Improvement Districts: The Case of the Grand Central Partnership," 15 *Yale L. & Policy Rev.* 283, 285–93 (1996) (discussing rise of BIDs).

7 See, e.g., Mark S. Davies, "Business Improvement Districts," 52 *Wash. U. J. Urb. & Contemp. L.* 187 (1997) (generally favorable assessment of BIDs); Lawrence O. Houstoun Jr., "Gotham Gets Civil," *Urb. Land*, Oct. 1997, at 80 (on contributions of New York City's forty BIDs); but cf. Kennedy, supra note 6 (criticizing amount of power that property owners have over BIDs).

8 I borrow *face-block* from Gerald D. Suttles, *The Social Construction of Community* 55–57 (1972). Suttles asserts that urbanites regard these as the smallest residential collectivities.

9 See Howard W. Hallman, *Neighborhoods: Their Place in Urban Life* 68–69 (1984) (discussing efficiencies of scale and scope in provision of public goods). A neighborhood-wide entity, it should be noted, has some potential advantages over a block-level organization. The block is too small a unit for provision of a public good that involves either significant scale efficiencies or positive externalities that cannot be dealt with at the block level. In addition, a block-level government may be prone to render decisions that are good for the block but bad for the neighborhood.

10 See James Q. Wilson and George L. Kelling, "Broken Windows: The Police and Neighborhood Safety," *Atlantic Monthly*, Mar. 1982, at 29, 31–32.

11 See Matthew A. Crenson, *Neighborhood Politics* 114–20 (1983) (reporting survey results indicating that lower-income people strongly dislike dirt, dilapidation, and crime); Wesley G. Skogan, *Disorder and Decline: Crime and the Spiral of Decay in American Neighborhoods* 56 (1990) (reporting +.88 correlation in assessments of street disorder between higher- and lower-income respondents, and +.87 correlation between blacks and whites).

12 See, e.g., Craig Horowitz, "The Suddenly Safer City," *New York Magazine*, Aug. 14, 1995, at 20; Dan M. Kahan, "Social Influence, Social Meaning, and Deterrence," 83 *Va. L. Rev.* 349, 367–69 (1997).

13 On the theory of public goods, see Harvey S. Rosen, *Public Finance* 61–74 (4th ed. 1995); Robert Jay Dilger, *Neighborhood Politics: Residential Community Associations in American Governance* 105–15 (1992) (discussing the free-riding problem in context of community governance). But cf. Fred Foldvary, *Public Goods and Private Communities: The Market Provision of Social Services* 1–16 (1994) (arguing that most commentators exaggerate risks of free-riding).

14 This evidence is not conclusive because new neighborhoods tend to have somewhat different physical layouts and social dynamics than old ones do.

15 On the history of RCAs in the United States, see Dilger, supra note 13, at 41–60.

16 See id. at 89–90.

17 Id. at 20. RCAs tend to be somewhat less populous than the ancient Athenian *deme*, which had an average adult population of about four hundred. See Liebmann, supra note 3, at 372–73.

18 The sizing of private street associations in St. Louis County also supports this infer-
    ence. A survey of four St. Louis suburbs found that the average size of associations
    ranged from 21 to 102 dwelling units. See Ronald J. Oakerson, "Private Street Associa-
    tions in St. Louis County," in Advisory Commission on Intergovernmental Relations,
    Residential Community Associations 55, 56 (1989).

19 See Eugene L. Meyer, "Love It or Leave It . . . Why I Decided to Go," Wash. *Post*, Apr.
    21, 1996, at C1: "In the Blizzard of '96, on 17th Street, we saw our first plow a full nine
    days after the snow fell. Trash wasn't picked up for almost a month." See generally
    Fred Siegel, *The Future Once Happened Here* (1997) (on the woes of New York City,
    Los Angeles, and District of Columbia).

20 See Stephen Coate and Stephen Morris, "On the Form of Transfers to Special Inter-
    ests," 103 *J. Pol. Econ.* 1210 (1995) (attributing inefficiency of transfers to voters' im-
    perfect information). Relatedly, some city administrations may deliberately discrimi-
    nate in delivering services, particularly against neighborhoods whose residents have
    declined to support the incumbent political party.

21 Most members of RCA boards consider local governments to be no more efficient
    than RCAs in providing local services (with the possible exceptions of street lighting
    and street repair). See Dilger, supra note 13, at 22–23.

22 On the optimal size of territorial clubs engaging in Tiebout-style competition, see
    Foldvary, supra note 13, at 62–78.

23 See Liebmann, supra note 3, at 336–39; see also id. at 372–79 (reviewing the views of
    Rousseau, Jefferson, de Tocqueville, and others on the advantages of decentralized
    government).

24 A survey conducted in a random sample of Baltimore neighborhoods found that the
    great majority of respondents regarded most neighbors on the same block as either
    "friends" or "acquaintances." See Crenson, supra note 11, at 100.

25 See, e.g., Michael J. Sandel, *Democracy's Discontent* (1996); Robert D. Putnam,
    "Bowling Alone: America's Declining Social Capital," 6 *J. Democracy* 65 (1995).

26 There is a lively debate over whether an institution governed by property owners can
    provide true opportunities for meaningful participation in community life. See
    Dilger, supra note 13, at 36–40, 131–44, 153–54. For a skeptical view, see Gregory S.
    Alexander, "Dilemmas of Group Autonomy: Residential Associations and Commu-
    nity," 75 *Cornell L. Rev.* 1 (1990). Like many analysts, Alexander embraces the statist
    perspective that participation in the affairs of governments—"civic participation"
    —is inherently more fulfilling than participation in the myriad forms of collective
    social endeavor. See id. at 43–47; see also Sandel, supra note 25, at 331–33 (arguing
    that *private* territorial institutions such as RCAs diminish civic resources because
    they provide substitutes for the *public* places where the rich and poor might com-
    mingle). But see, e.g., Putnam, supra note 25 (stressing importance of a strong civil
    society, in which participation in governmental affairs is just one form of collective
    endeavor).

27 For a general overview, see Elinor Ostrom, *Governing the Commons: The Evolution
    of Institutions for Collective Action* (1990).

28 On the concept of social capital, see James S. Coleman, *Foundations of Social Theory*
    300–21 (1990); Robert D. Putnam, *Making Democracy Work* 161–85 (1993).

29 Jane Jacobs, *The Death and Life of Great American Cities* 35–37 (1961).

30 Laboratory experiments indicate that the ability to communicate significantly re-
    duces free-riding in the supply of public goods. See Gary J. Miller, "The Impact of Eco-

nomics on Contemporary Political Science," 35 *J. Econ. Lit.* 1173, 1179–81 (1997) (reviewing the literature).

31 See Oakerson, supra note 18, at 59–60 (concluding that the smallness of private street associations in St. Louis was essential to their success in smoothly solving collective action problems). See George W. Liebmann, *The Little Platoons: Sub-Local Governments in Modern History* 55–56 (1995) (noting that residents were more likely to participate in block-level, than neighborhood-level, organizations involved in War on Poverty programs).

32 See sources cited in Robert C. Ellickson, *Order without Law* 182 nn. 48–49 (1991).

33 See generally Crenson, supra note 11 (describing neighborhood organizations).

34 Frazier asserts (without citing authority) that the number of voluntary block associations operating in New York City increased from a few hundred to over one thousand between 1965 and 1980. See Mark Frazier, "Privatizing the City," 12 *Policy Rev.* 91, 95 (1980).

35 This calculus is an offshoot of one developed in Frank I. Michelman, "Property, Utility, and Fairness: Comments on the Ethical Foundations of Just Compensation Law," 80 *Harv. L. Rev.* 1165, 1214–15 (1967).

36 Coercion may be difficult to detect because a landowner might decline to join a movement to create a block association for a strategic reason (such as the prospect of a large payoff), not on account of disagreement over the association's desirability.

37 See John Rawls, *A Theory of Justice* 22–33 (1971).

38 See, e.g., N. C. Gen. Stat. §§ 120–163, 120–172 (1997) (authorizing 50 percent of registered voters within boundaries of proposed municipality to make decision for all its residents and landowners).

39 See John F. Hart, "Colonial Land Use Law and Its Significance for Modern Takings Doctrine," 109 *Harv. L. Rev.* 1252, 1268–72 (1996).

40 See Bruce M. Kramer and Patrick H. Martin, The Law of Pooling and Unitization (3d ed. 1980).

41 See *City of Seattle v. Rogers Clothing for Men,* 787 P.2d 39 (Wash. 1990) (upholding procedure authorizing businesses liable for 60 percent of assessments to create BID).

42 See Dilger, supra note 13, at 91–93.

43 See Robert C. Ellickson and A. Dan Tarlock, *Land-Use Controls* 693–94 (1981).

44 Crenson, supra note 11, at 173–74, 211.

45 Id. at 196, 260; Skogan, supra note 11, at 133.

46 A notion developed in Hallman, supra note 9, at 209–11.

47 Stability and homogeneity abet block mobilization by enhancing social cohesion. See Crenson, supra note 11, at 176 (presenting positive correlations between socioeconomic homogeneity and levels of informal efforts to improve streets); Skogan, supra note 11, at 17–18 (on failure of block clubs in heterogeneous, high-turnover neighborhoods); Suttles, supra note 8, at 21–43 (discussing social attributes of "defended neighborhoods"). For this reason, Herbert Gans, who opposes homogeneity at the level of the city, generally favors it at the block level. See Herbert Gans, "The Balanced Community: Homogeneity or Heterogeneity in Residential Areas?," in Jon Pynoos et al., eds., *Housing Urban America* 135, 137 (1973). See generally Henry Hansmann, *The Ownership of Enterprise* (1996) (passim) (on how homogeneity of interests facilitates governance).

48 See Crenson, supra note 11, at 112–13 (noting that black residents of inner-city areas are especially likely to identify with block-level territories); id. at 114–120 (asserting

that residents of poor and predominantly black areas tend to be greatly dissatisfied with neighborhood conditions); Skogan, supra note 11 (arguing that social and physical disorder demoralizes and angers all urban residents).

49 Robert B. Reich, "Secession of the Successful," *N.Y. Times Magazine*, Jan. 20, 1991, at 16.

A Contract Theory of Marriage

For a further elaboration of some of this essay's themes, see Elizabeth S. Scott and Robert E. Scott, "Marriage as Relational Contract," 84 *Va. L. Rev.* 1225 (1998).

1 1997 La. Sess. Law Serv. Act 1380 (H. B. 756) (West), amending and reenacting Civ. Code Art. 102–3, Rev. Stat. 9:234, 9:245(A)(1), 9:224(C), 9:225(A)(3), 9:272–75, 9:307–9 (divorce available only on fault ground or after a two-year separation).

2 Milton Regan, "Market Discourse and Moral Neutrality in Divorce Law," 1994 *Utah L. Rev.* 605, 620, 627; Bruce Hafen, "Individualism and Autonomy in Family Law: The Waning of Belonging," 1991 *B. Y. U. L. Rev.* 1, 2; Mary Ann Glendon, *Abortion and Divorce in Western Law* 78 (1987); Mary Ann Glendon, *Rights Talk: The Impoverishment of Political Discourse* 12 (1991); William Galston, "Divorce American Style," 1996 *Public Interest* 12, 13 (1996); Amitai Etzioni, *The Spirit of Community: Rights, Responsibilities, and the Communitarian Agenda* 3–4 (1993).

3 Margaret Brinig and Steven Crafton, "Marriage and Opportunism," 23 *J. Legal Stud.* 869, 871 (1994); Lloyd Cohen, "Marriage, Divorce, and Quasi-rents; Or 'I Gave Him the Best Years of My Life'," 16 *J. Legal Stud.* 267, 275, 289, 303 (1987); Elisabeth Landes, "The Economics of Alimony," 7 *J. Legal Stud.* 35, 44 (1978).

4 Martin Zelder, "Inefficient Dissolutions as a Consequence of Public Goods: The Case of No-Fault Divorce," 22 *J. Legal Stud.* 503 (1993).

5 Charles J. Goetz and Robert E. Scott, "Principles of Relational Contracts," 67 *Va. L. Rev.* 1089 (1981).

6 Robert E. Scott, "Conflict and Cooperation in Long-Term Contracts," 75 *Cal. L. Rev.* 2005 (1987).

7 Stephen Sugarman, "Dividing Financial Interests on Divorce," in Stephen Sugarman and Herma Hill Kay, eds., *Divorce Reform at the Crossroads* 130, 149 (1991); Greg Duncan and Saul Hoffman, "A Reconsideration of the Economic Consequences of Marital Dissolution," 22 *Demography* 485 (1985).

8 Jana Singer, "The Privatization of Family Law," 1992 *Wis. L. Rev.* 1443, 1445 (1992).

9 Carl Schneider, "Moral Discourse and the Transformation of American Family Law," 83 *Mich. L. Rev.* 1803, 1807–08 (1985).

10 Singer, supra note 8.

11 Sally Sharp, "Semantics as Jurisprudence: The Elevation of Form over Substance in the Treatment of Separation Agreements in North Carolina," 69 *N. C. L. Rev.* 319, 326–27 (1991); Regan, supra note 2.

12 Uniform Marriage and Divorce Act, 9A U. L. A. § 306 (b) (West 1987).

13 Robert Mnookin, "Divorce Bargaining: The Limits on Private Ordering," 18 *U. Mich. J. L. Reform* 1015 (1985); Robert Mnookin and Lewis Kornhauser, "Bargaining in the Shadow of the Law: The Case for Divorce," 88 *Yale L. J.* 950, (1979).

14 American Law Institute, *Principles of the Law of Family Dissolution: Analysis and Recommendations*, Proposed Final Draft, part 1 §5.02 (1997).

15 Under the language of the Uniform Act, the only basis for setting aside a fairly exe-

cuted contract which greatly disadvantages one party is if support terms result in one party's eligibility for public assistance. Uniform Premarital Agreement Act, 9B U.L.A. §6(b) (West 1987). The comment to §6, on enforcement of premarital agreements, expressly refers to the "standard of unconscionability . . . used in commercial law, [and adopted by §306(b) of UMDA,] whose meaning includes protection against one-sidedness, oppression, or unfair surprise." The statute provides in §3(b) that "[t]he right of a child to support may not be adversely affected by a premarital agreement."

16 Jeffrey Stake, "Mandatory Planning for Divorce," 45 *Vand. L. Rev.* 397 (1992).

17 18 Cal.3d 660, 665, 557 P.2d 106, 110, 134 Cal. Rptr. 815, 819 (1976) (in a suit for "palimony," which followed the dissolution of the parties' long-term unmarried cohabitation, the court established that cohabiting couples' agreements regarding their property and support rights are enforceable under express and implied contract theories).

18 Hafen, supra note 2; Regan, supra note 2.

19 Schneider, supra note 9, at 1859.

20 John Robertson, *Children of Choice: Freedom and the New Reproductive Technologies* (1994).

21 Regan, supra note 2; Milton Regan, *Family Law and the Pursuit of Intimacy* 650, 635, 637 (1993); Galston, supra note 2.

22 Brinig and Crafton, supra note 3; Cohen, supra note 3; Jeffrey Stake, supra note 16.

23 Jana Singer, supra note 8, at 1445; Herma Kay, "An Appraisal of California's No-Fault Divorce Law," 75 *Cal. L. Rev.* 291, 318 (1987); Martha Fineman, "The Uses of Social Science Data in Legal Policymaking: Custody Determinations at Divorce," 1987 *Wis. L. Rev.* 107, 121, 140, 147–48.

24 Stephen Sugarman, "Dividing Financial Interests on Divorce," in Stephen Sugarman and Herma Hill Kay, eds., *Divorce Reform at the Crossroads* 130, 149 (1991); Greg Duncan and Saul Hoffman, "A Reconsideration of the Economic Consequences of Marital Dissolution," 22 *Demography* 485 (1985).

25 Kay, supra note 23.

26 Elizabeth S. Scott, "Rational Decisionmaking about Marriage and Divorce," 76 *Va. Law Rev.* 9, 25 (1990).

27 Katherine Bartlett, "Re-expressing Parenthood," 98 *Yale L. J.* 293, 3111 (1988); Martha Minow, "Forming underneath Everything that Grows: Toward a History of Family Law," 1985 *Wis. L. Rev.* 819, 894; Elizabeth S. Scott, "Rehabilitating Liberalism in Modern Divorce Law," 1994 *Utah L. Rev.* 687, 715–17.

28 Amy Wax, "Egalitarian Marriage: Bargaining in the Shadow of the Market," 84 *Va. L. Rev.* 509 (1998).

29 Id.; Mary Becker, "Problems with the Privatization of Heterosexuality," 73 *Denv. U. L. Rev.* 1169 (1996); Carol Rose, "Women and Property: Gaining and Losing Ground," 78 *Va. L. Rev.* 421, 429–30 (1992).

30 Sara MacLanahan and Gary Sandefur, *Growing Up with a Single Parent: What Hurts, What Helps* 1–2 (1994); R. Emery, *Marriage, Divorce, and Children's Adjustment* (1988).

31 Elizabeth S. Scott, supra note 26, at 9, 25; Regan, supra note 2.

32 Lynn Baker and Robert Emery, "When Every Relationship Is Above Average: Perceptions and Expectations of Divorce at the Time of Marriage," 17 *Law & Hum. Behav.* 439, 443 (1993); Alrand Thornton and Deborah Freedman, "Changing Attitudes toward Marriage and Single Life," 14 *Fam. Plan. Persp.* 297, 300 (1982).

33 Robert Scott and Douglas Leslie, *Contract Law and Theory* 17 (2d ed. 1993).

34 Eric Posner, "The Decline of Formality in Contract Law," this volume; Michael Trebilcock and Rosemin Keshani, "The Role of Private Ordering in Family Law: A Law and Economics Perspective," 41 *U. Toronto L. J.* 533, 535 (1991); Brinig and Crafton, supra note 3; Cohen, supra note 3.

35 Goetz and Scott, supra note 5.

36 Lisa Bernstein, "Social Norms and Default Rules Analysis," 3 *S. Cal. Interdisc'y L. J.* (1993).

37 Charles J. Goetz and Robert E. Scott, "The Limits of Expanded Choice: An Analysis of the Interactions between Express and Implied Contract Terms," 73 *Cal. L. Rev.* 261, 289–93 (1985).

38 Robert E. Scott, "A Relational Theory of Default Rules for Commercial Contracts," 19 *J. Legal Stud.* 597, 613–15 (1990).

39 Scott, supra note 6.

40 Steven L. Nock, "A Comparison of Marriages and Cohabiting Relationships," 16 *J. of Fam. Issues* 53, 54 (1995); John Cunningham and John Antill, "Current Trends in Nonmarital Cohabitation: In Search of the POSSLQ," in Julia Wood and Steve Duck, eds., *Under-Studied Relationships: Off the Beaten Track*, 148, 158, 161 (1995).

41 Baker and Emery, supra note 32; Thornton and Freedman, supra note 32.

42 Nock, supra note 40; Cunningham and Antill, supra note 40.

43 Scott, supra note 26.

44 Nock, supra note 40; Cunningham and Antill, supra note 40.

45 Nock, supra note 40; Jan E. Stets, "The Link between Past and Present Intimate Relationships," 14 *J. of Fam. Issues* 236, 240 (1993).

46 Robert E. Scott and William J. Stuntz, "Plea Bargaining as Contract," 101 *Yale L. J.* 1909, 1918–35 (1992).

47 See generally Ira Ellman, Paul Kurtz, and Elizabeth Scott, *Family Law: Cases, Text, Problems*, ch. 2 (3d ed. 1998).

48 Lon Fuller, "Consideration and Form," 41 *Colum. L. Rev.* 799, 800–802 (1941).

49 Scott, supra note 26.

50 Scott, supra note 38; Baker and Emery, supra note 32; Melvin Eisenberg, "The Limits of Cognition and the Limits of Contract," 47 *Stan. L. Rev.* 211, 217 (1995).

51 Scott and Stuntz, supra note 46; Gerd Gigerenzer, "How to Make Cognitive Illusions Disappear: Beyond 'Heuristics and Biases'," 2 "Eur. Rev. Soc. Psychol." 83 (1991).

52 Fuller, supra note 48.

53 See Michael Trebilcock, "External Critiques of Laissez-Faire," in this volume.

54 Cohen, supra note 3; Brinig and Crafton, supra note 3; Goetz and Scott, supra note 5.

55 Goetz and Scott, supra note 5.

56 Id.

57 Scott, supra note 6.

58 See Derek Parfit, "Later Selves and Moral Principles," in Alan Montefiore, ed., *Philosophy and Personal Relations* (1973) (discussing the implications of changing personal identity over time).

59 In other words, each would have the right to the full enjoyment and possession of the marital surplus, subject to the other's equal rights to enjoy the same surplus.

60 Margaret F. Brinig and June Carbone, "The Reliance Interest in Marriage and Divorce," 62 *Tulane L. Rev.* 855 (1988); Michael Trebilcock and Rosemin Keshani, "The Role of Private Ordering in Family Law: A Law and Economics Perspective," 41 *U. Toronto L. J.* 533, 535 (1991).

61 Margaret F. Brinig and F. H. Buckley, "Joint Custody: Bonding and Monitoring Theories," 73 *Ind. L. J.* 393 (1998).

62 Elizabeth S. Scott, "Pluralism, Parental Preference, and Child Custody," 80 *Cal. L. Rev.* 615 (1992).

63 Scott, supra note 26.

64 Id.; Christine Joll, "Contracts as Bilateral Commitments: A New Perspective in Contract Modification," 26 *J. Legal Stud.* 203, 204 (1997).

65 Scott, supra note 6.

66 Empirical studies of cooperative interactions indicate that lock-in effects are very strong. See sources cited in Scott, id., at 2026–27. These effects tend to make the parties behave like each other; the tendency is intensified as the interactions continue. Thus, if a pattern of cooperation can be established initially, a cooperative equilibrium will emerge. Each spouse's self-interest will induce him or her to maintain this productive pattern.

67 Scott, supra note 6.

68 Robert Ellickson, *Order without Law: How Neighbors Settle Disputes* (1991); Eric A. Posner, "Law, Economics, and Inefficient Norms," 144 *U. Pa. L. Rev.* 1697 (1996); Eric A. Posner, "Norms, Formalities, and the Statute of Frauds: A Comment," 144 *U. Pa. L. Rev.* 1971 (1996); Eric A. Posner, "The Regulation of Groups: The Influence of Legal and Nonlegal Sanctions on Collective Action," 63 *U. Chi. L. Rev.* 133 (1996); Lisa Bernstein, supra note 36; Robert Cooter, "Decentralized Law for a Complex Economy: The Structural Approach to Adjudicating the New Law Merchant," 144 *U. Pa. L. Rev.* 1643 (1996); Stewart MacCaulay, "Non-Contractual Relations in Business: A Preliminary Study," 28 *Am. Soc. Rev.* 55 (1963); Lawrence Lessig, "Social Meaning and Social Norms," 144 *U. Pa. L. Rev.* 2181 (1996); Cass R. Sunstein, "Social Norms and Social Roles," 96 *Colum. L. Rev.* 903, 910 (1996).

69 Richard H. MacAdams, "The Origin, Development, and Regulation of Norms," 96 *Mich. L. Rev.* 338 (1997).

70 Steven L. Nock, *Marriage in Men's Lives* (1998).

71 Scott, supra note 6.

72 Cooter, supra note 68; MacAdams, supra note 69.

73 Russell Hardin, "Trustworthiness," 107 *Ethics* 26, 35 (1996).

74 Ellickson, supra note 68; Richard Posner, "Social Norms and the Law: An Economic Approach," 87 *Am. Econ. Rev.* 365 (1997).

75 James Bowers and John Bigelow, "The Economics of Relationships and the Limits of the Law" (manuscript on file) (1998).

76 Martin Siegel, "For Better or Worse: Adultery, Crime, and the Constitution," 30 *J. Fam. L.* 45, 55–56 (1991–92); P. Pittman, *Private Lies: Infidelity and the Betrayal of Intimacy* 29 (1989); Joan Zorza, "Must We Stop Arresting Batterers?: Analysis and Policy Implications of New Police Domestic Violence Studies," 28 *New Eng. L. Rev.* 929, 936 (1994).

77 See Eric Posner, "Family Law and Social Norms," in this volume.

78 See the discussion of premarital contracts in section 1 supra. Parties can execute a contract that will determine property distribution and spousal support on divorce. The Uniform Premarital Agreement Act makes the standard contract defenses of fraud, duress, unconscionability, and incompetency available to the party who seeks to avoid enforcement, but does not (at least in theory) permit agreements to be set aside simply because enforcement is disadvantageous to one party. In jurisdictions that have not adopted the UPAA, premarital contracts are recognized, but equity at the

time of enforcement is a basis for setting aside the agreement. See *Button v. Button*, 388 N. W.2d 546 (Wis. 1986) (changed circumstances after execution warrant setting agreement aside); *Gross v. Gross* 464 N. E.2d 500 (Ohio 1984) (husband's assets increased from $500,000 to $6 million).

79 See, e.g., *Borelli v. Brusseau*, 16 Cal.Rptr.2d 16 (Cal.App. 1993) (refusing to enforce the parties' contract under which wife was supposed to receive compensation for the nursing services to her husband); *Koch v. Koch*, 232 A.2d 157 (N.J.Super. 1967) (oral agreement providing that husband's mother would come and live in the parties' household unenforceable); In re Marriage of Bennett, 587 N. E.2d 577 (Ill.App. 1992) (agreement to raise children in Jewish faith unenforceable).

80 See *McGuire v. McGuire*, 59 N. W.2d 336 (Neb. 1953).

81 Eric A. Posner, "The Regulation of Groups: The Influence of Legal and Nonlegal Sanctions on Collective Action," 63 *U. Chi. L. Rev.* 133 (1996); Temple, "Freedom of Contract and Intimate Relationships," 8 *Harv. J. L. & Pub. Pol.* 121 (1985); Robert Emery and Melissa Wyer, "Divorce Mediation," 42 *Am. Psychologist* 472, 474, 477 (1987).

82 Scott, supra note 38.

83 Carol Rose, "Women and Property: Gaining and Losing Ground," 78 *Va. L. Rev.* 421, 429–30 (1992); Wax, supra note 28.

84 See generally Ellman, Kurtz, and Bartlett, supra note 47, at 229–42. See also Idaho Code § 32–712.1(1); W.Va. Code §48–2-32 (Supp. 1985); Ore.Rev.Stat. §107.105(1)(f).

85 Robert Mnookin, "Child Custody Adjudication: Judicial Functions in the Face of Indeterminacy," 39 *L. & Contemp. Probs.* 226 (1976).

86 Martha Fineman, "The Uses of Social Science Data in Legal Policymaking: Custody Determinations at Divorce," 1987 *Wis. L. Rev.* 107, 121, 140, 147–48.

87 Scott, supra note 26.

88 Scott, supra note 62.

89 See e.g., UMDA §§302, 305 (divorce on ground of irretrievable breakdown).

90 Theodore F. Haas, "The Rationality and Enforceability of Contractual Restrictions on Divorce," 66 *N. C. L. Rev.* 879 (1988).

91 Anthony Kronman, "Paternalism and the Law of Contracts," 92 *Yale L. J.* 673, 775–82 (1983).

92 *MacFarlane v. Rich* 567 A.2d. 585 (N. H. 1989); *Stadler v. Stadler*, 526 So.2d 598 (Ala. App. 1988) (upholding premarital agreement providing for payments on divorce if husband engages in heavy drinking or causes bodily injury leading to divorce).

Marriage as a Signal

1 Michael Trebilcock and Rosemin Keshvani, "The Role of Private Ordering in Family Law: A Law and Economics Perspective," 41 *U. of Toronto L. J.* 533 (1991).

2 See, e.g., Amy Wax, "Bargaining in the Shadow of the Market: Is There a Future for Egalitarian Marriage?," 84 *Va. L. Rev.* 509 (1998).

3 William Bishop, " 'Is He Married?' Marriage as Information," 34 *U. of Toronto L. J.* 24 (1984).

4 Elizabeth Landes, "The Economics of Alimony," 7 *J. Legal Studies* 35 (1978).

5 See Robert Mnookin and Lewis Kornhauser, "Bargaining in the Shadow of the Law: The Case of Divorce," 88 *Yale L. J.* 1015 (1979).

6 For extensive discussions of bargaining inequalities in marital relationships, see Wax, supra note 2; Robert Mnookin, "Divorce Bargaining: The Limits on Private Ordering," in Eekelaar and Katz, eds., *The Resolution of Family Conflict: Comparative Legal Per-*

spectives (1984); Michael Trebilcock and Steven Elliot, "The Scope and Limits of Legal Paternalism: Altruism and Coercion in Intrafamilial Financial Arrangements," mimeo, University of Toronto Law School, October 1997.

Family Law and Social Norms

My thanks to Peg Brinig, Richard Craswell, Emlyn Eisenach, Jeff Stake, and the editor for their comments.

1 Eric A. Posner, *Law, Cooperation, and Rational Choice*, ch. 5 (unpublished manuscript, 1998).

2 See Robert C. Ellickson, *Order without Law* (1991); "Symposium: Law, Economics, and Norms," 144 *U. Pa. L. Rev.* 1643 (1996); "Symposium: Social Norms, Social Meanings, and the Law," 28 *J. Legal Stud.* 537 (1998).

3 For a related signaling model of marriage vows, see William Bishop, "'Is He Married?': Marriage as Information," 34 *U. Toronto L. Rev.* 245 (1984), in which parties signal their desire for an exclusive relationship. A brief discussion of bonding mechanisms can be found in Lloyd Cohen, "Marriage, Divorce, and Quasi Rents: Or, 'I Gave Him the Best Years of My Life,'" 26 *J. Legal Stud.* 267 (1987).

4 Signaling continues during the relationship, as the parties must show each other that they remain committed. A common signal is ritualistic gift giving. See Eric A. Posner, "Altruism, Status, and Trust in the Law of Gifts and Gratuitous Promises," 1997 *Wisc. L. Rev.* 567.

5 See id.; a formal model can be found in Colin Camerer, "Gifts as Economic Signals and Social Symbols," 94 *Am. J. Soc.* S180 (1988).

6 Different legal and normative regimes solve this tension in different ways. One is to avoid premarital sex but allow annulment of marriages when one partner is not sexually healthy. Another is to allow sex during engagement or an engagement period, which can be broken only if one partner is not sexually healthy. A third is to allow premarital sexual activity short of intercourse ("bundling" may have been an example of this). One finds all three patterns in various times and cultures.

7 Jianzhong Wu and Robert Axelrod, "How to Cope with Noise in the Interated Prisoner's Dilemma," in Robert Axelrod, ed., *The Complexity of Cooperation* (1997).

8 See Posner, supra note 4.

9 See also Shelly Lundberg and Robert Pollak, "Separate Spheres Bargaining and the Marriage Market," 101 *J. Pol. Econ.* 988, 993–95 (1993).

10 The idea that spouses may take on certain roles that enable them to monitor each other effectively, or, more generally, that spouses will resolve disputes along general principles that are set up in advance, has interesting parallels with Kreps's theory of corporate culture. See David Kreps, "Corporate Culture and Economic Theory," in James E. Alt and Kenneth A. Shepsle, eds., *Perspectives on Positive Political Theory* (1990).

11 See Natalie Zemon Davis, *Society and Culture in Early Modern France* 97–123 (1975); Bertram Wyatt-Brown, *Southern Honor: Ethics and Behavior in the Old South* 435–61 (1982); Martin Ingram, "Ridings, Rough Music, and the Reform of Popular Culture in Early Modern England," 105 *Past and Present* 79 (1984); E. P. Thompson, *Customs in Common* 467–538 (1993).

12 See Eric A. Posner, "Symbols, Signals, and Social Norms in Politics and the Law," 28 *J. Legal Stud.* 765 (1998); Posner, supra note 1, at ch. 2.

13 See Ingram, supra note 11; Wyatt-Brown, supra note 11.

14 See Bishop, supra note 3, at 252–54, for a related argument.

15 Marriage reform by ecclesiastical and civil authorities was often a response to the chaos that existed in the absence of requirements that marriages be licensed and weddings be public—the endless disputes about whether or not one person married another; for examples and discussion, see Richard Helmholz, *Marriage Litigation in Medieval England* (1974). Authorities frequently punished marital opportunism, such as adultery, so long as sufficiently openly practiced that problems of proof could be overcome. See Joel Harrington, *Reordering Marriage and Society in Reformation Germany* 249–50 (1995).

16 For historical evidence, see David Levine and Keith Wrightson, "The Social Control of Illegitimacy in Early Modern England," in Peter Laslett et al., eds., *Bastardy and Its Comparative History* 174 (1980).

17 A similar point is made in Michael J. Trebilcock and Rosemin Keshvani, "The Role of Private Ordering in Family Law," 41 *U. Toronto L. J.* 533, 558 (1991). See also Lundberg and Pollak, supra note 9.

18 For historical evidence on efforts by parents to control the marital choices of their children, see Harrington, supra note 15.

19 This is also true if the costs of entering marriage are too high; for an example from nineteenth-century Germany, where wealth and citizenship requirements for marriage resulted in a great deal of cohabitation and illegitimacy, see Lynn Abrams, "Concubinage, Cohabitation, and the Law: Class and Gender Relations in Nineteenth-Century Germany," 5 *Gender and History* 81 (1993).

20 A possible legal response is through the use of tax advantages for married people, etc.

21 See Posner, supra note 1, at ch. 5, which makes two main points. (1) The Scotts do not adequately explain why courts cannot verify instances of opportunism in a marital relationship, a conclusion that makes laws against spousal abuse and abandonment difficult to understand. (2) The Scotts' argument that social and relational norms deter opportunism conflicts with standard game theory models which show that cooperation in the two-person iterated prisoner's dilemma may be suboptimal, and with the signaling model discussed earlier, which suggests that social norms will often undermine cooperation rather than enforce it.

Contracting around No-Fault Divorce

1 La. Civ. Code Art. 9, §102.

2 Id. §307(B).

3 See generally Katherine Silbaugh, in "Turning Work into Love: Legal Responses to Home Labor," 91 *Nw. U. L. Rev.* 1 (1995).

4 Margaret F. Brinig and F. H. Buckley, "Joint Custody: Bonding and Monitoring Theories," 73 *Indiana L. J.* 393 (1998).

5 William Murchison, *Reclaiming Morality in America* 43 (1994).

6 Margaret F. Brinig and Steven M. Crafton, "Marriage and Opportunism," 23 *J. Legal Stud.* 869 (1994); Elisabeth S. Landes, "The Economics of Alimony," 7 *J. Legal Stud.* 35 (1978).

7 Brinig and Crafton, supra note 6, at 880. "Property Distribution Physics: The Talisman of Time and Middle-Class Law," 31 *Family L. Q.* 93 (1997); also Gary S. Becker, *Human Capital* (3d ed. 1993); Allen Parkman, *No-fault Divorce: What Went Wrong?* (1992); Allen M. Parkman, "Human Capital as Property in Celebrity Divorces," 29 *Fam. L. Q.* 141 (1995).

8 Margaret F. Brinig, "The Family Franchise," 1996 *Utah L. Rev.* 393.

9 Gary S. Becker, *A Treatise on the Family*, 30–42 (1991).

10 Lynn Baker and Robert Emery, "When Every Relationship Is Above Average: Perceptions and Expectations of Divorce at the Time of Marriage," 17 *L. & Hum. Beh.* 439 (1993).

11 Gary S. Becker, Elisabeth M. Landes, and Robert T. Michael, "An Economic Analysis of Marital Instability," 85 *J. Pol. Econ.* 85, 1141–1187 (1978).

12 See Amy L. Wax, "Bargaining in the Shadow of the Market: Is There a Future for Egalitarian Marriage?" 84 *Va. L. Rev.* 509 (1998); Jana Singer, "Husbands, Wives, and Human Capital: Why the Shoe Won't Fit," 31 *Fam. L. Q.* 119 (1997).

13 See, e.g., Wendy Williams, "The Equality Crisis: Some Reflections on Culture, Courts, and Feminism," in Katherine Bartlett and Roseann Kennedy, eds., *Feminist Legal Theory* 15, 22–25 (1991); Herma Hill Kay, "An Appraisal of California's No-fault Divorce Law," 20 *Cal. L. Rev.* 299 (1987).

14 Steven L. Nock, "Commitment and Dependency in Marriage," 57 *Journal of Marriage and the Family* 503 (1995).

15 Brinig and Crafton, supra note 6, at 887–92. But see Ira Ellman, "Marriage as Contract, Opportunistic Violence, and Other Bad Arguments for Fault Divorce," 1997 *U. Ill. L. Rev.* 719 (1997).

16 See Steven L. Nock, *Marriage in Men's Lives* (1998).

17 Paul R. D'Amato, "Life-Span Adjustment of Children to Their Parents' Divorce," in *The Future of Children: Children and Divorce* 4(1): 143, 145 (1994).

18 John Guideubaldi et al., "The Impact of Parental Divorce on Children: Report of the Nationwide NASP Study," paper presented at the annual convention of the National Association for School Psychologists, 1983.

19 David Popenoe, *Life without Father: Compelling New Evidence that Fatherhood and Marriage are Indispensable for the Good of Children and Society* (1995); see also Hillary Rodham Clinton, *It Takes a Village: And Other Lessons Children Teach Us* (1996).

20 Margaret F. Brinig, "The Family Franchise," 1996 *Utah L. Rev.* 393 (1996); Ira Lupu, "The Separation of Powers and the Protection of Children," 61 *U. Chi. L. Rev.* 1317 (1994); Popenoe, supra note 19.

21 Sara McLanahan and Gary D. Sandefer, *Growing Up with a Single Parent: What Hurts, What Helps* 30–31 (1994).

22 Janet R. Johnston, "High-Conflict Divorce," in *The Future of Children: Children and Divorce* 4(1): 165, 175 (1994).

23 La Civ. Code, Art. 9, §§ 307(4) and 308(4).

24 W. Va. Code §40-2-3(9).

25 *Williams v. North Carolina*, 317 U.S. 287, 299, 63 S.Ct. 207, 213–14, 87 L.Ed. 279 (1942).

Contracting for Bankruptcy Systems

This essay benefited from comments by Barry Adler, Frank Buckley, and the participants at the 1997 European Association of Law and Economics Meeting.

1 The existence of these costs is evidenced by the difficulty of conducting private workouts after insolvency. See Alan Schwartz, "Bankruptcy Workouts and Debt Contracts," 36 *J. Law & Econ.* 595 (1993) (summarizing studies showing that workouts fail about half the time).

2 Tort and environmental victims of the firm's activities do not bargain with the firm ex ante but do have current bankruptcy claims against it. These claims should be protected in bankruptcy, but just how is beyond this essay's scope.

3 Good reviews are Donald R. Korobkin, "The Role of Normative Theory in Bankruptcy Debates," 82 *Iowa L. Rev.* 75 (1996), and Christopher W. Frost, "Bankruptcy, Redistribution Policies, and the Limits of the Judicial Process," 74 *N. Car. L. Rev.* 75 (1995).

4 See, e.g., Barry Adler, "Financial and Political Theories of Corporate Bankruptcy," 45 *Stanford L. Rev.* 311 (1993); Robert K. Rasmussen, "Debtor's Choice: A Menu Approach to Corporate Bankruptcy," 71 *Tex. L. Rev.* 51 (1992).

5 A thorough summary of the economic literature developing this view is Jean-Jacques Laffont and David Martimort, "The Firm as a Multi-contract Organization," 6 *J. of Econ. & Management Strategy* 201 (1997).

6 Douglas Baird, "Bankruptcy's Uncontested Axioms," forthcoming *Yale L. J.*, argues that many traditional bankruptcy scholars implicitly assume that bankruptcy is special, in the sense that economic actors do not respond to bankruptcy-related incentives as they would respond to the incentives other bodies of law create.

7 This essay uses the phrases "solve the creditors' coordination problem" and "maximize the ex post value of the insolvent firm" interchangeably because the point of solving the problem is to maximize value.

8 The leading proponents of this view are Douglas Baird and Thomas Jackson. See, e.g., Douglas G. Baird and Thomas H. Jackson, *Cases, Problems, and Materials on Bankruptcy* (2d ed. 1990); Douglas G. Baird, "Revisiting Auctions in Chapter 11," 36 *J. Law & Econ.* 633 (1993); Douglas G. Baird and Thomas H. Jackson, "Corporate Reorganization and the Treatment of Diverse Ownership Interests: A Comment on Adequate Protection of Secured Creditors in Bankruptcy," 51 *U. Chi. L. Rev.* 97 (1984). A more technical argument to the same effect is Phillipe Aghion, Oliver Hart, and John Moore, "The Economics of Bankruptcy Reform," 8 *J. Law, Econ. & Organization* 523 (1992). Jackson's views heavily influenced the new German Insolvency Act. See Klaus Kamlah, "The New German Insolvency Act: Insolvenzordnung," 70 *American Bktcy. L. J.* 417 (1996).

9 That bankruptcy systems should prevent parties from using a system strategically is strongly argued in Baird and Jackson, supra note 9 (casebook). The question of whether bankruptcy systems should strictly follow absolute priority becomes complex when the effect of a firm's capital structure on its behavior is taken into account. For a summary of the issues, see Alan Schwartz, "The Absolute Priority Rule and the Firm's Investment Policy," 72 *Wash. U. L. Q* 1213 (1994).

10 Ponoroff and Knippenberg typically remark that bankruptcy law allocates losses from insolvency "according to a set of principles, none of which is preeminent by definition." Lawrence Ponoroff and F. Stephen Knippenberg, "The Implied Good Faith Filing Requirement: Sentinel of an Evolving Bankruptcy Policy," 85 *Nw. Univ. L. Rev.* 919, 960 (1991).

11 See Elizabeth Warren, "Bankruptcy Policy in an Imperfect World," 92 *Mich. L. Rev.* 336 (1993).

12 Arguments in favor of protecting employees are found in Donald R. Korobkin, "Employee Interests in Bankruptcy," 4 *American Bankruptcy Institute L. Rev.* 5 (1996); Jean Braucher, "Bankruptcy Reorganization and Economic Development," 23 *Capital U. L. Rev.* 499 (1994) (Braucher adds the qualification that a bankruptcy system should not protect jobs if this would cause job loss in general, but he does not pursue

this possibility); Raymond T. Nimmer, "Negotiated Bankruptcy Reorganization Plans: Absolute Priority and New Value Contributions," 36 *Emory L. Rev.* 1009 (1987). The commitment of these authors to employee protection is pallid compared to the current French bankruptcy system, which enumerates job protection as the first goal of the system and creditor payment as the last. See Richard L. Koral and Marie-Christine Sordino, "The New Bankruptcy Reorganization Law in France: Ten Years Later," 70 *American Bktcy. L. J.* 437 (1996).

13 See Warren, supra note 11; Ponoroff and Knippenberg, supra note 10. Warren's views seem to change, however. For example: "Bankruptcy procedures should be evaluated in terms of whether they enhance the value of the estate." Elizabeth Warren, "A Theory of Absolute Priority," 1 *N.Y.U. Annual Survey of American Law* 9, 47 (1991).

14 See Braucher, supra note 12, at 5–7-18 (1994); Nimmer, supra note 12, at 1028.

15 Warren, supra note 11.

16 For an exception with regard to employees, see Korobkin, supra note 12.

17 According to Warren, the Bankruptcy Code seeks "to redistribute the benefits that would stem from some creditors' collection rights to other parties who did not enjoy those rights." See Warren, supra note 11, at 357.

18 A sample of current scholarly views on the security interest priority is in "Symposium," 87 *Cornell L. Rev.* (1997). My position is in "Priority Contracts and Priority in Bankruptcy," 87 *Cornell L. Rev.* 101 (1997).

19 See Ponoroff and Knippenberg, Korobkin, Braucher, and Warren; Thomas H. Jackson, "Bankruptcy, Non-Bankruptcy Entitlements, and the Creditors' Bargain," 91 *Yale L. J.* 857 (1982).

20 Robert Rasmussen reaches the same conclusions as this essay does, but for different reasons. He argues that the requirements of social justice only imply a bankruptcy system that efficiently maximizes creditor returns. See Robert Rasmussen, "An Essay on Optimal Bankruptcy Rules and Social Justice," 1994 *Univ. Illinois L. Rev.* 1 (1994).

21 Frost makes a similar point. See Frost, supra note 3, at 118–19. It sometimes is mistakenly claimed that not to protect employees in bankruptcy can be inefficient because the workers' firm specific human capital will be lost. To see why this argument is incorrect, assume that much of a firm's wealth is in the firm specific human capital of its managers and employees. This implies that the firm's value as a going concern exceeds its value in liquidation. An efficient bankruptcy system continues firms in operation when their going concern values exceed their liquidation values.

22 Firms today are legally entitled to make the initial choice about which of the existing bankruptcy systems to use (liquidation or reorganization), but a bankruptcy court can overrule the firm's choice. Courts delegate substantial discretion to insolvent firms in practice. A creditor coalition also is legally entitled to choose the bankruptcy system if the coalition acts before the firm does, but high coalition costs ensure that firms almost always act first. Thus the analysis here assumes that only insolvent firms choose bankruptcy systems.

23 The analysis that follows is drawn from Alan Schwartz, "Contracting about Bankruptcy," 13 *J. Law, Econ., & Org.* 127 (1997).

24 A firm is reorganized when it is sold to current claimants, that is, creditors receive new equity in the firm or new forms of debt and the old equity receives nothing (if absolute priority is followed). A firm is liquidated when it is sold to the market either as a unit or piecemeal, with the proceeds distributed to the creditors. A reorganization takes more time to conduct than a liquidation.

25 Contracts that permit creditors to choose the bankruptcy system are not considered for two reasons. First, creditor coalition costs ex post would make it difficult for creditors jointly to enforce a contract. Second, an insolvent firm sometimes would be unable to bribe creditors to choose the efficient system when they would choose an inefficient system if unconstrained. As will appear, bribes are an essential part of optimal bankruptcy contracts.

26 The bargaining power assumption is made because it is analytically convenient and also because it is realistic to endow the firm with considerable bargaining power ex post. If the bargaining power assumption is relaxed to give creditors a share of renegotiation rents, then renegotiation would become a more attractive alternative relative to ex ante contract than the text above permits, but none of the analytical results would change.

27 It is questionable whether the firm's private benefits should count in a normative bankruptcy analysis because the purpose of a business bankruptcy system should be to maximize the creditors' monetary return. See Yeon-Koo Che and Alan Schwartz, "Section 365, Mandatory Bankruptcy Rules and Inefficient Continuance," 15(2) *J. Law, Econ., & Org.* (July 1999). Under the current mandatory system, the firm can consume private benefits without maximizing the creditors' monetary return, however. This essay will show that permitting freedom of contract respecting the choice of a bankruptcy system will generate higher returns for creditors than is now possible. This seems the best that can be done because a directive system that would maximize the creditors' return while eliminating the firm's private benefit has not been identified.

28 The situation modeled here is realistic. Today, a substantial minority of firms that file for bankruptcy choose the Chapter 11 reorganization process, but a very large fraction of these Chapter 11s are ultimately dismissed (the firm is then liquidated). Bankruptcy courts nevertheless dismiss too few Chapter 11 petitions. A recent study showed that over 40 percent of firms emerging from Chapter 11 experience operating losses in the three years following bankruptcy, and 32 percent of reorganized firms either reenter bankruptcy or restructure their debt. See Edith Shwalb Hotchkiss, "Postbankruptcy Performance and Management Turnover," 50 *J. of Finance* 3 (1995).

29 Respecting the notation, the monetary return is denoted y. The first subscripted capital letter denotes the ex post state and the second capital letter denotes the firm's choice of a bankruptcy system. Thus $y_{L,L}$ denotes the monetary return that is generated when the set of insolvency circumstances summarized by θ_L occurs and the firm chooses bankruptcy system L. And $y_{L,R}$ denotes the monetary return in state θ_L if the firm inefficiently chooses system R then.

30 When the firm keeps one-third of the insolvency monetary return, and will then choose the optimal system, the maximum expected return available for creditors becomes:

$$E(R) = .8 \times 260 + \frac{2}{3}.2(.3 \times 180 + .7 \times 120) = \$226.49$$

The terms in brackets reflect the firm's choice of the optimal bankruptcy system, but the monetary return that creditors receive must be multiplied by two-thirds because the firm is given one-third of that return to choose optimally.

31 This conclusion should be explained. Investment is suboptimal compared to the full information case. The more relevant question, since information seldom can be made perfect, is whether a particular contract is "constrained efficient": that is, whether the contract produces the best result given the information structure. To answer this

question for the text's example requires an analysis of the firm's contractual alternatives, which the text next makes.

32 The complex equation from which this value is derived is set out in Schwartz, supra note 23, at 237 n. 21.

33 The unique equilibrium when bankruptcy contracts are unenforceable has parties not writing these contracts. To see why, let parties use the renegotiation proof contract described above, which pays the firm one-third of the total bankruptcy monetary return to choose the optimal system. When this contract does not legally bind, a creditor would have the right to ignore the deal and file a bankruptcy claim for the full amount that it is owed rather than two-thirds of that amount. If the firm actually chose the system that maximized monetary returns and creditors generally adhered to the contract, a particular creditor could increase its bankruptcy payoff by exercising its legal right to claim the full amount it is owed. Since many creditors would reason in this way, many full claims would be filed, and there would not be enough left to pay the firm's bribe. Anticipating this, the firm itself would ignore the contract and choose the system that maximized its private benefits. And anticipating this, creditors would not agree to bankruptcy contracts.

34 Put formally, the estimated value of the optimal bribe equals the expected value at t^0 plus an error term with mean zero: $E(s^*(t^2)) = s^*(t^0) + \epsilon$, where $E(\epsilon) = 0$.

35 Trade creditors are either suppliers or customers of the insolvent firm.

36 Bankruptcy Code §1126(c).

37 The text's reference to "default" provisions is not strictly correct because a default applies in the absence of a contractual choice. When the state provides a set of procedures, particular parties will have to choose one. Thus it might be more appropriate to use Rasmussen's phrase, that the state should supply a "menu" of choices. See Rasmussen, supra note 4. The text uses the word "default" to account for the possibility that parties may want to (and should be allowed to) design their own procedure or materially alter a state-supplied procedure.

Free Contracting in Bankruptcy

1 F. H. Buckley, "The American Fresh Start," 4 *So. Cal. Interdisciplinary L. J.* 67 (1994).

2 The underinvestment costs Schwartz identifies are to be distinguished from the underinvestment costs that arise under "pecking order" theories. Myers and Majluf, "Corporate Financing and Investment Decisions When Firms Have Information that Investors Do Not Have," 13 *J. Fin. Econ.* 187 (1984).

3 The contractual solution would be stronger still if firm managers could sell their reorganization gain $b_{LR} - b_{LL}$ to creditors. However, I follow Schwartz in assuming that these values are unobservable.

4 Michael C. Jensen and William H. Meckling, "Theory of the Firm: Managerial Behavior, Agency Costs, and Ownership Structure," 3 *J. Fin. Econ.* 305 (1976).

5 Thomas H. Jackson and Robert E. Scott, "On the Nature of Bankruptcy: An Essay on Bankruptcy Sharing and the Creditors' Bargain," 75 *Va. L. Rev.* 155 (1989). See also Barry E. Adler, "Bankruptcy and Risk Allocation," 77 *Cornell L. Rev.* 439 (1992).

6 In theory, debt claims in Chapter 11 are valued as at the date of bankruptcy; but in practice postbankruptcy residual value that arises during the course of reorganization may accrue to shareholders through a judicial fiction that subsequent gains represent hidden value on bankruptcy.

7 F. H. Buckley, "The Termination Decision," 61 *U. M. K.C. L. Rev.* 243 (1992).

8 Claims that a stay of repossessory remedies should be mandated to strengthen debtor and management incentives to produce firm-specific assets are also unpersuasive. F. H. Buckley, "The American Stay," 3 *So. Cal. Interdisciplinary L. J.* 738, 760–61 (1994).

9 See, e.g., F. H. Buckley, Mark Gillen, and Robert Yalden, *Corporations: Principles and Policies* (3d ed. 1995).

10 Bankruptcy Act, R. S. C., c. B-3, §69(2). L. W. Houlden and C. H. Morawetz, 1 *Bankruptcy Law of Canada* F§54, 3–112–3–114 (3d ed. 1989).

11 See generally Buckley, supra note 8.

12 11 U.S.C. (1995).

13 Lynn LoPucki and William Whitford, "Bargaining over Equity's Share in the Bankruptcy Reorganization of Large, Publicly Held Companies," 139 *U. Pa. L. Rev.* 125 (1990).

14 F. H. Buckley, "The Canadian Keiretsu," 9 *J. App. Corp. Fin.* 46 (1997). The fragmented American economy is sometimes contrasted with the more concentrated German and Japanese ones. The three largest American banks have assets equal to 7 percent of GNP, while the comparable German and Japanese figures are 36 percent and 39 percent, respectively. But the three largest Canadian banks have assets equal to 55 percent of Canadian GDP, 50 percent higher than the German figure and nine times higher than the American one. The figure is 80 percent for the top five Canadian banks. Sources: *Globe and Mail Report on Business*, July 1993, at 114; *Statistical Abstract of the United States* 1994. This number will soon drop to four banks after a new round of bank mergers. One understands, of course, why the American figure is so low. From a Canadian perspective, however, the puzzle is why the German and Japanese economies are so fragmented.

15 R. M. Breckenridge, "The Canadian Banking System 1817–1890," *Am. Econ. Ass'n. Pub.* 366, 370, 446 (1895).

16 Peter C. Newman, 1 *The Canadian Establishment* 120–90 (1975).

17 Seymour Martin Lipset, *Continental Divide: The Values and Institutions of the United States and Canada* 129–30 (1990).

18 Raghuram G. Rajan and Luigi Zingales, "What Do We Know about Capital Structure? Some Evidence from International Data," 50 *J. Fin.* 1421 (1995). Canada is an exception to the Rajan-Zingales claim that "countries where the ex ante contract is most strictly enforced are also ones where firms have the least debt."

19 Bank Act, R. S. C. c. B-1.01 §§ 10, 466(1).

20 *White v. Bank of Toronto*, 3 D. L. R. 118 (Ont. C. A.) (1953).

21 *Canada Gaz. Supp.*, 24 Feb. 1996, at 19.

22 Mark J. Roe, "Some Differences in Corporate Structure in Germany, Japan, and the United States," 102 *Yale L. J.* 1927, 1955 (1993).

23 Buckley, supra note 8.

24 Stuart C. Gilson, "Management Turnover and Financial Stress," 25 *J. Fin. Econ.* 241 (1989); Lynn M. LoPucki and William C. Whitford, "Corporate Governance in the Bankruptcy Reorganization of Large, Publicly Held Companies," 141 *U. Penn. L. Rev.* 669 (1993); Stuart C. Gilson and Michael R. Vetsuypens, "Creditor Control in Financially Distressed Firms: Empirical Evidence," 72 *Wash. U. L. Q.* 1005 (1994).

25 Michael C. Jensen, "Corporate Control and the Politics of Finance," *J. Applied Corp. Fin.* 13 (Summer 1991); Michael Jensen, "Eclipse of the Public Corporation," *Harv. Bus. Rev.* 61 (Sept.–Oct. 1989).

26 Mark J. Roe, *Strong Managers, Weak Owners: The Political Roots of American Corporate Finance* (1994).

27   As they would have if the costs of inefficient liquidations under a private receivership exceeded the costs of inefficient reorganizations under a private stay. Robert M. Mooradian, "The Effect of Bankruptcy Protection on Investment: Chapter 11 as a Screening Device," 49 *J. Fin.* 1403 (1994).

28   Erik Berglof and Enrico Perotti, "The Governance Structure of the Japanese Financial Keiretsu," 36 *J. Fin. Econ.* 259 (1994); Takeo Hoshi, Anil Kashyap, and David Scharfstein, "The Role of Banks in Reducing the Costs of Financial Distress in Japan," 27 *J. Fin. Econ.* 67 (1990).

29   Douglas Diamond, "Monitoring and Reputation: The Choice between Bank Loans and Directly Placed Debt," 99 *J. Pol. Econ.* 689 (1991); Mitchell A. Petersen and Raghuram G. Rajan, "The Benefits of Lending Relationships: Evidence from Small Business Data," 49 *J. Fin.* 3 (1994).

30   Phillipe Aghion and Patrick Bolton, "An Incomplete Contract Approach to Financial Contracting," 59 *Rev. Econ. Stud.* 473 (1992); Steven Sharpe, "Asymmetric Information, Bank Lending, and Implicit Contracts: A Stylized Model of Customer Relationships," 45 *J. Fin.* 1069 (1990).

31   Raghuram G. Rajan, "Insiders and Outsiders: The Choice between Informed and Arm's-Length Debt," 48 *J. Fin.* 1367 (1992).

32   Newman, supra note 16, at 105.

33   Thomas H. Jackson, "Bankruptcy, Nonbankruptcy Entitlements, and the Creditors' Bargain," 91 *Yale L. J.* 857 (1982).

34   Michael Jensen and William Meckling, "Theory of the Firm: Managerial Behavior, Agency Costs, and Capital Structure," 3 *J. Fin. Econ.* 305 (1976).

35   Buckley, supra note 14.

36   Alan Schwartz, "Security Interests and Bankruptcy Priorities: A Review of Current Theories," 10 *J. Legal Stud.* 1 (1981).

37   Lucian A. Bebchuk and Jesse M. Fried, "The Uneasy Case for the Priority of Secured Claims in Bankruptcy," 105 *Yale L. J.* 857 (1996).

38   Robert K. Rasmussen, "Debtor's Choice: A Menu Approach to Corporate Bankruptcy," 71 *Tex. L. Rev.* 51 (1992).

39   Bankruptcy and Insolvency Act, Stat. Can. 1992, c. 27, § 69(1) [hereafter "BIA"]. Even before the BIA was adopted, repossessory rights might have been stayed through a petition under the Companies' Creditors Arrangement Act., R. S. C. 1975, c. C-36, a depression-era statute that was rediscovered in the 1980s.

40   BIA §§ 50.4(8), 69, 50.4(9).

41   Through purchases of investment dealers, the six major Chartered Banks now own over 70 percent of the world's fifth largest securities industry. Banks may also set up networking arrangements with other financial institutions and distribute their products and services in their bank branches to their own customers. In addition, banks may now offer financial services outside of the traditional four pillars, such as information processing and management systems, and real estate management and development. Because of these changes, the Chartered Banks' share of the Canadian financial intermediary industry rose to 50 percent by 1994. Buckley, supra note 14.

Free Contracting in Bankruptcy At Home and Abroad

I thank Rebecca Brown and Frank Buckley for helpful comments on a previous draft of this piece. I also thank the Dean's Fund at Vanderbilt Law School for generous financial support.

1   For an argument that efficient bankruptcy rules promote social justice, see Robert K. Rasmussen, "An Essay on Optimal Bankruptcy Rules and Social Justice," 1994 *Ill. L. Rev.* 1.

2   Schwartz's argument proceeds via a formal model. For more informal arguments along similar lines, see Barry E. Adler, "Financial and Political Theories of American Corporate Bankruptcy," 45 *Stan. L. Rev.* 311, 322–23 (1993); Robert K. Rasmussen, "Debtor's Choice: A Menu Approach to Corporate Bankruptcy," 71 *Tex. L. Rev.* 51, 55–68 (1992).

3   This statement assumes that the private benefits that managers receive are to be included in calculating which procedure creates greater societal wealth.

4   I am assuming here that the parties who want to induce the firm to choose the more efficient procedure pick either a renegotiation proof contract or a partially renegotiation proof contract depending on whichever is the cheaper in the case at hand.

5   For such a proposal, see Douglas G. Baird and Randal C. Picker, "A Simple Noncooperative Bargaining Model of Corporate Reorganizations," 20 *J. Legal Stud.* 311 (1991). See also F. H. Buckley, "Free Contracting in Bankruptcy," in this volume (describing the Canadian private receivership under which the bank has the right to foreclose on the debtor).

6   For such a proposal, see Barry E. Adler, "Financial and Political Theories of American Corporate Bankruptcy," 45 *Stan. L. Rev.* 311, 322–23 (1993).

7   Specifically, if there are n possible bankruptcy contracts that offer a payout to the creditor of k, and p_n is the probability that the nth contract is enforced, then the creditor's participation constraint is given by $\Sigma p_n k_n$.

8   Schwartz calls his proposal one for creating a number of "default" provisions. Yet the core notion of a default is that it applies unless the parties specify otherwise. For this reason, I prefer saying that the government should provide a "menu of options" rather than "a set of defaults."

9   Work in this area includes Joseph Farrell and Garth Saloner, "Installed Base and Compatibility: Innovation, Product Preannouncements, and Predation," 76 *Am. Econ. Rev.* 940 (1996); Joseph Farrell and Garth Saloner, "Standardization, Compatibility, and Innovation," 16 *Rand J. Econ.* 70 (1985); Michael Katz and Carl Shapiro, "Network Externalities, Competition, and Compatibility," 75 *Am. Econ. Rev.* 424 (1985); Michael Katz and Carl Shapiro, "Systems Competition and Network Effects," 8 *J. Econ. Persp.* 93 (1994).

10   See Michael Klausner, "Corporations, Corporate Law, and Networks of Contracts," 81 *Va. L. Rev.* 757 (1995).

11   Klausner, supra note 10, at 839–41. I have elsewhere argued that having a menu increases efficiency as opposed to leaving the matter to private contract (see Rasmussen, supra note 2), and Ian Ayres has also suggested that legislatures provide menus for corporate contracts. See Ian Ayres, "Making a Difference: The Contractual Contributions of Easterbrook and Fischel," 59 *U. Chi. L. Rev.* 1391, 1416 (1992).

12   Klausner, supra note 10, at 782–84.

13   Id. at 785–86.

14   Of course, there is an optimal number of rules. At some point, the gain attributable to adding another rule to the menu is outweighed by the cost of having to learn the details of that rule.

15   For a more detailed elaboration and defense of this proposal, see Rasmussen, supra note 2.

16   This limit does not solve the transition amendment problem because, in that situation, the parties had no ability to contract at the time of lending for loan cove-

nants restricting changes in the bankruptcy procedure to which the firm is committed.

17 For recent attempts to fill this void, see Lucian Bebchuk and Andrew Guzman, "An Economic Analysis of Transnational Bankruptcies," working paper (Feb. 1996); Robert K. Rasmussen, "A New Approach to Transnational Insolvencies," draft.

18 See Restatement of Conflict of Laws (Second) § 6.

19 William L. Prosser, "Interstate Publication," 51 *Mich. L. Rev.* 959, 971 (1953).

20 See Conflict of Laws, section 187.

21 See Conflict of Laws, section 187(2)(b).

22 See Conflict of Laws, section 187 comment e.

23 *The Bremen v. Zapata Co.* 407 U.S. 1 (1972).

24 Id. at 3.

25 Id. at 8.

26 Id. at 12.

27 Like Schwartz, I do not address here the problem of involuntary claimants.

28 See William L. Cary, "Federalism and Corporate Law: Reflections upon Delaware," 83 *Yale L. J.* 663 (1974).

29 For an excellent extended discussion of this point, see David Skeel, "Rethinking the Line between Corporate Law and Corporate Bankruptcy," 72 *Tex. L. Rev.* 471, 512–54 (1994).

Contract and Jurisdictional Freedom

Thanks to the George Mason University Law and Economics Center and the Donner Foundation for funding; and to Frank Buckley, participants at a seminar at the George Mason University Center for the Study of Public Choice, and the commentators at the Donner Conference on Conflict of Laws for helpful comments.

1 See infra text accompanying notes 5–6.

2 The original statement of the competition point is Charles M. Tiebout, "A Pure Theory of Local Expenditures," 64 *J. Pol. Econ.* 416 (1956).

3 We identify a federal system as one in which constituent jurisdictions are bound by a common constitution under which some powers are reserved for the central government. The role of the central government is, in part, to minimize potentially destructive competition like that described in this essay by making and enforcing central laws or by promoting competition between the states. We show that the alternative the central government chooses is critical to the system's overall efficiency.

4 See generally, Mancur Olson, *The Logic of Collective Action* (1965); R. McCormick and R. Tollison, *Politicians, Legislations, and the Economy* 3–4 (1981); Robert Tollison, "Public Choice and Legislation," 74 *Va. L. Rev.* 339 (1988). Wealth transfers may eventually spur corrective action by losing interest groups. See Gary Becker, "A Theory of Competition among Pressure Groups for Political Influence," 98 *Quart. J. Econ.* 371 (1983).

5 Who actually bears the cost of these laws depends on such factors as consumers' ability to substitute unregulated products or suppliers and on manufacturers' ability to price discriminate between regulating and nonregulating states. It seems clear that consumers and manufacturers usually will share product liability costs while in-state lawyers and plaintiffs will get most of the benefits. Since people usually do not know in advance whether they are likely to be plaintiffs, lawyers emerge as the most potent beneficiary class. Though in-state consumers bear some product liability costs even in

the absence of manufacturers' ability to price discriminate between states, these consumers have a higher likelihood of being beneficiaries of the law. For discussions of externalization and jurisdictional competition in products liability law see Michael W. McConnell, "A Choice-of-Law Approach to Products Liability Reform," in W. Olsen, ed., *New Directions in Liability Law* 90 (1988); Bruce L. Hay, "Conflicts of Law and State Competition in the Product Liability System," 80 *Geo. L. J.* 617 (1992); Michael E. Solimine, "An Economic and Empirical Analysis of Choice of Law," 24 *Ga. L. Rev.* 49 (1989).

6 See Roberta Romano, *The Genius of American Corporate Law* 5–6 (1993); Frank H. Easterbrook, "Federalism and European Business Law," 14 *Int. Rev. L. & Econ.* 125 (1994); Frank H. Easterbrook, "Antitrust and the Economics of Federalism," 26 *J. L. & Econ.* 23 (1983); Daniel R. Fischel, "From MITE to CTS: State Anti-Takeover Statutes, the Williams Act, the Commerce Clause, and Insider Trading," *1987 Sup. Ct. Rev.* 47, 85; Saul Levmore, "Interstate Exploitation and Judicial Intervention," 69 *Va. L. Rev.* 563, 568–69 (1983); Sidak and Woodward, "Corporate Takeovers, the Commerce Clause, and the Efficient Anonymity of Shareholders," 84 *Nw. U. L. Rev.* 1092 (1990).

7 See Friedrich Hayek, "The Economic Conditions of Interstate Federalism" (1939), reprinted in F. Hayek, *Individualism and the Economic Order*, ch. 12 (1948) at 268. Barry Weingast, "The Economic Role of Political Institutions: Market-Preserving Federalism and Economic Development," 11 *J. L. Econ. & Org.* 1, 3 (1995) notes that "[f]or most of the last 300 years, the richest nation in the world has had a federal structure."

8 Thus, contrary to William W. Bratton and Joseph A. McCahery, "An Inquiry into the Efficiency of the Limited Liability Company: Of Theory of the Firm and Regulatory Competition," 54 *Wash. & Lee L. Rev.* 629 (1997), the role of interest groups in state law is not necessarily inconsistent with an efficiency explanation. Indeed, some interest groups, such as lawyers, may be essential to competition.

9 The impact of comity depends on actors' ability to determine which state's law will apply to their conduct at the time of engaging in it. See Erin O'Hara and Larry E. Ribstein, "Interest Groups, Contracts, and Interest Analysis," 48 *Mercer L. Rev.* 765 (1997).

10 See U.S. Constitution, art. 4, §1: "Full Faith and Credit shall be given in each State to the public Acts, Records, and judicial Proceedings of every other State. And the Congress may by general Laws prescribe the Manner in which such Acts, Records and Proceedings shall be proved, and the Effect thereof."

11 See Larry E. Ribstein, "Statutory Forms for Closely Held Firms: Theories and Evidence from LLCs," 73 *Wash. U. L. Q.* 369 (1995).

12 See Ian Ayres, "Supply-Side Inefficiencies in Corporate Charter Competition: Lessons from Patents, Yachting, and Bluebooks," 43 *Kan. L. Rev.* 541 (1995).

13 See infra text accompanying note 68.

14 See Larry E. Ribstein, "Choosing Law by Contract," 18 *J. Corp. L.* 245 (1993).

15 See Geoffrey P. Miller, "Choice of Law as a Precommitment Device," in this volume.

16 U.S. Constitution, article 1, section 10 provides: "No state shall . . . pass any . . . Law impairing the obligations of contracts." For a discussion of the application of the Contracts Clause to corporations, see Henry N. Butler and Larry E. Ribstein, "The Contract Clause and the Corporation," 55 *Brook. L. Rev.* 767 (1989).

17 See 2 J. Beale, Conflict of Laws § 332.2 (1935); H. Goodrich on Conflict of Laws 110, at 325–33 (3d ed. 1949); Minor, Conflict of Laws 401–2 (1901); Lorenzen, "Validity and Effects of Contracts in Conflict of Law," 30 *Yale L. J.* 655, 658 (1921).

18 See Ribstein, supra note 14.

19 See Gary M. Anderson et al., "On the Incentives of Judges to Enforce Legislative Wealth Transfers," 32 *J. L. & Econ.* 215 (1989); W. Mark Crain and Robert D. Tollison, "Constitutional Change in an Interest Group Perspective," 8 *J. Legal Stud.* 165 (1979) and "The Executive Branch in the Interest-Group Theory of Government," 8 *J. Legal Stud.* 555 (1979); William M. Landes and Richard A. Posner, "The Independent Judiciary in an Interest Group Perspective," 18 *J. L. & Econ.* 875 (1975).

20 See Richard Posner, *The Economic Analysis of Law*, 534–36 (4th ed. 1992); Richard Posner, "What Do Judges and Justices Maximize: The Same Thing as Everyone Else," 3 *Sup. Ct. Econ. Rev.* 1 (1993) (noting that judges may act to impose personal preferences); Robert D. Cooter, "The Objectives of Private and Public Judges," 41 *Pub. Choice* 107, 129–30 (1983).

21 Courts have the alternative of dismissing on *forum non conveniens* grounds or, in federal court, transferring the case to the jurisdiction whose law is chosen. See "Note, Forum Non Conveniens as a Substitute for the Internal Affairs Rule," 58 *Colum. L. Rev.* 234 (1958).

22 See *Klaxon Co. v. Stentor Elec. Mfg. Co.*, 313 U.S. 487 (1941) (holding that federal courts in diversity cases must apply the forum state's choice-of-law rule).

23 See Robert D. Cooter and Daniel L. Rubinfield, "Economic Analysis of Legal Disputes and Their Resolution," 27 *J. Econ. Lit.* 1067, 1093 (1989); Landes and Posner, supra note 19, at 239–40.

24 See Cooter, supra note 20, at 129.

25 See Gordon Tullock, *Trials on Trial* 129 (1980).

26 See Paul H. Rubin and Martin J. Bailey, "The Role of Lawyers in Changing the Law," 23 *J. Legal Stud.* 807 (1994); Paul H. Rubin, "Common Law and Statute Law," 11 *J. Legal Stud.* 205 (1982). See generally George L. Priest, "The Common Law Process and the Selection of Efficient Rules," 6 *J. Leg. Stud.* 65 (1977); Paul H. Rubin, "Why Is the Common Law Efficient?," 6 *J. Leg. Stud.* 51 (1977); William M. Landes and Richard A Posner, "Adjudication as a Private Good," 8 *J. Legal Stud.* 235 (1979); Bruce H. Kobayashi, "Case Selection, External Effects, and the Trial/Settlement Decision," in D. A. Anderson, ed., *Dispute Resolution: Bridging the Settlement Gap* (1996).

27 See Ribstein, supra note 14.

28 For discussions of the factors employed by courts in deciding whether to enforce forum-selection clauses, see Linda S. Mullenix, "Another Choice of Forum, Another Choice of Law: Consensual Adjudicatory Procedure in Federal Court," 57 *Ford. L. Rev.* 291 (1988).

29 See *National Equipment Rental, LTD. v. Szukhent*, 375 U.S. 311 (1964); *Burger King Corp. v. Rudzewicz*, 471 U.S. 462, 473 n. 14 (1985) (noting that due process is not offended by the enforcement of a consent-to-jurisdiction provision that is obtained through free negotiations and is not unreasonable or unjust).

30 See *Carnival Cruise Lines, Inc. v. Shute*, 499 U.S. 585 (1991); *M/S Bremen v. Zapata Off-Shore Co.*, 407 U.S. 1 (1972).

31 This commentary is collected and approved in Paul D. Carrington and Paul H. Haagen, "Contract and Jurisdiction," *1996 Sup. Ct. Rev.* 331.

32 See, e.g., *Gilmer v. Interstate/Johnson Lane Corp.*, 111 S.Ct. 1647 (1991) (employment discrimination); *Rodriguez de Quijas v. Shearson/American Express, Inc.*, 490 U.S. 477 (1989) (securities law claim).

33 U.S. Federal Arbitration Act, 9 U.S.C. §1 et seq.

34 See Larry E. Ribstein, "Delaware, Lawyers, and Choice of Law," 19 *Del. J. Corp. L.* 999 (1994).

35 Our story is complementary rather than inconsistent with other mechanisms for avoiding state law. Paul Rubin and Rubin and Bailey, supra note 26, stress actors' ability to influence state law through litigation ex post. We show that actors also may influence state law through choice of law ex ante.

36 The history is traced in William F. Shughart and Robert D. Tollison, "Corporate Chartering in the Economics of Legal Change," 23 *Econ. Inq.* 585, 587–88 (1985); and Henry N. Butler, "Nineteenth-Century Jurisdictional Competition in the Granting of Corporate Charters," 14 *J. Legal Stud.* 129 (1985).

37 See Bernard S. Black, "Is Corporate Law Trivial?: A Political and Economic Analysis," 84 *Nw. U. L. Rev.* 542 (1990).

38 The general rule is stated in Restatement (Second) of Conflicts, §302(2) (1971).

39 See, e.g., *Mansfield v. Hardwood Lumber Co.*, 268 F.2d 317 (5th Cir. 1959).

40 See *Greenspun v. Lindley*, 36 N.Y.2d 473, 369 N.Y.S.2d 123, 330 N.E.2d 79 (1975); *Means v. Limpia Royalties*, 115 S.W.2d 468 (Tex. Civ. App. 1938).

41 Restatement (Second) of Conflicts, §295(3).

42 See, e.g., *Model Business Corporation Code*, ch. 15 (1984).

43 See Larry E. Ribstein, "The Constitutional Conception of the Corporation," 4 *Sup. Ct. Econ. Rev.* 95 (1995).

44 See Ribstein, supra note 14.

45 See generally, Armen A. Alchian and Harold Demsetz, "Production, Information Costs, and Economic Organization," 62 *Am. Econ. Rev.* 777 (1972); Steven N.S. Cheung, "The Contractual Nature of the Firm," 26 *J. L. & Econ.* 1 (1983).

46 See infra note 112.

47 We therefore agree with Roberta Romano's ultimate conclusions that corporations are not inherently different from franchises despite apparent differences in the type of contract or regarding the need for a single law to govern a changing and multistate membership body. See Roberta Romano, "Corporate Law as the Paradigm for Contractual Choice of Law," in this volume.

48 See Butler, supra note 36; Shughart and Tollison, supra note 36.

49 The Constitution's main role in this regard has been facilitating the development of interstate firms rather than in directly protecting these firms' choice of law.

50 See *Paul v. Virginia* 75 U.S. (8 Wall.) 168, 181 (1869) (corporations are "mere creation of local law" and depend on principles of comity to be able to do business outside their states of incorporation); Ribstein, supra note 43.

51 Though the emphasis here is on the U.S., a similar story may apply to Canada, in which there is an internal affairs rule and some corporate competition. See Douglas J. Cumming and Jeffrey G. MacIntosh, "The Role of Interjurisdictional Competition in Shaping Canadian Corporate Law" (undated MS) (showing that Canadian jurisdictions compete on the basis of fees though not proactively on the terms of corporate statutes).

52 Riker argues that this common culture has caused a transfer of individual loyalty from the states to the federal government. See William H. Riker, *Federalism: Origin, Operation, and Significance* 108–10 (1964). However, as suggested in the text, the same feature actually makes state regulation more viable by strengthening the competitive conditions that provide an important check.

53 See Jonathan R. Macey and Geoffrey Miller, "Toward an Interest-Group Theory of Delaware Corporate Law," 65 *Tex. L. Rev.* 469 (1987); Ribstein, supra note 34.

54 See Alan R. Bromberg and Larry E. Ribstein, *Bromberg and Ribstein on Limited Liability Companies and the Revised Uniform Partnership Act*, ch. 6 (1997); Alan R. Bromberg and Larry E. Ribstein, 1 *Bromberg and Ribstein on Partnership*, §1.04 (1996); Larry E. Ribstein and Robert Keatinge, *Ribstein and Keatinge on Limited Liability Companies*, ch. 13 (1991 & supp.).

55 See Larry E. Ribstein, "Limited Liability and Theories of the Corporation," 50 *Md. L. Rev.* 80 (1991).

56 See supra text at note 54 (discussing state income taxes on corporations).

57 See Revised Uniform Limited Partnership Act, §303 (1985).

58 See supra note 40.

59 See Larry E. Ribstein, "The Deregulation of Limited Liability and the Death of Partnership," 70 *Wash. U. L. Q.* 417 (1992).

60 See Treas. Reg. §301.7701–2(a).

61 See Macey and Miller, supra note 53; Ribstein, supra note 34.

62 See Ribstein, supra note 11.

63 See Cumming and McIntosh, supra note 51.

64 See Ayres, supra note 12; Bratton and McCahery, supra note 8; Ronald J. Daniels, "Should Provinces Compete? The Case for a Competitive Corporate Law Market," 36 *McGill L. J.* 130, 149 (1991); Susan Rose-Ackerman, "Risk Taking and Reelection: Does Federalism Promote Innovation?," 9 *J. Legal Stud.* 593 (1980).

65 See Ribstein, supra note 59.

66 See Ribstein and Keatinge, supra note 54, §13.03.

67 See Ribstein, supra note 11.

68 See Michael Klausner, "Corporations, Corporate Law, and Networks of Contracts," 81 *Va. L. Rev.* 757 (1995); Mark A. Lemley and David McGowan, "Legal Implications of Network Economic Effects, 86 *Cal. L. Rev.* 479, 562–86 (1998). See Child Care of Irvine, L. L. C. v. Facchina, 1998 WL 409363 (Del.Ch. July 15, 1998) (stating that "unlike the rich body of corporate law decisions that often provide members of this Court with at least an intuitive sense about the parties' likelihood of prevailing in this matter, in this dispute I do not enjoy the luxury of interpretive decisions upon which to make a reasoned judgment regarding who ultimately will prevail). It has been argued that "lock-in" explains why relatively few firms chose to depart from the standard corporate form and adopt close corporation statutes. See Note, Tara Wortman, "Unlocking Lock-In: Limited Liability Companies and the Key to Underutilization of Close Corporation Statutes," 70 *N.Y.U. L. Rev.* 1362 (1995). There is, to be sure, anecdotal evidence that firms have been reluctant to use new business forms. See Joseph Bankman, "The Structure of Silicon Valley Start-Ups," 41 *UCLA L. Rev.* 1737 (1994) (showing that these firms were unlikely to abandon the corporate form despite tax advantages of partnership); Larry E. Ribstein and Mark Sargent, eds., "Check the Box and Beyond: The Future of Limited Liability Entities," 52 *Bus. Law.* 605 (1997); Robert R. Keatinge, "Corporations, Unincorporated Organizations, and Unincorporations: Check the Box and the Balkanization of Business Organizations," 1 *J. Sm. & Em. Bus. Law* 201 (1997). However, it is far from clear that "lock-in," rather than the unsuitability of the new form, explains this reluctance. For example, close corporation statutes did not solve the basic problem that corporate default rules such as the absence of dissolution at will did not fit closely held firms. See Larry E. Ribstein, "The Closely Held Firm: A View from the U.S." 19 *Melbourne L. Rev.* 950 (1995).

69 See Ian Ayres, "Judging Close Corporations in the Age of Statutes," 70 *Wash. U. L. Q.* 365 (1992); Bratton and McCahery, supra note 8. Romano makes other arguments for

reduced competition here, including such firms' lack of reliance on standard forms. See Roberta Romano, "State Competition for Close Corporation Charters: A Commentary," 70 *Wash. U. L.Q.* 409 (1992).

70 See Ribstein, supra note 34.

71 See Ribstein, supra note 11.

72 This development is traced in Larry E. Ribstein, "Politics, Adaptation, and Change in Corporate Law," 8 *Aust. J. Corp. L.* 246 (1998).

73 See Rev. Rul. 88-76, 1988-2 C. B. 361 (1988).

74 See Larry E. Ribstein, "The Emergence of the Limited Liability Company," 51 *Bus. Law.* 1 (1995).

75 See Larry E. Ribstein, "Possible Futures for Closely Held Firms," 64 *U. Cin. L. Rev.* 319 (1996).

76 The history is traced in Ribstein and Keatinge, supra note 54, at §17.20. All but a handful of states (including large states such as Florida and Texas) ultimately followed the federal government in classifying LLCs as tax partnerships. See Bruce P. Ely and Joseph K. Beach, "State Tax Treatment of LLCs and RLLPs," 3 *J. Limited Liabilities Co.* 45 (1996).

77 Statutes are analyzed and tabulated in Ribstein and Keatinge, supra note 54, App. 13-1.

78 See Ribstein, supra note 11.

79 The data, available from the authors on request, was obtained largely from state secretaries of state, filling in some missing data from annual reports by the International Association of Corporation Administrators (IACA). The IACA data combines domestic and foreign unincorporated firms. The state formation data is confirmed by tax statistics showing a dramatic growth in LLCs between 1993 and 1995. See Keatinge, supra note 68 (summarizing data).

80 See supra text accompanying note 68.

81 See William J. Carney, "Limited Liability Companies: Origins and Antecedents," 66 *U. Colo. L. Rev.* 855 (1995); Carol Goforth, "The Rise of the Limited Liability Company: Evidence of a Race between the States, but Heading Where?," 45 *Syracuse L. Rev.* 1193 (1995). The data also show relatively few foreign LLCs. While this arguably suggests that lawyers had relatively little to worry about in terms of clients' going to lawyers in other states, it is inconclusive, since states may have preempted moves by enacting their statutes. The data on foreign firms in itself says little about whether revenues from firms based in other states were worth competing for, because it is possible that one or two states, such as Delaware, did earn significant revenue by competing for most of the foreign formation business.

82 See Robert Hamilton, "Registered Limited Liability Partnerships: Present at the Birth (Nearly)," 66 *Colo. L. Rev.* 1065, 1068-74 (1995).

83 For example, anecdotal information indicates that the LLP is used to avoid the Pennsylvania corporate tax.

84 LLPs theoretically also erode limits on limited liability, at least in jurisdictions that permit a full shield without restrictions on payouts. See Bromberg and Ribstein, supra note 54, §4.04(d). LLCs' main difference from LLPs—the restriction on payouts—is probably not a significant restriction in addition to what is imposed by fraudulent conveyance law.

85 Data is available by request from the authors.

86 We were unable to obtain data from other states that impose corporate taxes on LLCs, Florida and Pennsylvania.

87 Michael Klausner, in his comment in this volume, suggests that the availability of the LLP form indicates that "lock-in" is a potential problem. However, as noted in the text, the popularity of the LLC despite the availability of the LLP suggests that lock-in is not as much of a problem as might initially have been supposed.

88 The data show that corporations were down more than 10 percent in 1996 only in Oregon and Tennessee. Data from Oregon is probably unreliable, as noted on the source table. Limited partnerships were down more than 10 percent in 1996 only in Maryland, Massachusetts, New Hampshire, Ohio, Virginia, and Washington.

89 The data answers the question posed by Bratton and McCahery, supra note 8, at 662–63 as to whether firms that became LLCs were existing partnerships, Subchapter S or Subchapter C corporations, limited partnerships, or new firms that would not have been organized except as LLCs. Bratton and McCahery contend that this bears on the benefits of developing the LLC form. However, it is not clear how the benefits of each type of switch can be measured.

90 This may change as states adopt conversion procedures that make it easier to move from corporate and other forms to the LLC form. See infra text accompanying note 97.

91 See Keatinge, supra note 68.

92 The earlier trend in this direction is shown in Ribstein, supra note 11.

93 See "Simplification of Entity Classification Rules," 26 C. F. R. pt. 1, 301, 602 (10 December 1996, effective 1 January 1997); Ribstein, supra note 72 (discussing role of state statutory developments in development of federal "check-the-box" tax rule).

94 Subchapter S has also been liberalized, most notably by increasing the maximum number of shareholders from 35 to 75. See I. R. C. § 1361(b)(1)(A) as amended by the Small Business Job Protection Act of 1996, PL 104–188, 110 Stat. 1755. However, the onerous one-class capital structure mandated by Subchapter S remains.

95 Fourteen states now include this provision. See Ribstein and Keatinge, supra note 54, app. 11–1. This is in stark contrast to the original rule for dissolution on member dissociation in all states, and the rule in many states that prohibited firms from altering the dissolution-at-will rule by contrary agreement. See Ribstein, supra note 11.

96 See Rev. Rul. 95–37 (classifying conversion of partnership into LLC as partnership-to-partnership conversion); Rev. Rul. 84–52 (ruling that there is no recognition of gain or liquidation tax on partnership-to-partnership conversion).

97 Four states permit any business entity to convert to the LLC form while another seven permit conversion by general and limited partnerships. See Ribstein and Keatinge, supra note 54 (tabulating enactment of conversion provisions). Most of these provisions have been enacted within the last few months.

98 See Robert Thompson, "Piercing the Corporate Veil: An Empirical Study," 76 Cornell L. Rev. 1036 (1991).

99 Nine states currently have provisions precluding veil-piercing solely for nonobservance of formalities. See Ribstein and Keatinge, supra note 54, app. 12–1. Two states also have enacted provisions explicitly allowing firms with related parts to separate the liabilities of each part without being concerned about potential veil-piercing. See Del Code Ann. §18–215 and Iowa Code §490A.305, discussed in Ribstein and Keatinge, supra note 54, at §4.16a.

100 A study as of the end of 1994 showed that only 14 of the first 48 LLC statutes permitted one-member LLCs. See Ribstein, supra note 11. Currently only nine of the 51 LLC statutes require two members. See Ribstein and Keatinge, supra note 54, app. 4–1.

101 The International Franchise Association has 850 members, including the largest

franchisors. See W. John Moore, "Policy and Politics in Brief," 17(6) *National Journal* 340 (1992).

102 See Michael Hartnett, "Franchisors Miffed at Iowa Action, Fear Further Empowerment of Franchisees Nationally," 91(8) *Restaurant Business Magazine* 20 (1992) (stating that the attorney for a franchisees' association was advised to amend franchise regulations one state at a time rather than pursue a single piece of federal legislation because "[t]he closer the decision making is to home, the more impact people living at home can have on the legislation"); Richard Martin, "McD Fights to Overturn Iowa Franchise Law," 26(21) *Restaurant News Newspaper* 1 (1992) (legislation was drafted by a Des Moines attorney, Douglas Gross, on behalf of a franchisee coalition including Burger King, Pizza Hut, KFC, TacoBell, and Dairy Queen operators); Moore, supra note 101. See also James A. Brickley, Frederick H. Dark, and Michael S. Weisbach, "The Economic Effects of Franchise Termination Laws," 34 *J. L. & Econ.* 101, 115–16 (1991).

103 Smith, examining state regulation of automobile franchises, found evidence that much of the harm from such regulations was imposed on consumers rather than the automobile manufacturers. See Richard L. Smith II, "Franchise Regulation: An Economic Analysis of State Restrictions on Automobile Distribution," 25 *J. L. & Econ.* 125 (1982).

104 Sixteen states passed franchise regulation statues in the 1970s. Only the District of Columbia and Iowa have passed new statutes since then. However, the Iowa statute, passed in 1992, has been uniformly regarded as the most unfavorable to franchisors.

105 In 1995, franchisors secured favorable revisions to the Iowa statute. See Dennis E. Wieczorek, "The Iowa Franchise Law: 1995 Amendments and Some Proposals for 1996," 15 *Fran. L. J.* 43 (1996). See also Anne Scott, "Big Macs in Chains," B.13 *Business Record* 1 (1997) (describing efforts by franchisor and current McDonald's franchisees to repeal the Iowa statute).

106 States that require cause for termination include AR, CA, CT, DC, DE, HI, IA, IL, IN, MI, MN, NE, NJ, VA, WA, and WI. AR, CA, DC, DE, HI, IA, IN, NE, NJ, and WI also require cause for nonrenewal.

107 AR, CA, DC, HI, IA, IL, MI, MN, WA, and WI give a right to cure. In addition, IA and IN limit the franchisor's ability to prevent independent sourcing by franchisees, and make franchisors liable for encroachment.

108 See generally, Benjamin Klein, "Transactions Costs Determinants of "Unfair" Contractual Arrangements," 70 *Am. Econ. Rev. Papers & Proc.* 356 (1980), Benjamin Klein and Keith B. Leffler, "The Role of Market Forces in Assuring Contractual Performance," 89 *J. Pol. Econ.* 615 (1981).

109 Some of these statutes changed franchise contracts that were currently in force. See *Reinders Brothers, Inc. v. Rain Bird Eastern Sales Corp.* 627 F.2d 44 (7th Cir. 1980); James A. Brickley and Fredrick H. Dark, "The Choice of Organizational Form: The Case of Franchising," 18 *J. Fin. Econ.* 401 (1987). However, the retroactive application of the 1992 Iowa statute was successfully challenged on constitutional grounds. See *McDonald's Corp v. Nelson*, 822 F. Supp. 597 (S. D. Iowa 1993) (retroactive application of act violated contract clauses of state and federal constitutions); aff'd in *Holiday Inns Franchising, Inc. v. Branstad*, 29 F.3d 383 (8th Cir. 1994). See also Butler and Ribstein, supra note 16.

110 See Patrick J. Kaufmann and Francine Lafontaine, "Costs of Control: The Source of Economic Rents for McDonald's Franchisees," 37 *J. L. & Econ.* 417 (1994).

111   Our analysis does not directly examine the twenty-four statutes regulating the sale of new business opportunities and fourteen statutes requiring disclosure and registration of companies that sell franchises. In states that require registrations, franchisors are required by law to register Uniform Franchise Offering Circulars (UFOCs) before they can sell franchises. The regulation of sales and the imposition of registration requirements are a direct way to mitigate problems arising from ex-ante asymmetric information problems in franchise contracts, and may be more efficient than statutes that interfere with the franchisor-franchisee relationship. For a discussion of these issues, see Gillian K. Hadfield, "Problematic Relations: Franchising and the Law of Incomplete Contracts," 42 *Stan. L. Rev.* 927 (1990).

112   This insight underlies much of the data supporting the monitoring theory of franchising. See Brickley and Dark, supra note 109; Seth W. Norton, "Franchising, Labor Productivity, and the New Institutional Economics," 145 *J. Inst. & Theor. Econ.* 578 (1989); Paul H. Rubin, "The Theory of the Firm and the Structure of the Franchise Contract," 21 *J. L. & Econ.* 223 (1978); G. Frank Matthewson and Ralph A. Winter, "The Economics of Franchise Contracts," 28 *J. L. & Econ.* 503 (1985).

113   See Robert E. Martin, "Franchising and Risk Management," 78 *Amer. Econ. Rev.* 954 (1988).

114   See Brickley et al., supra note 102, at 115–16.

115   See Timothy Muris and Howard Beales, "State Regulation of Franchise Contracts, Working Paper," GMU Law School (1994).

116   The right to cure reduces deterrence by giving a franchisee one or more chances to cheat without fear of punishment for his actions.

117   See Brickley et al., supra note 102, at 126–30.

118   See Kaufmann and Lafontaine, supra note 110, at 447–48.

119   Attempts to affect existing contracts may be limited by the Contract Clause. See supra notes 16 and 109.

120   In a previous article one of us noted that federal courts wrote opinions in 151 cases citing the §187(1) of the Restatement (Second) of Conflicts since its final adoption in 1971, compared to 65 state opinions. The federal courts refused to enforce the clauses in 22.5 percent of these cases, while state courts refused to do so in 44 percent of the cases—this despite the fact that there are fewer total federal opinions. See Ribstein, supra note 14 at 285.

121   471 U.S. 462 (1985).

122   The agreement provided: "This Agreement shall become valid when executed and accepted by BKC at Miami, Florida; it shall be deemed made and entered into in the State of Florida and shall be governed and construed under and in accordance with the laws of the state of Florida. The choice of law designation does not require that all suits concerning this Agreement be filed in Florida." See *Burger King*, 471 U.S. at 481.

123   See id. at 483. The Michigan Franchise Investment Law requires cause for termination and allows the franchisee thirty days to cure any defects. Florida does not have a statute regulating the relationship between the franchisor and franchisee.

124   See Thomas M. Pitegoff, "Choice of Law in Franchise Agreements," 9 *Franch L. J.* 1, 20 (1989).

125   *Modern Computer Systems, Inc. v. Modern Banking Systems, Inc.*, 871 F.2d 734 (8th Cir. 1989); *Tele-Save Merchandising v. Consumers Distributing*, 814 F.2d 1120 (6th Cir. 1987).

126 814 F.2d 1120 (1987). See also *Banek v. Yogurt Ventures*, 6 F.3d 357 (1993).

127 871 F.2d 734, 738 (1989).

128 See Restatement (Second) of Conflicts §187, discussed above.

129 For some relatively recent cases refusing to enforce contractual choice of law, see *Electrical & Magneto Service Co. Inc. v. AMBAC Intern. Corp.* 941 F.2d 660 (8th Cir. 1991); *Solman Distributors, Inc. v. Brown-Forman Corp.*, 888 F.2d 170 (1st Cir. 1989); *Economou v. Physicians Weight Loss Centers of America;* 1991 WL 185217, (N.D.-Ohio 1991); *High Life Sales Co. v. Brown-Forman Corporation*, 823 S. W.2d 493 (1992); *Rutter v. BX of Tri-Cities Inc.*, 60 Wash. App. 743, 806 P.2d 1266 (1991).

130 908 F.2d 128 (7th Cir. 1991).

131 52 F.3d 734 (8th Cir. 1985).

132 Id. at 725, 740.

133 This shows that states are motivated to compete, pace the argument by Roberta Romano in her comment that the states need to impose an analogue to the corporate franchise tax in order to encourage such competition.

134 See *Entrepreneur Magazine*, 1996 Franchise 500, at *http://www.entrepreneurmag .com.*

135 See supra text accompanying notes 108–112.

136 Note that this choice of a favorable jurisdiction can be the result of migration of a franchisor's principal place of business from a regulated to an unregulated state. It also can be the result of successful lobbying by the existing set of in-state franchisors that prevents passage of unfavorable state legislation.

137 Examining the *Entrepreneur Magazine* sample, only 22 franchisors have located in states that prevent termination at will and fail to limit the application of these laws to in-state franchisees, and these have significantly lower levels of company ownership. Data available from authors on request.

138 For an economic analysis of the uniform law process, see Larry E. Ribstein and Bruce H. Kobayashi, "An Economic Analysis of Uniform State Laws," 25 *J. Legal Stud.* (1996).

139 FTC Trade Regulation Rule, Disclosure Regulation and Prohibitions Concerning Franchise and Business Opportunity Ventures, 16 C. F. R. §436.1–3 (1979).

140 For a discussion of this issue, see, e.g., Boyd Allan Byers, "Making a Case for Federal Regulation of Franchise Termination," 19 *J. Corp. L.* 607 (1994).

141 15 U.S.C. §§1221–25. The act was enacted in 1956, and imposes a duty of good faith. See Smith, supra note 103 at 132.

142 15 U.S.C. §§2801–6. The act was enacted in 1978 and requires cause for termination and nonrenewal, and allows for notice and limited ability to cure.

143 See Federal Fair Franchising Practices Act of 1997, 1997 Cong. U.S. H. R. 1083, 104th Cong., 1st Session (introduced 17, March 1997). This bill does not contain provisions allowing a franchisee right to cure. However, the bill, as introduced, would regulate the franchisor's ability to prevent independent sourcing of inputs by the franchisee, and would also limit the franchisor's ability to open new outlets near existing outlets (encroachment) even when the existing franchisee did not contract for an exclusive territory. Only two states currently regulate independent sourcing and encroachment. See supra note 107. For an economic analysis of these issues, see Benjamin Klein and Lester Saft, "The Law and Economics of Franchise Tying Contracts," 28 *J. L. & Econ.* 345 (1985); Benjamin Klein and Kevin M. Murphy, "Vertical Restraints as Contract Enforcement Mechanisms," 31 *J. L. & Econ.* 265 (1988).

144 FADFA only requires good faith. See the discussion in supra note 141. PMPA does not give the franchisee a broad right to cure. See 15 U.S.C.A §§2082: "Congress intended to give franchisees the right to cure for some types of conduct or conditions which, if continued, would warrant termination of franchise by oil company but did not intend to require a second chance for other kinds of conduct or conditions." *Wisser Co., Inc. v. Mobil Oil Corp.*, C.A.2 (N.Y.) 1984, 730 F.2d 54.

145 In contrast to general franchise regulation, which is limited to fewer than twenty states, forty-nine states (all but Alaska) have enacted state regulation of auto franchises. See Smith, supra note 103, at 141.

146 Md. Ann Code Art. 56 §157E(b). The regulations were upheld by the Supreme Court in *Exxon Corp. v. Governor of Maryland*, 437 U.S. 117 (1978). See Ribstein, supra note 14, at 289. For an economic analysis of these regulations, see John M. Barron and John R. Umbeck, "The Effects of Different Contractual Arrangements: The Case of Retail Gasoline Markets," 27 *J. L. & Econ.* 313 (1984) (finding that the Maryland law resulted in higher prices and shorter operating hours). See also Howard P. Marvel, "Tying, Franchising, and Gasoline Service Stations," 2 *J. Corp. Fin.* 199 (1997).

147 Delaware and the District of Columbia have enacted similar laws. See 6 D.C.A. §2905(a), D.C. St. §10–212. See also Jeffrey L. Spears, "Arguments for and against Legislative Attacks on Downstream Vertical Integration in the Oil Industry," 80 *Ky. L. J.* 1075 (1991) (describing numerous efforts to pass similar laws in other states).

148 See Federal Fair Franchising Practices Act of 1997, supra note 143.

149 For theory and evidence on the "race to the top" in corporate law, see Frank H. Easterbrook and Daniel R. Fischel, *The Economic Structure of Corporate Law*, ch. 8 (1991); Roberta Romano, supra note 6, at 14–24; Ralph Winter, *Government and the Corporation* (1978); Ronald J. Daniels, "Should Provinces Compete? The Case for a Competitive Corporate Law Market," 36 *McGill L. J.* 130 (1991); Peter Dodd and Richard Leftwich, "The Market for Corporate Charters: 'Unhealthy Competition' versus Federal Regulation," 53 *J. Bus.* 259 (1980); Jonathan Macey and Geoffrey Miller, "Toward an Interest-Group Theory of Delaware Corporate Law," 65 *Tex. L. Rev.* 469 (1987); Bayless Manning and Andrew G. T. Moore, "State Competition: Panel Response," 8 *Cardozo L. Rev.* 779 (1987); Elliott Weiss and Lawrence J. White, "Of Econometrics and Indeterminacy: A Study of Investors' Reactions to 'Changes' in Corporate Law," 75 *Cal. L. Rev.* 551 (1987).

150 For summaries and critiques of their specific arguments, see Ribstein, supra note 14.

151 See Alan Schwartz and Louis L. Wilde, "Intervening in Markets on the Basis of Imperfect Information: A Legal and Economic Analysis," 127 *U. Pa. L. Rev.* 630 (1979); Alan Schwartz and Louis L. Wilde, "Imperfect Information in Markets for Contract Terms: The Examples of Warranties and Security Interests," 69 *Va L. Rev.* 1387 (1983).

152 The choice-of-law rules discussed above do "catch" these transactions, but they also regulate many others. For example, the requirement that the chosen law have some connection with the transaction prevents the sort of perverse choice discussed in the text, but also the choice of legitimate jurisdictions. Whether the law is adequately connected with a particular transaction says little about whether the law is the product of a legitimate political process.

153 This is analogous to Ian Ayres's point about excessive revision, or "bluebooking," in corporate law. See Ayres, supra note 12. The structure of the legal profession inhibits clients' ability to obtain disinterested advice about the need for these legal services.

See Larry E. Ribstein, "Ethical Rules, Agency Cost, and Law Firm Structure," 84 *Va. L. Rev.* 1707 (1998). However, allocating rents to lawyers may be the best way to encourage their beneficial participation in producing efficient laws. See Ribstein, supra note 34. Lawyers' benefits from participating in the lawmaking process are partially attributable to state control of lawyer licensing which gives lawyers in a state a kind of property right in the state's law. This answers Ayres's point, supra note 69, about free-riding in the state provision of law. State licensing of lawyers provides a kind of "patent" protection that Ayres, who relies on provision of laws by legislators, says is missing in this context.

154 Such changes are constrained by the Constitution and by state competition itself. See supra notes 16 and 109.

155 See Robert K. Rasmussen, "Free Contracting in Bankruptcy at Home and Abroad," this volume.

156 See Roberta Romano, "Corporate Law as the Paradigm for Contractual Choice of Law," this volume.

157 See Margaret Brinig and Steven M. Crafton, "Marriage and Opportunism," 23 *J. Legal Stud.* 869 (1994); Lloyd Cohen, "Marriage, Divorce, and Quasi Rents; or, 'I Gave Him the Best Years of My Life,'" 16 *J. Legal Stud.* 267 (1987).

158 See Jennifer G. Brown, "Competitive Federalism and the Legislative Incentives to Recognize Same-Sex Marriage," 68 *S. Cal. L. Rev.* 745 (1995).

159 For example, marriage laws permitting free contracting, for example over divorce, might have external effects by weakening the signal that marriage conveys. See Michael Trebilcock, "Marriage as a Signal," in this volume.

160 We refer here to accident law. Many torts, including product liability and legal and medical malpractice, arise out of consensual relationships and arguably should be treated like contracts. As to product liability, see Paul H. Rubin, "Courts and the Tort-Contract Boundary in Product Liability," in this volume.

161 See O'Hara and Ribstein, supra note 9.

162 See Miller, supra note 15.

163 This is a possible answer to the question in Roberta Romano's comment as to why other countries use different approaches to choice of law.

164 See supra note 10 and accompanying text.

165 See supra note 112 and accompanying text.

166 See Jonathan Macey, "Promoting Public-Regarding Legislation through Statutory Interpretation: An Interest Group Model," 86 *Colum. L. Rev.* 223 (1986). As noted above, the proposed federal law to make uniform the regulation of franchises would not preempt state franchise law. See supra note 143.

A Comment on Contract and Jurisdictional Competition

1 Although Kobayashi and Ribstein discuss the scenario in which a state enacts a law that regulates contracts already in existence, the trivializing dynamic that they describe entails new contracts formed in response to regulation, in which the parties escape the regulation by choosing another state's law.

2 See, e.g., Roberta Romano, "Law as a Product: Some Pieces of the Incorporation Puzzle," 1 *J. L. Econ. & Org.* 225 (1985); Ralph Winter, "State Law, Shareholder Protection, and the Theory of the Corporation," 6 *J. Leg. Stud.* 251 (1977).

3 Kobayashi and Ribstein recognize that such legal restrictions are relevant. They do not

seem to recognize, however, that this is a necessary condition for a regulatory redistribution to stick.

4　Kobayashi and Ribstein's discussion of regulating states' willingness to allow choice of law but not waiver in franchise contracts provides a sense of how limiting joint conditions (b) and (c) may be.

5　See Marcel Kahan and Michael Klausner, "Path Dependence in Corporate Contracting: Increasing Returns, Herd Behavior, and Cognitive Biases," 74 *Wash. U. L. Rev.* 347 (1996), and "Standardization and Innovation in Corporate Contracting (or 'The Economics of Boilerplate')" [hereinafter referred to as 'Boilerplate'], 83 *Va. L. Rev.* 713 (1997); Michael Klausner, "Corporations, Corporate Law, and Networks of Contracts," 81 *Va. L. Rev.* 757 (1995).

6　If the specification of these relationships were left entirely to ad hoc contracting as each firm formed, de facto standardization might occur, since firms copy each other's contracts, but the degree of standardization would be purely a matter of chance, as would the terms that became standardized. By establishing a business form, the state performs a de jure standardization function.

7　Of course, within business forms there is leeway to customize. By customizing the parties can accomplish their particular aims, but to the extent they do so they forgo some benefits of standardization.

8　On increasing returns generally, see W. Brian Arthur, "Competing Technologies, Increasing Returns, and Lock-In by Historical Events," 99 *Econ. J.* 116 (1989). On increasing returns in the context of corporations, see sources cited at n. 5.

9　Kahan and Klausner, "Boilerplate," supra note 5, at 719.

10　The VHS format may have been inherently superior, but the decline in the value of the Beta format surely reflected the loss of complementary products as well.

11　This is one type of network product. The other type, exemplified by the telephone, is physically connected to other products in the network.

12　Other suboptimal equilibria include suboptimal uniformity, suboptimal diversity, standardization on an inferior product, and suboptimal abandonment of a product. See Klausner, supra note 5.

13　For the other side of the story, see S. J. Liebowitz and Stephen Margolis, "Path Dependence, Lock-In, and History," 11 *J. L. Econ. & Org.* 205, 218–22 (1995) (Beta VCR); S. J. Liebowitz and Stephen Margolis, "The Fable of the Keys," 22 *J. L. & Econ.* 1 (1990).

14　S. J. Liebowitz and Stephen Margolis, "Path Dependence, Lock-In, and History" (supra note 13); "Are Network Externalities a New Source of Market Failure?" 17 *Res. L. & Econ.* 1 (1995); and "Network Externality: An Uncommon Tragedy," 8 *J. Econ. Persp.* 133 (1994).

15　In "Boilerplate," supra note 5, Kahan and I consider and reject the possibility that lawyers will be able to internalize the costs and benefits entailed in a collective switch from one form of contract to another. We are more optimistic about underwriters, but we conclude that there is no reason to expect these agents to produce optimal contracts in the way that Leibowitz and Margolis argue will occur in the product market. Roberta Romano argues that well-informed experts will prevent suboptimal contracting. Romano, "Corporate Law and Corporate Governance," 5 *Industrial and Corporate Change* 277 (1996). The increasing-returns phenomenon, however, does not arise out of information imperfections. It arises out of externalities from early to later users of a product—or in the present context, users of a contract or business form.

16　Kobayashi and Ribstein refer to "transition costs" to explain this, but from what they report, newly formed firms are declining to opt for the LLC over the corporation. Those firms do not have transition costs.

As further support for their proposition that business forms are not subject to lock-in, Kobayashi and Ribstein cite the experience with LLPs. They explain that despite the fact that LLPs are backward compatible with traditional partnerships, and despite certain inherent advantages over LLCs, the LLP has not gained wide acceptance. This seems indeed to be a puzzle, but the puzzle exists for those that focus on the inherent benefits of business forms just as it exists for those of us interested in increasing returns. More information is apparently needed before we can understand the evolution of the LLP.

17　For an in-depth analysis of this, see Tara Wortman, "Unlocking Lock-In: Limited Liability Companies and the Key to Underutilization of Close Corporation Statutes," 70 *N.Y.U. L. Rev.* 1362 (1995). Wortman predicts that the inherent value of the LLC will be sufficient to avoid lock-in.

18　In an empirical study of change-of-control covenants in bonds, Marcel Kahan and I found evidence that weakly supported an inference of suboptimal contracting. Kahan and Klausner, supra note 5, at 751.

19　Of course, suboptimal diversity is possible as well. See sources cited at note 5.

20　I am assuming that Nevada would require its own lawyers to serve Nevada corporations. Delaware lawyers, however, could serve as consultants to Nevada lawyers.

21　This is an idea that I suggested in an earlier paper, Klausner, supra note 5. Larry Kramer and I may develop the idea in more detail, and in doing so address potential constitutional issues that might be implicated (but that, Larry tells me, would not be a barrier to such a regime).

Choice of Law as a Precommitment Device

1　The mechanism posited by Kobayashi and Ribstein works only if the parties have the ability to contract out of a state's legal regime; it has little or no application to the tort situation in which there is no ex ante contracting by the parties. One implication of their work, not explored in this comment, is that we are likely to see both greater variation among the states, and less appropriate regulation overall, in the tort area than in the contract area, because the corrective mechanism of contractual choice of law and forum is not available in the former context.

2　I use the term *legislation* throughout this comment to include all forms of lawmaking or regulation by the state government, including administrative action.

3　Michael Klausner, "A Comment on Contract and Jurisdictional Competition," in this volume.

4　Hence the title of this comment.

5　See generally Walter O. Weyrauch, "Romaniya: An Introduction to Gypsy Law," 45 *Am. J. Comp. L.* 225 (1997).

6　A could go to the government either to obtain a new regulation when none is on the books, or to strengthen existing rules to make them even more favorable to in-state residents.

7　For this reason, as Kobayashi and Ribstein observe, states uniformly apply the internal affairs doctrine in applying the law of the chartering state to conflicts among the constituencies of out-of-state corporations. The states give up the power to apply their law to out-of-state corporations in order to encourage such corporations to do business in the state.

8   Maria S. Haro, "Legal Guarantees for Foreign Investment in Peru" (1997) (on file with the author).

9   Id.

10 See, e.g., Howell Jackson, "A Concept Paper on Setting Up a Capital Markets Center in Nepal" (1998) (on file with the author).

Corporate Law as the Paradigm for Contractual Choice of Law

I have benefited from the comments of Henry Hansmann on an earlier draft.

1   This section draws from Roberta Romano, *The Genius of American Corporate Law* (1993) [hereinafter *Genius*], and Roberta Romano, "Competition for State Corporate Law," in Peter Newman, ed., *The New Palgrave Dictionary of Economics and the Law* (1998).

2   Roberta Romano, "State Competition for Corporate Charters," in John Ferejohn and Barry R. Weingast, eds., *The New Federalism: Can the States Be Trusted* 129, 132 (1997) (table 1).

3   *Genius*, supra note 1, at 7–8 (table 1–1).

4   See Roberta Romano, "Law as a Product: Some Pieces of the Incorporation Puzzle," 1 *J. L. Econ. & Org.* 225, 233–41, 246–47 (1985).

5   Ralph K. Winter, "State Law, Shareholder Protection, and the Theory of the Corporation," 6 *J. Leg. Stud.* 251 (1977).

6   For a critic of state competition advancing such a position see Lucian A. Bebchuk, "Federalism and the Corporation: The Desirable Limits on State Competition in Corporate Law," 105 *Harv. L. Rev.* 1437 (1992). Although lawyers have a significant interest in the output of the competitive process for charters (see Jonathan R. Macey and Geoffrey P. Miller, "Toward an Interest-Group Theory of Delaware Corporate Law," 65 *Tex. L. Rev.* 469 [1987], as discussed in *Genius*, supra note 2, at 29–31) it is not plausible that lawyers' interests dictate the overall content of corporate codes to the detriment of shareholders.

7   The results are summarized in *Genius*, supra note 1, at 17–18; Romano, supra note 2, at 141–42.

8   Romano, supra note 4, at 272.

9   E.g., Frank H. Easterbrook and Daniel R. Fischel, *The Economic Structure of Corporate Law* 220–22 (1991).

10 The most comprehensive study, which finds a small but significant negative stock price effect, is Jonathan Karpoff and Paul Malatesta, "The Wealth Effects of Second-Generation State Takeover Legislation," 25 *J. Fin. Econ.* 291 (1989) (study of forty statutes). *Genius*, supra note 1, at 60–69, reviews the empirical research on takeover statutes.

11 See Karpoff and Malatesta, supra note 10, at 315 (insignificant over two-day event interval); John S. Jahera and William N. Pugh, "State Takeover Legislation: The Case of Delaware," 7 *J. L. Econ. & Org.* 410, 416–19 (1991) (insignificant or significantly positive over eight two-day event intervals).

12 *Edgar v. MITE*, 457 U.S. 624 (1982).

13 This section draws from *Genius*, supra note 1, at 118–40.

14 In addition to the choice-of-law rule distinction emphasized in this comment, differences in ownership structure—U.S. corporations are typically diffusely held whereas EU and Canadian firms have controlling shareholders—diminish the incentive for sovereigns in these federations to compete for corporate charters because, as dis-

cussed in id., at 124–27, 138–39, differences in legal regime are less important to shareholders who exercise direct control over their firms.

15 William J. Carney, "Federalism and Corporate Law: A Non-Delaware View of the Results of Competition," in Joseph McCahery, William W. Bratton, Sol Picciotto, and Colin Scott, eds., *International Regulatory Competition and Coordination* 152, 169–70 (1996).

16 See, e.g., Katharina Pistor, "Co-determination in Germany: A Socio-Political Model with Governance Externalities" (unpublished manuscript 1997); Theodor Baums and Bernd Frick, "Co-determination in Germany: The Impact on the Market Value of the Firm" (unpublished manuscript 1997).

17 Klaus J. Hopt, "Directors' Duties to Shareholders, Employees, and Other Creditors: A View from the Continent," in Ewan McKendrick, ed., *Commercial Aspects of Trusts and Fiduciary Obligations* 115, 116 (1992).

18 See Ronald J. Daniels, "Should Provinces Compete? The Case for a Competitive Corporate Law Market," 36 *McGill L. J.* 130, 183 (1991).

19 It is plausible to assume investors are informed about liability rules, given the sophistication of institutional investors who comprise the majority of stock market investors and whose actions determine market prices on which uninformed investors can rely. There is, moreover, substantial evidence that differences in legal regimes are priced. For references see Roberta Romano, "Empowering Investors: A Market Approach to Securities Regulation," 107 *Yale L. J.* 2359 (1998) (reincorporation event studies and studies indicating creditor protections in bond indentures are positively priced).

20 See, e.g., Robert A. Leflar, Luther L. Mc Dougal III, and Robert L. Felix, *American Conflicts Law* 416–17 (4th ed. 1986); cf. *The Breman v. Zapata Off-Shore Co.*, 407 U.S. 1, 15–16 (1972) (circumstances when choice-of-forum clause rejected).

21 See, e.g., *CTS Corp. v. Dynamics Corp. of America*, 481 U.S. 69 (1987); Leflar et al., supra note 20, at 700; Restatement (Second) of Conflicts of Law § 302 cmt. e (American Law Institute, 1971) [hereinafter Restatement].

22 E.g., Del. Code Ann. tit. 6, § 1547 (Limited Liability Partnership Act); Del. Code Ann. tit. 6, §18–901 (Limited Liability Company Act).

23 See, e.g., Uniform Securities Act § 414, as codified at Cal. Corp. Code § 25008 (West 1997).

24 Pub. L. No. 104–67, 109 Stat. 737 (Dec. 22, 1995) (to be codified at 15 U.S.C. §§ 77a et seq.).

25 See *Oak Technology v. Superior Court of Santa Clara County*, No. HO16141 (Cal. Ct. App. Aug. 14, 1997), noted in "Calif. Court Finds No Error in Refusal to Stay State Litigation," 29 Sec. Reg. & L. Rep. (BNA) 1214 (29 Aug. 1997).

26 See Securities Litigation Uniform Standard Act of 1998, Pub. L. No. 105–353 (1998).

27 See Romano, supra note 19. The discussion that follows is drawn from the discussion of the choice-of-law rule in that article.

28 See *Restatement*, supra note 21, § 302 cmt. e; P. John Kozyris, "Some Observations on State Regulation of Multistate Takeovers—Controlling Choice of Law through the Commerce Clause," 14 *Del. J. Corp. L.* 499, 520–21 (1989).

29 Kozyris, supra note 28, at 521.

30 See *Basic, Inc. v. Levinson*, 485 U.S. 224 (1988).

31 See Leflar et al., supra note 20, at 416–17.

32 Although firms could presently try to come under only one state's securities laws by

refusing to sell their securities in any state but the state with the preferred regime, it is extraordinarily difficult to restrict sales in today's global markets.

33 For analysis of the states' financial incentives and the choice of securities domicile in a competitive securities regime see Romano, supra note 19 at 2388–92, 2408–10.

34 See Oliver E. Williamson, "Corporate Governance," 93 *Yale L. J.* 1197 (1984).

35 See Francine LaFontaine and Margaret E. Slade, "Retail Contracting: Theory and Practice," 45 *J. Indus. Econ.* 1, 16–17 (1997).

36 See Benjamin Klein, "The Economics of Franchise Contracts," 2 *J. Corp. Fin.* 9, 28–29 (1995); Antony W. Dnes, "The Economic Analysis of Franchise Contracts," 152 *J. Institutional & Theoretical Econ.* 297, 318 (1996).

37 Francine LaFontaine and Scott E. Masten, "Franchise Contracting, Organization, and Regulation: Introduction," 2 *J. Corp. Fin.* 1, 6 (1995).

38 See Gillian K. Hadfield, "Problematic Relations: Franchising and the Law of Incomplete Contracts," 42 *Stan. L. Rev.* 927 (1990).

39 For a theoretical model of opportunistic behavior in which shareholders breach implicit employment contracts in hostile takeovers see Andrei Shleifer and Lawrence H. Summers, "Breach of Trust in Hostile Takeovers," in Alan Auerbach, ed., *Corporate Takeovers: Causes and Consequences* 33 (1988). Such potential breaches are of far less serious concern than franchisors' potential breaches because hostile takeovers are much more expensive and require the action of a third party outside of the contracting relationship (the bidder) to be accomplished. Moreover, there is scant empirical support for Shleifer and Summers's implicit breach explanation of hostile takeovers. See Roberta Romano, "A Guide to Takeovers: Theory, Evidence, and Regulation," 9 *Yale J. on Reg.* 119, 140–42 (1992).

40 See J. Howard Beales III and Timothy J. Muris, "The Foundations of Franchise Regulation: Issues and Evidence," 2 *J. Corp. Fin.* 157 (1995). Hadfield, supra note 38, at 970–76, however, discusses several cases which she considers illustrative of significant franchisor opportunism.

41 See Henry Hansmann, *The Ownership of Enterprise* 159–60 (1996). Hansmann suggests that the franchises in which franchisees do not own the franchise, such as fast food chains, are more prone to franchisee than franchisor opportunism than those that franchisees own, such as hardware stores: they tend to be businesses where "important product production" is undertaken at the franchisee level and where a significant part of the product offered is "standardized service to travelers."

42 See Klein, supra note 36. The termination threat, Klein contends, is not the loss of a sunk investment in specific assets but the loss of the stream of future rents generated by the assets.

43 Courts may not make this mistake as often as legislators. Gillian Hadfield contends that courts fail to recognize the possibility of franchisor opportunism (which legislators attempt to constrain) and instead, recognizing only the possibility of franchisee opportunism, mistakenly enforce termination clauses too strictly. See Hadfield, supra note 38.

44 See LaFontaine & Slade, supra note 35, at 15–16.

45 Modern economic analyses of franchising have rejected older theories that franchising serves a capital-raising function and instead view franchisors as having adequate alternative sources of capital, explaining the use of the franchise form in terms of its ability to resolve organizational monitoring and control problems. See Dnes, supra note 36, at 298–99; LaFontaine and Masten, supra note 37, at 3–4.

46 Hadfield, supra note 38, at 983, who is concerned about franchisor opportunism, advocates judicial adaptation of the contract doctrine of good faith in interpreting franchise contract clauses. Such an adaptation would be followed in the regime franchisors choose if her analysis of the significance of franchisor opportunism and of the ability of courts to distinguish between legitimate and illegitimate terminations is correct. For the adaptation would then maximize the total value of the franchise: where the probability of opportunistic termination is high, franchisees will pay more for their units under a regime that protects them from illegitimate expropriation.

47 Firms may substitute internally owned units for franchise units in states with inefficient franchising laws, which, given the suboptimal organizational arrangement, will generate lower taxable income to a state than were the units franchises. But this opportunity loss is likely to be less visible to the state than a decrease in business franchise tax revenue that is directly attributed to a lower number of locally domiciled firms, as the income tax paid by franchise organizations is not separately reported and thus not easily comparable across states.

48 Once the franchisor becomes subject to a regime that prevents it from terminating a relationship, thereby facilitating franchisee opportunism, the franchisor will charge a higher price for subsequent units and future franchisees will therefore not be able to benefit financially from the extension of franchisee rights.

Contributors

Gregory S. Alexander is Professor of Law at Cornell Law School.

Margaret F. Brinig is Professor of Law at George Mason University.

F. H. Buckley is Professor of Law at George Mason University and author (with Mark Gillen and Robert Yalden) of *Corporations: Principles and Policies* (1995).

Robert Cooter is Herman F. Selvin Professor of Law at the University of California at Berkeley.

Steven J. Eagle is Professor of Law at George Mason University.

Robert C. Ellickson is Walter E. Meyer Professor of Property and Urban Law at the Yale Law School.

Richard A. Epstein is James Parker Hall Distinguished Service Professor of Law at the University of Chicago.

William A. Fischel is Professor of Economics at Dartmouth College.

Michael Klausner is Professor of Law at Stanford University.

Bruce H. Kobayashi is Associate Professor of Law at George Mason University.

Geoffrey P. Miller is Professor of Law at New York University.

Timothy J. Murtis is Foundation Professor of Law at George Mason University.

Robert H. Nelson is Professor of Public Affairs at the University of Maryland and Senior Fellow of the Competitive Enterprise Institute.

Eric A. Posner is Professor of Law at the University of Chicago.

Robert K. Rasmussen is Professor of Law at Vanderbilt University.

Larry E. Ribstein is Foundation Professor of Law at George Mason University.

Roberta Romano is Allen Duffy/1960 Professor of Law at Yale Law School.

Paul H. Rubin is Professor of Economics at Emory University.

Alan Schwartz is Sterling Professor of Law at Yale Law School.

Elizabeth S. Scott is University Professor and Robert C. Taylor Research Professor at the University of Virginia.

Robert E. Scott is Dean and Lewis F. Powell Jr. Professor of Law at the University of Virginia.

Michael J. Trebilcock is Professor of Law at the University of Toronto.

Acceptance. *See* Offer and acceptance

Adhesion contracts. *See* Standard form contracts

Agency costs, 3, 190, 265–66, 288–89; governance strategies, 303–10; incentive strategies, 290–97, 301–3; monitoring, 309–10

Bankruptcy, 12–13, 20–21, 281–324

Bargain theory, 63–66

Best efforts terms. *See* Opportunism

Block improvement districts. *See* Neighborhood associations

Bonding. *See* Self-binding gains

Breach of contract, 53–58

Choice of forum. *See* Choice of law

Choice of law: in bankruptcy, 319–24; bargaining freedom and, 21–22, 327–31. *See also* Jurisdictional competition

Commodification. *See* Externalities; Social conservatism

Common pool problem, 157, 309

Communitarianism: bankruptcy and communities, 284–86; marriage law and, 205–8

Conditions. *See* Impossibility

Condominiums, 161

Consent theories, 4–6, 80–82

Consequentialist account of contract law, 6–7, 12

Consideration, 43–48

Contingent claims, 139–40

Contracts clause, 327

Conventions, contracts as, 4–6

Corporation as a nexus of contracts, 282, 332–34, 352, 370–71

Covenant marriage, 201, 272, 275–79

Damages, 124–26. *See also* Breach of contract; Efficient breach

"Death of contract," 1, 25–31, 61–63, 93–94

Default contract terms, 238–41, 245–48, 316–19

Deregulation, 166–67

Divorce, 17–20, 225–27

Duress, 46–47

Efficiency norms, 6–7, 127–28

Efficient breach, 56–58

End-state preferences. *See* Social conservatism

Exit strategies, 199–200, 326–27. *See also* Jurisdictional competition

Expanded choice: assigning tort claims, 15, 139–54; "menus" in bankruptcy, 21, 312–19; waiving tort law claims, 14–15, 119–39. *See also* Choice of law; Covenant marriage; Default contract terms

Externalities, 13, 86–90; aesthetic, 157–60; choice of law, 360–61; land development, 178–83; marriage contracts and children, 209, 271; social norms, 269–72; stakeholders and bankruptcy, 281–86. *See also* Network externalities; Penalty default terms; Social conservatism

"Fatal conceit," 191

Fixed preferences. *See* Self-binding gains

Formalism and neoformalism, 2–4, 7–8, 9–10, 27–29, 35–61, 63–72

Franchises as contracts, 97–100, 339–46, 381–86

Frustration. *See* Impossibility

Gap-filling. *See* Default contract terms

Good faith duties. *See* Opportunism

Hands-tying. *See* Self-binding gains

Holdouts, 190–91, 198–99. *See also* NIMBY homeowners

Homeowners' associations, 162

Humean analysis of contracts. *See* Conventions

Impossibility, 49–53
Information failures, 10–12, 82–86
Iterated games, 228, 262–63. *See also* Reciprocal altruism

Judicial incentives, 9, 70–77
Jurisdictional competition, 323–24, 325–86. *See also* Choice of law

Kaldor-Hicks efficiency, 326

Laissez-faire, 7–9, 25–35, 67–70, 94–97
Land use controls, government. *See* Zoning
Lochner era, 103–18
Lock-in effects, 22, 229, 263, 337, 354–56. *See also* Network externalities

Mailbox rule. *See* Offer and acceptance
Markets and contract terms, 144–54, 319; stock and debt market discipline, 323–24, 373
Mistake, 84–86
Monitoring. *See* Agency costs
Monopolies, 59–61, 96–100
Moral hazard, 264, 383. *See also* Overinvestment; Underinvestment

Neighborhood associations, 159–66, 171–75, 179–83, 185, 187–91, 193–99
Network externalities, 316, 337, 351–56. *See also* Lock-in effects
NIMBY homeowners, 177–83
"Nirvana" fallacy, 14, 120

Objective theory of consent, 35–39. *See also* Bargain theory
Offer and acceptance, 35–43
Opportunism, 202–3, 218–20, 276, 309, 364; bankruptcy, 290–97; best efforts terms, 219–20. *See also* Underinvestment
Overinvestment, 304, 310. *See also* Opportunism

Paternalism, 10–13, 90–92, 214–15, 128–39; delegation to agents as a response, 265–66; divorce law as paternalistic, 203–4, 227, 241–44, 253–55, 269–72, 279; ex ante bargaining freedom and,

208–9; freedom of contract and, 58–62; judgment biases, 12, 128–33, 181, 215–16; weakness of the will, 12. *See also* Externalities
Penalty default terms, 252
Precommitment. *See* Self-binding gains
Progressive movement, 167–68
Promissory estoppel, 47–48
Public goods, 192. *See* NIMBY homeowners

Quasi-rents, 359

"Race to the bottom." *See* Jurisdictional competition
"Race to the top." *See* Jurisdictional competition
Reciprocal altruism, 228, 260–62
Relational contracts, 202, 211–12
Rent extraction. *See* Rent seeking
Rents, 359
Rent seeking, 190, 195, 326–27, 349–51
Residential community association (RCA), 185, 190–91, 194, 195, 197, 200. *See* Neighborhood association
Rights theories, 4–6. *See also* Consent theories
Risk sharing strategies, 221–22

Securities law as a contract, 378–80
Self-binding gains, 6–7, 12–13, 213–14, 230–31; fixed preferences, 230, 260–62
Self-enforcing contracts, 226
Signaling: in marriage, 19–20, 216–18, 249–55, 259–65, 269. *See also* Self-binding gains
Situational monopoly, 309
Social conservatism, 13–14, 20, 105–6, 115–18, 187, 253, 270. *See also* Communitarianism
Social constructs. *See* Conventions
Social norms, 196–97; marriage and, 229–35, 237–38, 254–68
Solidarity, 196
Stakeholders. *See* Externalities
Standard form contracts, 11, 83–84, 97–100, 149–51
Subjective value, 32–34
Subsidiarity, 187

Takings, 171, 188–89
Third-party beneficiary, 69
Tit-for-tat. *See* Reciprocal altruism

Transaction cost barriers, 17, 297–300
Transitional gains, 190–91

Unconscionability, 68–69, 97–100
Underinvestment: in bankruptcy, 20–21,

290–97, 301–3; in marriage, 222–25, 235,
259, 264. *See also* Opportunism
Unincorporated firms as a contract, 334–36

Zoning, government, 15–17, 157–58, 166–
76, 181–83, 184–86, 192, 196, 197

Library of Congress Cataloging-in-Publication Data

The fall and rise of freedom of contract / edited by Francis H.
Buckley.

p.   cm.

Includes index.

ISBN 0-8223-2333-8 (cloth : alk. paper)

1. Liberty of contract—United States.   2. Torts—United States.
3. Domestic relations—United States.   4. Bankruptcy—United
States.

I. Buckley, F. H. (Francis H.), 1948–   .

KF807.F35   1999

346.7302—dc21   99-13956   CIP